Prentice Hall

MATHEMATICS

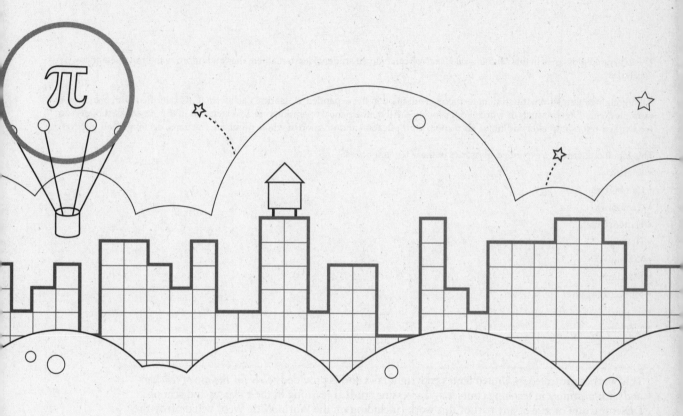

Multilingual Handbook

PEARSON

D1318527

...ton, Massachusetts • Chandler, Arizona • Glenview, Illinois • Upper Saddle River, New Jersey

The expanded glossaries in this *Multilingual Handbook* can help all students learn mathematics and improve their mathematics vocabulary.

All highlighted terms from the student textbook are defined in the expanded glossaries. Each term is also clarified with one or more examples with diagrams and/or worked-out problems. All mathematical operations are also included in the glossary. Students can see worked-out examples of addition, subtraction, multiplication and division of whole numbers, fractions, decimals, and integers.

This handbook provides expanded glossaries in these ten languages:
• English
• Cambodian
• Cantonese
• Haitian Creole
• Hmong
• Korean
• Mandarin
• Pilipino (Tagalog)
• Spanish
• Vietnamese

ISBN-13: 978-0-13-372193-5
ISBN-10: 0-13-372193-0

5 6 7 8 9 10 V011 13 12 11

Teaching Strategies for the Multilingual Classroom

Today's classrooms often have students with limited English skills. Many of these students have learned English as a second language. These students, as well as all other students in the classroom, can benefit from the following teaching strategies that are aimed at improving both their language and mathematics skills.

1. Use slow, clear speech that avoids idioms and slang. Use short sentences.

2. Act out the meaning with gestures, facial expressions, and other body language as well as any appropriate props, graphs, overhead transparencies, and other visual aids.

3. Have students use manipulatives so they can learn by doing.

4. Involve students rather than isolate them.

5. Do not require students to respond until they feel ready to speak before the group.

6. Employ cooperative learning strategies.

7. Relate instruction to students' prior experiences

8. Include multicultural activities to create a welcoming environment in the classroom.

9. Provide a focus on vocabulary, where new words are repeated often and are introduced in context.

10. Provide material where some of it is translated for students.

11. Encourage students to bring to class an English/native language dictionary to enable them to look up words as needed.

Table of Glossary Terms

A Table of Glossary Terms begins on page v. Students and teachers can use this quick reference to make it easier for them to look up terms.

- Pages v-xviii list each English term with its equivalent in Cambodian, Cantonese, Haitian Creole, Korean, Spanish, and Vietnamese.

- Pages xix-xxxii list each English term with its equivalent in Hmong, Pilipino (Tagalog), and Mandarin.

TABLE OF GLOSSARY TERMS

English	Cambodian	Cantonese	Haitian Creole	Korean	Spanish	Vietnamese
absolute position	ទីតាំងដាច់ខាត	絕對位置	pózisyon absólou	절대위치	posición absoluta	vị trí tuyệt đối
absolute value	តម្លៃដាច់ខាត	絕對值	valèr absólou	절대값	valor absoluto	trị số tuyệt đối
acute angle	មុំស្រួច	銳角	ang aygou	예각	ángulo agudo	góc nhọn
acute triangle	ត្រីកោណមុំស្រួច	銳角三角形	triang aygou	예각삼각형	triángulo acutángulo	tam giác nhọn
addend	ចំនួនបូក	加數	nouméró ajouté	가수	sumando	số cộng
addition	សេចក្ដីបូក	加法	adisyon	더하기	suma	phép cộng
Addition Property of Equality	លក្ខណៈនៃបូកប្រើស្មើសមភាព	等加屬性	Própriyété d'Égalité Adisyon	등식의 덧셈 성질	Propiedad de igualdad de la suma	Tính Chất Cộng Một Lượng Bằng Nhau
additive inverse	ចំនួនបញ្ច្រាសបូក	相反數（加性逆元素）	aditif invérs	덧셈에 대한 역원	inverso aditivo	số nghịch đảo cộng
adjacent leg	ជ្រុងជាប់	鄰邊	janm kontigou	인접 빗변	lado adyacente	cạnh kề
algebra	ពិជគណិត	代數	aljéb	대수	álgebra	đại số
algebraic expression	កន្សោមពិជគណិត	代數式	egspresyon aljebrik	대수 표기법	expresión algebraica	biểu thức đại số
alternate angles	មុំឆ្លាស់	交錯角	ang altèrné yo	상대각	ángulos alternos	những góc so le
angle	មុំ	角	ang	각	ángulo (angle)	góc
angle bisector	បន្ទាត់ពុះមុំ	角平分線	bisektris d'ang	각의 이등분선	bisectriz de un ángulo	đường phân giác
angle of rotation	មុំបង្វិល	旋轉角	ang de rótasyon	회전각	ángulo de rotación	góc quay
Angle-Side-Angle (ASA)	មុំ-ជ្រុង-មុំ	角邊角定理	Ang-Bó-Ang	한변과 두각	Angulo-Lado-Angulo	Góc-Cạnh-Góc
area	ផ្ទៃក្រឡា	面積	arya	면적	área	diện tích
arithmetic sequence	ថ្នាក់នព្វន្តកម្ម	算術序列	sékans aritmetik	등차수열	progresión aritmética	dãy số học
arrangement	ចំណាត់ថ្នាក់	排列	aranjman	순열	ordenación	sự sắp xếp
Associative Property of Addition	លក្ខណៈផ្គុំនៃបូក	加法結合律	Própriyété d'Adisyon Asósyatif	덧셈의 결합 법칙	Propiedad asociativa de la suma	Tính Chất Nhóm Của Phép Cộng
Associative Property of Multiplication	លក្ខណៈផ្គុំនៃគុណ	乘法結合律	Própriyété Moultiplikasyon Asósyatif	곱셈의 결합 법칙	Propiedad asociativa de la multiplicación	Tính Chất Nhóm Của Phép Nhân
average	មធ្យមភាគ	平均數	mouyen	평균	promedio	số trung bình
axes	អ័ក្ស	坐標軸	aks	축	ejes	trục tọa độ
bar graph	ក្រាបចង្កោម	柱狀圖	grafik bar	막대 그래프	gráfica de barras	biểu đồ thanh
base (of an exponent)	គោលគុណ (នៃស្វ័យគុណ)	（指數的）底數	baz (de youn egspózant)	(지수의) 밑	base (de un exponente)	cơ số (của một số mũ)
base (of a polygon)	បាត (នៃពហុកោណ)	（多邊形的）底邊	baz (pour youn póligon)	(도형의) 밑변	base (de un polígono)	cạnh đáy (của một đa giác)
base (of a solid)	បាត (នៃរូបសូលីដ)	（立體的）底面	baz (pour youn solid)	(입방체의) 밑면	base (de un sólido)	mặt đáy (của một hình khối)
binary number system	ប្រព័ន្ធទ្វេភាគ	二進制	sistem nouméró binér	2진법	sistema binario de numeración	hệ thống số nhị phân (binary number system)

English	Cambodian	Cantonese	Haitian Creole	Korean	Spanish	Vietnamese
binomial	ទ្វេធា	二項式	binomyal	이항식	binomio	nhị thức
bisect	ពុះពីរ	平分	bisekt	이등분	bisecar	chia đôi
boundary line	បន្ទាត់កំណត់ដែន	界線	lin lizyé	경계선	línea de límite	đường ranh
box-and-whisker plot	តារាងប្រអប់	框線圖	grafik bouat-é-lin	상자-수염 그림	gráfica de mediana y rango	biểu đồ box-and-whisker
capacity	ចំណុះ	容量	kapasité	용량	capacidad	dung tích
center	ផ្ចិត	中心	sant	중심	centro	tâm
center of rotation	ផ្ចិតបង្វិល	旋轉中心	sant de rótasyon	회전의 중심	centro de rotación	tâm của vòng quay
centi-	សង់ទី-	厘	santi-	센티	centi-	bách phân-
central angle	មុំផ្ចិត	中心角	ang santral	중심각	ángulo central	góc trung tâm
circle	រង្វង់	圓	sérk	원	círculo	vòng tròn
circle graph	ក្រាហ្វ រង្វង់	圓形圖	grafik sérk	원 그래프	gráfica circular	biểu đồ hình tròn
circumference	បរិមាត្ររង្វង់	圓週	sérkonfèrans	원둘레	circunferencia	chu vi
circumscribed figure	រូបចារឹករង្វង់	外切圖	figour sérkonskrir	외접도형	figura circunscrita	hình ngoại tiếp
clockwise	ទិសស្របទ្រនិច នាឡិកា	順時針	direksyon	시계방향	en el sentido de las manecillas del reloj	chiều kim đồng hồ
clustering	កក្រមុំ	估算	groupman	집락	agrupación	đồng hóa
coefficient	មេគុណ	系數	kóèfisyant	계수	coeficiente	hệ số
combination	បន្សំ	組合	kounmbinasyon	조합	combinación	kết hợp
common denominator	ភាគបែងរួម	公分母	dénominateur konmun	공통분모	denominador común	mẫu số chung
common factor	កត្តារួម	公因數	fakteur konmun	공약수	factor común	thừa số chung
common multiple	ពហុគុណរួម	公倍數	moultip konmun	공배수	múltiplo común	bội số chung
Commutative Property of Addition	លក្ខណៈ:ផ្លាស់ប្តូរបូកបាន	加法交換律	Própriyété Egschanjif à Adisyon	덧셈의 교환 법칙	Propiedad conmutativa de la suma	Tính Chất Giao Hoán của Phép Cộng
Commutative Property of Multiplication	លក្ខណៈ:ផ្លាស់ប្តូរគុណបាន	乘法交換律	Própriyété Egschanjif à Moulitplikasyon	곱셈의 교환 법칙	Propiedad conmutativa de la multiplicación	Tính Chất Giao Hoán của Phép Nhân
compatible numbers	លេខសមស្រប	整合數	nouméro konmpatib	순서운 수	números compatibles	những số tương hợp
compensation	ការទូទាត់	補償	konmpansasyon	보정	compensación	bù trừ
complementary angles	មុំបំពេញ	餘角	ang konmplèmèntèr	여각	ángulos complementarios	những góc bù
composite number	លេខសមាសភាគ	合數	nouméro konmpózit	합성수	número compuesto	số phức hợp
compound event	ព្រឹត្តិការណ៍សមាសភាគ	複合事件	évanman kounmbiné	곱사건	suceso compuesto	sự kiện kép
compound interest	ការប្រាក់បូករួម	複利	interet	복리	interés compuesto	lãi kép
compound statement	ការអះអាងរួម	複合語句	deklarasyon kounmbiné	복합 명제	afirmación compuesto	lời nói kép
concave polygon	ពហុកោណផត	凹多邊形	póligon kónkav	오목다각형	polígono cóncavo	đa giác lõm

English	Cambodian	Cantonese	Haitian Creole	Korean	Spanish	Vietnamese
conditional probability	សេចក្ដីប្រូបាប តាម លក្ខខ័ណ្ឌ	條件概率	probabilitye kóndisyonal	조건부 확률	probabilidad condicional	xác xuất có điều kiện
cone	កោន ឬសាជី	圓錐體	kón	원뿔	cono	hình nón
congruent	សមភាព	全等	konfórmé	합동	congruente	đồng dạng
conic projection	ទំរង់បញ្ចាំងកោន	圓錐投影	prójeksyon kónik	원추 투영법	proyección cónica	phóng hình theo dạng hình nón
conjunction	សម្ព័ន្ធ	聯言判斷	konjónksyon	명제의 교집합	conjunción	sự liên kết
constant	ថេរ	常數	kónstan	상수	constante	hằng số
constant graph	ក្រាហ្វ ថេរ	常量圖	grafik kónstan	상수 그래프	gráfica de una constante	đồ thị bất biến
constant of proportionality	ថេរៈនៃលក្ខណៈសមាមាត្រ	比例常數	kónstan de próporsyonalityé	비례상수	constante de proporcionalidad	hằng số tỷ lệ
conversion factor	កត្តាបម្លែង	換算因子	fakteur kónvèrzyon	환산인수	fórmula de conversión	hệ số chuyển đổi
convex polygon	ពហុកោណកុម្ព័ន្ធ	凸多邊形	poligón kónveks	볼록다각형	polígono convexo	đa giác lồi
coordinates	និយាមា	坐標	kóordinat	좌표	coordenadas	những tọa độ
coordinate plane, coordinate system	តំរុយកាយ័ន្ត, ប្រព័ន្ធតំរុយកាយ័ន្ត	坐標平面，坐標系	plèn kóordinat, sistem kóordinat	좌표면, 좌표체계	plano de coordenadas, sistema de coordenadas	mặt phẳng tọa độ, hệ thống tọa độ
corresponding angles (for lines)	មុំដែលត្រូវគ្នា	（直線中的）同位角	ang kórèspondé (pour lin)	(선의) 동위각	ángulos correspondientes (de rectas)	những góc đồng vị (trên những đường thẳng)
corresponding angles (in similar figures)	មុំដែលត្រូវគ្នា	（相似圓形中的）同位角	ang kórèspondé (nan figour similar)	(비슷한 도형들)동위각	ángulos correspondientes (de figuras similares)	những góc đồng vị (trong những hình tương tự)
corresponding sides	ប្រវែងដែលត្រូវ	對應邊	bó kórèspondé	동위변	lados correspondientes	những cạnh đồng vị
cosine	កូស៊ីនុស	餘弦	kósinus	코싸인	coseno (cosine)	cô-sin
counterclockwise	ខ្វែងបញ្ច្រាស	逆時針	dirèksyon ópózé kom youn aygoui sou youn eur	시계 반대방향	en sentido contrario de las manecillas del reloj	ngược chiều kim đồng hồ
counterexample	នាទស្សន៍ឧទាហរណ៍	反例	kontra egzanmp	반증	contraejemplo	ví dụ phản bác
Counting Principle	គោលការណ៍រាប់ចាប់	計數法則	Prinsip Konté	개수의 원리	Principio de conteo	Nguyên Tắc Đếm
cross product	ផលគុណបន្ធ័ង	交叉乘積	prodoui kouazé	교차 곱	producto cruzado	tích số chéo
cube	គូប	立方體	koub	입방체	cubo	hình lập phương
cubed	គូបឬស៊ុប្ប៊ុយ័ស្រាណថ្លា	立方	koubé	3승	elevado al cubo	khối
cubic unit	ឯកតាគូប	立方單位	younit koubik	입방 단위	unidad cúbica	đơn vị khối
customary system of measurement	វិធីសាស្ដ្រវាស់វែងទម្លាប់	英制度量單位	sistem de mézirman nórmal	관습적 측정법	sistema usual de medidas	hệ thống đo lường thông dụng
cylinder	ស៊ីឡាំង	圓柱體	silind	원통	cilindro	hình trụ
cylindrical projection	ទំរង់បញ្ចាំងស៊ីឡាំង	柱面投影	projeksyon silindrikal	원통 투영법	proyección cilíndrica	phóng hình theo dạng hình trụ
decagon	ទសកោណ	十邊形	dekagon	10각형	decágono	hình thập giác

English	Cambodian	Cantonese	Haitian Creole	Korean	Spanish	Vietnamese
deci-	ដេស៊ី-	十分之一	desi-	데시-	deci-	đề xi-
decimal	លេខទសភាគ	小數	desimal	소수	decimal	số thập phân
decimal addition	បូកលេខទសភាគ	小數的加法	adisyon desimal	소수 덧셈	adición decimal	phép cộng số thập phân
decimal division	ចែកលេខទសភាគ	小數的除法	divizyon desimal	소수 나눗셈	división decimal	phép chia số thập phân
decimal multiplication	គុណលេខទសភាគ	小數的乘法	moultiplikasyon desimal	소수 곱셈	multiplicación decimal	phép nhân số thập phân
decimal subtraction	ដកលេខទសភាគ	小數的減法	desimal soustraksyon	소수 뺄셈	sustracción decimal	phép trừ số thập phân
decimal system	ប្រព័ន្ធទសភាគ	十進制	sistem desimal	10진법	sistema decimal	hệ thống thập phân
decreasing graph	ក្រាហ្វចុះ:	下降圖形	grafik diminyé	감소 그래프	gráfica decreciente	đồ thị giảm
deductive reasoning	អនុមានវិធាន	演繹推理	rézonman dédouktif	연역적 사고	deducción	lý luận suy diễn
degree (°)	ដឺក្រេ	度	dégré	도	grado	độ
degree	ដឺក្រេ	最高次幂	dégré	차수	grado	cấp
deka-	ដេកា-	十	deka-	데카	deka-	đề ka-
denominator	កាត់ចែក	分母	dénóminateur	분모	denominador	mẫu số
dependent events	ព្រឹត្តិការណ៍កាត់ផ្ដៃ	相關事件	évanman dépandan	종속 경우	sucesos dependientes	những sự kiện phụ thuộc
dependent variable	អថេរកាត់ផ្ដៃ	相關變量	varyab dépandan	종속변수	variable dependiente	biến số phụ thuộc
diagonal	អង្កត់ទ្រូង ឬ វិញ្ញាសាផ្ដៃ	對角線	diagónal	대각선	diagonal	đường chéo
diameter	វិជ្ជមាត្រ	直徑	diamet	지름	diámetro	đường kính
difference	ផលដក	差	diférans	차	diferencia	hiệu số
digit	លេខកង្ក	數字	dijit	수자	dígito	con số
dilation	ការពង្រីក	縮放	dilasyon	확대/축소	dilación	sự co giãn
direct variation	កាប្រែប្រួលក្រង់	正變分	varasyon direk	비례식	variación directa	sự biến thiên trực tiếp
disjunction	ឌីឌ្សុងសយុង	邏言判斷	disjonksyon	이점	disyunción	sự tách biệt
Distributive Property	លក្ខណៈបែងចែក	分配律	Própèrityé Distriboutif	분배 법칙	Propiedad distributiva	Tính Chất Phân Phối
dividend	តំណែងចែក	被除數	dividand	피제수/나뉨수	dividendo	số bị chia
divisible	ចែកជ្ជែក	可除盡的	divisib	나누어 떨어지는	divisible	chia chẵn
division	លេខចែក	除法	divisyon	나눗셈	división	phép chia
divisor	ចំនួនចែក	除數	diviseur	제수/나눗수	divisor	ước số
dodecagon	ខាងសកោណ	十二邊形	dódekagón	12각형	dodecágono	đa giác 12 cạnh
double bar graph	ក្រាហ្វ ទ្វេកន្លះ	雙柱狀圖	grafik bar doublè	2중 막대그래프	gráfica de doble barra	đồ thị thanh đôi
double line graph	ក្រាហ្វឆ្នូបទ្វេ	雙線圖	grafik lin doublè	2중 선그래프	gráfica de doble línea	đồ thị biểu diễn đôi
double stem-and-leaf diagram	ដ្យាក្រាម គំនិតព្រ័ក្ដ្រាប	雙莖雙葉圖表	bòk-é-fé doublè diagram	이중 줄기-잎도표	diagrama doble de tallo y hoja	biểu đồ thân-và-lá đôi
edge	ប្រម៉ុខនាង	邊	rebó	모서리	arista	cạnh
endpoint	ចំណុចចុង	端點	pouint bout	끝점	extremo	điểm cuối
equality	សមភាព	相等	égalité	상등	igualdad	sự cân bằng

viii

© Scott Foresman Addison Wesley 6-8

English	Cambodian	Cantonese	Haitian Creole	Korean	Spanish	Vietnamese
equally-likely outcomes	កម្មផលដែលប្រហែលគ្នា	同概率	probabilité de rézoult égal	동등확률들	resultados igualmente probables	những kết quả có khả năng bằng nhau
equal ratios	ផលធៀបស្មើ	等比	próporsyon égal	등비	razones iguales	tỷ số bằng nhau
equation	សមីការ	等式	ékouézyon	등식	ecuación	phương trình
equilateral triangle	ត្រីកោណ សមបាត្រ	等邊三角形	triang ekouilateral	등변 삼각형	triángulo equilátero	tam giác đều
equivalent equations	សមីការសមមូល	等價方程式	ékouézyon ékivalan	동치 등식	ecuaciones equivalentes	những phương trình tương đương
equivalent expressions	កន្សោមសមមូល	等價表達式	égspresyon ékivalan	동치식	expresiones equivalentes	những biểu thức tương đương
equivalent fractions	ប្រភាគសមមូល	等值分數	fraksyon ékivalan	동치 분수	fracciones equivalentes	những phân số tương đương
equivalent rates	អត្រាសមមូល	等比率	tó ékivalan	동치율	relaciones equivalentes	những tỷ lệ tương đương
equivalent ratios	ផលធៀបសមមូល	等比	próporsyon ékivalan	동치비율	razones equivalentes	những tỷ số tương đương
estimate	ប្រមាណ	估算值	évalyasyon	어림내기	estimación	ước tính
Euler's formula	រូបមន្ត Euler	歐拉公式	formoul Euler	올러의 공식	Fórmula de Euler	công thức Euler
evaluate	វាយតម្លៃ	賦值	évalyoué	수치 구하기	evaluar	đánh giá
even number	លេខគូ	偶數	nouméró pér	짝수	número par	số chẵn
event	ព្រឹត្តិការណ៍	事件	évanman	경우	suceso	sự kiện
expanded form	សណ្ឋាន:ពង្រាយ	擴展形式	fórm egspansé	확장식	notación multiplicativa	dạng triển khai
experiment	ការពិសោធន៍	試驗	egspèriman	실험	experimento	thử nghiệm
experimental probability	ឥប្បធាតា ដោយពិសោធន៍	試驗概率	próbabilité egspèrimantal	실험 확률	probabilidad experimental	xác xuất thử nghiệm
exponent	និទស្សន្ត	指數	egspózant	지수	exponente	số mũ
exponential function	អនុគមន៍និទស្សន្ត	指數函數	fonksyon egspózantsyal	지수 함수	función exponencial	hàm số mũ
exponential notation	កំណត់សញ្ញាទ្វេនិទស្សន្ត	指數記號	fonksyon egspózantsyal	지수 기수법	forma exponencial	ký hiệu số mũ
expression	កន្សោម	表達式	notasyon egspózantsyal	식	expresión	biểu thức
exterior angles	មុមក្រៅ	外角	ang egztèryeur	외각	ángulos externos	những góc ngoài
face	មុខ	面	figi	면	cara	mặt
factor	កត្តា	因數	fakteur	인수	factor	thừa số
factorial	កត្តា:	階乘	faktueuryal	계승	factorial	giai thừa
factor tree	កត្តាបំបែក	因數樹	pyé boua fakteur	인수 체계	árbol de factores	cây thừa số
fair game	ល្បែងឧត្តិធ៌ម	公正遊戲	jouèt ekitab	공정한 게임	juego justo	trò chơi công bình
flip	ផ្លិកប្រ:	反射	pyé	뒤집기	inversión	lật ngược lại
foot	ហ្វីត	呎	pyé	푸트	pie	bộ
formula	រូបមន្ត	公式	fórmoul	공식	fórmula	công thức

English	Cambodian	Cantonese	Haitian Creole	Korean	Spanish	Vietnamese
fractal	ប្រភាគ	自相似圖形	fraktal	fractal	fractal	mẫu thức tự giống
fraction	ប្រភាគ	分數	fraksyon	분수	fracción	phân số
fraction addition	បូកប្រភាគ	分數的加法	adisyon fraksyon	분수의 덧셈	adición de fracciones	phép cộng phân số
fraction division	ចែកប្រភាគ	分數的除法	divisyon fraksyon	분수의 나눗셈	división de fracciones	phép chia phân số
fraction multiplication	គុណប្រភាគ	分數的乘法	moultipikasyon fraksyon	분수의 곱셈	multiplicación de fracciones	phép nhân phân số
fraction subtraction	ដកប្រភាគ	分數的減法	soustraksyon fraksyon	분수의 뺄셈	sustracción de fracciones	phép trừ phân số
frequency	ប្រេកង់	頻率	frèkans	빈도	frecuencia	tần số
frequency chart or table	តារាងប្រេកង់	頻率表	grafik oubyin tab frèkans	빈도표	tabla de frecuencia	biểu đồ hay bảng tần số
front-end estimation	ការប្រមាណខ្ទង-ខ្ពស់	高位估計	evalyouasyon avant	선취 어림내기	estimación por los primeros dígitos	ước tính số đầu
function	អនុគមន៍	函數	fonksyon	함수	función	hàm số
Fundamental Theorem of Arithmetic	គោលបទគ្រឹះ នៃនព្វន្តគណិត	算術基本定理	Térèm Fondèmantal pour	연산의 기본이론	Teorema fundamental de la aritmética	Định Lý Căn Bản của Số Học
gallon	ហ្កាឡុង	加侖	galon	갈론	galón	ga lông
geometry	ធរណីមាត្រ	幾何學	jéómetrik	기하학	geometría	hình học
geometric probability	សេរីធរណី ធរណីមាត្រ	幾何概率	probabilité jéómetrik	기하학적 확률	probabilidad geométrica	xác xuất hình học
geometric sequence	លំដាប់ធរណីមាត្រ	幾何序列/等比序列	sékan jéómetrik	기하학적 수열	progresión geométrica	dãy số hình học
gram	ក្រាម	克	gram	그램	gramo	gam
graph	ក្រាហ្វ	圖表	grafik	그래프	gráfica	biểu đồ
greatest common factor (GCF)	កត្តារួមធំបំផុត	最大公約數	fakteur pi gro komen	최대공약수	máximo factor común	thừa số chung lớn nhất
hecto–	ហិកតូ	百–	hektó–	헥토	hecto–	héc tô–
height	កម្ពស់	高	tay	높이	altura	chiều cao
heptagon	សត្តកោណ	七邊形	èptagon	7각형	heptágono	hình thất giác
hexadecimal number system	ប្រព័ន្ធលេខ ឆៅទសភាគ	十六進制	sistem nouméró eksadèsimal	16진법	numeración hexadecimal	hệ thống số thập lục phân
hexagon	ឆកោណ	六邊形	eksagon	6각형	hexágono	hình lục giác
histogram	ជាលំដាប់ក្រាម	直方圖	istógram	도수 분포도	histograma	biểu đồ ngang
horizontal axis	អ័ក្សផ្ដេក	水平軸	aks orizontal	수평축	eje horizontal	trục hoành
hypotenuse	អ៊ីប៉ូតេនុស	斜邊	ipotenous	사변	hipotenusa	cạnh huyền
identity	ភាពដូចគ្នាពេញ	恆等	idantité	항등수	identidad	đồng nhất thức
if-then statement	ការនាង "ប្រសិនបើ....នោះ"	條件語句	deklarasyon si-alor	조건 –결과 명제	enunciado condicional	lời nói nếu-thì
improper fraction	ប្រភាគទីទៃគ្នា	假分數	fraksyon déplasé	가분수	fracción impropia	phân số không hợp cách

English	Cambodian	Cantonese	Haitian Creole	Korean	Spanish	Vietnamese
increasing graph	ក្រាភិចកើន	上升圖形	grafik ranjé	증가 그래프	gráfica creciente	đồ thị tăng
inch	អិញ	吋	pous	인치	pulgada	in
independent events	ព្រឹត្តិការណ៍មិនពាក់ព័ន្ធ	獨立事件	évanman indépandan	독립 경우	sucesos independientes	những sự kiện độc lập
independent variable	អថេរ មិនពាក់ព័ន្ធ	自變量	varyab indépandan	독립 변수	variable independiente	biến số độc lập
inductive reasoning	វិសេសសាងុខាន វិចារ	歸納推理	rézonman indouktif	귀납적 사고	razonamiento inductivo	lý luận quy nạp
inequality	វិសមភាព	不等式	inékalité	부등식	desigualdad	sự bất bình đẳng
inscribed figure	រូបទារិកក្នុង	內接圖形	figour inskribé	내접도형	figura inscrita	hình nội tiếp
integers	ចំនួនគត់	整數	antyé	정수	números enteros	những số nguyên
integer addition	បូកចំនួនគត់	整數的加法	adisyon antyé	정수의 덧셈	adición entera	cộng số nguyên
integer division	ចែកចំនួនគត់	整數的除法	divisyon antyé	정수의 나눗셈	división entera	chia số nguyên
integer multiplication	គុណចំនួនគត់	整數的乘法	moultipkasyon antyé	정수의 곱셈	multiplicación entera	nhân số nguyên
integer subtraction	ដកចំនួនគត់	整數的減法	soustraksyon antyé	정수의 뺄셈	sustracción entera	trừ số nguyên
interest	ប្រាក់ចុងការ	利息	interet	이자	interés	lãi
interior angles	មុមក្នុង	內角	ang intéryeur	내각	ángulos internos	những góc trong
intersect	ប្រសព្វមុម	相交	koupé	교차	intersecarse	giao nhau
interval	ចន្លោះ	區間	intèrval	간격	intervalo	khoảng cách
inverse operations	ប្រមាណវិធីឆ្លាស់	逆運算驗算	prosédour invérs	역	operaciones inversas	những phép toán nghịch đảo
inverse variation	បន្លាស់ប្តូរឆ្លាស់	逆變分	varasyon invérs	역변동	variación inversa	sự biến thiên nghịch đảo
irrational number	ចំនួនអសនិទាន	無理數	nouméró irasyonal	무리수	número irracional	số vô tỷ
isometric drawing	គំនូរសមមាត្រ	等距畫法	désin isómètrik	등거리법	perspectiva isométrica	vẽ không theo luật xa gần
isosceles triángle	ត្រីកោនសមបាត	等腰三角形	triang isóselis	이등변 삼각형	triángulo isósceles	tam giác cân
kilo-	គីឡូ-	千-	kiló-	킬로	kilo-	kí lô-
latitude	រយៈខ្សែស្រប	緯度	latitoud	위도	latitud	vĩ tuyến
least common denominator (LCD)	ភាគបែងតូចមួយតូចបំផុត	最小公分母	mouenn dénóminateur komen	최소 공분모	mínimo común denominador	mẫu số chung nhỏ nhất
least common multiple (LCM)	លេខផលគុណរួមតូចបំផុត	最小公倍數	mouenn moultip komen	최소 공배수	mínimo común múltiplo	bội số chung nhỏ nhất
leg	ជ្រុងអមម	直角邊	janm	빗변	cateto	cạnh
like denominators	ភាគបែងស្មើ	同分母	dénóminateur mem	공분모	igual denominador	những mẫu số giống nhau
like terms	អង្គស្មើ	同類項	tèrm mem	같은 항	términos similares	những số hạng giống nhau
line	បន្លាត់	直線	lin	선	recta	đường thẳng
line graph	ក្រាភិចខ្សែ	線條圖	grafik lin	선 그래프	gráfica lineal	đồ thị đường thẳng
line of symmetry	ខ្សែបន្លាត់ឆ្លុះ	對稱軸	lin de simètri	대칭선	eje de simetría	đường cắt đối xứng
line plot	បន្លាត់ជេដ	線陣	plan lin	선 도면	diagrama de puntos	biểu đồ đường thẳng
line segment	បន្លាត់អង្គត់	線段	segman lin	선분	segmento de recta	đoạn thẳng

English	Cambodian	Cantonese	Haitian Creole	Korean	Spanish	Vietnamese
line symmetry	បន្ទាត់ឆ្លុះ	線對稱	simètri lin	선 대칭	simetría axial	đường đối xứng
linear equation	សមីការលីនេអ៊ែរ	線性方程	ékouézyon linyar	1차 방정식	ecuación lineal	phương trình tuyến
linear function	អនុគមន៍លីនេអ៊ែរ	線性函數	fonksyon linyar	선형 함수	función lineal	hàm số tuyến
linear inequality	វិសមភាពលីនេអ៊ែរ	線性不等式	orinégalité linyar	1차 부등식	desigualdad lineal	bất đẳng thức tuyến
liter	លីត្រ	升	lit	리터	litro	lít
longitude	រយៈបណ្ដោយ	經度	lonjitoud	경도	longitud	kinh tuyến
lower quartile	ការ៉ូទីចត្វាគ	下四分位	pi ba kartyé	하위 4분위	cuartil inferior	phần tư thấp
lowest terms	សញ្ញាតូចបំផុត	最簡分數	tèrm pi ba	최소항	mínima expresión	những số hạng thấp nhất
mass	ម៉ាស់	質量	mas	질량	masa	khối lượng
mean	មធ្យមភាគ	平均	mouyen	평균	media	số bình vị
measurement error	ខុសឆ្គងក្នុងការវាស់	測量誤差	éreur mézirman	측정오차	error en la medición	sai số đo lường
measure of central tendency	ទំហំនៃទំនោរកណ្ដាល	集中趨勢度量	mézir pour tandans santral	중심 경향성 측정치	medida de tendencia central	đo lường theo xu hướng trung tâm
median	មេដ្យាន	中位數	midyan	중앙값	mediana	số giữa
mental math	គណិតក្នុងចិត្ត	心算	matèmatik mental	암산	cálculo mental	tính nhẩm
meter	ម៉ែត្រ	米	mèt	미터	metro	mét
metric system	ប្រព័ន្ធមេទ្រិក	公制/十進制/米制	sistem metrik	미터법	sistema métrico decimal	hệ thống mét
midpoint	ចំណុចកណ្ដាល	中點	mid pouint	중점	punto medio	điểm giữa
mile	ម៉ៃល៍	哩	mil	마일	milla	dặm
milli-	មីលី-	千分之一	mili-	밀리	mili-	mi li-
mixed number	ចំនួនចម្រុះ	帶分數	nouméró melanjé	대분수	número mixto	số hỗn hợp
mode	ម៉ូត	眾數	mod	최빈값	moda	số thường xảy ra
monomial	ឯកធា	單項式	monòmyal	단항식	monomio	đơn thức
multiple	ពហុគុណ	倍數	moultip	배수	múltiplo	bội số
multiplication	គុណ	乘法	moultiplikasyon	곱셈	multiplicación	phép nhân
multiplication property	លក្ខណៈគុណ	乘法法則	próprityé moultiplikasyon	곱셈의 성질	propiedad multiplicativa	tính chất của phép nhân
Multiplication Property of Equality	លក្ខណៈសមភាពនៃគុណ	乘法相等定理	Próprityé de Égalité Moultiplikasyon	상등 곱셈의 속성	Propiedad de multiplicativa de la igualdad	Tính Chất Bình Đẳng của Phép Nhân
multiplicative inverse	គុណច្រាសប្រាណ	倒數	moultiplikativ invèrs	곱셈의 역수	inverso multiplicativo	số nhân đảo ngược
mutually exclusive	ឝ្ដិតឯកឯងមិនព្រមជាមួយ	互斥事件	egskloussif moutouèlman	배반사건	mutuamente exclusivos	độc quyền hỗ tương
negative numbers	ចំនួនអវិជ្ជមាន	負數	nouméró negatif	음수	números negativos	những số âm
negative relationship	ទំនាក់ទំនងអវិជ្ជមាន	負相關	rélasyon negatif	반비례 관계	correlación negativa	sự liên hệ nghịch chiều
negative slope	ជម្រាលអវិជ្ជមាន	負斜率	pant negatif	기울기	pendiente negativa	độ dốc âm
negative square root	ប្ញសការេអវិជ្ជមាន	負平方根	rasin karé negatif	루트	raíz cuadrada negativa	căn bậc hai âm
net	ប្រ៉ិលេ	網格	filé	전개도	desarrollo de un sólido	mạng

English	Cambodian	Cantonese	Haitian Creole	Korean	Spanish	Vietnamese
nonagon		九邊形	nónagon	9각형	nonágono	hình cửu giác
nonlinear equation		非線性方程	ékouézyon linyar	비선형 방정식	ecuación no lineal	phương trình cong (phi tuyến)
nonlinear function		非線性函數	fonksyon nonlinyar	비선형 함수	función no lineal	hàm số cong (phi tuyến)
no relationship		無關聯	pa de rélasyon	관계 없음	sin relaciones	không có sự liên hệ
number line		數軸	lin nouméró	수직선	recta numérica	hàng số
number-word form		數字-文字形式	fórm nouméró-mo	수-문자 형식	forma de numérica-verbal	hình thức số-chữ
numeral		數字	noumérál	수자	numeral	chữ số
numerator		分子	noumérateur	분자	numerador	tử số
obtuse angle		鈍角	ang obtous	둔각	ángulo obtuso	góc tù
obtuse triangle		鈍角三角形	triang obtous	둔각 삼각형	triángulo obtusángulo	tam giác tù
octagon		八邊形	óktagon	8각형	octágono	hình bác giác
odd number		奇數	nouméró anmpér	홀수	número impar	số lẻ
odds		可能性	kót	가망성	probabilidades	tỷ số
operation		運算	prósédour	연산	operación	phép toán
opposite leg		對邊	janm an fas	마주보는 빗변	lado opuesto	cạnh đối
opposite numbers		相反數	nouméró an fas	반대자리 수	números opuestos	những số đối nghịch
order of operations		運算次序	sékans à prósédour	연산의 순서	orden de las operaciones	thứ tự của các phép toán
ordered pair		有序偶	pèr sékansé	좌표쌍	par ordenado	cặp số thứ tự
origin		原點	orijin	원점	origen	gốc
orthographic drawing		正投影視圖	désin ortografik	정사영 그림	dibujo ortogonal	phép vẽ trực giao
ounce		盎司	ons	온스	onza	lạng
outcome		結果	rézoult	결과	resultado	kết quả
outlier		舍棄值	nouméró déró	이상점	valor extremo	số ngoại hạng
parabola		拋物線	parabóla	포물선	parábola	ba ra bol
parallel		平行線	paralel	평행	paralelo	song song
parallelogram		平行四邊形	paralelógram	평행사변형	paralelogramo	hình bình hành
pentagon		五邊形	pentagon	5각형	pentágono	hình ngũ giác
percent		百分比	poursan	퍼센트	por ciento	phần trăm
percent change		百分比換算	poursan shanj	변화율	porcentaje de cambio	số phần trăm thay đổi
percent decrease		百分比降	poursan diminyé	감소율	disminución porcentual	phần trăm giảm
percent increase		百分比增	poursan ranjé	증가율	incremento porcentual	phần trăm tăng
perfect square		完全平方	karé parfet	완전제곱	cuadrado perfecto	số bình phương hoàn chỉnh
perimeter		週長	périmet	주변길이	perímetro	chu vi

English	Cambodian	Cantonese	Haitian Creole	Korean	Spanish	Vietnamese
permutation		排列	pérmoutasyon	순열	permutación	phép hoán vị
perpendicular		垂直	pérpandikoular	수직	perpendicular	đường trực giao
perpendicular bisector		中垂線	bisektris pérpandikoular	수직 이등분선	mediatriz	đường trung trực
pi (π)		圓週率	pi	파이	pi	pi
pictograph		象形圖表	piktógram	그림그래프	pictografía	biểu đồ hình
place value		位值	valèr plas	자리값	valor posicional	trị số vị trí
plane		平面	plèn	평면	plano	mặt phẳng
point symmetry		點對稱	pouint simètri	점대칭	simetría central	điểm đối xứng
polygon		多邊形	póligon	다각형	polígono	đa giác
polyhedron		多面體	póliyedron	다면체	poliedro	khối đa diện
polynomial		多項式	pólinómyal	다항식	polinomio	đa thức
population		總體	popoulasyon	모집단	población	dân số
positive numbers		正數	nouméró pózitif	양수	números positivos	số dương
positive relationship		正相關	rélasyon pozitif	정비례관계	correlación positiva	sự liên hệ thuận chiều
positive slope		正斜率	pant pozitif	기울기	pendiente positiva	độ dốc dương
pound		磅	pouad	파운드	libra	cân Anh
power		乘方	pouvoua	승	potencia	lũy thừa
precision		精度	présizyon	정도	precisión	sự chính xác
prime factor		素因數	fakteur prèmyé	소인수	factor primo	thừa số nguyên tố
prime factorization		因式分解	fakteurizasyon prèmyé	소인수분해	descomposición factorial	thừa số hóa nguyên tố
prime number		素數	nouméró prèmyé	소수	número primo	số nguyên tố
principal		本金	kapital	원금	principal	tiền vốn
principal square root		主平方根	rasin karé prinsipal	루트	raíz cuadrada principal	căn số bậc hai chính
prism		棱柱	prizm	프리즘	prisma	hình lăng trụ
probability		概率	próbabilité	확률	probabilidad	xác xuất
product		積	prodoui	곱	producto	tích số
proportion		比例式	próporsyon	비례	proporción	tỷ lệ thức
protractor		量角器	raporteur	각도기	transportador	thước đo góc
pyramid		棱錐	piramid	피라미드	pirámide	hình tháp
Pythagorean Theorem		畢達哥拉斯定理	Térom Pythagorean	피타고라스의 정리	Teorema de Pitágoras	Định Lý Pytago
quadrants		象限	kadrant	4분면	cuadrantes	những góc phần tư
quadratic equation		二次方程	ékouézyon kadratik	2차 방정식	ecuación cuadrática	phương trình bậc hai
quadratic function		二次函數	fonksyon kadratik	2차 함수	función cuadrática	hàm số bậc hai
quadrilateral		四邊形	kadrilateral	사변형	cuadrilátero	hình tứ giác
quart		夸脫	kart	쿼트	cuarto	quạt

English	Cambodian	Cantonese	Haitian Creole	Korean	Spanish	Vietnamese
quartile		四分位	kartyé	4분위	cuartil	phần tư
quotient		商	kuósyent	몫	cociente	thương số
radical sign		根號	sin radikal	근호	radical	dấu căn
radius		半徑	radyous	반지름	radio	bán kính
random sample		隨機樣本	éshantiyon aza	무작위 견본	muestra aleatoria	mẫu ngẫu nhiên
range		區域	póté	범위	rango	khoảng biến thiên
rate		比率	tó	율	relación	tỷ suất
ratio		比	próporsyon	비율	razón	tỷ số
rational number		有理數	nouméró rasyonel	유리수	número racional	số hữu tỷ
ray		射線	douat de fazó	반직선	rayo	nửa đường thẳng
real numbers		實數	nouméró aktoual	실수	números reales	những số thực
reciprocals		倒數	résiprók	역수	recíprocos	những số đảo
rectangle		矩形	rektang	직사각형	rectángulo	hình chữ nhật
reflection		反射	réfleksyon	반향	reflexión	phản chiếu
regular polygon		正多邊形	póligon regoulèr	정다각형	polígono regular	đa giác đều
relative position		相對位置	pózisyon relatif	상대적 위치	posición relativa	vị trí tương đối
remainder		餘數	rest	나머지	residuo	số dư
repeating decimal		循環小數	desimal rèpété	순환소수	decimal periódico	số thập phân lặp lại với số lẻ
rhombus		菱形	ronmbus	마름모꼴	rombo	hình thoi
right angle		直角	ang douat	직각	ángulo recto	góc vuông
right triangle		直角三角形	triang douat	직각삼각형	triángulo rectángulo	tam giác vuông
rise		矢高	óteur	y의 변화량	variación vertical	sự tăng lên
rotation		旋轉	rótasyon	회전	rotación	quay
rotational symmetry		旋轉對稱	simètri rótasyonal	회전대칭	simetría rotacional	đối xứng quay
rounding		四舍五入	arondi	반올림/반내림	redondeo	quy tròn
run		矢長	trajet	x의 변화량	variación horizontal	sự tiến tới
sample		樣本	anshantiyon	표본	muestreo	mẫu
sample space		樣本空間	éspas anshantiyon	표본공간	espacio muestral	mẫu cách khoảng
scale (graphical)		(圖形的) 圖尺/標尺	èshel (grafikal)	(그래프의) 눈금	escala (gráfica)	chia độ (trong đồ thị)
scale (in scale drawings)		(按比例繪圖中的) 圖尺/標尺	èshel (nan désin èshel)	(비례도의) 축척	escala (en dibujos a escala)	tỷ lệ vẽ (trong việc vẽ theo tỷ lệ)
scale drawing		比例圖形	désin à èshel	비례도	dibujo a escala	vẽ theo tỷ lệ
scale factor		比例因子	fakteur èshel	척도	factor de escala	thừa số tỷ lệ
scalene triangle		不規則三角形	triang skalèn	부등변 삼각형	triángulo escaleno	tam giác lệnh

English	Cambodian	Cantonese	Haitian Creole	Korean	Spanish	Vietnamese
scatterplot	ប្រកឹចោតករ	散佈圖	plan gayé	점그래프	diagrama de dispersión	biểu đồ rải rác
scientific notation	កំណត់ត្រីវិទ្យាសាស្ត្រ	科學記數法	nótasyon siantifik	과학적 표기방법	notación científica	ký hiệu khoa học
sector	ចម្រៀកកង្វិល់	扇形	sekteur	부채꼴	sector circular	hình quạt
segment	អង្គត់	段	segman	선분	segmento	đoạn
segment bisector	អង្គត់ចែកពាក់កណ្តាល	線段平分線	bisektris segman	선분의 이등분선	bisectriz del segmento	đường trung đoạn
sequence	បំដាប់	序列	sékans	수열	progresión	dãy số
side	ប្រវែងជ្រុង	邊	bó	변	lado	cạnh
Side-Angle-Angle (SAA)	ជ្រុង-មុម-មុម	邊角角	Bó-Ang-Ang	두 각과 끼인 한 변	Lado-ángulo-ángulo	Cạnh-Góc-Góc
Side-Angle-Side (SAS)	ជ្រុង-មុម-ជ្រុង	邊角邊	Bó-Ang-Bó	세 변	Lado-ángulo-lado	Cạnh-Góc-Cạnh
Side-Side-Side (SSS)	ជ្រុង-ជ្រុង-ជ្រុង	邊邊邊	Bó-Bó-Bó	세 변	Lado-lado-lado	Cạnh-Cạnh-Cạnh
significant digits	តួលេខចំាបាច់	有效數字	shif signifikan	주요 자리수	dígitos significativos	những con số có ý nghĩa
similar	ប្រហាក់ប្រហែល (សាមញ្ញ)	相似	similar	닮은꼴	similar	tương tự
similarity ratio	សមាមាត្រដោយប្រៀប	相似比	próporsyon similar	닮은 비율	relación de similaridad	tỷ lệ tương tự
simple interest	ប្រាក់ការធម្មតា	單利	interet sanmp	단순이자	interés simple	lãi đơn
simplified	សម្រួបបង្រួបហើយ	最簡多項式	sanmplifiyé a	정리된 식	simplificado	đã đơn giản hoá
simplify	សម្រួប	化簡	sanmplifiyé	정리	simplificar	đơn giản hoá
simulation	ទង្វើក្លែង	模擬	simoulasyon	시뮬레이션	simulación	giả cách
sine	ស៊ីនុស	正弦	sinus	싸인	seno	sin
slant height	អោប់ទ្រេត	斜高	tay shiré	경사면의 높이	altura oblicua	chiều cao nghiêng
slide	បន្លាស	平移	bais	미끄러짐	trasladar	trượt
slope	ជម្រាលជ្រុង	斜率	inklinasyon	기울기	pendiente	độ nghiêng
solid	សូលីត	立體	solid	입방체	sólido	khối
solutions of an equation or inequality	ចម្លើយសង្ការ ឫ វិសមការ	等式或不等式的解	sólousyon yo pour youn ékouézyon ou inégalité	등식 혹은 부등식의 해법	soluciones de una ecuación o desigualdad	những lời giải của một phương trình hay bất đẳng thức
solution of a system	ចម្លើយប្រព័ន្ធ	方程組的解	soulousyon you pour youn sistem	공식의 해	solución de un sistema	lời giải của một hệ thống
solve	ដោះស្រាយ	求解	rézolvé	풀기	resolver	giải
sphere	ស្វ៊ែរ	球面	sfér	구	esfera	khối cầu
square	កាេ៉	正方形	karé	정사각형	cuadrado	hình vuông
squared	ការេស្វ៊ែររណៈទី២	平方	karé	제곱	elevado al cuadrado	bình phương
square centimeter	សង់ទីម៉ែត្រការេ	平方厘米	santimet karé	평방센티미터	centímetro cuadrado	xen ti mét vuông
square inch	អ៊ិញការេ	平方吋	pous karé	평방인치	pulgada cuadrada	in vuông
square root	ឫសការេ	平方根	rasin karé	평방근	raíz cuadrada	căn số bậc hai

English	Cambodian	Cantonese	Haitian Creole	Korean	Spanish	Vietnamese
standard form		標準型	fòrm nórmal	표준 양식	forma usual	hình thức tiêu chuẩn
stem-and-leaf diagram		莖-葉圖表	bòk-é-fé diagram	줄기-잎 도표	diagrama de tallo y hojas	đồ hình thân-và-lá
step function		階梯函數	fonksyon mash	계단식 함수	función por partes	hàm số thang bậc
straight angle		直線角	ang toudouat	평각	ángulo llano	góc bẹt
substitute		代換	ranmplasé	대입	sustituir	thế trị
subtraction		減法	soustraksyon	뺄셈	la resta	trừ
sum		和	tótal	합	suma	tổng số
supplementary angles		補角	ang souplimantèr	보각	ángulos suplementarios	những góc phụ
surface area (SA)		表面積	arya anlè	표면 면적	área del superficie	diện tích bề mặt
survey		調查	étoud	설문조사	encuesta	cuộc thăm dò
symmetry		對稱	simètri	대칭	simetría	đối xứng
system of linear equations		線性方程組	sistem ékouézyon linyar	1차 방정식 제계	sistema de ecuaciones lineales	hệ thống của những phương trình tuyến
T-table		T形表	tab-T	T-도표	tabla de valores	bảng-T
tally		計數	konmpt	빗줄 눈금	conteo	kiểm đếm
tally marks		計數符號	mark konmpt	빗줄 표시	marcas de conteo	dấu đếm
tangent line		切線	lin tanjant	접선	la tangente	đường tiếp tuyến
tangent ratio		正切	próporsyon*tanjant	탄젠트 비율	la tangente	tỷ số tan
term		項	tèrm	항	término	số hạng
terminating decimal		有限小數	desimal tèrminé	유한소수	decimal finito	số thập phân chấm dứt
tessellation		棋盤圖形	an mózéyik	모자이크식	teselado	sự lát hoa
theoretical probability		理論概率	próbabilité téyoretik	이론상 확률	probabilidad teórica	xác xuất lý thuyết
transformation		平移	transfórmasyon	변형	transformación	phép biến đổi
translation		平移	tradouksyon	이동	traslación	sự tịnh tiến
transversal		橫穿	transvèrsal	횡단선	transversal	đường cắt chéo
trapezoid		梯形	trapèzoidal	사다리꼴	trapecio	hình thang
tree diagram		樹狀圖表	diagram pyé boua	수형도	diagrama de árbol	biểu đồ cây
trend		趨勢	tandans	경향	tendencia	xu hướng
trend line		相關曲線	lin tandans	경향선	la tendencia	đường hướng
trial		試	test	시도	de prueba	thử
triangle		三角形	triang	삼각형	triángulo	hình tam giác
trigonometric ratios		三角函數	próporsyon trigónométrik	삼각법비율	razones trigonométricas	những tỷ số lượng giác
trinomial		三項式	trinómyal	3항식	trinomio	tam thức
turn		轉動	tourné	돌기	giro	xoay
unfair game		不公平游戲	jouet pa ékitab	불공평한 게임	juego no limpio	trò chơi bất công

English	Cambodian	Cantonese	Haitian Creole	Korean	Spanish	Vietnamese
unit price	ឯកតាតម្លៃ	單價	pri younit	단가	precio unitario	giá đơn vị
unit	ឯកតា	單位	younit	단위	unidad	đơn vị
unit fraction	ឯកតាប្រភាគ	單分數	fraksyon younit	단위분수	fracción integrante	phân số đơn vị
unit rate	ឯកតានល្បឿន	單位比率	tó younit	단위율	razón unitaria	tỷ lệ đơn vị
unlike denominators	តាវ៉ាង់ម៌ីសភ្នៈ	異分母	dénóminateur pa mem	서로다른 분모	distinto denominador	những mẫu số khác nhau
upper quartile	ការធ្វើផល	上四分位	kartyé pi ró	상위 4분위	cuartil superior	phần tư cao
variable	អថេរ	變數	varyab	변수	variable	biến số
Venn diagram	គ្រោងក្រាមវេន	馮氏圖圖表	Diagram Venn	벤다이어그램	diagrama de Venn	biểu đồ Venn
vertex	កំពូល	頂點	vèrteks	꼭지점	vértice	đỉnh
vertical angles	មុំបញ្ឈរ	對頂角	ang vèrtikal	마주보는 각	ángulos opuerstos por el vértice	những góc đối đỉnh
vertical axis	អ័ក្សបញ្ឈរ	立軸	aks vèrtikal	수직 축	eje vertical	trục tung
volume	មាឌ (ម៉ាឌ)	體積	vólounm	부피	volumen	thể tích
weight	ទម្ងន់	重力	poua	중량	peso	trọng lượng
whole number	លេខពេញ	整數	nouméró antyé	0과 자연수	número entero positivo	số nguyên
word form	ប្រើអក្សរ	文字形式	fórm mó	문자형식	forma verbal	dạng chữ
x-axis	អ័ក្ស-x	x 軸	aks-x	x 축	eje de las x	trục-x
x-coordinate	ប្រ៉ង់កូអរដោនេ-x	x 坐標	kóordinat-x	x 좌표	la abscisa	tọa độ-x
x-intercept	ចំណុចប្រសព្វ-x	x 截距	intérsepsyon-x	x 축 교차점	punto de intersección de x	điểm chấn-x
y-axis	អ័ក្ស-y	y 軸	aks-y	y 축	eje de las y	trục-y
y-coordinate	ប្រ៉ង់កូអរដោនេ-y	y 坐標	kóordinat-y	y 좌표	ordenada	tọa độ-y
y-intercept	ចំណុចប្រសព្វ-y	y 截距	intérsepsyon-y	y 축 교차점	punto de intersección de y	điểm chấn-y
yard	ម៉ាត	碼	yad	야드	yarda	thước Anh
zero pair	គូសូន្យ	相反數對	pér zéró	0을 이루는 쌍	par cero	cặp số triệt tiêu
Zero Property of Addition	បណ្តោះ៖តម៌ិសោនយ៉ូក	和爲零的加法定律	Própriyété pour Adisyon Zéró	덧셈의 0의 법칙	Propiedad cero de la suma	Tính Chất Triệt Tiêu của Phép Cộng

6-8

TABLE OF GLOSSARY TERMS

English	Hmong	Pilipino (Tagalog)	Mandarin
absolute position	qhov chaw tseeb ntsiab	tiyak na posisyon	绝对位置
absolute value	tus nqi tu nrho	tiyak na halaga	绝对值
acute angle	ntsais kaum ti	anggulong agudo	锐角
acute triangle	lub duab peb ceg ti	tatsulok na agudo	锐角三角形
addend	tus los ntxiv	addend	加数
addition	kev sib txiv	pagdaragdag	加法
Addition Property of Equality	Yam Ntxwv kev Tso Ntxiv kom Sib Npaug	Katangiang Pagdaragdag ng Pagkakatumbas	方程式的加法性质
additive inverse	tus los ntxiv tig rov	kabaligtaran ng pagdaragdag	加法逆元
adjacent leg	txoj ces nyob sib ze	katabing binti	直角边
algebra	algebra	alhebra	代数
algebraic expression	kev sau leb raws algebraic	pagpapahayag sa alhebra	代数式
alternate angles	ntsais kaum hloov tau	mga halinhinang anggulo	错角
angle	ntsais kaum	anggulo	角
angle bisector	txoj kab phua ntshais kaum	anggulong humahati	角平分线
angle of rotation	ntsais kaum kiv tig	anggulo ng pag-ikot	旋转角
Angle-Side-Angle (ASA)	Ntsais kaum-Sab-Ntsais kaum	Anggulo-Panig-Anggulo	角边角
area	npoo av	lawak	面积
arithmetic sequence	leb sib raws	aritmetikang pagkakasunod-sunod	等差数列
arrangement	kev teeb tsa	pagsasaayos	排列
Associative Property of Addition	Yam Ntxwv Raws ntawm kev Ua Leb Sib ntxiv	Pagsama-samang Katangian ng Pagdaragdag	加法结合律
Associative Property of Multiplication	Yam Ntxwv Raws ntawm kev Ua leb npaug	Pagsama-samang Katangian ng Multiplikasyon	乘法的结合律
average	pes nrab	karaniwan	平均数
axes	cov kab sib lig	axes	轴
bar graph	daim graph ua ib tug	talaguhitang may baras	条形图
base (of an exponent)	hauv paus pib (ntawm ib tug exponent)	base (ng isang exponent)	（指数的）底数
base (of a polygon)	hauv paus pib (ntawm ib lub duab ces kaum)	base (ng isang polygon)	（多边形的）底边
base (of a solid)	hauv paus pib (ntawm ib yam khoom tawv)	base (ng isang solid)	（立体的）地面
binary number system	kabke siv leb lav ob pib qab	binary na sistema ng bilang	二进制
binomial	muaj ob lub npe	binomial	二项式
bisect	ua ob tog	hatiin sa gitna	平分
boundary line	txoj kab npoo	linyang hanggahan	分界线

xix

English	Hmong	Pilipino (Tagalog)	Mandarin
box-and-whisker plot	box-and-whisker plot	box-and-whisker plot	盒须图
capacity	ntim tau ntau tsawg	kapasidad	容量
center	teev plawv	sentro, gitna	球心
center of rotation	nrab plawv kiv tig	sentro o gitna ng pag-ikot	旋转中心
centi-	centi-	senti-	厘
central angle	ntsais kaum plawv	panggitnang anggulo	圆心角
circle	voj voog	bilog	圆
circle graph	txoj kab graph voj voog	talaguhitang bilog	圆形图
circumference	txoj kab ncig ntug voj voog	sirkumperensiya	圆周
circumscribed figure	lub duab sib qhwv	katawang nakapaikot	外切图形
clockwise	mus raws li koob moos khiav	pakanan	顺时针
clustering	kev tso yam sib xws nyob ua ke	pagkumpul-kumpol	归类
coefficient	tus leb siv los npuab	katuwang	系数
combination	kev koom ua ke	kombinasyon	组合
common denominator	tus leb zoo ib yam hauv qab	panlahat na panghatimbilang	公分母
common factor	tus factor sib koom	panlahat na factor	公因数
common multiple	tus leb koom ua npaug	panlahat na multiple	公倍数
Commutative Property of Addition	Tus Yam Ntxwv kev muab Sib ntxiv	Pagpalit-palit na Katangian ng Pagdaragdag	加法交换律
Commutative Property of Multiplication	Yam Ntxwv kev Ua leb Tshooj Npaug	Pagpalit-palit na Katangian ng Multiplikasyon	乘法交换律
compatible numbers	cov leb nyob tau ua ke	mga magkabagay na bilang	相配的数
compensation	kev them rau	pagpupunan	补偿法
complementary angles	ntsais kaum sib txhawb	mga magkakabagay na anggulo	互余角
composite number	leb muaj tus tshooj	composite na bilang	合数
compound event	txheej xwm sib tshooj	pinagsama-samang pangyayari	复合事件
compound interest	paj sib tshooj	pinagsama-samang interes	复利
compound statement	zaj lus tshooj	pinagsama-samang pahayag	复合语句
concave polygon	lub duab ces kaum	malukong na polygon	凹多边形
conditional probability	kev tej zaum yuav tshim sim tau	may-pasubaling probabilidad	条件概率
cone	duab ua yias yeeb	kono	圆锥
congruent	sib xws	magkatumbas	全等
conic projection	tsom ua duab yias yeeb	conic projection	圆锥投影
conjunction	lus txuas	pagkakasabay	合取词

English	Hmong	Pilipino (Tagalog)	Mandarin
constant	qhov tsis hloov pauv	palagian	常数
constant graph	txoj kab graph tsis hloov	palagiang talaguhitan	常数图
constant of proportionality	qhov tsis hloov pauv yam los sib piv	palagian ng proporsiyonalidad	比例常数
conversion factor	tus leb siv cia ntxeev	paktor ng pagpapalit	换算因子
convex polygon	duab ces kaum muaj kab lo	maumbok na polygon	凸多边形
coordinates	cov kab los sib txiav	mga coordinate	坐标
coordinate plane, coordinate system	daim npoo cov kab sib txiav, ntsauv kab sib txiav	coordinate plane, coordinate system	坐标平面、坐标系
corresponding angles (for lines)	cov ntsais kaum sib xws (rau cov kab)	mga magkatugong na anggulo (para sa mga linya)	同位角 (对于多条线来说)
corresponding angles (in similar figures)	cov ntsais kaum sib xws (nyob rau cov duab yuav luag zoo ib yam)	mga magkatugong na anggulo (sa mga magkatulad na pigura)	对应角 (在相似图形中)
corresponding sides	cov sab sib xws	mga magkatugong na panig	对应边
cosine	cosine	cosine	余弦
counterclockwise	mus raws sab rov qab tus koob moos	pasaliwa	逆时针
counterexample	piv txwv ntaus rov qab	halimbawang panlaban	反例
Counting Principle	Tus Kab ke Suav	Prinsipyo ng Pagbilang	计数原理
cross product	yam tau txais sib tig	kinalabasang resulta ng pagmultiplika	交叉乘积
cube	lub duab rau fab	cube	立方体
cubed	peb tshooj	cubed	三次方
cubic unit	ntsuas txog yam nruab nrog	cubic unit	立方单位
customary system of measurement	yam kev ntsuas raws li yav thaud	kinaugaliang sistema ng pagsusukat	常用测量系统
cylinder	lub duab ua tog raj	silindro	圆柱体
cylindrical projection	kev tsom duab ua voj voog	cylindrical projection	圆柱投影
decagon	duab muaj kaum ces	dekagon	十边形
deci-	deci-	desi-	十分之一
decimal	lub teev quas	decimal	小数
decimal addition	kev ntxiv rau tom qab teev quas	decimal addition	小数加法
decimal division	kev faib leb muaj teev quas	decimal division	小数除法
decimal multiplication	kev tso npaug ntxiv	decimal multiplication	小数乘法
decimal subtraction	kev rho tawm tom qab teev quas	decimal subtraction	小数减法
decimal system	kev sau leb tom qab teev quas	decimal na sistema	十进制
decreasing graph	txoj kab qhia nqis zuj zus	talaguhitang lumiliit	递减图

English	Hmong	Pilipino (Tagalog)	Mandarin
deductive reasoning	kev muab tswv yim los ntawm lwm qhov	pangangatwirang may-batayan	演绎推理
degree (°)	teev cim siab qis (°)	grado (°)	度(°)
degree	teev cim siab qis	antas	最高次幂
deka-	deka-	deka-	十
denominator	tus leb nyob sab hauv leb faib	panghatimbilang	分母
dependent events	xwm txheej sib rub	mga nababatay ng pangyayari	相依事件
dependent variable	tus hloov pauv sib rub	nababatay na variable	因变量
diagonal	txoj kab hla kaum	diyagonal	对角线
diameter	txoj kab hla plawv voj voog	diyametro	直径
difference	qhov sib txawv	pagkakaiba	差
digit	cov zauv	tambilang	阿拉伯数字
dilation	kev txav loj me	pagluwang	伸缩
direct variation	kev txawv txav raws ncaj	tuwirang pagkakaiba	正变分
disjunction	kev xaiv ib qho	disjunction	析取
Distributive Property	Yam ntxwv nthuav tawm	Katangian ng Pamamahagi	分配律
dividend	tus cia faib	ang hahatiin	被除数
divisible	faib tu tau	mahahati	整除
division	kev faib	paghahati	除法
divisor	tus faib	ang panghati	除数
dodecagon	duab kaum ob ces	dodecagon	十二边形
double bar graph	daim graph qhia ob tshooj	talaguhitang may dobleng baras	双条图
double line graph	daim graph ob txog kab	talaguhitang may dobleng linya	双线图
double stem-and-leaf diagram	daim diagram ob tshooj ceg thiab nplooj	dobleng dayagram na may sanga't dahon	双茎叶图
edge	npoo	gilid	边
endpoint	tw xaus	dulo	端点
equality	kev sib npaug	pagkakatumbas	等式
equally-likely outcomes	qhov yam li yuav muaj tawm sib npaug	mga kinalalabasang pantay-pantay ang pagiging malamáng na mangyari	等可能的结果
equal ratios	cov ratios sib npaug	mga pantay-pantay na pagkakaugnay	等比
equation	tus sau ob sab sib npaug	equation	等式
equilateral triangle	duab peb ceg muaj sab sib npaug	equilateral triangle	等边三角形
equivalent equations	cov sau ob sab sib npaug sib xws	mga magkatumbas na equation	等价方程
equivalent expressions	zaj sau sib xws	mga magkatumbas na pagpapahayag	等价表达式

English	Hmong	Pilipino (Tagalog)	Mandarin
equivalent fractions	fractions sib xws	mga magkatumbas ng hatimbilang	相等的分数
equivalent rates	cov rates sib xws	mga magkatumbas na halaga	等同速率
equivalent ratios	cov ratios sib xws	mga magkatumbas na pagkakaugnay	等比率
estimate	kev kwv yees	pagtantiya	估计
Euler's formula	Euler's formula	pormula ni Euler	欧拉方程
evaluate	ntaus nqi	suriin	求值
even number	leb khub	bilang na tukol	偶数
event	xwm txheej	pangyayari	事件
expanded form	kev nthuav dav	pinalalawak na anyô	展开式
experiment	kev sim paub	eksperimento	试验
experimental probability	kev sim paub txog qhov tuaj yeem tshwm sim tau	pang-eksperimentong probabilidad	试验概率
exponent	exponent	exponent	指数
exponential function	exponential function	exponential function	指数函数
exponential notation	tus sau cim exponential	exponential notation	指数计数法
expression	kev sau expression	pagpapahayag	表达式
exterior angles	cov ntsais kaum sab nraud	mga angulong panlabas	外角
face	phab	mukha	面
factor	factor	paktor	因数
factorial	factorial	factorial	阶乘
factor tree	ceg ncau factor	puno ng paktor	因数树图
fair game	kev sib tw ncaj nrab	makatarungang laro	公平游戏
flip	pov	pitikin	翻转
foot	foot	talampakan	英尺
formula	formula	pormula	公式
fractal	fractal	fractal	分形体
fraction	ib qho me	hatimbilang	分数
fraction addition	kev muab qhov me los sib ntxiv	pagdaragdag ng hatimbilang	分数加法
fraction division	kev muab qho me sib faib	paghahati ng hatimbilang	分数除法
fraction multiplication	kev muab qhov me ua tshooj	multiplikasyon ng hatimbilang	分数乘法
fraction subtraction	kev muab qhov me rho tawm	pagbabawas ng hatimbilang	分数减法
frequency	kev ntxug	kadalasan	频率
frequency chart or table	daim chart los yog table kev ntxug	talangguhit ng kadalasan o talaan ng kadalasan	频率图或频率表

English	Hmong	Pilipino (Tagalog)	Mandarin
front-end estimation	kev kwm yees tom hauv ntej-tom qab	pagtantiya ng nasa harapang dulo	前端估计
function	function	function	函数
Fundamental Theorem of Arithmetic	tus Theorem	Saligang Teyoriya ng Aritmetika	算术基础理论
gallon	gallon	galon	加仑
geometry	geometry	heometriya	几何
geometric probability	kev tuaj yeem tshwm sim geometric	geometric probability	几何概率
geometric sequence	kev sib txuas geometric	geometric sequence	等比数列
gram	gram	gramo	克
graph	graph	talaguhitan	图表
greatest common factor (GCF)	greatest common factor	pinakamalaking sangkap na panlahat	最大公因数
hecto-	hecto	hekto-	百
height	ncua siab	taas	高
heptagon	heptagon	pituhang-gilid	七边形
hexadecimal number system	hexadecimal number system	heksadesimal na sistema ng bilang	十六进制
hexagon	hexagon	animang-gilid	六边形
histogram	histogram	histogram	柱形图
horizontal axis	txoj kab tav toj	pahalang na aksis	水平轴
hypotenuse	hypotenuse	hypotenuse	斜边
identity	kev qhia	pagkakakilanlan	单位元素
if-then statement	zaj lus hais yog tias-thaum ntawd	pahayag na kung-samakatwid	如果–那么语句
improper fraction	leb fraction tsis yog	hindi nararapat na hatimbilang	假分数
increasing graph	daim graph nce zuj zus	tumataas na talaguhitan	递增图
inch	inch	pulgada	英寸
independent events	xwm txheej ywj siab	mga nagsasariling pangyayari	独立事件
independent variable	tus hloov pauv ywj siab	nagsasariling variable	自变量
inductive reasoning	kev muab tswv yim	pangangatwirang batay sa partikular na katotohanan	归纳推理
inequality	kev tsis koob pheej	di-pagkakatumbas	不等式
inscribed figure	lub duab pw sab hauv ib lub	iniukit na pigura	内接图形
integers	integers	mga numerong buo	整数
integer addition	kev ntxiv integer	pagdaragdag ng numerong buo	整数加法
integer division	kev ntxiv integer	paghahati ng numerong buo	整数除法

English	Hmong	Pilipino (Tagalog)	Mandarin
integer multiplication	kev tshooj npaug integer	multiplikasyon ng numerong buo	整数乘法
integer subtraction	kev rho tawm integer	pagbabawas ng numerong buo	整数减法
interest	paj	tubo	利息
interior angles	ntsais kaum sab hauv	mga anggulong panloob	内角
intersect	kab txiav koom	bumagtas	相交
interval	kem sib luag	pagitan	同隔
inverse operations	kev ua leb rov qab	mga operasyong pabaligtad	逆运算
inverse variation	kev hloov rov	pabaligtad na pag-iiba-iba	逆变分
irrational number	leb 'tsis yog tiag	di-napangangatwirang bilang	无理数
isometric drawing	kev kos duab isometric	isometric drawing	等距画法
isosceles triangle	duab peb ceg sab sib nte	triyanggulong isosiles	等腰三角形
kilo-	kilo-	kilo-	千
latitude	kab ib ntxaig	latitude	纬度
least common denominator (LCD)	least common denominator	pinakamaliit na panghatimbilang na panlahat	最小公分母
least common multiple (LCM)	least common multiple	pinakamaliit na multiple na panlahat	最小公倍数
leg	ces	binti	直角边
like denominators	leb denominators sib xws	mga katulad na panghatimbilang	同分母
like terms	tus leb sib xws	mga katulad na termino	同类项
line	txoj kab	linya	线
line graph	graph kab	talaguhitang linya	线形图
line of symmetry	txoj kab sib xws	linya ng simetriya	对称线
line plot	kab nraj	line plot	线图
line segment	ib ntu ntawm txoj kab	bahagi ng linya	线段
line symmetry	sib xws raws txoj kab	simetriya sa linya	线对称
linear equation	equation ua kab	linear equation	线性方程
linear function	function ua kab	linear function	线性函数
linear inequality	kev tsis koob pheej ua kab	di-pagkakatumbas-tumbas ng guhit	线性不等式
liter	liter	litro	升
longitude	txoj kab nqi raws lub ntiaj teb	longitude	经度
lower quartile	ib feem plaub ncua nqis	mas mababang quartile	下四分位数
lowest terms	tus leb qis tshaj plaws	mga pinakamababang termino	最低项
mass	ntau tsawg	mass	质量

English	Hmong	Pilipino (Tagalog)	Mandarin
mean	qhov nrab	mean	平均值
measurement error	kev ntsuas txhaum	kamalian sa pagsusukat	测量误差
measure of central tendency	measure of central tendency	sukat ng gitnang pagkahilig	集中趋势数
median	qhov nrab	median	中值
mental math	leb siv kev cim xeeb	matematika sa isip	心算
meter	meter	metro	米
metric system	metric system	metrikong sistema	公制
midpoint	teev nrab	gitnang puntos	中点
mile	mile	milya	英里
milli-	milli-	milli-	千分之一
mixed number	najnpawb sib xyaws	magkahalong bilang	带分数
mode	mode	mode	众数
monomial	monomial	monomial	单项式
multiple	tus tau txais tshooj npaug	multiple	倍数
multiplication	kev tshooj npaug	multiplikasyon	乘法
multiplication property	yam ntxwv kev ua tshooj npaug	katangiang multiplikasyon	乘法的性质
Multiplication Property of Equality	Yam Ntxwv kev Ua Tshooj Npaug	Multiplikasyon na Katangian ng Pagkakatumbas	等式的乘法性质
multiplicative inverse	tus tshooj npaug rov qab	kabaligtaran ng multiplikasyon	乘法逆元
mutually exclusive	sib nyom	kapwa kumakansela	互斥
negative numbers	cov leb nqis	mga negatibong bilang	负数
negative relationship	kev sib tshuam xeeb nqis	negatibong kaugnayan	负相关
negative slope	txoj kab nqis	negatibong tarik	负斜率
negative square root	tus cag ob xab xeeb kaum nqis	negatibong square root	负平方根
net	net	net	网格
nonagon	nonagon	nonagon	九边形
nonlinear equation	equation tsis ua kab ncaj	nonlinear equation	非线性方程
nonlinear function	function tsis ua kab ncaj	nonlinear function	非线性函数
no relationship	tsis muaj kev sib tshuam xeeb	walang kaugnayan	不相关
number line	txoj kab muaj najnpawb	linya ng bilang	数轴
number-word form	kev siv najnpawb-lus	anyô ng bilang at salita	数-字形式
numeral	sau ua najnpawb	pambilang	数字
numerator	tus leb saum toj	kabilangan	分子

English	Hmong	Pilipino (Tagalog)	Mandarin
obtuse angle	ntsais kaum nthuav	anggulong bika	钝角
obtuse triangle	duab peb ceg nthuav	tatsulok na bika	钝角三角形
octagon	octagon	octagon	八边形
odd number	leb tab	bilang na may butal kapag pinagdalawa	奇数
odds	odds	kalamangan	机率
operation	kev ua	operasyon	运算
opposite leg	ces tim cuab	kasalungat na binti	相对的直角边
opposite numbers	leb sib tig	mga kasalungat na bilang	相反数
order of operations	kab ke ua leb	ayos ng mga operasyon	运算顺序
ordered pair	nkawm leb teeb cia	pinag-ayus-ayos na pares	有序对
origin	chiv keeb	pinagsimulan	原点
orthographic drawing	daim duab cov sab ncaj	ortograpikong larawang-guhit	正投影图
ounce	fiab	onsa	盎司
outcome	qhov tshwm tawm	kinalabasan	结果
outlier	outlier	outlier	异常值
parabola	txoj kab parabola	parabola	抛物线
parallel	txoj kab ib ntxaig	paralelo	平行线
parallelogram	lub duab parallelogram	paralelogramo	平行四边形
pentagon	lub duab tsib ces kaum	pentagon	五边形
percent	feem pua	porsiyento	百分比
percent change	qhov txawv raws feem pua	porsiyentong pagbabago	百分比变化
percent decrease	feem pua nqis	porsiyentong pagbaba	百分比下降
percent increase	feem pua nce	porsiyentong pagtaas	百分比上升
perfect square	xab xeeb kaum zoo	perfect square	完全平方
perimeter	cheeb tsam ncig ntug	perimeter	周长
permutation	kev teeb tso	permutation	排列
perpendicular	txoj kab sawv ntsug ncaj	patayo	垂直
perpendicular bisector	txoj kab teeb ncaj txiav nruab nrab	patayong tagahati	垂直平分
pi (π)	pi (π)	pi (π)	圆周率 (π)
pictograph	daim graph siv duab	pictograph	象形图
place value	tus nqi qhov chaw	halaga ng puwesto	位值
plane	daim npoo	patag	平面
point symmetry	teev sib xwsπ	point symmetry	点对称

English	Hmong	Pilipino (Tagalog)	Mandarin
polygon	polygon	polygon	多边形
polyhedron	polyhedron	polyhedron	多面体
polynomial	polynomial	polynomial	多项式
population	population	populasyon	对象总体
positive numbers	cov leb nce	mga positibong bilang	正数
positive relationship	kev tshuam xeeb nce	positibong kaugnayan	正相关
positive slope	txoj kab qaij nce	positibong tarik	正斜率
pound	pound	libra	磅
power	tus leb tshooj	antas	幂
precision	qhov tseeb	pagkatiyak	精度
prime factor	prime factor	gansal na factor	质因数
prime factorization	prime factorization	prime factorization	质因数分解
prime number	prime number	gansal na bilang	质数
principal	peev chiv qab	puhunan	本金
principal square root	tus cag xab xeeb kaum nce	pangunahing square root	主平方根
prism	prism	prisma	棱柱
probability	kev tuaj yeem tshwm sim tau	probabilidad	概率
product	qhov tau txais	resulta ng pagmultiplika	乘积
proportion	proportion	proporsiyon	比例
protractor	protractor	protractor	量角器
pyramid	pyramid	piramide	棱锥
Pythagorean Theorem	Pythagorean Theorem	Pythagorean Theorem	勾股定理
quadrants	quadrants	mga quadrant	象限
quadratic equation	equation ob tshooj	quadratic equation	二次方程
quadratic function	function ob tshooj	quadratic function	二次函数
quadrilateral	duab plaub sab kaum	quadrilateral	四边形
quart	quart	quart	夸脱
quartile	ib feem plaub	quartile	四分位数
quotient	qhov tau los ntawm kev faib	quotient	商
radical sign	tus cim cag	radical sign	根号
radius	radius	radius	半径
random sample	kev lam cia li xaiv	sapalarang muwestra	随机样本
range	ncua	hanay	值域

English	Hmong	Pilipino (Tagalog)	Mandarin
rate	rate	rate	比率
ratio	ratio	pagkakaugnay	比
rational number	rational number	rational na bilang	有理数
ray	ray	ray	射线
real numbers	real numbers	mga totoong bilang	实数
reciprocals	reciprocals	reciprocals	倒数
rectangle	duab plaub ces ob sab ntev	rektanggulo	矩形
reflection	pom rov qab	larawan	反射
regular polygon	regular polygon	regular polygon	正多边形
relative position	thaj chaw sib piv	may-kaugnayang posisyon	相对位置
remainder	qhov seem	ang natitira	余数
repeating decimal	repeating decimal	umuulit-ulit na decimal	循环小数
rhombus	rhombus	rombus	菱形
right angle	ntsais kaum ncaj	anggulong kwadrado	直角
right triangle	duab peb ces ncaj	tatsulok na may anggulong kwadrado	直角三角形
rise	pauv sawv ntsug	rise	上升的高度
rotation	kiv tig	pag-ikot	旋转
rotational symmetry	kev sib xws kiv tig	simetriya sa pag-ikot	轴向对称
rounding	rounding	pagbubuo	四舍五入
run	pawv tav toj	run	跨度
sample	piv txwv khaws sim	muwestra	样本
sample space	cov piv txwv tau txais tag nrho	halimbawang espasyo	样本空间
scale (graphical)	cim suav (nyob rau graphical)	iskala (sa talaguhitan)	（图形的）刻度
scale (in scale drawings)	ntu ntev luv	iskala (sa mga larawang-guhit na may iskala)	比例（在比例图中）比例
scale drawing	tus ntsuas kev kos duab	iskalang larawang-guhit	比例图
scale factor	tus txav loj me	iskalang factor	比例因数
scalene triangle	duab peb ces sab tsis sib luag	scalene triangle	不等边三角形
scatterplot	kev tso ri	scatterplot	散点图
scientific notation	scientific notation	siyentipikong pagtatala	科学记数法
sector	txauj	sektor	扇形
segment	ntu txoj kab	bahagi	线段
segment bisector	txoj kab los txiav nruab nrab	segment bisector	线段平分线
sequence	kev sib txuas	pagkakasunod-sunod	数列

English	Hmong	Pilipino (Tagalog)	Mandarin
side	sab	panig	边
Side-Angle-Angle (SAA)	Sab-Ntshais Kaum-Ntsais Kaum	Panig-Anggulo-Anggulo	边角角
Side-Angle-Side (SAS)	Sab-Ntsais Kaum-Sab	Panig-Anggulo-Panig	边角边
Side-Side-Side (SSS)	Sab-Sab-Sab	Panig-Panig-Panig	边边边
significant digits	cov zauv tseem ceeb	mga makahulugang tambilang	有效数字
similar	sib xws	magkatulad	相似
similarity ratio	tus ratio uas sib xws	pagkakaugnay ng pagkakatulad	相似比
simple interest	paj ncaj	simpleng tubo	单利
simplified	muab sib sau	pinasimple	化简
simplify	ua kom tsawg	gawing simple	简化
simulation	kev xyaum raws	simulasyon	模拟
sine	sine	sine	正弦
slant height	ncua siab qaij	pahilig na taas	斜高
slide	swb	ipadausdos	滑动
slope	phab qaij	tarik	斜率
solid	lub duab khov	solido	立方体
solutions of an equation or inequality	kev daws rau tus equation los yog qhov tsis sib npaug	mga kalutasan ng isang equation o inequality	方程式或不等式的解
solution of a system	kev daws rau tus system	kalutasan ng isang sistema	方程组的解
solve	daws	lutasin	解答
sphere	duab pob kheej khauv	globo	球体
square	duab plaub fab xab xeeb kaum	parisukat	正方形
squared	tshooj npaug	squared	平方
square centimeter	centimeter xwm fab xwm meem	sentimetrong parisukat	平方厘米
square inch	inch xwm fab xwm meem	pulgadang parisukat	平方英寸
square root	cag tshooj ob	square root	平方根
standard form	daim foo standard	pamantayang paraan	标准形式
stem-and-leaf diagram	daim diagram Kav-thiab-Nplooj	sanga-at-dahong dayagram	茎叶图
step function	function txawv tu	step function	阶梯函数
straight angle	ntsais kaum ncaj	anggulong tuwid	平角
substitute	tus hloov	kahilili	替代
subtraction	kev rho tawm	pagbabawas	减法
sum	tag nrho	kabuuan	总数

English	Hmong	Pilipino (Tagalog)	Mandarin
supplementary angles	ntsais kaum ntxiv	supplementary angles	互朴角
surface area (SA)	npoo	lawak ng kalatagan	表面积
survey	kev rhiav paub	palatanungan	调查
symmetry	kev sib xws teeb tim	simetriya	对称
system of linear equations	tus system ntawm cov equations ua kab	sistema ng mga linear equation	线性方程组
T-table	lub T-table	talaang T	T 形表
tally	tus cim	talaan	短线
tally marks	tsiaj cim	mga marka ng talaan	短线标记
tangent line	txoj kab tangent	tangent line	切线
tangent ratio	tangent ratio	tangent na pagkakaugnay	正切比
term	tus leb	termino	项
terminating decimal	tus leb kawg	nagwawakas na decimal	有限小数
tessellation	kev tso ua tseej leej	tessellation	镶嵌
theoretical probability	kev xav tias tuaj yeem tshwm sim tau	teoretikal na probabilidad	理论概率
transformation	kev hloov txauv	pagpapanibagong-anyô	变换
translation	txhais mus	pagsalin	平移
transversal	txoj kab tav toj	transversal	截线
trapezoid	lub duab	trapezoid	梯形
tree diagram	diagram tsob ntoo	dayagram ng puno	树图
trend	xws li	pagkahilig	趋势
trend line	txoj kab xws li	linya ng pagkahilig	趋势线
trial	kev sim	pagsubok	试验
triangle	duab buab peb ceg	tatsulok	三角形
trigonometric ratios	trigonometric ratios	mga pagkakaugnay pang-trigonometriya	三角比
trinomial	peb lub npe	trinomial	三项式
turn	tig rov	ibaligtad	转动
unfair game	kev sib tw tsis ncaj nrab	di-makatarungang laro	不公平游戏
unit price	hauv paus nqi	presyo ng isa	单价
unit	hauv paus chiv	unit	单位
unit fraction	fraction pib	unit na hatimbilang	单分数
unit rate	rate pib	unit rate	单位比率
unlike denominators	denominators tsis sib thooj	mga di-magkatulad na panghatimbilang	不同分母
upper quartile	ib feem plaub sab saud	itaas na quartile	上四分位数

English	Hmong	Pilipino (Tagalog)	Mandarin
variable	tus hloov pauv	variable	变量
Venn diagram	Venn diagram	Venn diagram	维恩图
vertex	hau sib cob	vertex	顶点
vertical angles	ntsais kaum sawv ntsug	mga patayong anggulo	对顶角
vertical axis	txoj kab sawv ntsug	patayong aksis	垂直轴
volume	qhov ntim tau	bolumen	体积
weight	nyhav sib	bigat	重量
whole number	leb pauv	buong bilang	整数
word form	hom lus	anyô ng salita	字格式
x-axis	txoj kab x	x-aksis	x 轴
x-coordinate	txoj kab x-sib txiav	x-coordinate	x 坐标
x-intercept	txoj kab x- mus txiav	x-intercept	x 轴截距
y-axis	txoj kab y	y-aksis	y 轴
y-coordinate	txoj kab y-sib txiav	y-coordinate	y 坐标
y-intercept	txoj kab y-mus txiav	y-intercept	y 轴截距
yard	nrab daj	yarda	码
zero pair	txwm zej	serong pares	成零对
Zero Property of Addition	Yam Ntxwv Kev Sib Ntxiv ntawm lub Zej	Katangiang Sero ng Pagdaragdag	加法的成零特性

English Glossary

absolute position Location given as coordinates.

Example:

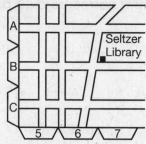

B7 is the absolute position for the Seltzer Library.

absolute value A number's distance from zero. The symbol for absolute value is $|\ |$.

Examples:

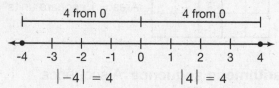

$|-4| = 4$ $|4| = 4$

acute angle An angle measuring less than 90°.

Examples:

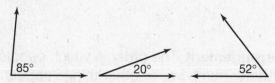

acute triangle A triangle with three acute angles.

Example:

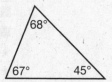

addend A number added to one or more other numbers.

Example: $12 + 19 = 31$
                    addend   addend

addition An operation that gives the total number when two or more numbers are put together.

Example:

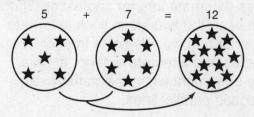

Addition Property of Equality If $a = b$, then $a + c = b + c$.

Example:

In the second line of the example below, 1 is added to both sides of the equation.

$$\begin{aligned} \text{If} \quad x - 1 &= 2 \\ \text{then} \quad x - 1 + \mathbf{1} &= 2 + \mathbf{1} \\ x &= 3 \end{aligned}$$

additive inverse A number's opposite.

Examples: The additive inverse of -2 is 2.
               The additive inverse of 5 is -5.

adjacent leg For an acute angle on a right triangle, the leg lying on one of the angle's sides.

Examples:

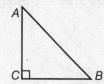

$\overline{AC}$ is the adjacent leg to $\angle CAB$.

$\overline{BC}$ is the adjacent leg to $\angle ABC$.

algebra A branch of mathematics in which arithmetic relations are explored using variables to represent numbers.

algebraic expression An expression that contains at least one variable.

Examples: $n - 7$ $2y + 17$ $5(x - 3)$

1

alternate angles Two angles formed by two lines and a transversal that are on opposite sides of the transversal that are either (1) between the two given lines (alternate interior angles) or (2) not between the two given lines (alternate exterior angles). Alternate interior angles and alternate exterior angles are congruent when the transversal crosses parallel lines.

Examples:
alternate exterior angles:
 ∠1 and ∠8
 ∠2 and ∠7

alternate interior angles:
 ∠3 and ∠6
 ∠4 and ∠5

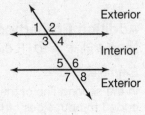

angle Two rays with a common endpoint.

Example:

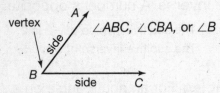

∠ABC, ∠CBA, or ∠B

angle bisector A ray that divides an angle into two congruent angles.

Example:

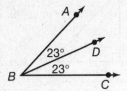

$\overrightarrow{BD}$ is the angle bisector of ∠ABC.

angle of rotation The angle through which a figure turns during a rotation.

Example:

The angle of rotation is 90°.

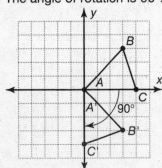

Angle-Side-Angle (ASA) A rule used to determine whether triangles are congruent by comparing corresponding parts.

Example:

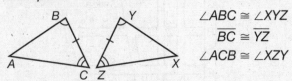

∠ABC ≅ ∠XYZ
$\overline{BC} \cong \overline{YZ}$
∠ACB ≅ ∠XZY

△ABC ≅ △XYZ by the ASA rule.

area The amount of surface a figure covers.

Example:

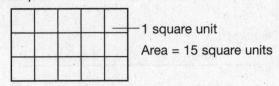

1 square unit
Area = 15 square units

arithmetic sequence A sequence where the difference between consecutive terms is always the same.

Example:

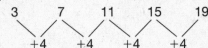

arrangement The order in which people, letters, numbers, or other things appear.

Example:
All possible arrangements of three shapes:

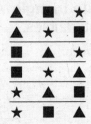

Associative Property of Addition The fact that changing the grouping of addends does not change the sum.

Examples: $a + (b + c) = (a + b) + c$
$5 + (3 + 7) = (5 + 3) + 7$

Associative Property of Multiplication
The fact that changing the grouping of factors does not change the product.

Examples: $a(bc) = (ab)c$
$$3 \times (4 \times 2) = (3 \times 4) \times 2$$

average See *mean.*

axes See *x-axis* and *y-axis.*

bar graph A graph that uses vertical or horizontal bars to display data.

Examples:

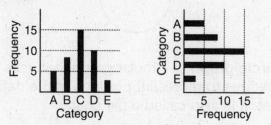

base (of an exponent) A number multiplied by itself the number of times shown by an exponent.

Example: base $\quad$ exponent
$$6^2 = 6 \times 6 = 36$$

base (of a polygon) Any side (usually the one at the bottom), or the length of that side.

Examples:

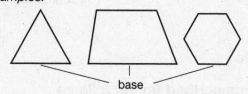

base

base (of a solid) In a prism or cylinder, one of the two parallel and congruent faces. In a pyramid, the face opposite the vertex. In a cone, the circular face.

Examples:

base $\quad$ base $\quad$ base

binary number system A base-2 place value system.

Example:
In the binary number system, 1011 is equal to 11 in the decimal (base 10) number system.

	Eights place	Fours place	Twos place	Ones place
Base 2	1	0	1	1
Place value	8	4	2	1
Product	$1\times8=8$	$0\times4=0$	$1\times2=2$	$1\times1=1$

$(1 \times 8) + (0 \times 4) + (1 \times 2) + (1 \times 1) = 8 + 0 + 2 + 1 = 11$

binomial A two-term polynomial.

Examples: $\quad 4x^3 - 2x^2 \quad\quad 2x + 5$

bisect To divide an angle or segment into two congruent angles or segments.

Examples:

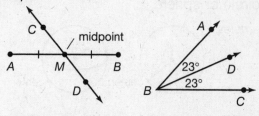

$\overleftrightarrow{CD}$ bisects $\overline{AB}$. $\quad\quad$ $\overrightarrow{BD}$ bisects $\angle ABC$.

boundary line On a graph of a linear inequality, the line separating points that are solutions from points that are not.

Example:

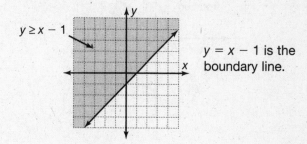

$y \geq x - 1$

$y = x - 1$ is the boundary line.

3

box-and-whisker plot A visual way of showing how a collection of data is distributed. The example below is based on the following ten test scores: 52, 64, 75, 79, 80, 80, 81, 88, 92, 99.

Example:

capacity The volume of a figure, given in terms of liquid measure.

Examples:

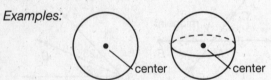

500 ml   1 L   1 cup   1 quart   1 gallon

center The point at the exact middle of a circle or sphere.

Examples:

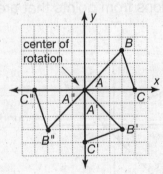

center   center

center of rotation The point about which a rotation turns a figure.

Example:

The origin is the center of rotation.

centi- A prefix meaning $\frac{1}{100}$.

Example: 1 centimeter = $\frac{1}{100}$ meter

central angle An angle whose vertex is at the center of a circle.

Example:

Point *C* is the center of the circle.

∠*BCA* is a central angle

circle A plane figure whose points are all the same distance from its center.

Example:

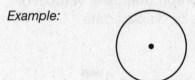

circle graph A circular graph that uses wedges to represent portions of the data set. It is also called a pie chart.

Example:

Favorite Pets

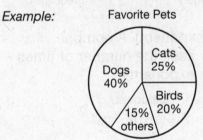

Cats 25%
Dogs 40%
Birds 20%
15% others

circumference The distance around a circle.

Example:

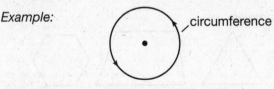

circumference

circumscribed figure A figure containing another. A polygon is circumscribed around a circle if the circle touches each of its sides.

Example:

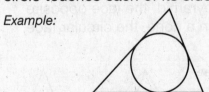

The triangle is circumscribed about the circle.

clockwise The direction of rotation when the top of a figure turns to the right.

Example:

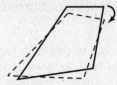

clustering An estimation method where numbers that are approximately equal are treated as if they were equal.

Example:

26 + 24 + 23 is about 25 + 25 + 25, or 3 × 25.

coefficient A constant by which a variable is multiplied.

Example:
coefficient ╲ ╱ variable
$12y$

combination A selection of items in which order is not important.

Example:

Two students from this group will be selected to be on a committee: David, Juanita, Kim.

The possible combinations are:
David, Juanita   David, Kim   Juanita, Kim
Note: The combination "David, Juanita" is the same as the combination "Juanita, David."

common denominator A denominator that is the same in two or more fractions.

Example:

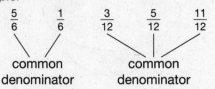

common factor A number that is a factor of two or more numbers.

Example:

4 is a common factor of 8, 12, and 20.

$$8 = 4 \times 2$$
$$12 = 4 \times 3$$
$$20 = 4 \times 5$$

common multiple A number that is a multiple of each of two or more given numbers.

Example:

multiples of 3: 3 6 9 **12** 15 18 21 **24** 27...

multiples of 4: 4 8 **12** 16 20 **24** 28...

12 and 24 are two of the common multiples of 3 and 4.

Commutative Property of Addition The fact that order does not affect the sum of two or more numbers.

Examples:
$$a + b = b + a$$
$$18 + 23 = 23 + 18$$

Commutative Property of Multiplication The fact that order does not affect the product of two or more numbers.

Examples:
$$ab = ba$$
$$4 \times 7 = 7 \times 4$$

compatible numbers Pairs of numbers that can be computed easily.

Examples: 30 + 70   40 ÷ 4   25 + 75

compensation The mental math strategy of choosing numbers close to the numbers in a problem, and then adjusting the answer to compensate for the numbers chosen.

Example:
$$99 \times 4 = (100 - 1) \times 4$$
$$= (100 \times 4) - (1 \times 4)$$
$$= 400 - 4$$
$$= 396$$

complementary angles Two angles whose measures add up to 90°.

Example:

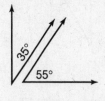

35° + 55° = 90°

composite number A whole number greater than 1 that has more than two factors.

Examples:

factors of 15: 1, 3, 5, 15
    15 is a composite number.

factors of 7: 1, 7
    7 is not a composite number.

compound event Event that is the combination of two or more single events.

Example:

 and

Getting heads on a coin toss and rolling a 1 with a number cube is a compound event.

compound interest Interest based on both principal and previous interest.

Example:

If you deposit $100 in a savings account which earns 6% interest compounded annually, you will have $100 + (0.06 × 100) = $106 the first year and $106 + (0.06 × 106) = $112.36 the second year.

compound statement A logical statement formed by joining two or more statements.

Examples:

10 is greater than 5 *and* 10 is less than 21.

10 is greater than 5 *or* 10 is less than 5.

concave polygon A polygon with one or more diagonals lying outside the figure.

Example:

conditional probability The probability that an event B will occur, given that event A has already occurred.

Example:

If you know the first of two coin tosses is tails, the probability of tossing two heads is zero. However, if you know the first toss is heads, the probability of getting two heads is $\frac{1}{2}$.

cone A solid with one circular base.

Example:

congruent Having the same size and shape.

Examples:

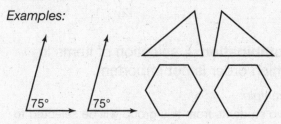

conic projection A map projection that uses a cone shape to represent a spherical surface.

Example:

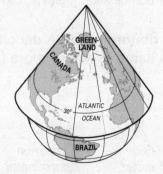

conjunction A logical set of statements joined by the word *and*.

Examples:

   $x > -2$ and $x < 5$

   A square has 4 sides of equal length *and* a square is a rectangle.

constant A quantity that does not change.

Example:

In the algebraic expression $x + 7$, 7 is a constant.

constant graph A graph in which the height of the line does not change.

Example:

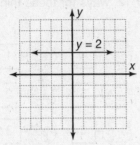

constant of proportionality The quantity $\frac{y}{x}$ for two variables x and y whose ratio is constant. It is usually denoted by k.

Example:

x	3	6	9	12
y	5	10	15	20

$k = \frac{5}{3}$

conversion factor A measurement equivalence used to convert quantities from one unit to another. It is often expressed as a fraction.

Examples:

12 inches = 1 foot; $\frac{12 \text{ inches}}{1 \text{ foot}}$

4 quarts = 1 gallon; $\frac{4 \text{ quarts}}{1 \text{ gallon}}$

convex polygon A polygon with all diagonals lying inside the figure.

Examples:

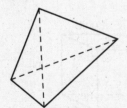

coordinates A pair of numbers in an ordered pair which is used to locate a point on a coordinate plane.

Example:

(5, 6)

coordinates

coordinate plane, coordinate system A system of intersecting horizontal and vertical number lines used to locate points.

Example:

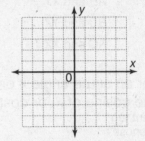

corresponding angles (for lines) The angles on the same side of a transversal which intersects two or more lines. Corresponding angles are congruent when the transversal crosses parallel lines.

Example:

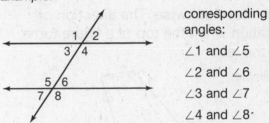

corresponding angles:

∠1 and ∠5

∠2 and ∠6

∠3 and ∠7

∠4 and ∠8

corresponding angles (in similar figures) Matching angles on similar figures.

Example:

$\triangle ABC \sim \triangle XYZ$

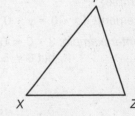

corresponding angles:

∠ABC and ∠XYZ

∠BCA and ∠YZX

∠CAB and ∠ZXY

corresponding sides Matching sides on similar figures.

Example:
$\triangle ABC \sim \triangle XYZ$

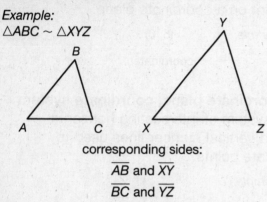

corresponding sides:
$\overline{AB}$ and $\overline{XY}$
$\overline{BC}$ and $\overline{YZ}$
$\overline{AC}$ and $\overline{XZ}$

cosine For an acute angle x on a right triangle, the cosine of x, or $\cos(x)$, is the ratio $\frac{\text{adjacent leg}}{\text{hypotenuse}}$.

Example:

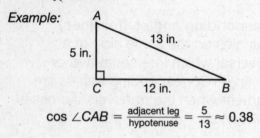

$\cos \angle CAB = \frac{\text{adjacent leg}}{\text{hypotenuse}} = \frac{5}{13} \approx 0.38$

counterclockwise The direction of rotation when the top of a figure turns to the left.

Example:

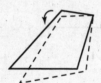

counterexample An example that shows a statement is false.

Example:
statement: If $x \cdot 0 = y \cdot 0$, then $x = y$.
counterexample: $3 \cdot 0 = 0$ and $5 \cdot 0 = 0$, but $3 \neq 5$.

Counting Principle If a situation can occur in m ways, and a second situation can occur in n ways, then these things can occur together in $m \times n$ ways.

Example:
There are 2 outcomes for flipping a coin and 6 outcomes for rolling a number cube. So there are 2×6, or 12, ways for these things to occur together.

cross product The product of the numerator of one ratio with the denominator of another.

Example:

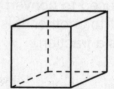

cross products:
$1 \times 5 = 5$
$3 \times 2 = 6$

cube A 6-sided prism whose faces are congruent squares.

Example:

cubed Raised to the third power.

Example: 2 cubed $= 2^3 = 2 \times 2 \times 2 = 8$

cubic unit A unit measuring volume, consisting of a cube with edges one unit long.

Example:

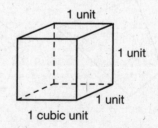

customary system of measurement
The measurement system often used in the United States: inches, feet, miles, ounces, pounds, tons, cups, quarts, gallons, etc.

Examples:

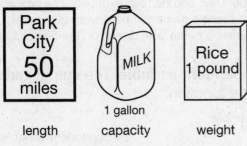

length   capacity   weight

cylinder A solid with two parallel, circular bases.

Example:

cylindrical projection A map projection that uses a cylinder shape to represent a spherical surface.

Example:

decagon A polygon with 10 sides.

Example:

deci- A prefix meaning $\frac{1}{10}$.

Example: 1 decimeter = $\frac{1}{10}$ meter

decimal Any base-10 numeral written using a decimal point.

Examples: 6.21   0.59   12.2   5.0

decimal addition Adding two or more decimals.

Example:

$$\begin{array}{r} 1 \\ 12.65 \\ +\ 29.10 \\ \hline 41.75 \end{array}$$

decimal division Dividing two decimals.

Example:

$$\begin{array}{r} 1.25 \\ 0.24\overline{)0.3\,0\,0\,0} \\ -\ 24 \\ \hline 60 \\ -\ 48 \\ \hline 120 \\ -\ 120 \\ \hline 0 \end{array}$$

decimal multiplication Multiplying two or more decimals.

Example:

$$\begin{array}{rl} \overset{2}{}\ & \\ 0.13 & \text{2 decimal places} \\ \times\ 0.7 & \text{1 decimal place} \\ \hline 0.091 & \text{3 decimal places} \end{array}$$

decimal subtraction Subtracting two decimals.

Example

$$\begin{array}{r} 13\ 12 \\ 4\ \cancel{3}\ \cancel{2}10 \\ \cancel{5}\cancel{4}.\cancel{3}\cancel{0} \\ -\ 16.58 \\ \hline 37.72 \end{array}$$

decimal system A base-10 place value system.

Example:

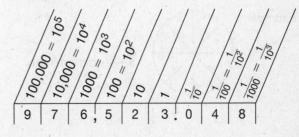

decreasing graph A graph in which the height of the line decreases from left to right.

Example:

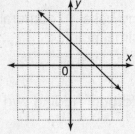

deductive reasoning Using logic to draw a conclusion.

Example:

When one diagonal is added to any quadrilateral, two triangles are formed. You know that the sum of the measures of the angles of a triangle is 180°. Therefore, the sum of the measures of the angles of a quadrilateral is twice that of a triangle, or $2 \times 180° = 360°$.

degree (°) A unit of angle measure.

Example: 1° is $\frac{1}{360}$ of a complete circle.

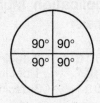

degree For a polynomial, the value of the largest exponent of a variable.

Example: The degree of $5x^3 - 2x^2 + 7x$ is 3.

deka- A prefix meaning 10.

Example: 1 dekameter = 10 meters

denominator The bottom number in a fraction which tells how many parts the whole is divided into.

Example:

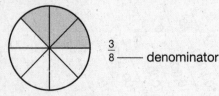

$\frac{3}{8}$ ——— denominator

dependent events Events for which the outcome of one affects the probability of the other.

Example:
The names Therese, Diane, and José are written on separate slips of paper. One slip is drawn and kept. Then another slip is drawn. The probability that Diane's name will be drawn, given that Therese's name was drawn on the first slip, is $\frac{1}{2}$.

dependent variable The output variable for a function.

Example:

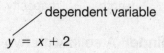

dependent variable

$y = x + 2$

diagonal On a polygon, a segment connecting two vertices that do not share a side.

Example:

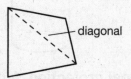

diagonal

diameter A line segment, or its length, that passes through the center of a circle and has both endpoints on the circle.

Example:

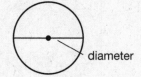

diameter

difference The result of subtracting one number from another.

Example: $28 - 15 = 13$

difference

digit The symbols used to write the numerals 0, 1, 2, 3, 4, 5, 6, 7, 8, and 9.

Example:
In 5,847, the digits are 5, 8, 4, and 7.

dilation A proportional reduction or enlargement of a figure.

Example:

The scale factor for the dilation from the small rectangle to the large rectangle is 3.

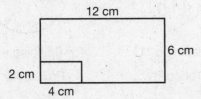

12 cm
6 cm
2 cm
4 cm

direct variation When two variables are related by a constant ratio.

Example:

time in hours (x)	1	2	3	4
distance in miles (y)	55	110	165	220

$$\frac{y}{x} = 55$$

disjunction A logical set of statements joined by the word *or.*

Examples:

$x > 4$ or $x < -1$

We went to the movie or we watched TV.

Distributive Property The fact that $a(b + c) = ab + ac$.

Example: $3(6 + 5) = 3 \cdot 6 + 3 \cdot 5$

dividend The number to be divided in a division problem.

Example:

dividend
$8 \div 4 = 2$

divisible Can be divided by another number without leaving a remainder.

Example: 18 is divisible by 6, since $18 \div 6 = 3$.

division An operation that tells how many equal sets or how many in each equal set.

Examples:

$18 \div 6 = 3$ $18 \div 3 = 6$

18 divided into 6 groups puts 3 in each group.   18 divided into 3 groups puts 6 in each group.

divisor A number that another number is being divided by.

Example:

divisor
$8 \div 4 = 2$

dodecagon A polygon with 12 sides.

Example:

double bar graph A combination of two bar graphs, comparing two related data sets.

Example:

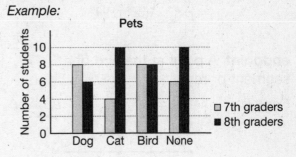

Pets

Number of students

Dog   Cat   Bird   None

□ 7th graders
■ 8th graders

double line graph A combination of two line graphs, comparing two related data sets.

Example:

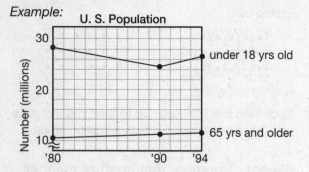

U. S. Population

double stem-and-leaf diagram A stem-and-leaf comparison of two sets of data in a single diagram.

Example:

Leaf	Stem	Leaf
7 2 1	3	0 1 3
5 0 0	4	2 3
9	5	5 6 8
5 2 0	6	1 4

edge A segment where two faces of a polyhedron meet.

Example:

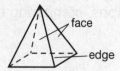

face

edge

endpoint A point at the end of a segment or ray.

Examples:

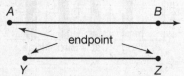

A   B

endpoint

Y   Z

equality A mathematical relation of being exactly the same.

Examples: $16 + 8 = 24$ $25 \div 5 = 5$

equally-likely outcomes Outcomes that have the same probability.

Examples:

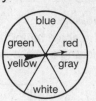

blue
green   red
yellow   gray
white

Rolling a "1"   Spinning red
Probability: $\frac{1}{6}$ Probability: $\frac{1}{6}$

equal ratios Ratios naming the same amount.

Example: $\frac{2}{6}$, $\frac{1}{3}$, and $\frac{4}{12}$

equation A mathematical sentence stating that two expressions are equal.

Examples:

$14 = 2x$ $3 + y = 81$ $3 + 4 = 7$

equilateral triangle A triangle whose sides are all the same length.

Example:

4   4

4

equivalent equations Equations that are true for exactly the same variable replacements.

Example: $x - 5 = 10$ and $x = 15$

equivalent expressions Two expressions that always have the same value for the same substitutions.

Example: $5(x + 1)$ and $5x + 5$

equivalent fractions Two fractions representing the same number.

Example: $\frac{1}{2}$ and $\frac{8}{16}$

equivalent rates Rates naming the same amount.

Example: $\frac{40 \text{ miles}}{2 \text{ hours}}$ and $\frac{20 \text{ miles}}{1 \text{ hour}}$

equivalent ratios See *equal ratios.*

estimate An approximation for the result of a calculation.

Example: 99×21

Estimate: $100 \times 20 = 2000$

$99 \times 21 \approx 2000$

Euler's formula A formula about the number of faces (F), vertices (V), and edges (E) of a polyhedron which states that $F + V - E = 2$.

Example:

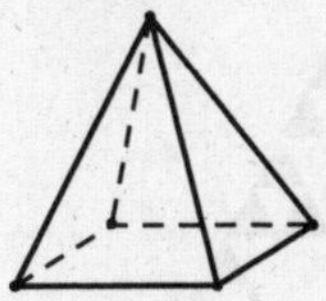

For the triangular pyramid shown,

$5 + 5 - 8 = 2$

faces vertices edges

evaluate To substitute values for variables in an expression and then simplify by applying the order of operations.

Example: Evaluate $8(x - 3)$ for $x = 10$.

$8(x - 3) = 8(10 - 3)$

$= 8(7)$

$= 56$

even number A whole number that has 0, 2, 4, 6, or 8 in the ones place.

Examples: 16 28 34 112 3000

event An outcome or set of outcomes of an experiment or situation.

Example:

Event: Obtaining a 3 or higher when one number cube is rolled.

Possible outcomes for this event: 3, 4, 5, 6

expanded form A way of writing an exponential number showing all of the factors individually.

Example: exponential number 9^3

expanded form $9 \times 9 \times 9$

experiment In probability, any activity involving chance.

Examples:

coin toss number cube roll spinner spin

experimental probability A probability based on data from experiments or surveys.

Example:

A bean bag is tossed into a ring 100 times. There are 23 hits. The experimental probability of a hit is $\frac{23}{100} = 23\%$.

exponent A raised number showing repeated multiplication.

Example: exponent

$4^3 = 4 \times 4 \times 4 = 64$

exponential function A nonlinear function in which an exponent is a variable.

Example: $y = 4^x$

exponential notation A way of writing repeated multiplication of a number using exponents.

Examples: 2^8 5^2 9^3

expression A mathematical phrase made up of variables and/or numbers and operations.

Examples: $5(8 + 4)$ $x - 3$ $2x + 4$

exterior angles When a transversal crosses two lines, the angles outside those two lines are called exterior angles.

Example:

exterior angles: ∠1, ∠2, ∠7, ∠8

face A flat surface on a solid.

Example:

face

factor A number that divides another number without leaving a remainder.

Example: Since $30 \div 5 = 6$, 5 is a factor of 30.

factorial The factorial of a number is the product of all whole numbers from 1 to that number. The symbol for factorial is "!".

Example:

6 factorial $= 6! = 6 \times 5 \times 4 \times 3 \times 2 \times 1 = 720$

factor tree A diagram showing how a whole number breaks down into its prime factors.

Example:

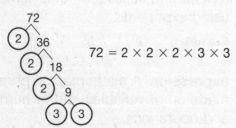

$72 = 2 \times 2 \times 2 \times 3 \times 3$

fair game A game in which all players have the same probability of winning.

Example:

Fair game: Two players take turns rolling a number cube. Player A gets a point for rolls of 1, 3, or 5. Player B gets a point for rolls of 2, 4, or 6. The probability of getting a point is $\frac{1}{2}$ for both players.

flip See *reflection*.

foot A unit in the customary system of measurement equal to 12 inches.

Example:

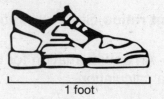

1 foot

formula A rule showing relationships among quantities.

Examples: $A = bh$ $p = 4s$

fractal A pattern with self-similarity. If a small part of a fractal is enlarged, the enlarged region looks similar to the original figure.

Example:

fraction A number in the form $\frac{a}{b}$ which describes part of a whole when the whole is cut into equal pieces.

Examples: $\frac{3}{5}$ $\frac{2}{7}$ $\frac{1}{4}$ $\frac{7}{10}$

fraction addition Adding two or more fractions.

Example: $\frac{1}{3} + \frac{1}{4}$

$$\frac{1}{3} = \frac{1 \times 4}{3 \times 4} = \frac{4}{12}$$

$$\frac{1}{4} = \frac{1 \times 3}{4 \times 3} = \frac{3}{12}$$

$$\frac{1}{3} + \frac{1}{4} = \frac{4}{12} + \frac{3}{12} = \frac{4+3}{12} = \frac{7}{12}$$

fraction division Dividing two fractions.

Example: $\frac{1}{6} \div \frac{3}{4} = \frac{1}{6} \times \frac{4}{3}$

$$= \frac{1 \times 4}{6 \times 3}$$

$$= \frac{4}{18} \text{ or } \frac{2}{9}$$

14

fraction multiplication Multiplying two or more fractions.

Example:
$$1\tfrac{1}{2} \times \tfrac{1}{4} = \tfrac{3}{2} \times \tfrac{1}{4}$$
$$= \tfrac{3 \times 1}{2 \times 4}$$
$$= \tfrac{3}{8}$$

fraction subtraction Subtracting two fractions.

Example:
$$\tfrac{3}{4} - \tfrac{2}{3}$$
$$\tfrac{3}{4} = \tfrac{3 \times 3}{4 \times 3} = \tfrac{9}{12}$$
$$\tfrac{2}{3} = \tfrac{2 \times 4}{3 \times 4} = \tfrac{8}{12}$$
$$\tfrac{3}{4} - \tfrac{2}{3} = \tfrac{9}{12} - \tfrac{8}{12} = \tfrac{9-8}{12} = \tfrac{1}{12}$$

frequency The number of times something occurs in a survey. See *frequency chart*.

frequency chart or table A table showing classes of things and the frequency with which things occur.

Example:

Color of Shirt	Frequency
Black	8
Tan	2
White	5
Blue	4

front-end estimation An estimation method where only the first or second digit of each number is used for computation, and the result is adjusted based on the remaining digits.

Example: One-digit front-end estimation

```
  2,485
+ 3,698
  5,000   Add first digits.
+ 1,200   485 + 698 is about 1,200.
  6,200
```

function An input-output relationship giving only one output for each input.

Examples:
$$y = x + 4 \qquad y = 2x \qquad y = x^2$$

Fundamental Theorem of Arithmetic All integers greater than 1 can be written as a unique product of prime numbers.

Examples:
$$24 = 2 \times 2 \times 2 \times 3$$
$$35 = 5 \times 7$$

gallon A unit in the customary system of measurement equal to 4 quarts.

Example:

1 gallon

geometry A branch of mathematics in which the relations between points, lines, figures, and solids are explored.

geometric probability A probability based on comparing measurements of geometric figures.

Example:

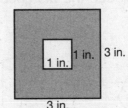

Area of large square = $3 \cdot 3$ or 9 in^2

Shaded area = $9 \text{ in}^2 - 1 \text{ in}^2 = 8 \text{ in}^2$

Probability of landing in shaded area = $\tfrac{8}{9}$

geometric sequence A sequence where the ratio between consecutive terms is always the same.

Example:

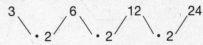

gram The basic unit of mass in the metric system.

Example:

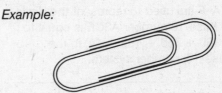

The mass of a large paperclip is about 1 gram.

graph A diagram that shows information in an organized way.

Examples:

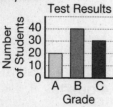

Stem	Leaf
3	0 1 3
4	2 2
5	6 7 9

greatest common factor (GCF) The greatest whole number that divides two or more whole numbers without leaving a remainder.

Example: 6 is the GCF of 12, 18, and 24.

hecto- A prefix meaning 100.

Example: 1 hectometer = 100 meters

height On a triangle, quadrilateral, or pyramid, the perpendicular distance from the base to the opposite vertex or side. On a prism or cylinder, the distance between the bases.

Examples:

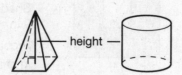

heptagon A polygon with 7 sides.

Example:

hexadecimal number system A base-16 place value system.

Example:

The letters A–F are used to represent the digits 10–15. The base-16 number A3CE is equal to 41,934 (40,960 + 768 + 192 + 14) in the decimal (base-10) number system.

Base 16	A	3	C	E
Place value	4096	256	16	1
Product	10 × 4096 = 40,960	3 × 256 = 768	12 × 16 = 192	14 × 1 = 14

16

hexagon A polygon with 6 sides.

Examples:

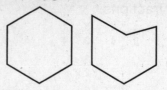

histogram A type of bar graph where the categories are equal ranges of numbers.

Example:

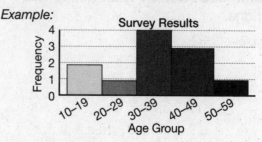

horizontal axis The horizontal line of the two lines on which a bar graph or a coordinate plane is built.

Examples:

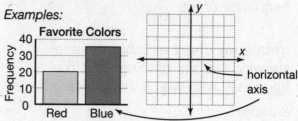

hypotenuse The side opposite the right angle in a right triangle.

Example:

A

hypotenuse

C

B

identity For any operation, the number that keeps another number the same. 0 is the additive identity, since $a + 0 = a$, 1 is the multiplicative identity since $a \times 1 = a$.

Examples: $6 + 0 = 6$
    $5 \times 1 = 5$

if-then statement A logical statement that uses *if* and *then* to show a relationship between two conditions.

Example:

If a triangle is scalene, *then* none of its sides are congruent.

improper fraction A fraction whose numerator is greater than or equal to its denominator.

Examples: $\frac{5}{2}$ $\frac{8}{8}$ $\frac{14}{3}$

increasing graph A graph in which the height of the line increases from left to right.

Example:

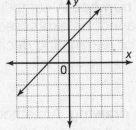

inch A unit of length in the customary measurement system.

Example: The paperclip measures $1\frac{3}{8}$ in. or $1\frac{3}{8}"$.

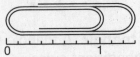

independent events Events for which the outcome of one does not affect the probability of the other.

Example:
The names Therese, Diane, and José are written on separate slips of paper. One slip is drawn and returned. Then another slip is drawn. The probability that Diane's name will be drawn, given that Therese's name was drawn on the first slip, is $\frac{1}{3}$.

independent variable The input variable for a function.

Example:

independent variable
/
$y = x + 2$

inductive reasoning Using a pattern to draw a conclusion.

Example:
Many quadrilaterals are drawn and their angles are measured. Each time the sum of the angles is 360°. The conclusion drawn is that the sum of the angles of a quadrilateral is 360°.

inequality A mathematical sentence involving $<$, $>$, $\leq$, or $\geq$.

Examples:

$6 < 9$ $x + 3 \geq 21$ $2x - 8 > 0$

inscribed figure A figure that is contained inside another. A polygon is inscribed in a circle if all of its vertices lie on the circle.

Example:

The triangle is inscribed in the circle.

integers The set of positive whole numbers, their opposites, and 0.

Examples: ..., $-3, -2, -1, 0, 1, 2, 3, ...$

$$\begin{array}{ccccccccc} \shortmid & \shortmid & \shortmid & \shortmid & \shortmid & \shortmid & \shortmid & \shortmid & \shortmid \\ -4 & -3 & -2 & -1 & 0 & 1 & 2 & 3 & 4 \end{array}$$

integer addition Adding two or more integers.

Examples:

$-5 + 8 = 3$ $-5 + (-8) = -13$
$5 + (-3) = 2$ $5 + 8 = 13$

integer division Dividing two integers.

Examples:

$-40 \div 8 = -5$ $40 \div (-8) = -5$
$-40 \div (-8) = 5$ $40 \div 8 = 5$

integer multiplication Multiplying two or more integers.

Examples:

$-5 \cdot 8 = -40$ $-5 \cdot (-8) = 40$
$5 \cdot (-8) = -40$ $5 \cdot 8 = 40$

integer subtraction Subtracting two integers.

Examples:

$-5 - 8 = -13$ $-5 - (-8) = 3$
$5 - (-3) = 8$ $5 - 8 = -3$

interest Money paid for the use of money.

Example:
Dave deposited $300 in a savings account. After 1 year the balance of his account was $315. He earned $15 in interest on his savings account.

interior angles When a transversal crosses two lines, the angles inside those two lines are called interior angles.

Example:

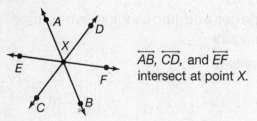

interior angles:
$\angle 3$, $\angle 4$, $\angle 5$, and $\angle 6$

intersect To cross through the same point.

Example:

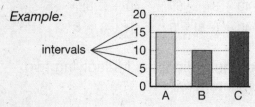

$\overleftrightarrow{AB}$, $\overleftrightarrow{CD}$, and $\overleftrightarrow{EF}$ intersect at point X.

interval One of the equal-sized divisions on a bar graph or line graph scale.

Example:

intervals

inverse operations Operations that "undo" each other.

Examples:
addition and subtraction $2 + 3 = 5$ $5 - 3 = 2$
multiplication and division $2 \cdot 3 = 6$ $6 \div 3 = 2$

inverse variation When two variables are related by a constant product.

Example:

x	1	2	3	4	5	6
y	60	30	20	15	12	10

$$x \cdot y = 60$$

irrational number A number, such as $\sqrt{2}$, that cannot be expressed as a repeating or terminating decimal.

Examples: $\sqrt{5}$ π $-\sqrt{\frac{1}{2}}$

isometric drawing A method used to give perspective to a drawing.

Example:

isosceles triangle A triangle with at least two congruent sides.

Example:

18   18

14

kilo- A prefix meaning 1000.

Example: 1 kilometer = 1000 meters

latitude A measurement in degrees north or south from the equator.

Example:

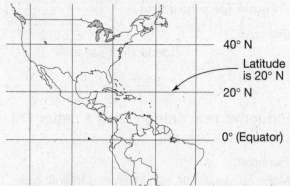

40° N

Latitude is 20° N

20° N

0° (Equator)

least common denominator (LCD) The least common multiple (LCM) of two or more denominators.

Example: $\frac{1}{2}$ $\frac{2}{3}$ $\frac{3}{4}$

The LCM of 2, 3, and 4 is 12, so the LCD of the fractions is 12.

The fractions written with the LCD are $\frac{6}{12}$, $\frac{8}{12}$, and $\frac{9}{12}$.

least common multiple (LCM) The smallest number that is a common multiple.

Example:
multiples of 3: 3 6 9 **12** 15 18 21 **24** ...
multiples of 4: 4 8 **12** 16 20 **24** 28 32 ...
12 is the LCM of 3 and 4.

leg A side of a right triangle other than the hypotenuse.

Example:

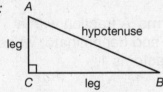

like denominators Denominators that are the same in two or more fractions.

Example: $\frac{1}{8}$ $\frac{3}{8}$ $\frac{6}{8}$

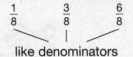
like denominators

like terms Terms in which the same variable is raised to the same exponent.

Example: $3x^2$ and $9x^2$ $10y$ and $2y$

line A one-dimensional figure that extends without end in both directions. Two points name a line.

Example:

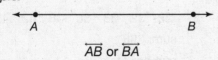

$\overleftrightarrow{AB}$ or $\overleftrightarrow{BA}$

line graph A graph in which a line shows changes in data, often over time.

Example:

line of symmetry The line that divides a figure with line symmetry into two identical halves.

Examples:

1 line of symmetry   4 lines of symmetry

line plot A plot that shows the shape of a data set by stacking x's above each value on a number line.

Example:

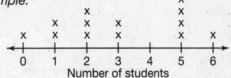

line segment Part of a straight line, with two endpoints. Two points name a segment.

Example:

$\overline{AB}$ or $\overline{BA}$

line symmetry A figure has line symmetry if it can be divided into two identical halves.

Example:

Figure with   Figure with no
line symmetry   line symmetry

linear equation An equation whose graph is a straight line.

Example:

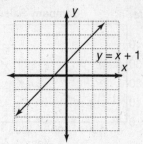

$y = x + 1$

linear function A function whose graph is a straight line.

Example:

Input	Output
x	y
−2	3
−1	2
0	1
1	0
2	−1
3	−2

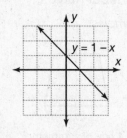

$y = 1 - x$

linear inequality A mathematical sentence involving $<$, $>$, $\leq$ or $\geq$ whose graph is a region with a straight-line boundary.

Example:

$y \geq x - 1$

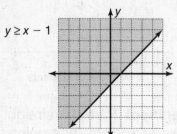

liter The basic unit of volume in the metric system.

Example:

2-liter bottle

longitude A measurement in degrees east or west from the prime meridian.

Example:

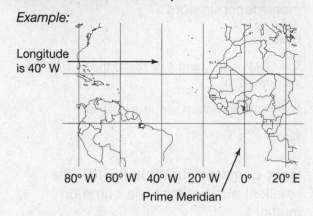

Longitude is 40° W

80° W   60° W   40° W   20° W   0°   20° E

Prime Meridian

lower quartile The median of the lower half of a data set.

Example:

27   27   27   29   32   33   36   38   42   43   62

lower quartile   median   upper quartile

lowest terms A fraction with a numerator and denominator whose only common factor is 1.

Examples: $\dfrac{1}{2}$ $\dfrac{3}{5}$ $\dfrac{21}{23}$

mass The amount of matter that something contains.

Examples:

A raisin has a mass of 1 gram.

A pair of athletic shoes has a mass of 1 kilogram.

mean The sum of the values in a data set divided by the number of values. Also known as the average.

Example:

27   27   27   29   32   33   36   38   42   43   62

sum: 396

number of values: 11

mean: 396 ÷ 11 = 36

measurement error The uncertainty in a measurement. The greatest possible error in a measurement is half the smallest unit used.

Example:

Since inch is the smallest unit, the greatest possible error is $\frac{1}{2}$ inch. So the actual height is between $5'5\frac{1}{2}"$ and $5'6\frac{1}{2}"$.

5' 6"

measure of central tendency A single value summarizing a set of numerical data.

Example:

Mean, median, and mode are common measures of central tendency.

27 27 27 29 32 33 36 38 42 43 62

mode   median

Mean = 396 ÷ 11 = 36

median The middle value of a data set when the values are arranged in numerical order.

Example:

27 27 27 29 32 33 36 38 42 43 62

median

mental math Performing calculations in your mind, without using pencil and paper or a calculator.

Example:

2000 × 30

3 zeros + 1 zero = 4 zeros

Think: 2 × 3 = 6, annex 4 zeros

2000 × 30 = 60,000

meter The basic unit of length in the metric system.

Example:

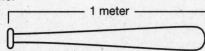

1 meter

The baseball bat is about 1 meter long.

metric system A system of measurement based on the meter, the gram, and the liter.

Examples:

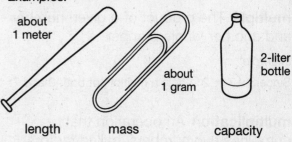

about 1 meter

about 1 gram

2-liter bottle

length   mass   capacity

midpoint The point that divides a segment into two congruent smaller segments.

Example: C is the midpoint of $\overline{AB}$.

A   C   B

Length of $\overline{AC}$ = Length of $\overline{CB}$

mile A unit in the customary system of measurement equal to 5280 feet.

Example:

A mile is the distance you can walk in 15 to 20 minutes or run in about 10 minutes.

milli- A prefix meaning $\frac{1}{1000}$.

Example: 1 millimeter = $\frac{1}{1000}$ meter

mixed number A number made up of a whole number and a fraction.

Examples: $3\frac{1}{2}$ $1\frac{3}{4}$ $13\frac{3}{8}$

mode The value(s) that occur most often in a data set.

Example:

27 27 27 29 32 33 36 38 42 43 62

For the given set of data, 27 is the mode.

21

monomial An algebraic expression that has exactly one term.

Examples: $2x^2$ $5y$ x^3 -3

multiple The product of a given number and another whole number.

Example:

Since $3 \times 7 = 21$, 21 is a multiple of both 3 and 7.

multiplication An operation that combines two numbers, called factors, to give one number, called the product.

Example:

3 rows of 6

$3 \times 6 = 18$
factors   product

multiplication property If *A* and *B* are independent events, then the probability of both occurring is given by $P(A \text{ and } B) = P(A) \times P(B)$.

Example:

1st spin: $P(\text{red}) = \frac{1}{4}$

2nd spin: $P(\text{red}) = \frac{1}{4}$

1st and 2nd spins: $P(\text{red and red}) = \frac{1}{4} \times \frac{1}{4} = \frac{1}{16}$

Multiplication Property of Equality
If $a = b$, then $ac = bc$.

Example:

In the second line of the example below, 2 is multiplied on both sides of the equation.

If $\frac{1}{2}y = 4$

then $2 \times \frac{1}{2}y = 2 \times 4$

multiplicative inverse If the product of two numbers is 1, each number is the multiplicative inverse of the other.

Example:

$\frac{1}{6}$ and 6 are multiplicative inverses since $\frac{1}{6} \times 6 = 1$.

mutually exclusive If either event *A* or *B* occurs, then the other cannot occur.

Examples:

If the temperature outside is 90°, it is not snowing.

If a polygon has only three sides, it cannot have 4 angles.

negative numbers Numbers less than zero.

Example:

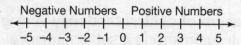

Negative Numbers   Positive Numbers

negative relationship Two data sets have a negative relationship when the data values in one set increase as the values in the other decrease.

Example:

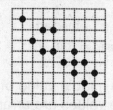

negative slope The slope of a line slanting downward.

Example:

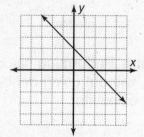

negative square root The opposite of the principal square root of a number.

Example:

principal square root: negative square root:

$\sqrt{25} = 5$ $-\sqrt{25} = -5$

net A flat pattern that can be folded to create a three-dimensional figure such as a prism.

Example:

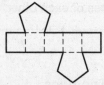

Net for pentagonal prism

Pentagonal prism

nonagon A polygon with 9 sides.

Examples:

nonlinear equation An equation whose graph is a curve rather than a line.

Example:

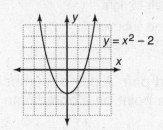

$y = x^2 - 2$

nonlinear function A function whose graph is not a straight line because equal changes in *x* do not result in equal changes in *y*.

Examples:

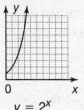 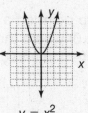 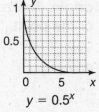

$y = 2^x$ $y = x^2$ $y = 0.5^x$

no relationship Two data sets have no relationship when there is no positive or negative relationship.

Example:

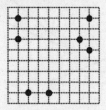

number line A line that shows numbers in order.

Examples:

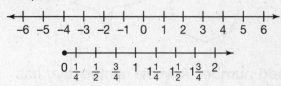

number-word form A way of writing a number using digits and words.

Examples: 45 trillion   9 thousand

numeral A symbol for a number.

Examples: 7   58   234

numerator The top number in a fraction which tells how many parts of the whole are being named.

Example:

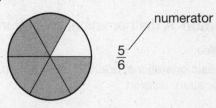

numerator

$\dfrac{5}{6}$

obtuse angle An angle that measures more than 90° and less than 180°.

Examples:

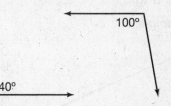

100°

140°

obtuse triangle A triangle with an obtuse angle.

Examples:

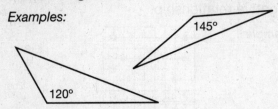

octagon A polygon with 8 sides.

Examples:

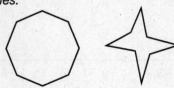

odd number A whole number that has 1, 3, 5, 7, or 9 in the ones place.

Examples:

43   225   999   8,007

odds The ratio of the number of ways an event can happen to the number of ways it cannot.

Example:

Odds of rolling a 3: 1 to 5

Odds against rolling a 3: 5 to 1

operation A mathematical procedure.

Examples:

Four basic operations: addition, subtraction, multiplication, division

opposite leg For an acute angle on a right triangle, the leg lying across from the angle.

Example:

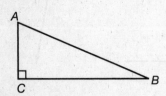

$\overline{CB}$ is the opposite leg to $\angle CAB$.

$\overline{AC}$ is the opposite leg to $\angle ABC$.

opposite numbers Numbers that are the same distance on a number line from zero but are on opposite sides.

Example:

7 and −7 are opposites of each other.

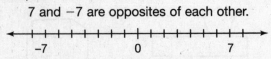

order of operations The rules telling what order to do operations in: (1) simplify inside parentheses, (2) simplify exponents, (3) multiply and divide from left to right, and (4) add and subtract from left to right.

Example:

Evaluate $2x^2 + 4(x - 2)$ for $x = 3$.

(1) simplify inside parentheses	$2 \cdot 3^2 + 4(3 - 2)$ $2 \cdot 3^2 + 4(1)$
(2) simplify exponents	$2 \cdot 9 + 4$
(3) multiply and divide from left to right	$18 + 4$
(4) add and subtract from left to right	22

ordered pair A pair of numbers used to locate a point on a coordinate plane.

Example:

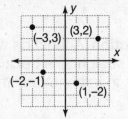

origin The zero point on a number line, or the point (0, 0) where the axes of a coordinate system intersect.

Examples:

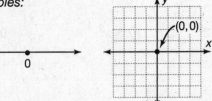

orthographic drawing A drawing of an object using front, side, and top views.

Example:

Front　　Side　　Top

ounce A unit of weight in the customary measurement system.

Example:

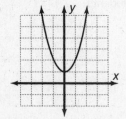

A letter weighs about one ounce.

outcome One way an experiment or situation could turn out.

Example:

Outcomes for Tossing 2 Coins:

coin 1	coin 2
head	tail
head	head
tail	head
tail	tail

There are 4 outcomes. One outcome is head, head.

outlier An extreme value in a data set, separated from most of the other values.

Example:

27　27　27　29　32　33　36　38　42　43　62

↑
outlier

parabola A U-shaped or upside-down U-shaped curve which is the graph of a quadratic function.

Examples:

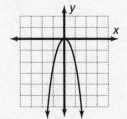

parallel Two lines, segments, or rays in the same plane that do not intersect.

Examples:

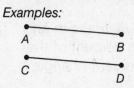 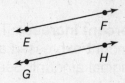

parallelogram A four-sided figure whose opposite sides are parallel and congruent.

Examples:

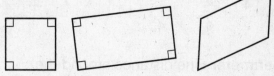

pentagon A polygon with 5 sides.

Examples:

percent A ratio comparing a number to 100.

Example:

$$\frac{58}{100} = 0.58 = 58\%$$

percent change The amount of a change, increase or decrease, divided by the original amount, expressed as a percent of the original amount.

Examples:

Find the percent change if $1500 is invested and $75 is earned in interest.

$\frac{75}{1500} = 0.05 = 5\%$　　$75 is a 5% increase.

Find the percent change if an item that costs $50 is on sale for $10 off.

$\frac{10}{50} = 0.20 = 20\%$　　$10 off is a 20% decrease.

percent decrease The decrease in an amount expressed as a percent of the original amount. See *percent change*.

percent increase The increase in an amount expressed as a percent of the original amount. See *percent change*.

perfect square The square of a whole number.

Examples:

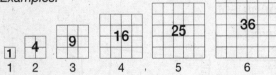

perimeter The distance around the outside of a figure.

Example: $P = 5 + 2 + 6 + 4 + 11 + 6$
$= 34$ units

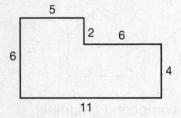

permutation An arrangement of items in which order is important.

Example:

One student from this group will be elected president and one will be elected vice president: Wendy, Alex, Carlos. The possible permutations are:

Wendy—president, Alex—vice president
Wendy—president, Carlos—vice president
Alex—president, Wendy—vice president
Alex—president, Carlos—vice president
Carlos—president, Wendy—vice president
Carlos—president, Alex—vice president

Note: Each of the above is a different permutation.

perpendicular Lines, rays, or line segments that intersect at right angles.

Examples:

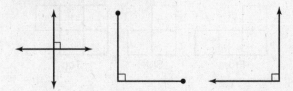

perpendicular bisector A line, ray, or segment that intersects a segment at its midpoint and is perpendicular to it.

Example:

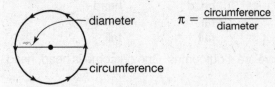

$\overrightarrow{DE}$ is the perpendicular bisector of $\overline{AB}$.

pi (π) The ratio of a circle's circumference to its diameter: 3.14159265….

Example:

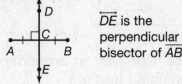

$$\pi = \frac{\text{circumference}}{\text{diameter}}$$

pictograph A graph using symbols to represent data.

Example:

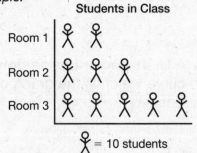

Students in Class

Room 1
Room 2
Room 3

= 10 students

place value The value given to the place a digit occupies.

Example:

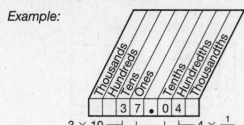

3×10
7×1
$0 \times \frac{1}{10}$
$4 \times \frac{1}{100}$

plane A flat surface that extends forever.

Example:

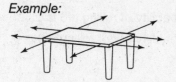

To visualize a plane, think of extending the table surface in all directions.

point symmetry A figure has point symmetry if it looks unchanged after a 180° rotation.

Example:

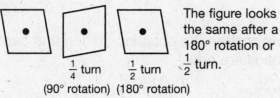

$\frac{1}{4}$ turn (90° rotation) $\frac{1}{2}$ turn (180° rotation)

The figure looks the same after a 180° rotation or $\frac{1}{2}$ turn.

polygon A closed figure in a plane made of line segments that intersect only at their endpoints.

Examples:

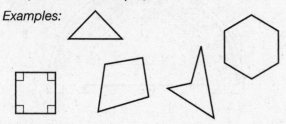

polyhedron A solid whose faces are polygons.

Examples:

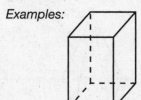

polynomial An algebraic expression that is the sum of one or more terms.

Examples: $x^2 + 2x - 3$ $5y - 15$

population The collection of all things to be studied in a survey.

Example:

All 1000 names of a club's membership were put on cards and the cards were shuffled. Then 100 cards were drawn and these members were given a phone survey. The population of the survey is all 1000 of the club members.

positive numbers Numbers greater than zero.

Example:

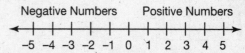

Negative Numbers   Positive Numbers

$-5\ -4\ -3\ -2\ -1\ 0\ 1\ 2\ 3\ 4\ 5$

positive relationship Two data sets have a positive relationship when their data values both increase or both decrease.

Example:

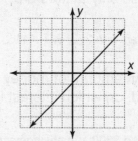

positive slope The slope of a line slanting upward.

Example:

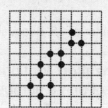

pound A unit in the customary system of measurement equal to 16 ounces.

Example:

Rice 1 pound

power An exponent or the number produced by raising a base to the exponent.

Example:

$16 = 2^4$ 2 is raised to the 4th power.

16 is the 4th power of 2.

precision The exactness of a measurement, determined by the unit of measure.

Example:

5'1" 61"

The smaller unit of measure, inches, is more precise than the larger unit of measure, feet.

prime factor A prime number that divides another integer without leaving a remainder.

Example:

5 is a prime factor of 35, because $35 \div 5 = 7$.

prime factorization Writing a number as a product of prime numbers.

Example: $70 = 2 \times 5 \times 7$

prime number A whole number greater than 1 whose only factors are 1 and itself.

Example:

The primes start with 2, 3, 5, 7, 11, ...

principal An amount of money deposited or borrowed, on which interest is paid.

Example:

Dave deposited $300 in a savings account. After 1 year the balance of his account was $315. $300 is the amount of principal.

principal square root The positive square root of a number.

Example:

principal square root   negative square root

$\sqrt{25} = 5$ $-\sqrt{25} = -5$

prism A polyhedron whose bases are congruent and parallel.

Example:

probability A ratio of the number of ways an event can happen to the total number of possible outcomes.

Example:

The probability of rolling a 3 is $\frac{1}{6}$.

The probability of not rolling a 3 is $\frac{5}{6}$.

product The result of multiplying two or more numbers.

Example:

product

$2 \times 3 \times 5 = 30$

proportion An equation stating that two ratios are equal.

Example: $\frac{12}{34} = \frac{6}{17}$

protractor A tool for measuring angles.

Example:

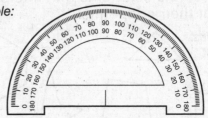

pyramid A solid with one polygonal base and whose other sides are all triangles meeting at a single point.

Examples:

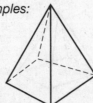

28

Pythagorean Theorem In a right triangle where c is the length of the hypotenuse and a and b are the lengths of the legs, $a^2 + b^2 = c^2$.

Example:

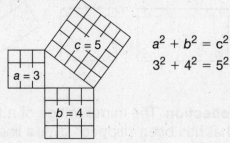

$$a^2 + b^2 = c^2$$
$$3^2 + 4^2 = 5^2$$

quadrants The four regions determined by the axes of a coordinate plane.

Example:

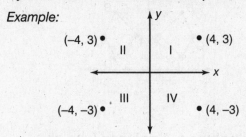

quadratic equation An equation with a squared term like x^2.

Examples:

$$y = x^2 + 3x - 12 \qquad y = 2x^2 + 7$$

quadratic function A function where the highest power of x is 2. The graph of a quadratic function is a parabola.

Example:

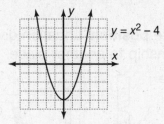

$y = x^2 - 4$

quadrilateral A polygon with 4 sides.

Examples:

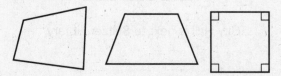

quart A unit of volume in the customary measurement system.

Example:

A quart of milk

quartile One of the numbers dividing a data set into equal fourths.

Example:

27 27 27 29 32 33 36 38 42 43 62

lower quartile   median   upper quartile

27, 33, and 42 are the three quartiles for this data set.

quotient The result of dividing one number by another.

Example:

$$8 \div 4 = 2 \quad \text{quotient}$$

radical sign $\sqrt{}$, used to represent the square root of a number.

Example: $\sqrt{49} = 7$

radius A line from the center of a circle to any point on the circle.

Example:

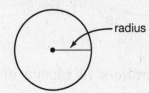

radius

random sample A sample chosen in such a way that every member of the population has an equal chance of being included.

Example:

All 1000 names of a club's membership were put on cards and the cards were shuffled. Then 100 cards were drawn and these members were given a phone survey. All the members of the club had an equal chance of being called so this was a random sample.

range The difference between the highest and lowest values in a data set.

Example:

27 27 27 29 32 33 36 38 42 43 62

The range is 62 − 27 = 35.

rate A ratio showing how quantities with different units are related.

Examples: $\frac{72 \text{ dollars}}{28 \text{ hours}}$ $\frac{55 \text{ miles}}{1 \text{ hour}}$

ratio A comparison of two quantities, often written as a fraction.

Examples: $\frac{2}{1}$ 2 to 1   2:1

rational number A number that can be written as a ratio of two integers. Integers, fractions, and many decimals are rational numbers.

Examples:

Integer	Fraction	Decimal
$-27 = \frac{-27}{1}$	$\frac{7}{8}$	$3.1 = 3\frac{1}{10} = \frac{31}{10}$

ray A part of a line that has one endpoint and extends forever in the other direction. A ray is named by its endpoint first.

Example:

 $\overrightarrow{AB}$

real numbers All rational and irrational numbers.

Examples:

-27 $\frac{1}{2}$ 3.1

$\sqrt{5}$ π $-\sqrt{\frac{1}{2}}$

reciprocals Two numbers whose product is 1.

Example:

$\frac{3}{5}$ and $\frac{5}{3}$ are reciprocals since $\frac{3}{5} \cdot \frac{5}{3} = 1$.

rectangle A parallelogram with opposite sides the same length and all angles measuring 90°.

Examples:

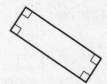

reflection The mirror image of a figure that has been "flipped" over a line. Also, the name for the transformation that flips the figure over the line.

Example:

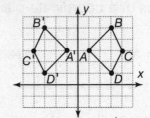

regular polygon A polygon with all sides and angles congruent.

Examples:

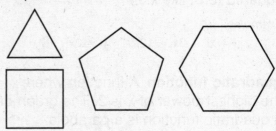

relative position Location given in relationship to another place.

Example:

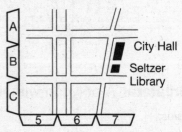

City Hall is next to Seltzer Library.

remainder The number less than the divisor that remains after the division process is completed.

Example:

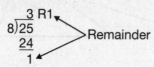

repeating decimal A decimal with a repeating digit or group of digits to the right of the decimal point.

Examples: $0.\overline{6}$ $0.1\overline{23}$ $2.\overline{18}$

rhombus A parallelogram with four sides of equal length.

Examples:

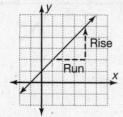

right angle An angle that measures 90°.

Example:

right triangle A triangle with one right angle.

Examples:

rise For a line on a graph, the vertical change for a given horizontal change.

Example:

rotation The image of a figure that has been "turned," as if on a wheel. Also, the name for the transformation that turns the figure.

Example:

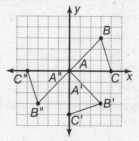

rotational symmetry A figure has rotational symmetry if it can be rotated less than a full circle and exactly match its original image.

Examples:

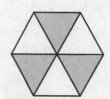

Each figure has rotational symmetry.

rounding Estimating a number to a given place value.

Example:

2153 rounded to	
nearest hundred: 2200	nearest ten: 2150

run For a line on a graph, the horizontal change used to find the vertical change, or rise.

Example:

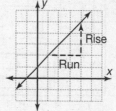

sample A set of data used to predict how a particular situation might happen.

Example:

All 1000 names of a club's membership were put on cards and the cards were shuffled. Then 100 cards were drawn and these members were given a phone survey. The sample is the 100 members that took the phone survey.

31

sample space The set of all possible outcomes of an experiment.

Example:

Outcomes for Tossing 2 Coins:

coin 1	coin 2
head	tail
head	head
tail	head
tail	tail

The sample space is head, tail; head, head; and tail, tail.

scale (graphical) The evenly spaced marks on a bar graph's or line graph's vertical axis, used to measure the heights of the bars or lines.

Example:

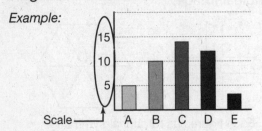

scale (in scale drawings) The ratio of measurements in a scale drawing to the measurements of the actual object. See *scale drawing*.

scale drawing A drawing that uses a scale to make an enlarged or reduced picture of an object.

Example:

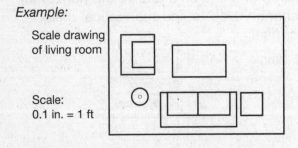

Scale drawing of living room

Scale: 0.1 in. = 1 ft

scale factor The ratio used to enlarge or reduce similar figures.

Example:

$$\frac{10}{5} = 2$$

$$\frac{6}{3} = 2$$

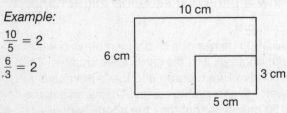

10 cm
6 cm
3 cm
5 cm

The scale factor is 2 for the enlargement.

scalene triangle A triangle whose sides have different lengths.

Examples:

scatterplot A graph using paired data values as points to show the relationship between the two data sets.

Example:

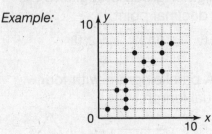

scientific notation A number written as a decimal greater than or equal to 1 and less than 10, multiplied by a power of 10.

Example: $350,000 = 3.5 \times 10^5$

sector A wedge-shaped part of a circle, used in a circle graph to show how portions of a set of data compare with the whole set.

Examples:

segment See *line segment*.

segment bisector A line, ray, or segment through the midpoint of a segment.

Example:

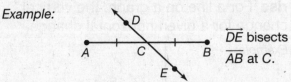

$\overleftrightarrow{DE}$ bisects $\overline{AB}$ at *C*.

32

sequence An arrangement of numbers that follows a pattern.

Examples:

arithmetic sequence

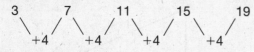

geometric sequence

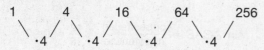

side Each of the rays forming an angle. Also, the line segments that make up a polygon.

Examples:

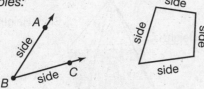

Side-Angle-Angle (SAA) A rule used to determine whether triangles are congruent by comparing corresponding parts.

Example:

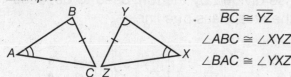

$\overline{BC} \cong \overline{YZ}$
$\angle ABC \cong \angle XYZ$
$\angle BAC \cong \angle YXZ$

$\triangle ABC \cong \triangle XYZ$ by the SAA rule.

Side-Angle-Side (SAS) A rule used to determine whether triangles are congruent by comparing corresponding parts.

Example:

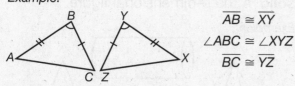

$\overline{AB} \cong \overline{XY}$
$\angle ABC \cong \angle XYZ$
$\overline{BC} \cong \overline{YZ}$

$\triangle ABC \cong \triangle XYZ$ by the SAS rule.

Side-Side-Side (SSS) A rule used to determine whether triangles are congruent by comparing corresponding parts.

Example:

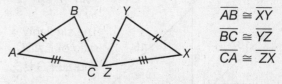

$\overline{AB} \cong \overline{XY}$
$\overline{BC} \cong \overline{YZ}$
$\overline{CA} \cong \overline{ZX}$

$\triangle ABC \cong \triangle XYZ$ by the SSS rule.

significant digits In a measured quantity, the digits representing the actual measurement.

Examples:

380.6700   All digits are significant.

0.0038   3 and 8 are significant, but none of the zeros are significant.

similar Having the same shape but not necessarily the same size.

Examples:

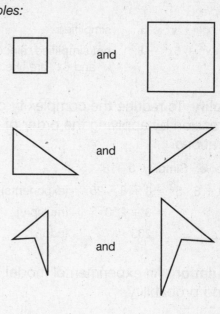

similarity ratio The ratio between corresponding side lengths on similar figures.

Example:

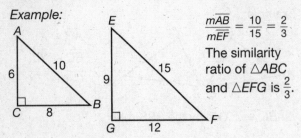

$$\frac{m\overline{AB}}{m\overline{EF}} = \frac{10}{15} = \frac{2}{3}$$

The similarity ratio of $\triangle ABC$ and $\triangle EFG$ is $\frac{2}{3}$.

simple interest Interest based on principal alone.

Example: Ramon invests $240 in an account which earns 6% interest per year for 5 years.

He will earn $240 \cdot 0.06 \cdot 5 = 72$; $72 in simple interest after 5 years.

simplified A polynomial containing no like terms.

Example:

$4x^4 + x^3 + x^2 - 8$ simplified

$4x^4 + x^2 + 6x^2 - 8$ not simplified, since x^2 and $6x^2$ are like terms

simplify To reduce the complexity of an expression by applying the order of operations.

Example: Simplify $3 + 8 \cdot 5^2$.

$$\begin{aligned} 3 + 8 \cdot 5^2 &= 3 + 8 \cdot 25 &\text{(exponents)} \\ &= 3 + 200 &\text{(multiply)} \\ &= 203 &\text{(add)} \end{aligned}$$

simulation An experimental model used to find probability.

Example:

A baseball player bats .250. To simulate how this player might bat, a 4-section spinner is spun. The simulation can be used to predict how often the batter would hit 2 in a row or 3 in a row.

sine For an acute angle x on a right triangle, the sine of x, *or* $\sin(x)$, is the ratio $\frac{\text{opposite leg}}{\text{hypotenuse}}$.

Example:

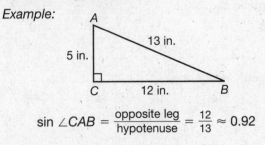

$$\sin \angle CAB = \frac{\text{opposite leg}}{\text{hypotenuse}} = \frac{12}{13} \approx 0.92$$

slant height On a pyramid, the perpendicular distance from one edge of the base to the vertex.

Example:

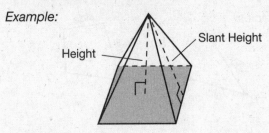

slide See *translation*.

slope For a line on a graph, slope is the rise divided by the run, used to describe the steepness of a line.

Example:

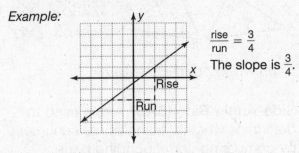

$$\frac{\text{rise}}{\text{run}} = \frac{3}{4}$$

The slope is $\frac{3}{4}$.

solid A three-dimensional figure.

Examples:

solutions of an equation or inequality
Values of a variable that make an equation or inequality true.

Examples:

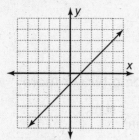 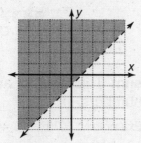

The line represents the solutions to $y = x - 1$.

The shaded area represents the solutions to $y > x - 1$.

solution of a system The variable replacements making all equations in a system true.

Example:
$$y = x + 4$$
$$y = 3x - 6$$

The ordered pair (5, 9) solves both equations. So, (5, 9) is a solution of the system.

solve To find the solutions of an equation or inequality.

Example: Solve $x + 6 = 13$.

$$x + 6 = 13$$
$$x + 6 + (-6) = 13 + (-6)$$
$$x + 0 = 7$$
$$x = 7$$

sphere A solid whose points are all the same distance from the center.

Example:

square A quadrilateral with all sides the same length and all angles measuring 90°.

Example:

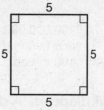

squared Raised to the second power.

Example: 3 squared is written 3^2.
$$3^2 = 3 \times 3 = 9$$

square centimeter The area of a square with 1-centimeter sides.

Example:

1 square centimeter

square inch The area of a square with 1-inch sides.

Example:

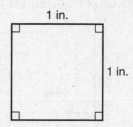

1 square inch

square root The square root of *N* is the number that when multiplied by itself gives *N*. Also, the square root of a given number is the length of one side of a square with an area equal to the given number.

Example:
$9 \times 9 = 81$, so 9 is the square root of 81.
$9 = \sqrt{81}$

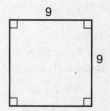

Area is 81 square units.

standard form A way of writing a number using digits.

Example:

Standard form:	100,000,000
Word form:	one hundred million
Number-word form:	100 million

stem-and-leaf diagram A display of data that uses the digits of the data numbers to show the shape and distribution of the data set.

Example:

The diagram shows the data set: 33, 34, 34, 35, 40, 41, 46, 51, 51, 52, 53, 55, 58.

Stem	Leaf
3	3 4 4 5
4	0 1 6
5	1 1 2 3 5 8

step function A function in which different rules are applied to different input values. The graph of a step function is made up of unconnected pieces.

Example:

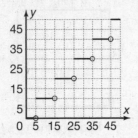

straight angle An angle measuring 180°.

Example:

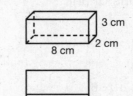

substitute To replace a variable with a specific value.

Example:

Use the formula $A = l \cdot w$ to find the area of a rectangle with length 12 cm and width 8 cm.

$A = l \cdot w$

$A = 12 \cdot 8$ Substitute values for
$A = 96$ length and width.

Area is 96 cm².

subtraction An operation that tells the difference between two numbers, or how many are left when some are taken away.

Example: $12 - 5 = 7$

⊠ ⊠ ⊠ ⊠ ⊠
○ ○ ○ ○ ○
○ ○

sum The result of adding two or more numbers.

Example: $30 + 18 = 48$ ⟋ sum

supplementary angles Two angles whose measures add up to 180°.

Example:

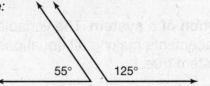

surface area (SA) The sum of the areas of each face of a polyhedron.

Example:

Two faces are 8 cm by 3 cm.
$A = b \cdot h = 8 \cdot 3 = 24$ cm²

Two faces are 8 cm by 2 cm.
$A = b \cdot h = 8 \cdot 2 = 16$ cm²

Two faces are 2 cm by 3 cm.
$A = b \cdot h = 2 \cdot 3 = 6$ cm²

The surface area of the rectangular prism is:

$SA = 2(24 + 16 + 6)$
$= 92$ cm²

survey A study that requires collecting and analyzing information.

Example:

A survey was conducted to determine what sport was the most popular among students.

symmetry See *line symmetry, point symmetry,* and *rotational symmetry.*

system of linear equations Two or more linear equations considered together.

Example: $y = x + 3$
$y = 4x - 15$

T-table A table showing corresponding *x*- and *y*-values for an equation.

Example: $y = 2x + 1$

x	y
−2	−3
−1	−1
0	1
1	3
2	5

tally A record, using tally marks, of a count taken during a survey.

Example:

Vehicle	Tally
Sedan	IIII III
Station Wagon	IIII
Suburban	IIII I
Truck	IIII
Van	III

tally marks Marks used to organize a large set of data. Each mark indicates one time a value appears in the data set.

Example: | One   IIII Five

tangent line A line that touches a circle at only one point.

Examples:

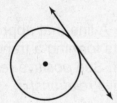

tangent ratio For an acute angle *x* on a right triangle, the tangent of *x*, or $\tan(x)$, is $\frac{\text{opposite leg}}{\text{adjacent leg}}$.

Example:

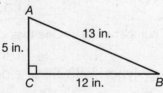

$\tan \angle CAB = \frac{\text{opposite leg}}{\text{adjacent leg}} = \frac{12}{5} = 2.4$

term One number in a sequence. Also, a part of a polynomial that is a signed number, a variable, or a number multiplied by a variable or variables. The variables can have whole-number exponents.

Examples:

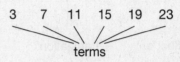
sequence   3   7   11   15   19   23
terms

polynomial $2x^3 - x^2 + 3x - 5$
terms

terminating decimal A decimal with a fixed number of digits.

Examples: 3.5   0.599992   4.05

tessellation A repeating pattern of figures that covers a plane without gaps or overlaps.

Examples:

theoretical probability The ratio of the number of ways an event can happen to the total number of possible outcomes.

Example:

$\frac{\text{Number of ways to spin white}}{\text{Total ways}} = \frac{3}{6} = \frac{1}{2}$

Since half of the sections on the spinner are white, the theoretical probability of spinning white is $\frac{1}{2}$.

transformation A change in the position of a figure.

Example:

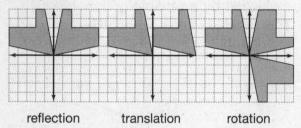

reflection   translation   rotation

translation The image of a figure that has been slid to a new position without flipping or turning. Also, the name for the transformation that slides the figure.

Example:

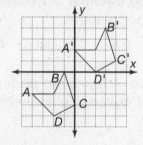

transversal A line that crosses two or more other lines.

Example:

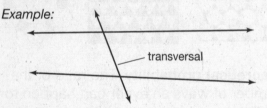

transversal

trapezoid A quadrilateral with exactly two sides parallel.

Examples:

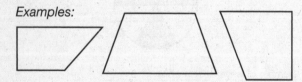

tree diagram A branching, tree-like diagram showing all possible outcomes of a situation.

Example:

Tossing 3 coins:

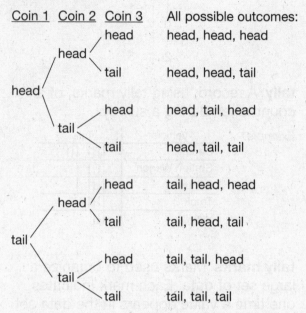

Coin 1	Coin 2	Coin 3	All possible outcomes:
		head	head, head, head
	head		
		tail	head, head, tail
head			
		head	head, tail, head
	tail		
		tail	head, tail, tail
		head	tail, head, head
	head		
		tail	tail, head, tail
tail			
		head	tail, tail, head
	tail		
		tail	tail, tail, tail

trend A relationship between two sets of data that shows up as a pattern in a scatterplot. See *positive relationship, negative relationship, no relationship.*

trend line A line that approximately "fits" points forming a trend in a scatterplot. See *positive relationship* and *negative relationship.*

trial One experiment.

Examples:

One roll of a number cube   One toss of a coin

triangle A polygon with three sides.

Examples:

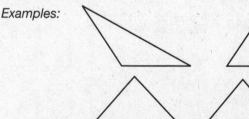

trigonometric ratios Ratios of the side lengths of a right triangle, related to the measures of the triangle's acute angles.

Examples:

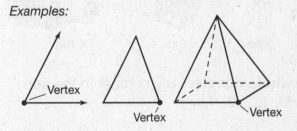

$$\cos \angle CAB = \frac{\text{adjacent leg}}{\text{hypotenuse}} = \frac{3}{5} = 0.6$$

$$\sin \angle CAB = \frac{\text{opposite leg}}{\text{hypotenuse}} = \frac{4}{5} = 0.8$$

$$\tan \angle CAB = \frac{\text{opposite leg}}{\text{adjacent leg}} = \frac{4}{3} \approx 1.3$$

trinomial A polynomial with three terms.

Examples: $2x^3 - x^2 + 3x$ $3x^2 + 2x - 4$

turn See *rotation*.

unfair game A game in which not all players have the same probability of winning.

Example:

Unfair game: A pair of number cubes is rolled and each player is assigned a sum from 2 to 12. Each player gets a point when his/her sum is rolled. Since the sums from 2 to 12 do not have equal chances of being rolled, the players do not have equal chances of winning and thus the game is unfair.

unit price A unit rate giving the cost of one item.

Examples:

$3.00 per pound $5.75 per box

unit One of something. An amount or quantity used as a standard of measurement.

unit fraction A fraction with a numerator of 1.

Examples: $\frac{1}{4}$ $\frac{1}{2}$ $\frac{1}{7}$

unit rate A rate in which the second number in the comparison is one unit.

Examples: 25 gallons per minute $\frac{55 \text{ miles}}{1 \text{ hour}}$

unlike denominators Denominators that are different in two or more fractions.

Example: $\frac{1}{2}$ $\frac{2}{5}$ $\frac{2}{9}$

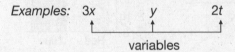

unlike denominators

upper quartile The median of the upper half of a data set.

Example:

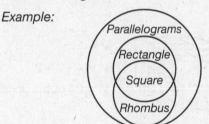

27 27 27 29 32 33 36 38 42 43 62

lower quartile   median   **upper quartile**

variable A quantity that can change or vary, often represented by a letter.

Examples: $3x$ y $2t$

variables

Venn diagram A diagram that uses regions to show relationships between sets of things.

Example:

Parallelograms
Rectangle
Square
Rhombus

vertex On an angle or a polygon, the point where two sides intersect. On a polyhedron, the intersection point of three or more faces.

Examples:

Vertex   Vertex   Vertex

vertical angles Angles on opposite sides of the intersection of two lines.

Example:

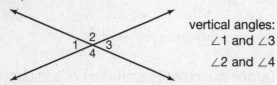

vertical angles:
∠1 and ∠3
∠2 and ∠4

vertical axis The vertical line of the two lines on which a bar graph or a coordinate plane is built.

Examples:

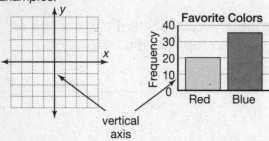

vertical axis

volume The amount of space taken up by a solid.

Example:

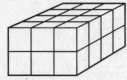

$V = lwh$
$V = 4 \cdot 3 \cdot 2$
$V = 24$ cubic units

weight A measure of the force that gravity exerts on a body.

Examples:

1 oz   1 lb   1 ton

whole number Any number in the set {0, 1, 2, 3, 4, ...}.

word form A way of writing a number using only words.

Examples:

forty-five trillion   one billion   six

x-axis The horizontal axis on a coordinate plane.

Example:

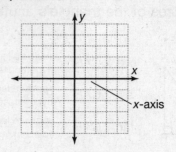

x-axis

x-coordinate The first number in an ordered pair.

Example:

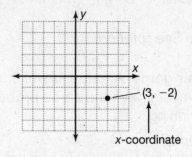

(3, −2)

x-coordinate

x-intercept A point where the graph of an equation crosses the x-axis.

Example:

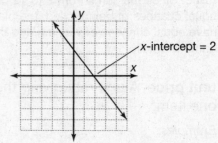

x-intercept = 2

y-axis The vertical axis on a coordinate plane.

Example:

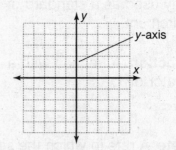

y-axis

y-coordinate The second number in an ordered pair.

Example:

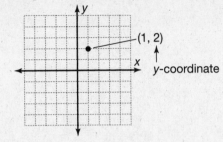

(1, 2)

↑ y-coordinate

y-intercept A point where the graph of an equation crosses the y-axis.

Example:

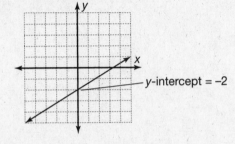

y-intercept = −2

yard A unit in the customary system of measurement equal to 3 feet.

Example:

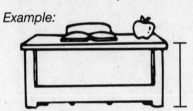

The height of a desk is about a yard.

zero pair A number and its opposite.

Examples: 7 and −7   23 and −23

Zero Property of Addition The sum of an integer and its additive inverse is 0.

Examples: 3 + (−3) = 0
                 −8 + 8 = 0

Cambodian Glossary

ទីតាំងដាច់ខាត (absolute position)
កន្លែងឡ្យៃជា និយាមកា ។

ឧទាហរណ៍:

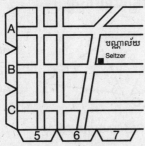

B7 ជាទីតាំងដាច់ខាតរបស់បណ្ណាល័យ Seltzer ។

ចំនួនដាច់ខាត (absolute value)
ចម្ងាយនៃចំនួនមួយពីសូន្យ, បង្ហាញដោយ | | ។

ឧទាហរណ៍:

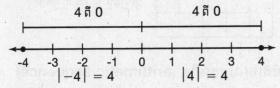

មុមស្រួច (acute angle) មុមមួយទំហំតិចជាង
90° ។

ឧទាហរណ៍:

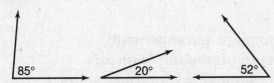

ត្រីកោណស្រួច (acute triangle) ត្រីកោណមួយ
មុមស្រួចបី ។

ឧទាហរណ៍:

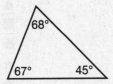

ជើងបូក (addend) ចំនួនមួយបូកជាមួយនឹង
ចំនួនមួយ ឬច្រើនទៀត ។

ឧទាហរណ៍: $12 + 19 = 31$
ជើងបូក   ជើងបូក

លេខបូក (addition) ការធ្វើលេខ
ដែលឡ្យៃចំនួនទាំងអស់ កាលបើចំនួនពីរ
ឬចំនួនច្រើនទៀត ដាក់បញ្ចូលគ្នា ។

ឧទាហរណ៍:

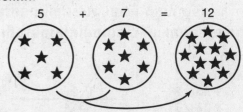

$5 \qquad + \qquad 7 \qquad = \qquad 12$

លក្ខណៈលេខបូកនៃសមភាព (Addition Property of Equality) បើ $a = b$, ដូច្នេះ
$a + c = b + c$ ។

ឧទាហរណ៍:
នៅបន្ទាត់ទី២ នៃឧទាហរណ៍ ខាងក្រោម ។
1 បូកបញ្ចូលនៅផ្នែកសងខាងនៃសមីការ ។

បើ	$x - 1$	$=$	2
ដូច្នេះ:	$x - 1 + 1$	$=$	$2 + 1$
	x	$=$	3

ចំនួនថែមប្រច្រាស (additive inverse)
ចំនួនផ្ទុយមួយ ។

ឧទាហរណ៍:   ចំនួនថែមប្រច្រាសនៃ -2 គឺ 2.
ចំនួនថែមប្រច្រាសនៃ 5 គឺ -5.

ជ្រុងជាប់គ្នា (adjacent leg) ក្នុងមុមស្រួចនៃត្រី
កោណកែង គឺជ្រុងដែលភ្ជាប់នៅលើផ្នែកខាង
ណាមួយនៃមុម ។

ឧទាហរណ៍:

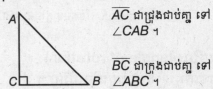

$\overline{AC}$ ជាជ្រុងជាប់គ្នា ទៅ $\angle CAB$ ។

$\overline{BC}$ ជាក្រុងជាប់គ្នា ទៅ $\angle ABC$ ។

ពិជគណិត (algebra) មែកធាងមួយនៃគណិត
សាស្ត្រ ដែលក្នុងនោះ ទំនាក់ទំនងលេខគណិត
ត្រូវបានស្រាវជ្រាវរកដោយយក អថេរ ទៅតំណាង
ចំនួនទាំងនោះ ។

កន្សោមពិជគណិត (algebraic expression)
កន្សោមដែលមាន យ៉ាងហោចណាស់ អថេរ
មួយដែរ ។

ឧទាហរណ៍: $n - 7 \qquad 2y + 17 \qquad 5(x - 3)$

មុមឆ្លាស់ **(alternate angles)** មុមពីរកើតឡើង ដោយ បន្ទាត់ត្រង់ពីរ និងបន្ទាត់កាត់មួយ ជាបែប (1) នៅចន្លោះបន្ទាត់ត្រង់អោយពីរ (មុមឆ្លាស់ក្នុង) ឬ (2) មិននៅចន្លោះបន្ទាត់ត្រង់អោយពីរទេ (មុមឆ្លាស់ ក្រៅ) ។ មុមឆ្លាស់ក្នុង និងមុមឆ្លាស់ក្រៅ មានតម្លៃ ស្មើគ្នាកាលបើបន្ទាត់កាត់បានពុះបន្ទាត់ស្របទាំងពីរ ។

ឧទាហរណ៍:
មុមឆ្លាស់ក្រៅ
   $\angle 1$ និង $\angle 8$
   $\angle 2$ និង $\angle 7$
មុមឆ្លាស់ក្នុង
   $\angle 3$ និង $\angle 6$
   $\angle 4$ និង $\angle 5$

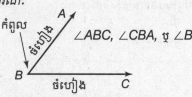

មុម (angle) រស្មីពីរ ដែលមានចំណុចប្រសព្វមួយ ។
ឧទាហរណ៍:

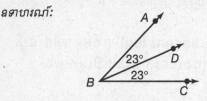

$\angle ABC, \angle CBA$, ឬ $\angle B$

បន្ទាត់ពុះចែកមុម (angle bisector) មួយដែល ពុះចែកមុមមួយអោយទៅជា មុម មានតម្លៃស្មើគ្នា ។
ឧទាហរណ៍:

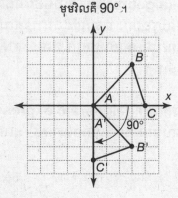

$\overline{BD}$ ជាបន្ទាត់ពុះចែកមុម ក្នុង $\angle ABC$.

មុមវិល (angle of rotation) មុមកើតឡើងដោយរូបវិលជុំវិញ ។
ឧទាហរណ៍:

មុមវិលគឺ 90° ។

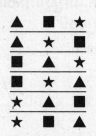

មុម-ចំហៀង-មុម (Angle-Side-Angle (ASA)) ក្បួនប្រើសំរាប់កំណត់ពីត្រីកោណ មានតម្លៃស្មើគ្នា ដោយប្រៀបធៀបធ្នែកស្មើគ្នា ។

ឧទាហរណ៍:

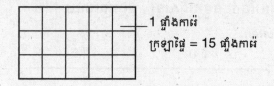

$\angle ABC \cong \angle XYZ$
$\overline{BC} \cong \overline{YZ}$
$\angle ACB \cong \angle XZY$

$\triangle ABC \cong \triangle XYZ$ ដោយក្បួន ASA ។

ក្រឡាផ្ទៃ (area) ចំនួនផ្ទៃមុខដែលពាសលើរូប ។
ឧទាហរណ៍:

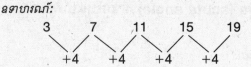

1 ឯកតាការ៉េ
ក្រឡាផ្ទៃ = 15 ឯកតាការ៉េ

លំដាប់លេខគណិត (arithmetic sequence) លំដាប់នៅតែដដែល រវាងផលដក នៃគូលេខរៀងគ្នា ។

ឧទាហរណ៍:

3   7   11   15   19
 +4   +4   +4   +4

ចំណាត់ថែង (arrangement) គឺជារបៀបដែលមនុស្ស-អក្សរ-លេខ ឬក្នុងទៃទៀតបាន លេច បង្ហាញចេញមក ។

ឧទាហរណ៍:
ចំណាត់ថែងអាចមានច្រើនបែប
ក្នុងសភាពរូប ទាំងបីនេះ

▲ ■ ★
▲ ★ ■
■ ▲ ★
■ ★ ▲
★ ▲ ■
★ ■ ▲

លក្ខណៈផ្គុំនៃលេខបូក (Associative Property of Addition) ការដែលបូរកញ្ចុំជើងបូក និងមិន ផ្លាស់បូរផលបូក ទេ ។

ឧទាហរណ៍: $a + (b + c) = (a + b) + c$
              $5 + (3 + 7) = (5 + 3) + 7$

លក្ខណៈផ្គុំនៃលេខគុណ (Associative Property of Multiplication) ការដែលប្ដូរកញ្ចុំកត្តា និងមិនផ្លាស់ប្ដូរផលគុណទេ ។

ឧទាហរណ៍:
$$a(bc) = (ab)c$$
$$3 \times (4 \times 2) = (3 \times 4) \times 2$$

មធ្យមភាគ (average) មើលពាក្យ *mean* ។

អ័ក្ស (axes) មើលពាក្យ *x-axis* និងពាក្យ *y-axis* ។

ក្រាភិចរនុក (bar graph) ក្រាភិចដែលប្រើរនុកបញ្ឈរ ឬរនុកផ្ដេក ដើម្បីនឹងបង្ហាញទិន្នន័យ ។

ឧទាហរណ៍:

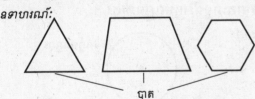

ធាតុគុណ (របស់និទស្សន្ត) (base of an exponent) លេខដែលគុណនឹងខ្លួនឯង ទៅតាមចំនួនដង ប្រាប់ដោយ និទស្សន្ត មួយ ។

ឧទាហរណ៍: ធាតុគុណ និទស្សន្ត
$$6^2 = 6 \times 6 = 36$$

ឋាត (របស់ពហុកោណ) (base of a polygon) ជ្រុងណាមួយ (ជាធម្មតា ជ្រុងខាងក្រោម), ឬរង្វាស់ប្រវែងនៃជ្រុងនោះ ។

ឧទាហរណ៍:

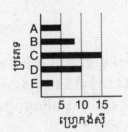

ឋាត (របស់ សូលីត) (base of a solid) ចំពោះព្រិស ឬស៊ីឡាំង គឺមុខមួយ នៃមុខទាំងពីរ ដែលស្របគ្នានិងសមភាព ។ ចំពោះ ពីរ៉ាមិត គឺមុខឈមនឹង កំពូល ។ ចំពោះ កោន គឺមុខ បរិវត្ត ។

ឧទាហរណ៍:

ប្រព័ន្ធទ្វិភាគ (binary number system) ប្រព័ន្ធប្រើក្បួន-២ នៃខ្ទង់លេខ ។

ឧទាហរណ៍:
ក្នុងប្រព័ន្ធទ្វិភាគ, 1011 ស្មើនឹង 11 ក្នុងប្រព័ន្ធលេខទសភាគ (ក្បួន-10) ។

	ខ្ទង់ 8	ខ្ទង់ 4	ខ្ទង់ 2	ខ្ទង់ 1
ក្បួន-២	1	0	1	1
ខ្ទង់លេខ	8	4	2	1
ផលគុណ	1×8=8	0×4=0	1×2=2	1×1=1

$(1 \times 8) + (0 \times 4) + (1 \times 2) + (1 \times 1) = 8 + 0 + 2 + 1 = 11$

ទ្វិធា (binomial) គឺអង្គ-ពីរ នៃពហុធា ។

ឧទាហរណ៍: $4x^3 - 2x^2$ $2x + 5$

ពុះចែក (bisect) គឺចែកមុមមួយ ឬអង្កត់មួយ ឱ្យបានជាមុមពីរ ឬអង្កត់ពីរសមភាព ។

ឧទាហរណ៍:

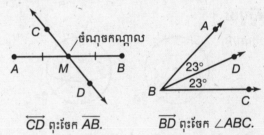

$\overline{CD}$ ពុះចែក $\overline{AB}$. $\overrightarrow{BD}$ ពុះចែក $\angle ABC$.

បន្ទាត់កំណត់ដែន (boundary line) ក្នុងក្រាភិច នៃបន្ទាត់ អសមភាព គឺបន្ទាត់បែងចែកចំណុចទាំងឡាយ ដែលជាចម្លើយ និង មិនចំលើយនោះ ។

ឧទាហរណ៍:

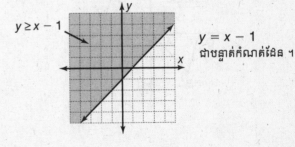

$y \geq x - 1$

$y = x - 1$ ជាបន្ទាត់កំណត់ដែន ។

តារាងប្រអប់ (box-and-whisker plot) ការបង្ហាញឲ្យមើលឃើញ ពីរបៀបប្រមូលទិន្នន័យ និង បែងចែក ។ ឧទាហរណ៍ខាងក្រោម សំអាងលើពិន្ទុប្រឡង តេស្ត ទាំងដប់ដូចតទៅ: 52, 64, 75, 79, 80, 80, 81, 88, 92, 99.

ឧទាហរណ៍:

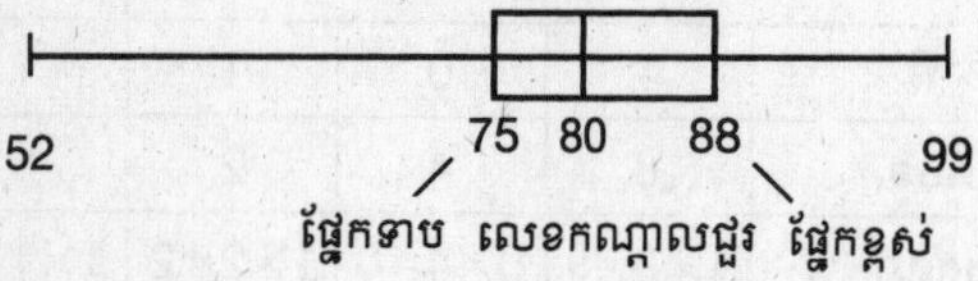
ពិន្ទុប្រឡងតេស្ត
52
75
80
88
99
ផ្នែកទាប
លេខកណ្តាលជួរ
ផ្នែកខ្ពស់

ចំណុះ (capacity) មាឌនៃរបស់មួយ ដែលគិតជារង្វាស់វត្ថុរាវ ។

ឧទាហរណ៍:

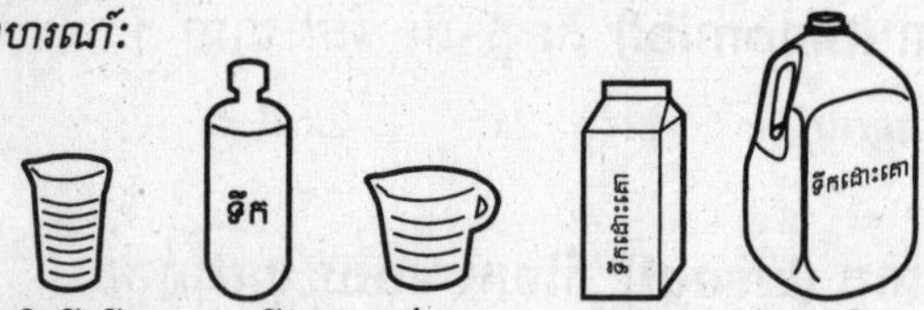
ទឹក
ទឹកដោះគោ
ទឹកដោះគោ

500 មិល្លីលីត្រ 1 លីត្រ 1 ពែង 1 ក្វាត 1 ហ្គាឡិន

ផ្ចិត (center) ចំណុចនៅកណ្តាលមណ្ឌល ឬស្វ៊ែមួយ ។

ឧទាហរណ៍:

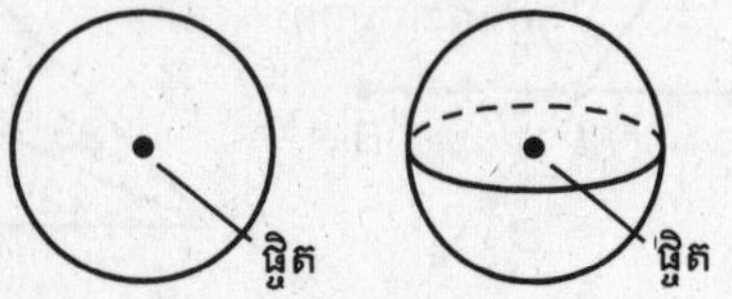
ផ្ចិត
ផ្ចិត

ផ្ចិតរង្វិល (center of rotation) ចំណុចដែលរូបមួយ វិលព័ទ្ធជុំវិញ ។

ឧទាហរណ៍:

ចំណុចដែលរូបមួយ វិលព័ទ្ធជុំវិញ ។

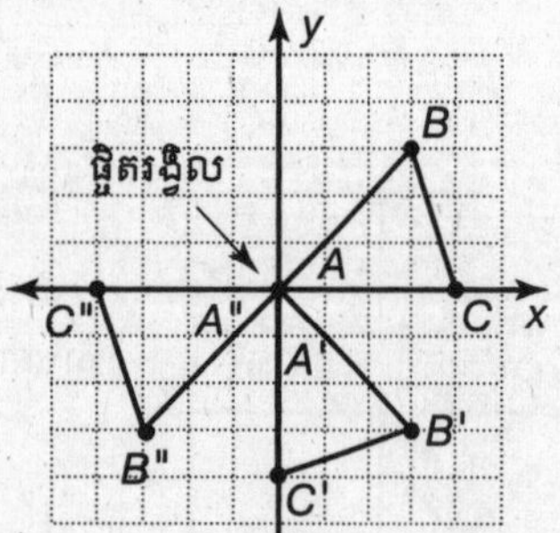
y
x
B
A
C
ផ្ចិតរង្វិល
C"
A"
A'
B'
B"
C'

សង្ទី- (centi-) បុព្វបទ មានន័យថា ភាគមួយរយ $\frac{1}{100}$ ។

ឧទាហរណ៍: 1 សង្ទីម៉ែត្រ = $\frac{1}{100}$ ម៉ែត្រ

មុមផ្ចិត (central angle) មុមដែលមានកំពូលនៅត្រង់ផ្ចិតរបស់មណ្ឌល ។

ឧទាហរណ៍:

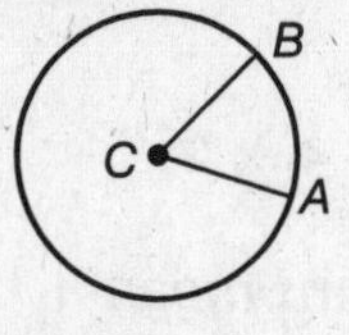
B
C
A

ចំណុច *C* ជាផ្ចិតរបស់មណ្ឌល ។ ∠*BCA* គឺជាមុមផ្ចិត

រង្វង់ (circle) រូបប្លង់ ដែលមានចំណុចទាំងអស់មានចម្ងាយដូចគ្នា ពីផ្ចិត ។

ឧទាហរណ៍:

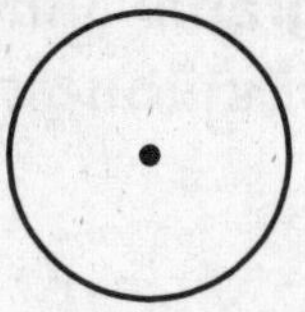

ក្រាភិច មណ្ឌល (circle graph) ក្រាភិចមណ្ឌលដែលប្រើផ្ទាំងចម្រៀកជាតំណាង ផ្នែកសំណុំទិន្នន័យ ។ ក្រាភិចមណ្ឌល អាចហៅថាជាតារាងនំផែបានដែរ ។

ឧទាហរណ៍:

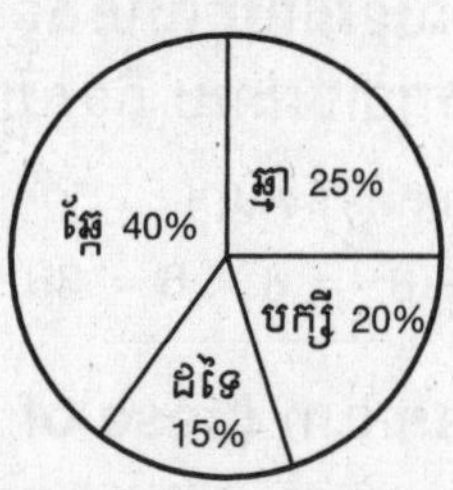
សត្វពេញចិត្តជាងគេ
ឆ្មា 25%
ឆ្កែ 40%
បក្សី 20%
ដទៃ 15%

វណ្ឌមណ្ឌល (circumference) រយៈចម្ងាយព័ទ្ធជុំវិញមណ្ឌលមួយ ។

ឧទាហរណ៍:

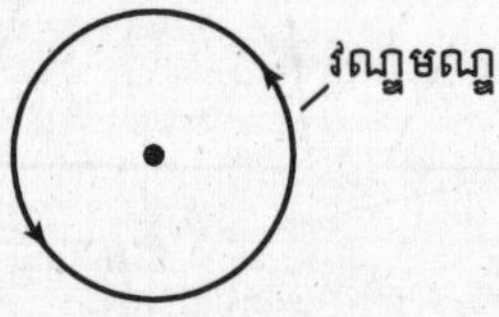
វណ្ឌមណ្ឌល

រូបចារឹកក្នុង (circumscribed figure) រូបភាពដែលមានរូបមួយទៀត នៅខាងក្នុង ។ ពហុកោណមួយ មានមណ្ឌលចារឹកក្នុង ប្រសិនបើមណ្ឌល ប៉ះជ្រុងរបស់វា ។

ឧទាហរណ៍:

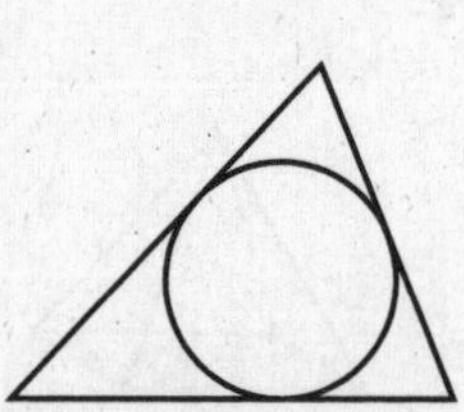

ត្រីកោណមានមណ្ឌលចារឹកក្នុង ។

រង្វិលឆ្វេង-ស្ដាំ (clockwise) ទិសរង្វិល
កាលបើកំពូលលើនៃរូបរាងអ្វីមួយបាន
វិលទៅខាងស្ដាំ ។

ឧទាហរណ៍:

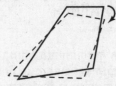

កញ្ចុំ (clustering) របៀបប្រមាណដោយយកចំនួន
ប្រហាក់ប្រហែលគ្នា ចាត់ទុកទាំងអស់ថា ស្មើគ្នា ។

ឧទាហរណ៍:
26 + 24 + 23 ប្រហែលនឹង 25 + 25 + 25, ឬ 3 × 25 ។

មេគុណ (coefficient) គូផេរ មួយ
ដែលត្រូវបានចំនួនអថេរ យកមក គុណាជាមួយ ។

ឧទាហរណ៍:

មេគុណ   អថេរ

$12y$

បន្សំ (combination)
ជម្រើសរបស់ដោយមិនគិតលំដាប់ ។

ឧទាហរណ៍:
សិស្សពីរនាក់ក្នុងក្រុមនេះ នឹងត្រូវបានជ្រើសរើសចូលក្នុង
គណៈកម្មការ: ដេវីង, ចននីតា, គីម ។
បន្សំអាចធ្វើបានគឺ : ដេវីង, ចននីតា   ដេវីង, គីម   ចននីតា, គីម
កំណត់សំគាល់: បន្សំ "ដេវីង, ចននីតា" ដូចគ្នានឹង បន្សំ "ចននីតា,
ដេវីង" ។

ភាគបែងរួម (common denominator)
ភាគបែងដែលដូចគ្នានឹងភាគបែងនៃប្រភាគពីរ
ឬច្រើនទៀត ។

ឧទាហរណ៍:

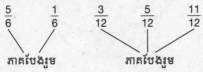

$$\frac{5}{6} \quad \frac{1}{6} \quad \frac{3}{12} \quad \frac{5}{12} \quad \frac{11}{12}$$

ភាគបែងរួម   ភាគបែងរួម

កត្តារួម (common factor) លេខដែលជាកត្តា
នៃចំនួនពីរ ឬច្រើនទៀត ។

ឧទាហរណ៍:

4 ជាកត្តារួម របស់ 8, 12, និង 20.

$$8 = \mathbf{4} \times 2$$
$$12 = \mathbf{4} \times 3$$
$$20 = \mathbf{4} \times 5$$

ពហុគុណរួម (common multiple)
លេខដែលជាពហុគុណនៃចំនួនពីរ ឬច្រើនទៀត ។

ឧទាហរណ៍:
ពហុគុណរបស់ 3: 3 6 9 **12** 15 18 21 **24** 27...
ពហុគុណរបស់ 4: 4 8 **12** 16 20 **24** 28...
12 និង 24 គឺជាពហុគុណរួមទាំងពីររបស់ 3 និង 4 ។

លក្ខណៈបន្លាស់ប្ដូរនៃលេខបូក (Commutative Property of Addition) ការដែលដាក់ជា
លំដាប់ (order) និងមិនបន្លាស់ប្ដូរផលបូកនៃចំនួនពីរ
ឬច្រើនទេ ។

ឧទាហរណ៍: $a + b = b + a$
                $18 + 23 = 23 + 18$

លក្ខណៈបន្លាស់ប្ដូរនៃលេខគុណ (Commutative Property of Multiplication) ការដែល
ដាក់ជាលំដាប់ និងមិនបន្លាស់ប្ដូរផលគុណនៃចំនួនពីរ
ឬច្រើនទេ ។

ឧទាហរណ៍: $ab = ba$
                $4 \times 7 = 7 \times 4$

លេខឆបគ្នា (compatible numbers) គូលេខ
(pairs of numbers) ដែលអាចងាយនឹងគិតគូរ ។

ឧទាហរណ៍:   30 + 70   40 ÷ 4   25 + 75

ការទូទាត់លេខ (compensation) វិធីគិតមាត់ទទេ
ដោយប្រើលេខមានចំនួនក្បែរលេខក្នុង ចំណោទ
រួចបន្ថែមមក តម្រឹមចំឡើយដោយទូទាត់ទៅចំនួនលេខ
ដែលជ្រើសនោះ ។

ឧទាហរណ៍: $99 \times 4 = (100 - 1) \times 4$
             $= (100 \times 4) - (1 \times 4)$
             $= 400 - 4$
             $= 396$

មុមបំពេញ (complementary angles)
មុមពីរដែលរង្វាស់មុមបូកចូលគ្នា ស្មើនឹង 90° ។

ឧទាហរណ៍:

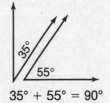

$35° + 55° = 90°$

លេខសមាសភាគ (composite number)
ចំនួនគត់ 1 ហើយមានកត្តា ច្រើនលើសពីពីរទៅ ។

ឧទាហរណ៍:

កត្តារបស់ 15: 1, 3, 5, 15
    15 ជាលេខសមាសភាគ ។

កត្តា របស់ 7: 1, 7
    7 មិនមែនជាលេខសមាសភាគទេ ។

ព្រឹត្តិការណ៍លាយគ្នា (compound event)
ព្រឹត្តិការណ៍ ដែលជាបន្សំ នៃ ព្រឹត្តិការណ៍ទោល ពីរ ឬច្រើនឡើត ។

ឧទាហរណ៍:

 និង

បោះកាក់ធ្លាក់បានខាងមុខ និងក្រឡុកគូបធ្លាក់បានលេខ 1 គឺជាព្រឹត្តិការណ៍លាយគ្នា ។

ការប្រាក់ប្រផូន (compound interest)
ការប្រាក់ដែលគិតទាំងប្រាក់ដើម និងការប្រាក់ពីមុន រួម ចូលគ្នា ។

ឧទាហរណ៍:

ប្រសិនបើអ្នកដាក់ប្រាក់ $ 100 ក្នុងគណនីសន្សំ ដែលបានការ ប្រាក់ប្រផូន 6% រៀងរាល់ឆ្នាំ អ្នកនឹងបាន $100 + (0.06 × 100) = $106 នៅឆ្នាំទីមួយ និង $106 + (0.06 × 106) = $112.36 នៅឆ្នាំទីពីរ ។

ការអះអាងរួម (compound statement)
ការអះអាងជាក់លាក់ កើតឡើងដោយការអះអាងពីរ ឬច្រើនរួមគ្នា ។

ឧទាហរណ៍:

10 ច្រើនជាង 5 និង 10 គិតជាង 21 ។
10 ច្រើនជាង 5 ឬ 10 គិតជាង 50 ។

ពហុកោណថត (concave polygon)
ពហុកោណដែលមានអង្គត់ខ្លួង មួយ ឬច្រើនឡើត ចិតក្រៅរូប ។

ឧទាហរណ៍:

អវនិយភាព មាន លក្ខខណ្ឌ (conditional probability)
អវនិយភាព ដែលថា ព្រឹត្តិការណ៍ B នឹងកើតមានឡើង បានបង្ហាញថា ព្រឹត្តិការណ៍ A បានកើតមានរួចទៅហើយ ។

ឧទាហរណ៍:

បើប្រសិនជាអ្នកដឹងថា ការបោះកាក់មួង ឬពីរដង បានខាងខ្នង អវនិយភាព ក្នុងការបោះកាក់ឲ្យ បានខាងមុខ ពីរដង គឺសូន្យ ។ ក៏ប៉ុន្តែ បើអ្នកដឹងថា ការបោះកាក់លើកដំបូងបានខាងមុខ, អវនិយភាពនឹងបានខាងមុខពីរដង គឺ $\frac{1}{2}$ ។

កោន ឬសាជី (cone) សូលីតមានរង្វាស់បាត ។

ឧទាហរណ៍:

សមភាព (congruent) មានទំហំ និងរាងដូចគ្នា ។

ឧទាហរណ៍:

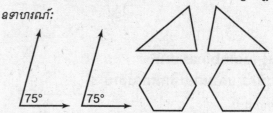

ចំណោលកោន (conic projection)
ចំណោលផែនទី ដែលប្រើរាងកោន ដើម្បីកំណត់ផ្ទៃស្វ៊ែ មួយ ។

ឧទាហរណ៍:

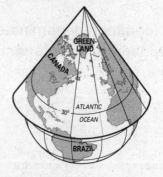

សន្ធាន (conjunction) សំណុំជាក់លាក់ នៃការអះអាង ភ្ជាប់ដោយពាក្យ "និង" ។

ឧទាហរណ៍:

$x > -2$ និង $x < 5$

ការំម្មួយមានផ្ទៃ 4 ប្រវែងស្មើគ្នា និង ការំជាបួនផ្ទៃទ្រវែង ។

ថេរ (constant) បរិមាណមួយ ដែលមិនផ្លាស់ប្តូរ ។

ឧទាហរណ៍:

នៅក្នុងកន្សោមពិជគណិត x + 7, 7 គឺជាថេរមួយ ។

ក្រាភិច ថេរ (constant graph) ក្រាភិចមួយ ដែលកម្ពស់របស់បន្ទាត់ មិនប្តូរផ្លាស់ ។

ឧទាហរណ៍:

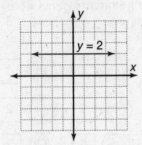

ថេរៃនៃលក្ខណៈសមាមាត្រ (constant of proportionality) $\frac{y}{x}$ បរិមាណ y របស់អថេរ x និង y ដែលមានអនុបាត ជាថេរ ។ ជាធម្មតា ច្រើនតំណាង ដោយ អក្សរ k ។

ឧទាហរណ៍:

x	3	6	9	12
y	5	10	15	20

$k = \frac{5}{3}$

កត្តាបន្លាស់ (conversion factor) ខ្នាតស្មើគ្នា ច្រើសំរាប់ បន្លាស់បរិមាណពី ខ្នាតវង្វាស់មួយ ទៅមួយទៀត ។ កត្តាបន្លាស់ច្រើនច្រើជាបែបប្រភាគ ។

ឧទាហរណ៍:

12 អ៊ិញ = 1 ហ្វ៊ីត; $\frac{12\ \text{អ៊ិញ}}{1\ \text{ហ្វ៊ីត}}$

4 ក្វាត = 1 ហ្គាឡុន; $\frac{4\ \text{ក្វាត}}{1\ \text{ហ្គាឡុន}}$

ពហុកោណប៉ោង (convex polygon) ពហុកោណដែលអង្កត់ទ្រូង ទាំងអស់ចិត នៅក្នុងរូប ។

ឧទាហរណ៍:

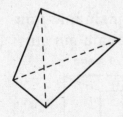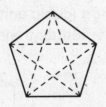

និយាមកា (coordinates) លេខមួយនៃលេខ ទាំងឡាយ ក្នុងលំដាប់គូ ដែលច្រើ សំរាប់បញ្ជាក់ទីតាំង និយាមកា នៅក្នុងប្លង់ ។

ឧទាហរណ៍:

(5, 6)

និយាមកា

និយាមកាប្លង់, ប្រព័ន្ធនិយាមកា (coordinate plane, coordinate system) សំណុំបន្ទាត់មួយ ច្រើបញ្ជាក់ទីតាំងចំណុចទាំងឡាយ នៅក្នុងប្លង់ មួយ ។

ឧទាហរណ៍:

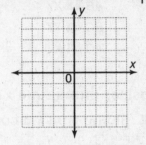

មុមតថានុរូប (corresponding angles for lines) (សម្រាប់បន្ទាត់) មុមនៅលើជ្រុងតែមួយ នៃបន្ទាត់ទទឹង ដែលកាត់បន្ទាត់ពីរ ឬច្រើនទៀត ។ មុមតថានុរូប មាន សមភាព កាលបើបន្ទាត់ទទឹង កាត់បន្ទាត់ស្របគ្នា ។

ឧទាហរណ៍:

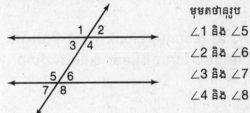

មុមតថានុរូប
∠1 និង ∠5
∠2 និង ∠6
∠3 និង ∠7
∠4 និង ∠8

មុមតថានុរូប (corresponding angles in similar figures) (ក្នុងរូបស្របជ្រៀងគ្នា) ការផ្គូមុម ក្នុងរូបស្របជ្រៀងគ្នា ។

ឧទាហរណ៍:

$\triangle ABC \sim \triangle XYZ$

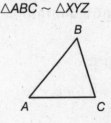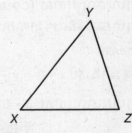

មុមតថានុរូប
∠ABC និង ∠XYZ
∠BCA និង ∠YZX
∠CAB និង ∠ZXY

ជ្រុងថាន្ទុរូប (corresponding sides)
ការផ្គូផ្ជងជ្រុង ក្នុងរូបស្រដៀងគ្នា ។

ឧទាហរណ៍:
$\triangle ABC \sim \triangle XYZ$

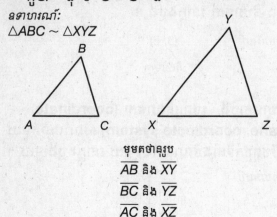

មុមគថាន្ទុរូប
$\overline{AB}$ និង $\overline{XY}$
$\overline{BC}$ និង $\overline{YZ}$
$\overline{AC}$ និង $\overline{XZ}$

កូស៊ីនុស (cosine) ចំពោះមុមស្រួច x ក្នុង
ត្រីកោណកែង កូស៊ីនុស របស់ x ឬ $\cos(x)$
គឺជាអនុបាត $\frac{\text{ជ្រុងជាប់គ្នា}}{\text{អ៊ីប៉ូតេនុស}}$ ។

ឧទាហរណ៍:

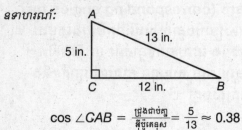

$$\cos \angle CAB = \frac{\text{ជ្រុងជាប់គ្នា}}{\text{អ៊ីប៉ូតេនុស}} = \frac{5}{13} \approx 0.38$$

រង្វិលប្រច្រាស (counterclockwise) ទិសរង្វិល
កាលបើកំពូលលើ នៃរូបវរាងអ្វីមួយ បានរិលទៅខាង
ឆ្វេង ។

ឧទាហរណ៍:

ឧទាហរណ៍ប្រច្រាស (counterexample)
ឧទាហរណ៍ ដែលបង្ហាញការអះអាងថាជាការខុស ។

ឧទាហរណ៍:

ការអះអាង: បើ $x \cdot 0 = y \cdot 0$, ដូច្នេះ $x = y$.

ឧទាហរណ៍ប្រច្រាស: $3 \cdot 0 = 0$ និង $5 \cdot 0 = 0$,
ប៉ុន្តែ $3 \neq 5$.

គោលការណ៍រាប់ (Counting Principle)
បើក្នុងស្ថានភាពមួយអាចកើតមាន m យ៉ាង
ហើយក្នុងស្ថានភាពទីពីរ អាចកើតមាន n យ៉ាង
ដូច្នេះ រឿងទាំងនេះ អាចកើតមានឡើងជា មួយគ្នា
ក្នុង $m \times n$ យ៉ាង ។

ឧទាហរណ៍:
មានលទ្ធផល ពីរ ក្នុងការបោះត្រឡប់កាក់ និងលទ្ធផលប្រាំមួយ
ក្នុងការបង្វិល ត្រឡប់គូប ។ ដូច្នេះ មាន 2×6 ឬ 12 យ៉ាង
ក្នុងទម្រើម្មទាំងពីរ ។

ផលគុណខ្នែង (cross product) ផលគុណ
ភាគយក នៃអនុបាតមួយជាមួយ
និងភាគបែងនៃអនុបាតមួយទៀត ។

ឧទាហរណ៍:

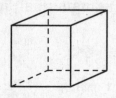

ផលគុណខ្នែង
$1 \times 5 = 5$
$3 \times 2 = 6$

គូប (cube) ព្រិស- 6 ជ្រុង ដែលមុខទាំងអស់
ជាការ៉េ សមភាព ។

ឧទាហរណ៍:

តម្លើងស្ទួយគុណទី៣ (cubed) តម្លើងស្ទួយគុណ
ដល់កម្រិតទី៣ ។

ឧទាហរណ៍: 2 ស្ទួយគុណទី៣ $= 2^3 = 2 \times 2 \times 2 = 8$

ឃ្លាតគូប (cubic unit) ឃ្លាតសំរាប់វាស់ វ៉ូល្យម
(មាឌ) ដែលជាគូប មានទ្រនុងខាង ឃ្លាត មួយ ។

ឧទាហរណ៍:

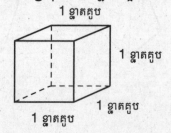

1 ឃ្លាតគូប
1 ឃ្លាតគូប
1 ឃ្លាតគូប
1 ឃ្លាតគូប

រង្វាស់តាមបែបទម្លាប់ (customary system of measurement) រង្វាស់ប្រពៃណី ដែលញឹកញាប់ប្រើនៅសហរដ្ឋអាមេរិក គឺ : អ៊ិញ, ហ្វីត, ម៉ែល, អោនស្ស, ផោន, គោន, ផែង, ក្វាត, ហ្គាឡ្យិន ។ល។

ឧទាហរណ៍:

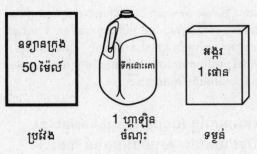

ទឹកដោះគោ

ខឱ្យានក្រុង 50 ម៉ែល

ប្រដែង

1 ហ្គាឡ្យិន ចំណុះ

អង្ករ 1 ផោន

ទម្ងន់

ស៊ីឡ្យាំង (cylinder) សូលីត ដែលមានមុខកាត់បរិវត្ត ពីរស្របគ្នា ។

ឧទាហរណ៍:

ចំណោលស៊ីឡ្យាំង (cylindrical projection) ចំណោលផែនទី ដែលប្រើទ្រង់ទ្រាយ ស៊ីឡ្យាំង ដើម្បីតំណាងជាផែល្ហ្វា ។

ឧទាហរណ៍:

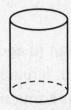

ទសកោណ (decagon) ពហុកោណ ដែលមាន 10 ជ្រុង ។

ឧទាហរណ៍:

ដេស្ស៊ី- (deci-) បុព្វបទ មានន័យថា មួយភាគដប់ $\frac{1}{10}$ ។

ឧទាហរណ៍: 1 ដេស្ស៊ីម៉ែត្រ = $\frac{1}{10}$ ម៉ែត្រ

លេខទសភាគ (decimal) លេខទសភាគ ក្បួន-10 ឯណា ដែល សរសេររប្រើចំណុចទសភាគ ។

ឧទាហរណ៍: 6.21   0.59   12.2   5.0

បូកលេខទសភាគ (decimal addition) ការបូកលេខទសភាគពី ពីរ និងច្រើនឡើងទៅៗត ។

ឧទាហរណ៍:
$$\begin{array}{r} 1 \\ 12.65 \\ +\ 29.10 \\ \hline 41.75 \end{array}$$

ចែកលេខទសភាគ (decimal division) ការចែកលេខទសភាគពីរ ។

ឧទាហរណ៍:
$$\begin{array}{r} 1.25 \\ 0.24\overline{)0.3000} \\ -24 \\ \hline 60 \\ -48 \\ \hline 120 \\ -120 \\ \hline 0 \end{array}$$

គុណលេខទសភាគ (decimal multiplication) ការគុណលេខទសភាគ ពីរ ឬច្រើនថែមទៀត ។

ឧទាហរណ៍:
$$\begin{array}{r} 2 \\ 0.13 \\ \times\ 0.7 \\ \hline 0.091 \end{array}$$
2 ខ្ទង់ទសភាគ
1 ខ្ទង់ទសភាគ
3 ខ្ទង់ទសភាគ

ដកលេខទសភាគ (decimal subtraction) ការដកលេខទសភាគពីរ ។

Example
$$\begin{array}{r} 13\ 12 \\ 4\ \cancel{5}\ \cancel{2}10 \\ 5\cancel{4}.3\cancel{0} \\ -16.58 \\ \hline 37.72 \end{array}$$

ប្រព័ន្ធទសភាគ (decimal system) ប្រព័ន្ធខ្ទង់ គោល-10 (ក្បួន-10) ។

ឧទាហរណ៍:

$100{,}000 = 10^5$	$10{,}000 = 10^4$	$1000 = 10^3$	$100 = 10^2$	10	1	$\frac{1}{10}$	$\frac{1}{100} = \frac{1}{10^2}$	$\frac{1}{1000} = \frac{1}{10^3}$
9	7	6,	5	2	3.	0	4	8

ក្រាភិចចុះ (decreasing graph) ក្រាភិច ដែលមានកម្លស់របស់បន្ទាត់ ថយចុះពីឆ្វេងទៅស្ដាំ ។

ឧទាហរណ៍:

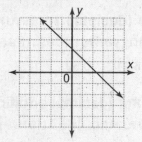

អនុមានវិចារ (deductive reasoning) ប្រើ ឡូសុិច ដើម្បីទាញសេចក្ដីសន្និដ្ឋាន ។

ឧទាហរណ៍:

កាលបើវិជ្ជុរកោណ (ឬអង្កត់ទ្រូង) ណាមួយ កូសបន្ថែមទៅលើ ចតុរង្គ (quadrilateral) ត្រីកោណពីរនឹងកើតឡើង ។ អ្នកដឹងថា ផលបូកនៃរង្វាស់មុម ក្នុងត្រីកោណមួយ មាន 180 ។ ដូច្នេះ ផលបូកនៃរង្វាស់មុម ក្នុងចតុរង្គ គឺមានពីរដងមុមត្រីកោណ, ឬ $2 \times 180° = 360°$ ។

ដឺក្រេ (degree (°)) គឺខ្នាតរង្វាស់មុម ។

ឧទាហរណ៍: 1° មាន $\frac{1}{360}$ របស់មណ្ឌលពេញមួយ ។

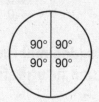

ដឺក្រេ (degree) ក្នុងពហុធា គឺតម្លៃនិទស្សន្ត ធំបំផុត របស់អថេរ ។

ឧទាហរណ៍: ដឺក្រេ របស់ $5x^3 - 2x^2 + 7x$ គឺ 3 ។

ដេកា- (deka-) បុព្វបទ មានន័យថា 10 ។

ឧទាហរណ៍: 1 ដេកាម៉ែត្រ = 10 ម៉ែត្រ

ភាគបែង (denominator) លេខផ្នែកខាងក្រោម របស់ប្រភាគ ដែលប្រាប់ថាចំនួនប៉ុន្មានចំណែក របស់ទាំងមូល ត្រូវចែកនោះ ។

ឧទាហរណ៍:

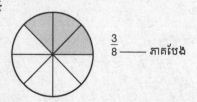

ព្រឹត្តិការណ៌ពាក់ព័ន្ធ (dependent events) ព្រឹត្តិការណ៌ទាំងឡាយ ដែលលទ្ធផលរបស់ ព្រឹត្តិការណ៌មួយ ធ្វើអោយប្រែប្រួលដល់ ភវនិយភាព នៃព្រឹត្តិការណ៌ងទៀតៗ ។

ឧទាហរណ៍:

ឈ្មោះ Therese, Diane, និង Jose បានសរសេរក្នុងកូនក្រដាស ដាច់ពីគ្នា ។ គេចាប់ហ្គួយក គ្រដាសសម្ងួយមកទុក ។ បន្ទាប់មក គេចាប់ហ្គួយកម្ងួយទៀត ។ ភវនិយភាព នៃឈ្មោះ Diane ដែលនឹងត្រូវហ្គួយកនោះ បានអោយដឹងថា ឈ្មោះ Therese បានហ្គួតនៅសន្លឹកទីមួយនោះ, គឺ $\frac{1}{2}$ ។

អថេរពាក់ព័ន្ធ (dependent variable) លទ្ធផលអថេរ សម្រាប់អនុគមន៌ មួយ ។

ឧទាហរណ៍:

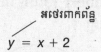

អង្កត់ទ្រូង ឬ វិជ្ជុរកោណ (diagonal) ក្នុង ពហុកោណ អង្កត់មួយ ដែលភ្ជាប់ កំពូលទាំងពីរ មិនទាក់ទងគ្នាដោយជ្រុងណាមួយទេ ។

ឧទាហរណ៍:

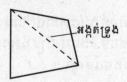

វិជ្ជុមាត្រ (diameter) អង្កត់បន្ទាត់ ឬ រង្វាស់ប្រវែងរបស់វា ដែលកាត់តាម រង្វង់ផ្ចិត ហើយចុងទាំងសងខាងនៅលើខ្សែរង្វង់ ។

ឧទាហរណ៍:

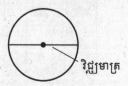

ផលដក (difference) លទ្ធផល ធ្វើលេខសង ដោយដកលេខ ពីចំនួនមួយទៀត ។

ឧទាហរណ៍: $28 - 15 = 13$

លេខសញ្ញា (digit) សញ្ញាសម្រាប់សរសេរលេខ 0, 1, 2, 3, 4, 5, 6, 7, 8, និង 9 ។

ឧទាហរណ៍:

ក្នុង 5,847 លេខសញ្ញាមាន 5, 8, 4, និង 7 ។

ការរីក (dilation) ការអូញ ឬ រីកចេញទៅតាម សមាមាត្រនៃរូបមួយ ។

ឧទាហរណ៍:

កត្តាកម្រិតរង្វាស់ការរីកចតុកោណកែង ពីតូចទៅធំ មាន 3 ។

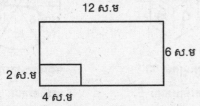

ការប្រែប្រួលត្រង់ (direct variation) កាលបើ អថេរពីរទាក់ទងនឹងគ្នា ដោយអនុបាត (ផលធៀប) ថេរ:មួយ ។

ឧទាហរណ៍:

ពេលគិតជាម៉ោង (x)	1	2	3	4
រយៈចម្ងាយគិតជាម៉ែល (y)	55	110	165	220

$$\frac{y}{x} = 55$$

មិនចុះសម្រុង (disjunction) ឃ្លាសុីកមួយសំណុំ នៃការអះអាងបញ្ជាក់ ភ្ជាប់គ្នាដោយពាក្យ "ឬ" ។

ឧទាហរណ៍:

$x > 4$ ឬ $x < -1$

យើងទៅមើលកុន ឬ យើងមើលទូរទស្សន៍

លក្ខណៈបំបែក (Distributive Property) ការណ៍ដែល $a(b + c) = ab + ac$ ។

ឧទាហរណ៍: $3(6 + 5) = 3 \cdot 6 + 3 \cdot 5$

តំណាងចែក (dividend) លេខដែលត្រូវចែក ក្នុងចំណោមលេខចែក ។

ឧទាហរណ៍:

តំណាងចែក

$8 \div 4 = 2$

ចែកដាច់ (divisible) (ចែកគត់) អាចចែកនឹងលេខ ណាមួយ ដោយគ្មានសេស ។

ឧទាហរណ៍:   18 អាចចែកដាច់នឹង 6, ព្រោះ $18 \div 6 = 3$.

លេខចែក (division) ប្រមាណវិធី ដែលប្រាប់ថាតើ ចំនួនប៉ុន្មាន កើតបានជា សំណុំ ឬ ចំនួនប៉ុន្មាន ក្នុងមួយសំណុំ ។

ឧទាហរណ៍:

$18 \div 6 = 3$ $18 \div 3 = 6$

18 ចែកពី 6 ក្រុម   18 ចែកពី 3 ក្រុម
ដាក់ 3 ក្នុងមួយក្រុម ។   ដាក់ 6 ក្នុងមួយក្រុម ។

មេចែក (divisor) លេខដែលត្រូវយកទៅចែក ជាមួយលេខណាមួយ ។

ឧទាហរណ៍:

មេចែក

$8 \div 4 = 2$

ទ្វាទសកោណ (dodecagon) ពហុកោណ ដែលមានជ្រុង 12 ។

ឧទាហរណ៍:

ក្រាភិច រនុកឌុប (double bar graph) ការរួម បញ្ចូលគ្នា នៃក្រាភិចរនុកពីរ ដោយប្រៀបធៀប ទិន្នន័យ ទាំងពីរ ក្នុងសំណុំ ដែលទាក់ទងគ្នា នោះ ។

ឧទាហរណ៍:

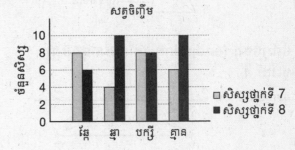

ក្រាភិចខ្សែទ្វេ (double line graph)

ការរួមបញ្ចូលគ្នា នៃក្រាភិចខ្សែពីរ ដោយប្រៀបធៀប ទិន្នន័យ ទាំងពីរក្នុងសំណុំ ដែលទាក់ទងគ្នានោះ ។

ឧទាហរណ៍:

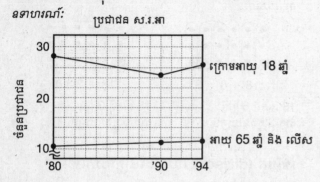

ប្រជាជន ស.រ.អា

ក្រោមអាយុ 18 ឆ្នាំ

អាយុ 65 ឆ្នាំ និង លើស

ឌីយ៉ាក្រាម និងស្ទឹកទ្វេ (double stem-and-leaf diagram)

ការប្រៀបធៀប និងស្ទឹក ក្នុង ទិន្នន័យ នៃសំណុំទាំងពីរ នៅលើឌីយ៉ាក្រាមទោល ។

ឧទាហរណ៍:

ស្ទឹក	ទង	ស្ទឹក
7 2 1	3	0 1 3
5 0 0	4	2 3
9	5	5 6 8
5 2 0	6	1 4

ទ្រនុងខាង (edge)

អង្កត់ កើតឡើងដោយ មុខខាងពីរ របស់សូលីត ពហុមុខ មកជួបគ្នា ។

ឧទាហរណ៍:

មុខខាង

ទ្រនុងខាង

ចំណុចចុង (endpoint)

ចំណុចនៅចុងអង្កត់ ឬរ៉េយ៍ ។

ឧទាហរណ៍:

A   B

ចំណុចចុង

Y   Z

សមភាព (equality)

ក្នុងទំនាក់ទំនងគណិត ដែលស្មើគ្នាបេះបិទ ។

ឧទាហរណ៍:   16 + 8 = 24   25 ÷ 5 = 5

លទ្ធផលប្រហែលគ្នា (equally-likely outcomes)

លទ្ធផល ដែលមាន ភវនិយភាព ដូចគ្នា ។

ឧទាហរណ៍:

ក្រឡុករក "1"

ភវនិយភាព: $\frac{1}{6}$

បង្វិលរក ក្រហម

ភវនិយភាព: $\frac{1}{6}$

ផលធៀបស្មើគ្នា (equal ratios) (អនុបាត)

ផលធៀបទាំងឡាយ ដែលមានចំនួនដូចគ្នា ។

ឧទាហរណ៍: $\frac{2}{6}$, $\frac{1}{3}$, និង $\frac{4}{12}$

សមីការ (equation)

ប្រយោគគណិត ដែលបញ្ជាក់ថា កន្សោមពីរ ស្មើគ្នា ។

ឧទាហរណ៍:

$$14 = 2x \qquad 3 + y = 81 \qquad 3 + 4 = 7$$

ត្រីកោណ សមង្ស (equilateral triangle)

ត្រីកោណដែលមានជ្រុងទាំងអស់ស្មើគ្នា ។

ឧទាហរណ៍:

4   4

4

សមីការសមមូល (equivalent equations)

សមីការដែលពិត កាលបើបូរកន្លែងអថេរដដែល ។

ឧទាហរណ៍: $x - 5 = 10$ និង $x = 15$

កន្សោមសមមូល (equivalent expressions)

កន្សោមពីរដែលតែងតែមានតម្លៃដដែល កាលបើមានការយកមកជំនួស ដដែល ។

ឧទាហរណ៍: $5(x + 1)$ និង $5x + 5$

ប្រភាគសមមូល (equivalent fractions)

ប្រភាគពីរ តំណាងចំនួនដដែល ។

ឧទាហរណ៍: $\frac{1}{2}$ និង $\frac{8}{16}$

អត្រាសមមូល (equivalent rates)
អត្រាដែលឱ្យឈ្មោះចំនួនដងដែល ។

ឧទាហរណ៍: $\dfrac{40 \text{ ម៉ៃល៍}}{2 \text{ ម៉ោង}}$ និង $\dfrac{20 \text{ ម៉ៃល៍}}{1 \text{ ម៉ោង}}$

ផលធៀបសមមូល (equivalent ratios)
មើលផលធៀបស្មើគ្នា ។

ម្រមាណ (estimate)
ចំនួនប្រហាក់ប្រហែល ក្នុងលទ្ធផលនៃការគណនា ។

ឧទាហរណ៍:

$$99 \times 21$$
ប្រមាណ: $100 \times 20 = 2000$
$$99 \times 21 \approx 2000$$

រូបមន្ត Euler (Euler's formula)
រូបមន្តអំពីចំនួនមុខ (F), កំពូល (V) និង ទ្រុង ខាង (E) របស់ សូលីតពហុមុខ ដែលបញ្ជាក់ថា
$$F + V - E = 2.$$

ឧទាហរណ៍:

ចំពោះពីរ៉ាមីតត្រីកោណ បង្ហាញនេះ:

$$\underset{\text{មុខ}}{5} + \underset{\text{កំពូល}}{5} - \underset{\text{ទ្រុង}}{8} = 2$$

វាយតម្លៃ (evaluate)
គឺដើម្បីបូរតម្លៃរបស់ អថេរ នៅក្នុងកន្សោម រួចហើយ សម្រួល ដោយរៀបលំដាប់ របស់ប្រមាណវិធី ។

ឧទាហរណ៍: វាយតម្លៃ $8(x - 3)$ ដោយ $x = 10$.
$$\begin{aligned} 8(x - 3) &= 8(10 - 3) \\ &= 8\,(7) \\ &= 56 \end{aligned}$$

លេខគូ (even number)
គឺលេខគត់ ដែលមាន 0, 2, 4, 6, ឬ 8 នៅក្នុងខ្ទង់រាយ ។

ឧទាហរណ៍: 16 28 34 112 3000

ព្រឹត្តិការណ៍ (event)
គឺជាលទ្ធផលលេខចេញមក ឬ លទ្ធផលលេខចេញមកមួយឃុត ពីការពិសោធន៍ ឬ ស្ថានការណ៍មួយ ។

ឧទាហរណ៍:

ព្រឹត្តិការណ៍ — បោះដុំគូបបានលេខ 3 ឬចំជាងនេះ កាលណាលេខណាមួយរម្យៀលគ្រឡប់ឡើង ។

លទ្ធផលលេខចេញមក ដែលអាចកើតមានបាន សម្រាប់ព្រឹត្តិការណ៍នេះ គឺ 3, 4, 5, 6

លក្ខណៈពង្រាយ (expanded form)
គឺជារបៀបសរសេរលេខមាន និទស្សន្ត ដោយបង្ហាញកត្តាគុណ មួយម្តងៗ ។

ឧទាហរណ៍:
លេខមាននិទស្សន្ត	9^3
លក្ខណៈពង្រាយ	$9 \times 9 \times 9$

ការពិសោធន៍ (experiment)
ក្នុង ភវនិយភាព សកម្មភាពណានីមួយដែល ទាក់ទង និងចែដន្យ ។

ឧទាហរណ៍:
បោះគ្រឡប់កាក់ ក្រឡុកគូបមានលេខ បង្វិលរង្វាស់ថាស

ភវនិយភាព ដោយពិសោធន៍ (experimental probability)
គឺ ភវនិយភាព ដែលឆ្អាងទៅលើ ទិន្នន័យ បានមកពីការពិសោធន៍ ឬសម្រង់ ។

ឧទាហរណ៍:
កញ្ចប់សណ្ណែកបានបោះគ្រឡប់ចុះឡើង 100 ដង អោយកើតបាន ជា ទម្រង់តម្រៀបគ្នា គេបានប៉ះបែបនោះ គឺ 23 ដង ។ ភវនិយភាព នៃការពិសោធន៍ ដើម្បីអោយបានប៉ះបែបនោះ គឺ $\dfrac{23}{100} = 23\%.$

និទស្សន្ត (exponent)
គឺចំនួនដែលកើតឡើង បង្ហាញនូវការផ្ទួនមេគុណ ។

ឧទាហរណ៍:
$$\overset{\text{និទស្សន្ត}}{4^3} = 4 \times 4 \times 4 = 64$$

អនុគមន៍បង្កើនផ្គូន (exponential function)
គឺមិនមែនជាអនុគមន៍ខ្សែរបត់ ដែលមាននិទស្សន្ត ជាអថេរមួយទេ ។

ឧទាហរណ៍: $y = 4^x$

កំណត់សញ្ញាបង្កើនផ្គូន (exponential notation)
គឺជារបៀបសរសេរ កត់សម្គាល់លេខ គុណាផ្គូន នៃចំនួនណាមួយដោយប្រើ និទស្សន្ត ។

ឧទាហរណ៍: 2^8 5^2 9^3

កន្សោម (expression)
គឺជាប្រយោគគណិត កើតឡើងដោយមាន អថេរ និង/ ឬ លេខ និងប្រមាណវិធី ។

ឧទាហរណ៍: $5(8 + 4)$ $x - 3$ $2x + 4$

មុមក្រៅ (exterior angles)
មុមកើតឡើងដោយ បន្ទាត់កាត់ទទឹងមួយ (transversal) និង ខ្សែរបន្ទាត់ ដែល ប៉ះពីក្រៅខ្សែរបន្ទាត់ទាំងនោះ ។

ឧទាហរណ៍:

មុមក្រៅ
∠1, ∠2, ∠7, ∠8

មុខ (face)
(ខាងមុខ) គីថ្ងៃសំប៉ែតនៅលើសូលិតមួយ ។

ឧទាហរណ៍:

កត្តា (factor)
គីលេខដែលចែកនឹងលេខមួយទៀត ដោយមិនអោយមានសេស ។

ឧទាហរណ៍: ដោយហេតុថា $30 \div 5 = 6$,
5 គីជាកត្តាចែករបស់ 30 ។

កត្តាចុះ (factorial)
កត្តាចុះនៃចំនួនណាមួយ គីជាផលគុណនៃលេខគត់ ចាប់ពីលេខ 1 ទៅទល់នឹងលេខនោះ ។ សញ្ញារបស់កត្តាចុះ គី "!" ។

ឧទាហរណ៍:

$6 \text{ កត្តាចុះ } = 6! = 6 \times 5 \times 4 \times 3 \times 2 \times 1 = 720$

កត្តាស្វែង (factor tree)
គី ឌីយ៉ាក្រាម ដែល បង្ហាញពីលេខគត់ បំបែក ចេញជាកត្តាដំបូង ។

ឧទាហរណ៍:

```
      72
    2   36
      2   18
        2   9
          3   3
```

$72 = 2 \times 2 \times 2 \times 3 \times 3$

ល្បែងស្មើ (fair game)
គីជាល្បែង ដែលអ្នកលេងទាំងអស់ឈ្នះ ដោយបាន ភវនយភាព ប្រហែលស្មើគ្នា ។

ឧទាហរណ៍:
ល្បែងស្មើ: អ្នកលេងពីរនាក់ ចែកវេនគ្នាក្រឡុកគូបលេខ ។
អ្នកលេង A ទទួលបានពិន្ទុក្រឡុក 1, 3 ឬ 5 ។ អ្នកលេង B ទទួលបានពិន្ទុក្រឡុក 2, 4 ឬ 6 ។ ភវនយភាពពិន្ទុគឺ $\frac{1}{2}$ ចំពោះអ្នកលេងទាំងពីរ ។

ផ្ទាប់ចុះ (flip)
មើលពាក្យឆ្លុះ ។

ហ្វីត (foot)
គីជាឯកតា រង្វាស់តាមបែបទម្លាប់ ស្មើនឹង 12 អ៊ិញ ។

ឧទាហរណ៍:

1 ហ្វីត

រូបមន្ត (formula)
គីជាក្បួនបង្ហាញពីទំនាក់ទំនងរវាងបរិមាណ ។

ឧទាហរណ៍: $A = bh$ $p = 4s$

វិរូបភាព (fractal)
គីជាតម្រៀលនាំ ដោយមានសមរូបផ្ទាល់ ។ ប្រសិនបើផ្នែកតូចរបស់ វិរូបភាព ពង្រីកធំឡើង រូបធំនេះនឹងដូចរូបដើមរបស់វា ។

ឧទាហរណ៍:

ប្រភាគ (fraction)
គីលេខដែលមានទម្រង់ $\frac{a}{b}$ រៀបរាប់ប្រាប់ពីផ្នែកតូចៗ ក្នុងដុំទាំងមូល កាលបើដុំទាំងមូល ចុះចែកជាដុំស្មើៗគ្នា ។

ឧទាហរណ៍: $\frac{3}{5}$ $\frac{2}{7}$ $\frac{1}{4}$ $\frac{7}{10}$

បូកប្រភាគ (fraction addition)
ការបូកប្រភាគ ពីរ ឬប្រភាគច្រើនទៀត ។

ឧទាហរណ៍: $\frac{1}{3} + \frac{1}{4}$

$$\frac{1}{3} = \frac{1 \times 4}{3 \times 4} = \frac{4}{12}$$

$$\frac{1}{4} = \frac{1 \times 3}{4 \times 3} = \frac{3}{12}$$

$$\frac{1}{3} + \frac{1}{4} = \frac{4}{12} + \frac{3}{12} = \frac{4 + 3}{12} = \frac{7}{12}$$

ចែកប្រភាគ (fraction division)
ការចែកប្រភាគ ពីរ ។

ឧទាហរណ៍:
$$\frac{1}{6} \div \frac{3}{4} = \frac{1}{6} \times \frac{4}{3}$$
$$= \frac{1 \times 4}{6 \times 3}$$
$$= \frac{4}{18} \text{ ឬ } \frac{2}{9}$$

គុណប្រភាគ (fraction multiplication) គឺការគុណប្រភាគពីរ ឬ ប្រភាគច្រើនទៀត ។

ឧទាហរណ៍:
$$1\frac{1}{2} \times \frac{1}{4} = \frac{3}{2} \times \frac{1}{4}$$
$$= \frac{3 \times 1}{2 \times 4}$$
$$= \frac{3}{8}$$

ដកប្រភាគ (fraction subtraction) គឺការដកប្រភាគពីរ ។

ឧទាហរណ៍:
$$\frac{3}{4} - \frac{2}{3}$$
$$\frac{3}{4} = \frac{3 \times 3}{4 \times 3} = \frac{9}{12}$$
$$\frac{2}{3} = \frac{2 \times 4}{3 \times 4} = \frac{8}{12}$$
$$\frac{3}{4} - \frac{2}{3} = \frac{9}{12} - \frac{8}{12} = \frac{9-8}{12} = \frac{1}{12}$$

ប្រេកង់ (frequency) គឺចំនួនដងនៃអ្វីដែលកើតមានឡើង នៅក្នុងសម្រង់ ។ មើលតារាង ប្រេកង់ ។

តារាងប្រេកង់ (frequency chart or table) គឺតារាងបង្ហាញប្រាប់ពីក្រុមនៃវត្ថុនិង ប្រេកង់ កើតឡើងនៃវត្ថុទាំងនោះ ។

ឧទាហរណ៍:

ពណ៌អាវ	ប្រេកង់
ខៀ	8
ដាំដែង	2
ស	5
ខៀវ	4

ការប្រមាណចុង-ដើម (front-end estimation) គឺការប្រមាណវិធី ដែលគិតតែពីខ្ទង់ ទីមួយ ឬ ទីពីរ នៃចំនួននីមួយៗ ក្នុងការធ្វើលេខ ហើយលទ្ធផល ចុងក្រោយ គឺតម្រឹមទៅតាមខ្ទង់ ដែលសល់នោះ ។

ឧទាហរណ៍: ការប្រមាណចុង-ដើម ខ្ពង់រាយ
```
      2,485
    + 3,698
    ──────
      5,000     ឬកខ្ពង់ទីមួយ
    + 1,200     485 + 698 គឺប្រហែល 1,200 ។
    ──────
      6,200
```

អនុគមន៍ (function) គឺជាទំនាក់ទំនង នៃការដាក់ចូល-ដកចេញ ហើយទទួលបានផលនៃការដក ចេញមួយ ចំពោះតែការដាក់ចូល មួយប៉ុណ្ណោះ ។

ឧទាហរណ៍:
$$y = x + 4 \qquad y = 2x \qquad y = x^2$$

គោលទ្រឹស្ដីបទ នៃលេខគណិត (Fundamental Theorem of Arithmetic) ចំនួនគត់ ទាំងអស់ ដែលធំជាង 1 អាចចាត់ទុកជា ផលគុណតែម្លួយគត់ នៃចំនួនដើម ។

ឧទាហរណ៍: $24 = 2 \times 2 \times 2 \times 3$
$35 = 5 \times 7$

ហ្គាឡ្វិន (gallon) គឺជាឯកតា រង្វាស់តាមបែបទម្លាប់ ស្មើនិង 4 ក្វាត ។

ឧទាហរណ៍:

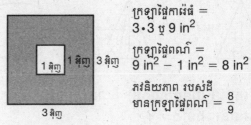

1 ហ្គាឡ្វិន

ធរណីមាត្រ (geometry) គឺជាមែកធាងមួយ នៃគណិតសាស្ត្រ ដែលសិក្សាពីទំនាក់ទំនងរវាង ចំណុច, បន្ទាត់, រូប, និង សូលីត ។

អវនិយភាព ធរណីមាត្រ (geometric probability) គឺអវនិយភាពមួយ ដែលចិតនៅលើ រង្វាស់ប្រៀបធៀបនៃរូបធរណីមាត្រ ។

ឧទាហរណ៍:

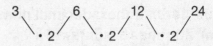

ក្រឡាផ្ទៃការ៉េធំ =
3 • 3 ឬ 9 in^2

ក្រឡាផ្ទៃពណ៌ =
9 in^2 − 1 in^2 = 8 in^2

អវនិយភាព របស់ជី
មានក្រឡាផ្ទៃពណ៌ = $\frac{8}{9}$

3 អិញ

1 អិញ   1 អិញ   3 អិញ

លំដាប់ធរណីមាត្រ (geometric sequence) គឺលំដាប់ដែលតែងតែមានផលធៀប ដូចដែល នៅចន្លោះគូបន្តបន្ទាប់នោះ ។

ឧទាហរណ៍:

3 ⌐ 6 ⌐ 12 ⌐ 24
•2   •2   •2

ក្រាម (gram) គឺជាឯកតាគោល របស់ ម៉ាស់ ក្នុងមាត្រាប្រព័ន្ធ ។

ឧទាហរណ៍:

ម៉ាស់ របស់ដង្កៀបក្រដាសធំប្រហែល 1 ក្រាម ។

ក្រាភិច **(graph)** គឺឌីយ៉ាក្រាម ដែលប្រាប់ពត៌មាន
ទៅតាមរបៀបរៀបរយមួយ ។

ឧទាហរណ៍:

លទ្ធផលតេស្ត

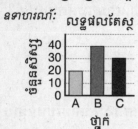

3	0 1 3
4	2 2
5	6 7 9

កត្តារួមធំបង្អស់ **(greatest common factor
(GCF))** លេខតត់គូធំបំផុត ដែលចែកលេខតត់គូពីរ
ឬច្រើនទៀត មិនអោយមានសេស ។

ឧទាហរណ៍: 6 គឺជា GCF របស់ 12, 18 និង 24 ។

ហិកតូ **(hecto-)** គឺជាបុព្វបទ មានន័យថា 100 ។

ឧទាហរណ៍: 1 ហិកតូម៉ែត្រ = 100 ម៉ែត្រ

កម្ពស់ **(height)** ក្នុងត្រីកោណ, ចតុរង្គ ឬ ពីរ៉ាមីត
របៈប្រវែងកែង ពីបាត ឈមទៅ កំពូល ឬជ្រុងខាង
នោះ ។

ឧទាហរណ៍:

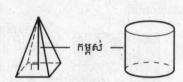

កម្ពស់ — កម្ពស់ —

សត្តកោណ **(heptagon)** គឺជាពហុកោណ
ដែលមានជ្រុងខាង 7 ។

ឧទាហរណ៍:

ប្រព័ន្ធលេខ ឋទសភាគ **(hexadecimal number
system)** គឺជាប្រព័ន្ធខ្ទង់ ប្រើក្បួន-16 ។

ឧទាហរណ៍:

អក្សរ A-F ប្រើសម្រាប់តំណាងតត់គូលេខ 10-15 ។ លេខក្បួន-16
A3CE ស្មើនឹង 41, 934 (40,960 + 768 + 192 + 14)
នៅក្នុងប្រព័ន្ធលេខ ទសភាគ (ក្បួន-10) ។

ក្បួន- 16	A	3	C	E
ខ្ទង់	4096	256	16	1
ផលគុណ	10 × 4096 = 40,960	3 × 256 = 768	12 × 16 = 192	14 × 1 = 14

ឆកោណ **(hexagon)** គឺជាពហុកោណ
ដែលមានជ្រុងខាង 6 ។

ឧទាហរណ៍:

ជាលិកាក្រាម **(histogram)** គឺជាប្រភេទនៃក្រាភិចរនុក
ដែលប្រភេទទាំងអស់ មានលេខកំណត់បាន ស្មើគ្នា ។

ឧទាហរណ៍:

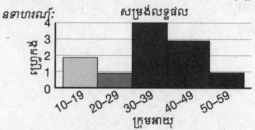

សម្រងលទ្ធផល

អ័ក្សរផ្ដេក **(horizontal axis)** ខ្សែរផ្ដេក របស់
បន្ទាត់ទាំងពីរ នៅលើក្រាភិច រនុក ឬលើ
(កូអរដោនេ) និយាមកា ប្លង់ ដែលកើតឡើងនោះ ។

ឧទាហរណ៍:

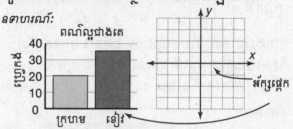

ពណ៌ល្បាងគេ

អ័ក្សផ្ដេក

អ៊ីប៉ូតេនុស **(hypotenuse)** គឺជ្រុងឈម និងមុម
កែង ក្នុងត្រីកោណកែង ។

ឧទាហរណ៍:

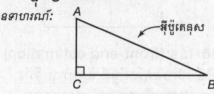

អ៊ីប៉ូតេនុស

ឯកលគុណភាព **(identity)** គឺចំពោះប្រមាណវិធី
ណាមួយក៏ដោយ លេខដែលធ្វើអោយលេខ មួយ
ទៀត នៅដដែល ។ 0 គឺជា ឯកលគុណភាពបូក,
ព្រោះ $a + 0 = a$, គឺជាឯកលគុណភាពគុណ ព្រោះ
$a \times 1 = a$ ។

ឧទាហរណ៍: $6 + 0 = 6$
$5 \times 1 = 5$

ការអះអាង "ប្រសិនបើ....ដូច្នេះ" **(if-then
statement)** គឺជាការអះអាងឡូស៊ិកមួយ ដែល
ប្រើពាក្យ ប្រសិនបើ និង ដូច្នេះ ដើម្បីបញ្ជាក់ពីទំនាក់
ទំនងរវាងលក្ខខ័ណ្ឌពីរ ។

ឧទាហរណ៍:

ប្រសិនបើ ត្រីកោណមួយ ជាត្រីកោណ វិសមង្ស ដូច្នេះ ជ្រុងទាំង
អស់មិនស្មើគ្នាទេ ។

ប្រភាគមិនទៀង (improper fraction) គឺប្រភាគ ដែលមានភាគយក ធំជាង ឬ ស្មើនឹងភាគបែង ។

ឧទាហរណ៍: $\dfrac{5}{2}$ $\dfrac{8}{8}$ $\dfrac{14}{3}$

ក្រាភិចកើន (increasing graph) ក្រាភិច ដែលមានកម្ពស់នៃខ្សែបន្ទាត់ កើនឡើងពីឆ្វេងទៅ ស្ដាំ ។

ឧទាហរណ៍:

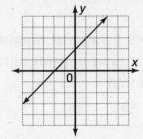

អ៊ិញ (inch) គឺជាឯកតា រយៈប្រវែង តាមបែប ទម្លាប់នៃប្រព័ន្ធរង្វាស់ ។

ឧទាហរណ៍: ដង្កៀបក្រដាសប្រវែង $1\frac{3}{8}$ អ៊ិញ ឬ $1\frac{3}{8}"$ ។

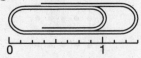

ព្រឹត្តិការណ៍មិនពាក់ព័ន្ធ (independent events) ព្រឹត្តិការណ៍ទាំងឡាយ ដែលលទ្ធផល របស់ ព្រឹត្តិការណ៍មួយ មិនធ្វើឱ្យប្រែប្រួលដល់ ភវនិយភាព នៃ ព្រឹត្តិការណ៍ងទៀតៗ ។

ឧទាហរណ៍:
ឈ្មោះ Therese, Diane, និង Jose
បានសរសេរក្នុងកូនក្រដាសដាច់ពីគ្នា ។
គេចាប់ហ្នឹងយកក្រដាសមួយមក ហើយទុកទៅវិញ ។ បន្ទាប់មក
គេចាប់ហ្នឹងយកកម្ចុយទៀត ។ ភវនិយភាព នៃឈ្មោះ Diane
ដែលនឹងត្រូវហ្នឹងយកនោះ បានអោយដឹងថា ឈ្មោះ Therese
បានហ្នឹតនៅសន្លឹកទីមួយនោះ គឺ $\frac{1}{3}$ ។

អថេរ មិនពាក់ព័ន្ធ (independent variable) គឺការអោយតម្លៃអថេរនៃអនុគមន៍ ។

ឧទាហរណ៍:

អថេរមិនពាក់ព័ន្ធ
／
$y = x + 2$

វិសេសានុមាន វិចារ (inductive reasoning) ប្រើដិតក្រម្បលំនាំ ដើម្បីទាញសេចក្ដី សន្និដ្ឋាន ។

ឧទាហរណ៍:
គេគូរចតុរង្គ ជាច្រើន និងវាស់មុមរបស់វា ។ រាល់ដងគេរាស់មុម
ផលបូកនៅតែ 360° ។ គេទាញសេចក្ដីសន្និដ្ឋានថា ផលបូកមុម
របស់ចតុរង្គ មាន 360° ។

វិសមភាព (inequality) គឺប្រយោគគណិត ទាក់ទងនឹង $<$, $>$, $\le$, ឬ $\ge$ ។

ឧទាហរណ៍:
$6 < 9$ $x + 3 \ge 21$ $2x - 8 > 0$

រូបចារិកក្នុង (inscribed figure) គឺរូបដែលនៅ ក្នុងរូបមួយទៀត ។ បើពហុកោណមួយចារិក ក្នុង រង្វង់, កំពូលទាំងអស់ (vertices) របស់វាជាប់នៅលើ រង្វង់នោះ ។

ឧទាហរណ៍:

ត្រីកោណចារិកក្នុងរង្វង់ ។

ចំនួនគត់ (integers) គឺសំណុំនៃលេខគត់គូរិជ្ជមាន, លេខប្រច្រាស របស់វា និងលេខសូន្យ 0 ។

ឧទាហរណ៍:   ..., -3, -2, -1, 0, 1, 2, 3, ...

<!-- number line -->
-4 -3 -2 -1 0 1 2 3 4

បូកចំនួនគត់ (integer addition) គឺការបូកចំនួន គត់ពីរ ឬច្រើនទៀត ។

ឧទាហរណ៍:
$-5 + 8 = 3$ $-5 + (-8) = -13$
$5 + (-3) = 2$ $5 + 8 = 13$

ចែកចំនួនគត់ (integer division) គឺការចែកចំនួន គត់ពីរ ។

ឧទាហរណ៍:
$-40 \div 8 = -5$ $40 \div (-8) = -5$
$-40 \div (-8) = 5$ $40 \div 8 = 5$

គុណចំនួនគត់ (integer multiplication) គឺការគុណចំនួនគត់ពីរ ឬច្រើនទៀត ។

ឧទាហរណ៍:
$-5 \cdot 8 = -40$ $-5 \cdot (-8) = 40$
$5 \cdot (-8) = -40$ $5 \cdot 8 = 40$

ដកចំនួនគត់ (integer subtraction) គឺការដក ចំនួនគត់ពីរ ។

ឧទាហរណ៍:
$-5 - 8 = -13$ $-5 - (-8) = 3$
$5 - (-3) = 8$ $5 - 8 = -3$

ប្រាក់ចុងការ (interest) គឺប្រាក់ត្រូវបង់ឱ្យ កាលបើខ្ចីប្រាក់ទៅប្រើការ ។

ឧទាហរណ៍:
ជេរ បានដាក់ប្រាក់ $300 ក្នុងគណនីសន្សំ ។ បន្ទាប់ពេល 1 ឆ្នាំ ក ការទូទាត់គណនីរបស់ គាត់ គឺមាន $315 ។ គាត់បាន $15 ជាប្រាក់ចុងការ ក្នុងគណនីសន្សំរបស់គាត់ ។

មុមក្នុង (interior angles) គឺមុមកើតឡើងដោយ បន្ទាត់កាត់ទទឹងមួយ និង ខ្សែបន្ទាត់ដែលប៉ះនៅ ចន្លោះខ្សែបន្ទាត់ទាំងនោះ ។

ឧទាហរណ៍:

មុមក្នុង

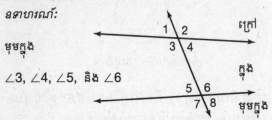

$\angle 3, \angle 4, \angle 5,$ និង $\angle 6$

ប្រសព្វមុម (intersect) គឺកាត់មកជួបនឹងចំណុច តែមួយ ។

ឧទាហរណ៍:

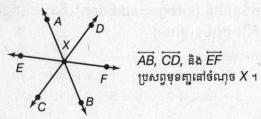

$\overrightarrow{AB}, \overrightarrow{CD},$ និង $\overrightarrow{EF}$
ប្រសព្វមុខគ្នានៅចំណុច X ។

ចន្លោះ (interval) គឺខ្នាតបែងចែកប្រវែងស្មើគ្នា ក្នុងក្រាភិករនុក ឬក្រាភិចខ្សែ ។

ឧទាហរណ៍:

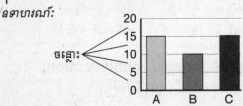

ចន្លោះ

ប្រមាណវិធីផ្ទាស់ (inverse operations) គឺប្រមាណវិធី ដែលដោះស្រាយលេខទៅវិញទៅមក ។

ឧទាហរណ៍:

ការបូកលេខ និងដកលេខ	$2 + 3 = 5 \quad 5 - 3 = 2$
ការគុណលេខ និងចែកលេខ	$2 \cdot 3 = 6 \quad 6 \div 3 = 2$

បន្ថាស់បួរឆ្នាស់ (inverse variation) គឺកាលបើអថេរៈពីរ ទាក់ទិននឹងផលគុណថេរមួយ ។

ឧទាហរណ៍:

x	1	2	3	4	5	6
y	60	30	20	15	12	10

$$x \cdot y = 60$$

ចំនួនអសនិទាន (irrational number) គឺចំនួន ដូចជា $\sqrt{2}$ ដែលមិនអាចសរសេរ បន្តទៅ ឡើត ឬ មានចុងជាទសភាគ ។

ឧទាហរណ៍: $\sqrt{5}$ $\quad$ π $\quad$ $-\sqrt{\dfrac{1}{2}}$

គំនូរសមមាត្រ (isometric drawing) គឺជារបៀបមួយ ប្រើក្នុងគំនូរ យថាទស្សរន៍ ។

ឧទាហរណ៍:

ត្រីកោនសមបាត (isosceles triangle) គឺជាត្រីកោណ ដែលមានយ៉ាងហោចណាស់ផ្ជែង សមបាតពីរ ។

ឧទាហរណ៍:

18 $\quad$ 18

14

គីឡូ- (kilo-) គឺជាបុព្វបទ មានន័យថា 1000 ។
ឧទាហរណ៍: 1 គីឡូម៉ែត្រ = 1000 ម៉ែត្រ

រយៈខ្សែស្រប (latitude) គឺជារង្វាស់ប្រវែង គិតជាដឺក្រេ ខាងជើង ឬ ខាងត្បូង ពីខ្សែអេក្វាទ័រ ។

ឧទាហរណ៍:

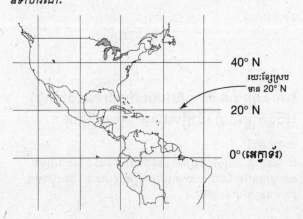

40° N

រយៈខ្សែស្រប
មាន 20° N

20° N

0° (អេក្វាទ័រ)

ភាគបែងរួមតូចបំផុត (least common denominator (LCD)) គឺជាលេខផលគុណ រួមតូចបំផុត (LCM) របស់ភាគបែងពីរឬច្រើនទៀត ។

ឧទាហរណ៍: $\frac{1}{2}$ $\frac{2}{3}$ $\frac{3}{4}$

ផលគុណ រួមតូចបំផុតរបស់ 2, 3, និង 4 គឺ 12, ដូច្នេះ LCD នៃប្រភាគនេះ គឺ 12.

ប្រភាគសរសេរជា LCD គឺ $\frac{6}{12}, \frac{8}{12},$ និង $\frac{9}{12}.$

លេខផលគុណរួមតូចបំផុត (least common multiple (LCM)) គឺជាចំនួនតូចបំផុត ដែលជា លេខផលគុណរួម ។

ឧទាហរណ៍:
ផលគុណនៃ 3: 3 6 9 **12** 15 18 21 **24** ...
ផលគុណនៃ 4: 4 8 **12** 16 20 **24** 28 32 ...
12 គឺជា LCM របស់ 3 និង 4 ។

ជ្រុងម្ខាង (leg) គឺជាជ្រុងរបស់ត្រីកោណកែង ដែលមិនមែន អ៊ីប៉ូតេនុស ។

ឧទាហរណ៍:

ភាគបែងស្មើ (like denominators) គឺភាគដែលដូចគ្នា ក្នុងប្រភាគពីរ ឬច្រើនទៀត ។

ឧទាហរណ៍: $\frac{1}{8}$ $\frac{3}{8}$ $\frac{6}{8}$

ភាគបែងស្មើ

អង្គស្មើ (like terms) គឺអង្គទាំងឡាយ ដែល អថេរ មានកម្រិត និងស្វ័យគុណ ស្មើគ្នា ។

ឧទាហរណ៍: $3x^2$ និង $9x^2$ $10y$ និង $2y$

បន្ទាត់ (line) គឺជារូបបរិមាត្រ-ទោលមួយ ដែលពន្លាត ចេញគ្មាន ទីបំផុត ទៅទាំងពីរទិស ។ ចំណុចពីរកើត បានជាបន្ទាត់មួយ ។

ឧទាហរណ៍:

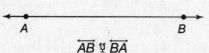

$\overline{AB}$ ឬ $\overline{BA}$

ក្រាភិចខ្សែ (line graph) គឺជាក្រាភិច ដែលមាន ខ្សែរូបបន្ទាត់ប្រាប់បង្ហាញពីការផ្លាស់ប្តូរ ទិន្នផល (data) ញឹកញាប់ទៅតាមពេលវេលា ។

ឧទាហរណ៍:

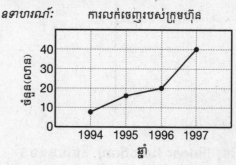
ការលក់ចេញរបស់ក្រុមហ៊ុន

ខ្សែបន្ទាត់ឆ្លុះ (line of symmetry) គឺជាខ្សែ បន្ទាត់ ដែលចែករូបមួយ ដោយបន្ទាត់ឆ្លុះ អោយ បានជាពីរភាគបេះបិទ ។

ឧទាហរណ៍:

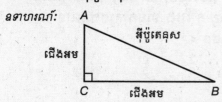

បន្ទាត់ឆ្លុះមួយ 1   បន្ទាត់ឆ្លុះមួយ 4

បន្ទាត់ដៅ (line plot) ចំណុចដៅ ដែលបង្ហាញពី រាងរៅ នៃទិន្នផល កើតឡើងដោយបន្តុប x's ពីលើតម្លៃ និមួយៗ ក្នុងខ្សែលេខ ។

ឧទាហរណ៍:

```
                              x
              x               x
        x     x     x         x
  x     x     x     x         x     x
──┼─────┼─────┼─────┼─────┼─────┼─────┼──
  0     1     2     3     4     5     6
              ចំនួនសិស្ស
```

បន្ទាត់អង្គត់ (line segment) គឺជាផ្នែកនៃបន្ទាត់ ត្រង់ ដែលមានចំណុចបំផុត ពីរ ។ ចំណុចពីរកើត បានជាអង្គត់មួយ ។

ឧទាហរណ៍:

$\overline{AB}$ ឬ $\overline{BA}$

បន្ទាត់ឆ្លុះ (line symmetry) រូបដែលមានបន្ទាត់ ឆ្លុះ ប្រសិនបើអាចចែកបានជាពីរភាគបេះបិទ ។

ឧទាហរណ៍:

រូបមានបន្ទាត់ឆ្លុះ   រូបគ្មានបន្ទាត់ឆ្លុះទេ

សមីការខ្សែ (linear equation) គឺជាសមីការមួយ ដែលមានក្រាភិចជាបន្ទាត់ត្រង់ ។

ឧទាហរណ៍:

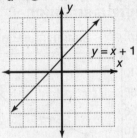

$$y = x + 1$$

អនុគមន៍ខ្សែ (linear function) គឺជាអនុគមន៍ មួយ ដែលមានក្រាភិច ជាបន្ទាត់ត្រង់ ។

ឧទាហរណ៍:

អោយតម្លៃ	ផលតម្លៃ
x	y
-2	3
-1	2
0	1
1	0
2	-1
3	-2

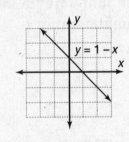

$$y = 1 - x$$

វិសមភាពខ្សែ (linear inequality) គឺជាកម្រេង គណិត ដែលទាក់ទងនឹង $<, >, \leq$ ឬ $\geq$ ៤ ក្រាភិច មានបន្ទាត់ត្រង់ ជាប្រាំដែនថែកភាគ ។

ឧទាហរណ៍:

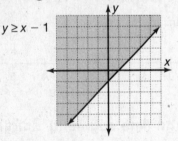

$$y \geq x - 1$$

លីត្រ (liter) គឺជាឯកតាគោលរបស់ រ៉ូលុម នៃមាត្រាប្រព័ន្ធ ។

ឧទាហរណ៍:

ដបពីរលីត្រ

រយៈខ្សែរូបណ្តោយ (longitude) គឺជារង្វាស់ប្រវែង គិតជា ដឺក្រេ ខាងកើត ឬខាងលិច ពីខ្សែ ដើម មេរីខាន ។

ឧទាហរណ៍:

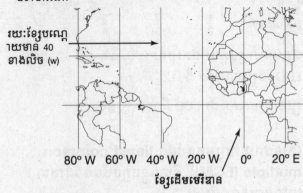

រយៈខ្សែរូបណ្តោ យមាន 40 ខាងលិច (w)

80° W 60° W 40° W 20° W 0° 20° E

ខ្សែដើមមេរីខាន

ភាគបួនតូច (lower quartile) គឺជាលេខកណ្តាល នៃផ្នែកខាងតូចរបស់សំណុំ ទិន្នផល ។

ឧទាហរណ៍:

27 27 27 29 32 33 36 38 42 43 62

↑ ភាគបួនតូច   ↑ លេខកណ្តាល   ↑ ភាគបួនធំ

អង្គតូចបំផុត (lowest terms) ប្រភាគ ដែល ភាគយក និងភាគ បែង មានកត្តារួមជាលេខ 1 ក្នុងអង្គតូចបំផុត ។

ឧទាហរណ៍:

$$\frac{1}{2} \qquad \frac{3}{5} \qquad \frac{21}{23}$$

ម៉ាស់ (mass) គឺចំនួនរូបធាតុ ដែលវត្ថុអ្វីនិមួយៗ ទ្រទ្រង់នោះ ។

ឧទាហរណ៍:

គ្រាប់ទំពាំងបាយជូរក្រៀម   ស្បែកជើងកីឡាមួយគូ
មានម៉ាស់ 1 ក្រាម ។   មានម៉ាស់ 1 គីឡូក្រាម ។

ផលធម្យម (mean) គឺផលបូក របស់តម្លៃក្នុងសំណុំ ទិន្នផល ចែកនឹងចំនួនតម្លៃ ។ ហៅម៉្យាងទៀតថា ចំនួនមធ្យម ។

ឧទាហរណ៍:

27 27 27 29 32 33 36 38 42 43 62

ផលបូក: 396

ចំនួនតម្លៃ: 11

ផលធម្យម: $396 \div 11 = 36$

រង្វាស់ល្អៀង (measurement error) គឺការចុំ
ជាក់លាក់ក្នុងរង្វាស់ ។ ល្អៀងធំបំផុត ក្នុង រង្វាស់
ដែលអាចមានឡើង គឺពាក់កណ្ដាល នៃឯកតា តូច
បំផុត ដែលប្រើនោះ ។

ឧទាហរណ៍:

បើអ្នកញជាឯកតាតូចបំផុត ល្អៀងធំបំផុត
ដែលអាចមានឡើងនោះ គឺមាន $\frac{1}{2}$ អ៊ីញ ។
ដូច្នេះ កម្ពស់ពិតប្រាកដ គីរវាងពី
$5'5\frac{1}{2}"$ និង $5'6\frac{1}{2}"$ ។

ទំហំនៃទំនងកណ្ដាល (measure of central
tendency) គឺជាតម្លៃទោលសង្ខេបប្រាប់ពី
សំណុំមួយរបស់លេខទិន្នផល ។

ឧទាហរណ៍:
ផលមធ្យម, លេខកណ្ដាល, និងលេខញឹកញាប់ ជាទំហំធម្មតា
នៃទំនងកណ្ដាល ។

27   27   27   29   32   33   36   38   42   43   62

លេខញឹកញាប់   លេខកណ្ដាល

ផលមធ្យម: = 396 ÷ 11 = 36

លេខកណ្ដាល (median) គឺជាតម្លៃកណ្ដាលនៃ
សំណុំទិន្នផលមួយ កាលបើតម្លៃទាំងនោះ តម្រៀប
តាមលេខរៀង ។

ឧទាហរណ៍:
27   27   27   29   32   33   36   38   42   43   62

លេខកណ្ដាល

មុឃាគណិត (mental math) ការគិតគណនា
តែក្នុងខួរក្បាល ដោយពុំប្រើ ខ្មៅដៃ និងក្រដាស ឬ
ប្រដាប់គិតលេខ ។

ឧទាហរណ៍:

2000   ×   30

3 សូន្យ   +   1 សូន្យ = 4 សូន្យ

គិត: 2   ×   3 = 6, ថែមសូន្យ 4 ទៀត

2000   ×   30 = 60,000

ម៉ែត្រ (meter) គឺជាឯកតាគោល នៃរង្វាស់ប្រវែង
ក្នុងមាត្រាប្រព័ន្ធ ។

ឧទាហរណ៍:

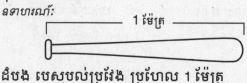
1 ម៉ែត្រ

ដំបង បេសបល់ប្រវែង ប្រហែល 1 ម៉ែត្រ

មាត្រាប្រព័ន្ធ (metric system) គឺជាប្រព័ន្ធ
នៃរង្វាស់ ដែលប្រើម៉ែត្រ, ក្រាម និងលីត្រ ។

ឧទាហរណ៍:

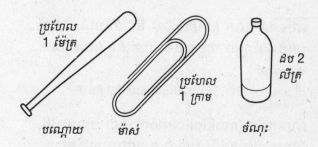

ប្រហែល
1 ម៉ែត្រ

ប្រហែល
1 ក្រាម

ឬ ច 2
លីត្រ

បណ្ដោយ   ម៉ាស់   ចំណុះ

ចំណុចកណ្ដាល (midpoint) គឺចំណុចដែលបែង
ចែកអង្កត់ សមភាគខ្លីពីរ ។

ឧទាហរណ៍:   C ជាចំណុចកណ្ដាលរបស់ $\overline{AB}$.

A   C   B

រង្វាស់ប្រវែង $\overline{AC}$ = រង្វាស់ប្រវែង $\overline{CB}$

ម៉ៃល៍ (mile) គឺជាឯកតារង្វាស់តាមបែបបទម្លាប់
ស្មើនឹង 5280 ហ្វីត ។

ឧទាហរណ៍:

1 ម៉ៃល៍ គឺជាចម្ងាយ ដែលអ្នកអាច
ដើរក្នុងរយៈពេល 15 ទៅ 20 មីនុត ឬ
រត់ក្នុង 10 មីនុត ។

មីល្លី- (milli-) ជាបុព្វបទ មានន័យថា $\frac{1}{1000}$ ។

ឧទាហរណ៍:   1 ម៉ែត្រ = $\frac{1}{1000}$ ម៉ែត្រ

លេខចម្រុះ (mixed number) គឺលេខកើតឡើង
ដោយលេខគត់គូ និង ប្រភាគ ។

ឧទាហរណ៍: $3\frac{1}{2}$ $1\frac{3}{4}$ $13\frac{3}{8}$

លេខញឹកញាប់ (mode) គឺតម្លៃដែលលេចមក
ច្រើនជង ក្នុងសំណុំទិន្នផល ។

ឧទាហរណ៍:
27   27   27   29   32   33   36   38   42   43   62

ក្នុងសំណុំទិន្នផលនេះ 27 គឺជាលេខញឹកញាប់ ។

ឯកធា (monomial) គឺជាកន្សោមពិជគណិត ដែលមានអង្គតែមួយ គត់ ។

ឧទាហរណ៍: $2x^2$ $5y$ x^3 -3

លេខផលគុណ (multiple) គឺជាផលគុណនៃលេខ ឲ្យណាមួយ ជាមួយនឹងលេខគត់គូ មួយទៀត ។

ឧទាហរណ៍:
បើ $3 \times 7 = 21$, គឺជាលេខផលគុណរបស់ 3 និង 7 ។

លេខគុណ (multiplication) គឺជាប្រមាណវិធី ដែលរួមផ្សំចំនួនពីរ ហៅថា កត្តាគុណ បង្កើតបាន ជាចំនួនមួយ ហៅថា ផលគុណ ។

ឧទាហរណ៍:

3 ជួរនៃ 6

$$3 \times 6 = 18$$
កត្តាគុណ   ផលគុណ

លក្ខណៈលេខគុណ (multiplication property) ប្រសិន A និង B ជាព្រឹត្តិការណ៍ មិនពាក់ ព័ន្ធគ្នា ដូច្នេះ ភវនិយភាព របស់ចំនួនទាំងពីរ ដែលកើតឡើង ឲ្យជា:

$P(A$ និង $B) = P(A) \times P(B)$ ។

ឧទាហរណ៍:

បង្វិលទីមួយ: P(ក្រហម) $= \frac{1}{4}$

បង្វិលទីពីរ: P(ក្រហម) $= \frac{1}{4}$

P(ក្រហម និងក្រហម) $= \frac{1}{4} \times \frac{1}{4} = \frac{1}{16}$

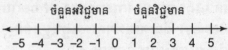

លក្ខណៈសមភាពនៃលេខគុណ (Multiplication Property of Equality) ប្រសិនបើ $a = b$,

ដូច្នេះ: $ac = bc$ ។

ឧទាហរណ៍:

នៅលើបន្ទាត់ទីពីរនៃឧទាហរណ៍ខាងក្រោម, 2 គឺ ត្រូវបានគុណជាមួយផ្នែកទាំងពីរនៃសមីការ

ប្រសិនបើ $\frac{1}{2}y = 4$

ដូច្នេះ $2 \times \frac{1}{2}y = 2 \times 4$

ចំនួនគុណប្រច្រាស (multiplicative inverse) ប្រសិនបើផលគុណ របស់ចំនួនពីរ ស្មើ 1 ចំនួននីមួយៗ គឺជា ចំនួនគុណប្រច្រាស របស់ចំនួនមួយទៀត ។

ឧទាហរណ៍:
$\frac{1}{6}$ និង 6 គឺជាចំនួនគុណប្រច្រាស ព្រោះ $\frac{1}{6} \times 6 = 1$ ។

មិនកំណត់ក្នុងទេវិញទៅមក (mutually exclusive) ប្រសិនបើព្រឹត្តិការណ៍ ណាមួយ A ឬ B កើតឡើង ព្រឹត្តិការណ៍មួយទៀត មិនកើតឡើងទេ ។

ឧទាហរណ៍:
ប្រសិនបើ សិតុណ្ហភាព ខាងក្រៅឡើងដល់ 90° និងមិនមានធ្លាក់ព្រិលទេ ។
ប្រសិនបើ ពហុកោណមួយ មានតែ 3 ជ្រុង វាមិនអាចមានមុម 4 ទេ ។

ចំនួនអវិជ្ជមាន (negative numbers) គឺចំនួន ដែលតិចជាងសូន្យ ។

ឧទាហរណ៍:

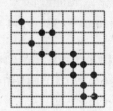

ទំនាក់ទំនងអវិជ្ជមាន (negative relationship) សំណុំទិន្នផលពីរ ដែលមានទំនាក់ទំនង អវិជ្ជមាន កាលបើតម្លៃទិន្នផល នៅក្នុងសំណុំមួយកើតឡើង ហើយតម្លៃទិន្នផលមួយទៀត ថយចុះ ។

ឧទាហរណ៍:

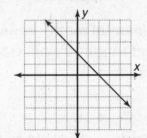

ជម្រាលអវិជ្ជមាន (negative slope) គឺជម្រាលរបស់បន្ទាត់ទេរ ចុះក្រោម ។

ឧទាហរណ៍:

ប្រុសការ៉ េ អវិជ្ជមាន (negative square root) គឺចំនួនផ្ទុយនឹងគោលការណ៍ ប្រុសការ៉ េ នៃចំនួនណាមួយ ។

ឧទាហរណ៍:
គោលការណ៍ប្រុសការ៉ េ   ប្រុសការ៉ េ អវិជ្ជមាន
$\sqrt{25} = 5$ $-\sqrt{25} = -5$

ផ្ទាំងត (net) គឺផ្ទាំងសំប៉ែត មានលក្ខណៈលំនាំ ដែលអាចបត់បញ្ចូលគ្នា បង្កើតជា រូបពិត ដូចជាព្រីស ជាដើម ។

ឧទាហរណ៍:

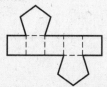

ផ្ទាំងត សម្រាប់ធ្វើជា ព្រីសបញ្ចកោណ   ព្រីសបញ្ចកោណ

នវកោណ (nonagon) គឺជាពហុកោណ មានជ្រុងខាង 9 ។

ឧទាហរណ៍:

សមីការមិនមែនខ្សែ (nonlinear equation) គឺជាសមីការដែលមានក្រាភិច ច្រើនជារបត់ ជាងជា ខ្សែបន្ទាត់ ។

ឧទាហរណ៍:

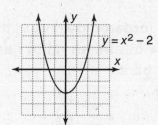

$y = x^2 - 2$

អនុគមន៍មិនមែនខ្សែ (nonlinear function) គឺជាអនុគមន៍មានក្រាភិច មិនមែនជាខ្សែបន្ទាត់ត្រង់ ពីព្រោះ កាលបើ បន្លាស់ស្មើ នៅលើ x មិនបង្កើត ជាបន្លាស់ស្មើនៅ y ទេ ។

ឧទាហរណ៍:

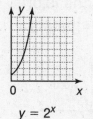 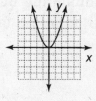 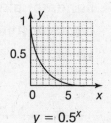

$y = 2^x$ $y = x^2$ $y = 0.5^x$

គ្មានទំនាក់ទំនង (no relationship) សំណុំ ទិន្នផលពីរ គ្មានទំនាក់ទំនងនឹងគ្នា កាលបើគ្មាន ទំនាក់ទំនងវិជ្ជមាន ឬ អវិជ្ជមាន ។

ឧទាហរណ៍:

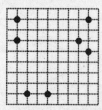

បន្ទាត់លេខ (number line) គឺជាខ្សែបន្ទាត់ ដែលបង្ហាញពីចំនួនលេខតាមលំដាប់ ។

ឧទាហរណ៍:

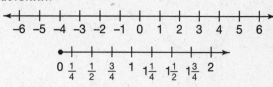

លេខអក្សរ (number-word form) គឺជា របៀប សរសេរលេខ ដោយប្រើតួលេខ និង ពាក្យ ។

ឧទាហរណ៍:   45 សែនលាន   9 ពាន់

លេខសញ្ញា (numeral) គឺជានិមិត្តរូប សំគាល់ ចំនួនលេខមួយៗ ។

ឧទាហរណ៍:   7   58   234

ភាគយក (numerator) គឺលេខខាងលើ ក្នុង ប្រភាគ ដែលប្រាប់ពីចំនួននៃផ្នែកយកចេញពីដុំ ទាំងមូល ។

ឧទាហរណ៍:

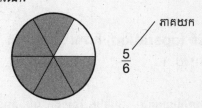

ភាគយក

$\dfrac{5}{6}$

មុមទាល (obtuse angle) គឺជាមុម ដែលមាន រង្វាស់ច្រើនជាង 90° និង តិចជាង 180° ។

ឧទាហរណ៍:

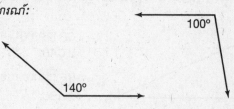

100°

140°

ត្រីកោណទាល (obtuse triangle)
គឺជាត្រីកោណ ដែលមានមុមទាលមួយ ។

ឧទាហរណ៍:

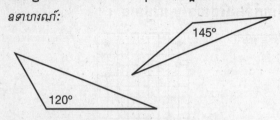

អដ្ឋកោណ (octagon) គឺជាពហុកោណមួយ
ដែលមានជ្រុងខាង 8 ។

ឧទាហរណ៍:

លេខសេសសគូ (odd number) គឺជាលេខគត់គូ
ដែលមាន 1, 3, 5, 7 ឬ 9 នៅក្នុងខ្ទង់រាយ ។

ឧទាហរណ៍:

    43   225   999   8,007

សេស (odds) គឺផលធៀប នៃចំនួនរបៀប ដែល
ព្រឹត្តិការណ៍មួយអាចកើតមានឡើង ទៅនឹងចំនួន
របៀប ដែលព្រឹត្តិការណ៍ មិនអាចកើតមានឡើង
នោះ ។

ឧទាហរណ៍:

 សេស ក្នុងការបោះគ្រឡប់រកលេខ 3: 1 ទៅ 5
សេស ក្នុងការបោះមិនឱ្យប៉ះលេខ 3វិញ: 5 ទៅ 1 ។

ប្រមាណវិធី (operation) គឺជារបៀបប្រើក្នុង
គណិតសាស្ត្រ ។

ឧទាហរណ៍:
គោលប្រមាណវិធីបួនយ៉ាង : លេខបូក, លេខដក, លេខគុណ,
លេខចែក

ជ្រុងអមលម្មុខ (opposite leg) ចំពោះមុមស្រួច
ក្នុងត្រីកោណកែង គឺជ្រុងអមផ្នែកកាត់មុខ មុមនោះ ។

ឧទាហរណ៍:

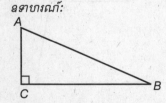

$\overline{CB}$ ជ្រុងអមលម្មុខនឹង
∠CAB.

$\overline{AC}$ ជ្រុងអមលម្មុខនឹង
∠ABC.

លេខផ្ទុយគ្នា (opposite numbers)
គឺលេខដែលមានរយៈចម្ងាយ ពីសូន្យប៉ុនគ្នា នៅលើ
បន្ទាត់លេខ ប៉ុន្តែនៅជ្រុងម្ខាងម្នាក់ ។

ឧទាហរណ៍:

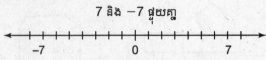

7 និង −7 ផ្ទុយគ្នា

លំដាប់នៃប្រមាណវិធី (order of operations)
គឺក្បួន ដែលប្រាប់ពីលំដាប់ក្នុងប្រមាណវិធី មាន:
(1) សម្រួលខាងក្នុងវង់ក្រចក, (2) សម្រួលនិទស្សន្ត,
(3) គុណនឹងចែក ពីឆ្វេងទៅស្តាំ និង, (4) បូក និងដក
ពីឆ្វេងទៅស្តាំ ។

ឧទាហរណ៍:
កំណត់តម្លៃ $2x^2 + 4(x − 2)$ សម្រាប់ $x = 3$.

(1) សម្រួលខាងក្នុងវង់ក្រចក	$2 \cdot 3^2 + 4(3 − 2)$
	$2 \cdot 3^2 + 4(1)$
(2) សម្រួលនិទស្សន្ត	$2 \cdot 9 + 4$
(3) គុណនឹងចែក ពីឆ្វេងទៅស្តាំ	$18 + 4$
(4) បូក និងដក ពីឆ្វេងទៅស្តាំ	22

លំដាប់គូ (ordered pair) លេខមួយគូប្រើសម្រាប់
កំណត់ទីតាំងចំណុចមួយ នៅលើ កូរដោនេ
(តម្រុយ) ប្លង់ ។

ឧទាហរណ៍:

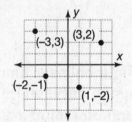

ចំណុចគល់ (origin)
ចំណុចសូន្យនៅលើបន្ទាត់លេខ ឬចំណុច (0,0)
ដែលខ្សែអក្សរបស់ប្រព័ន្ធតម្រុយ បានប្រសព្វគ្នា ។

ឧទាហរណ៍:

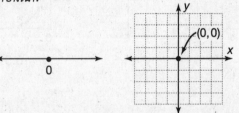

គំនូរមើលចំត្រង (orthographic drawing)

គឺជាការគូររូបមើលចំត្រងពីមុខ - ពីចំហៀង និង ពីលើ ។

ឧទាហរណ៍:

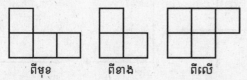

ពីមុខ   ពីខាង   ពីលើ

អោនស្យ (ounce) គឺជាឯកតា រង្វាស់ទម្ងន់តាមបែប ទម្លាប់ ។

ឧទាហរណ៍:

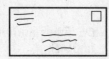

សំបុត្រទម្ងន់ប្រហែល មួយអោនស្យ

លទ្ធផល (outcome) គឺជារបៀបមួយ ដែលការ ពិសោធន៍ ឬស្ថានការណ៍ណាមួយ អាចនឹងបង្កើត បាន នោះ ។

ឧទាហរណ៍:

លទ្ធផលការបោះកាក់ 2

ភាក់ទី ១	ភាក់ទី ២
មុខ	ខ្នង
មុខ	មុខ
ខ្នង	មុខ
ខ្នង	ខ្នង

លទ្ធផលមាន 4 ។ លទ្ធផលមួយគឺ មុខ-មុខ ។

លេខដាច់ប៉ែក (outlier) គឺជាតម្លៃចុងផុត នៅក្នុងសំណុំទិន្នផល ដាច់ចេញពីតម្លៃឡៀៗ ។

ឧទាហរណ៍:

27 27 27 29 32 33 36 38 42 43 62

↑
លេខដាច់ប៉ែក

ប៉ារ៉ាបូល (parabola) គឺជារបស់កោង រាង ∪ ឬ ∩ ក្រឡាប់ចុះក្រោម ដែលជាក្រាភិច នៃអនុគមន៍ ដឺក្រេទី 2 ។

ឧទាហរណ៍:

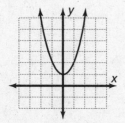 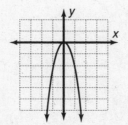

ខ្សែស្រប (parallel) បន្ទាត់ពីរ, អង្កត់ ឬ រ៉េយ៍ ដែលមិនកាត់គ្នា ទោះបីពន្លាតវែងឆ្ងាយ យ៉ាង ណាក៏ដោយ ។

ឧទាហរណ៍:

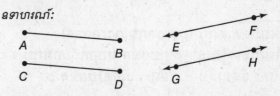

ប្រលេឡូក្រាម (parallelogram) ជារូបមាន ជ្រុងខាង 4 ដែលមានជ្រុងឈមមុខ ស្របគ្នា និង មានសមភាព ។

ឧទាហរណ៍:

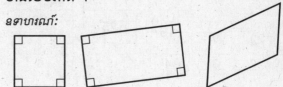

បញ្ចកោណ (pentagon) ជាពហុកោណ មាន ជ្រុងខាង 5 ។

ឧទាហរណ៍:

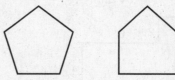

ភាគរយ (percent) ជាផលធៀប ដែលប្រៀបចំនួន ណាមួយទៅ 100 ។

ឧទាហរណ៍:

$$\frac{58}{100} = 0.58 = 58\%$$

បន្លាស់ប្ដូរភាគរយ (percent change) ចំនួន បន្លាស់ប្ដូរ, កើនឬថយចុះ, ចែកនឹងចំនួនដើមដំបូង ហើយ និងចាត់ទុកថា ជាភាគរយនៃចំនួន ដើមដំបូង នោះ ។

ឧទាហរណ៍:

ចូររកបន្លាស់ប្ដូរភាគរយ ប្រសិនបើប្រាក់ $1500 យកទៅប្រើបាន ចុងការ $75 ។

$$\frac{75}{1500} = 0.05 = 5\%$$ $75 ជាកំណើន 5% ។

ចូររកបន្លាស់ប្ដូរភាគរយ ប្រសិនបើរបស់មួយថ្ងៃ $50 ហើយលក់ចុះ ថ្លៃ $10 ។

$$\frac{10}{50} = 0.20 = 20\%$$ $10 ចុះថ្លៃគឺជា 20% ថយចុះ ។

ឥនភាពភាគរយ (percent decrease) ការថយ
ចុះ នៅក្នុងមួយចំនួន បញ្ជាក់ជាភាគរយរបស់
ចំនួនដើម ។ មើល "បន្ថយស់បូរភាគរយ" ។

កំណើនភាគរយ (percent increase)
កំណើនឡើងនៅក្នុងមួយចំនួន បញ្ជាក់ជាភាគរយ
របស់ ចំនួនដើម ។ មើល "បន្ថយស់បូរភាគរយ" ។

ការៃសុក្រិត (perfect square) គឺការៃរបស់
លេខគត្តគូ ។

ឧទាហរណ៍:

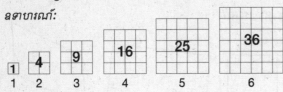

1	4	9	16	25	36
1	2	3	4	5	6

បរិមាត្រ (perimeter) រយៈចម្ងាយព័ទ្ធជុំវិញពី
ក្រៅរូបមួយ ។

ឧទាហរណ៍: $P = 5 + 2 + 6 + 4 + 11 + 6$
$= 34$ ឯកតា

5
2 6
6
4
11

ការរៀបលំដាប់ (permutation) ការរៀបរយៈរបស់
ទៅតាមលំដាប់ធំតូច ។

ឧទាហរណ៍:

សិស្សម្នាក់ក្នុងក្រុមនេះ នឹងត្រូវជ្រើសតាំងជាប្រធាន
និងម្នាក់ឡើតជាអនុប្រធាន: Wendy, Alex, Carlos ។
ការរៀបលំដាប់អាចមានដូចតទៅនេះ:

Wendy—ប្រធាន, Alex—អនុប្រធាន
Wendy—ប្រធាន, Carlos—អនុប្រធាន
Alex—ប្រធាន, Wendy—អនុប្រធាន
Alex—ប្រធាន, Carlos—អនុប្រធាន
Carlos—ប្រធាន, Wendy—អនុប្រធាន
Carlos—ប្រធាន, Alex—អនុប្រធាន

កត់សំគាល់: ការរៀបនិមួយៗខាងលើនេះ មានការរៀបលំដាប់ខុសគ្នា ។

កែង (perpendicular) បន្ទាត់, រំយ៍, ឬ
អង្គត់បន្ទាត់ ដែលប្រសព្វមុខ កើតបានជាមុមកែង ។

ឧទាហរណ៍:

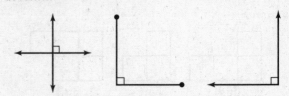

បន្ទាត់ពុះកែង (perpendicular bisector)
បន្ទាត់, រំយ៍, ឬអង្គត់ ដែលប្រសព្វមុខនិងអង្គត់មួយ
ឡើត នៅចំណុចកណ្ដាល និងកែងទៅអង្គត់នោះ ។

ឧទាហរណ៍:

D
C
A   B
E

$\overrightarrow{DE}$ គឺជាបន្ទាត់ពុះចែកកែង
របស់ $\overline{AB}$.

ជាយ៍ pi (π) ផលធៀបរង្វាស់វង្វង់ក្រៅ
ទៅនឹងវិជ្ជមាត្រ: 3.14159265....

ឧទាហរណ៍:

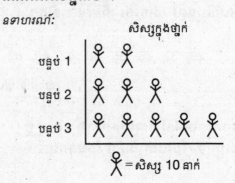

វិជ្ជមាត្រ
រង្វង់ក្រៅ

$$\pi = \frac{\text{រង្វង់ក្រៅ}}{\text{វិជ្ជមាត្រ}}$$

ក្រាភិចរូប (pictograph) គឺក្រាភិចប្រើរូបសញ្ញា
ជាតំណាងទិន្នផល ។

ឧទាហរណ៍:

សិស្សក្នុងថ្នាក់

បន្ទប់ 1	🧍 🧍
បន្ទប់ 2	🧍 🧍 🧍
បន្ទប់ 3	🧍 🧍 🧍 🧍 🧍

🧍 = សិស្ស 10 នាក់

ខ្ទង់លេខ (place value) តម្លៃអោយទៅតាមខ្ទង់ ដែលតួលេខ នោះចិតនៅ ។

ឧទាហរណ៍:

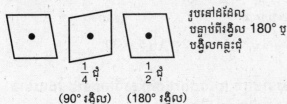

$$3 \times 10 \qquad 4 \times \frac{1}{100}$$
$$7 \times 1 \qquad 0 \times \frac{1}{10}$$

ប្លង់ (plane) គឺផ្ទៃរាប ដែលពន្លាតឆ្ងាយទីបំផុត ។

ឧទាហរណ៍:

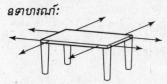

គិតប្រមាណមើលទៅផ្ទៃតុ ដែលពន្លាត់វែងទៅគ្រប់ទិស ដែលគិតបានជាប្លង់ ។

ចំណុចឆ្លុះ (point of symmetry) រូបមានចំណុចឆ្លុះ កាលបើមិនបូរផ្លាស់ បើឃើងផ្ទេររឆ្លិល180° ។

ឧទាហរណ៍:

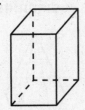

$\frac{1}{4}$ ជុំ
(90° រឆ្លិល)

$\frac{1}{2}$ ជុំ
(180° រឆ្លិល)

រូបនៅខាងដែល បន្ទាប់ពីរឆ្លិល 180° ឬ បន្ទិលកន្លះជុំ

ពហុកោណ (polygon) រូបជិតជ្រុង បង្កើតអោយ មានអង្កត់បន្ទាត់ ។

ឧទាហរណ៍:

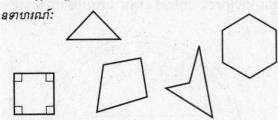

សូលីតពហុមុខ (polyhedron) សូលីត ដែលមាន មុខខាងជាពហុកោណ ។

ឧទាហរណ៍:

ពហុធា (polynomial) គឺជាកន្សោមពិជគណិត ដែលមានផលបូក កើតឡើងដោយអង្គ មួយ ឬច្រើន ទៀត ។

ឧទាហរណ៍: $x^2 + 2x - 3$ \qquad $5y - 15$

ចង្កោម (population) ជម្រើសរក របស់ទាំង អស់សម្រាប់សិក្សា ដែលមាននៅក្នុងសម្រង់ ។

ឧទាហរណ៍:

ឈ្មោះ 1000 ដែលជាសមាជិកក្លិប បានចុះក្នុងក្រដាសឆ្នោត ដើម្បីនឹងហ្គូតចាប់យក ។ បន្ទាប់មក ក្រដាសឆ្នោត 100 បានហ្គូតចេញ ហើយត្រូវបានគេទូរស័ព្ទទៅប្រាប់ ធ្វើជា សម្រង់ ។ ចង្កោមនៃ សម្រង់ គឺ ចំនួន 1000 នៃសមាជិកក្លិបនោះ ។

ចំនួនវិជ្ជមាន (positive numbers) គឺចំនួនទាំង ឡាយ ដែលធំជាងសូន្យ ។

ឧទាហរណ៍:

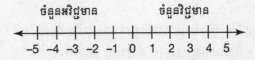

ចំនួនអវិជ្ជមាន \qquad ចំនួនវិជ្ជមាន

$$-5 \;\; -4 \;\; -3 \;\; -2 \;\; -1 \;\; 0 \;\; 1 \;\; 2 \;\; 3 \;\; 4 \;\; 5$$

ទំនាក់ទំនងវិជ្ជមាន (positive relationship) សំណុំទិន្នផលពីរ មានទំនាក់ទំនងវិជ្ជមាន កាលណា តម្លៃទិន្នផលទាំងពីរ កើនឡើង ឬថយចុះ ។

ឧទាហរណ៍:

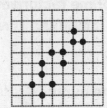

ខ្សែជម្រាលវិជ្ជមាន (positive slope) គឺខ្សែ ជម្រាលទៅឡើងលើ ។

ឧទាហរណ៍:

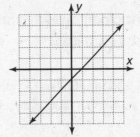

ផោន (pound) គឺជាឯកតារង្វាស់ ក្នុងប្រព័ន្ធតាម ទម្លាប់ស្មើនឹង 16 អោនស្យ ។

ឧទាហរណ៍:

អង្ករ
1 ផោន

ស្វ័យគុណ (power) និទស្សន្ត ឬ ចំនួនដែលកើន ឡើងដោយ បង្កើនគោល ទៅតាម និទស្សន្ត ។

ឧទាហរណ៍:

$16 = 2^4$ 2 បង្កើនស្វ័យគុណទី 4
16 គឺជាស្វ័យគុណទី 4 របស់ ។

ជាក់លាក់ (precision) គឺភាពពិតប្រាកដនៃរង្វាស់ ប្រវែង បញ្ជាក់ដោយឯកតារង្វាស់ ។

ឧទាហរណ៍:

ឯកតាខ្នាតតូច, អ៊ីញ្ច,
ជាក់លាក់ពិតប្រាកដ
ជាងឯកតាខ្នាតធំ, ហ្វីត

5'1" 61"

កត្តាដើម (prime factor) លេខដើមដែលចែកនឹង ចំនួនគត់ណាមួយទៀត មិនមាន សេស ។

ឧទាហរណ៍:

5 គឺជាកត្តាដើមរបស់ 35, ព្រោះ 35 ÷ 5 = 7.

គុណកត្តាដើម (prime factorization) ការ សរសេរលេខ ជាបែបផលគុណ របស់លេខដើម ។

ឧទាហរណ៍:

$70 = 2 \times 5 \times 7$

លេខដើម (prime number) លេខគត់គូ ដែលធំជាង 1 មានកត្តា 1 និង ខ្លួនវា ។

ឧទាហរណ៍:

លេខដើម សរសេរនៅដើមលេខ 2, 3, 5, 7, 11, ...

ប្រាក់ដើម (principal) ចំនួនទឹកប្រាក់ដាក់ធនាគារ ឬអោយខ្ចី ដែលទទួលបានចុងការ ។

ឧទាហរណ៍:

ដេវ បានដាក់ប្រាក់ $300 ក្នុងគណនីសន្សំ ។ មួយឆ្នាំក្រោយមក ការទូទាត់គណនី មាន $315 ។ $300 គឺជាប្រាក់ដើម ។

ឬសការ៉េធំ (principal square root) គឺជាឬសការ៉េវិជ្ជមាន នៃចំនួនណាមួយ ។

ឧទាហរណ៍:

ឬសការ៉េធំ   ឬសការ៉េអវិជ្ជមាន
$\sqrt{25} = 5$ $-\sqrt{25} = -5$

ព្រីស (prism) គឺជាសូលីតពហុកោណ មានបាតសមភាព និងស្របគ្នា ។

ឧទាហរណ៍:

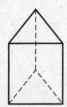

ភវនិយភាត (probability) ផលធៀបចំនួនរបៀប ច្រើនយ៉ាង នៃព្រឹត្តិការណ៍ ដែលអាចកើត មានឡើង ទៅនឹងចំនួនទាំងអស់នៃលទ្ធផល ដែលអាចមាននោះ ។

ឧទាហរណ៍:

ភវនិយភាត ក្រឡុកយក 3 គឺ $\frac{1}{6}$
ភវនិយភាត មិនក្រឡុក 3 គឺ $\frac{5}{6}$

ផលគុណ (product) គឺលទ្ធផលនៃការគុណលេខ ពីរចំនួន ឬច្រើនទៀត ។

ឧទាហរណ៍:

ផលគុណ
|
$2 \times 3 \times 5 = 30$

សមាមាត្រ (proportion) សមីការ មួយ ដែលមាន ផលធៀប ពីរស្មើគ្នា ។

ឧទាហរណ៍:

$\frac{12}{34} = \frac{6}{17}$

បន្ទាត់មុម (protractor) សម្ភារៈប្រើសម្រាប់វាស់មុម ។

ឧទាហរណ៍:

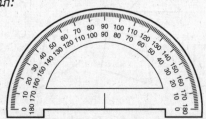

ពីរ៉ាមីត (pyramid) គឺជាសូលីតមួយ មានបាត និងមុខទាំងអស់ជាត្រីកោណ រួមជាកំពូលមួយ ។

ឧទាហរណ៍:

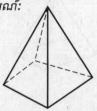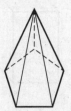

ទ្រឹស្តីបទ ពីតាគ័រ (Pythagorean Theorem)

ត្រីកោណកែង c ជារង្វាស់ប្រវែង អ៊ីប៉ូតេនុស និង a និង b ជារង្វាស់ប្រវែងជ្រុងអម, $a^2 + b^2 = c^2$ ។

ឧទាហរណ៍:

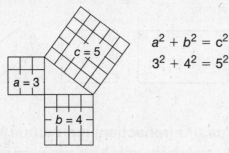

$$a^2 + b^2 = c^2$$
$$3^2 + 4^2 = 5^2$$

កាដ្រង់ (quadrants)

សំរុំចំណុចទាំង 4, កំណត់បានដោយ អ័ក្សនៃខ្សែកូអរដោនេ ពីរ ។

ឧទាហរណ៍:

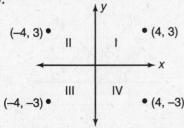

សមីការដឺក្រេទីពីរ (quadratic equation)

គឺជាសមីការ ដែលមានអង្គការ៉េ ដូចជា x^2 ។

ឧទាហរណ៍:

$$y = x^2 + 3x - 12 \qquad y = 2x^2 + 7$$

អនុគមន៍ដឺក្រេទីពីរ (quadratic function)

គឺអនុគមន៍ ដែលមានស្វ័យគុណារបស់ x ធំបំផុត ស្មើ 2 ។ ក្រាហ្វិចរបស់អនុគមន៍ ដឺក្រេទីពីរ គឺជា ប៉ារ៉ាបូល ។

ឧទាហរណ៍:

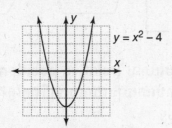

$$y = x^2 - 4$$

ចតុរង្គ (quadrilateral)

គឺបហុកោណដែលមាន ជ្រុងខាង 4 ។

ឧទាហរណ៍:

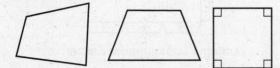

ក្វាត (quart)

គឺជាឯកតាការរបស់វ៉ូលុម (មាឌ) ក្នុងប្រព័ន្ធរង្វាស់ តាមបែបទម្លាប់ ។

ឧទាហរណ៍:

ទឹកដោះគោ មួយក្វាត

ភាគបួន (quartile)

ចំនួនមួយនៃចំនួនដែលបែងចែក សំណុំទិន្នផល ជាភាគបួនស្មើគ្នា ។

ឧទាហរណ៍:

27 27 27 29 32 33 36 38 42 43 62

ភាគបួនតូច   លេខកណ្តាល   ភាគបួនធំ

27, 33 និង 42 គឺភាគបួនទាំងបីនៃសំណុំទិន្នផលនេះ ។

ផលចែក (quotient)

គឺជាលទ្ធផលបាន ដោយចែកចំនួនមួយ និងចំនួនមួយទៀត ។

ឧទាហរណ៍:

ផលចែក
$$8 \div 4 = 2$$

សញ្ញា រ៉ាឌីកាល់ (radical sign $\sqrt{}$)

ប្រើសម្រាប់តំណាងឫសការ៉េ របស់ចំនួនមួយ ។

ឧទាហរណ៍:

$$\sqrt{49} = 7$$

កាំរង្វង់ (radius)

គឺជាបន្ទាត់ឆ្នាប់ពីផ្ចិតរង្វង់ ទៅចំណុចណាមួយនៃរង្វង់ ។

ឧទាហរណ៍:

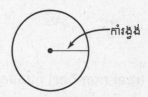

កាំរង្វង់

សំណាកនៃសេចម្រុះ (random sample)

គឺជាសំណាកជ្រើសរើស ក្នុងបែបមួយ ដែលសមាជិក ម្នាក់ៗ ក្នុងចង្គោម ដោយភាពចៃដន្យស្មើៗគ្នា អាចត្រូវរើសយក ។

ឧទាហរណ៍:

ឈ្មោះ 1000 ដែលជាសមាជិកភ្ជិប បានចុះក្នុងក្រដាសឆ្នោត ដើម្បីនឹងហូតរបស់យក ។ បន្ទាប់មក ក្រដាសឆ្នោត 100 បានហូតចេញ ហើយត្រូវបានគេទួរសួរពួកទៅប្រាប់ធ្វើសម្រេង ។ សមាជិកទាំងអស់របស់ភ្ជិប មានភាពចៃដន្យស្មើៗគ្នា និងត្រូវបានគេហៅនេះ គឺជាសំណាកនៃរើស ចម្រុះ ។

រង្វាត (range) ផលដករវាងតម្លៃខ្ពស់ និងទាបបំផុត នៅក្នុងសំណុំទិន្នផល ។

ឧទាហរណ៍:

27 27 27 29 32 33 36 38 42 43 62

រង្វាតមាន 62 − 27 = 35.

អត្រា (rate) ផលធៀបបង្ហាញពីទំនាក់ទំនងរវាង បរិមាណ ដែលមានឯកតាខុសគ្នា ។

ឧទាហរណ៍: $\dfrac{72 \text{ ដុល្លារ}}{28 \text{ ម៉ោង}}$ $\dfrac{55 \text{ ដុល្លារ}}{1 \text{ ម៉ោង}}$

ផលធៀប (ratio) ការប្រៀបធៀប បរិមាណពីរ ដែលធម្មតា ប្រើនសរសេរជាប្រភាគ ។

ឧទាហរណ៍: $\dfrac{2}{1}$ 2 ទៅ 1   2:1

ចំនួនសនិទាន (rational number) ចំនួនដែល អាចសរសេរជាផលធៀប របស់ចំនួន គត់ពីរ ។ ចំនួនគត់, ប្រភាគ និងទសភាគជាច្រើន ជាចំនួន សនិទាន ។

ឧទាហរណ៍:

ចំនួនគត់	ប្រភាគ	ទសភាគ
$-27 = \dfrac{-27}{1}$	$\dfrac{7}{8}$	$3.1 = 3\dfrac{1}{10} = \dfrac{31}{10}$

រេយ៍ (ray) ផ្នែកនៃបន្ទាត់ ដែលមានចំណុចចុង ហើយពន្លាតគ្មានទីបំផុត នៅទិស ម្ខាងទៀត ។ រេ៍យ មានឈ្មោះ រាប់ពីចំណុចចុងទៅ ។

ឧទាហរណ៍:

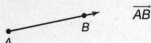

$\overrightarrow{AB}$

ចំនួនពិត (real number) គឺចំនួនសនិទាន និង ចំនួន អសនិទាន ទាំងអស់ ។

ឧទាហរណ៍:

−27 $\dfrac{1}{2}$ 3.1

$\sqrt{5}$ π $-\sqrt{\dfrac{1}{2}}$

លេខឆ្នាស់ (reciprocals) ចំនួនពីរដែលផលគុណស្មើនឹង 1 ។

ឧទាហរណ៍:

$\dfrac{3}{5}$ និង $\dfrac{5}{3}$ ឆ្នាស់គ្នា ដូច្នេះ: $\dfrac{3}{5} \cdot \dfrac{5}{3} = 1.$

ចតុកោណកែង (rectangle) ប្រលេឡូក្រាម ដែលមានជ្រុងឈមប្រវែងស្មើគ្នា និងរង្វាស់មុម ទាំងអស់ មួយៗមាន 90° ។

ឧទាហរណ៍:

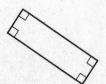

លេខឆ្លាស់ (reflection) រូបភាពឆ្លុះរបស់រូបមួយ ដែលបានផ្តាច់ចុះ ទៅម្ខាងខ្សែ មួយ ។ ឆ្លុះកជាឈ្មោះ ប្រើសម្រាប់សម្គាល់ បន្ទាស់រូប ដែលផ្តាច់រូបចុះទៅ ម្ខាងខ្សែ ។

ឧទាហរណ៍:

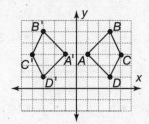

ពហុកោណនិយ័ត (regular polygon) ពហុកោណ ដែលមានជ្រុងខាង និង មុមទាំងអស់ សមភាពគ្នា ។

ឧទាហរណ៍:

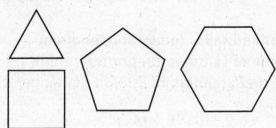

ទីតាំងប្រយោល (relative position) ទីកន្លែង ដែលប្រាប់ដោយប្រយោលទៅនឹកកន្លែងដទៃទៀត ។

ឧទាហរណ៍:

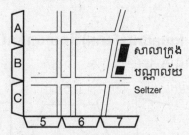

សាលាក្រុង នៅជិតបណ្ណាល័យ Seltzer ។

សេស (remainder) គឺចំនួនតូចជាងតួចែក ដែលនៅសល់ បន្ទាប់ពីធ្វើលេខចែកក្បួច ។

ឧទាហរណ៍: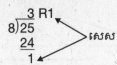
សេស

ទសភាគជ្រំបន្ត (repeating decimal) ទសភាគ ដែលមានតួលេខ ជ្រំបន្ត ឬ ក្រុមតួលេខនៅខាងស្ដាំ ចំណុចទសភាគ ។

ឧទាហរណ៍: $0.\overline{6}$ $0.\overline{123}$ $2.\overline{18}$

រ៉ុមប៊ីស (rhombus) ប្រលេឡូក្រាមមួយ ដែលមាន ជ្រុងទាំងបួន ប្រវែងស្មើគ្នា ។

ឧទាហរណ៍:

មុំកែង (right angle) មុំមួយដែលមានរង្វាស់ ប្រវែង 90° ។

ឧទាហរណ៍:

ត្រីកោណកែង (right triangle) ត្រីកោណដែល មានមុំកែងមួយ ។

ឧទាហរណ៍:

ទោល (rise) ចំពោះបន្ទាត់នៅក្នុងក្រាភិច បន្ទាត់ បញ្ឈរបូរផ្លាស់ បើកាលណាបន្ទាត់បូរផ្លាស់ ដែរ ។

ឧទាហរណ៍: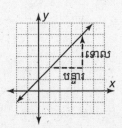
ទោល
បន្ទារ

រង្វិល (rotation) រូបភាពរបស់រូប ដែលត្រូវបានបង្វិលនៅលើថាស ។ ពាក្យរង្វិល ក៏សំដៅ ទៅលើការបង្វាស់រូប ដោយបង្វិលរូបដែរ ។

ឧទាហរណ៍: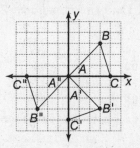

រង្វិលឆ្លុះ (rotational symmetry) រូបមួយដែល មានបង្វិលឆ្លុះ ប្រសិនបើវាត្រូវបានបង្វិលពុំបានពេញ មួយ ហើយនៅមានរូបភាពបេះបិទនឹងភាពដើម ។

ឧទាហរណ៍: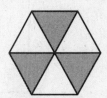

រូបនីមួយៗមានរង្វិលឆ្លុះ៖

ផ្គត់លេខ (rounding) ការប្រមាណាប៉ាន់ចំនួន អោយត្រូវតាមខ្ទង់លេខ ។

ឧទាហរណ៍:

2153 ផ្គត់ទៅខ្ទង់	
គិតតាមខ្ទង់ រយ: 2200	គិតតាមខ្ទង់ ដប់: 2150

បន្ទារ (run) ចំពោះបន្ទាត់នៅក្នុងក្រាភិច បន្ទាស់បូរ បន្ទាត់ផ្ដេក ប្រើសម្រាប់រកបន្ទាស់បូរ បន្ទាត់ បញ្ឈរ ឬទោល ។

ឧទាហរណ៍: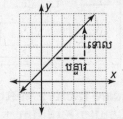
ទោល
បន្ទារ

សំណាក (sample) សំណុំទិន្នផលដែលប្រើការសម្រាប់ ទស្សន៍ទាយ អំពីស្ថានការណ៍ពិសេស ណាមួយ ដែលអាចនឹងកើតឡើងបាននោះ ។

ឧទាហរណ៍:
ឈ្មោះ 1000 ដែលជាសមាជិកក្ដិច បានចុះក្នុងក្រដាសឆ្នោត ដើម្បី នឹងធ្វើតាចាប់យក ។ បន្ទាប់មក ក្រដាសឆ្នោត 100 បានហូតចេញ ហើយ ត្រូវបានគេទុរសព្ទទៅប្រាប់ ធ្វើជា សម្រង់ ។ សំណាកចំនួន នសមាជិក 100 នាក់ ដែលគេទុរសព្ទទៅប្រាប់ធ្វើជាសម្រង់នោះ ។

សំណាកលំហ (sample space) សំណុំនៃលទ្ធផល ដែលនឹងអាចកើតមានឡើង ក្នុងការ ពិសោធន៍ម្តួយ ។

ឧទាហរណ៍:

លទ្ធផលក្នុងការបោះត្រឡុប់កាក់ 2:

កាក់ទី 1	កាក់ទី 2
មុខ	ខ្នង
មុខ	មុខ
ខ្នង	មុខ
ខ្នង	ខ្នង

សំណាកលំហ គឺ មុខ, ខ្នង; មុខ, មុខ; និង ខ្នង, ខ្នង

ស្កាមក្រិត (ក្នុងក្រាភិច) (scale (graphical))
ចន្លោះស្កាមក្រិតគត់គូ នៅក្នុងក្រាភិចរនុក ឬ
ក្រាភិចខ្នៀរបញ្ឈរ ប្រើសម្រាប់វាស់កម្ពស់រនុក ។

ឧទាហរណ៍:

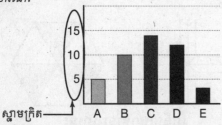

ខ្នាតរង្វាស់ (scale (in scale drawing))
ផលធៀបរបស់រង្វាស់ នៅក្នុងខ្នាតគំនូរ ឬមាត្រដ្ឋាន
ទៅនឹងរង្វាស់របស់ពិតប្រាកដ ។ *មើលមាត្រដ្ឋាន ។*

មាត្រដ្ឋាន (scale drawing) គំនូរដែលប្រើខ្នាត
ដើម្បីពង្រីក ឬពង្រួញ រូបវត្ថុម្តួយ ។

ឧទាហរណ៍:

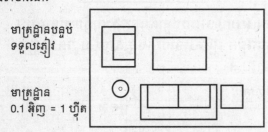

កត្តាមាត្រដ្ឋាន (scale factor) ផលធៀបប្រើ
សម្រាប់ពង្រីកឬបន្ថយរូបស្រដៀងគ្នា ។

ឧទាហរណ៍:

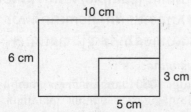

$$\frac{10}{5} = 2$$
$$\frac{6}{3} = 2$$

កត្តាមាត្រដ្ឋាន គឺ 2 សំរាប់ពង្រីក ។

ត្រីកោណវិសមង្ស្ (scalene triangle) ត្រីកោណ
ដែលជ្រុងខាង មានរង្វាស់ប្រវែងខុសគ្នា ទាំងអស់ ។

ឧទាហរណ៍:

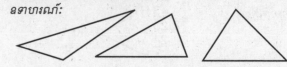

ក្រភិចពាស (scatterplot) ក្រាភិចប្រើតម្លៃទិន្ន
ផលគូ ជាចំណុចដើម្បីបង្ហាញពីទំនាក់ទំនង រវាង
សំណុំទិន្នផលពីរ ។

ឧទាហរណ៍:

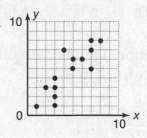

កំណត់ប្រើបែបវិទ្យាសាស្ត្រ (scientific
notation) លេខសរសេរមានទសភាគ ធំជាង ឬស្មើ
1 គុណនឹង ស្វ័យគុណ 10 ។

ឧទាហរណ៍: $350{,}000 = 3.5 \times 10^5$

ចម្រៀករង្វង់ (sector) ផ្នែកម្តួយជ្រុងរបស់រង្វង់
ប្រើក្នុងក្រាភិចរង្វង់ បង្ហាញពីសំណុំទិន្នផល មួយ
ប្រៀបទៅសំណុំទាំងមូល ។

ឧទាហរណ៍:

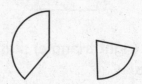

អង្កត់ (segment) *មើលអង្កត់ខ្សែ (line segment) ។*

អង្កត់ពុះ (segment bisector) បន្ទាត់, រ៉េយ៍
ឬអង្កត់ ដែលនៅលើចំណុចកណ្តាល របស់ អង្កត់ ។

ឧទាហរណ៍:

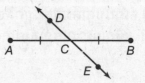

$\overrightarrow{DE}$ ពុះចែក
$\overline{AB}$ នៅត្រង់
C.

លំដាប់ (sequence) ការតម្រៀបលេខ ទៅតាម លក្ខណៈសំនាំ ។

ឧទាហរណ៍:

លំដាប់លេខគណិត

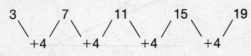

លំដាប់ធរណីមាត្រ

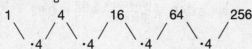

ជ្រុងខាង (side) រ៉េយ៍ និមួយៗ ជួយបង្កើតអោយ

ចានជាមុមម្មួយ ។ អង្កត់ខ្សែរ៍ក៏ជួយបង្កើតអោយមាន ចានជាពហុកោណដែរ ។

ឧទាហរណ៍:

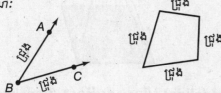

ជ្រុង-មុម-មុម (Side-Angle-Angle (SAA))

ក្បួនប្រើសម្រាប់បញ្ជាក់ត្រីកោណសមភាព ដោយប្រៀបធៀប ផ្ទេកតថានុរូប ។

ឧទាហរណ៍:

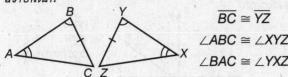

$\overline{BC} \cong \overline{YZ}$

$\angle ABC \cong \angle XYZ$

$\angle BAC \cong \angle YXZ$

$\triangle ABC \cong \triangle XYZ$ ដោយក្បួន SAA .

ជ្រុង-មុម-ជ្រុង (Side-Angle-Side (SAS))

ក្បួនប្រើសម្រាប់បញ្ជាក់ត្រីកោណសមភាព ដោយប្រៀបធៀប ផ្ទេកតថានុរូប ។

ឧទាហរណ៍:

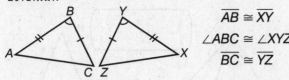

$\overline{AB} \cong \overline{XY}$

$\angle ABC \cong \angle XYZ$

$\overline{BC} \cong \overline{YZ}$

$\triangle ABC \cong \triangle XYZ$ ដោយក្បួន SAS.

ជ្រុង-ជ្រុង-ជ្រុង (Side-Side-Side (SSS))

ក្បួនប្រើសម្រាប់បញ្ជាក់ត្រីកោណសមភាព ដោយប្រៀបធៀប ផ្ទេកតថានុរូប ។

ឧទាហរណ៍:

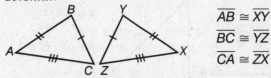

$\overline{AB} \cong \overline{XY}$

$\overline{BC} \cong \overline{YZ}$

$\overline{CA} \cong \overline{ZX}$

$\triangle ABC \cong \triangle XYZ$ ដោយក្បួន SSS.

គួលេខចាំបាច់ (significant digits) នៅក្នុង

រង្វាស់បរិមាណ, គួលេខតំណាងរង្វាស់ពិតប្រាកដ ។

ឧទាហរណ៍:

380.6700 គួលេខទាំងអស់ ជាគួលេខចាំបាច់ ។

0.0038 3 និង 8 ជាគួលេខចាំបាច់ - តែគ្មានលេខសូន្យណា មួយ ជាគួលេខចាំបាច់ទេ ។

ស្រដៀងគ្នា ឬសមរូប (similar) មានរូបរងដូចគ្នា

តែមិនចាំបាច់មាន ទំហំប៉ុនគ្នាទេ ។

ឧទាហរណ៍:

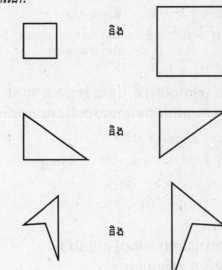

 និង

និង

និង

ផលធៀបសមរូប **(similarity ratio)** ផលធៀប
រវាងប្រវែងជ្រុង តថានុរូប ក្នុងរូបស្រដៀងគ្នា ។

ឧទាហរណ៍:

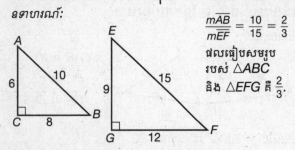

$$\frac{m\overline{AB}}{m\overline{EF}} = \frac{10}{15} = \frac{2}{3}$$

ផលធៀបសមរូប
របស់ △ABC
និង △EFG គឺ $\frac{2}{3}$.

ប្រាក់ការទោល **(simple interest)** ប្រាក់ចុងការ
ដែលកើតឡើងដោយប្រាក់ដើមមួយគត់ ។

ឧទាហរណ៍: Ramon ធ្វើវិនិយោគប្រាក់ $240 ក្នុងគណនី
ដែលបានចុងការ 6% ក្នុងមួយឆ្នាំ អស់ រយៈពេល
5 ឆ្នាំ ។

តាត់និងបាន 240 · 0.06 · 5 = 72;
$72 គឺជាប្រាក់ការទោល ក្នុងរយៈពេល 5 ឆ្នាំ ។

សម្រួលហើយ **(simplified)** ពហុធា ដែលមាន
អង្គមិនដូចគ្នា ។

ឧទាហរណ៍:

$4x^4 + x^3 + x^2 - 8$ សម្រួលហើយ

$4x^4 + x^2 + 6x^2 - 8$ មិនទាន់សម្រួល ព្រោះ x^2 និង
$6x^2$ ជាអង្គដូចគ្នា

សម្រួល **(simplify)** គឺ បន្លយមិនសុភាព របស់
កន្សោមដោយអនុវត្តទៅតាមលំដាប់នៃប្រមាណវិធី ។

ឧទាហរណ៍: សម្រួល $3 + 8 · 5^2$.

$$3 + 8 · 5^2 = 3 + 8 · 25 \quad \text{(និទស្សន្ត)}$$
$$= 3 + 200 \quad \text{(គុណ)}$$
$$= 203 \quad \text{(បូក)}$$

ទង្វើគ្រាប់ **(simulation)** គំរូបពិសោធ
ប្រើសំរាប់រក ភវនិយភាព ។

ឧទាហរណ៍:

អ្នកលេង បេសបល់ ម្នាក់ វាយ .250 ។ ដើម្បីធ្វើគ្រាប់
តើអ្នកលេងអាចវាយបានប៉ុន្មាន បើគេបង្វិលរង្វង់ផ្នែក-4 ។
ទង្វើគ្រាប់អាចប្រើសម្រាប់គន់គូរ ថាតើ អ្នកវាយអាចវាយត្រូវ 2
ឬត្រូវ 3 ក្នុងមួយពេលៗ ។

ស៊ីនុស **(sine)** ចំពោះមុមស្រួច x ក្នុងត្រីកោណកែង,
ស៊ីនុសរបស់ x ឬ sin(x) គឺជាផលធៀប $\frac{\text{ជ្រុងអមឈម}}{\text{អ៊ីប៉ូតេនុស}}$ ។

ឧទាហរណ៍:

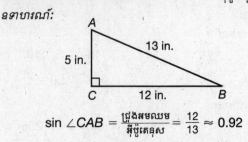

$$\sin \angle CAB = \frac{\text{ជ្រុងអមឈម}}{\text{អ៊ីប៉ូតេនុស}} = \frac{12}{13} \approx 0.92$$

អាប៉ូតែម **(slant height)** ក្នុងពីរ៉ាមីត រយៈចម្ងាយ
កែង ពីជ្រុងបាតទៅកំពូល ។

ឧទាហរណ៍:

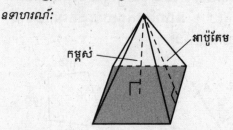

កម្ពស់   អាប៉ូតែម

បន្តិល **(slide)** មើលពាក្យបំលែង **(translation)**។

ខ្សែជម្រាល **(slope)** ចំពោះបន្ទាត់ក្នុងក្រាភិច,
ខ្សែជម្រាល កើតឡើងដោយយកទោលទៅចែក និង
បន្ធារ សម្រាប់បញ្ជាក់ពីលក្ខណៈផ្អែករបស់បន្ទាត់ ។

ឧទាហរណ៍:

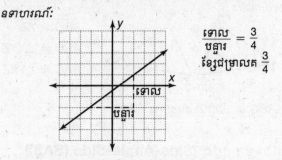

$$\frac{\text{ទោល}}{\text{បន្ធារ}} = \frac{3}{4}$$

ខ្សែជម្រាលគឺ $\frac{3}{4}$

សូលីត **(solid)** គឺរូបភាព ត្រីមាត្រ ។

ឧទាហរណ៍:

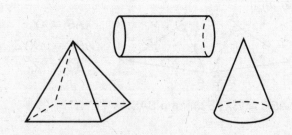

ចម្លើយសមីការ ឬ វិសមីការ (solutions of an equation or inequality) តម្លៃរបស់ អថេរ ដែលបង្កើតបាន ជាសមីការមួយ ឬវិសមីការពិត ។

ឧទាហរណ៍:

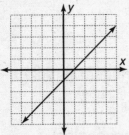
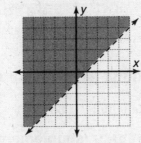

បន្ទាត់ជាតំណាងសមីការ
$y = x - 1$

ផ្នែកពណ៌តំណាង
$y > x - 1$

ចម្លើយប្រព័ន្ធ (solution of a system) បន្ទាស់ប្ដូរ អថេរ បានឆ្លើយតបគ្រប់សមីការ ជាប្រព័ន្ធ ពិត ។

ឧទាហរណ៍:

$$y = x + 4$$
$$y = 3x - 6$$

លំដាប់គូ (5,9) ឆ្លើយតបសមីការទាំងពីរ ដូច្នេះ (5,9) គឺជាចម្លើយ ប្រព័ន្ធ ។

ដោះស្រាយ (solve) ដើម្បីរកចម្លើយសមីការមួយ ឬវិសមីការមួយ ។

ឧទាហរណ៍: ដោះស្រាយ $x + 6 = 13$.

$$x + 6 = 13$$
$$x + 6 + (-6) = 13 + (-6)$$
$$x + 0 = 7$$
$$x = 7$$

ស្វ៊ែរ (sphere) គឺជាសូលីត ដែលចំណុចទាំងអស់ មានរយៈចម្ងាយស្មើគ្នា ពីផ្ចិត ។

ឧទាហរណ៍:

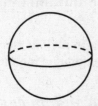

ការ៉េ (square) គឺជាចតុរង្គ ដែលជ្រុងទាំងអស់ មាន រង្វាស់ស្មើគ្នា និងមុម ទាំងអស់មានរង្វាស់ 90° ។

ឧទាហរណ៍:

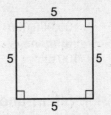

តម្លើងស្វ៊យគុណទីពីរ (squared) តម្លើង ស្វ៊យគុណ ដល់កម្រិតទីពីរ ។

ឧទាហរណ៍: 3 ការ៉េ $= 3^2$
$$3^2 = 3 \times 3 = 9$$

សង្ទីម៉ែត្រការ៉េ (square centimeter) ក្រឡា ផ្ទៃរបស់ការ៉េដែលជ្រុងនីមួយៗប្រវែង 1 សង្ទីម៉ែត្រ ។

ឧទាហរណ៍:

1 សង្ទីម៉ែត្រការ៉េ

អ៊ិញការ៉េ (square inch) ក្រឡាផ្ទៃរបស់ការ៉េ ដែលជ្រុងនីមួយៗ ប្រវែង 1 អ៊ិញ ។

ឧទាហរណ៍:

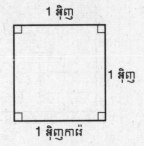

1 អ៊ិញការ៉េ

ឫសការ៉េ (square root) ឫសការ៉េ របស់ N គឺជាចំនួនដែលអោយទៅ N គុណនឹងខ្លួនឯង ។ ម្យ៉ាងទៀត ឫសការ៉េ របស់ចំនួនអោយណាមួយ គឺជាការ៉េ ប្រវែងរបស់ជ្រុង ដែលកើតបានជា ក្រឡាផ្ទៃមួយ ។

ឧទាហរណ៍:
$9 \times 9 = 81$, ដូច្នេះ 9
ជាឫសការ៉េ របស់ 81
$9 = \sqrt{81}$

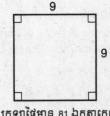

ក្រឡាផ្ទៃមាន 81 ឯកតាកេរ៉េ

ទម្រង់ខ្នាត (standard form) របៀបសរសេរ លេខ ដោយប្រើតួលេខ ។

ឧទាហរណ៍:

ទម្រង់ខ្នាត:	100,000,000
ទម្រង់ខ្នាត:	មួយរយលាន
ទម្រង់លេខ-ពាក្យ:	100 លាន

និយាយក្រាមទង និងស្ទឹក (stem-and-leaf diagram) ការបង្ហាញទិន្នផល ដោយប្រើតួលេខ របស់ចំនួនទិន្នផល ប្រាប់បញ្ជាក់ពីរាងនៅ និងការ ចែកចាយរបស់សំណុំទិន្នផល ។

ឧទាហរណ៍:

និយាយក្រាមបង្ហាញពីសំណុំទិន្នផល: 33, 34, 34, 35, 40, 41, 46, 51, 51, 52, 53, 55, 58.

ទង	ស្ទឹក					
3	3	4	4	5		
4	0	1	6			
5	1	1	2	3	5	8

អនុគមន៍ល្បាក់ (step function) អនុគមន៍ ដែលប្រើក្បូនផ្សេងៗ ទាក់ទងទៅនឹងការដាក់តម្លៃ ។ ក្រាភិចរបស់អនុគមន៍ល្បាក់ ផ្សំដោយកំណាត់បន្ទាត់ មិនតគ្នាជាប់គ្នា ។

ឧទាហរណ៍:

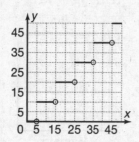

មុមរាប (straight angle) គឺមុមមានរង្វាស់ 180° ។

ឧទាហរណ៍:

ជំនួស (substitute) ផ្លាស់ប្ដូរ អថេរ ដោយតម្លៃ យថាប្រភេទ ។

ឧទាហរណ៍:

ចូរប្រើរូបមន្ត $A = l \cdot w$ ដើម្បីរកក្រឡាផ្ទៃរបស់ចតុកោណកែង ដែលមានបណ្ដោយ 12 ស.ម និង ទទឹង 8 ស.ម ។

$A = l \cdot w$

$A = 12 \cdot 8$ ជំនួសតម្លៃ បណ្ដោយ

$A = 96$ និងទទឹង

ក្រឡាផ្ទៃមាន 96 ស.ម

លេខដក (subtraction) ប្រមាណវិធី ដែលប្រាប់ការខុសគ្នារវាងចំនួនពីរ ឬ ចំនួនដែលនៅ សល់ បន្ទាប់ពីចំនួនខ្លះ បានដកចេញ ។

ឧទាហរណ៍:
$12 - 5 = 7$

⊠ ⊠ ⊠ ⊠ ⊠
○ ○ ○ ○ ○
○ ○

ផលបូក (sum) លទ្ធផល ឬបូកចំនួនពីរ ឬច្រើនទៀត ។

ឧទាហរណ៍:
$30 + 18 = 48$ ← ផលបូក

មុមបន្ថែម (supplementary angles) មុមពីរដែលបូកបញ្ចូលគ្នា មាន 180° ។

ឧទាហរណ៍:

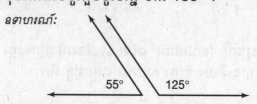

55° 125°

ក្រឡាផ្ទៃរួម (surface area (SA)) ផលបូកក្រឡាផ្ទៃមុខនីមួយៗ របស់សូលីតពហុមុខ ។

ឧទាហរណ៍:

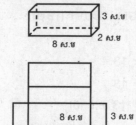

មុខពីរ មាន 8 ស.ម និង 3 ស.ម
$A = b \cdot h = 8 \cdot 3 = 24$ ស.ម

មុខពីរ មាន 8 ស.ម និង 2 ស.ម
$A = b \cdot h = 8 \cdot 2 = 16$ ស.ម

មុខពីរ មាន 2 ស.ម និង 3 ស.ម
$A = b \cdot h = 2 \cdot 3 = 6$ ស.ម

ក្រឡាផ្ទៃរួមរបស់ព្រិសចតុកោណ កែងមាន

$SA = 2(24 + 16 + 6)$
$= 92$ ស.ម

សម្រង់ (survey) ការសិក្សាតម្រូវអោយមានការ ប្រមូលសន្លឹ និងការធ្វើវិភាគពត៌មាន ។

ឧទាហរណ៍:

សម្រង់មួយបានរៀបចំឡើង ដើម្បីកំណត់បញ្ជាក់ថាតើ គឺឡាណាមួយ ដែលមានប្រជាប្រិយ ជាង គេចំពោះសិស្ស ។

ឆ្លុះ (symmetry) ចូរមើលបន្ទាត់ឆ្លុះ (line symmetry), ចំណុចឆ្លុះ និងរង្វិលឆ្លុះ (rotational symmetry) ។

ប្រព័ន្ធសមីការខ្សែ (system of linear equations) សមីការខ្សែពីរ ឬច្រើនទៀត ដែលប្រើការ ជាមួយគ្នា ។

ឧទាហរណ៍:
$y = x + 3$
$y = 4x - 15$

តារាងជ្រុងបញ្ច្រាស (T-table) គឺជាតារាងបង្ហាញប្រាប់ x និង តម្លៃ-y ជា គូជានុរូប របស់សមីការមួយ ។

ឧទាហរណ៍:
$$y = 2x + 1$$

x	y
−2	−3
−1	−1
0	1
1	3
2	5

ចម្រឹង (tally) កំណត់ត្រា ប្រើក្រិតចម្រឹង ជារបាប់ ក្នុង ពេលធ្វើសម្រង់ ។

ឧទាហរណ៍:

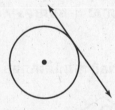

របៀបន	ចម្រឹង
ឆុនគូច	||||| |||
គ្រូសារ	||||
� ឡានដឹកឆុនគូច	|||||	
ឡានដឹក	|||||
ឡានថ្មើងគូច	|||

ក្រិតចម្រឹង (tally marks) ក្រិត ប្រើសម្រាប់រៀប ផ្ទៃសំណុំទិន្នផលធំ ។ ក្រិតនីមួយៗ បញ្ជាក់តម្លៃមួយ ដំង ដែលលេចចេញនៅក្នុងសំណុំទិន្នផល ។

ឧទាហរណ៍:

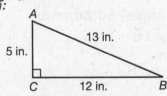

| មួយ ||||| ប្រាំ

ខ្សែប៉ះ: (tangent line) (ឬខ្សែតង់ហ្សង់) ខ្សែរដែលបានប៉ះរង្វង់តែមួយចំណុច ។

ឧទាហរណ៍:

ផលធៀបតង់ហ្សង់ (tangent ratio) ចំពោះ មុមស្រួច x ក្នុងត្រីកោណកែង, តង់ហ្សង់របស់ x ឬ $\tan(x)$, គឺ $\frac{\text{ជ្រុងអមឈមម}}{\text{ជ្រុងអមជាប់}}$ ។

ឧទាហរណ៍:

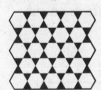

$$\tan \angle CAB = \frac{\text{ជ្រុងអមឈមម}}{\text{ជ្រុងអមជាប់}} = \frac{12}{5} = 2.4$$

អង្គ (term) ចំនួនមួយនៅក្នុងលំដាប់ ។ ម្យ៉ាងទៀត ផ្នែកមួយនៃពហុធា ដែលជាចំនួនមានសញ្ញាមុខមួយ, អថេរមួយ, ឬចំនួនមួយ ដែលគុណជាមួយ អថេរមួយ ឬអថេរជាច្រើនទៀត ។ អថេរទាំងនោះ មាននិទស្សន្ត ជាលេខគត់គូ បាន ។

ឧទាហរណ៍:

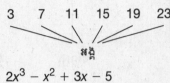

លំដាប់   3   7   11   15   19   23

អង្គ

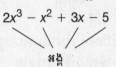

ពហុធា $2x^3 - x^2 + 3x - 5$

អង្គ

កំណត់ចុងលេខទសភាគ (terminating decimal) ទសភាគមួយ ដែលមានចំនួនគត់លេខ មិនបូរផ្លាស់ ។

ឧទាហរណ៍:   3.5   0.599992   4.05

ក្បាច់បណ្តាក់ក្តា (tessellation) លក្ខណៈលំនាំ ច្រំបន្ត របស់រូបដែល ពាសបូងមួយ គ្មានចន្លោះទទេ ឬត្រួតលើគ្នា ។

ឧទាហរណ៍:

 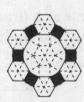

ទ្រឹស្ដី ភវនិយភាព (theoretical probability) ផលធៀប នៃចំនួនរបៀបដែលស្ថានការណ៍ អាចកើត ឡើង ទៅនឹងចំនួនលទ្ធផល ដែលអាចមាននោះ ។

ឧទាហរណ៍:

$$\frac{\text{ចំនួនរបៀបបង្ហើលយកផ្នែក ស}}{\text{ចំនួនរបៀបទាំងអស់}} = \frac{3}{6} = \frac{1}{2}$$

ដោយហេតុថា ពាក់កណ្តាលផ្នែករង្វង់បង្ហើលពណ៌ស ទ្រឹស្ដីភវនិយភាពក្នុងការបង្ហើលយកផ្នែក ស គឺ $\frac{1}{2}$ ។

បន្លាស់រូប (transformation) គឺការផ្លាស់ប្ដូរ ទំហំ ឬ ទីតាំងរបស់រូប ។

ឧទាហរណ៍:

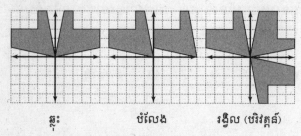

ឆ្លុះ   បំលែង   រង្វិល (បរិវត្តន៍)

បំលែង (translation) រូបភាព របស់រូបមួយ ដែលបានបង្វិលទៅទីតាំងថ្មីមួយទៀត ដោយមិនផ្លាប់ចុះ ឬត្រឡប់ ។ គេប្រើពាក្យនេះ សម្រាប់បន្លាស់រូប ក្នុងការបង្វិលរា ។

ឧទាហរណ៍:

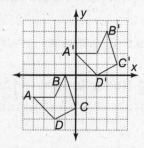

កាត់ទទឹង (tranversal) បន្ទាត់មួយដែលឆ្លងកាត់ បន្ទាត់ពីរ ឬច្រើនទៀត ។

ឧទាហរណ៍:

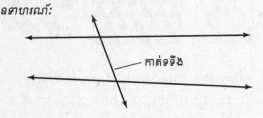

កាត់ទទឹង

ចតុកោណព្នាយ (trapezoid) គឺចតុរង្គ ដែលមានជ្រុងខាងពីរស្របគ្នា ។

ឧទាហរណ៍:

ឌីយ៉ាក្រាម (tree diagram) គឺការបែបមេកសាខា – ឌីយ៉ាក្រាម ស្វែងបង្ហាញនូវលទ្ធផល ទាំងអស់ ដែលមានលេខចេញមក របស់ស្ថានការណ៍ណាមួយ ។

ឧទាហរណ៍:
ការបោះត្រឡប់កាក់ 3:

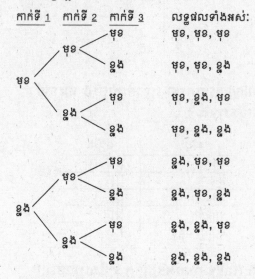

ទំនោរ (trend) គឺជាទំនាក់ទំនងរវាងសំរុំពីរ នៃ ទិន្នផល ដែលបង្ហាញជាលក្ខណៈលំនាំ នៅក្នុង ឌីយ៉ាក្រាមចំណុចរាយ ។ *មើលទំនាក់ទំនងវិជ្ជមាន និងទំនាក់ ទំនងអវិជ្ជមាន ។*

បន្ទាត់ទំនោរ (trend line) បន្ទាត់មួយ ដែល ទំនង ជា "សិ" និងចំណុចទាំងឡាយ ដែលបង្កើតជាទំនោរ នៅក្នុងក្រាទិចពាស ។ *មើលទំនាក់ទំនងវិជ្ជមាន និង អវិជ្ជមាន*

សាកល្បង (trial) ការធ្វើពិសោធន៍ ។

ឧទាហរណ៍:

បោះត្រឡប់គូបលេខ   បោះត្រឡប់កាក់

ត្រីកោណ (triangle) គឺជាពហុកោណ ដែលមានជ្រុងខាងបី ។

ឧទាហរណ៍:

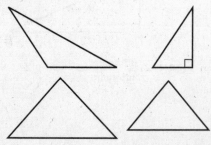

ផលធៀប ត្រីកោណមាត្រ (trigonometric ratios)
ផលធៀប រង្វាស់ប្រវែងនៃជ្រុងអម ក្នុង ត្រីកោណកែង ទាក់ទងទៅនឹងរង្វាស់មុំស្រួចរបស់ ត្រីកោណ ។

ឧទាហរណ៍:

$$\cos \angle CAB = \frac{\text{កូស៊ីនុស}}{\text{អ៊ីប៉ូតេនុស}} = \frac{3}{5} = 0.6$$

$$\sin \angle CAB = \frac{\text{ជ្រុងអមឈម}}{\text{អ៊ីប៉ូតេនុស}} = \frac{4}{5} = 0.8$$

$$\tan \angle CAB = \frac{\text{ជ្រុងអមឈម}}{\text{កូស៊ីនុស}} = \frac{4}{3} \approx 1.3$$

ត្រីធា (trinomial)
គឺពហុធា ដែលមានអង្គបី ។

ឧទាហរណ៍: $2x^3 - x^2 + 3x$ $3x^2 + 2x - 4$

ត្រឡប់ (turn)
មើលពាក្យរង្វិល (បរិវត្តន៍) (rotation) ។

ល្បែងមិនស្មើ (unfair game)
គឺជាល្បែងដែល អ្នកលេងទាំងអស់ មិនឈ្នះ ដោយបាន ភវនីយភាព ស្មើគ្នាទេ ។

ឧទាហរណ៍:

ល្បែងមិនស្មើ: គូបលេខ មួយគូ បានបោះត្រឡប់ឡើង ។ អ្នកលេង ម្នាក់ៗត្រូវបូករួមលេខពី 2 ទៅ 12 ។ ពិន្ទុអ្នកលេងម្នាក់ៗ គឺផលបូក លេខ ដែលបានបោះនោះ ។ ដូច្នេះផលបូកពីលេខ 2 ទៅ 12 ពុំស្មើគ្នា ទេ ក្នុងការផ្សេងបោះត្រឡប់ ហើយអ្នកលេងទាំងអស់ មិនអាច ស្មើគ្នា បាន ក្នុងការ ដំណើ‌មឈ្នះ - នេះហើយជាល្បែងមិនស្មើគ្នា ។

ឯកតាថ្លៃ (unit price)
គឺឯកតាអត្រា តម្លៃរបស់នីមួយៗ ។

ឧទាហរណ៍:
    $3.00 ក្នុងមួយដោន $5.75 ក្នុងមួយប្រអប់

ឯកតា (unit)
ចំនួនមួយនៃវត្ថុអ្វីមួយនោះ ។ ចំនួន ឬបរិមាណ ប្រើជាខ្នាតរង្វាស់ ។

ឯកតាប្រភាគ (unit fraction)
គឺប្រភាគដែលមានភាគយកស្មើ ១ ។

ឧទាហរណ៍: $\frac{1}{4}$ $\frac{1}{2}$ $\frac{1}{7}$

ឯកតាអត្រា (unit rate)
គឺអត្រា ក្នុងការប្រៀបធៀប ដែលចំនួនទីពីរ គឺជាមួយឯកតា ។

ឧទាហរណ៍:   25 ហ្គាឡុន ក្នុងមួយមិនុត $\frac{55 \text{ ម៉ៃល}}{1 \text{ ម៉ោង}}$

ភាគបែងមិនភ្លោះ (unlike denominators)
គឺភាគ បែងក្នុងប្រភាគពីរ ឬច្រើនទៀត ដែលមិនដូច គ្នា ។

ឧទាហរណ៍: $\frac{1}{2}$ $\frac{2}{5}$ $\frac{2}{9}$

ភាគបែងមិនភ្លោះ

ភាគបួនធំ (upper quartile)
គឺជាលេខកណ្តាល នៃផ្នែកខាងធំរបស់សំណុំ ទិន្នផល ។

ឧទាហរណ៍:

27   27   27   29   32   33   36   38   42   43   62

ភាគបួនតូច   កណ្តាល   ភាគបួនធំ

អថេរ (variable)
គឺបរិមាណ ដែលអាចផ្លាស់ប្តូរ ឬ រ ហើយភាគច្រើនយកអក្សរជាតំណាង ។

ឧទាហរណ៍:   3x   y   2t

អថេរ

ឌីយ៉ាក្រាមតំបន់ (Venn diagram)
គឺជាឌីយ៉ាក្រាម ដែលប្រើផ្នែកតំបន់ ដើម្បីបង្ហាញពីទំនាក់ ទំនង រវាងសំណុំនៃរបស់ ។

ឧទាហរណ៍:

កំពូល (vertex)
នៅក្នុងមុំ ឬពហុកោណ ចំណុច ដែលជ្រុងខាងពីរ បានមកប្រសព្វមុខ ។ ក្នុងសូលីត ពហុមុខ គឺចំណុចប្រសព្វ របស់មុខបី ឬ ច្រើនទៀត ។

ឧទាហរណ៍:

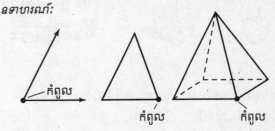

កំពូល   កំពូល   កំពូល

មុមឈម (vertical angles) មុមឈមទល់មុខគ្នា កើតឡើងដោយ បន្ទាត់ប្រសព្វមុខពីរ ។

ឧទាហរណ៍:

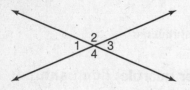

មុមឈម:
∠1 និង ∠3
∠2 និង ∠4

អ័ក្សបញ្ឈរ (vertical axis) គឺបន្ទាត់បញ្ឈរ ក្នុងបន្ទាត់ទាំងពីរ ដែលកើតឡើងដោយក្រាភិច ឬ ដោយតម្រុយបច្ឆង (កូអរដោណេ) ។

ឧទាហរណ៍:

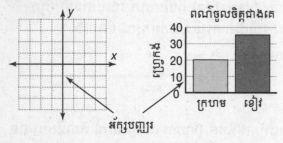

ពណ៌ចូលចិត្តជាងគេ

អ័ក្សបញ្ឈរ

មាឌ (រ៉ូល្យម) (volume) គឺទំហំល្វែង ដែលសូលីត មួយអាចក្តោបបាន ។

ឧទាហរណ៍:

$V = lwh$
$V = 4 \cdot 3 \cdot 2$
$V = 24$ ឯកតាគីប

ទម្ងន់ (weight) គឺរង្វាស់នៃកម្លាំង ដែលទំនាញ ផែនដី សង្កត់ទៅលើគ្រាប់អង្គអ្វីមួយ ។

ឧទាហរណ៍:

1 អោនខ្ស   1 ផោន   1 តោន

លេខគត់គូ (whole number) លេខណាមួយ នៅក្នុងសំណុំ {0, 1, 2, 3, 4, ...}.

ប្រើអក្សរ (word form) គឺរបៀបសរសេរលេខណា មួយ ដោយប្រើអក្សរជាពាក្យសំគាល់ ។

ឧទាហរណ៍:

សែសិបប្រាំបែសែន-សាន   មួយរយលាន   ប្រាំមួយ

អ័ក្ស-x (x-axis) គឺអ័ក្សផ្ដេក ក្នុងតម្រុយបច្ឆង ។

ឧទាហរណ៍:

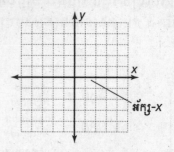

អ័ក្ស-x

កូអរដោណេ-x (x-coordinate) គឺចំណុចទីមួយ នៅក្នុងលំដាប់គូ ។

ឧទាហរណ៍:

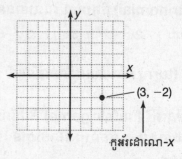

(3, −2)

កូអរដោណេ-x

ចំណុចប្រសព្វ-x (x-intercept) គឺជាចំណុចនៅ ក្នុងក្រាភិច នៃសមីការមួយ ដែលអ័ក្ស x មកប៉ះ ។

ឧទាហរណ៍:

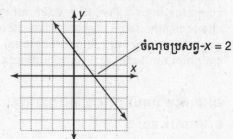

ចំណុចប្រសព្វ-x = 2

អ័ក្ស-y (y-axis) គឺអ័ក្សបញ្ឈរ ក្នុងតម្រុយបច្ឆង ។

ឧទាហរណ៍:

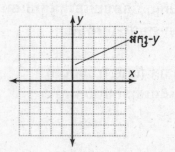

អ័ក្ស-y

កូអរដោណេ-y **(y-coordinate)** គឺចំណុចទីពីរ
នៅក្នុងលំដាប់គូ ។

ឧទាហរណ៍:

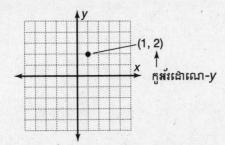

ចំណុចប្រសព្វ-y **(y-intercept)** គឺជាចំណុចនៅ
ក្នុងក្រាភិច នៃសមីការមួយ ដែលអក្ស-y មកប៉ះ ។

ឧទាហរណ៍:

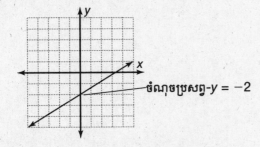

ចំណុចប្រសព្វ-y = −2

 យ៉ាត **(yard)** គឺជាឯកតានៃរង្វាស់ប្រវែងតាមទម្ងាប់
ស្មើនឹង 3 ហ្វីត ។

ឧទាហរណ៍:

កម្ពស់តុ ប្រហែល
1 យ៉ាត

គូតគត់ **(zero pair)** គឺចំនួនណាមួយ
និងចំនួនផ្ទុយរបស់វា ។

ឧទាហរណ៍: 7 និង −7   23 និង −23

លក្ខណៈគត់នៃលេខបូក **(Zero Property of
Addition)** ផលបូកនៃចំនួនគត់ ណា មួយ
និងជើងបូកបញ្ច្រាស់របស់វា ស្មើនឹងសូន្យ ។

ឧទាហរណ៍:   3 + (−3) = 0
                −8 + 8 = 0

Cantonese Glossary

絕對位置 (absolute position) 由坐標確定的位置。

例如：

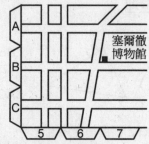

B7是塞爾徹博物館的絕對坐標。

絕對值 (absolute value) 一個數與零之間的距離，絕對值用符號 | | 表示。

例如：

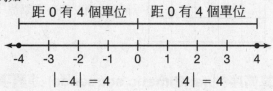

$|-4| = 4$　　　　$|4| = 4$

銳角 (acute angle) 小於 90°的角。

例如：

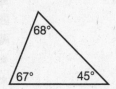

85°　　　20°　　　52°

銳角三角形 (acute triangle) 三個角都是銳角的三角形。

例如：

68°
67°　　45°

加數 (addend) 加到一個或幾個數上的數。

例如：　　$12 + 19 = 31$
　　　　　　加數　加數

加法 (addition) 兩個或兩個以上的數放在一起能夠得出和的運算。

例如：

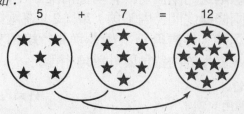

5　　+　　7　　=　　12

等加屬性 (Addition Property of Equality) 如果 $a = b$，
則 $a + c = b + c$。

例如：
在下面例子中的第二行，1加到等式的兩邊。

如果　　$x - 1 = 2$
則　　$x - 1 + 1 = 2 + 1$
　　　　$x = 3$

相反數（加性逆元素）(additive inverse) 一個數的相對數。

例如：　　-2 的相反數是 2。
　　　　　　5 的相反數是 -5。

鄰邊 (adjacent leg) 對於直角三角形的兩個銳角來說，位於該角下面的那條邊。

例如：

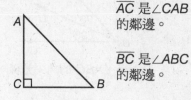

$\overline{AC}$ 是 $\angle CAB$ 的鄰邊。

$\overline{BC}$ 是 $\angle ABC$ 的鄰邊。

代數 (algebra) 數學的一個分支，它的四則運算關係是通過使用變量代替數字進行的。

代數式 (algebraic expression) 至少包含一個變量的表達式。

例如：　　$n - 7$　　　$2y + 17$　　　$5(x - 3)$

交錯角 (alternate angles) 兩條直線與一條直線相交所形成的，並且位於這條相交直線兩邊的兩個角。有兩種情況：（1）在兩條線之間（內錯角）或（2）在兩條線之外（外錯角）。相交線與平行線相交時，對頂的內錯角與外錯角相等。

例如：

外錯角：
$\angle 1$ 和 $\angle 8$
$\angle 2$ 和 $\angle 7$

內錯角：
$\angle 3$ 和 $\angle 6$
$\angle 4$ 和 $\angle 5$

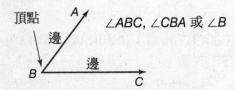

角 (angle) 具有同一個端點的兩條射線。

例如：

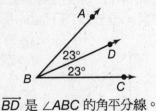

頂點
邊
邊

$\angle ABC$, $\angle CBA$ 或 $\angle B$

角平分線 (angle bisector) 將一個角分成兩個相等角的射線。

例如：

$\overline{BD}$ 是 $\angle ABC$ 的角平分線。

旋轉角 (angle of rotation) 旋轉時使一個圖形轉動的角。

例如：

旋轉角為 90°。

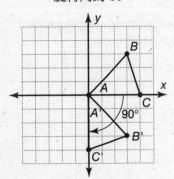

角邊角定理 (Angle-Side-Angle (ASA)) 通過比較三角形的相應部份來確定三角形是否全等的定理。

例如：

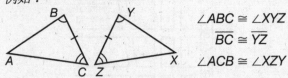

$\angle ABC \cong \angle XYZ$
$\overline{BC} \cong \overline{YZ}$
$\angle ACB \cong \angle XZY$

$\triangle ABC \cong \triangle XYZ$ 根據角邊角定理。

面積 (area) 一個圖形表面的總和。

例如：

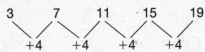

一個平方單位
面積 = 15 個平方單位

算術序列 (arithmetic sequence) 連續項之間的差總是相同的序列。

例如：

3   7   11   15   19
  +4   +4   +4   +4

排列 (arrangement) 人、字母、數字或其它事物的順序。

例如：

三種形狀的
所有可能排列：

加法結合律 (Associative Property of Addition) 改變加數的組合，其和不變。

例如：
$a + (b + c) = (a + b) + c$
$5 + (3 + 7) = (5 + 3) + 7$

乘法結合律 (Associative Property of Multiplication) 改變乘數因子的組合，其乘積不變。

例如：
$$a(bc) = (ab)c$$
$$3 \times (4 \times 2) = (3 \times 4) \times 2$$

平均數 (average) 見其詞義。

坐標軸 (axes) 見 x 軸和 y 軸。

柱狀圖 (bar graph) 使用豎向或橫向的柱條來表示數據的圖形。

例如：

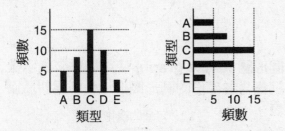

（指數的）底數 (base of an exponent) 以指數的次數使其自身相乘的數。

例如：
底數　　指數
$$6^2 = 6 \times 6 = 36$$

（多邊形的）底邊 (base of a polygon) 任何一條邊（通常爲下面的邊），或該邊的長。

例如：

底邊

（立體的）底面 (base of a solid) 在棱柱體或圓柱體中，兩個平行並且全等的面中的一個。在棱錐體中，與頂點相對的面。在圓錐中的圓形面。

例如：

底面　　　底面　　　底面

二進制 (binary number system) 以二位值爲基礎的系統。

例如：
在二進制中，1011等於十進制（以十位值爲基礎）中的11。

	八位	四位	二位	一位
二進制	1	0	1	1
位值	8	4	2	1
積	1×8=8	0×4=0	1×2=2	1×1=1

$(1 \times 8) + (0 \times 4) + (1 \times 2) + (1 \times 1) = 8 + 0 + 2 + 1 = 11$

二項式 (binomial) 含有兩項的多項式。

例如：
$$4x^3 - 2x^2 \qquad 2x + 5$$

平分 (bisect) 將一個角或線段分爲兩個全等的角或相等的兩條線段。

例如：

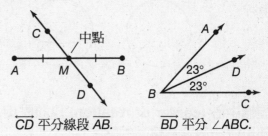

$\overrightarrow{CD}$ 平分線段 $\overline{AB}$.　　$\overrightarrow{BD}$ 平分 $\angle ABC$.

界線 (boundary line) 在線性不等式的圖形中，將不等式的解和不包含在解內的點分開的那條線。

例如：

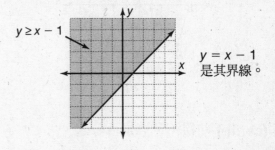

$y \geq x - 1$

$y = x - 1$ 是其界線。

框線圖 (box-and-whisker plot) 一種形象化地表示統計數據分佈的方法。下面的例子是以十個考分為基礎的：52, 64, 75, 79, 80, 80, 81, 88, 92, 99。

例如：

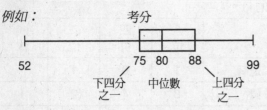

考分

下四分之一　中位數　上四分之一

容量 (capacity) 一個物體的體積，用來給出液體的度量。

例如：

500毫升　1升　1杯　1夸脫　1加侖

中心 (center) 在一個圓或球的正中心的點。

例如：

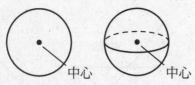

中心　　中心

旋轉中心 (center of rotation) 以該點旋轉可使一個圖形轉動的點。

例如：　原點是旋轉中心。

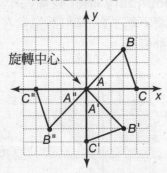

旋轉中心

厘 (centi-) 前綴，意思是百分之一。

例如：　　$1厘米 = \dfrac{1}{100}$ 米

中心角 (central angle) 角的頂點位於圓心的角。

例如：

點 C 是圓心。
∠BCA 是中心角。

圓 (circle) 所有點與其中心的距離都相等的平面圖形。

例如：

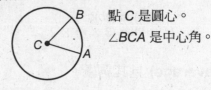

圓形圖 (circle graph) 使用楔形來表示數據集合各部份的圓形圖形。也稱為餅狀圖表。

例如：

可愛的寵物

貓 25%
狗 40%
鳥 20%
其它 15%

圓週 (circumference) 圓的一週的長度。

例如：

圓週

外切圖 (circumscribed figure) 圖形中包含另一個圖形。如果一個圓接觸到一個多邊形的每一條邊，那麼這個多邊形外切該圓。

例如：

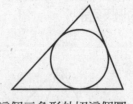

這個三角形外切這個圓。

順時針 (clockwise) 一個圖形的頂部向右轉動時的旋轉方向。

例如：

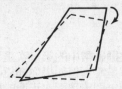

估算 (clustering) 一種近似計算方法。如果各個數字大致相等，則認爲它們是相等的。

例如：

26 + 24 + 23 大約等於 25 + 25 + 25, 或 3 × 25。

系數 (coefficient) 與一個變量相乘的常數。

例如：

常數　變量

12*y*

組合 (combination) 項的集合，其順序已經不重要。

例如：

這組學生中將有兩人入選委員會：David, Juanita, Kim。

可能的組合爲：

David, Juanita　　David, Kim　　Juanita, Kim

註：組合"David, Juanita"與組合"Juanita, David"相同。

公分母 (common denominator) 兩個或兩個以上分數中分母相同，其分母叫公分母。

例如：

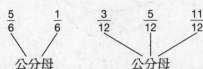

$\frac{5}{6}$　$\frac{1}{6}$　$\frac{3}{12}$　$\frac{5}{12}$　$\frac{11}{12}$

公分母　　　　公分母

公因數 (common factor) 一個數，它是兩個或兩個以上數的因數。

例如：

4是8、12和20的公因數。

8 = **4** × 2

12 = **4** × 3

20 = **4** × 5

公倍數 (common multiple) 一個數，它是給定的兩個或兩個以上數的倍數。

例如：

3的倍數：3 6 9 **12** 15 18 21 **24** 27…

4的倍數：4 8 **12** 16 20 **24** 28…

12和24是3和4的兩個公倍數。

加法交換律 (Commutative Property of Addition) 兩個或兩個以上的數，改變它們的順序，其和不變。

例如：

$a + b = b + a$

$18 + 23 = 23 + 18$

乘法交換律 (Commutative Property of Multiplication) 兩個或兩個以上的數，改變它們的順序，其乘積不變。

例如：

$ab = ba$

$4 × 7 = 7 × 4$

整合數 (compatible numbers) 容易計算的一對數。

例如：　　30 + 70　　40 ÷ 4　　25 + 75

補償 (compensation) 智力算術，就是選擇與問題中相近的數，然後調整答案以對所選擇的數進行補償。

例如：

$$99 × 4 = (100 - 1) × 4$$
$$= (100 × 4) - (1 × 4)$$
$$= 400 - 4$$
$$= 396$$

餘角 (complementary angles) 兩個角的值相加爲 90°。

例如：

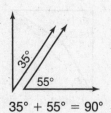

35° + 55° = 90°

合數 (composite number) 整個數大於 1，並至少具有兩個因數。

例如：

15 的因數：1, 3, 5, 15

　　15 是合數。

7 的因數：1, 7

　　7 不是合數。

複合事件 (compound event) 由兩個或兩個以上的單獨事件合成的事件。

例如：

 和

拋硬幣得到正面和擲數字立方體得到1是複合事件。

複利 (compound interest) 以本金和以前的利息為基礎所得到的利息。

例如：

如果你在儲蓄帳號上存入100圓，每年得到的複利利率為6%。

第一年你將得到100圓＋ 0.06 × 100 = 106 圓，

第二年為 0.06 × 106 = 112.36 圓。

複合語句 (compound statement) 由兩個或兩個以上的語句複合而成的邏輯語句。

例如：

10 大於 5 和 10 小於21。

10 大於 5 或 10 小於 5。

凹多邊形 (concave polygon) 一條或一條以上的對角線位於圖形之外的多邊形。

例如：

條件概率 (conditional probability) 祇要給定的條件甲已經發生，條件乙就發生的概率。

例如：

如果你知道兩次拋硬幣中的第一次是背面，則拋出兩次正面的概率是零。但如果你知道兩次拋硬幣中的第一次是正面，則出現兩次正面的概率就是 $\frac{1}{2}$。

圓錐體 (cone) 有一個圓形底面的實心體。

例如：

全等 (congruent) 形狀和大小都相等。

例如：

圓錐投影 (conic projection) 一種地圖投影方法，用圓錐形狀來表示一個球形表面。

例如：

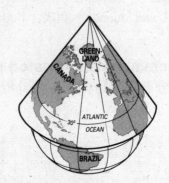

聯言判斷 (conjunction) 用 "和"、"與" 或 "並且" 等連接起來的一組邏輯語句。

例如：

$x > -2$ 並且 $x < 5$

正方形有相等的四條邊并且正方形是矩形。

常數 (constant) 一個值不變的數。

例如：
在代數式 $x + 7$ 中，7 是一個常數。

常量圖 (constant graph) 線的高度不變的圖形。

例如：

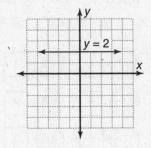

比例常數 (constant of proportionality) 兩個變量 x 與 y 的比值 $\frac{y}{x}$ 為常數。常用 k 表示。

例如：

x	3	6	9	12
y	5	10	15	20

$k = \frac{5}{3}$

換算因子 (conversion factor) 用於將數量從一種單位轉換成另一種單位的等價度量。通常以分數表示。

例如：

12 吋 = 1 呎　　$\frac{12 \text{ 吋}}{1 \text{ 呎}}$

4 夸脫 = 1 加侖　　$\frac{4 \text{ 夸脫}}{1 \text{ 加侖}}$

凸多邊形 (convex polygon) 所有對角線都在圖形之內的多邊形。

例如：

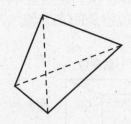 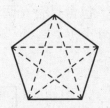

坐標 (coordinates) 有序數值中的一對，在坐標平面中用來確定一個點的位置。

例如：　　　　(5, 6)
　　　　　　　　／　＼
　　　　　　　坐標

坐標平面，坐標系 (coordinate plane, coordinate system) 用於確定點在平面中位置的縱橫交叉數軸體系。

例如：

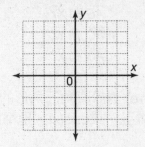

（直線中的）同位角 (corresponding angles for lines) 一條直線穿過兩條或兩條以上的直線，位於該直線同一側的角。當穿過的這些直線為平行線時，同位角全等。

例如：

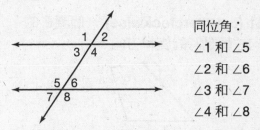

同位角：
∠1 和 ∠5
∠2 和 ∠6
∠3 和 ∠7
∠4 和 ∠8

（相似圖形中的）同位角 (corresponding angles in similar figures) 相似圖形中對應的角。

例如：
△ABC ～ △XYZ

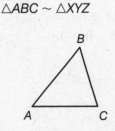 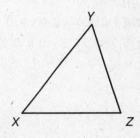

同位角：
∠ABC 和 ∠XYZ
∠BCA 和 ∠YZX
∠CAB 和 ∠ZXY

對應邊 (corresponding sides) 相似圖形中對應的邊。

例如： △ABC ~ △XYZ

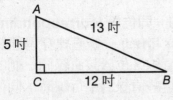

對應邊：

$\overline{AB}$ 和 $\overline{XY}$

$\overline{BC}$ 和 $\overline{YZ}$

$\overline{AC}$ 和 $\overline{XZ}$

餘弦 (cosine) 對於直角三角形的一個銳角 x 來說，其餘弦，或 $\cos(x)$，是鄰邊與斜邊的比值。

例如：

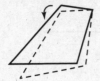

$$\cos \angle CAB = \frac{\text{鄰邊}}{\text{斜邊}} = \frac{5}{13} \approx 0.38$$

逆時針 (counterclockwise) 一個圖形的頂部向左轉動時的旋轉方向。

例如：

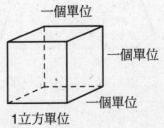

反例 (counterexample) 證明一個命題錯誤的例子。

例如：

命題：如果 $x \cdot 0 = y \cdot 0$，則 $x = y$。

反例：例如：$3 \cdot 0 = 0$ 並且 $5 \cdot 0 = 0$，但是 $3 \neq 5$。

計數法則 (Counting Principle) 如果第一種情況可由 m 種方法產生，第二種情況可由 n 種方法產生，那麼它們一起產生的方法有 $m \times n$ 種。

例如：

拋投硬幣產生兩種結果，擲數字立方體產生六種結果。所以有 2×6 種，或12種一起產生的方法。

$6 \times 2 = 12$

交叉乘積 (cross product) 一個比值的分子與另一個比值的分母的乘積。

例如：

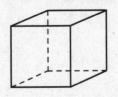

交叉乘積：

$1 \times 5 = 5$

$3 \times 2 = 6$

立方體 (cube) 所有面均全等的六面體。

例如：

立方 (cubed) 增加到三次方。

例如：

2 的立方 $= 2^3 = 2 \times 2 \times 2 = 8$

立方單位 (cubic unit) 一種體積度量單位，包含具有一個單位邊長的立方體。

例如：

一個單位

一個單位

一個單位

1立方單位

英制度量單位 (customary system of measurement) 這種單位制常用於美國：吋、呎、哩、盎司、磅、噸、杯、夸脫、加侖等。

例如：

長度　　　容量　　　重量

圓柱體 (cylinder) 具有兩個平行的圓形底面的立體。

例如：

柱面投影 (cylindrical projection) 一種地圖投影方法。用一個柱面表示一個球形表面。

例如：

十邊形 (decagon) 有十條邊的多邊形。

例如：

十分之一 (deci-) 前綴，意思為十分之一。

例如：　　1 分米 $= \frac{1}{10}$ 米

小數 (decimal) 以十為基礎的數字，用一個小數點寫出。

例如：　　6.21　　0.59　　12.2　　5.0

小數的加法 (decimal addition) 兩個或兩個以上的小數相加。

例如：
$$\begin{array}{r} 1 \\ 12.65 \\ +\ 29.10 \\ \hline 41.75 \end{array}$$

小數的除法 (decimal division) 兩個小數相除。

例如：

$$\begin{array}{r} 1.25 \\ 0.24\overline{)0.3000} \\ -24 \\ \hline 60 \\ -48 \\ \hline 120 \\ -120 \\ \hline 0 \end{array}$$

小數的乘法 (decimal multiplication) 兩個或兩個以上的小數相乘。

例如：
$$\begin{array}{rl} 2 & \\ 0.13 & \text{2 兩位小數} \\ \times\ 0.7 & \text{1 一位小數} \\ \hline 0.091 & \text{3 三位小數} \end{array}$$

小數的減法 (decimal subtraction) 兩個小數相減。

例如：
$$\begin{array}{r} {}^{13\ 12} \\ 4\ 3\ 2\ 10 \\ 5\,4.3\,0 \\ -\ 16.58 \\ \hline 37.72 \end{array}$$

十進制 (decimal system) 以十位數值為基礎的系統。

例如：

$100{,}000 = 10^5$	$10{,}000 = 10^4$	$1000 = 10^3$	$100 = 10^2$	10	1	$\frac{1}{10}$	$\frac{1}{100} = \frac{1}{10^2}$	$\frac{1}{1000} = \frac{1}{10^3}$
9	7	6,	5	2	3.	0	4	8

下降圖形 (decreasing graph) 從左至右縱坐標逐漸減小的直線圖形。

例如：

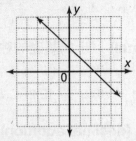

演繹推理 (deductive reasoning) 運用邏輯得出一個結論。

例如：

任何一個四邊形加入一條對角線之後，就形成兩個三角形。我們知道，一個三角形的各個角之和為180°。因此，四邊形各個角的和為三角形的兩倍，或 $2 \times 180° = 360°$。

度 (degree) (°) 角的度量單位。

例如： 1° 是一個完整圓的 $\frac{1}{360}$。

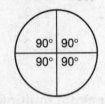

最高次冪 (degree) 對一個多項式來說，最高次冪是變量的最大指數。

例如： $5x^3 - 2x^2 + 7x$ 的最高次冪為3。

十 (deka-) 前綴，意思為十。

例如： 十米 = 10 米

分母 (denominator) 分數線下面的數字，它說明一個整體被分成多少<u>部份</u>。

例如：

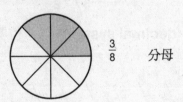

$\frac{3}{8}$　分母

相關事件 (dependent events) 一個事件的結果可能影響另一個事件出現概率的事件。

例如：

Therese，Diane和José的名字分別寫在一張小紙條上。一張小紙條被抽走並放了起來。然後，又抽走了另外一張小紙條。Diane的名字被抽走的概率，與Therese的名字被第一個抽走的概率均是$\frac{1}{2}$。

相關變量 (dependent variable) 一個函數的因變量。

例如：

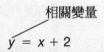

相關變量

$y = x + 2$

對角線 (diagonal) 多邊形中連接兩個不在一條邊上的頂點的線段。

例如：

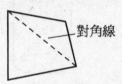

對角線

直徑 (diameter) 一條線段，或其長度。該線段穿過圓心並且兩個端點都在圓上。

例如：

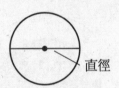

直徑

差 (difference) 從另一個數值中減去一個數值之後得到的結果。

例如：　　　28 - 15 = 13

差

數字 (digit) 用來書寫數字0，1，2，3，4，5，6，7，8，9的符號。

例如：

在5847中，有數字5，8，4和7。

© Scott Foresman Addison Wesley 6-8

縮放 (dilation) 一個圖形按比例放大或縮小。

例如：

從小矩形到大矩形的比例因子為3。

正變分 (direct variation) 兩個變量的關系為比例常數。

例如：

時間以小時計 (x)	1	2	3	4
距離以哩計 (y)	55	110	165	220

$$\frac{y}{x} = 55$$

選言判斷 (disjunction) 由 "或" 連接起來的一組邏輯語句。

例如：

$x > 4$ 或 $x < -1$

我們看電影或我們看電視。

分配律 (Distributive Property) $a(b + c) = ab + ac$ 的運算法則。

例如：$3(6 + 5) = 3 \cdot 6 + 3 \cdot 5$

被除數 (dividend) 在除式中被分開的數。

例如：

被除數

$8 \div 4 = 2$

可除儘的 (divisible) 可被另一個數整除而沒有餘數。

例如： 18 可被 6 除儘，因此 $18 \div 6 = 3$。

除法 (division) 一種運算，表明有多少相等的集合或每一個相等的集合中有多少部份。

例如：

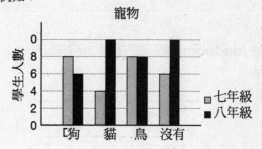

$18 \div 6 = 3$ $18 \div 3 = 6$

將 18 分成 6 組，   將 18 分成 3 組，
每組分得 3 個。   每組分得 6 個。

除數 (divisor) 使另一個數被除的數。

例如：

除數

$8 \div 4 = 2$

十二邊形 (dodecagon) 有十二條邊的多邊形。

例如：

雙柱狀圖 (double bar graph) 由兩個柱狀圖合成，比較兩個相關的數據集合。

例如：

寵物

學生人數

狗　貓　鳥　沒有

七年級
八年級

雙線圖 (double line graph) 由兩個線條圖合併而成，比較兩個相關的數據集合。

例如：

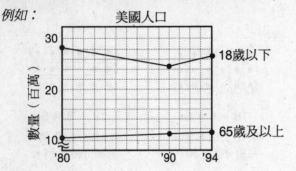

美國人口

雙莖葉圖表 (double stem-and-leaf diagram) 在一個圖表中比較兩個數據集合。

例如：

葉	莖	葉
7 2 1	3	0 1 3
5 0 0	4	2 3
9	5	5 6 8
5 2 0	6	1 4

邊 (edge) 多面體中兩個面相交所形成的線段。

例如：

面
邊

端點 (endpoint) 線段的終點或射線的起點。

例如：

端點

相等 (equality) 一種精確相等的數學關系。

例如：
$$16 + 8 = 24 \qquad 25 \div 5 = 5$$

同概率 (equally-likely outcomes) 具有相同概率的結果。

例如：

擲出一個 "1"　　　　旋轉到紅

概率：$\frac{1}{6}$　　　　概率：$\frac{1}{6}$

等比 (equal ratios) 具有相同比值的比例。

例如：　$\frac{2}{6}, \frac{1}{3},$ 和 $\frac{4}{12}$

等式 (equation) 描述兩個表達式完全相等的算式。

例如：
$$14 = 2x \qquad 3 + y = 81 \qquad 3 + 4 = 7$$

等邊三角形 (equilateral triangle) 三條邊的邊長都相等的三角形。

例如：

等價方程式 (equivalent equations) 使用相同的變量進行代換而成立的方程。

例如：　$x - 5 = 10$ 和 $x = 15$

等價表達式 (equivalent expressions) 同一代換情況下，兩個表達式總是具有相同的值。

例如：　$5(x + 1)$ 和 $5x + 5$

等值分數 (equivalent fractions) 兩個分數表示同一個數值。

例如：　$\frac{1}{2}$ 和 $\frac{8}{16}$

等比率 (equivalent rates) 比率的值相等。

例如： $\dfrac{40哩}{2小時}$ 和 $\dfrac{20哩}{1小時}$

等比 (equivalent ratios) 見等比率。

估算值 (estimate) 計算後得到的近似值。

例如：
$$99 \times 21$$
估算值：$100 \times 20 = 2000$
$$99 \times 21 \approx 2000$$

歐拉公式 (Euler's formula) 一個多面體的面 (F)、頂點 (V) 和邊 (E) 的數目具有關係式 $F + V - E = 2$。

例如：

對於所示的三棱錐，
$$5 + 5 - 8 = 2$$
面　頂點　邊

賦值 (evaluate) 將一個表達式中的變量用數值代換，然後按照運算關係進行簡化計算。

例如：　對 $8(x - 3)$ 賦值 $x = 10$。
$$8(x - 3) = 8(10 - 3)$$
$$= 8(7)$$
$$= 56$$

偶數 (even number) 個位數是 0，2，4，6 和 8的整數。

例如：　16　28　34　112　3000

事件 (event) 一次試驗或一種狀態的一個或一組結果。

例如：
事件：　　當擲一個數字立方體時，得到 3 或比 3 大的數。

該事件的
可能結果：　3, 4, 5, 6

擴展形式 (expanded form) 一種指數書寫方法，可以分別顯示所有因子。

例如：　　指數　　　　　9^3
　　　　　擴展形式　　$9 \times 9 \times 9$

試驗 (experiment) 在概率中，含有機會的任何活動。

例如：　抛投硬幣　擲數字立方體　轉動轉盤

試驗概率 (experimental probability) 以試驗或測量爲基礎得到的概率。

例如：

將豆袋投向圈中100次，有23次擊中，擊中的試驗概率爲 $\dfrac{23}{100} = 23\%$.

指數 (exponent) 一個被提高位置的數字，表示重複相乘的次數。

例如：　　　　　指數
$$4^3 = 4 \times 4 \times 4 = 64$$

指數函數 (exponential function) 指數爲變量的非線性函數。

例如：　　　　　$y = 4^x$

指數記號 (exponential notation) 用指數表示一個數連乘的一種書寫方法。

例如：　　　2^8　　　5^2　　　9^3

表達式 (expression) 由變量和/或數字及運算符號組成的數學詞語。

例如：　$5(8 + 4)$　　　$x - 3$　　　$2x + 4$

外角 (exterior angles) 一條線穿過兩條線時，位於這兩條線外部的角。

例如：

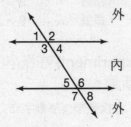

外角：
∠1, ∠2, ∠7, ∠8

面 (face) 立體的一個平面。

例如：

面

因數 (factor) 一個數除另一個數後沒有餘數，這個數爲因數。

例如： 因爲 $30 ÷ 5 = 6$，所以5是30的因數。

階乘 (factorial) 一個數的階乘是從1到該數所有整數的乘積。其符號爲"!"。

例如：
6 的階乘 $= 6! = 6 × 5 × 4 × 3 × 2 × 1 = 720$

因數樹 (factor tree) 表示一個數如何分解爲素因數的圖表。

例如：

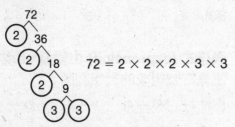

$72 = 2 × 2 × 2 × 3 × 3$

公正遊戲 (fair game) 所有參加遊戲者均有相同獲勝概率的遊戲。

例如：

公正的遊戲：兩個遊戲者擲數字立方體。A得到1、3或5，B得到2、4或6。對於兩個遊戲者來說，獲勝的概率都是50%。

反射 (flip) 見反射。

呎 (foot) 一種英制單位，等於12吋。

例如：

呎

公式 (formula) 表示數量之間關係的一種規則。

例如： $A = bh$ $p = 4s$

自相似圖形 (fractal) 自我相似的一種圖形。如果它的一部份被放大，放大區域與原始圖形相似。

例如：

分數 (fraction) 形式爲 $\frac{a}{b}$ 的一個數，當整體被分成相等的部份時，表示整體中的部份。

例如： $\frac{3}{5}$ $\frac{2}{7}$ $\frac{1}{4}$ $\frac{7}{10}$

分數的加法 (fraction addition) 兩個或兩個以上的分數相加。

例如： $\frac{1}{3} + \frac{1}{4}$

$$\frac{1}{3} = \frac{1 × 4}{3 × 4} = \frac{4}{12}$$

$$\frac{1}{4} = \frac{1 × 3}{4 × 3} = \frac{3}{12}$$

$$\frac{1}{3} + \frac{1}{4} = \frac{4}{12} + \frac{3}{12} = \frac{4 + 3}{12} = \frac{7}{12}$$

分數的除法 (fraction division) 兩個分數相除。

例如：
$$\frac{1}{6} ÷ \frac{3}{4} = \frac{1}{6} × \frac{4}{3}$$

$$= \frac{1 × 4}{6 × 3}$$

$$= \frac{4}{18} \text{ 或 } \frac{2}{9}$$

分數的乘法 (fraction multiplication) 兩個或兩個以上的分數相乘。

例如：
$$1\frac{1}{2} \times \frac{1}{4} = \frac{3}{2} \times \frac{1}{4}$$
$$= \frac{3 \times 1}{2 \times 4}$$
$$= \frac{3}{8}$$

分數的減法 (fraction subtraction) 兩個分數相減。

例如： $\frac{3}{4} - \frac{2}{3}$

$$\frac{3}{4} = \frac{3 \times 3}{4 \times 3} = \frac{9}{12}$$
$$\frac{2}{3} = \frac{2 \times 4}{3 \times 4} = \frac{8}{12}$$
$$\frac{3}{4} - \frac{2}{3} = \frac{9}{12} - \frac{8}{12} = \frac{9-8}{12} = \frac{1}{12}$$

頻率 (frequency) 調查中一定時間內事物出現的次數。見頻率表。

頻率表 (frequency chart or table) 表明事物分類及其出現概率的表。

例如：

襯衣的顏色	頻率
黑色	8
桔紅色	2
白色	5
藍色	4

高位估計 (front-end estimation) 一種估算方法，在這種估算方法中只有每個數的第一位或第二位參與計算，其結果則根據餘數進行調整。

例如：　一位數高位估計
```
   2,485
 + 3,698
 ───────
   5,000    加第一位
 + 1,200    485 + 698 約等於1,200。
 ───────
   6,200
```

函數 (function) 一種輸入輸出關係。對於一個輸入值來說，只有一個輸出值。

例如：
$$y = x + 4 \qquad y = 2x \qquad y = x^2$$

算術基本定理 (Fundamental Theorem of Arithmetic) 所有大於1的整數都可以寫成一個單一的素數的乘積。

例如：
$$24 = 2 \times 2 \times 2 \times 3$$
$$35 = 5 \times 7$$

加侖 (gallon) 一種英制單位，等於4夸脫。

例如：

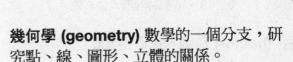

牛奶

1夸脫

幾何學 (geometry) 數學的一個分支，研究點、線、圖形、立體的關係。

幾何概率 (geometric probability) 一種以比較幾何圖形的量度為基礎的概率。

例如：

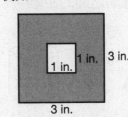

1 in. 1 in. 3 in.

3 in.

大正方形的面積 = 3 · 3 或9吋^2

陰影面積 = 9吋^2 − 1吋^2 = 8吋^2

陰影面積的概率為 = $\frac{8}{9}$

幾何序列/等比序列 (geometric sequence) 兩個連續項之間的比值始終相等的序列。

例如：

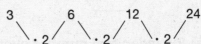

3　·2　6　·2　12　·2　24

克 (gram) 公制質量的基本單位。

例如：

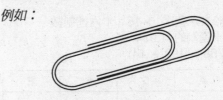

一個大曲別針的質量大約1克。

圖表 (graph) 表示整理好的資訊的一種圖表。

例如：

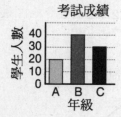

最大公約數 (greatest common factor (GCF)) 除以兩個或兩個以上的整數而沒有餘數的最大整數叫最大公約數。

例如：　6是12、18和24的最大公約數。

百- (hecto-) 前綴，意思為100。

例如：　1 百米 = 100 米

高 (height) 在三角形、四邊形或棱錐體中，從底面到頂點或對邊的垂直距離。在棱柱或圓柱體中，兩個底面之間的距離。

例如：

七邊形 (heptagon) 有七條邊的多邊形。

例如：

十六進制 (hexadecimal number system) 以十六位數值為基礎的系統。

例如：

字母A–F用於表示數字10–15。十六進制數A3CE 等於十進制的41,934
(40,960 + 768 + 192 + 14)。

十六進制	A	3	C	E
位值	4096	256	16	1
積	10 × 4096 = 40,960	3 × 256 = 768	12 × 16 = 192	14 × 1 = 14

六邊形 (hexagon) 有六條邊的多邊形。

例如：

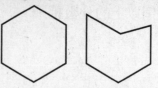

直方圖 (histogram) 一種柱狀圖，其範疇等於數值的區域。

例如：

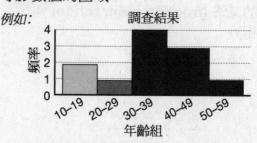

水平軸 (horizontal axis) 建立直方圖或坐標平面時，兩條線中的水平線。

例如：

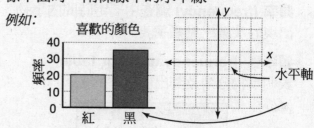

斜邊 (hypotenuse) 直角三角形中與直角相對應的邊。

例如：

恆等 (identity) 對於任何一種運算，使另外一個數保持不變的數。0是加法恆等，因為 $a + 0 = a$；1是乘法恆等，因為 $a \times 1 = a$。

例如：　6 + 0 = 6
　　　　5 × 1 = 5

條件語句 (if-then statement) 使用"如果"和"那麼"表示兩個事物之間關係的邏輯語句。

例如：如果一個三角形是不規則三角形，那麼沒有任何邊相等。

假分數 (improper fraction) 分數的分子大於或等於分母的分數。

例如:　　　$\frac{5}{2}$　　　　$\frac{8}{8}$　　　　$\frac{14}{3}$

上升圖形 (increasing graph) 從左至右縱坐標逐漸增大的直線圖形。

例如:

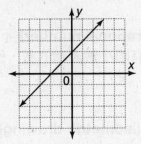

吋 (inch) 一種英制長度單位。

例如:　這個曲別針長 $1\frac{3}{8}$ 吋，或 $1\frac{3}{8}''$。

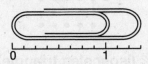

獨立事件 (independent events) 一個事件的結果不對另一個事件的概率產生影響的事件。

例如:
Therese，Diane和José的名字分別寫在一張小紙條上。一張小紙條被抽走，後又還了回來。然後，又抽走了另外一張小紙條。Diane的名字被抽走的概率，與Therese的名字被第一個抽走的可能性都是 $\frac{1}{3}$。

自變量 (independent variable) 一個函數的輸入變量。

例如:

　　　　　　自變量
　　　　　　/
　　　$y = x + 2$

歸納推理 (inductive reasoning) 運用典型事例得出結論。

例如:
畫出很多四邊形並測量它們的角。每次得到各角之和均為360°。因此得出結論:四邊形的所有角之和為360°。

不等式 (inequality) 包含 $<$，$>$，$\leq$，或 $\geq$ 符號的算式。

例如:

　　　$6 < 9$　　　$x + 3 \geq 21$　　　$2x - 8 > 0$

內接圖形 (inscribed figure) 一個圖形被包含在另一個圖形內。如果一個多邊形的所有頂點均在一個圓上，則這個多邊形內接該圓。

例如:

這個三角形內接這個圓。

整數 (integers) 所有正整數、負整數及零的集合。

例如:　　　$..., -3, -2, -1, 0, 1, 2, 3, ...$

整數的加法 (integer addition) 兩個或兩個以上的整數相加。

例如:

　　　$-5 + 8 = 3$　　　　$-5 + (-8) = -13$
　　　$5 + (-3) = 2$　　　　$5 + 8 = 13$

整數的除法 (integer division) 兩個整數相除。

例如:

　　　$-40 \div 8 = -5$　　　$40 \div (-8) = -5$
　　　$-40 \div (-8) = 5$　　　$40 \div 8 = 5$

整數的乘法 (integer multiplication) 兩個或兩個以上的整數相乘。

例如:

　　　$-5 \cdot 8 = -40$　　　　$-5 \cdot (-8) = 40$
　　　$5 \cdot (-8) = -40$　　　$5 \cdot 8 = 40$

整數的減法 (integer subtraction) 兩個整數相減。

例如:

　　　$-5 - 8 = -13$　　　$-5 - (-8) = 3$
　　　$5 - (-3) = 8$　　　　$5 - 8 = -3$

利息 (interest) 對使用的款項所支付的金錢。

例如:

Dave 在存款帳戶中存入300圓。一年後,他的存款餘額為315圓。他從存款中得到15圓的利息。

內角 (interior angles) 由一條直線與另外一些直線相交所形成的,位於每兩條直線之間的角。

例如:

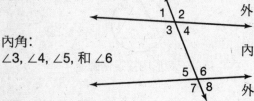

內角:
∠3, ∠4, ∠5, 和 ∠6

相交 (intersect) 穿過同一點。

例如:

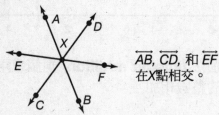

$\overleftrightarrow{AB}$, $\overleftrightarrow{CD}$, 和 $\overleftrightarrow{EF}$ 在X點相交。

區間 (interval) 在一個柱狀圖或線條圖中,被分成相同大小的部份。

例如:

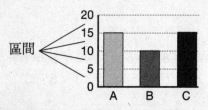

逆運算驗算 (inverse operations) 由結果逆推回來的運算。

例如:

加法和減法 $2 + 3 = 5$ $5 - 3 = 2$

乘法和除法 $2 \cdot 3 = 6$ $6 \div 3 = 2$

逆變分 (inverse variation) 兩個變量的關係通過一個常數積產生。

例如:

x	1	2	3	4	5	6
y	60	30	20	15	12	10

$$x \cdot y = 60$$

無理數 (irrational number) 不能用無限循環小數或有限小數表示的數,例如$\sqrt{2}$。

例如: $\sqrt{5}$ π $-\sqrt{\frac{1}{2}}$

等距畫法 (isometric drawing) 一種圖形透視畫法。

例如:

等腰三角形 (isosceles triangle) 至少有兩條邊相等的三角形。

例如:

千- (kilo-) 前綴,意思為一千。

例如: 1 千米 = 1000 米

緯度 (latitude) 由赤道向南北方向以度表示的一種度量。

例如:

最小公分母 (least common denominator (LCD)) 兩個或兩個以上分母的最小公倍數 (LCM)。

例如:　$\frac{1}{2}$　　$\frac{2}{3}$　　$\frac{3}{4}$

2、3和4最小公倍數 (LCM) 是12，因此這些分數的最小公分母 (LCD) 是12。

這些分數按最小公分母書寫成$\frac{6}{12}$、$\frac{8}{12}$和$\frac{9}{12}$。

最小公倍數 (least common multiple (LCM)) 公倍數中的最小數。

例如:

3的倍數有：3　6　9　**12**　15　18　21　**24** ...
4的倍數有：4　8　**12**　16　20　**24**　28　32 ...
12是3和4的最小公倍數。

直角邊 (leg) 直角三角形中斜邊以外的邊。

例如:

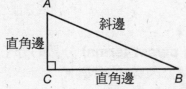

同分母 (like denominators) 兩個或兩個以上的分數中的分母相同。

例如:

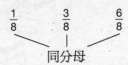

同類項 (like terms) 相同的變量，其指數相同的項。

例如:　$3x^2$ 和 $9x^2$　　$10y$ 和 $2y$

直線 (line) 向兩個方向延伸，沒有盡頭的一維圖形。兩點決定一條直線。

例如:

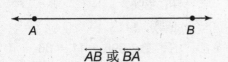

$\overleftrightarrow{AB}$ 或 $\overleftrightarrow{BA}$

線條圖 (line graph) 用一條線表示數據變化的圖形（常隨時間而變化）。

例如:

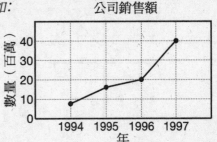

對稱軸 (line of symmetry) 利用線對稱軸將一個圖形分成兩個完全相等的兩部份的線叫對稱軸。

例如:

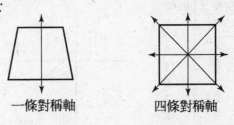

一條對稱軸　　　　　四條對稱軸

線陣 (line plot) 在數軸上用疊加x的方法表示數據集合的形狀。

例如:

學生數量

線段 (line segment) 直線的一部份，具有兩個端點。兩點決定一條線段。

例如:

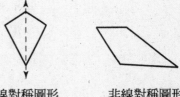

$\overline{AB}$ 或 $\overline{BA}$

線對稱 (line symmetry) 如果一個圖形可以被分成完全相等的兩部份，這個圖形是線對稱。

例如:

線對稱圖形　　　　　非線對稱圖形

線性方程 (linear equation) 其圖形是一條直線的方程。

例如:

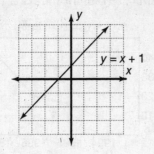

$$y = x + 1$$

線性函數 (linear function) 其圖形是一條直線的函數。

例如:

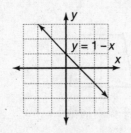

自變量	因變量
x	y
-2	3
-1	2
0	1
1	0
2	-1
3	-2

$$y = 1 - x$$

線性不等式 (linear inequality) 包含有 $<$，$>$，$\le$ 或 $\ge$ 的數學算式，其圖形是一個以一條直線為邊界的區域。

例如:

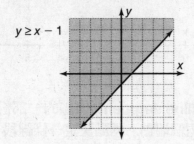

$$y \ge x - 1$$

升 (liter) 公制單位中的基本容量單位。

例如:

2升的瓶子

經度 (longitude) 由本初子午線向東西方向以度表示的一種度量。

例如:

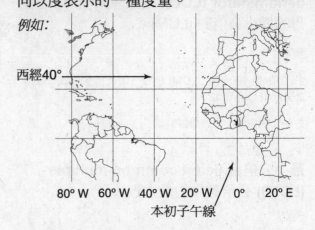

西經40°

80° W 60° W 40° W 20° W 0° 20° E

本初子午線

下四分位 (lower quartile) 數據集合下半部份的中位數。

例如:

27 27 27 28 31 33 36 38 42 43 62

下四分位　　　中位數　　　上四分位

最簡分數 (lowest terms) 分數的分子和分母只有一個公因數1的分數。

例如: $\dfrac{1}{2}$　　$\dfrac{3}{5}$　　$\dfrac{21}{23}$

質量 (mass) 物體所含有的量。

例如:

一顆葡萄乾的質量為1克。

一雙田徑鞋的質量為1千克。

平均 (mean) 一個數據集合的和被其個數相除。也叫平均數。

例如:

27 27 27 29 32 33 36 38 42 43 62

和: 396

個數: 11

平均數: $396 \div 11 = 36$

測量誤差 (measurement error) 測量中的不確定值。測量中的最大可能誤差是其使用的最小單位的二分之一。

例如：

由于吋是最小單位，最大可能誤差是 $\frac{1}{2}$ 吋。所以實際高度在 $5'5\frac{1}{2}"$ 和 $5'6\frac{1}{2}"$ 之間。

5' 6"

集中趨勢度量 (measure of central tendency) 概括一個數據集合的一個數值。

例如：

平均數、中位數和眾數是普通集中趨勢度量。

27 27 27 29 32 33 36 38 42 43 62

眾數　　　　　中位數

平均數 = 396 ÷ 11 = 36

中位數 (median) 當數據集合中數據的值按大小順序排列時，指數據集合的中間值。

例如：

27 27 27 29 32 33 36 38 42 43 62

中位數

心算 (mental math) 不用鉛筆和紙或計算器，使用頭腦進行計算的數學。

例如：

　　　2000　×　30

　　3 個零　+　1 個零 = 4 個零

　　思考：2　×　3 = 6，再加 4 個零

　　　2000　×　30 = 60,000

米 (meter) 公制的基本長度單位。

例如：

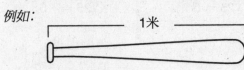

1米

這根棒球棒大約1米長。

公制/十進制/米制 (metric system) 一種以米、克和升爲基礎的度量體系。

例如：

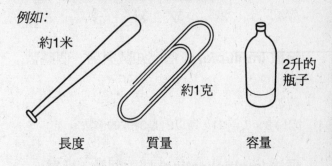

約1米

約1克

2升的瓶子

長度　　　　質量　　　　容量

中點 (midpoint) 將一條線段分成兩條完全相等的較短線段的點。

例如：　　　C 是線段 $\overline{AB}$ 的中點。

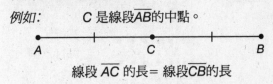

A　　　　　C　　　　　B

線段 $\overline{AC}$ 的長 = 線段 $\overline{CB}$ 的長

哩 (mile) 一種英制單位，等於5280呎。

例如：

一哩是你步行15到20分鐘，或跑步10分鐘的路程。

千分之一 (milli-) 前綴，意思爲 $\frac{1}{1000}$。

例如：　　1 毫米 = $\frac{1}{1000}$ 米

帶分數 (mixed number) 由一個整數和一個分數組成的數。

例如：　　　$3\frac{1}{2}$　　　$1\frac{3}{4}$　　　$13\frac{3}{8}$

眾數 (mode) 最常出現於數據集合中的數。

例如：

27 27 27 29 32 33 36 38 42 43 62

在給定的數據集合中，27是眾數。

單項式 (monomial) 只含有一項的代數式。

例如:　　　$2x^2$　　$5y$　　x^3　　-3

倍數 (multiple) 一個已知數與另一個整數的積。

例如:

因為 $3 \times 7 = 21$，所以21是3和7的倍數。

乘法 (multiplication) 將兩個數（稱為因數）合並在一起，得出一個數（稱為積）的一種運算。

例如:

```
• • • • • •
• • • • • •        三行，
• • • • • •        每行六個
```

$$3 \times 6 = 18$$
　　因數　　積

乘法法則 (multiplication property) 如果A和B是獨立事件，則兩件事同時發生的概率由 $P(A \text{ 和 } B) = P(A) \times P(B)$ 給出。

例如:

第一次轉動:　$P(紅) = \frac{1}{4}$

第二次轉動:　$P(紅) = \frac{1}{4}$

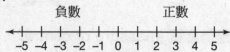

第一次和第二次轉動:　$P(紅和紅) = \frac{1}{4} \times \frac{1}{4} = \frac{1}{16}$

乘法相等定理 (Multiplication Property of Equality) 如果 $a = b$，那麼 $ac = bc$。

例如:

在下面例子的第二行中，等式兩邊都乘以2。

如果　　　$\frac{1}{2}y = 4$

那麼　　$2 \times \frac{1}{2}y = 2 \times 4$

倒數 (multiplicative inverse) 如果兩個數的乘積為1，則一個數是另一個數的倒數。

例如:

因為 $\frac{1}{6} \times 6 = 1$，所以 $\frac{1}{6}$ 和6互為倒數。

互斥事件 (mutually exclusive) 如果事件A和B中的任一個發生，另一個就不會發生。

例如:

如果外面的溫度為90°，就不可能下雪。

如果多邊形只有三條邊，它不可能有四個角。

負數 (negative numbers) 小於零的數。

例如:

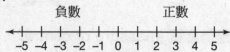

負數　　　　　　正數

$-5\ -4\ -3\ -2\ -1\ 0\ 1\ 2\ 3\ 4\ 5$

負相關 (negative relationship) 兩個數據集合負相關時，一個數據集合的值增大，則另一個數據集合的值減小。

例如:

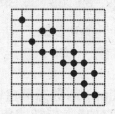

負斜率 (negative slope) 一條線的坡向下傾斜。

例如:

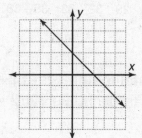

負平方根 (negative square root) 一個數的正平方根的負數。

例如:

正平方根:　　　　　　負平方根:

$\sqrt{25} = 5$　　　　　$-\sqrt{25} = -5$

網格 (net) 可以折疊成為三維圖形（如棱柱體）的平面圖案。

例如：

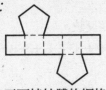

五面棱柱體的網格　　　　五面棱柱體

九邊形 (nonagon) 有九條邊的多邊形。

例如：

非線性方程 (nonlinear equation) 其圖形是曲線而不是直線的方程。

例如：

$y = x^2 - 2$

非線性函數 (nonlinear function) 函數的圖形不是一條直線的函數。因為 x 的變化，不會使 y 具有相同的變化。

例如：

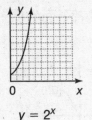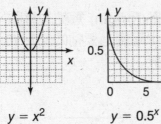

$y = 2^x$　　　　$y = x^2$　　　　$y = 0.5^x$

無關聯 (no relationship) 當兩個數據集合既沒有肯定關係又沒有否定關係時，這兩個數據集合無關聯。

例如：

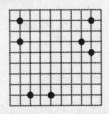

數軸 (number line) 表示數的順序的一條直線。

例如：

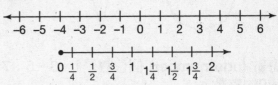

數字-文字形式 (number-word form) 用數字和文字表示數的一種方法。

例如：　45 兆　　　9 千

數字 (numeral) 數的表示符號。

例如：　7　　　　58　　　　234

分子 (numerator) 分數中分數線上面的數字，表示從總體內選擇了多少。

例如：

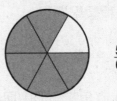

分子

$\frac{5}{6}$

鈍角 (obtuse angle) 大於90°，小於180°的角。

例如：

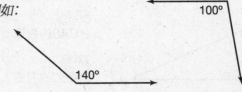

100°

140°

鈍角三角形 (obtuse triangle) 有一個角為鈍角的三角形。

例如:

八邊形 (octagon) 有八條邊的多邊形。

例如:

奇數 (odd number) 個位數是1、3、5、7或9的整數。

例如:

43   225   999   8,007

可能性 (odds) 一個事件可能發生的途徑與其不可能發生的途徑的數量的比。

例如:

 擲出一個3的可能性: 1比5。

不可能擲出一個3的可能性: 5比1。

運算 (operation) 一種數學過程。

例如:

四種基本運算: 加、減、乘、除。

對邊 (opposite leg) 直角三角形中與銳角相對應的邊。

例如:

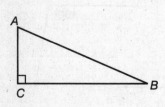 $\overline{CB}$ 是 ∠CAB的對邊。

$\overline{AC}$ 是 ∠ABC的對邊。

相反數 (opposite numbers) 在數軸上,與零的距離相等但在零點兩邊的數。

例如:

7 和 −7 是相反數。

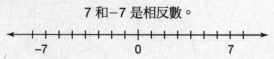

運算次序 (order of operations) 說明運算順序的規則: (1) 運算括號內的項 (2) 指數運算 (3) 從左至右進行乘除運算 (4) 從左至右進行加減運算。

例如:

給 $2x^2 + 4(x - 2)$ 賦值 $x = 3$。

(1) 運算括號內的項	$2 \cdot 3^2 + 4(3 - 2)$
	$2 \cdot 3^2 + 4(1)$
(2) 指數運算	$2 \cdot 9 + 4$
(3) 從左至右進行乘除運算	$18 + 4$
(4) 從左至右進行加減運算	22

有序偶 (ordered pair) 用於確定坐標平面上點的位置的一對數。

例如:

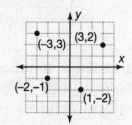

原點 (origin) 數軸的零點,或者平面坐標系中兩個坐標軸的交點 (0,0)。

例如:

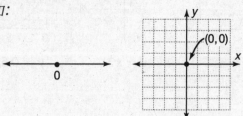

正投影視圖 (orthographic drawing) 對一個物體的正面、側面和上面進行投影所得到的視圖。

例如:

正面　　　　側面　　　　上面

盎司 (ounce) 一種英制重量單位。

例如:

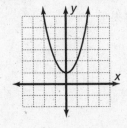

一封信大約一盎司重。

結果 (outcome) 一次試驗或一種狀態所能得到的結論。

例如:

拋投兩枚硬幣的結果:

第一枚	第二枚
正面	背面
正面	正面
背面	正面
背面	背面

有四種結果。一種結果是正面和正面。

舍棄值 (outlier) 數據集合中的一個異常值,該值從其它數值中分離開。

例如:

27　27　27　29　32　33　36　38　42　43　62

↑
舍棄值

拋物線 (parabola) 二次函數的圖形,是一條U形或倒U形曲線。

例如:

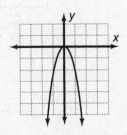

平行線 (parallel) 無論如何延伸都不會相交的兩條直線、線段或射線。

例如:

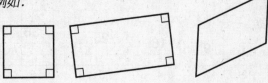

平行四邊形 (parallelogram) 對邊平行且相等的四邊形為平行四邊形。

例如:

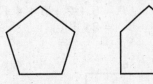

五邊形 (pentagon) 有五條邊的多邊形。

例如:

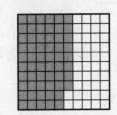

百分比 (percent) 一個數與100的比值。

例如:

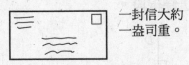

$$\frac{58}{100} = 0.58 = 58\%$$

百分比換算 (percent change) 被原始數據相除之後的數量變化,增大或減小,並以原始數的百分比表示。

例如:

如果投資1500圓,得到75圓的利息,求出其百分比換算。

$$\frac{75}{1500} = 0.05 = 5\%$$　　　75圓為增長了5%。

如果一件價值50圓的商品被削價10圓出售,求出其百分比換算。

$$\frac{10}{50} = 0.20 = 20\%$$　　　10圓為降低了20%。

百分比降 (percent decrease) 降低的數值除以原始數量的百分數表示。見*百分比換算*。

百分比增 (percent increase) 增加的數值除以原始數量的百分數表示。見*百分比換算*。

完全平方 (perfect square) 一個整數的平方。

例如:

1	4	9	16	25	36
1	2	3	4	5	6

週長 (perimeter) 一個圖形週邊的長度。

例如:

$P = 5 + 2 + 6 + 4 + 11 + 6$
$= 34$ 單位

```
    5
      2   6
6             4
     11
```

排列 (permutation) 一種項的安排方法，其中順序是重要的。

例如:

從下面一組學生中選出一位主席和一位副主席: Wendy, Alex, Carlos。可能的順序為:

Wendy —— 主席，Alex —— 副主席
Wendy —— 主席，Carlos —— 副主席
Alex —— 主席，Wendy —— 副主席
Alex —— 主席，Carlos —— 副主席
Carlos —— 主席，Wendy —— 副主席
Carlos —— 主席，Alex —— 副主席

註: 上面的每一例均是一種不同的排列。

垂直 (perpendicular) 直線、射線或線段相交成直角。

例如:

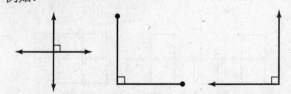

中垂線 (perpendicular bisector) 一條直線、射線或線段相交於另一條線段的中點並垂直於這條線段。

例如:

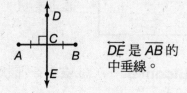

$\overrightarrow{DE}$ 是 $\overline{AB}$ 的中垂線。

圓週率 (pi (π)) 圓的週長與它的直徑的比值: 3.14159265…

例如:

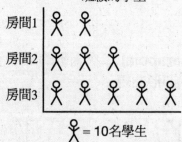

$$\pi = \frac{圓週長}{直徑}$$

象形圖表 (pictograph) 使用符號表示數字的圖形。

例如:

　　　　　　　班級的學生

房間1　👤 👤
房間2　👤 👤 👤
房間3　👤 👤 👤 👤 👤

👤 = 10名學生

位值 (place value) 給予一個數字所佔位置的值。

例如:

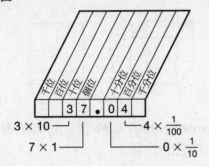

3×10 —
7×1 —
$4 \times \frac{1}{100}$
$0 \times \frac{1}{10}$

平面 (plane) 向外無限擴展的一個平的表面。

例如:

設想將一個桌面向所有方向擴展就可以看到一個平面。

點對稱 (point symmetry) 如果一個圖形旋轉180° 後沒有變化，則這個圖形是點對稱。

例如:

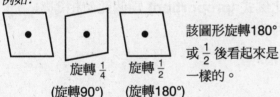

旋轉 $\frac{1}{4}$
(旋轉90°)

旋轉 $\frac{1}{2}$
(旋轉180°)

該圖形旋轉180° 或 $\frac{1}{2}$ 後看起來是一樣的。

多邊形 (polygon) 由線段組成的封閉圖形。

例如:

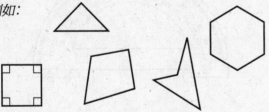

多面體 (polyhedron) 表面爲多邊形的立體。

例如:

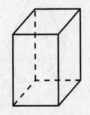

多項式 (polynomial) 一種數學表達式，是一項或多項的和。

例如:

$$x^2 + 2x - 3 \qquad 5y - 15$$

總體 (population) 在一項調查中，所有被研究對象的集合。

例如:

所有1000名俱樂部會員的名字寫在卡片上，將這些卡片混在一起。然後，從中抽出100張卡片，並對這些會員進行電話調查。調查的總體是1000名俱樂部會員。

正數 (positive numbers) 大於零的數。

例如:

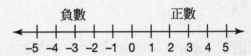

負數　　　　正數

$-5 \ -4 \ -3 \ -2 \ -1 \ 0 \ 1 \ 2 \ 3 \ 4 \ 5$

正相關 (positive relationship) 兩個數據集合正相關時，兩個數據集合的值同時增大或同時減小。

例如:

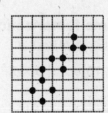

正斜率 (positive slope) 一條線的坡向上傾斜。

例如:

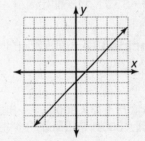

磅 (pound) 一種英制度量單位，等於16盎司。

例如:

米
1 磅

乘方 (power) 即指數，或將底數乘以指數次的數。

例如：

$$16 = 2^4 \quad 2 \text{ 自乘四次。}$$

$$16 \text{ 是 2 的四次冪。}$$

精度 (precision) 度量的精確度，決定於度量的單位。

例如：

較小的單位吋，比較大的單位呎更精確。

5'1" 61"

素因數 (prime factor) 被另一個整數相除沒有餘數的數。

例如：

5 是 35 的素因數，因爲 35 ÷ 5 = 7。

因式分解 (prime factorization) 將一個數寫成素因數的乘積的形式。

例如：　　　$70 = 2 \times 5 \times 7$

素數 (prime number) 大於1並且只有1和本身爲其因數的整數。

例如：

素數從2，3，5，7，11…開始。

本金 (principal) 存入或借出的一筆需要支付利息的款項。

例如：

Dave在存款賬戶上存入300圓。一年以後他的賬戶餘額爲315圓。300圓是這筆款的本金。

主平方根 (principal square root) 一個數的正平方根。

例如：

主平方根　　　負平方根

$\sqrt{25} = 5$ 　　 $-\sqrt{25} = -5$

棱柱 (prism) 底面平行且全等的多面體。

例如：

概率 (probability) 事件發生的方法與總的可能性結果的比值。

例如：

擲出 3 的概率爲 $\frac{1}{6}$。

不能擲出 3 的概率爲 $\frac{5}{6}$。

積 (product) 兩個或兩個以上的數相乘所得到的結果。

例如：

積

$2 \times 3 \times 5 = 30$

比例式 (proportion) 兩個比值相等的等式。

例如：　　　$\dfrac{12}{34} = \dfrac{6}{17}$

量角器 (protractor) 一種測量角度的工具。

例如：

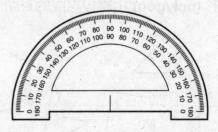

棱錐 (pyramid) 有一個底，其它面爲相交於同一點的三角形的立體。

例如：

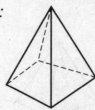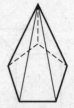

畢達哥拉斯定理 (Pythagorean Theorem)
在直角三角形中，c為斜邊，a和b為直角
邊，則 $a^2 + b^2 = c^2$。

例如：

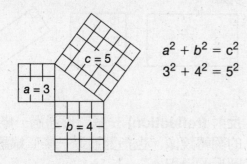

$$a^2 + b^2 = c^2$$
$$3^2 + 4^2 = 5^2$$

象限 (quadrants) 由平面坐標中的坐標軸
決定的四個區域。

例如：

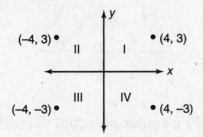

二次方程 (quadratic equation) 含有二次
項（平方項）的等式，如 x^2。

例如：

$$y = x^2 + 3x - 12 \qquad y = 2x^2 + 7$$

二次函數 (quadratic function) 函數
中x的最高次方為2。二次函數的圖形為
拋物線。

例如：

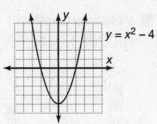

四邊形 (quadrilateral) 有四條邊的
多邊形。

例如：

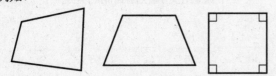

夸脫 (quart) 一種英制容積度量單位。

例如：

四分位 (quartile) 將一個數據集合分為相
等的四部份的數。

例如：

27　27　27　29　32　33　36　38　42　43　62
　　　　↑　　　　　　↑　　　　　　↑
　　　　下　　　　中位數　　　　　上
　　四分位　　　　　　　　　　四分位

27，33，和 42 是這個數據集合的三個四分位。

商 (quotient) 一個數被另一個數相除所得
到的結果。

例如：

　　　　　　　　　　　　　　商
$$8 \div 4 = 2$$

根號 (radical sign) $\sqrt{}$ ，用來表示一個數
的平方根的符號。

例如：

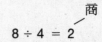

$$\sqrt{49} = 7$$

半徑 (radius) 從圓心到圓上任一點的一條
線段。

例如：

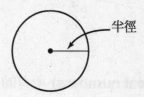

隨機樣本 (random sample) 一種樣本抽
選方法。在這種方法中，總體中的任何一
個元素被包含在樣本內的機會相等。

例如：

所有1000名俱樂部會員的名字寫在卡片上，將這
些卡片混在一起。然後，從中抽出100張卡片，並
對這些會員進行電話調查。俱樂部中的所有會員均
有被打電話的相等機會，因此這是一個隨機樣本。

區域 (range) 數據集合中最大值和最小值之差。

例如:

27 27 27 29 32 33 36 38 42 43 62

區域是 62 − 27 = 35。

比率 (rate) 表示不同單位數量之間相互關係的比例。

例如: $\dfrac{72圓}{28小時}$ $\dfrac{55哩}{1小時}$

比 (ratio) 兩個數相比校,常寫成分數形式。

例如: $\dfrac{2}{1}$ 2 to 1 2:1

有理數 (rational number) 可以寫成兩個整數之比的數。整數、分數和許多小數都是有理數。

例如:

整數	分數	小數
$-27 = \dfrac{-27}{1}$	$\dfrac{7}{8}$	$3.1 = 3\dfrac{1}{10} = \dfrac{31}{10}$

射線 (ray) 直線的一部份,具有一個端點並向另一個方向無限延伸。射線是由其端點命名的。

例如:

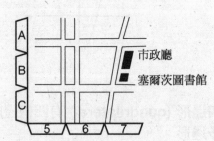

$\overrightarrow{AB}$

實數 (real numbers) 所有的有理數和無理數。

例如:

-27 $\dfrac{1}{2}$ 3.1

$\sqrt{5}$ π $-\sqrt{\dfrac{1}{2}}$

倒數 (reciprocals) 積為1的兩個數。

例如:

$\dfrac{3}{5}$ 和 $\dfrac{5}{3}$ 互為倒數,因為 $\dfrac{3}{5} \cdot \dfrac{5}{3} = 1$。

矩形 (rectangle) 對邊相等並且四個角都是90°的平行四邊形。

例如:

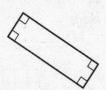

反射 (reflection) 一個圖形通過一條直線的翻轉鏡像。也指對通過一條直線翻轉該圖形的過程。

例如:

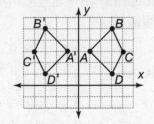

正多邊形 (regular polygon) 所有邊和角均相等的多邊形。

例如:

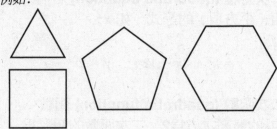

相對位置 (relative position) 一個位置是由與另一個位置的相互關係所決定的。

例如:

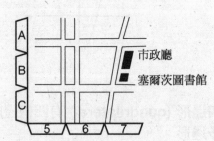

■ 市政廳
■ 塞爾茨圖書館

市政廳在塞爾茨圖書館的旁邊。

餘數 (remainder) 除法運算完成後，餘下的比除數小的數。

例如：

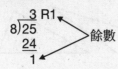

餘數

循環小數 (repeating decimal) 小數點後有一位或一組數字循環的小數。

例如：　0.$\overline{6}$　　0.$\overline{123}$　　2.1$\overline{8}$

菱形 (rhombus) 四條邊都相等的平行四邊形。

例如：

直角 (right angle) 角度為90°的角。

例如：

直角三角形 (right triangle) 有一個角為直角的三角形。

例如：

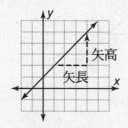

矢高 (rise) 對於圖形中的一條線，水平變化所引起的豎直變化。

例如：

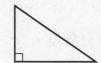

矢高
矢長

旋轉 (rotation) 一個圖形像在輪子上一樣被轉動。也指轉動圖形時的變化過程。

例如：

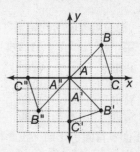

旋轉對稱 (rotational symmetry) 如果一個圖形旋轉小於一週就能和原始圖形完全精確的重合，則這個圖形是旋轉對稱。

例如：

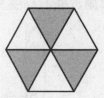

每一個圖形都是旋轉對稱。

四捨五入 (rounding) 根據給定的位數得出一個數的近似值。

例如：

2153 約等於	
精確到百位：2200	精確到十位：2150

矢長 (run) 對於圖形中的一條線，豎直變化，或矢高，所引起的水平變化。

例如：

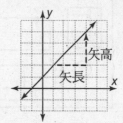

矢高
矢長

樣本 (sample) 用於預測一種典型情況如何發生的數據集合。

例如：

所有1000名俱樂部會員的名字寫在卡片上，將這些卡片混在一起。然後，從中抽出100張卡片，並給這些會員打電話進行調查。樣本為這些被打電話的100名會員。

樣本空間 (sample space) 一個試驗所有可能結果的集合。

例如:

拋投兩枚硬幣的結果:

第一枚	第二枚
正面	背面
正面	正面
背面	正面
背面	背面

樣本空間是正面、背面，正面、正面和背面、背面。

（圖形的）圖尺/標尺 (scale (graphical)) 柱狀圖或線條圖軸上的相等的空間記號，用於測量柱的高度。

例如:

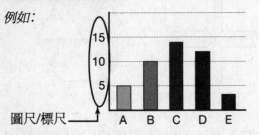

（按比例繪圖中的）圖尺/標尺 (scale (in scale drawings)) 按比例所畫圖形中圖形的尺寸與圖形實際尺寸的比值。見*比例圖形*。

比例圖形 (scale drawing) 按一定比例繪製的一個物體放大或縮小後的圖形。

例如:

起居室的
比例圖

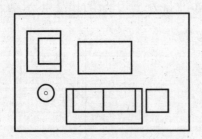

比例尺:
0.1吋=1呎

比例因子 (scale factor) 放大或縮小相似圖形的比值。

例如:

$\frac{10}{5} = 2$ $\frac{6}{3} = 2$

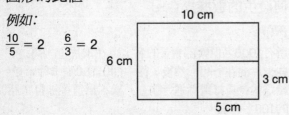

放大比例因子為2。

不規則三角形 (scalene triangle) 各邊都不相等的三角形。

例如:

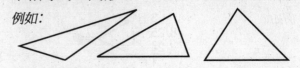

散佈圖 (scatterplot) 使用具有成對坐標值的點表示兩個數據集合相互關係的圖形。

例如:

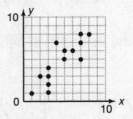

科學記數法 (scientific notation) 一個數被寫成一個大於等於1且小於10的數和以十為底的乘方的積。

例如: $350,000 = 3.5 \times 10^5$

扇形 (sector) 圓的一個楔形部份，用於在圓形圖中表示一個數據集合的一部份在數據集合整體中所佔的比例。

例如:

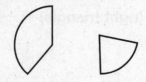

段 (segment) 見*線段*。

線段平分線 (segment bisector) 一條直線、射線或線段通過另一條線段的中點。

例如:

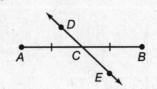

$\overline{DE}$ 在 C 點平分 $\overline{AB}$

序列 (sequence) 具有一定規律的數字排列。

例如：

等差序列：

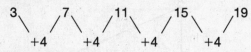

等差序列：

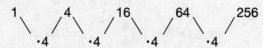

邊 (side) 形成一個角的每一條射線。也指組成多邊形的線段。

例如：

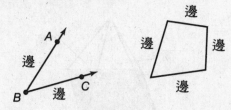

邊角角 (Side-Angle-Angle (SAA)) 比較三角形的相應部份，判斷三角形是否全等的一個定理。

例如：

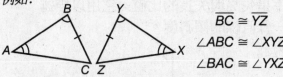

由邊角角定理得出 △ABC ≅ △XYZ。

邊角邊 (Side-Angle-Side (SAS)) 比較三角形的相應部份，判斷三角形是否全等的一個定理。

例如：

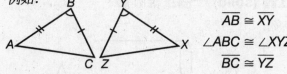

由邊角邊定理得出 △ABC ≅ △XYZ。

邊邊邊 (Side-Side-Side (SSS)) 比較三角形的相應部份，判斷三角形是否全等的一個定理。

例如：

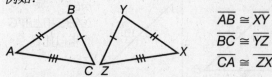

由邊邊邊定理得出△ABC ≅ △XYZ。

有效數字 (significant digits) 在測量數值中，該數字表示實際測量值。

例如：

380.6700　所有數字均是有效數字。

0.0038　　3和8是有效數字，但沒有一個零是有效數字。

相似 (similar) 形狀相同大小不同的圖形。

例如：

和

和

和

相似比 (similarity ratio) 相似圖形相應邊長的比值。

例如：

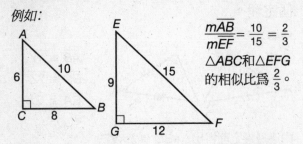

$$\frac{m\overline{AB}}{m\overline{EF}} = \frac{10}{15} = \frac{2}{3}$$

△ABC和△EFG的相似比爲$\frac{2}{3}$。

單利 (simple interest) 僅以本金爲基礎的利息。

例如：　Ramon在一個帳號中存入240圓，5年內每年得到的利息爲6%。他將得到 240・0.06・5 = 72，5年後單利爲72圓。

最簡多項式 (simplified) 沒有同類項的多項式。

例如：

$4x^4 + x^3 + x^2 - 8$　　　最簡多項式

$4x^4 + x^2 + 6x^2 - 8$　　不是最簡多項式，因爲x^2和$6x^2$是同類項。

化簡 (simplify) 按運算順序簡化一個表達式。

例如：　化簡：$3 + 8・5^2$

$3 + 8・5^2 = 3 + 8・25$　　（冪）

$= 3 + 200$　　（乘）

$= 203$　　（加）

模擬 (simulation) 用於求解概率的一種實驗模型。

例如：

一個棒球隊員的擊球概率爲0.250。爲了模擬他如何擊球，轉動一個有四部份的轉盤。這種模擬可用於預測他多長時間能夠連續2次和連續3次擊中。

正弦 (sine) 對於直角三角形中的一個銳角x，x的正弦，或sin(x)，爲對邊與斜邊的比值。

例如：

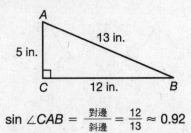

$$\sin \angle CAB = \frac{對邊}{斜邊} = \frac{12}{13} \approx 0.92$$

斜高 (slant height) 棱錐體中，從底面的一條邊到頂點的垂直高度。

例如：

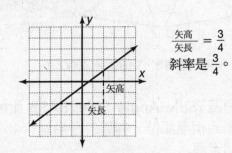

平移 (slide) 見平移。

斜率 (slope) 對於一個直線圖形來說，斜率是矢高與矢長的比值。它用以描述一條直線的傾斜度。

例如：

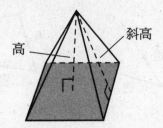

$$\frac{矢高}{矢長} = \frac{3}{4}$$

斜率是$\frac{3}{4}$。

立體 (solid) 一個三維圖形。

例如：

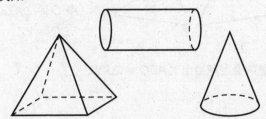

等式或不等式的解 (solutions of an equation or inequality) 使一個等式或不等式成立的變量的值。

例如：

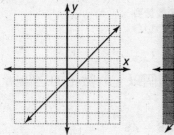

這條直線是
$y = x - 1$
的解。

這個陰影區域是
$y > x - 1$
的解。

方程組的解 (solution of a system) 使方程組中的所有方程均成立的變量代換。

例如：

$$y = x + 4$$
$$y = 3x - 6$$

有序數組 (5,9) 能使兩個等式都成立。所以，(5,9) 是方程組的一個解。

求解 (solve) 尋找等式或不等式的解的過程。

例如：

Solve $x + 6 = 13$.
$$x + 6 = 13$$
$$x + 6 + (-6) = 13 + (-6)$$
$$x + 0 = 7$$
$$x = 7$$

球面 (sphere) 所有點與中心的距離均相等的立體。

例如：

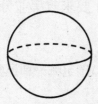

正方形 (square) 所有邊長均相等，並且所有角均為90°的四邊形。

例如：

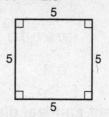

平方 (squared) 升為二次冪。

例如：　3 的平方 = 3^2
$$3^2 = 3 \times 3 = 9$$

平方厘米 (square centimeter) 邊長為一厘米的正方形的面積。

例如：

1 厘米

1 厘米

1 平方厘米

平方吋 (square inch) 邊長為一吋的正方形的面積。

例如：

1 吋

1 吋

1 平方吋

平方根 (square root) N的平方根是其自身相乘等於N的一個數。也可以說，一個數的平方根是面積等於該數的正方形一條邊的長。

例如：
$9 \times 9 = 81$，
所以9是81的平方根。
$9 = \sqrt{81}$

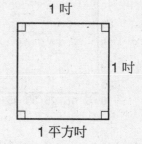

面積是81個平方單位。

標準型 (standard form) 使用數字書寫數的方法。

例如:

標準形式	100,000,000
文字形式	一億
數字-文字形式	1 百萬

莖-葉圖表 (stem-and-leaf diagram) 一種使用數據中的數字來表示數據集合的形狀和分佈的方法。

例如:

這個圖表表示數據集合:33, 34, 34, 35, 40, 41, 46, 51, 51, 52, 53, 55, 58。

莖	葉					
3	3	4	4	5		
4	0	1	6			
5	1	1	2	3	5	8

階梯函數 (step function) 在一個函數中,不同的自變量具有不同的函數值規則。階梯函數的圖形爲各個不連續的線段所組成。

例如:

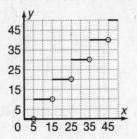

直線角 (straight angle) 角度爲180°的角。

例如:

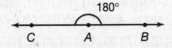

代換 (substitute) 用一個特殊值替換一個變量。

例如:

利用公式 $A = l \cdot w$ 計算一個長12cm,寬8cm的長方形的面積。

$A = l \cdot w$
$A = 12 \cdot 8$ 將長和寬代換
$A = 96$ 爲數值。

面積是 96 cm²。

減法 (subtraction) 一種運算方法,它能給出兩個數之間的不同,或從其中取出一部份後還剩餘多少。

例如: $12 - 5 = 7$

⊠⊠⊠⊠⊠
○○○○○
○○

和 (sum) 兩個或兩個以上的數相加之後所得的結果。

例如: $30 + 18 = 48$ ← 和

補角 (supplementary angles) 兩個角的值相加爲180°的角。

例如:

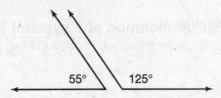

表面積 (surface area (SA)) 多面體每一個面的面積的和。

例如:

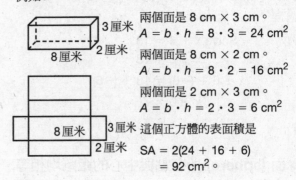

兩個面是 8 cm × 3 cm。
$A = b \cdot h = 8 \cdot 3 = 24 \text{ cm}^2$

兩個面是 8 cm × 2 cm。
$A = b \cdot h = 8 \cdot 2 = 16 \text{ cm}^2$

兩個面是 2 cm × 3 cm。
$A = b \cdot h = 2 \cdot 3 = 6 \text{ cm}^2$

這個正方體的表面積是

$SA = 2(24 + 16 + 6)$
$= 92 \text{ cm}^2$

調查 (survey) 要求收集並分析資訊的一種研究。

例如:

進行一項調查以確定哪一種運動在學生中最受歡迎。

對稱 (symmetry) 見線對稱、點對稱和旋轉對稱。

線性方程組 (system of linear equations) 兩個或兩個以上的線性方程被放在一起。

例如: $y = x + 3$
             $y = 4x - 15$

T形表 (T-table) 表示一個方程相應的*x*值和*y*值的表。

例如:

$$y = 2x + 1$$

x	y
−2	−3
−1	−1
0	1
1	3
2	5

計數 (tally) 在調查中,使用計數符號進行計數的記錄。

例如:

汽車	清算
Sedan	⊯ |||
Station Wagon	||||
Suburban	⊯	
Truck	⊯
Van	|||

計數符號 (tally marks) 用以組織一個大數據集合的符號。每一個符號表示一個值在數據集合中出現了一次。

例如:

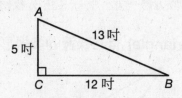

切線 (tangent line) 與一個圓只有一個交點的直線。

例如:

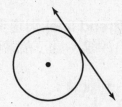

正切 (tangent ratio) 對於直角三角形中的銳角*x*,*x*角的正切,或tan(*x*),是對邊與鄰邊的比值。

例如:

A，13 吋，5 吋，C，12 吋，B

$$\tan \angle CAB = \frac{對邊}{鄰邊} = \frac{12}{5} = 2.4$$

項 (term) 序列中的一個數。也可以是多項式中的一部份,該部份是一個帶正負號的數、一個變量,或一個數和一個或多個變量的乘積。變量可以是整數指數。

例如:

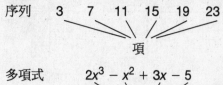

序列　3　7　11　15　19　23
　　　　　　　　項

多項式　　$2x^3 - x^2 + 3x - 5$
　　　　　　　　項

有限小數 (terminating decimal) 具有有限位數的小數。

例如:　　3.5　　0.599992　　4.05

棋盤圖形 (tessellation) 重複圖案形成的圖形。該圖形覆蓋一個區域,沒有縫隙,也沒有重疊。

例如:

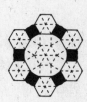

理論概率 (theoretical probability) 一個事件可能發生的次數與總的可能結果之間的比值。

例如:

$$\frac{轉到白色的次數}{總次數} = \frac{3}{6} = \frac{1}{2}$$

因為轉盤上有一半區域是白色的,所以轉到白色的概率為 $\frac{1}{2}$。

平移 (transformation) 圖形大小和位置的一種變化。

例如:

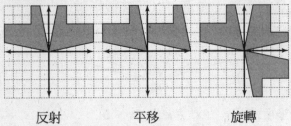

反射　　　　平移　　　　旋轉

平移 (translation) 一個已經被平移到新位置,並且沒有被反轉和轉動的圖形。也指平移一個圖形的過程。

例如:

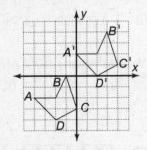

橫穿 (transversal) 穿過另外兩條或兩條以上直線的直線。

例如:

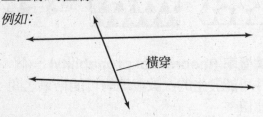

橫穿

梯形 (trapezoid) 只有兩條邊平形的四邊形。

例如:

樹狀圖表 (tree diagram) 其分枝像樹一樣的圖形,表示一種情況的所有可能結果。

例如:

拋投3枚硬幣:

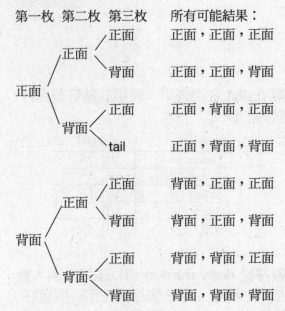

第一枚	第二枚	第三枚	所有可能結果:
正面	正面	正面	正面,正面,正面
		背面	正面,正面,背面
	背面	正面	正面,背面,正面
		tail	正面,背面,背面
背面	正面	正面	背面,正面,正面
		背面	背面,正面,背面
	背面	正面	背面,背面,正面
		背面	背面,背面,背面

趨勢 (trend) 兩個數據集合之間的一種關係,可以以一個圖案的形式在一個散佈圖中表現出來。見*正相關*、*負相關*和*無關聯*。

相關曲線 (trend line) 與趨勢散佈圖中的點基本吻合的線。見*正相關*和*負相關*。

試 (trial) 一種試驗。

例如:

擲一個數字立方體一次　　　　拋投一枚硬幣一次

三角形 (triangle) 有三條邊的多邊形。

例如:

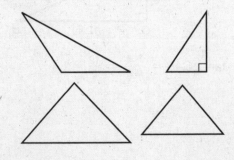

三角函數 (trigonometric ratios)

直角三角形邊長的比，與三角形中的銳角有關。

例如：

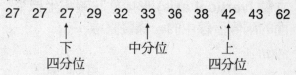

$$\cos \angle CAB = \frac{鄰邊}{斜邊} = \frac{3}{5} = 0.6$$

$$\sin \angle CAB = \frac{對邊}{斜邊} = \frac{4}{5} = 0.8$$

$$\tan \angle CAB = \frac{對邊}{鄰邊} = \frac{4}{3} \approx 1.3$$

三項式 (trinomial) 有三個項的多項式。

例如：　　$2x^3 - x^2 + 3x$　　　$3x^2 + 2x - 4$

轉動 (turn) 見*旋轉*。

不公平游戲 (unfair game) 一種並非所有參加游戲者都有相同獲勝機會的游戲。

例如：

不公平游戲：擲一對數字立方體，每一個游戲者給予一個從2到12的和。當他/她的和被擲出時，將得到一點。因為從2到12的和被擲出的機會不相等，所以沒有相同的獲勝機會。因此這個游戲是不公平游戲。

單價 (unit price) 一個項目價格的單位比。

例如：　3.00圓一磅　　　　5.75圓一盒

單位 (unit) 事物中的一個。計算數量的一個標準量度。

單分數 (unit fraction) 分子是1的分數。

例如：　　$\frac{1}{4}$　　　　$\frac{1}{2}$　　　　$\frac{1}{7}$

單位比率 (unit rate) 在一個比率中，相比較的兩個數中的第二個數是一個單位。

例如：　　每分鐘29加侖　　$\frac{55\,哩}{1\,小時}$

異分母 (unlike denominators) 兩個或兩個以上分數中的分母不同。

例如：

上四分位 (upper quartile) 一個數據集合中上二分之一的中點。

例如：

27　27　27　29　32　33　36　38　42　43　62

下四分位　　　中分位　　　上四分位

變量 (variable) 一個可以改換或變化的量，常用一個字母表示。

例如：　　　$3x$　　　　　y　　　　　$2t$

變量

馮氏圖表 (Venn diagram) 用區域來表示兩事物之間關係的圖表。

例如：

平行四邊形
長方形
正方形
菱形

頂點 (vertex) 在一個角或多邊形中，兩條邊相交所形成的點。在多面體中，三個或三個以上的面相交所形成的點。

例如：

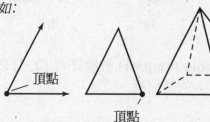

頂點　　　　頂點　　　　頂點

對頂角 (vertical angles) 兩條相交直線形成的相對角。

例如:

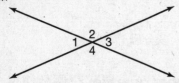

對頂角:
∠1 和 ∠3
∠2 和 ∠4

立軸 (vertical axis) 形成柱狀圖和坐標平面的兩條直線中的一條豎直線。

例如:

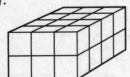

喜歡的顏色

立軸

體積 (volume) 一個立體所佔有的空間數量。

例如:

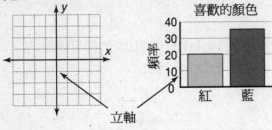

$V = lwh$

$V = 4 \cdot 3 \cdot 2$

$V = 24$ 立方單位

重力 (weight) 地心對任何物體引力的度量。

例如:

1盎司　　　1磅　　　1噸

整數 (whole number) 數據集合 {0, 1, 2, 3, 4, ...} 中的任何數。

文字形式 (word form) 只使用文字的數字表示方法。

例如:

四十五兆　　　十億　　　六

x 軸 (x-axis) 坐標平面中的水平軸。

例如:

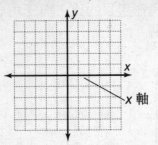

x 軸

x 坐標 (x-coordinate) 有序數組中的第一個數。

例如:

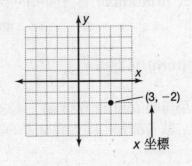

(3, −2)

x 坐標

x 截距 (x-intercept) 方程的圖形與x軸的交點。

例如:

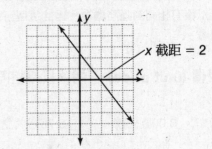

x 截距 = 2

y 軸 (y-axis) 坐標平面中的垂直軸。

例如:

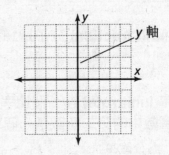

y 軸

y 坐標 (y-coordinate) 有序數組中的第二個數。

例如:

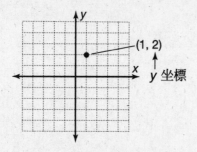

y 截距 (y-intercept) 方程的圖形與y軸的交點。

例如:

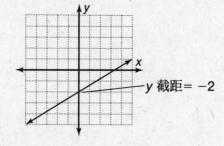

碼 (yard) 一種英制單位，等於三呎。

例如:

桌子大約
有一碼高。

相反數對 (zero pair) 一個數與他的相反數。

例如:　7 和 −7　　23 和 −23

和爲零的加法定律 (Zero Property of Addition) 一個整數與它的相反數相加，和爲零。

例如:
$$3 + (-3) = 0$$
$$-8 + 8 = 0$$

Haitian Creole Glossary

pózisyon absólou (absolute position)
N'ap bay pózisyon kom kóordinat.

Egzanmp:

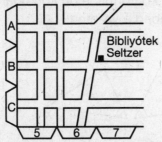

B7 pozisyon absólou pour Bibliyótek Seltzer la.

valèr absólou (absolute value) Youn
distans nouméró de zéró. Simból la pour
valèr absólou sé | |.

Egzanmp yo:

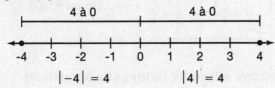

$|-4| = 4$ $|4| = 4$

ang aygou (acute angle) Youn ang ki
méziré mouens de 90°.

Egzanmp yo:

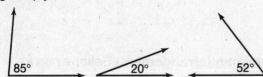

triang aygou (acute triangle) Youn triang
ak toua ang aygou.

Egzanmp:

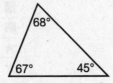

nouméró ajouté (addend) Youn nouméró ki
ou adisyonin á oun ou ou plous lót nouméró.

Egzanmp: $12 + 19 = 31$

nouméró ajouté   nouméró ajouté

adisyon (addition) Youn prósédour ki bay
nouméró tótal la le ou mèté dou ou plous de
nouméró ansanmb.

Egzanmp:

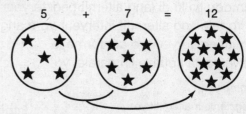

**Própriyèté d'Égalité Adisyon
(Addition Property of Equality)**
Si $a = b$, alor $a + c = b + c$.

Egzanmp:

Nan lin sékond de égznamp la an ba, 1 sé adisyonnin
à toulèdé bó d'ékouézion.

Si	$x - 1$	$= 2$
alor	$x - 1 + 1$	$= 2 + 1$
	x	$= 3$

aditif invérs (additive inverse) Opposé de
youn nouméró.

Egzanmp yo: Aditif invérs la de -2 sé 2.

Aditif invérs la de 5 sé -5.

janm kontigou (adjacent leg) Pour youn
ang aygou nan youn triang douat, sé janm la
ka'p koushé à youn bó d'ang la.

Egzanmp yo: $\overline{AC}$ sé pyé kontigou
à $\angle CAB$.

$\overline{BC}$ sé pyé kontigou
à $\angle ABC$.

aljéb (algebra) Youn seksyon de matèmatik
nan ki yo egsploré rélasyon aritmetik yo outilizè
varyab yo pour rèprézanté noumèró yo.

**egspresyon aljebrik (algebraic
expression)** Youn egspresyon ki ginyin youn
varyab ou plous.

Egzanmp yo: $n - 7$ $2y + 17$ $5(x - 3)$

ang altèrné yo (alternate angles) Dou ang ki fé par dou lin é youn tranzvèrsal ki rèté anfas bó tranzvèrsal la ki: (1) mitan dou lin ki di (ang altèrnitif intéryeur yo) oubyin (2) pa mitan dou lin ki di (ang altèrnitif egztèryeur yo). Yo rélé ang altèrnitif intèryeur yo é ang altèrnitif egztèryeur yo conformé le tranzvèrsal la kouazé lin paralèl yo.

Egzanmp yo:

ang egztèryeur altèrnitif yo:
∠1 é ∠8
∠2 é ∠7

ang intèryeur altèrnitif yo:
∠3 é ∠6
∠4 é ∠5

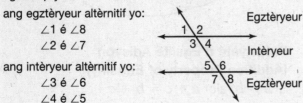

Egztèryeur

Intèryeur

Egztèryeur

ang (angle) Dou douat de fazó avek mem pouint a fini.

Egzanmp:

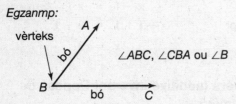

vèrteks

∠ABC, ∠CBA ou ∠B

bisektris d'ang (angle bisector) Youn douat de fazó ki divisé youn ang à dou ang égal.

Egzanmp:

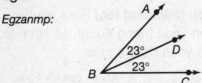

$\overrightarrow{BD}$ ang bisektris la de ∠ABC.

ang de rótasyon (angle of rotation) Ang la nan ki youn figour tourné pandan youn rotasyon.

Egzanmp:

Ang la de rótasyon 90°.

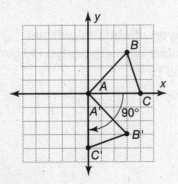

Ang-Bó-Ang (Angle-Side-Angle) (ASA) Youn règ nou outilizè pour détèrminé si triang yo konformé le ou konmparé pyès yo ki kórespond à yo-mem.

Egzanmp:

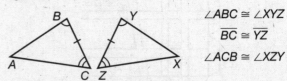

∠ABC ≅ ∠XYZ

$\overline{BC} ≅ \overline{YZ}$

∠ACB ≅ ∠XZY

△ABC ≅ △XYZ par reg ASA la.

arya (area) Anlé tótal youn figour kouvri.

Egzanmp:

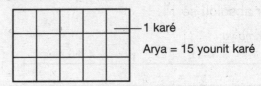

1 karé

Arya = 15 younit karé

sékans aritmetik (arithmetic sequence) Youn sékans koté diferans la pour tèrm konsekoutif toujou lamem.

Egzanmp:

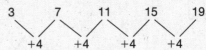

3   7   11   15   19

+4   +4   +4   +4

aranjman (arrangement) Sèkans nan ki moun, nouméró, ou bagay vini.

Egzanmp:

Tout aranjman ki pósib pour toua figour:

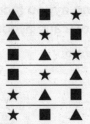

Própriyèté d'Adisyon Asósyatif (Associative Property of Addition) Fè la ki si ou shanjé kom ou groupé nouméró adjouté yo, li pa shanjé tótal la.

Egzanmp yo: $a + (b + c) = (a + b) + c$

$5 + (3 + 7) = (5 + 3) + 7$

Própriyèté Moultiplikasyon Asósyatif (Associative Property of Multiplication) Fè la ki si ou shanjé kom ou groupé fakteur yo, li pa shanjé prodoui a.

Egzanmp yo:
$$a(bc) = (ab)c$$
$$3 \times (4 \times 2) = (3 \times 4) \times 2$$

mouyen (average) Régardé *mouyen*.

aks (axes) Régardé aks-*x* é aks-*y*.

grafik bar (bar graph) Youn grafik ki sèrvi bar vértikal ou orizantal yo pour montré doné yo.

Egzanmp yo:

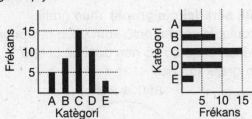

baz (de youn egspózant) (base of an exponent) Youn nouméró ki moultipliyé par li-mem nouméró de tanmp la par youn egspózantt.

Egzanmp: baz egspózant
$$6^2 = 6 \times 6 = 36$$

baz (pour youn póligon) (base of a polygon) Kek bó (nórmalman bó a à bounda a), oubyin longèr la pour bó sa-a.

Egzanmp yo:

baz

baz (pour youn solid) (base of a solid) Nan youn prizim ou silind, li oun de dou figi ki paralel é konformé. Nan youn piramid, figi a an fas somèt la. Nan youn kón, sé figi sèrkoular a.

Egzanmp yo:

baz
baz

baz

baz

sistem nouméró binér (binary number system) Youn plas baz-2 sistem valèr.

Egzanmp:

Nan sistem binér a, 1011 égal 11 nan baz desimal (baz 10) sistem nouméró.

	Plas ouit	Plas kat	Plas dou	Plas oun
Baz 2	1	0	1	1
Valèr plas	8	4	2	1
Prodoui	1×8=8	0×4=0	1×2=2	1×1=1

$(1 \times 8) + (0 \times 4) + (1 \times 2) + (1 \times 1) = 8 + 0 + 2 + 1 = 11$

binomyal (binomial) Youn polinómyal doutèrm.

Egzanmp yo: $4x^3 - 2x^2$ $2x + 5$

bisekt (bisect) À divisé youn ang ou segman nan dou ang ou segman égal.

Egzanmp yo:

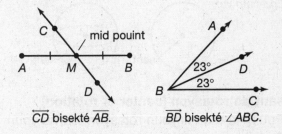
$\overrightarrow{CD}$ bisekté $\overline{AB}$. $\overrightarrow{BD}$ bisekté $\angle ABC$.

lin lizyé (boundary line) Sou youn grafik pour youn inégalité linyar, sé lin la káp sèparé pouint yo ki sé sólousyon yo de pouint yo ki pa solousyon.

Egzanmp:

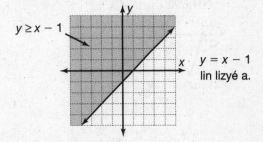
$y \geq x - 1$
$y = x - 1$ lin lizyé a.

Haitian Creole 3

grafik bouat-é-lin (box-and-whisker plot)
Youn mouyen pour montré koman ou kapab
distriboué youn kólèksyon doné. Egazamp la
an ba bazé sou dis mark ki vini apré sa-a:
52, 64, 75, 79, 80, 80, 81, 88, 92, 99.

Egzanmp:

kapasité (capacity) Volyounm la pour youn
figour, ki bay nan nom yo de mézir likid.

Egzanmp:

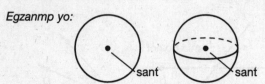

500 ml   1 L   1 tas   1 kart   1 galon

sant (center) Pouint la à midi egzakt la nan
youn sérk ou sfèr.

Egzanmp yo:

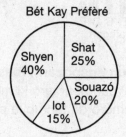

sant de rótasyon (center of rotation)
Pouint la otou ki youn rótasyon tourné youn
figour.

Egzanmp:

orijin la sé sant de rótasyon.

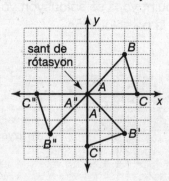

santi- (centi-) Youn préfiks ki gin dèfiniyson
de $\frac{1}{100}$.

Egzanmp: 1 santimet $= \frac{1}{100}$ met

ang santral (central angle) Youn ang ki
vèrteks sé à sant la nan youn sérk.

Egzanmp:

Pouint C sant la nan sérk.

∠BCA es un ángulo central

sérk (circle) Youn figour plèn nan ki pouint li
yo mem distans de sant la.

Egzanmp:

grafik sérk (circle graph) Youn grafik
sérkoular ki sèrvi morsó kom youn tart pour
rèprésanté morsó yo nan doné a. Li rèlé
youn grafik tart ósi.

Egzanmp:

Bét Kay Préfèré

Shyen 40%   Shat 25%   Souazó 20%   lot 15%

sérkonfèrans (circumference) Distans la
ótou youn sérk.

Egzanmp:

sérkonfèrans

figour sérkonskrir (circumscribed figure)
Youn figour k'ap kinmbé youn lot. Youn
póligon sirkonsriyé ótou youn sérk si sérk la
toushé chak bó li.

Egzanmp:

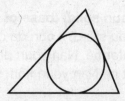

Triang la ki sérkonmskriyé ótou sérk la.

4   Haitian Creole

direksyon (clockwise) kom youn aygoui sou youn lè Direksyon na nan rótasyon nan ki anró a de youn figour tourné a douat.

Egzanmp:

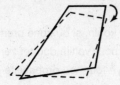

groupman (clustering) Youn metod pour èstimasyon na ki nouméró yo ki piti preskè égal, ou regardé yo kom yo égal aktyoualman.

Egzanmp:

26 + 24 + 23 preskè 25 + 25 + 25, oubyin 3 × 25.

kóèfisyant (coefficient) Youn konstan ki moultipliyé par youn varyab.

Egzanmp:

$$\underset{12y}{\text{kóèfisyant \quad varyab}}$$

kounmbinasyon (combination) Youn sélèksyon de bagay nan ki sékans pa zimportan.

Egzanmp:

Nou va shouazi dou étoudyon de groups pour youn kónmité: David, Jaunita, Kim.

Kounmbinasyon pósib sé:
David, Juanita David, Kim Jaunita, Kim

Nót: Kounmbinasyon na « David, Juanita » mem bagay kom konmbinasyon « Juanita, David ».

dénominateur konmun (common denominator) Youn dénominateur ki mem nan dou ou plous fraksyon.

Egzanmp:

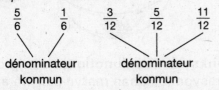

$$\frac{5}{6} \quad \frac{1}{6} \quad \frac{3}{12} \quad \frac{5}{12} \quad \frac{11}{12}$$

dénominateur konmun \qquad dénominateur konmun

fakteur konmun (common factor) Youn nouméró nan ki youn fakteur nan dou ou plous nouméró.

Egzanmp:

4 youn fakteur konmun nan 8, 12, é 20.

$$8 = \mathbf{4} \times 2$$
$$12 = \mathbf{4} \times 3$$
$$20 = \mathbf{4} \times 5$$

moultip konmun (common multiple) Youn nouméró ki youn moultip pour shak de dou ou plous nouméró.

Egzanmp:

moultip de 3: 3 6 9 **12** 15 18 21 **24** 27...

moultip de 4: 4 8 **12** 16 20 **24** 28...

12 é 24 dou moultip konmun nan 3 é 4.

Própriyété Egschanjif à Adisyon (Commutative Property of Addition) Fè la ki sékans pa afekté tótal la de dou ou plous nouméró.

Egzanmp yo:

$$a + b = b + a$$
$$18 + 23 = 23 + 18$$

Própriyèté Egschanjif à Moulitplikasyon (Commutative Property of Multiplication) Fé la ki sékans pa afekté prodoui la pour dou ou plous nouméró.

Egzanmp yo:

$$ab = ba$$
$$4 \times 7 = 7 \times 4$$

nouméro konmpatib (compatible numbers) Pèr nouméró ki ou kapab kalkoulé fasilman.

Egzanmp yo: 30 + 70 40 ÷ 4 25 + 75

konmpansasyon (compensation) Stratèjé nan tet la pour shouazi nouméró pré nouméró yo nan youn problem, alor ajousté sólousyon pour konmpansé pour nouméró yo ou té shouazi.

Egzanmp:
$$99 \times 4 = (100 - 1) \times 4$$
$$= (100 \times 4) - (1 \times 4)$$
$$= 400 - 4$$
$$= 396$$

ang konmplèmèntèr (complementary angles) Dou ang nan ki mézirman fé tótal 90°.

Egzanmp:

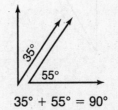

35° + 55° = 90°

nouméró konmpózit (composite number)
Youn nouméró antyé pi gró à 1 ginyin plous de fakteur dou.

Egzanmp yo:

fakteur de 15: 1, 3, 5, 15
   15 sé youn nouméró konmpózit.

fakteur de 7: 1, 7
   7 pa youn nouméró konmpózit.

évanman kounmbiné (compound event)
Youn évanman ki youn kounmbinasyon dou ou plous évanman.

Egzanmp:

 é

Youn evanman kounmbiné sé si ou volitijé youn kouin épi li vini tét oubyion ou roulé youn koub nouméró épi li vini 1.

interet (compound interest) Kounmbiné interet bazé nan kapital é interet prévyouz.

Egzanmp:

Si ou dépózé $100 nan youn konmpt sou livret ki ginyin interet 6% ki kounmbiné pa ané, ou va ginyin $100 + (0.06 × 100) = $106 prémyé ané a épi $106 + (0.06 × 106) = $112.26 ané sekond la.

deklarasyon kounmbiné (compound statement) Youn deklarasyon lojikman ki fórmé le ou maryé dou ou plous deklarasyon.

Egzanmp yo:

10 pi gró 5 *épi* 10 mouens de 21.

10 pi gró 5 *oubyin* 10 mouens de 5.

póligon kónkav (concave polygon) Youn póligon avek youn ou plous diagónal yo ka'p rèté déró figour a.

Egzanmp:

probabilityé kóndisyonal (conditional probability) Probabilityé a ki youn évanman B va pasé, si nou koné évanman A pasé déja.

Egzanmp:

Le ou voltijé oun kouin, si ou koné premyé a pour dou foua, próbabilité pour voltijé dou tet zéró. Min, si ou kone koné premyé foua tet, probabilité $\frac{1}{2}$.

kón (cone) Youn sólid avek oun baz sèrkoular.

Egzanmp:

konfórmé (congruent) Figour yo ki ginyin mem grandèr é fórm.

Egzanmp yo:

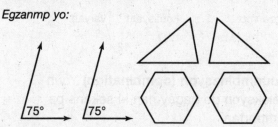

prójeksyon kónik (conic projection) Youn prójeksyon kartografik ki sèrvi youn figour kon pour rèprésanté youn sourfis sfèrikal.

Egzanmp:

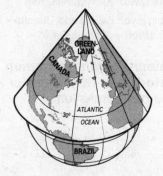

konjónksyon (conjunction) Youn group de deklarasyon lojikman maryé par mó a épi.

Egzanmp yo:

$x > -2$ épi $x < 5$

Youn karé ginyin 4 bó longèr égal épi youn karé youn rektang.

kónstan (constant) Youn kantité ki pa shanjé.

Egzanmp:

Nan egspresyon aljèbrik $x + 7$, 7 youn kónstan.

grafik kónstan (constant graph) Youn grafik nan ki roté a de lin na pa shanjé.

Egzanmp:

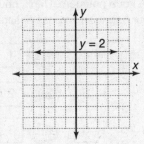

kónstan de próporsyonalityé (constant of proportionality) Kantité a pour $\frac{y}{x}$ pour dou varyab x é y nan ki próporsyon pa rèté konstan. Nórmalman li noté par k.

Egzanmp:

x	3	6	9	12
y	5	10	15	20

$k = \frac{5}{3}$

fakteur kónvèrzyon (conversion factor) Youn ékivanlans mézirman sèrvi pour konvèrté kantité yo pour youn younit à youn lot. Yo souvan di li kom youn fraksyon.

Egzanmp yo:

12 pous = 1 pyé $\frac{12 \text{ pous}}{1 \text{ pyé}}$

4 kart = 1 galon $\frac{4 \text{ kart}}{1 \text{ galon}}$

poligón kónveks (convex polygon) Youn póligon avek tout diagonal nan intèryeur de figour.

Egzanmp yo:

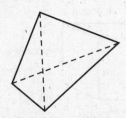

kóordinat (coordinate) Youn pér nouméró nan youn pér sékans ki sèrvi pour sharshé youn pouint sou youn plèn kóordinat.

Egzanmp: (5, 6)

kóordinat

plèn kóordinat, sistem kóordinat (coodinate plane, coordinate system) Youn sistem lin órizontal é lin nouméró vèrtikal outilizé pour sharshé pouint yo.

Egzanmp:

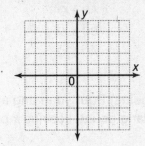

ang kórèspondé (pour lin) (corresponding angles for lines) Ang yo sou mem bó youn transvèrsal ki kouazé dou ou plous lin. Ang kórespondé yo rélé égal le transvèrsal la kouazé lin paralèl yo.

Egzanmp:

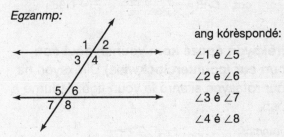

ang kórèspondé:

$\angle 1$ é $\angle 5$

$\angle 2$ é $\angle 6$

$\angle 3$ é $\angle 7$

$\angle 4$ é $\angle 8$

ang kórèspondé (nan figour similar) (corresponding angles in similar figures) Ang ki mézire mem sou figour similar yo.

Egzanmp:
$\triangle ABC \sim \triangle XYZ$

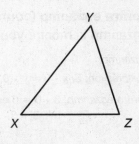

ang kórèspondé:

$\angle ABC$ é $\angle XYZ$

$\angle BCA$ é $\angle YZX$

$\angle CAB$ é $\angle ZXY$

bó kórèspondé (corresponding sides)
Bó ki méziré mem sou figour similar.

Egzanmp:

$\triangle ABC \sim \triangle XYZ$

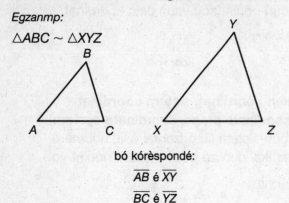

bó kórèspondé:

$\overline{AB}$ é $\overline{XY}$

$\overline{BC}$ é $\overline{YZ}$

$\overline{AC}$ é $\overline{XZ}$

kósinus (cosine) Pour youn ang aygou *x* sou youn triang douat, kósinus *x* próporsyon $\frac{\text{janm ajasant}}{\text{ipótènous}}$.

Egzanmp:

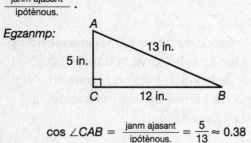

$$\cos \angle CAB = \frac{\text{janm ajasant}}{\text{ipótènous}} = \frac{5}{13} \approx 0.38$$

dirèksyon ópózé kom youn aygoui sou youn eur (counterclockwise) Dirèksyon na pour rótasyon si anró la youn figour tourné à gósh.

Egzanmp:

kontra egzanmp (counterexample) Youn egzanmp ki montré youn dèklarasyon fó.

Egzanmp:

dèklarasyon: Si $x \cdot 0 = y \cdot 0$, alor $x = y$.

kontra egzanmp: $3 \cdot 0 = 0$ épi $5 \cdot 0 = 0$, min $3 \neq 5$.

Prinsip Konté (Counting Principle) Si sitouasyon kapab pasé nan *m* mouyen yo, épi youn sitouasyon sèkondèr kapab pasé nan *n* mouyen yo, alor bagay sa yo kapab pasé ansanmb nan $m \times n$ mouyen yo.

Egzanmp:

Nou gin 2 rézoult pour voltijé youn kouin épi 6 rézoult for roulé youn koub nouméró. Donk, nou gin 2×6, ou 12 rezoult pour bagay sa yo pasé ansanmb.

prodoui kouazé (cross product) Prodoui la noumérateur nan youn próporsyon avek dènóminateur de youn lot.

Egzanmp:

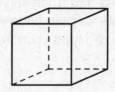

prodoui kouazé yo:

$1 \times 5 = 5$

$3 \times 2 = 6$

koub (cube) Youn prizm ki gin figi yo ki karé kóngrouan.

Egzanmp:

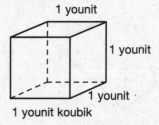

koubé (cubed) Èlèvé à pouvoua touazyem.

Egzanmp: 2 koubé = $2^3 = 2 \times 2 \times 2 = 8$

younit koubik (cubic unit) Youn younit pour méziré vóloumn ki sé youn koub avek rebó yo ki méziré oun younit.

Egzanmp:

1 younit

1 younit

1 younit

1 younit koubik

sistem de mézirman nórmal (customary system of measurement) Sistem de mézirman anmpolyé souvan Ózétaz Uni: pous, pyé, mil, óns, pouad, ton, tas, kart, galón, é plous.

Egzanmp yo:

longèr   kapasité   poua

silind (cylinder) Youn solid ak dou baz ki paralel é sèrkoular.

Egzanmp:

projeksyon silindrikal (cylindrical projection) Youn projeksyon kartógrafik ki outilzé youn fórm silind pour rèprèsanté youn anlé sfèrikal.

Egzanmp:

dekagon (decagon) Youn póligon avek 10 bó.

Egzanmp:

desi- (deci-) Youn préfiks pour $\frac{1}{10}$.

Egzanmp: 1 desimet $= \frac{1}{10}$ met

desimal (decimal) Kek baz-10 nouméró ki ékri sèrvi youn vérgoul.

Egzanmp yo: 6.21   0.59   12.2   5.0

adisyon desimal (decimal addition) Lè ou adisyonin dou ou plous desimal.

Egzanmp:
$$\begin{array}{r} 1 \\ 12.65 \\ +\ 29.10 \\ \hline 41.75 \end{array}$$

divizyon desimal (decimal division) Lè ou divizé dou desimal.

Egzanmp:
$$0.24\overline{)0.3000}$$
$$\begin{array}{r} 1.25 \\ -24 \\ \hline 60 \\ -48 \\ \hline 120 \\ -120 \\ \hline 0 \end{array}$$

moultiplikasyon desimal (decimal multiplication) Lè ou moulipliyé dou ou plous desimal.

Egzanmp:

$$\begin{array}{rl} 2 & \\ 0.13 & \text{2 plas desimal} \\ \times\ 0.7 & \text{1 plas desimal} \\ \hline 0.091 & \text{3 plas desimal} \end{array}$$

desimal soustraksyon (decimal subtraction) Soutraksyon dou desimal.

Example
$$\begin{array}{r} 13\ 12 \\ 4\ \cancel{3}\ \cancel{2}10 \\ \cancel{5}\cancel{4}.\cancel{3}\cancel{0} \\ -\ 16.58 \\ \hline 37.72 \end{array}$$

sistem desimal (decimal system) Youn 10-baz sistem de valèr plas.

Egzanmp:

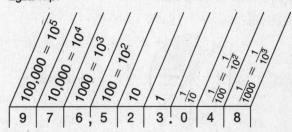

grafik diminyé (decreasing graph)
Youn grafik nan ki roté lin na diminyé
gósh à douat.

Egzanmp:

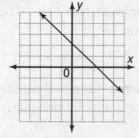

rézonman dédouktif (deductive reasoning)
Outilizé lójik pour fórmé youn kónklouzyon.

Egzanmp:

Le ou adisyonin youn diagónal à kek kouadrilatèral,
gin dou triang formé. Ou kóne tótal nan ang yo pour
youn triang 180°. Donk, tótal la mézir ang pour youn
kouadrilatèral doublè mézirman na nan youn triang,
oubyin 2 × 180° = 360°.

dégré (degree (°)) Youn younit de mézirman
pour ang yo.

Egzanmp: 1° sé $\frac{1}{360}$ youn sérk konmplet.

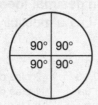

dégré (degree) Pour youn polinómyal,
valèr a pi gró a egspózant pour youn varyab.

Egzanmp: Dégré a pour $5x^3 - 2x^2 + 7x$ sé 3.

deka- (deka-) youn préfiks pour 10.

Egzanmp: 1 dekamèt = 10 mèt

dénóminateur (denominator) Nouméró pi
ba a nan youn fraksyon ki di nan konmbyin
pyés tótal la sé divisé.

Egzanmp:

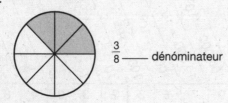

$\frac{3}{8}$ —— dénóminateur

évanman dépandan (dependent events)
Évanman pour ki rézoult youn afekté lot la.

Egzanmp:

Nom yo Therese, Diane, é José ékri sou oun pyés
papié pour shak. Yo shouazi oun papié épi kinmbé'l.
Alor yo shouazi oun lot. Probabilité a yo va shouazi
nom Diane sou premié papié $\frac{1}{2}$.

varyab dépandan (dependent variable)
Varyab sorti a pour youn fonksyon.

Egzanmp:

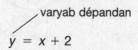

varyab dépandan

$y = x + 2$

diagónal (diagonal) Sou youn poligón,
youn sègman ka'p kónèkté dou vèrtik ki pa
patajé youn bó.

Egzanmp:

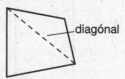

diagónal

diamet (diameter) Youn sègman lin, ou
longèr li, ki pasé pa sant la youn sérk épi li
ginyin pouint bout touledé sou sérk la.

Egzanmp:

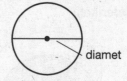

diamet

difèrans (difference) Rézoult la le ou
subtrakté youn nouméró à youn lot.

Egzanmp: 28 − 15 = 13

difèrans

shif (digit) Simból yo outilizè pour ékri
nouméró yo 0, 1, 2, 3, 4, 5, 6, 7, 8, é 9.

Egzanmp:

Nan 5,847 shif yo 5, 8, 4, é 7.

dilasyon (dilation) Youn rédouksyon própórsyonal oubyin agrandisman de youn figour.

Egzanmp:

Fakteur eshèl la pour dilasyon na pour ti rektang à gro rektang 3.

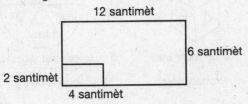

varasyon direk (direct variation) Le dou varyab relaté pa youn próporsyon kónstan.

Egzanmp:

tanmp nan eur (x)	1	2	3	4
distans nan mi (y)	55	110	165	220

$$\frac{y}{x} = 55$$

disjonksyon (disjunction) Youn group lójikal deklarasyon maryé par mó oubyin.

Egzanmp yo:

$x > 4$ oubyin $x < -1$

Nou té allé à sinema a oubyin nou té regardé télévizyon.

Própèrityé Distriboutif (Distributive Property) Fè la ki $a(b + c) = ab + ac$.

Egzanmp: $3(6 + 5) = 3 \cdot 6 + 3 \cdot 5$

dividand (dividend) Nouméró a ou va divisé nan youn problem divisyon.

Egzanmp:

dividand
$$8 \div 4 = 2$$

divisib (divisible) Ou kapab divisé nouméró sa par youn lot sans kité youn rest.

Egzanmp: Ou kapab divisé 18 par 6, parskè
18 ÷ 6 = 3.

divisyon (division) Youn fonksyon ki di ou konmbyin group égal oubyin konmbyin nan shak group égal.

Egzanmp yo:

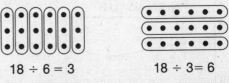

18 ÷ 6 = 3   18 ÷ 3 = 6

Le ou divisé 18 nan 6 group, li mèté 3 nan shak group.

Le ou divisé 18 nan 3 group, li mèté 6 nan shak group.

diviseur (divisor) Youn nouméró ka'p divisé par youn lot nouméró.

Egzanmp:

diviseur
$$8 \div 4 = 2$$

dódekagón (dodecagon) Youn póligon avek 12 bó.

Egzanmp:

grafik bar doublè (double bar graph) Youn konmbinasyon de dou grafik bar ka'p konmparé dou group ki liyé.

Egzanmp:

Bet kay

Nouméró étoudyan

7yem
8yem

Shyèn Shat Souazo Okèn

grafik lin doublè (double line graph)
Youn konbinasyon de dou grafik lin, ka'p konmparé dou group ki liyé.

Egzanmp:

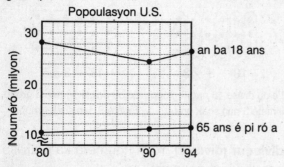

Popoulasyon U.S.

an ba 18 ans

65 ans é pi ró a

bòk-é-fé doublè diagram (double stem-and-leaf diagram)
Youn konmparison bòk-é-fé nan dou group de doné nan oun diagram.

Egzanmp:

fé	bòk	fé
7 2 1	3	0 1 3
5 0 0	4	2 3
9	5	5 6 8
5 2 0	6	1 4

rebó (edge)
Youn segman koté dou figi nan youn póliédron randévou.

Egzanmp:

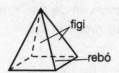

figi

rebó

pouint bout (endpoint)
Youn pouint à bout la pour youn segman oubyin réyon.

Egzanmp yo:

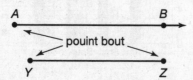

A   B

pouint bout

Y   Z

égalité (equality)
Youn rélasyon matèmatikal nan ki dou bagay mém egazkteman.

Egzanmp yo: $16 + 8 = 24$ $25 \div 5 = 5$

probabilité de rézoult égal (equally-likely outcomes)
Rézoult yo ki ginin mem probabilité.

Egzanmp yo:

blou

vér   rouj

jaun   gri

blank

si ou roulé oun

Probabilité: $\frac{1}{6}$

si ou lanse youn aygoui à rouj

Probabilité: $\frac{1}{6}$

próporsyon égal (equal ratios)
Próporsyon ki di mem valèr.

Egzanmp: $\frac{2}{6}$, $\frac{1}{3}$ é $\frac{4}{12}$

ékouézyon (equation)
Youn fraz matèmatikal nan ki di dou egspresyon égal.

Egzanmp yo:

$14 = 2x$ $3 + y = 81$ $3 + 4 = 7$

triang ekouilateral (equilateral triangle)
Youn triang nan ki bó yo égal longèr.

Egzanmp:

4   4

4

ékouézyon ékivalan (equivalent equations)
Ékouézyon yo ki vré pour mem ranmplasman varyab.

Egzanmp: $x - 5 = 10$ épi $x = 15$

égspresyon ékivalan (equivalent expressions)
Dou égspresyon ki toujou ginyin mem valèr a pour mem ranmplasman.

Egzanmp: $5(x + 1)$ épi $5x + 5$

fraksyon ékivalan (equivalent fractions)
Dou fraksyon ki rèprésanté mem nouméró a.

Egzanmp: $\frac{1}{2}$ é $\frac{8}{16}$

tó ékivalan (equivalent rates) Tó ki gin mem montan.

Egzanmp: $\dfrac{40\ mil}{2\ eur}$ épi $\dfrac{20\ mil}{1\ eur}$

próporsyon ékivalan (equivalent ratios) Regardé próporsyon égal.

évalyasyon (estimate) Youn aproksimasyon pour rézoult la nan youn kalkoulasyon.

Egzanmp: 99×21
Évalyasyon: $100 \times 20 = 2000$
$99 \times 21 \approx 2000$

formoul Euler (Euler's formula) Youn formoul apropó nouméró figi (*F*), somet (*V*), é rebó (*E*) nan youn pólièdron ki di $F + V - E = 2$.

Egzanmp:

Pour piramid triang montré,
$5\ +\ 5\ -\ 8\ =\ 2$
figi   somet   rébó

évalyoué (evaluate) Ránmplasé valèr yo pour varyab nan youn egspresyon épi sanmplifyé li paré ou fé sékans fonksyon.

Egzanmp: Évalyoué $8(x - 3)$ pour $x = 10$.
$8(x - 3) = 8(10 - 3)$
$= 8\ (7)$
$= 56$

nouméró pér (even number) Youn nouméro ki ginyin 0, 2, 4, 6, 8, nan plas oun yo.

Egzanmp yo: 16   28   34   112   3000

évanman (event) Youn rézoult oubyin youn group rézoult nan youn egspèriman oubyin youn sitouasyon.

Egzanmp:
Evanman: Si ou gin 3 ou pi ró a lè ou roulé youn koub nouméró.

Rézoult yo pósib pour evanman sa-a: 3, 4, 5, 6

fórm egspansé (expanded form) Koman ékri youn nouméró egspózantsyal pour montré youn fakteur individyoualman.

Egzanmp: nouméró egspózantsyal 9^3
fórm egspansé $9 \times 9 \times 9$

egspèriman (experiment) Nan próbabilité, kek aksion ki sèrvi shans.

Egzanmp yo:
voltijé youn kouin   roulé youn koub nouméró   lansé youn aygoui

próbabilité egspèrimantal (experimental probability) Youn próbabitlité ki bazé sou doné de egspèriman yo oubyin sondé.

Egzanmp:

Yo voltijé youn ti sashé plèn poua nan youn ti sérk 100 foua. Yo gin 23 pouint nan sérk. Probabilité egspérimantal pour pouint yo $\dfrac{23}{100} = 23\%$.

egspózant (exponent) Youn nouméró an ró a ka'p montré youn moultipikasyon repeté.

Egzanmp: egspózant
$4^3 = 4 \times 4 \times 4 = 64$

fonksyon egspózantsyal (exponential function) Youn fonksyon non-linyar nan ki youn egspózant youn varyab.

Egzanmp: $y = 4^x$

fonksyon egspózantsyal (exponential notation) Youn fonksyon non-linyar nan ki youn egspózant youn varyab.

Egzanmp yo: 2^8 5^2 9^3

notasyon egspózantsyal (expression) Koman ékri moultipikasyon repeté pour youn nouméró outilizè egspózant.

Egzanmp yo: $5(8 + 4)$ $x - 3$ $2x + 4$

ang egztèryeur (exterior angles) Si youn transvèrsal kouazé dou lin, ang yo déró dou lin sa yo rélé ang egztèryeur.

Egzanmp:

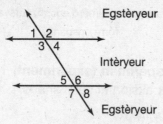

ang egztèryeur:
∠1, ∠2, ∠7, ∠8

Egstèryeur
Intèryeur
Egstèryeur

figi (face) Youn anlé plat sou youn sólid.

Egzanmp:

figi

fakteur (factor) Youn nouméró ki divisé youn lot sans kité youn dénóminateur.

Egzanmp: Depoui 30 ÷ 5 = 6, 5 youn fakteur nan 30.

faktueuryal (factorial) Fakteuryal de youn nouméró prodoui de tout nouméró à 1 à nouméró sa-a. Simból oubyin fakteuryal « ! ».

Egzanmp:

6 fakteuryal = 6! = 6 × 5 × 4 × 3 × 2 × 1 = 720

pyé boua fakteur (factor tree) Youn diagram ka'p montré koman youn nouméró dékanmpozé à fakteur priméri.

Egzanmp:

72
2 36
2 18   72 = 2 × 2 × 2 × 3 × 3
2 9
3 3

jouèt ekitab (fair game) Youn jouèt nan ki tout partisipan gin mem shans pour ginyin.

Egzanmp:

Jouèt ekitab: Dou partispipan roulé youn koub nouméro youn apré lot. Partisipan A va gin oun pouint for shak roulé à 1, 3, 5. Partisipan B va gin oun pouint for shak roulé à 2, 4, 6. Próbabilité a pour ginyin youn pouint $\frac{1}{2}$ pour shak.

baskilé (flip) Regardé *réfleksyon*.

pyé (foot) Youn younit nan ki sistem mézirman nórmal égal 12 pous.

Egzanmp:

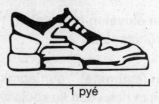

1 pyé

fórmoul (formula) Youn reg ka'p montré rélasyon ótou kantité.

Egzanmp yo: $A = bh$ $p = 4s$

fraktal (fractal) Youn patouan ki sanmblé li-mem. Si ou grandi youn pyès fraktal la, arya ki grandi sanmblé figour orijinal.

Egzanmp:

fraksyon (fraction) Youn nouméró nan fórm $\frac{a}{b}$ ki dékriyé pyès nan tótal si tótal koupé nan pyès égal.

Egzanmp yo: $\frac{3}{5}$ $\frac{2}{7}$ $\frac{1}{4}$ $\frac{7}{10}$

adisyon fraksyon (fraction addition) Adisyonin dou ou plous fraksyon.

Egzanmp: $\frac{1}{3} + \frac{1}{4}$

$$\frac{1}{3} = \frac{1 \times 4}{3 \times 4} = \frac{4}{12}$$

$$\frac{1}{4} = \frac{1 \times 3}{4 \times 3} = \frac{3}{12}$$

$$\frac{1}{3} + \frac{1}{4} = \frac{4}{12} + \frac{3}{12} = \frac{4 + 3}{12} = \frac{7}{12}$$

divisyon fraksyon (fraction division) Divisé dou fraksyon.

Egzanmp: $\frac{1}{6} \div \frac{3}{4} = \frac{1}{6} \times \frac{4}{3}$

$$= \frac{1 \times 4}{6 \times 3}$$

$$= \frac{4}{18} \text{ oubyin } \frac{2}{9}$$

moultipikasyon fraksyon (fraction multiplication) Moultipliyé dou ou plous fraksyon.

Egzanmp: $1\frac{1}{2} \times \frac{1}{4} = \frac{3}{2} \times \frac{1}{4}$

$$= \frac{3 \times 1}{2 \times 4}$$

$$= \frac{3}{8}$$

soustraksyon fraksyon (fraction subtraction) Soustrakté dou fraksyon.

Egzanmp: $\frac{3}{4} - \frac{2}{3}$

$$\frac{3}{4} = \frac{3 \times 3}{4 \times 3} = \frac{9}{12}$$

$$\frac{2}{3} = \frac{2 \times 4}{3 \times 4} = \frac{8}{12}$$

$$\frac{3}{4} - \frac{2}{3} = \frac{9}{12} - \frac{8}{12} = \frac{9 - 8}{12} = \frac{1}{12}$$

frèkans (frequency) Nouméró tanmp yo kek bagay pasé nan youn étoud. Régardé *grafik frèkans*.

grafik oubyin tab frèkans (frequency chart or table) Youn tab ka'p montré group bagay épi frèkans na ki yo pasé.

Egzanmp:

shemiz koulor	frekans
nouar	8
broun rouk	2
blank	5
blou	4

evalyouasyon avant (front-end estimation) Youn mètod evalyouasyon nan ki shif premyé oubyin sèkondèr pour shak nouméró sèrvi pour estimasyon, épi rezoult la ajousté bazé nan shif yo ka'p rèté.

Egzanmp: shif-oun evalyouasyon avant

```
   2,485
 + 3,698
 -------
   5,000   Adisyoné shif premyé.
 + 1,200   485 + 698 preskè 1,200.
 -------
   6,200
```

fonksyon (function) Youn antré-sorti rélasyon ki bay oun sorti pour chak antré selman.

Egzanmp yo:

$$y = x + 4 \qquad y = 2x \qquad y = x^2$$

Térèm Fondèmantal pour (Fundamental Theorem of Arithmetic) Matèmatik Tout antyé plous de 1 ou kakpab ékri kom youn prodoui nouméró premyé ounik yo.

Egzanmp yo: $24 = 2 \times 2 \times 2 \times 3$
$35 = 5 \times 7$

galon (gallon) Youn younit nan sistem nórmal pour mézirman ki égal 4 kart.

Egzanmp:

1 galon

jéómetrik (geometry) Youn branch matematik nan ki yo egsplóré relasyon pour dou pouint, lin, figour, oubyin sólid.

probabilité jéómetrik (geometric probability) Youn próbabilité ki bazé nan konmparé ézirman pour figour jéómetrik.

Egzanmp:

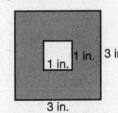

Arya à gró karé = $3 \cdot 3$ oubyin 9 pous^2

Arya gri = 9 pous^2 − 1 pous^2 = 8 pous^2

Próbabilté pour atéri nan ayra gri = $\frac{8}{9}$

sékan jéómetrik (geometric sequence) Youn sékans nan ki réasyon pour tèrm konsekoutif toujou limem.

Egzanmp:

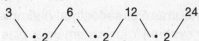

3   6   12   24
$\cdot 2$ $\cdot 2$ $\cdot 2$

gram (gram) Younit basik pour mas nan sistem metrik.

Egzanmp:

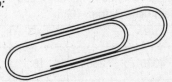

Mass la pour youn trnmbón preskè oun gram.

grafik (graph) Youn diagram ki montré infórmasyon nan youn fasón organizé.

Egzanmp yo:

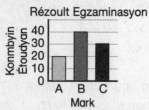

bòk	fé
3	0 1 3
4	2 2
5	6 7 9

fakteur pi gro komen (greatest common factor (GCF)) Nouméró antyé pi gro ki divisé dou ou plous nouméró sans kité youn rest.

Egzanmp: 6 sé GCF nan 12, 18 , é 24.

hektó- (hecto-) Youn préfiks pour 100.

Egzanmp: 1 hektómet = 100 met

tay (height) Sou youn triang, kadrilatèral, oubyin piramid, distans pèrpandikoulèr baz àq vèrteks anfas ou bó. Sou youn prizm oubyin silindar, distans mitan baz.

Egzanmp yo:

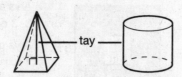

èptagon (heptagon) Youn poligon ak 7 bó.

Egzanmp:

sistem nouméró eksadèsimal (hexadecimal number system) Youn sistem valèr plas baz-16.

Egzanmp:

Lèt A à F sèrvi pour reprézanté shif 10 à 15. nouméró baz-16 A3CE egal à 41,934 (40,960 + 768 + 14) nan nouméró'sistem dèsimal (baz-10).

Baz-16	A	3	C	E
Valèr plas	4096	256	16	1
Prodoui	10 × 4096 = 40,960	3 × 256 = 768	12 × 16 = 192	14 × 1 = 14

eksagon (hexagon) Youn poligon ak 6 bó.

Egzanmp yo:

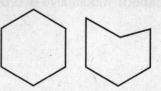

istógram (histogram) Youn tip grafik bar kotè katègóri yo ginyin transhé égal pour nouméró.

Egzanmp:

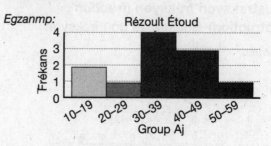

aks orizontal (horizontal axis) Lin orizontal la pour dou lin nan ki yo konstroui youn grafik bar oubyin youn plèn kóordinat.

Egzanmp yo:

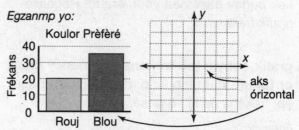

ipotenous (hypotenuse) Bó anfas ang douat nan youn triang douat.

Egzanmp:

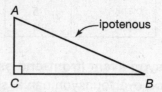

idantité (identity) Pour kek prósèdour, nouméró a ki kinmbé youn lot nouméró mem. 0 sé idantité aditif, paskè $a + 0 = a$, 1 idantité moultipikatif paskè $a \times 1 = a$.

Egzanmp yo:
$$6 + 0 = 6$$
$$5 \times 1 = 5$$

deklarasyon si-alor (if-then statement) Youn deklarasyon lójik ki sèrvi *si* é *alor* pou montré youn koneksyon pour dou kondisyon.

Egzanmp:

Si youn triang skalèn, *alor* yoyoun bo li égal.

fraksyon déplasé (improper fraction)

Youn fraksyon nan ki noumérateur plous de oubyin égal à dénóminateur li.

Egzanmp yo: $\frac{5}{2}$ $\frac{8}{8}$ $\frac{14}{3}$

grafik ranjé (increasing graph)

Youn grafik nan ki tay lin ranjé gósh à douat.

Egzanmp:

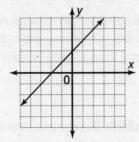

pous (inch)

Youn younit longèr nan sistem mézirman nórmal.

Egzanmp: Trombón na méziré $1\frac{3}{8}$ pous oubyin $1\frac{3}{8}''$.

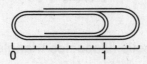

évanman indépandan (independent events)

Évanman yo nan ki rézoult de youn pa afèkté probabilité pour lót la.

Egzanmp:

Name yo Therese, Diane, é José ékri sou oun pyés papié pour shak. Yo shouazi youn papié épi rètourné'l. Alor yo shouazi you lot. Probabilité a yo va shouazi nom Diane, parskè yo koné nom Therese té shouazi prèmié foua sé $\frac{1}{3}$.

varyab indépandan (independent variable)

Varyab antré pour youn fonksyon.

Egzanmp:

$$\text{varyab indépandan}$$
$$y = \overset{/}{x} + 2$$

rézonman indouktif (inductive reasoning)

Le ou outilizé youn patouan pour fé youn konklouzyon.

Egzanmp:

Yo désiné anmpil kouadrilateral, épi yo méziré ang yo. Shak foua tótal la pou ang yo 360°. Yo fé Konklouzyon tótal la pour ang nan youn kouadrilateral 360°

inékalité (inequality)

Youn fraz matèmatikal ap outilizè $<$, $>$, $\leq$, oubyin $\geq$ 3.

Egzanmp yo:

$6 < 9$ $x + 3 \geq 21$ $2x - 8 > 0$

figour inskribé (inscribed figure)

Youn figour ki kinmbé nan youn lot. Youn póligon ki inskribé nan youn sérk si tout vértisi li touché sérk la.

Egzanmp:

Triang la inskribé nan sérk la.

antyé (integers)

Group la nouméró póztitif antyé, kontrèr yo, é 0.

Egzanmp yo: $..., -3, -2, -1, 0, 1, 2, 3, ...$

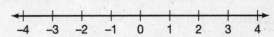

adisyon antyé (integer addition)

Adisyonin dou ou plous antyé.

Egzanmp yo:

$-5 + 8 = 3$ $-5 + (-8) = -13$

$5 + (-3) = 2$ $5 + 8 = 13$

divisyon antyé (integer division)

Divisé dou antyé.

Egzanmp yo:

$-40 \div 8 = -5$ $40 \div (-8) = -5$

$-40 \div (-8) = 5$ $40 \div 8 = 5$

moultipkasyon antyé (integer multiplication)

Moultipliyé dou ou plous antyé.

Egzanmp yo:

$-5 \cdot 8 = -40$ $-5 \cdot (-8) = 40$

$5 \cdot (-8) = -40$ $5 \cdot 8 = 40$

soustraksyon antyé (integer subtraction)

Soustrakté dou antyé.

Egzanmp yo:

$-5 - 8 = -13$ $-5 - (-8) = 3$

$5 - (-3) = 8$ $5 - 8 = -3$

interet (interest) Lajan ki payé pour sèrvi lajan.

Egzanmp:

Dave té mèté $300 nan youn kompt dépani. Apré 1 ané balans nan kompt li $315. Li té ginyin $15 nan interet nan kompt dépani li.

ang intéryeur (interior angles) Ang yo formé par youn transvèrsal é lin yo li kouazé, mitan lin sa yo.

Egzanmp:

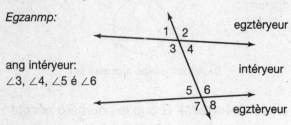

ang intéryeur:
∠3, ∠4, ∠5 é ∠6

koupé (intersect) Kouazé par mem pouint.

Egzanmp:

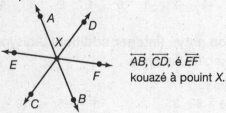

$\overrightarrow{AB}$, $\overrightarrow{CD}$, é $\overrightarrow{EF}$ kouazé à pouint X.

intèrval (interval) Oun de grandér-égal a nan youn grafik bar oubyin grafik lin.

Egzanmp:

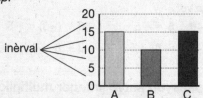

prosédour invérs (inverse operations) Prosédour yo ki anilé yo mem.

Egzanmp yo:

adisyon é soustraksyon	$2 + 3 = 5$	$5 - 3 = 2$
moultiplikasyon é divisyon	$2 \cdot 3 = 6$	$6 \div 3 = 2$

varasyon invérs (inverse variation) Le dou varyab relaté par oun prodoui kónstan.

Egzanmp:

x	1	2	3	4	5	6
y	60	30	20	15	12	10

$$x \cdot y = 60$$

nouméró irasyonal (irrational number) Youn nouméró $\sqrt{2}$, ki nou pa kapab di kom youn desimal k'ap repété ou tèrminé.

Egzanmp yo: $\sqrt{5}$ $\qquad$ π $\qquad$ $-\sqrt{\frac{1}{2}}$

désin isómètrik (isometric drawing) Youn mètod sèrvi pour bay pérspektif à youn désin.

Egzanmp:

triang isóselis (isosceles triangle) Youn triang ak dou bó égal.

Egzanmp:

kiló- (kilo-) Youn préfiks pour 1000.

Egzanmp: 1 kilomet = 1000 met

latitoud (latitude) Youn mézirman nan dégré nord ou soud à ékateur a.

Egzanmp:

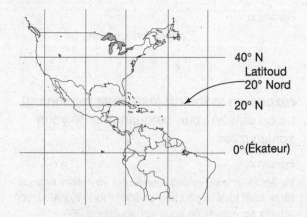

mouenn dénóminateur komen (least common denominator (LCD)) Mouenn moultip komen (LCD) pour dou ou plous dénóminateur.

Egzanmp: $\frac{1}{2}$ $\frac{2}{3}$ $\frac{3}{4}$

LCM pour 2,3 é 4 sé 12, donk LCD pour fraksyon yo 12.

Fraksyon yo ékri avek LCD a $\frac{6}{12}$, $\frac{8}{12}$ é $\frac{9}{12}$.

mouenn moultip komen (least common multiple (LCM)) Mouenn nouméró ki moultip komen.

Egzanmp:
moultip pour 3: 3   6   9   **12**   15   18   21   **24**   ...
moultip pour 4: 4   8   **12**   16   20   **24**   28   32   ...
12 sé LCM pour 3 é 4

janm (leg) Youn bó pour youn triang douat egsèpté pour youn ipotenous.

Egzanmp:

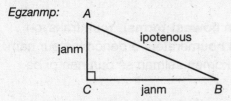

dénóminateur mem (like denominators) Dénóminateur ki mem nan dou ou plous fraksyon.

Egzanmp:

tèrm mem (like terms) Tèrm yo nan ki mem vayab ranjé à mem egspózant.

Egzanmp: $3x^2$ é $9x^2$ $10y$ é $2y$

lin (line) Youn figour oun-dimasyonal ki allé nan dou direksyon sans fini.

Egzanmp:

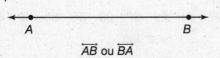

$\overleftrightarrow{AB}$ ou $\overleftrightarrow{BA}$

grafik lin (line graph) Youn grafik nan ki youn lin montré doné ki shanjé, souvan par tanmp.

Egzanmp:

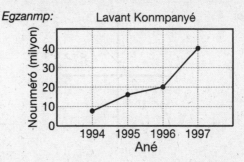

lin de simètri (line of symmetry) Lin na ki divisé youn figour ak lin de simèt nan dou mouatyé idantikal.

Egzanmp yo:

1 lin de simèt   4 lin de simèt

plan lin (line plot) Youn plan ki montré anfórm pour youn group doné par mèté x oun sou oun an ró shak valèr sou youn lin nouméró.

Egzanmp:

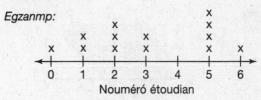

Nouméró étoudian

segman lin (line segment) Pyés nan lin toudouat avek dou pouint-bout. Dou pouints dèterminé youn segman.

Egzanmp:

$\overline{AB}$ ou $\overline{BA}$

simètri lin (line symmetry) Youn figour ginyin simètri lin si ou kapab divisé li nan dou mouatyé idantikal.

Egzanmp:

Figour avek   Figour sans
simètri lin   simètri lin

Haitian Creole   19

ékouézyon linyar (linear equation) Youn ékouzyon nan ki grafik youn lin toudouat.

Egzanmp:

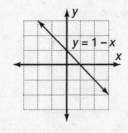

$y = x + 1$

fonksyon linyar (linear function) Youn fonksyon nan ki grafik youn lin toudouat.

Egzanmp:

antré	sorti
x	y
-2	3
-1	2
0	1
1	0
2	-1
3	-2

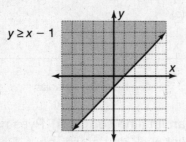

$y = 1 - x$

orinégalité linyar (linear inequality) Youn fraz matèmatik ki ginyin $<$, $>$, $\leq$ oubyin $\geq$ nan ki grafik youn arya ak lizyé lin touduat.

Egzanmp:

$y \geq x - 1$

lit (liter) Younit bazik pour vólounm nan sistem metrik.

Egzanmp:

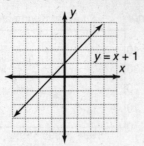

2-lit bouté

lonjitoud (longitude) Youn mézirman nan dégré lès ou ouest à mèridyan prinsipal.

Egzanmp:

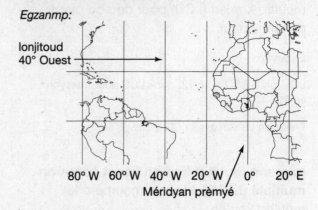

lonjitoud
40° Ouest

80° W   60° W   40° W   20° W   0°   20° E

Méridyan prèmyé

pi ba kartyé (lower quartile) Midyan pour pi ba mouatyé pour youn groupe doné.

Egzanmp:

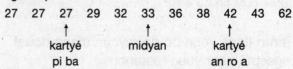

27   27   27   29   32   33   36   38   42   43   62

      ↑   ↑   ↑

kartyé   midyan   kartyé
pi ba   an ro a

tèrm pi ba (lowest terms) Youn fraksyon avek youn noumérateur é dénóminateur nan ki fakteur komen sèlman sé oun nan pi ba tèrm.

Egzanmp yo: $\dfrac{1}{2}$ $\dfrac{3}{5}$ $\dfrac{21}{23}$

mas (mass) Total la matyé youn bagay kinmbé.

Egzanmp yo:

Youn rézin ginyin   Youn pèr soulyé atlètik ginyin
mas à 1 gram.   youn mas à 1 kiló.

mouyen (mean) Total la à valèr nan youn group dóné divisé par nouméró a de valèr.

Egzanmp:

27   27   27   29   32   33   36   38   42   43   62

total: 396

nouméró valèr: 11

midyan: $396 \div 11 = 36$

éreur mézirman (measurement error)

Anbalanman na nan youn mézirman. Pi gró éreur possib sé oun demi piti younit.

Egzanmp:

Paskè oun pous younit pi ptit, pi gró éreur $\frac{1}{2}$ pous. Donk tay aktoual mitan $5'5\frac{1}{2}"$ é $5'6\frac{1}{2}"$.

5' 6"

mézir pour tandans santral (measure of central tendency)

Oun valèr ka'p rezoumé youn group doné noumérikal.

Egzanmp:

Mouyen, midyan, é mód, yo mezirman komen pour tandans santral.

27 27 27 29 32 33 36 38 42 43 62

mod   midyan

Mouyen = 396 ÷ 11 = 36

midyan (median)

Valèr mitan na pour youn group doné si ou mèté nouméró yo nan sékans.

Egzanmp:

27 27 27 29 32 33 36 38 42 43 62

midyan

matèmatik mental (mental math)

Lé ou'ap fé kalkoulasyon nan tet ou, sans youn kréyon é papyé oubyin youn kalkoulateur.

Egzanmp:

2000 × 30

3 zéró + 1 zéró = 4 zéró

Pansé: 2 × 3 = 6, meté 4 zéró an plous

2000 × 30 = 60,000

mèt (meter)

Younit basik pour longèr nan sistem metrik.

Egzanmp:

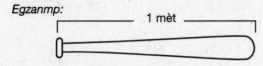

1 mèt

Bat bèzból la preskè 1 mèt.

sistem metrik (metric system)

Youn sistem baze sou mèt, gram, é lit la.

Egzanmp yo:

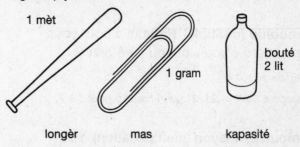

1 mèt

1 gram

bouté 2 lit

longèr   mas   kapasité

mid pouint (midpoint)

Pouint la ki divisé youn segman nan dou segman plous piti segman égal.

Egzanmp: C mid pouint na pour $\overline{AB}$.

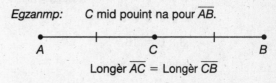

A   C   B

Longèr $\overline{AC}$ = Longèr $\overline{CB}$

mil (mile)

Younit nan sistem nórmal égal à 5,280 pyé.

Egzanmp:

Oun mil distans na ou kakpab marshé apré 15 à 20 minout ou kouri apré 10 minout.

mili- (milli-)

Youn préfiks pour $\frac{1}{1000}$.

Egzanmp: 1 milimèt = $\frac{1}{1000}$ mèt

nouméró melanjé (mixed number)

Youn nouméró konmpozé de youn nouméró antyé é youn fraksyon.

Egzanmp yo: $3\frac{1}{2}$ $1\frac{3}{4}$ $13\frac{3}{8}$

mod (mode)

Valèr ki ou jouin pi souvan nan youn group doné.

Egzanmp:

27 27 27 29 32 33 36 38 42 43 62

Pour group doné isit 27 mod la.

monòmyal (monomial) Youn egspresyon ajèbrik ki ginyin oun térm egzakteman.

Egzanmp yo: $2x^2$ $5y$ x^3 -3

moultip (multiple) Prodoui a pour youn nouméró é youn lót nouméró antyé.

Egzanmp:

Depoui $3 \times 7 = 21$, 21 youn moultip pour 3 é 7.

moultiplikasyon (multiplication) Youn prósèdour ki kounmbiné dou nouméró ki rèlé fakteur, à youn nouméró, ki rèlé prodoui a.

Egzanmp:

3 ranjé à 6

$$3 \times 6 = 18$$
fakteur   prodoui

própritiyé moultiplikasyon (multiplication property) Si A é B evanman inividoual, alor próbabilité a pour pèr ap pasé montré par $P(A$ é $B) = P(A) \times P(B)$. $P(A$ é $B) = P(A) \times P(B)$.

Egzanmp:

1yém lansé: $P(\text{rouj}) = \frac{1}{4}$

2yém lansé: $P(\text{rouj}) = \frac{1}{4}$

1yém é 2yém lansé: $P(\text{rouj é rouj}) = \frac{1}{4} \times \frac{1}{4} = \frac{1}{16}$

Própritiyé de Égalité Mouliplikasyon (Multiplication Property of Equality) Si $a = b$, alor $ac = bc$.

Egzanmp:

Nan lin sèkondèr an ba, 2 moultipliyé à toulèdé bó ékouézyon na.

$$\text{Si} \qquad \frac{1}{2}y = 4$$

$$\text{alor} \qquad \mathbf{2} \times \frac{1}{2}y = \mathbf{2} \times 4$$

moultiplikativ invèrs (multiplicative inverse) Si prodoui pour dou nouméró sé 1, shak nouméró moultiplikativ invèrs pour lot la.

Egzanmp:

$\frac{1}{6}$ yo yé moultiplikativ invèrs depoui $\frac{1}{6} \times 6 = 1$.

egsklousif moutouèlman (mutually exclusive) Si evenman A oubyin B pasé, alor lot la pa kapab pasé.

Egzanmp yo:

Si tanmperatour déró 90°, li pa'p fé lanéj.

Si youn póligon giyin 3 bó sèlman, li pa kapab ginyin 4 ang.

nouméró negatif (negative numbers) Nouméró mouens de zéró.

Egzanmp:

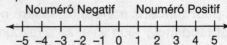

Nouméró Negatif   Nouméró Positif

rélasyon negatif (negative relationship) Dou group doné ginyin youn rélasyon negatif le valèr doné yo grandi kom valèr yo pour lot diminyé.

Egzanmp:

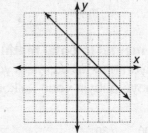

pant negatif (negative slope) Pant la pour youn lin k'ap shiré an ba.

Egzanmp:

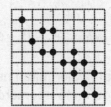

rasin karé negatif (negative square root) Opósé à rasin karè prinsipal pour youn nouméró.

Egzanmp:

rasin karé prinsipal: rasin Karé negatif:

$$\sqrt{25} = 5 \qquad\qquad -\sqrt{25} = -5$$

filé (net) Youn patouan plat ki ou kapab pilyé pour fé youn figour toua-dimasyonal kom youn prizm.

Egzanmp:

Filé pour prizm pentagonal   Prizm pentagonal

nónagon (nonagon) Youn póligon ak 9 bó.

Egzanmp yo:

ékouézyon linyar (nonlinear equation) Youn ékouézyon nan ki grafik li youn koub é pa youn lin.

Egzanmp:

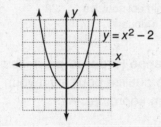

$y = x^2 - 2$

fonksyon nonlinyar (nonlinear function) Youn fonksyon nan ki grafik li pa youn li toudouat parskè shanj égal nan x pa rézoulté nan shanj égal nan y.

Egzanmp yo:

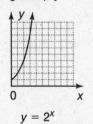 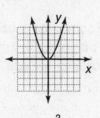 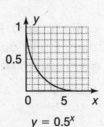

$y = 2^x$ $y = x^2$ $y = 0.5^x$

pa de rélasyon (no relationship) Dou group doné pa gin rélasyon si li pa egzisté youn rélasyon pózitif ou negatif.

Egzanmp:

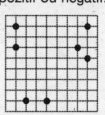

lin nouméró (number line) Youn lin ki montré nouméró nan sékans.

Egzanmp yo:

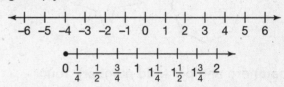

fórm nouméró-mo (number-word form) Youn mouyen pour ékri youn nouméró nan sékans.

Egzanmp yo: 45 trilyon   9 mil

nouméral (numeral) Youn sinmbol pour youn nouméró.

Egzanmp yo: 7   58   234

noumérateur (numerator) Nouméró an ro a nan youn fraksyon ki di konmbyin pyès pour antyé a ya'p rélé.

Egzanmp:

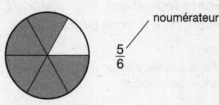

noumérateur

$\dfrac{5}{6}$

ang obtous (obtuse angle) Youn ang ki méziré plous de 90° mouens de 180°.

Egzanmp yo:

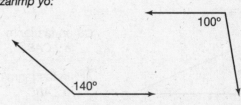

100°

140°

triang obtous (obtuse triangle) Youn triang ak youn ang obtous.

Egzanmp yo:

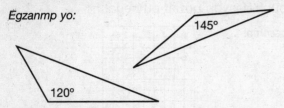

óktagon (octagon) Youn póligon avek 8 bó.

Egzanmp yo:

nouméró anmpér (odd number) Youn nouméró antyé ki gin 1, 3, 5, 7, ou 9 nan plas oun.

Egzanmp yo:

43   225   999   8,007

kót (odds) Próporsyon na pour konmbyin mouyen youn evanman kapab pasé à konmbyin mouyen li pa kapab.

Egzanmp:

Kót pour roulé youn 3: 1 à 5

Kót pour pa roule youn 3: 5 à 1

prósédour (operation) Youn mètod matematik pour fé youn bagay.

Egzanmp yo:

Kat prosédour basik: adisyon, soustraksyon, moultiplikasyon, divisyon.

janm an fas (opposite leg) Pour youn ang aygou nan youn triang douat, janm la an fas ang la.

Egzanmp:

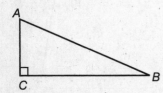

$\overline{CB}$ an fas janm à ∠CAB.

$\overline{AC}$ an fas janm à ∠ABC.

nouméró an fas (opposite numbers) Nouméró ki mem ditans nan youn lin noumèró à zéró min an fas yo.

Egzanmp:

7 é −7 an fas yo mem.

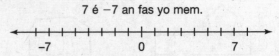

sékans à prósèdour (order of operations) Reg yo ki di ki sékans pour fé pósedour yo: (1) sanmplifiyé parantèsis intèryeur (2) sanmplifiyé egspózant (3) moulitpilyé épi divisé à gósh à douat (4) adisyonin épi soutriyé à gósh á douat.

Egzanmp:

Évaluoué $2x^2 + 4(x − 2)$ pour $x = 3$.

(1) sanmplifiyé parantèsis intèryeur	$2 \cdot 3^2 + 4(3 − 2)$ $2 \cdot 3^2 + 4(1)$
(2) sanmplifiyé egspózant	$2 \cdot 9 + 4$
(3) moulitpilyé épi divisé à gósh à douat	$18 + 4$
(4) adisyonin épi soutriyé à gósh á douat	22

pèr sékansé (ordered pair) Youn pèr nouméró outilizé pour jouin youn pouint sou youn plèn kóordinat.

Egzanmp:

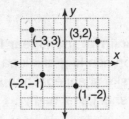

orijin (origin) Pouint zéró a nan youin nouméró lin ou pouint (0, 0) kote aks la pour youn sistem kóordinat kouazé.

Egzanmp yo:

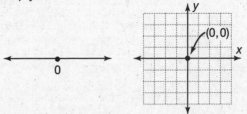

désin ortógrafik (orthographic drawing)
Youn désin à youn objet ka'p sévi vou dévan, bó, é tet yo.

Egzanmp:

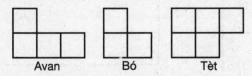

Avan   Bó   Tèt

ons (ounce) Youn younit poua nan sistem mézirman nórmal.

Egzanmp:

 Youn lèt pézé preskè oun ons.

rézoult (outcome) Oun mouyen nan ki youn ezpérimen kapab fini.

Egzanmp:

Rézoult pour voltijé dou kouin:

kouin 1	kouin 2
tèt	laké
tèt	tèt
laké	tèt
laké	laké

Yo gin 4 rézoult. Youn rézoult sé tèt, tèt.

nouméró déró (outlier) Youn valèr egstrèm nan youn group doné ki sèparé plous de lot valèr.

Egzanmp:

27   27   27   29   32   33   36   38   42   43   62
                                                         ↑
                                                nouméró déró

parabóla (parabola) Youn koub fórmé kom youn U oubyin youn koub kom youn U tet an ba ki grafik la pour youn fonksyon.

Egzanmp yo:

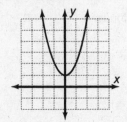

paralel (parallel) Dou lin, segman ou douat de fazó ka pa kouazé li fé fé diferans ki distans yo allé.

Egzanmp yo:

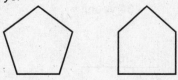

paralelógram (parallelogram) Youn figour avek kat bó nan ki bó an fas paralel é égal.

Egzanmp yo:

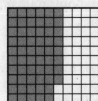

pentagon (pentagon) Youn póligon ak 5 bó.

Egzanmp yo:

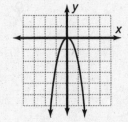

poursan (percent) Youn próporsyon ki konmparé youn nouméró avek 100.

Egzanmp:

$$\frac{58}{100} = 0.58 = 58\%$$

poursan shanj (percent change) Total la pour youn shanj, ranjé, ou diminyé moultipliyé par tótal original la, é nou di kom poursan à tótal orijinal.

Egzanmp yo:

Jouin poursan shanj si $1500 invèté épi $75 ginyin nan interet.

$\frac{75}{1500} = 0.05 = 5\%$ $75 youn 5% ranjé.

Jouin poursan shanj si youn bagay ki kouté $50 vand pour mouens $10.

$\frac{10}{50} = 0.20 = 20\%$ Mouens $10 youn 20% diminyé.

poursan diminyé (percent decrease) Si youn tótal diminyé nou di li kom youn poursan à tótal orijinal. Régardé *poursan shanj*.

poursan ranjé (percent increase) Si youn tótal ranjé nou di li kom youn poursan à tótal orijinal. Régardé *poursan shanj*.

karé parfet (perfect square) Youn karé pour youn nouméró antyé.

Egzanmp yo:

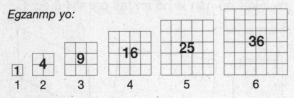

périmet (perimeter) Distans na outou youn figour déró.

Egzanmp: $P = 5 + 2 + 6 + 4 + 11 + 6$
$= 34$ younit

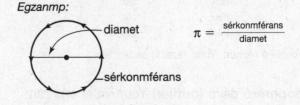

pérmoutasyon (permutation) Youn aranjman de bagay yo nan ki sékans zinmportan.

Egzanmp:

Nou va shouazi youn étoudyan nan group sa pour prezidan, épi nou va shouazi oun pour vis prezidan: Wendy, Alex, Carlos. Pérmoutasyon posib yo:

Wendy—prezidan, Alex—vic presidan
Wendy—prezidan, Carlos—vis presidan
Alex—prezidan, Wendy—vis presidan
Alex—prezidan, Carlos—vis presidan
Carlos—prezidan, Wendy—vis presidan
Carlos—prezidan, Alex—vis presidan

Nót: Shak egzanmp an ro a youn diféran pérmoutasyon.

pérpandikoular (perpendicular) Lin, douat de fazó, ou segman lin yo ki kouazé à ang douat.

Egzanmp yo:

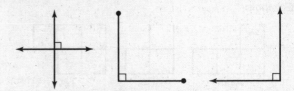

bisektris pérpandikoular (perpendicular bisector) Lin, douat de fazó, ou segman lin yo ki kouazé youn segman à mid pouint li épi li pérpandikoular à li.

Egzanmp:

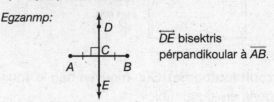

$\overleftrightarrow{DE}$ bisektris pérpandikoular à $\overline{AB}$.

pi (pi (π)) Próporsyon na pour youn sérkonmférans pour youn sérk à diamet li: 3.14159265...

Egzanmp:

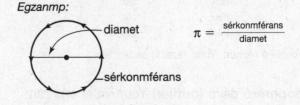

$$\pi = \frac{\text{sérkonmférans}}{\text{diamet}}$$

piktógram (pictograph) Youn grafik ka'p outilizé simbol pour rèprézanté doné.

Egzanmp:

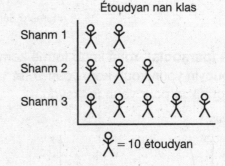

Étoudyan nan klas

Shanm 1

Shanm 2

Shanm 3

$\overset{\curlywedge}{\lambda}$ = 10 étoudyan

valèr plas (place value) Valèr a nou bay à plas la koté youn shif rèté.

Egzanmp:

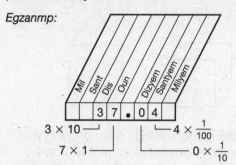

3×10 —
7×1 —
$4 \times \frac{1}{100}$
$0 \times \frac{1}{10}$

plèn (plane) Youn anlé plat ki egstandé ajamé.

Egzanmp:

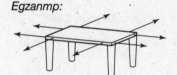

Pour vizoulizé youn plèn, pansé à egstandé youn soufas tab à tout dirèksyon.

pouint simètri (point symmetry) Youn figour ginyin pouint simètri si li sanmblé sans shanj apré youn rótasyon à 180° rótasyon.

Egzanmp:

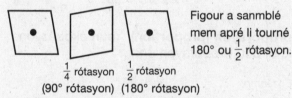

$\frac{1}{4}$ rótasyon
(90° rótasyon)

$\frac{1}{2}$ rótasyon
(180° rótasyon)

Figour a sanmblé mem apré li tourné 180° ou $\frac{1}{2}$ rótasyon.

póligon (polygon) Youn figour fèrmé ki fé ak segman lin.

Egzanmp yo:

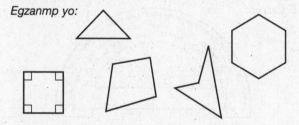

póliyèdron (polyhedron) Youn solid nan ki fig póligon yo.

Egzanmp yo:

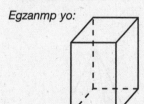

pólinómyal (polinomial) Youn egspresyon aljebrik ki tótal pour youn ou plous térm.

Egzanmp yo: $x^2 + 2x - 3$ $5y - 15$

popoulasyon (population) Kólètsyon na de tout bagay pour youn étoud.

Egzanmp:

Yo té ékri tout 1000 nom pour manmb yo nan youn kloub à kart épi yo té bat kart. Aklor yo shuoazi 100 kart épi yo tèléfoné manmb sa yo pour youn étoud. Popoulasyon na pour étoud la sé tout 1000 manmb nan kloub.

nouméró pózitif (positive numbers) Nouméró pi gro kom zéró.

Egzanmp:

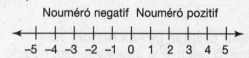

Nouméró negatif   Nouméró pozitif

rélasyon pozitif (positive relationship) Dou group doné ginyin youn relásyon pozitif si valèr doné yo ranjé ansanmb ou diminyé ansanmb.

Egzanmp:

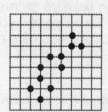

pant pozitif (positive slope) Pant la pour youn lin ka'p pant an ro a.

Egzanmp:

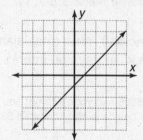

pouad (pound) Youn younit nan sistem nórmal pour mézirman ki égal 16 ons.

Egzanmp:

Diri
1 pouad

pouvoua (power) Youn egspózant oubyin nouméró a ki rézoulté le youn baz ranjé à egspózant na.

Egzanmp:

$$16 = 2^4$$ 2 ranjé à pouvoua 4yèm na.

16 sé 4yèm pouvoua pour 2.

présizyon (precision) Koman egzaktèman youn mézirman, détèrminé par younit à mézir.

Egzanmp:

Youn pi piti younit à mezir, pous par egzanmp, ginyin plous présizyon kom youn pi gró younit à mézir, pyé par egzanmp.

5'1" 61"

fakteur prèmyé (prime factor) Youn nouméró prèmyé ki divisé youn lot nouméró antyé sans ki'te youn rest.

Egzanmp:

5 youn fakteur prèmyé pour 35, pakskè 35 ÷ 5 = 7.

fakteurizasyon prèmyé (prime factorization) Le ou'ap ékri youn nouméró kom youn prodoui à nouméró prèmyé.

Egzanmp: $$70 = 2 \times 5 \times 7$$

nouméró prèmyé (prime number) Youn nouméró antyé pi gró kom 1 nan ki fakteur yo 1 é li mem.

Egzanmp:

Prèmyé yo komansé avek 2, 3, 5, 7, 11, ...

kapital (principal) Youn tótal lajan dépósé ou prèté, an ki yo payé ou intérèt.

Egzanmp:

Dave dépósé $300 nan youn konmpt sou livret. Apré youn ané balans la nan konmpt li $315. $300 kapital la.

rasin karé prinsipal (principal square root) Rasin karé pósitif pour youn no[uméró]().

Egzanmp:

rasin karé prinsipal   rasin karé negatif

$\sqrt{25} = 5$ $-\sqrt{25} = -5$

prizm (prism) Youn poilyèdron nan ki baz yo égal é paralel.

Egzanmp:

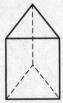

próbabilité (probability) Youn próporsyon pour konmbyin posibilité youn evenman kapab pasé à tótal nouméró pour rézoult ki possib.

Egzanmp:

Próbabilté a pour roulé youn 3 sé $\frac{1}{6}$.

Próbabilté a pour pa roulé youn 3 sé $\frac{5}{6}$.

prodoui (product) Rezoult la apré ou moultipliyé dou ou plous nouméró.

Egzanmp:

prodoui

$$2 \times 3 \times 5 = 30$$

próporsyon (proportion) Youn ékouézyon ki di dou próporsyon égal.

Egzanmp: $\frac{12}{34} = \frac{6}{17}$

raporteur (protractor) Youn zouti pour méziré ang.

Egzanmp:

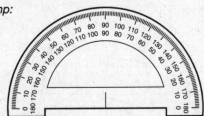

piramid (pyramid) Youn solid ak youn baz é nan ki lot bó yo triang ki randévou a oun pouint selman.

Egzanmp yo:

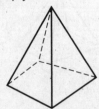
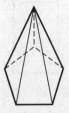

Térom Pythagorean (Pythagorean Theorem) Nan youn triang douat nan ki c longèr a à ipotenous épi a é b longèr pour janm yo, $a^2 + b^2 = c^2$.

Egzanmp:

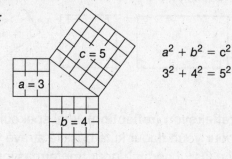

$a^2 + b^2 = c^2$
$3^2 + 4^2 = 5^2$

$c = 5$
$a = 3$
$b = 4$

kadrant (quadrants) Arya kat la ki détèrminé par aks yo nan youn plén kóordinat.

Egzanmp:

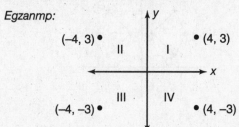

$(-4, 3)$ • II   I • $(4, 3)$

$(-4, -3)$ • III   IV • $(4, -3)$

ékouézyon kadratik (quadratic equation) Youn ékouézyon avek youn tèrm karé kom x^2.

Egzanmp yo:

$$y = x^2 + 3x - 12 \qquad y = 2x^2 + 7$$

fonksyon kadratik (quadratic function) Youn fonksyon nan ki pi ró pouvoua pour x sé 2. Grafik la pour youn fonksyon kadratik youn parbaból.

Egzanmp:

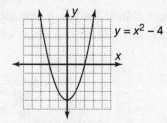

$y = x^2 - 4$

kadrilateral (quadrilateral) Youn póligon ak 4 bó.

Egzanmp yo:

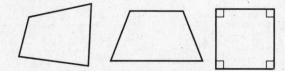

kart (quart) Youn younit pour vólounm nan sistem mézirman nórmal.

Egzanmp:

Lèt   Oun kart lèt

kartyé (quartile) Youn noumèró ki divisé youn group doné nan kartyé égal.

Egzanmp:

27 27 27 29 32 33 36 38 42 43 62

kartyé   midyan   kartyé
pi ba   an ro a

27, 33, é 42 sé toua kartyé pour group nouméró sa a.

kuósyent (quotient) Rezoult apré divisé youn nouméró par youn lot.

Egzanmp:

kuósyent
$8 \div 4 = 2$

sin radikal $\sqrt{}$ (radical sign) Pour rèprézanté rasin karé pour youn nouméró.

Egzanmp: $\sqrt{49} = 7$

radyous (radius) Youn lin ki orijiné nan sant la nan sérk à kek pouint sou sérk la.

Egzanmp:

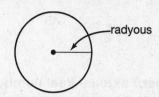

radyous

éshantiyon aza (random sample) Youn échantiyon yo shouazi alor ki shak manmb nan popoulasyon ginyin shans égal pour inklouzyon.

Egzanmp:

Tout 1000 nom manmb pour youn kloub yo té mètè sou kart, épi yo bat kart. Alor yo té shouazi 100 kart, épi yo fé youn étoud avek manmb sa yo par tèléfoné. Tout manmb nan kloub la té gin youn shans égal pour tèléfoné, donk sa youn éshantiyon aza.

póté (range) Difèrans la mitan valèr pi ró é pi ba nan groupe doné.

Egzamp:

27 27 27 29 32 33 36 38 42 43 62

Póté a 62 − 27 = 35.

tó (rate) Youn próporsyon ka'p montré koman kantité yo ak younit difèran gin rélasyon.

Egzanmp yo: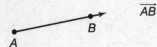

próporsyon (ratio) Youn konmparison pour dou kantité, nou souvan ékri kom youn fraksyon.

Egzanmp yo: $\frac{2}{1}$ 2 à 1   2:1

nouméró rasyonel (rational number) Youn nouméró ou kapab ékri kom youn próporsyon pou dou antyé. Antyé, fraksyon, é anmpil desimal nouméró rasyonel.

Egzanmp yo:

Antyé	Fraksyon	Desimal
$-27 = \frac{-27}{1}$	$\frac{7}{8}$	$3.1 = 3\frac{1}{10} = \frac{31}{10}$

douat de fazó (ray) Youn segman pour youn li ki gin oun pouint bout épi egstandé ajamé à lot dirèksyon. Youn douat a fazó rèlé par pouint bout li prèmyé.

Egzanmp:

$\overrightarrow{AB}$

nouméró aktoual (real numbers) Tout nouméró rasyonel é irasyonel.

Egzanmp yo:

-27 $\frac{1}{2}$ 3.1

$\sqrt{5}$ π $-\sqrt{\frac{1}{2}}$

résiprók (reciprocals) Dou nouméró ki gin prodoui 1.

Egzanmp:

$\frac{3}{5}$ é $\frac{5}{3}$ résiprók depoui $\frac{3}{5} \cdot \frac{5}{3} = 1$.

rektang (rectangle) Youn parlelógram avek bó anfas ki gin mem longèr é tout ang méziré 90°.

Egzanmp yo:

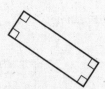

réfleksyon (reflection) Imaj spekoulér a pour youn figour ki té baskilé atravé youn lin. Ósi, li nom na pour tranfórmasyon na ki baskilé figour a atravé lin na.

Egzanmp:

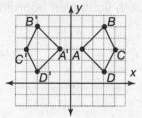

póligon regoulèr (regular polygon) Youn polygon nan ki tout bó é ang égal.

Egzanmp yo:

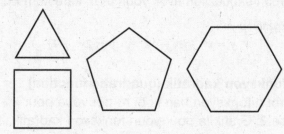

pózisyon relatif (relative position) Youn lókasyon nan rélasyon à youn lot bagay.

Egzanmp:

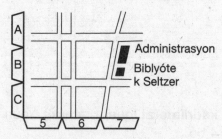

Administrasyon na pre à Biblyótek Seltzer.

rest (remainder) Nouméró a ki pi mouens de divisór a ki rèté apré divizyon fini.

Egzanmp:

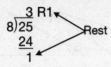

desimal rèpété (repeating decimal) Youn desimal avek youn shif ou group shif a douat pouint desimal la.

Egzanmp yo: $0.\overline{6}$ $0.\overline{123}$ $2.\overline{18}$

ronmbus (rhombus) Youn paralelógram avek kat bó égal.

Egzanmp yo:

ang douat (right angle) Youn ang ki méziré 90°.

Egzanmp:

triang douat (right triangle) Youn triang avek oun ang douat.

Egzanmp yo:

óteur (rise) Pour youn lin sou youn grafik, sé shanj vértik pour youn shanj órizontal.

Egzanmp:

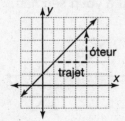

rótasyon (rotation) Imaj la pour youn figour ki yo té tourné, kom sou youn rou. Ósi, nom na pour transfórmasyon na ki tourné figour a.

Egzanmp:

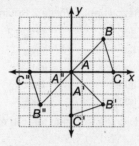

simètri rótasyonal (rotational symmetry) Youn figour ginyin simètri rótasyonal si ou kapab tourné li mouens de youn sérk konmplet épi kadré imaj orijinal li.

Egzanmp yo:

 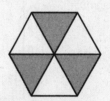

Shak figour ginyin simètri rótasyonal.

arondi (rounding) Estimasyon pour youn nouméró à youn valèr plas ki deklaré.

Egzanmp:

2153 arondi à	
pi pré sant: 2200	pi pré dis: 2150

trajet (run) Pour youn lin sou youn grafik, sé shanj órizontal outilizé pour jouin shanj vértikal.

Egzanmp:

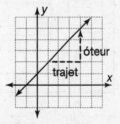

anshantiyon (sample) Youn group doné outilizé pour prèdi koman youn sitousayon partikoular petet va pasé.

Egzanmp:

Tout 1000 nom manmb pour youn kloub yo té mèté sou kart, épi yo bat kart. Alor yo té shouazi 100 kart, épi yo fé youn étoud avek manmb sa yo par tèléfoné. Anshantiyon sé 100 manmb ki partispé nan étoud la.

éspas anshantiyon (sample space) Group la pour tout rézoult pósib pour youn egspériman.

Egzanmp:

Rézoult pour Vóltijé 2 Kouin.

kouin 1	kouin 2
tèt	laké
tèt	tèt
laké	tèt
laké	laké

Éspas anshantiyon sé tèt, laké; tèt, tèt; épi laké, laké.

èshel (grafikal) (scale (graphical)) Mark yo ki espasé églman sou aks vértikal sou youn grafik bar ou grafik lin, épi li outilizè pour méziré roté pour bar yo.

Egzanmp:

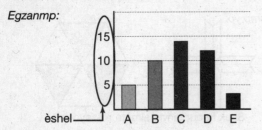

èshel (nan désin èshel) (scale (in scale drawings)) Próporsyon pour mézirman yo nan youn désin à èshel à mézirman you nan ojet aktoual. Regardé *désin à éshel.*

désin à èshel (scale drawing) Youn désin ki anmployé youn èshel pour fé youn désin pi gro ou pi piti pour youn objet.

Egzanmp:

Désin à èshel pour salon

Èshel: 0.1 pous = 1 pyé

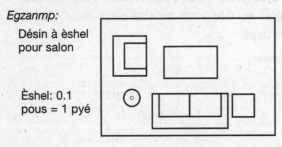

fakteur èshel (scale factor) Próporsyon na ki sèrvi pour grandi ou redoui figour similar.

Egzanmp:

$\frac{10}{5} = 2$

$\frac{6}{3} = 2$

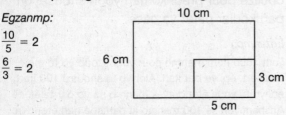

Fakteur èshel la 2 pour grandiman.

---

triang skalèn (scalene triangle) Youn triang nan ki bó gin longèr difèran.

Egzanmp yo:

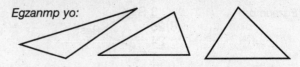

plan gayé (scatterplot) Youn grafik ka'p sèrvi doné valèr doné yo nan pér kom pouint pour montré rèlasyon pour group doné yo.

Egzanmp:

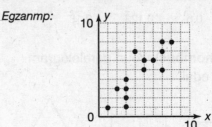

nótasyon siantifik (scientific notation) Youn nouméró ékri kom youn dèsimal pi gro ou égal à 1 épi mouens de 10, moultipliyé par pouvoua 10.

Egzanmp: $350{,}000 = 3.5 \times 10^5$

sekteur (sector) Youn yé à youn sérk ki an form de kouin épi ki sérvi nan youn grafik sérk pour móntré koman parti yo pour youn group doné mèté avek group antyé a.

Egzanmp yo:

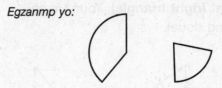

segman (segment) Régarde *segman lin.*

bisektris segman (segment bisector) Youn lin, douat de fazó, ou segman ki pasé nan mid pouint à youn segman.

Egzanmp:

$\overrightarrow{DE}$ bisekté $\overline{AB}$ à C.

sékans (sequence) Youn dispózisyon nouméró ki fé youn patouan.

Egzanmp yo:

sékans matèmatik

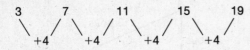

sékans jéómetrik

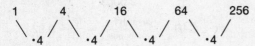

bó (side) Shak douat de fazó ka'p fórmé youn ang. Ósi, sègman lin yo ki fé youn póligon.

Egzanmp yo:

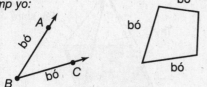

Bó-Ang-Ang (Side-Angle-Angle (SAA)) Youn reg ki sèrvi pour détèrminé si triang yo égal par konmparé parti ki mem.

Egzanmp:

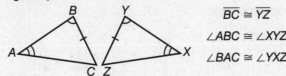

$\overline{BC} \cong \overline{YZ}$

$\angle ABC \cong \angle XYZ$

$\angle BAC \cong \angle YXZ$

$\triangle ABC \cong \triangle XYZ$ nan reg SAA.

Bó-Ang-Bó (Side-Angle-Side (SAS)) Youn reg ki sèrvi pour détèrminé si triang yo égal par konmparé parti ki mem.

Egzanmp:

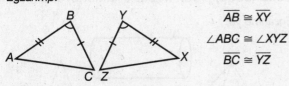

$\overline{AB} \cong \overline{XY}$

$\angle ABC \cong \angle XYZ$

$\overline{BC} \cong \overline{YZ}$

$\triangle ABC \cong \triangle XYZ$ nan reg SAS.

Bó-Bó-Bó (Side-Side-Side (SSS)) Youn reg ki sèrvi pour détèrminé si triang yo égal par konmparé parti ki mem.

Egzanmp:

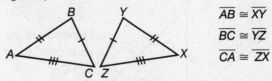

$\overline{AB} \cong \overline{XY}$

$\overline{BC} \cong \overline{YZ}$

$\overline{CA} \cong \overline{ZX}$

$\triangle ABC \cong \triangle XYZ$ nan reg SSS.

shif signifikan (significant digits) Nan youn kantité ki té méziré, yo shif ki rèprésanté mézirman aktouel.

Egzanmp yo:

380.6700   Tout shif signifkan.

0.0038   3 é 8 signifikan, min petet pa mem dimansyon.

similar (similar) Li ginyin mem fórm min petet pa mem dimansyon.

Egzanmp yo:

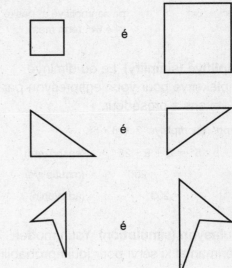

próporsyon simlilar (similarity ratio)
Próporsyon na pour bó longèr kórespondan sou figour similar.

Egzanmp:

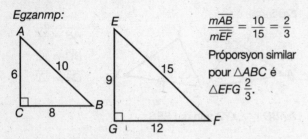

$$\frac{m\overline{AB}}{m\overline{EF}} = \frac{10}{15} = \frac{2}{3}$$

Próporsyon similar pour $\triangle ABC$ é $\triangle EFG$ $\frac{2}{3}$.

interet sanmp (simple interest)
Interet ki bazé sou kapital selman.

Egzanmp: Ramon invèté $240 nan youn kompt ki bay li 6% interet par ané pour 5 ané.

Li va rèsérvoua $240 \cdot 0.06 \cdot 5 = 72$; $72 nan interet apré 5 ané.

sanmplifiyé a (simplified)
Youn polinómyal ki ginyin pa tèrm mem yo.

Egzanmp:

$4x^4 + x^3 + x^2 - 8$ sanmplifiyé a

$4x^4 + x^2 + 6x^2 - 8$ pa sanmplifiyé a, paskè x^2 é $6x^2$ térm mem.

sanmplifiyé (simplify)
Le ou diminyé konmpleksityé pour youn egspresyon par mèté sékans à prósédour.

Egzanmp: sanmplifiyé $3 + 8 \cdot 5^2$.

$3 + 8 \cdot 5^2 = 3 + 8 \cdot 25$ (egspózant)

$= 3 + 200$ (moutipliyé)

$= 203$ (adisyonin)

simoulasyon (simulation)
Youn modèl egspérimantal ki sérvi pour jouin próbabilité.

Egzanmp:

Youn jouèr bèzból frapé ból .250. Pour simoulé koman jouèr sa petet frapé ból, yo lansé youn aygoui à lanseur. Simoulasyon na kapab di konmbyin tanmp jouèr ta frapé 2 nan sékans ou byin 3 nan sékans.

sinus (sine)
Pour youn ang aygou *x* nan youn triang douat , sinus la pour *x*, oubyin sin(*x*) sé próporsyon na $\frac{\text{janm an fas}}{\text{ipotenous}}$.

Egzanmp:

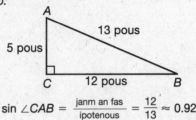

$$\sin \angle CAB = \frac{\text{janm an fas}}{\text{ipotenous}} = \frac{12}{13} \approx 0.92$$

tay shiré (slant height)
Nan youn piramid distance perpandikoular à oun rébó nan baz à vèrteks.

Egzanmp:

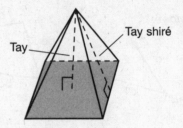

bais (slide)
Regardé *tradoukson*.

inklinasyon (slope)
Pour youn lin soun youn grafik, distans la de youn rébó nana baz à vèrteks.

Egzanmp:

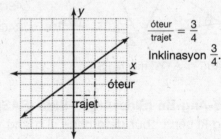

$$\frac{\text{óteur}}{\text{trajet}} = \frac{3}{4}$$

Inklinasyon $\frac{3}{4}$.

solid (solid)
Youn figour 3-dimansyonal.

Egzanmp yo:

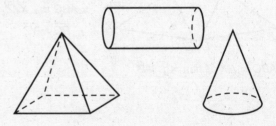

sólousyon yo pour youn ékouézyon ou inégalité (solutions of an equation or inequality) Valèr yo pour youn varyab ki fé vré youn ékouézyon oubyin inégalité.

Egzanmp yo:

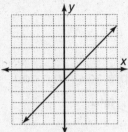

Lin na représanté solousyon à
$y = x - 1$.

Arya gri représanté la à $y > x - 1$.

soulousyon you pour youn sistem (solution of a system) Ranmplasman varyab la k'ap fé vré tout ékouézyon nan youn sistem.

Egzanmp:
$$y = x + 4$$
$$y = 3x - 6$$

Pér la nan sékans (5, 9) rézolvé ékouézyon touledé. Donk, (5, 9) youn rézólousyon pour sistem na.

rézolvé (solve) Pour jouin rézólousyon yo pour youn ékouézyon oubyin inégalité.

Egzanmp: Rézolvé $x + 6 = 13$.
$$x + 6 = 13$$
$$x + 6 + (-6) = 13 + (-6)$$
$$x + 0 = 7$$
$$x = 7$$

sfér (sphere) Youn solid nan ki tout pouint mem distans à sant.

Egzanmp:

karé (square) Youn kadrilateral avek tout bó mem longèr épi tout ang méziré 90°.

Egzanmp:

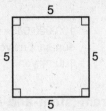

karé (squared) Ogmanté à pouvoua douzyem.

Egzanmp: 3 karé = 3^2.
$$3^2 = 3 \times 3 = 9$$

santimet karé (square centimeter) Arya nan youn karé bó yo ki mézire 1 santimet.

Egzanmp:

1 santimet karé

pous karé (square inch) Arya nan oun karé avek bó ki mézire 1 pous.

Egzanmp:

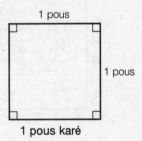

1 pous karé

rasin karé (square root) Rasin karé por *N* sé nouméró a ki si ou moulipiyé li par li mem bay *N*. Ósi, rasin karé a pour kek nouméró sé longèr a pour oun bó à youn karé avek youn arya égal pour kek nouméró.

Egzanmp:

$9 \times 9 = 81$, donk
9 rasin karé pour 81.

$9 = \sqrt{81}$

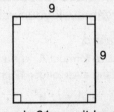

Arya la 81 younit karé.

fórm nórmal (standard form) Youn fason pour ékri youn nouméró avek shif yo.

Egzanmp:

Fórm nórmal: 100,000,000
Fórm mó: oun sant milyon
Form-nouméró-mó 100 milyon

bòk-é-fé diagram (stem-and-leaf diagram) Youn grafik pour doné ki sérvi shif yo á nouméró doné pour montré fòrm é distribousyon à group doné.

Egzanmp:

Diagram la montré group doné: 33, 34, 34, 35, 40, 41, 46, 51, 51, 52, 53, 55, 58.

Bòk	Fé				
3	3	4	4	5	
4	0	1	6		
5	1	1	2	3	5	8

fonksyon mash (step function) Youn fonksyon nan ki yo mèté règ diféran à valèr antré yo. Grafik la pour youn fonksyon mash konmpózé de pyés yo ki pa kónekté.

Egzanmp:

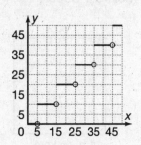

ang toudouat (straight angle) Youn ang ki méziré 180°.

Egzanmp:

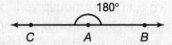

ranmplasé (substitute) À ranmplasé youn varyab avek youn valèr spesifik.

Egzanmp:

Outilizé fórmoul $A = l \cdot w$ pour jouin arya pour youn rektang avek longèr 12 cm é lajèr 8 cm.

$A = l \cdot w$

$A = 12 \cdot 8$ Ranmplasé valèr pour
$A = 96$ longèr è lajèr.

Arya 96 cm².

soustraksyon (subtraction) Youn prósédeur ki montré difèrans poue dou nouméró, oubyin konmbyin nouméró rèté ap're kek soustrèr.

Egzanmp: $12 - 5 = 7$

⊠⊠⊠⊠⊠
○○○○○
○○

tótal (sum) Rézoult la apré adisyonin dou ou plous nouméró.

Example: $30 + 18 = 48$ ← tótal

ang souplimantèr (supplementary angles) Dou ang ki mézirman fé tótal 180°.

Egzanmp:

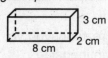

arya anlé (surface area (SA)) Total la pour arya pour shak figi à youn póliyèdron.

Egzanmp:

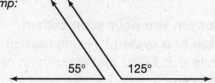

Dou figi 8 cm par 3 cm.
$A = b \cdot h = 8 \cdot 3 = 24 \text{ cm}^2$

Dou figi 8 cm par 2 cm.
$A = b \cdot h = 8 \cdot 2 = 16 \text{ cm}^2$

Dou figi 2 cm par 3 cm.
$A = b \cdot h = 2 \cdot 3 = 6 \text{ cm}^2$

Arya anlé la pour prizm rektangoular sé:

$SA = 2(24 + 16 + 6)$
$\quad\; = 92 \text{ cm}^2$

étoud (survey) Youn prósédour nan ki ou ranmasé é évalyoué infórmasyon.

Egzanmp:

Yo té fé youn étoud pour détèrminé ki èsport pi plous pópoular pour étoudyan.

simètri (symmetry) Regardé *simètri lin*, *simètri pouint*, é *simètri rótasyonal*.

sistem ékouézyon linyar (system of linear equations) Dou ou plous ékouézyon linyar ki ou kónsidèré ansanmb.

Egzanmp: $y = x + 3$
                $y = 4x - 15$

tab-T (T-table) Youn grafik tab ka'p montré valèr x é y pour youn ékouézyon.

Egzanmp:

$$y = 2x + 1$$

x	y
−2	−3
−1	−1
0	1
1	3
2	5

konmpt (tally) Youn rapor ka'p sèrvi mark konmpt pour youn tótal té fé nan youn étoud.

Egzanmp:

Mashin	Konmpt
ótó	١ЖT III
kamyonet	IIII
gró kamyonet	ЖT I
kamyon	ЖT
kamyonet	III

mark konmpt (tally marks) Mark yo pour organizé youn gró group doné. Shak mark di oun foua youn valèr vini nan group doné a.

Egzanmp:

I oun   ЖT sink

lin tanjant (tangent line) Youn lin ki toushé youn sérk à youn pouint selman.

Egzanmp yo:

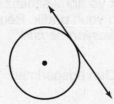

próporsyon tanjant (tangent ratio) Pour youn ang aygou x nan youn ang douat, tanjant la pour x, oubyin tan(x), se $\frac{\text{janm an fas}}{\text{janm kontigou}}$.

Egzanmp:

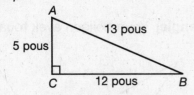

$$\tan \angle CAB = \frac{\text{janm an fas}}{\text{janm kontigou}} = \frac{12}{5} = 2.4$$

térm (term) Oun nouméró nan youn sékans. Ósi, youn pyès pólimóyal ki youn nouméró sinyé, youn varyab, oubyin youn nouméró moultipliyé par youn varyab ou varyab yo. Varyab yo kapab ginyin egspózant nouméró antyé.

Egzanmp yo:

sékans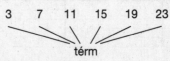

térm

pólinómyal $2x^3 - x^2 + 3x - 5$

térm

desimal tèrminé (terminating decimal) Youn desimal avek nouméró à shif fiksé.

Egzanmp yo: 3.5   0.599992   4.05

an mózéyik (tessellation) Youn patouan figour ki kouvri youn plèn sans èspas oubyin shevouaské.

Egzanmp yo:

próbabilité téyoretik (theoretical probability) Próporsyon na pour nouméró pósibilité nan ki youn evanman kapab pasé à nouméró tótal rèzoult.

Egzanmp:

$$\frac{\text{Pósibilité tótal pour lansé aygoui à blank}}{\text{Posibilité tótal}} = \frac{3}{6} = \frac{1}{2}$$

Depoui oun demi seksyon sou lanseur à blank, próbabilité téyoretik pour lansé aygoui à blank $\frac{1}{2}$.

transfórmasyon (transformation) Youn shanj nan dimansyon oubyin pózisyon pour youn figour.

Egzanmp:

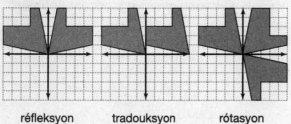

réfleksyon   tradouksyon   rótasyon

tradouksyon (translation) Imaj la pour youn figour ki té mèté nan youn pózisyon nouvó sans baskilé li oubyin tourné li.

Egzanmp:

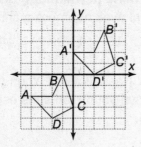

transvèrsal (transversal) Youn lin ki kouazé dou ou plous lot lin.

Egzanmp:

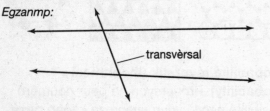

transvèrsal

trapèzoidal (trapezoid) Youn kadrilateral avek dou bó paralel.

Egzanmp yo:

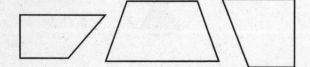

diagram pyé boua (tree diagram) Youn diagram ki ginyin bransh kom youn pyé boua ka'p montré tout rézoult pósib pour youn sitouasyon.

Egzanmp:

Voltijé 3 kouin:

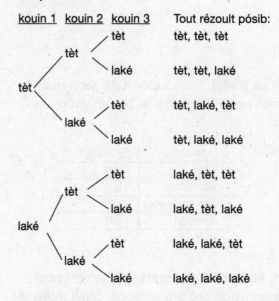

tandans (trend) Youn rélasyon pour dou group doné ki vini kom youn patouan nan youn grafik. Régardé *rélasyon pózitif, rélasyon negatif, pa de rélasyon*.

lin tandans (trend line) Youn lin nan ki souiv pouint yo apraksimatiz épi fórmé youn tandans nan youn grafik. Régardé *rélasyon pozitif épi rélasyon negatif*.

test (trial) Oun egspériman.

Egzanmp yo:

Oun roulé à koub nouméró   Oun voltijé kouin

triang (triangle) Youn póligon avek toua bó.

Egzanmp yo:

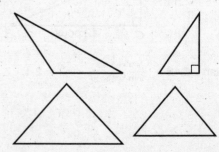

próporsyon trigónomètrik (trigonometric ratios) Próporsyon yo pour longèr bó nan youn triang douat nan rélasyon à mèzirman yo pour ang aygou nan triang la.

Egzanmp yo:

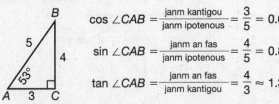

$$\cos \angle CAB = \frac{\text{janm kantigou}}{\text{janm ipotenous}} = \frac{3}{5} = 0.6$$

$$\sin \angle CAB = \frac{\text{janm an fas}}{\text{janm ipotenous}} = \frac{4}{5} = 0.8$$

$$\tan \angle CAB = \frac{\text{janm an fas}}{\text{janm kantigou}} = \frac{4}{3} \approx 1.3$$

trinómyal (trinomial) Youn póligon avek toua tèrm.

Egzanmp yo: $2x^3 - x^2 + 3x$ $3x^2 + 2x - 4$

tourné (turn) Régradé rótasyon.

jouet pa ékitab (unfair game) Youn jouet nan ki tout jouèr pa ginyin mem próbabilité pour ginyin.

Egzanmp:

Jouet pa ékitab: Yo roulé dou koub nouméró, épi you bay shak jouèr youn tótal 2 à 12. Shak jouèr va gin oun pouint si tótal li roulé. Depoui tótal 2 à 12 pa gin shans égal pour roulé, jouèr yo pa gin shans égal pour ginyin, donk jouet pa èkitab.

pri younit (unit price) Youn younit ka'p di konmbyin youn younit kouté.

Egzanmp yo:
$3.00 par pouad $5.75 par bouat

younit (unit) Oun bagay. Youn tó oubyin youn kantité outilizé kom youn étandard pour mézirman.

fraksyon younit (unit fraction) Youn fraksyon avek youn noumérateur 1.

Egzanmp yo: $\frac{1}{4}$ $\frac{1}{2}$ $\frac{1}{7}$

tó younit (unit rate) Youn tó nan ki nouméró sekond nan konmparison na sé 1.

Egzanmp yo: 25 galon par minout $\frac{55 \text{ mil}}{1 \text{ eur}}$

dénóminateur pa mem (unlike denominators) Dénóminateur ki difèran nan dou ou plous fraksyon.

Egzanmp:

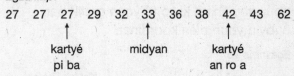

$$\frac{1}{2} \qquad \frac{2}{5} \qquad \frac{2}{9}$$

démóminateur pa mem

kartyé pi ró (upper quartile) Midyan na pour pi ró dèmi nan youn group doné.

Egzanmp:

27   27   27   29   32   33   36   38   42   43   62

kartyé pi ba   midyan   kartyé an ro a

varyab (variable) Youn kantité ki kapab shanjé, épi li souvan rèprésanté par youn lèt.

Egzanmp yo: $3x$ y $2t$

varyab

Diagram Venn (Venn diagram) Youn diagram ki sèrvi réjon pour montré rélasyon yo pour group bagay yo.

Egzanmp:

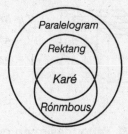

Paralelogram
Rektang
Karé
Rónmbous

vèrteks (vertex) Nan youn ang ou póligon, pouint la koté dou bó kouazé. Nan youn pólièdron, pouint la koté toua ou plous figi kouazé.

Egzanmp yo:

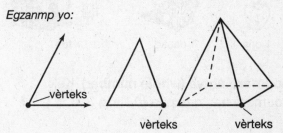

vèrteks   vèrteks   vèrteks

ang vèrtikal (vertical angles) Ang an fas à intèrseksyon à dou lin.

Egzanp:

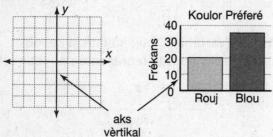

ang vèrtikal:
∠1 é ∠3
∠2 é ∠4

aks vèrtikal (vertical axis) Lin vèrtikal la pour dou lin an ki yo fé youn grafik bar oubyin youn plèn kóordinat.

Egzanp yo:

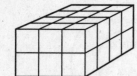

Koulor Préferé

aks vèrtikal

vólounm (volume) Total èpas ki òkoupé par youn solid.

Egzanp:

$V = lwh$
$V = 4 \cdot 3 \cdot 2$
$V = 24$ younit koubik

poua (weight) Youn mesirman pour fos fé osu youn bagay par gravité.

Egzanp yo:

1 ons   1 pouad   1 ton

nouméró antyé (whole number) Kek nouméró nan group la {0, 1, 2, 3, 4, ...}.

fórm mó (word form) Youn fason pour ékri youn nouméró avek mó selman.

Egzanp yo:

karant-sink trilyon   oun bilyon   sis

40 Haitian Creole

aks-x (x-axis) Aks órizontal la sou youn plèn kóordinat.

Egzanp:

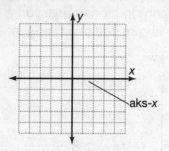

aks-x

kóordinat-x (x-coordinate) Premyé nouméró a nan youn pèr sékans.

Egzanp:

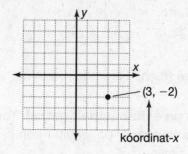

(3, −2)

kóordinat-x

intérsepsyon-x (x-intercept) Youn pouin koté grafik pour youn ékouézyon kouazé aks-x.

Egzanp:

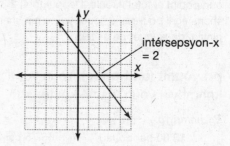

intérsepsyon-x = 2

aks-y (y-axis) Aks vèrtikal la sou youn plèn kóordinat.

Egzanp:

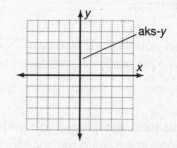

aks-y

kóordinat-y (y-coordinate) Noumèró
sekond nan youn pèr sékans.

Egzanmp:

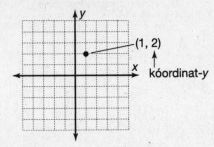

intérsepsyon-y (y-intercept) Youn pouint
koté grafik pour youn ékouézyon kouazé
aks-y.

Egzanmp:

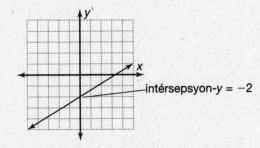

yad (yard) Youn younit nan sistem
mèzirman nórmal égal à 3 pyé.

Egzanmp:

Tay pour youn
biró preskè oun
yad.

pér zéró (zero pair) Youn nouméró é ópósit li.

Egzanmp yo: 7 é −7   23 é −23

**Própriyèté pour Adisyon Zèró (Zero
Property of Addition)** Total la pour youn
antyé épi aditif li sé zéró.

Egzanmp yo: $3 + (−3) = 0$
                    $−8 + 8 = 0$

Korean Glossary

Korean

절대위치 (absolute position) 좌표로 주어지는 위치.

보기:

B7은 셀저 도서관을 가르키는 절대위치이다.

절대값 (absolute value) 0에서부터 어떤 수 까지의 거리. 절대값의 기호는 $| \ |$ 이다.

보기:

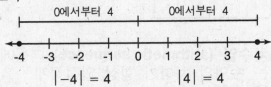

$|-4| = 4 \qquad |4| = 4$

예각 (acute angle) 각도가 90도 보다 적은 각.

보기:

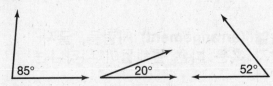

$85° \qquad 20° \qquad 52°$

예각삼각형 (acute triangle) 세개의 예각으로 이루어진 삼각형.

보기:

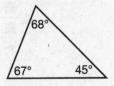

가수 (addend) 한개 혹은 그 이상의 다른 수에 더해지는 수.

보기:　　　　12 + 19 = 31

　　　　　　　가수　　가수

더하기 (addition) 두개 혹은 그 이상의 수를 합하여 총합이 나오도록 하는 것.

보기:

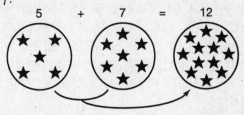

등식의 덧셈 성질 (Addition Property of Equality) a = b 면 a + c = b + c.

보기:
다음 보기의 두번째 줄에서 등식의 양쪽에 각각 1이 더해졌다.

$$\begin{aligned} 만일 \quad x - 1 &= 2 \\ 그러면 x - 1 + 1 &= 2 + 1 \\ x &= 3 \end{aligned}$$

덧셈에 대한 역원 (additive inverse) 한 수의 반대 수.

보기:　　　-2의 덧셈의 역수는 2이다
　　　　　　5의 덧셈의 역수는 -5이다

인접 빗변 (adjacent leg) 직각 삼각형의 한 예각의 어느 한쪽으로나 놓여 있는 변.

보기:

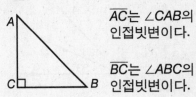

$\overline{AC}$는 ∠CAB의 인접빗변이다.

$\overline{BC}$는 ∠ABC의 인접빗변이다.

대수 (algebra) 숫자를 대신한 변수로 산수를 공부하는 수학의 한 분야.

대수 표기법 (algebraic expression) 최소한 한개의 변수를 가지고 있는 표기법.

보기:　$n - 7$　　$2y + 17$　　$5(x - 3)$

상대각 (alternate angles) 두 선과 이 두 선을 가로지르는 선에 의해 만들어지는 두개의 각으로 가로지르는 선의 반대편에 각각 있으며, (1) 주어진 두 선 사이에 있거나 (상대각의 내각) (2) 주어진 두 선 사이에 있지 않는 각 (상대각의 외각). 이 가로지르는 선이 수평선을 가로지르는 경우 상대각의 내각과 상대각의 외각은 합동이다.

보기:

상대각의 외각:
∠1 과 ∠8
∠2 과 ∠7

상대각의 내각:
∠3 과 ∠6
∠4 과 ∠5

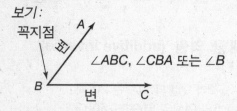

각 (angle) 같은 끝점을 가진 두개의 반직선.

보기:

꼭지점
변

∠ABC, ∠CBA 또는 ∠B

각의 이등분선 (angle bisector) 한 각을 두개의 동일한 각으로 나누는 반직선.

보기:

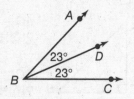

$\overrightarrow{BD}$ 는 ∠ABC의 이등분선이다.

회전각 (angle of rotation) 도형이 회전하는 각도.

보기:

회전각은 90도이다.

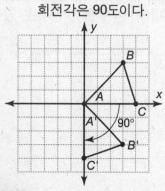

한변과 두각 (Angle-Side-Angle: ASA) 대응하는 부분을 비교하여 삼각형들이 합동인지를 판단하는데 사용하는 방법.

보기:

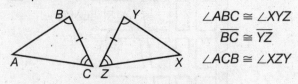

∠ABC ≅ ∠XYZ
$\overline{BC} \cong \overline{YZ}$
∠ACB ≅ ∠XZY

△ABC ≅ △XYZ 따라서 ASA 법칙에 의해.

면적 (area) 한 도형이 차지하는 표면.

보기:

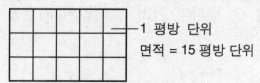

1 평방 단위

면적 = 15 평방 단위

등차수열 (arithmetic sequence) 다음에 오는 수와의 차이가 항상 일정하게 같은 수열.

보기:

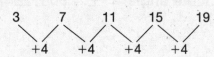

순열 (arrangement) 사람들, 글자, 숫자 혹은 다른 물체들이 나타나는 순서.

보기:

3가지 도형이 이룰 수 있는 모든 순열:

덧셈의 결합 법칙 (Associative Property of Addition) 가수의 집합을 변형시켜도 합은 같다는 법칙.

보기: $a + (b + c) = (a + b) + c$

$5 + (3 + 7) = (5 + 3) + 7$

2 Korean

곱셈의 결합 법칙 (Associative Property of Multiplication) 인수의 집합을 변형시켜도 곱은 같다는 법칙.

보기:
$$a(bc) = (ab)c$$
$$3 \times (4 \times 2) = (3 \times 4) \times 2$$

평균 (average) 평균을 참조한다.

축 (axes) x축과 y축을 참조한다.

막대 그래프 (bar graph) 자료를 표시하기위해 수직 막대나 수평 막대를 사용하는 그래프.

보기:

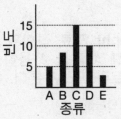 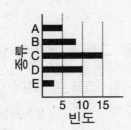

(지수의) 밑 (base of an exponent) 한 수를 반복해서 몇번 곱했는지를 표시하는 것이 지수이고 그 곱해진 원체의 수를 밑이라 한다.

보기: 밑　　지수
$$6^2 = 6 \times 6 = 36$$

(도형의) 밑변 (base of a polygon) 한 변 (보통 아래에 있는 변), 또는 그 변의 길이.

보기:

밑변

(입방체의) 밑면 (base of a solid) 프리즘이나 원통에서 평행 또는 합동인 두 면 중 하나. 피라미드의 경우 꼭지점을 바라보는 면. 원뿔의 경우에는 원형의 면.

보기:

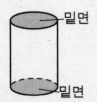 

밑면　밑면　밑면

2진법 (binary number system) 2진수를 사용하는 수의 체계.

보기:
이진법에서 1011은 10진법의 (10진수) 11과 같다.

	8의 자리	4의 자리	2의 자리	1의 자리
2진수	1	0	1	1
자리수	8	4	2	1
곱	1×8=8	0×4=0	1×2=2	1×1=1

$(1 \times 8) + (0 \times 4) + (1 \times 2) + (1 \times 1) = 8 + 0 + 2 + 1 = 11$

이항식 (binomial) 두항의 다항식.

보기:　　$4x^3 - 2x^2$　　$2x + 5$

이등분 (bisect) 각이나 선분을 합동인 두개의 각이나 선분으로 나누는 것.

보기:

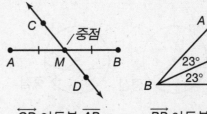

$\overrightarrow{CD}$ 이등분 $\overline{AB}$.　　$\overrightarrow{BD}$ 이등분 $\angle ABC$.

경계선 (boundary line) 1차 부등식 그래프에서 해법인 점들을 그렇지 않은 점들로부터 분리하는 선.

보기:

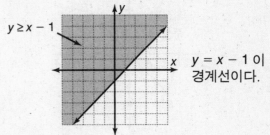

$y \geq x - 1$

$y = x - 1$ 이 경계선이다.

상자-수염 그림 (box-and-whisker plot)
자료들이 어떻게 분포되어있는지를
시각적으로 보여주는 방법. 아래의
보기는 10개의 시험 성적을 보여주고
있다: 52, 64, 75, 79, 80, 80, 81, 88,
92, 99.

보기:

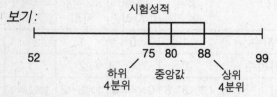

용량 (capacity) 도형의 부피. 액체
단위로 표시한다.

보기:

중심 (center) 원이나 구체의 정중앙에
있는 점.

보기:

회전의 중심 (center of rotation)
도형이 회전을 하는데 중심이 되는 점.

보기:

이 보기에서 원점은 회전의 중심이다.

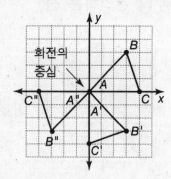

센티 (centi-) 100분의 1을 의미하는
접두어.

보기:　　1 센티미터 = $\frac{1}{100}$ 미터

중심각 (central angle) 꼭지점이 원의
중심에 있는 각.

보기:

점 C는 원의 중심이다.
∠BCA는 중심각이다.

원 (circle) 모든 점들이 중심에서 모두
같은 거리에 있는 평면 도형.

보기:

원 그래프 (circle graph) 자료 집합의
부분들을 보여주기 위해 쐐기를 사용하는
원형 그래프. 파이 차트라고도 부른다.

보기:

좋아하는 애완동물

원둘레 (circumference) 원 주위의
거리.

보기:

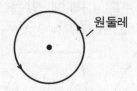

원둘레

외접도형 (circumscribed figure) 다른
도형을 포함하고 있는 도형. 한 원이
다른 다각형의 각 변과 닿아 있으면 이
다각형은 원에 외접해 있는것이다.

보기:

삼각형은 원에 외접해 있다.

시계방향 (clockwise) 도형의 윗부분이 오른쪽으로 회전하는 방향.

보기:

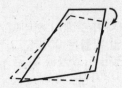

집락 (clustering) 어림수를 내는데 사용하는 방법으로, 값이 비슷한 수들을 모두 동일한 수로 가정하는 것.

보기:

26 + 24 + 23 은 약 25 + 25 + 25 또는 3 x 25이다.

계수 (coefficient) 변수에 곱해지는 0과 자연수.

보기:

계수 \ / 변수

12y

조합 (combination) 항목들이 같이 묶여 있는 것으로 순서는 중요하지 않다.

보기:

이 그룹에 있는 학생들인 데이비드, 화니타, 킴 중에서 2명이 위원회에 뽑힐 것이다.

가능한 조합은 다음과 같다:
데이비드, 화니타   데이비드, 킴   화니타, 킴

참고: "데이비드, 화니타" 조합은 "화니타, 데이비드" 조합과 같다.

공통분모 (common denominator) 두개 혹은 그 이상의 분수의 동일한 분모.

보기:

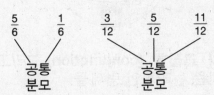

$\frac{5}{6}$ $\frac{1}{6}$ $\frac{3}{12}$ $\frac{5}{12}$ $\frac{11}{12}$

공통분모   공통분모

공약수 (common factor) 두개 혹은 그 이상의 수에 인수인 수.

보기:

4는 8, 12, 20의 공약수이다.

$8 = \mathbf{4} \times 2$

$12 = \mathbf{4} \times 3$

$20 = \mathbf{4} \times 5$

공배수 (common multiple) 주어진 두개 혹은 그 이상의 수 각각에 배수인 수.

보기:

3의 배수: 3 6 9 **12** 15 18 21 **24** 27...

4의 배수: 4 8 **12** 16 20 **24** 28...

12와 24는 3과 4의 공배수이다.

덧셈의 교환 법칙 (Commutative Property of Addition) 둘 혹은 그 이상의 수를 더하는 순서가 합에 영향을 미치지 않는다는 법칙.

보기: $a + b = b + a$

$18 + 23 = 23 + 18$

곱셈의 교환 법칙 (Commutative Property of Multiplication) 둘 혹은 그 이상의 수를 곱하는 순서가 곱에 영향을 미치지 않는다는 법칙.

보기: $ab = ba$

$4 \times 7 = 7 \times 4$

손쉬운 수 (compatible numbers) 쉽게 계산을 할 수 있는 수.

보기: 30 + 70   40 ÷ 4   25 + 75

보정 (compensation) 문제에 있는 수와 가까운 수를 사용하고나서 사용한 수를 보정하기 위해 답을 조정하는 암산 방법.

보기: $99 \times 4 = (100 - 1) \times 4$

$= (100 \times 4) - (1 \times 4)$

$= 400 - 4$

$= 396$

여각 (complementary angles) 합이 90도인 두개의 각.

보기:

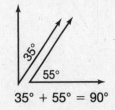

$35° + 55° = 90°$

합성수 (composite number) 1보다 큰 0과 자연수로 둘 이상의 약수를 가지고 있는 수.

보기:

15의 약수: 1, 3, 5, 15
    15는 합성수이다.

7의 약수: 1, 7
    7은 합성수가 아니다.

곱사건 (compound event) 둘 혹은 그 이상의 단일 결과가 합쳐진 결과.

보기:

동전을 던져서 앞면을 보고 주사위에서 1을 얻는 것은 복합 결과라 한다.

복리 (compound interest) 원금 및 이전의 이자에 대한 이자.

보기:

연 복리 이자율이 6%인 적금에 $100을 저금했으면 첫해에는 $100 + 0.06 x 100 = $106이 생길 것이고 두번째 해에는 $106 + 0.06 x 106 = $112.36이 생길 것이다.

복합 명제 (compound statement) 둘 혹은 그 이상의 명제를 합하여 만든 논리적인 명제.

보기:

10은 5보다 크다. 그리고 10은 21보다 작다.

10은 5보다 크다. 또는 10은 5보다 작다.

오목다각형 (concave polygon) 하나 혹은 그 이상의 대각선이 도형의 바깥쪽에 있는 다각형.

보기:

조건부 확률 (conditional probability) A가 이미 발생했을 경우 B가 발생할 확률.

보기:

두 번의 동전 던지기 중에서 첫번째가 뒷면인 경우 두번 모두 앞면일 확률은 0이다. 그러나 첫번째 던지기에서 앞면이 나왔음을 알 경우 두번 모두 앞면일 경우는 1/2이다.

원뿔 (cone) 밑면이 원형인 입방체.

보기:

합동 (congruent) 같은 크기와 모양을 갖는것.

보기:

원추 투영법 (conic projection) 구체의 표면을 원뿔로 나타내는 지도 투영법.

보기:

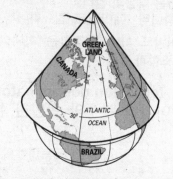

명제의 교집합 (conjunction) 그리고 로 이어지는 논리적인 명제들.

보기:

$x > -2$ 그리고 $x < 5$

정사각형은 4개의 변의 길이가 모두 같다. 그리고 정사각형은 사각형이다.

상수 (constant) 변하지 않는 수량.

보기 :
대수 표기법인 *x* + 7 에서 7은 자연수이다.

상수 그래프 (constant graph) 선의
높이가 변하지 않는 그래프.

보기 :

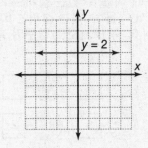

비례상수 (constant of proportionality)
*x*와 *y*인 두개의 변수를 위한 $\frac{y}{x}$ 비율은
일정하다. 보통 *k*로 표시한다.

보기 :

x	3	6	9	12
y	5	10	15	20

$k = \frac{5}{3}$

환산인수 (conversion factor) 한
단위에서 다른 단위로 환산하는데
사용하는 첫수. 보통 분수로 표시한다.

보기 :

12 인치 = 1 푸트 $\frac{12인치}{1푸트}$

4 쿼트 = 1 갈론 $\frac{4쿼트}{1갈론}$

볼록다각형 (convex polygon) 모든
대각선이 도형의 내부에 있는 다각형.

보기 :

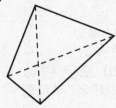
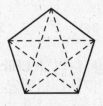

좌표 (coordinate) 좌표면상의 한 점의
위치를 나타나는데 사용하는 수의 집합
중 하나.

보기 :

(5, 6)
좌표

**좌표면, 좌표체계 (coordinate plane,
coordinate system)** 한 면에 있는 점의
위치를 나타내는데 사용하는 선들.

보기 :

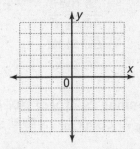

**(선의) 동위각 (corresponding angles
for lines)** 둘 혹은 그 이상의 선을 지나는
선의 같은 쪽에 있는 각. 평행선을
가로지르는 경우 동위각은 합동이다.

보기 :

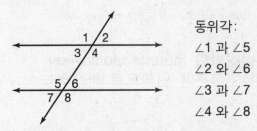

동위각:
∠1 과 ∠5
∠2 와 ∠6
∠3 과 ∠7
∠4 와 ∠8

**(비슷한 도형들에서의) 동위각
(corresponding angles in similar
figures)** 비슷한 도형들에서 서로
상응하는 각.

보기 :
△*ABC* ~ △*XYZ*

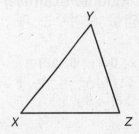

동위각:
∠*ABC* 와 ∠*XYZ*
∠*BCA* 와 ∠*YZX*
∠*CAB* 와 ∠*ZXY*

동위변 (corresponding sides) 비슷한 도형들에서 서로 상응하는 변.

보기:

△ABC ~ △XYZ

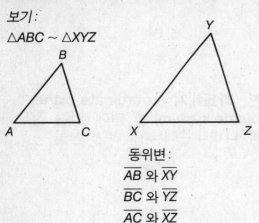

동위변:
$\overline{AB}$ 와 $\overline{XY}$
$\overline{BC}$ 와 $\overline{YZ}$
$\overline{AC}$ 와 $\overline{XZ}$

코싸인 (cosine) 직각삼각형에서 예각인 x의 코싸인, 즉 $\cos(x)$는 $\frac{\text{인접빗변}}{\text{사변}}$ 의 비율이다.

보기:

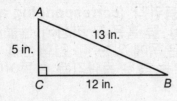

$$\cos \angle CAB = \frac{\text{인접빗변}}{\text{사변}} = \frac{5}{13} \approx 0.38$$

시계 반대방향 (counterclockwise) 도형의 윗부분이 왼쪽으로 회전하는 방향.

보기:

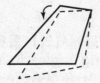

반증 (counterexample) 명제가 거짓임을 보여주는 예.

보기:

만일: $x \cdot 0 = y \cdot 0$, 그러면 $x = y$
반증: $3 \cdot 0 = 0$ 그리고 $5 \cdot 0 = 0$,
그러나 $3 \neq 5$

계수의 원리 (Counting Principle) 어떤 상황이 발생할 수 있는 경우의 수가 m이라면 두번째 상황이 발생할 수 있는 경우의 수는 n이고, 이 둘이 같이 발생할 수 있는 경우의 수는 $m \times n$이다.

보기:

동전을 던질 때 나올 수 있는 결과는 2가지이고 주사위를 던져 나올 수 있는 결과는 6가지이다. 그러므로 2×6, 즉 12가지의 경우가 발생할 수 있다.

$6 \times 2 = 12$

교차 곱 (cross product) 한 분수의 분자와 다른 분수의 분모를 곱하는 것.

보기:

$\frac{1}{3}$ ⤢ $\frac{2}{5}$

교차 곱:
$1 \times 5 = 5$
$3 \times 2 = 6$

입방체 (cube) 모든 면이 합동의 정사각형인 6면의 프리즘.

보기:

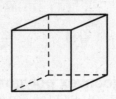

3승 (cubed) 3제곱.

보기:

2의 3승 = $2^3 = 2 \times 2 \times 2 = 8$

입방 단위 (cubic unit) 모든 변의 길이가 1 단위인 입방체의 부피를 측량하는 단위.

보기:

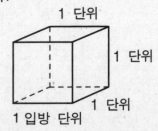

1 단위
1 단위
1 단위
1 입방 단위

관습적 측정법 (customary system of measurement) 보통 미국에서 사용하는 측량법: 인치, 피트, 마일, 온스, 파운드, 톤, 컵, 쿼트, 갈론 등.

보기:

길이　　　1 갤론 용량　　　무게

원통 (cylinder) 밑 면 두개가 평행이고 원형인 입방체.

보기:

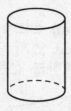

원통 투영법 (cylindrical projection) 구체의 표면을 원형으로 나타내는 지도 투영법.

보기:

10각형 (decagon) 10개의 변이 있는 다각형.

보기:

데시- (deci-) $\frac{1}{10}$ 을 의미하는 접두사.

보기: 1 데시미터 = $\frac{1}{10}$ 미터

소수 (decimal) 소수점을 사용하는 10진수.

보기:　6.21　0.59　12.2　5.0

소수 덧셈 (decimal addition) 둘 혹은 그 이상의 소수를 더하는 것.

보기:
$$\begin{array}{r} 1 \\ 12.65 \\ + 29.10 \\ \hline 41.75 \end{array}$$

소수 나눗셈 (decimal division) 두개의 소수를 나누는 것.

보기:
$$\begin{array}{r} 1.25 \\ 0.24 \overline{)0.3000} \\ -24 \\ \hline 60 \\ -48 \\ \hline 120 \\ -120 \\ \hline 0 \end{array}$$

소수 곱셈 (decimal multiplication) 둘 혹은 그 이상의 소수를 곱하는 것.

보기:
$$\begin{array}{r} 2 \\ 0.13 \\ \times 0.7 \\ \hline 0.091 \end{array}$$
소수점 2자리
소수점 1자리
소수점 3자리

소수 뺄셈 (decimal subtraction) 두개의 소수를 빼는 것.

보기:
$$\begin{array}{r} 13\ 12 \\ 4\ \not{3}\ \not{2}10 \\ \not{5}\not{4}\not{3}\not{0} \\ -16.58 \\ \hline 37.72 \end{array}$$

10진법 (decimal system) 10진수를 사용하는 수의 체계.

보기:

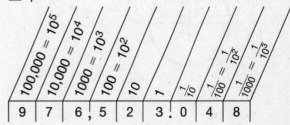

감소 그래프 (decreasing graph) 선의 높이가 왼쪽에서부터 오른쪽으로 감소하는 그래프.

보기:

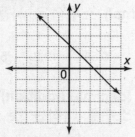

연역적 사고 (deductive reasoning) 논리를 이용하여 결론을 도출시키는 것.

보기:

사다리꼴에 대각선을 더하면 두개의 삼각형이 생긴다. 삼각형의 각의 합은 180도이다. 그러므로 사다리꼴의 각의 합은 삼각형의 두배, 즉 2 x 180° = 360° 이다.

도 (degree °) 각의 측량 단위.

보기: 1° 은 원의 $\frac{1}{360}$ 이다.

차수 (degree) 다항식에서 한 변수의 가장 큰 지수의 값.

보기: $5x^3 - 2x^2 + 7x$ 의 차수는 3이다.

데카 (deka-) 10을 의미하는 접두사.

보기: 1 데카미터 = 10 미터

분모 (denominator) 분수의 밑부분으로 전체가 모두 몇개의 부분으로 나뉘어졌는지를 보여준다.

보기:

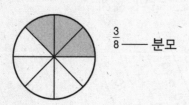

$\frac{3}{8}$ —— 분모

종속 경우 (dependent events) 하나의 결과가 다른 결과의 확률에 영향을 미치는 경우.

보기:

테레지, 다이앤 그리고 호세라는 이름이 각기 다른 종이에 적혀있다. 그 중에 한 장을 뽑는다. 그리고나서 또 다른 한 장을 뽑는다. 테레지의 이름이 처음에 뽑혔을 경우 다이앤의 이름이 뽑힐 확률은 $\frac{1}{2}$ 이다.

종속변수 (dependent variable) 함수에서의 결과 변수.

보기:

종속변수

$y = x + 2$

대각선 (diagonal) 다각형에서 같은 변을 서로 가지고 있지 않은 두개의 꼭지점들을 연결하는 선분.

보기:

대각선

지름 (diameter) 원의 중심을 지나고 양 끝점이 원에 있는 선분이나 그 선분의 길이.

보기:

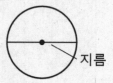

지름

차 (difference) 한 수에서 다른 수를 뺐을 때의 결과.

보기: 28 – 15 = 13

차

수자 (digit) 0, 1, 2, 3, 4, 5, 6, 7, 8, 9와 같은 번호를 쓰는데 사용하는 기호.

보기:

5,847 에서 수자는 5, 8, 4, 7 이다.

확대/축소 (dilation) 도형의 비례적 축소나 확대.

보기 :

작은 직사각형에서 큰 직사각형으로의 확대배율은 3이다.

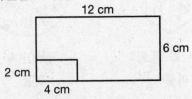

비례식 (direct variation) 두 변수간에 항상 같은 비율이 존재하는 경우.

보기 :

시간 (x)	1	2	3	4
마일 (y)	55	110	165	220

$$\frac{y}{x} = 55$$

이접 (disjunction) "또는" 이라는 단어로 연결되어있는 논리적인 명제들.

보기 :

$x > 4$ 또는 $x < -1$

우리는 영화를 보러갔다. 또는 우리는 TV를 봤다.

분배 법칙 (Distributive Property) $a(b + c) = ab + ac$ 라는 법칙.

보기 : $3(6 + 5) = 3 \cdot 6 + 3 \cdot 5$

피제수/나뉨수 (dividend) 나눗셈에서 나눔을 당하는 수.

보기 :

피제수

$8 \div 4 = 2$

나누어 떨어지는 (divisible) 다른 수로 나누었을 때 수가 남지 않는 것.

보기 : $18 \div 6 = 3$ 이므로 18은 6으로 나누어 떨어진다.

나눗셈 (division) 동일한 수의 집합이 몇개나 생기는지 또는 각 동일한 수의 집합에 몇이 들어가 있는지를 보여주는 것.

보기 :

$18 \div 6 = 3$ $18 \div 3 = 6$

18을 6으로 나누면 각 그룹에 3개가 들어가있다.

18을 3으로 나누면 각 그룹에 6개가 들어가있다.

제수/나눗수 (divisor) 한 수를 나누는 수.

보기 :

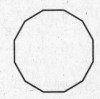

제수

$8 \div 4 = 2$

12각형 (dodecagon) 변이 12개인 다각형.

보기 :

2중 막대그래프 (double bar graph) 두개의 관련된 자료들을 비교하는데 쓸 수 있도록 막대를 두개씩 사용하는 그래프.

보기 :

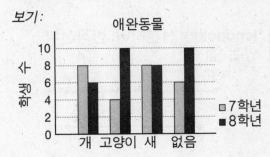

2중 선그래프 (double line graph)

두개의 관련된 자료들을 비교하는데 쓸 수 있도록 선을 두개씩 사용하는 그래프.

보기:

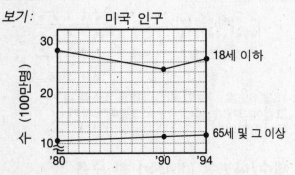

이중 줄기-잎 도표 (double stem-and-leaf diagram)

한 도표에서 두 종류의 자료를 비교하는 줄기-잎 도표.

보기:

잎	줄기	잎
7 2 1	3	0 1 3
5 0 0	4	2 3
9	5	5 6 8
5 2 0	6	1 4

모서리 (edge)

다면체의 두 면이 만나는 부분.

보기:

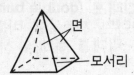

끝점 (endpoint)

선분이나 반직선의 끝에 있는 점.

보기:

상등 (equality)

완전히 같음을 의미하는 수학적 표현.

보기: 16 + 8 = 24   25 ÷ 5 = 5

동등확률 (equally-likely outcomes)

동일한 확률을 가지는 결과.

보기:

"1"을 굴림   적색이 나옴

확률: $\frac{1}{6}$ 확률: $\frac{1}{6}$

등비 (equal ratio)

같은 수량을 나타내는 비율들.

보기: $\frac{2}{6}$, $\frac{1}{3}$, 그리고 $\frac{4}{12}$

등식 (equation)

두개의 식이 같음을 보여주는 수학적 문장.

보기:

$14 = 2x$ $3 + y = 81$ $3 + 4 = 7$

등변 삼각형 (equilateral triangle)

모든 변의 길이가 같은 삼각형.

보기:

동치 등식 (equivalent equations)

똑같은 변수를 대치하면 참이 성립되는 식.

보기: $x - 5 = 10$ 그리고 $x = 15$

동치식 (equivalent expression)

같은 수를 대입했을 때 항상 같은 값을 갖는 두개의 식.

보기: $5(x + 1)$ 그리고 $5x + 5$

동치 분수 (equivalent fractions)

같은 수를 의미하는 두개의 분수.

보기: $\frac{1}{2}$ 그리고 $\frac{8}{16}$

동치율 (equivalent rates) 같은 값을 갖는 비율.

보기: $\dfrac{40 \text{ 마일}}{2 \text{ 시간}}$ 그리고 $\dfrac{20 \text{ 마일}}{1 \text{ 시간}}$

동치비율 (equivalent ratios) 동등비율 참조.

어림내기 (estimate) 계산의 결과를 어림잡아 보는것.

보기: 99×21
어림내기: $100 \times 20 = 2000$
           $99 \times 21 \approx 2000$

율러의 공식 (Euler's formula)
다면체의 면의 수 (F), 꼭지점의 수 (V) 그리고 모서리의 수 (E)에 대한 공식으로 $F + V - E = 2$임을 의미한다.

보기:

삼각형 피라미드에서
$5 + 5 - 8 = 2$
면   꼭지점   모서리

수치 구하기 (evaluate) 식에서 변수에 값을 대입하고 계산을 통해 이를 간단하게 하는 것.

보기: $x = 10$일 때, $8(x - 3)$의 수치 구하기
$8(x - 3) = 8(10 - 3)$
         $= 8\,(7)$
         $= 56$

짝수 (even number) 1자리수에 0, 2, 4, 6, 또는 8이 있는 0과 자연수.

보기: 16   28   34   112   3000

경우 (event) 실험이나 상황의 결과.

보기:
경우: 주사위를 던졌을 때
           3 혹은 그 이상의 수가
           나오는 것.

이 경우의
가능한 결과: 3, 4, 5, 6

확장식 (expanded form) 지수가 있는 수를 쓸 때 모든 인수를 각각 보여주는 식.

보기: 지수가 있는 수 9^3
          확장식 $9 \times 9 \times 9$

실험 (experiment) 확률에 있어서 기회와 관련된 그 어떤 행위.

보기:

     동전   주사위   돌림판
     던지기   던지기   돌리기

실험 확률 (experimental probability) 실험이나 설문조사를 통한 자료에 기초한 확률.

보기:

콩 주머니를 고리에 100번 던졌다, 고리에 들어간 수는 모두 23번이다. 고리에 들어갈 실험확률은 $\dfrac{23}{100} = 23\%$ 이다.

지수 (exponent) 연속적인 곱셈의 횟수.

보기: 지수
$4^3 = 4 \times 4 \times 4 = 64$

지수 함수 (exponential function) 지수가 변수로 작용하는 비선형 함수.

보기: $y = 4^x$

지수 기수법 (exponential notation) 지수를 사용하여 연속적인 곱셈을 표시하는 방법.

보기: 2^8 5^2 9^3

식 (expression) 변수 그리고/또는 수와 연산으로 이루어진 수학적 문구.

보기: $5(8 + 4)$ $x - 3$ $2x + 4$

외각 (exterior angles) 선들과 이 선을 가로지르는 선에 의해 생기는 각으로 선들의 바깥쪽에 있다.

보기:

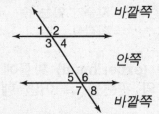

외각:
∠1, ∠2, ∠7, ∠8

면 (face) 입방체의 평평한 표면.

보기:

인수 (factor) 다른 수를 남김 없이 나누는 수.

보기: 30 ÷ 5 = 6, 이므로 5는 30의 인수이다.

계승 (factorial) 한 수의 계승은 1에서 부터 그 수까지의 모든 0과 자연수를 곱한 것으로 "!"으로 표시한다.

보기:

6 계승 = 6! = 6 × 5 × 4 × 3 × 2 × 1 = 720

인수 체계 (factor tree) 0과 자연수가 가장 적은 인수로 나누어지는 것을 보여주는 도표.

보기:

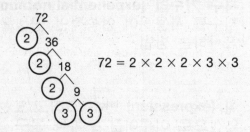

$72 = 2 \times 2 \times 2 \times 3 \times 3$

공정한 게임 (fair game) 게임의 모든 참가자가 같은 우승 확률을 가지는 게임.

보기:

F공정한 게임: 두명이 차례로 주사위를 던진다. A는 1, 3, 5가 나올 때 점수를 받을 수 있고 B는 2, 4, 6이 나올 때 점수를 받는다. 점수를 받을 수 있는 확률은 참가자 모두에게 $\frac{1}{2}$ 이다.

뒤집기 (flip) 반향 참조.

푸트 (foot) 관습적 측정법의 단위로 12인치와 같다.

보기:

푸트

공식 (formula) 수량간의 관계를 보여주는 법칙.

보기: $A = bh$ $p = 4s$

fractal 동일한 모양의 패턴으로 fractal의 일부를 확대했을 때 확대한 부분이 원체 도형과 모습이 같은 것.

보기:

분수 (fraction) $\frac{a}{b}$ 형식의 수. 전체를 동일한 조각으로 나누었을 때 전체의 부분을 나타내는 것.

보기: $\frac{3}{5}$ $\frac{2}{7}$ $\frac{1}{4}$ $\frac{7}{10}$

분수의 덧셈 (fraction addition) 둘 혹은 그 이상의 분수를 더하는 것.

보기: $\frac{1}{3} + \frac{1}{4}$

$$\frac{1}{3} = \frac{1 \times 4}{3 \times 4} = \frac{4}{12}$$

$$\frac{1}{4} = \frac{1 \times 3}{4 \times 3} = \frac{3}{12}$$

$$\frac{1}{3} + \frac{1}{4} = \frac{4}{12} + \frac{3}{12} = \frac{4+3}{12} = \frac{7}{12}$$

분수의 나눗셈 (fraction division) 두 분수를 나누는 것.

보기: $\frac{1}{6} \div \frac{3}{4} = \frac{1}{6} \times \frac{4}{3}$

$$= \frac{1 \times 4}{6 \times 3}$$

$$= \frac{4}{18} \text{ 또는 } \frac{2}{9}$$

분수의 곱셈 (fraction multiplication)
둘 혹은 그 이상의 분수를 곱하는 것.

보기:
$$1\frac{1}{2} \times \frac{1}{4} = \frac{3}{2} \times \frac{1}{4}$$
$$= \frac{3 \times 1}{2 \times 4}$$
$$= \frac{3}{8}$$

분수의 뺄셈 (fraction subtraction)
두 분수를 빼는 것.

보기: $\frac{3}{4} - \frac{2}{3}$

$$\frac{3}{4} = \frac{3 \times 3}{4 \times 3} = \frac{9}{12}$$
$$\frac{2}{3} = \frac{2 \times 4}{3 \times 4} = \frac{8}{12}$$
$$\frac{3}{4} - \frac{2}{3} = \frac{9}{12} - \frac{8}{12} = \frac{9-8}{12} = \frac{1}{12}$$

빈도 (frequency)
설문 조사 등에서 어떤 일이 발생하는 횟수. *빈도표 (frequency chart)* 참조.

빈도표 (frequency chart or table)
항목과 발생 횟수를 보여주는 표.

보기:

셔츠의 색	빈도
검정색	8
밤색	2
하얀색	5
파란색	4

선취 어림내기 (front-end estimation)
어림내기 방법의 하나로, 각 수의 첫째 자리 또는 둘째 자리만을 사용해서 계산을 하고 결과는 나머지 자릿수들로 조정하는 것.

보기: 첫째 자리 선취 어림내기

```
   2,485
 + 3,698
   5,000    첫째 자리를 더한다
 + 1,200    485 + 698 는 약 1,200.
   6,200
```

함수 (function)
입력과 결과 관계에서 각 입력에 단 하나의 결과만 나오는 것.

보기:
$$y = x + 4 \qquad y = 2x \qquad y = x^2$$

연산의 기본이론 (Fundamental Theorem of Arithmetic)
1보다 큰 모든 정수는 소수의 곱으로 표현될 수 있다.

보기:
$$24 = 2 \times 2 \times 2 \times 3$$
$$35 = 5 \times 7$$

갈론 (gallon)
관습적 측정법의 단위로 4 쿼트와 같다.

보기:

1갈론

기하학 (geometry)
점, 선, 도형 및 입방체간의 관계를 연구하는 수학의 한 분야.

기하학적 확률 (geometric probability)
기하학적 도형들의 치수간 비교에 기초한 확률.

보기:

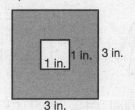

큰 정사각형의 면적 = 3·3 또는 9 평방인치

칠해진 부분 = $9 \text{ in}^2 - 1 \text{ in}^2 = 8 \text{ in}^2$

칠해진 부분에 다다를 확률 = $\frac{8}{9}$

기하학적 수열 (geometric sequence)
이어지는 수와의 비율이 항상 같은 수열.

보기:

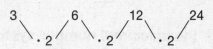

그램 (gram)
미터 체계의 질량 단위.

보기:

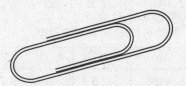

큰 종이 클립의 질량은 약 1그램이다.

그래프 (graph) 정보를 정리해서 보여주는 도표.

보기:

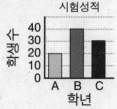

최대공약수 (greatest common factor GCF) 둘 혹은 그 이상의 0과 자연수를 남기지 않고 나눌 수 있는 가장 큰 0과 자연수.

보기: 6은 12, 18 24의 최대공약수이다.

헥토 (hecto-) 100을 의미하는 접두어.

보기: 1 헥토미터 = 100 미터

높이 (height) 삼각형, 사다리꼴 또는 피라미드에서 밑변 부터 마주보는 꼭지점이나 까지의 수직 거리. 프리즘이나 실린더의 경우에는 밑변간의 거리.

보기:

7각형 (heptagon) 7개의 변을 가진 다각형.

보기:

16진법 (hexadecimal number system) 16진수를 사용하는 수의 체계.

보기:

글자 A–F는 10–15 자리수를 의미한다. 16진수 A3CE는 10진법에서 41,934 (40,960 + 768 + 192 + 14) 와 같다.

진수16	A	3	C	E
자릿수	4096	256	16	1
곱	10 × 4096 = 40,960	3 × 256 = 768	12 × 16 = 192	14 × 1 = 14

6각형 (hexagon) 6개의 변을 가진 다각형.

보기:

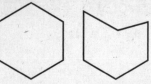

도수 분포도 (histogram) 막대그래프의 일종으로 항목들이 모두 같은 범위안에 있는 것.

보기:

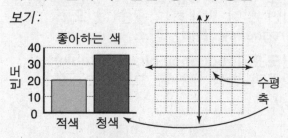

수평 축 (horizontal axis) 막대 그래프나 좌표면의 두 선들 중의 수평선.

보기:

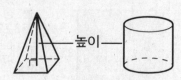

사변 (hypotenuse) 직각 삼각형에서 직각의 반대 방향에 있는 변.

보기:

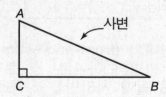

항등수 (identity) 어느 연산에서나 다른 수를 항상 같은 수로 있도록 하는 수. $a + 0 = a$이므로 0은 덧셈의 항등수이고 $a \times 1 = a$ 이므로 1은 곱셈의 항등수이다.

보기: $6 + 0 = 6$
                 $5 \times 1 = 5$

조건 - 결과 명제 (if-then statement) 두 상황의 관계를 보여주는데 있어 조건 *(if)* 과 결과 *(then)*를 사용하는 논리적 명제.

보기:

만일 삼각형이 부등변 삼각형이면 그 어떤 변도 합동이 아니다.

가분수 (improper fraction) 분자가 분모보다 크거나 같은 분수.

보기:
$$\frac{5}{2} \qquad \frac{8}{8} \qquad \frac{14}{3}$$

증가 그래프 (increasing graph) 선의 높이가 왼쪽에서 오른쪽으로 증가하는 그래프.

보기:

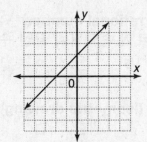

인치 (inch) 관습적 측정법의 길이 단위.

보기:
종이 클립의 길이는 $1\frac{3}{8}$ 인치 혹은 $1\frac{3}{8}''$ 이다.

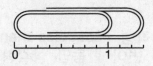

독립 경우 (independent events) 하나의 결과가 다른 결과의 확률에 영향을 미치지 않는 경우.

보기:
T테레지, 다이앤 그리고 호세라는 이름이 각기 다른 종이에 적혀있다. 그 중에 한 장을 뽑았다 다시 집어 넣는다. 그리고나서 또 다른 한 장을 뽑는다. 테레지의 이름이 처음에 뽑혔을 경우 다이앤의 이름이 뽑힐 확률은 $\frac{1}{3}$ 이다.

독립 변수 (independent variable) 함수에서의 입력 변수.

보기:
$$\text{독립 변수}$$
$$\diagup$$
$$y = x + 2$$

귀납적 사고 (inductive reasoning) 결론을 도출하는데 패턴을 사용하는 것.

보기:
사다리꼴을 많이 그리고나서 이들의 각도를 측정했다. 매번 각의 합이 360°도인 것으로 나왔다. 여기서 사다리꼴의 각의 합은 360°도라는 결론을 도출한다.

부등식 (inequality) $<, >, \le,$ 또는 $\ge$ 가 들어있는 수학적 문장.

보기:
$$6 < 9 \qquad x + 3 \ge 21 \qquad 2x - 8 > 0$$

내접도형 (inscribed figure) 다른 도형 속에 포함되어 있는 도형. 다각형의 모든 꼭지점들이 원에 닿아있으면 이 다각형은 원에 내접해 있는것이다.

보기:

삼각형은 원에 내접해 있다.

정수 (integers) 0과 자연수의 양수, 그 반대 수 그리고 0의 집합.

보기: ..., −3, −2, −1, 0, 1, 2, 3, ...

$$\begin{array}{ccccccccc} \bullet & \bullet & \bullet & \bullet & \bullet & \bullet & \bullet & \bullet & \bullet \\ -4 & -3 & -2 & -1 & 0 & 1 & 2 & 3 & 4 \end{array}$$

정수의 덧셈 (integer addition) 둘 혹은 그 이상의 정수를 더하는 것.

보기:
$$-5 + 8 = 3 \qquad\qquad -5 + (-8) = -13$$
$$5 + (-3) = 2 \qquad\qquad 5 + 8 = 13$$

정수의 나눗셈 (integer division) 두 정수를 나누는 것.

보기:
$$-40 \div 8 = -5 \qquad 40 \div (-8) = -5$$
$$-40 \div (-8) = 5 \qquad 40 \div 8 = 5$$

정수의 곱셈 (integer multiplication) 둘 혹은 그 이상의 정수를 곱하는 것.

보기:
$$-5 \cdot 8 = -40 \qquad -5 \cdot (-8) = 40$$
$$5 \cdot (-8) = -40 \qquad 5 \cdot 8 = 40$$

정수의 뺄셈 (integer subtraction) 두 정수를 빼는 것.

보기:
$$-5 - 8 = -13 \qquad -5 - (-8) = 3$$
$$5 - (-3) = 8 \qquad 5 - 8 = -3$$

이자 (interest) 돈을 사용하기 위해 지불하는 돈.

보기:
데이브는 적금 구좌에 $300을 저금했다. 1년 후 이 구좌의 잔금은 $315이 되었다. 이 적금 구좌를 통해 데이브는 $15의 이자를 받은 것이다.

내각 (interior angles) 선들과 이 선을 가로지르는 선에 의해 생기는 각으로 이 선들 사이에 있다.

보기:

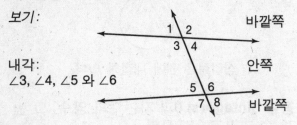

바깥쪽
안쪽
바깥쪽

내각:
∠3, ∠4, ∠5 와 ∠6

교차 (intersect) 같은 점을 통해서 서로 가로지르는 것.

보기:

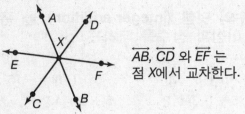

$\overrightarrow{AB}$, $\overrightarrow{CD}$ 와 $\overrightarrow{EF}$ 는 점 X에서 교차한다.

간격 (interval) 막대그래프나 선그래프에서 동일하게 나누어진 척도.

보기:

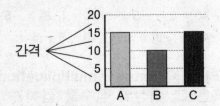

간격

역 (inverse operations) 서로의 연산을 각각 무효화 시키는 연산.

보기:
addition and subtraction $2 + 3 = 5$ $5 - 3 = 2$
multiplication and division $2 \cdot 3 = 6$ $6 \div 3 = 2$

역변동 (inverse variation) 두 변수가 일정한 곱으로 관련되어 있는 것.

보기:

x	1	2	3	4	5	6
y	60	30	20	15	12	10

$$x \cdot y = 60$$

무리수 (irrational number) $\sqrt{2}$ 와 같이 소수점으로 계속되거나 끝낼 수 없는 수.

보기: $\sqrt{5}$ π $-\sqrt{\frac{1}{2}}$

등거리법 (isometric drawing) 그림에 원근감을 주기 위한 기법.

보기:

이등변 삼각형 (isosceles triangle) 최소한 두 변이 합동인 삼각형.

보기:

18   18
14

킬로 (kilo-) 1000을 의미하는 접두사.

보기: 1 킬로미터 = 1000 미터

위도 (latitude) 적도에서 남북으로 정한 측량 단위. "도"로 표시한다.

보기:

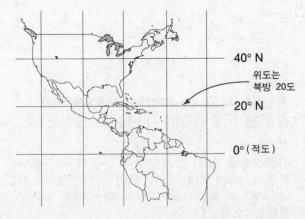

40° N
위도는 북방 20도
20° N
0° (적도)

최소 공분모 (least common denominator LCD) 둘 혹은 그 이상의 분모들의 최소 공배수 (LCM).

보기: $\frac{1}{2}$ $\frac{2}{3}$ $\frac{3}{4}$

2, 3 및 4의 LCM은 12이므로 분수의 LCD는 12이다.

최소 공분모 12로 표기된 분수들은 다음과 같다: $\frac{6}{12}$, $\frac{8}{12}$, $\frac{9}{12}$.

최소 공배수 (least common multiple LCM) 가장 적은 수의 공배수.

보기:

3의 배수: 3 6 **12** 15 18 21 **24** ...
4의 배수: 4 8 **12** 16 20 **24** 32 ...
12는 3과 4의 LCM이다.

빗변 (leg) 직각 삼각형에서 사변이 아닌 다른 변.

보기:

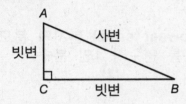

공분모 (like denominators) 둘 혹은 그 이상의 분수에서 같은 분모.

보기:

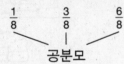

같은 항 (like terms) 같은 변수가 같은 지수로 올려지는 항.

보기: $3x^2$ 와 $9x^2$ $10y$ 와 $2y$

선 (line) 양 방향으로 끝없이 뻗어나가는 1차원적인 도형. 두개의 점으로 선의 이름을 정한다.

보기:

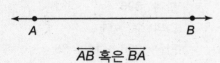

$\overrightarrow{AB}$ 혹은 $\overrightarrow{BA}$

선 그래프 (line graph) 보통 시간의 경과에 따른 자료의 변화를 보여주는데 사용하는 그래프.

보기:

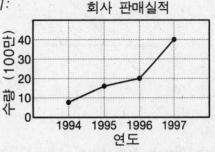

대칭선 (line of symmetry) 도형을 두개의 대칭되는 절반으로 나누는 선.

보기:

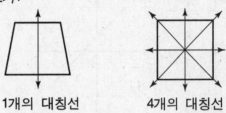

1개의 대칭선   4개의 대칭선

선 도면 (line plot) 번호가 적혀있는 선 위의 각 자리값위에 x를 쌓아올려 자료 집합의 모양을 보여주는 도면.

보기:

학생 수

선분 (line segment) 직선의 일부로, 두개의 끝점을 지닌다. 이 두개의 점으로 선분의 이름을 정한다.

보기:

A ●————————● B $\overline{AB}$ 또는 $\overline{BA}$

선 대칭 (line symmetry) 도형이 두개의 동일한 절반으로 나누어질 수 있으면 이 도형은 선 대칭이 된다.

보기:

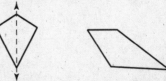

선 대칭이   선 대칭이
되는 도형   되지 않는 도형

1차 방정식 (linear equation) 그래프가 직선인 등식.

보기:

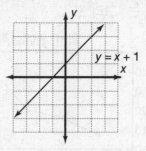

$y = x + 1$

선형 함수 (linear function) 그래프가 직선인 함수.

보기:

입력값	결과
x	y
-2	3
-1	2
0	1
1	0
2	-1
3	-2

$y = 1 - x$

1차 부등식 (linear inequality) $<, >, \leq$ 또는 $\geq$ 가 있는 수학 문장으로 그래프는 직선의 경계가 있는 영역으로 나온다.

보기:

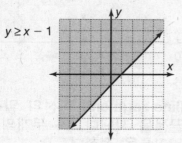

$y \geq x - 1$

리터 (liter) 미터법에서 부피를 측량하는 기본 단위.

보기:

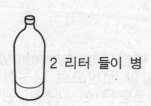

2 리터 들이 병

경도 (longitude) 본초 자오에서 동서로 정한 측량 단위. "도"로 표시한다.

보기:

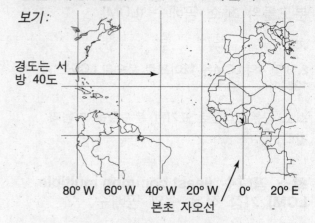

경도는 서방 40도

80° W 60° W 40° W 20° W 0° 20° E

본초 자오선

하위 4분위 (lower quartile) 자료의 집합에서 하위 절반의 중앙값.

보기:

27 27 27 29 32 33 36 38 42 43 62

하위 4분위   중앙값   상위 4분위

최소항 (lowest terms) 분자와 분모의 유일한 공통 인수가 1인 분수.

보기: $\frac{1}{2}$ $\frac{3}{5}$ $\frac{21}{23}$

질량 (mass) 물체가 내포하고 있는 물질의 양.

보기:

건포도는 1 그램의 질량을 지닌다.   운동화 한켤레는 1 킬로그램의 질량을 지닌다.

평균 (mean) 자료 집단의 값을 모두 더하여 값의 수로 나눈 것. 평균 (average) 이라고도 한다.

보기:

27 27 27 29 32 33 36 38 42 43 62

합계: 396

값의 수: 11

평균: 396 ÷ 11 = 36

측정오차 (measurement error) 측정의 불확실성. 가능한 최대 오차는 사용되는 최소 단위의 절반이다.

보기:

인치가 최소 단위이므로, 가능한 최대 오차는 $\frac{1}{2}$ 인치이다. 따라서 실재 키는 $5'5\frac{1}{2}"$에서 $5'6\frac{1}{2}"$이다.

5' 6"

중심 경향성 측정치 (measure of central tendency) 숫자로 나타나는 자료의 집합을 요약하는 단일 값.

보기:

평균값, 중앙값, 최빈값이 가장 보편적인 중심 경향성 측정치이다.

27 27 27 29 32 33 36 38 42 43 62

최빈값　　　　　중앙값

평균값 = 396 ÷ 11 = 36

중앙값 (median) 자료 집합에서 값을 순서별로 정리했을 때 중앙에 위치하는 값.

보기:

27 27 27 29 32 33 36 38 42 43 62

중앙값

암산 (mental math) 종이나 연필, 또는 계산기를 사용하지 않고 머리로 계산.

보기:

　　　2000 × 30

　0이 3개 + 0이 1개 = 0 이 4개

　생각: 2 × 3 = 6, 여기에 4개의 0을 달아준다.

　　2000 × 30 = 60,000

미터 (meter) 미터법에서 길이를 나타내는 기본 단위.

보기:

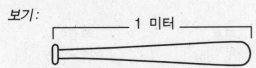

1 미터

야구 배트의 길이는 1 미터이다.

미터법 (metric system) 미터, 그램, 리터를 기본으로 하는 측정 단위.

보기:

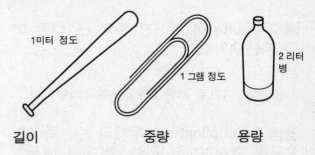

1미터 정도　　　1 그램 정도　　2 리터 병

길이　　　　　중량　　　　　용량

중점 (midpoint) 한 선분을 두개의 작고 합동인 선분으로 나누는 점.

보기:　　C 는 $\overline{AB}$의 중점이다.

$\overline{AC}$ 의 길이 = $\overline{CB}$ 의 길이

마일 (mile) 관습적 측정법의 단위로 5280 피트와 같다.

보기:

1 마일은 걸어서 15분에서 20분 거리, 또는 뛰어서 10분 정도 걸리는 거리이다.

밀리 (milli-) $\frac{1}{1000}$ 을 의미하는 접두사.

보기: 1 밀리미터 = $\frac{1}{1000}$ 미터

대분수 (mixed number) 0과 자연수와 분수로 이루어진 수.

보기:　　$3\frac{1}{2}$　　$1\frac{3}{4}$　　$13\frac{3}{8}$

최빈값 (mode) 자료의 집합에서 가장 많이 나오는 값.

보기:

27 27 27 29 32 33 36 38 42 43 62

주어진 이 자료의 집합에서 최빈값은 27이다.

단항식 (monomial) 단 한개의 항만을 가지고 있는 대수 표현법.

보기: $2x^2$ $5y$ x^3 -3

배수 (multiple) 주어진 수와 또 다른 0 과 자연수의 곱.

보기:

$3 \times 7 = 21$ 이므로, 21은 3과 7 모두의 배수이다.

곱셈 (multiplication) 두개의 수, 즉 인수들을 합하여 곱이라는 한 수를 내도록 하는 연산.

보기:

6이 3줄

$$3 \times 6 = 18$$

인수   곱

곱셈의 성질 (multiplication property) A 와 B가 독립 경우이면 이 둘 모두가 발생할 확률

$P(A$ 그리고 $B) = P(A) \times P(B)$.

보기:

첫번째 돌리기: P (빨간색) $= \frac{1}{4}$

두번째 돌리기: P (빨간색) $= \frac{1}{4}$

첫번째 돌리기와 두번째 돌리기: P (빨간색 그리고 빨간색) $= \frac{1}{4} \times \frac{1}{4} = \frac{1}{16}$

상등 곱셈의 속성 (Multiplication Property of Equality) 만일 $a = b$ 이면 $ac = bc$ 이다.

보기:

아래 보기의 두번째 선에서 2는 등식의 양쪽에 곱해졌다.

만일 $\frac{1}{2}y = 4$ 이면

$$2 \times \frac{1}{2}y = 2 \times 4 \text{ 이다}$$

곱셈의 역수 (multiplicative inverse) 두 수의 곱이 1이면 이 두 수는 서로의 역수이다.

보기:

$\frac{1}{6} \times 6 = 1$ 이므로 $\frac{1}{6}$ 과 6은 곱셈의 역수들이다.

배반사건 (mutually exclusive) A나 B 중에 하나가 발생할 경우, 나머지는 발생할 수 없다.

보기:

외부의 온도가 90도이면 눈이 내리지 않는다.

다각형에 3개의 면만 있다면 4개의 각을 지닐 수 없다.

음수 (negative numbers) 0 보다 적은 수.

보기:

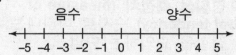

음수   양수

반비례 관계 (negative relationship) 두개의 자료 집합중 한 집합의 자료 값이 증가할 때 나머지 집합의 자료 값이 감소하면 이 집합들은 반비례 관계를 가지고 있다.

보기:

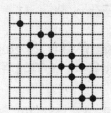

기울기 (negative slope) 아래쪽으로 기울어진 직선의 기울기.

보기:

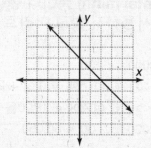

루트 (negative square root) 한 수의 루트의 반대.

보기:

루트   루트

$\sqrt{25} = 5$ $-\sqrt{25} = -5$

전개도 (net) 평평한 패턴으로 이것을 접으면 프리즘과 같은 입체 도형을 만들 수 있다.

보기:

5각형 프리즘 전개도   5각형 프리즘

9각형 (nonagon) 9개의 변을 가진 다각형.

보기:

비선형 방정식 (nonlinear equation) 그래프가 직선이 아닌 곡선인 방정식.

보기:

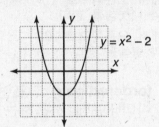

$y = x^2 - 2$

비선형 함수 (nonlinear function) x의 같은 변화가 y의 같은 변화를 초래하지 않으므로 그래프가 직선이 아닌 함수.

보기:

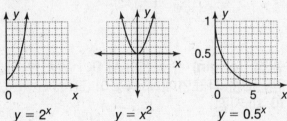

$y = 2^x$ $y = x^2$ $y = 0.5^x$

관계 없음 (no relationship) 두개의 자료 집합간에 비례 관계나 반비례 관계가 없으면 두 자료 집합간에는 관계가 없다.

보기:

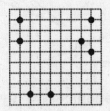

수직선 (number line) 차례대로 수를 나타내는 직선.

보기:

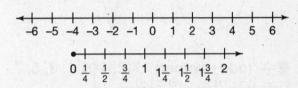

수-문자 형식 (number-word form) 수자와 글자를 사용해서 수를 나타내는 방법.

보기: 45조   9천

수자 (numeral) 수를 나타내는 기호.

보기: 7   58   234

분자 (numerator) 분수에서 윗부분에 있는 수로, 전체에서 얼마나 많은 부분이 담겨 있는지를 보여주는 것.

보기:

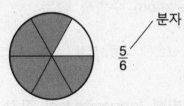

분자

$\dfrac{5}{6}$

둔각 (obtuse angle) 90도 보다 크고 180도 보다 적은 각.

보기:

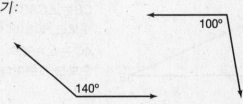

100°

140°

둔각 삼각형 (obtuse triangle) 둔각이 있는 삼각형.

보기:

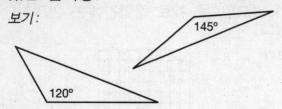

8각형 (octagon) 8개의 변을 가진 다각형.

보기:

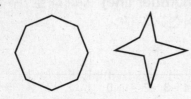

홀수 (odd number) 1자리수에 1, 3, 5, 7, 또는 9가 있는 0과 자연수.

보기:

43   225   999   8,007

가망성 (odds) 한 경우가 발생할 수 있는 길과 그 경우가 발생하지 못하는 길 사이의 비율.

보기:

3이 나올 가망성: 1 대 5

3이 나오지 않을 가망성: 5 대 1

연산 (operation) 수학적 절차.

보기:

4가지 기본 연산은 덧셈, 뺄셈, 곱셈, 나눗셈이다.

마주보는 빗변 (opposite leg) 직각 삼각형의 예각에서 그 각을 마주보는 빗변.

보기:

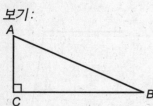

$\overline{CB}$는 ∠CAB의 마주보는 빗변이다.
$\overline{AC}$는 ∠ABC의 마주보는 빗변이다.

반대자리 수 (opposite numbers) 수직선에서 0에서 같은 거리에 있는 수이지만 자리가 반대인 수.

보기:

7과 −7은 서로 반대의 자리에 있다.

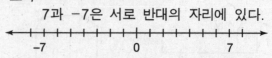

연산의 순서 (order of operations) 어떤 순서로 연산을 해야 하는지를 정해 놓은 규칙: (1) 괄호안을 간단히 정리한다, (2) 지수를 간단히 한다, (3) 왼쪽에서 오른쪽으로 곱셈과 나눗셈을 한다, 그리고 (4) 왼쪽에서 오른쪽으로 덧셈과 뺄셈을 한다.

보기:

$x = 3$인 경우 $2x^2 + 4(x − 2)$ 를 풀어라.

(1) 괄호안을 간단히 $2 \cdot 3^2 + 4(3 − 2)$
정리한다 $2 \cdot 3^2 + 4(1)$

(2) 지수를 간단히 한다 $2 \cdot 9 + 4$

(3) 왼쪽에서 오른쪽으로 $18 + 4$
곱셈과 나눗셈을 한다

(4) 왼쪽에서 오른쪽으로 22
덧셈과 뺄셈을 한다

좌표쌍 (ordered pair) 좌표면에서 점의 위치를 나타내는데 사용하는 한쌍의 번호.

보기:

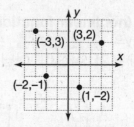

원점 (origin) 수직선에서 0이 위치한 지점, 또는 좌표면에서 축들이 교차하는 (0, 0) 지점.

보기:

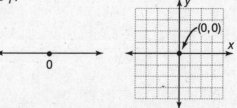

정사영 그림 (orthographic drawing)
앞에서 본 그림, 옆에서 본 그림, 그리고
위에서 본 그림으로 물체를 그리는 방법.

보기:

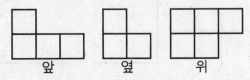

앞   옆   위

온스 (ounce) 관습적 측정법의 무게 단
위.

보기:

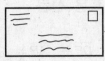 편지의 무게는 약
1 온스이다.

결과 (outcome) 실험이나 상황에서 일
어날 수 있는 것 중의 하나.

보기:

두개의 동전을 던졌을 때 생기는 결과

동전 1	동전 2
앞	뒤
앞	앞
뒤	앞
뒤	뒤

4가지 결과가 있다. 그중에 하나는 앞 앞이다.

이상점 (outlier) 자료 집합에서 대부분
의 다른 값과는 달리 극단적으로 나타
나는 값.

보기:

27 27 27 29 32 33 36 38 42 43 62
↑
이상점

포물선 (parabola) U 자형이거나 엎어진
U 자형의 곡선으로 2차 함수의 그래프.

보기:

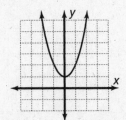

평행 (parallel) 아무리 뻗어나가도 절대
로 만나지 않는 두 직선, 선분 혹은 반
직선.

보기:

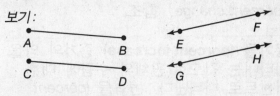

평행사변형 (parallelogram) 4개의 변을
가진 도형으로 서로 마주보는 변이 평
행이며 합동인 도형.

보기:

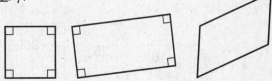

5각형 (pentagon) 5개의 변을 가진 다각형.

보기:

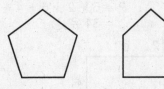

퍼센트 (percent) 수를 100에 비교한
비율.

보기:

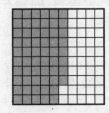 $\frac{58}{100} = 0.58 = 58\%$

변화율 (percent change) 감소 또는 증
가와 같은 변화량을 원체의 수량으로
나누어 원체의 수량에 대한 퍼센트로
나타낸 변화량.

보기:

$1500을 투자하여 $75의 이자를 받았을 경우의
변화율을 계산하라.

$\frac{75}{1500} = 0.05 = 5\%$ $75 는 5% 증가와 같다.

$50 짜리 상품이 $10 할인을 했을 경우 이 변화율
을 계산하라.

$\frac{10}{50} = 0.20 = 20\%$ $10 할인은 20% 감소와
같다.

감소율 (percent decrease) 감소의 양을 나타내는 것으로 원체의 수량에 대한 퍼센트로 나타낸다. *변화율 (percent change)* 참조.

증가율 (percent increase) 증가의 양을 나타내는 것으로 원체의 수량에 대한 퍼센트로 나타낸다. *변화율 (percent change)* 참조.

완전제곱 (perfect square) 0과 자연수의 제곱.

보기:

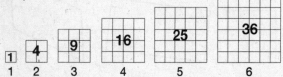

주변길이 (perimeter) 도형 둘레의 거리.

보기:

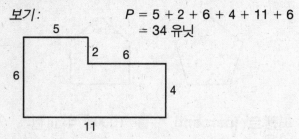

$$P = 5 + 2 + 6 + 4 + 11 + 6$$
$$= 34 \text{ 유닛}$$

순열 (permutation) 항목의 배열로, 순서가 중요성을 갖는다.

보기:

다음의 학생중에서 한 학생이 회장으로, 그리고 다른 한 학생이 부회장으로 뽑힐 것이다: 웬디, 알렉스, 카를로스. 가능한 순열은 다음과 같다:

웬디 — 회장, 알렉스 — 부회장
웬디 — 회장, 카를로스 — 부회장
알렉스 — 회장, 웬디 — 부회장
알렉스 — 회장, 카를로스 — 부회장
카를로스 — 회장, 웬디 — 부회장
카를로스 — 회장, 알렉스 — 부회장

참고:위의 보기들은 각각 다른 순열이다.

수직 (perpendicular) 서로 직각으로 교차하는 선들, 반직선들, 선분들.

보기:

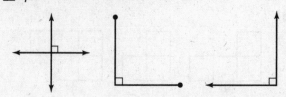

수직 이등분선 (perpendicular bisector) 선분의 중점에서 수직으로 교차하는 선, 반직선, 혹은 선분.

보기:

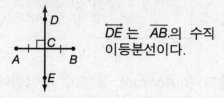

$\overrightarrow{DE}$ 는 $\overline{AB}$.의 수직 이등분선이다.

파이 (pi (π)) 원의 둘레와 지름간의 비율: 3.14159265...

보기:

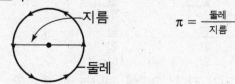

$$\pi = \frac{\text{둘레}}{\text{지름}}$$

그림그래프 (pictograph) 기호로 자료를 대신 나타내는 그래프.

보기:

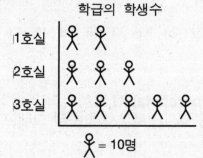

학급의 학생수

☺ = 10명

자리값 (place value) 각 자리수에 주어진 값.

보기:

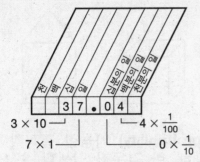

3×10 ─┐
7×1 ─┘
┌─ $4 \times \frac{1}{100}$
└─ $0 \times \frac{1}{10}$

평면 (plane) 무한대로 확장하는 평평한 표면.

보기:

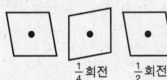

평면을 상상하려면 책상의 표면을 모든 방향으로 연장하는 것을 연상하면 된다.

점대칭 (point symmetry) 180도 회전 후에도 변형이 없을 경우에 이 도형은 점대칭이다.

보기:

$\frac{1}{4}$ 회전 $\frac{1}{2}$ 회전
(90도 회전) (180도 회전)

180도 회전, 혹은 절반 회전 후에도 도형은 동일하게 보인다.

다각형 (polygon) 선분으로 이루어진 닫혀진 도형.

보기:

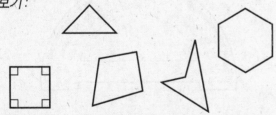

다면체 (polyhedron) 면들이 다각형인 입방체.

보기:

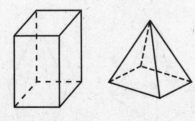

다항식 (polynomial) 한개나 그 이상의 항의 합인 대수 표현법.

보기:

$$x^2 + 2x - 3 \qquad 5y - 15$$

모집단 (population) 통계 조사에서 조사될 대상의 전체.

보기:

클럽 회원 1,000명의 이름을 각각 카드에 적어놓고 이 카드들을 섞었다. 이중에서 100 장의 카드를 뽑아서 이 회원들에게 전화 설문조사를 실시했다. 이 설문조사의 모집단은 1,000 명의 클럽 회원 모두이다.

양수 (positive numbers) 0 보다 큰 수

보기:

음수   양수

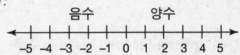

$-5 \ -4 \ -3 \ -2 \ -1 \ 0 \ 1 \ 2 \ 3 \ 4 \ 5$

정비례관계 (positive relationship) 두개의 자료 집합의 값이 같이 증가하거나 감소하면 이 두 자료 집합은 비례관계이다.

보기:

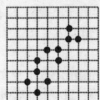

기울기 (positive slope) 위쪽으로 기울어진 선의 기울기.

보기:

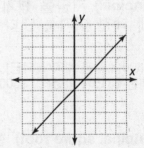

파운드 (pound) 관습적 측정법에서의 단위로 16 온스와 같다.

보기:

쌀
1파운드

승 (power) 지수 또는 지수의 밑을 지수만큼 올렸을 때 나오는 수.

보기:

$$16 = 2^4 \quad 2를 4승하다.$$

$$16은 2의 4승이다.$$

정도 (precision) 측정의 정확성. 측정단위로 결정된다.

보기:

작은 측정단위인 인치는 큰 측정단위인 피트보다 더 정확하다.

5'1" 61"

소인수 (prime factor) 다른 정수를 나누었을 때 나머지가 남지 않는 수.

보기:

$$35 \div 5 = 7 \text{ 이므로, 5는 35의 약수이다.}$$

소인수분해 (prime factorization) 한 수를 약수의 곱으로 표시하는 것.

보기: $70 = 2 \times 5 \times 7$

소수 (prime number) 1보다 큰 0과 자연수로 인수가 1과 그 자신밖에 없는 수.

보기:

소수는 2, 3, 5, 7, 11... 등으로 시작한다.

원금 (principal) 저금을 했거나 빌린 돈으로 이에 대한 이자를 낸다.

보기:

데이브는 $300을 적금 계좌에 저금했다. 1년 후 이 계좌의 잔액은 $315가 되었다. $300이 원금의 액수이다.

루트 (principal squre root) 한 수의 양수 루트.

보기:

루트   루트
$$\sqrt{25} = 5 \qquad -\sqrt{25} = -5$$

프리즘 (prism) 면들이 합동이고 평행인 다면체.

보기:

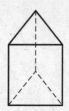

확률 (probability) 가능한 결과의 모든 수에 대해 한 경우가 발생할 수 있는 수의 비율.

보기:

3이 나올 확률은 $\frac{1}{6}$이다.

3이 나오지 않을 확률은 $\frac{5}{6}$이다.

곱 (product) 둘 혹은 그 이상의 수를 곱한 결과.

보기:

곱
$$2 \times 3 \times 5 = 30$$

비례 (proportion) 두 비율은 같음을 보여주는 등식.

보기:

$$\frac{12}{34} = \frac{6}{17}$$

각도기 (protractor) 각도를 측정하는 기구.

보기:

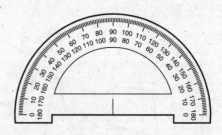

피라미드 (pyramid) 밑변이 하나이고 나머지 변들은 모두 삼각형으로 한 점에서 만나는 입방체.

보기:

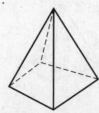
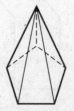

피타고라스의 정리 (Pythagorean Theorem) 직각삼각형에서 c는 사변의 길이이고 a와 b는 빗변의 길이라면, $a^2 + b^2 = c^2$.

보기:

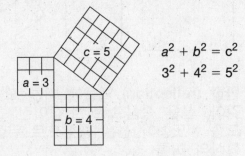

$$c = 5 \qquad a^2 + b^2 = c^2$$
$$a = 3 \qquad 3^2 + 4^2 = 5^2$$
$$b = 4$$

4분면 (quadrants) 좌표평면에서 축으로 결정되는 네개의 구역.

보기:

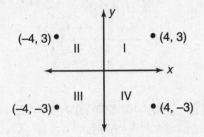

$(-4, 3)$ • II   I • $(4, 3)$

$(-4, -3)$ • III   IV • $(4, -3)$

2차 방정식 (quadratic equation) x^2와 같은 제곱항이 들어있는 방정식.

보기:

$$y = x^2 + 3x - 12 \qquad y = 2x^2 + 7$$

2차 함수 (quadratic function) x의 최대 승이 2인 함수. 2차 함수의 그래프는 포물선이다.

보기:

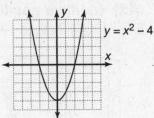

$$y = x^2 - 4$$

사변형 (quadrilateral) 4개의 변을 가진 다각형.

보기:

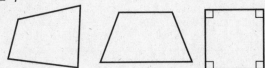

쿼트 (quart) 관습적 측정법에서 부피를 측정하는 단위.

보기:

우유   우유 한 쿼트

4분위 (quartile) 자료 집합을 4개의 동등한 부분으로 나누었을 때, 그 부분 중의 하나.

보기:

27 27 27 29 32 33 36 38 42 43 62
         ↑   ↑   ↑
        하위   중앙값   상위
        4분위   4분위

27, 33, 42는 이 자료 집합에 대한 세개의 4분위이다.

몫 (quotient) 한 수를 다른 수로 나누었을 때 나오는 결과.

보기:

몫
$$8 \div 4 = 2$$

근호 (radical sign) $\sqrt{}$, 한 수의 루트를 나타낼 때 쓰이는 기호.

보기:

$$\sqrt{49} = 7$$

반지름 (radius) 원의 중심에서 원의 한 점 까지의 선.

보기:

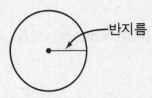

반지름

무작위 견본 (random sample) 모집단의 모든 구성원이 견본에 포함될 확률이 동일한 추출 견본.

보기:

클럽 회원 1,000명의 이름을 각각 카드에 적어놓고 이 카드들을 섞었다. 이중에서 100 장의 카드를 뽑아서 이 회원들에게 전화 설문조사를 실시했다. 이 클럽의 회원들 모두가 전화 설문조사의 대상이 될 수 있는 동일한 확률을 가지고 있었으므로 이것은 무작위 추출 견본이다.

범위 (range) 한 자료 집합에서 최고값과 최저값의 차이.

보기:

27 27 27 29 32 33 36 38 42 43 62

범위는 62 − 27 = 35.

율 (rate) 다른 단위를 가진 수량들이 어떻게 관계되는지를 보여주는 비율.

보기: $\dfrac{72 \text{ 달러}}{28 \text{ 시간}}$ $\dfrac{55 \text{ 마일}}{1 \text{ 시간}}$

비율 (ratio) 두 수량간의 비교. 보통 분수로 쓰여진다.

보기: $\dfrac{2}{1}$ 2 대 1   2:1

유리수 (rational number) 두 정수의 비율로 쓰일 수 있는 수. 정수, 분수, 그리고 많은 소수들이 유리수이다.

보기:

정수	분수	소수
$-27 = \dfrac{-27}{1}$	$\dfrac{7}{8}$	$3.1 = 3\dfrac{1}{10} = \dfrac{31}{10}$

반직선 (ray) 한쪽에는 끝점이 있고 나머지 방향으로는 무한대로 뻗어나가는 선의 일부. 반직선의 이름을 정할 때는 끝점을 먼저 부른다.

보기:

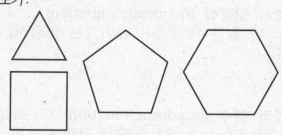

$\overrightarrow{AB}$

실수 (real number) 모든 유리수와 무리수.

보기:

-27 $\dfrac{1}{2}$ 3.1

$\sqrt{5}$ π $-\sqrt{\dfrac{1}{2}}$

역수 (reciprocals) 서로의 곱이 1인 두 수.

보기:

$\dfrac{3}{5} \cdot \dfrac{5}{3} = 1$ 이므로 $\dfrac{3}{5}$ 와 $\dfrac{5}{3}$ 은 역수이다.

직사각형 (rectangle) 마주보는 변이 같은 길이이고 모든 각이 90도인 평행 4변형.

보기:

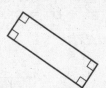

반향 (reflection) 거울에 비친 모습과 같이, 선을 중심으로 "뒤집어진" 도형의 모습. 도형이 선을 중심으로 뒤집어진 형상의 이름.

보기:

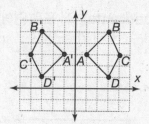

정다각형 (regular polygon) 모든 변과 각들이 합동인 다각형.

보기:

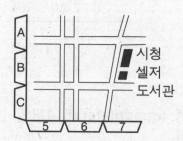

상대적 위치 (relative position) 다른 장소와 비교해서 상대적으로 주어진 위치.

보기:

A   B   C

■ 시청
■ 셀저
─ 도서관

5   6   7

시청은 셀저 도서관 바로 옆에 있다.

나머지 (remainder) 나눗셈이 끝난 후 제수보다 적게 남은 수.

보기:

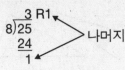

나머지

순환소수 (repeating decimal) 소수점 다음의 수나 수들이 계속 반복되는 소수.

보기: 0.6̄   0.1̄2̄3̄   2.1̄8̄

마름모꼴 (rhombus) 4변의 길이가 모두 같은 평행사변형.

보기:

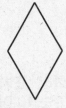

직각 (right angle) 각도가 90도인 각.

보기:

직각삼각형 (right triangle) 한 각이 직각인 삼각형.

보기:

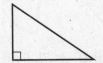

y의 변화량 (rise) 그래프의 선에서 주어진 수평 변화에 대한 수직 변화.

보기:

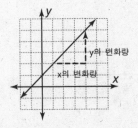

회전 (rotation) 도형의 모습이 마치 바퀴가 돌듯이 도는 것. 도형을 돌리는 변형 그 자체를 뜻하기도 한다.

보기:

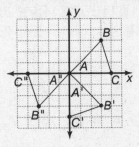

회전대칭 (rotational symmetry) 한 도형이 한 바퀴보다 적게 회전했을때도 원체의 모습과 같으면 이 도형은 회전 대칭이다.

보기:

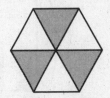

각 도형은 회전 대칭이다.

반올림/반내림 (rounding) 주어진 자리 값으로 수를 어림내는 것.

보기:

2153을 반올림/반내림 하면	
100의 자리로 한 경우: 2200	10의 자리로 한 경우: 2150

x의 변화량 (run) 그래프의 선에서 수직 변화, 또는 y의 변화량을 계산하는데 사용하는 수평변화.

보기:

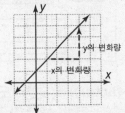

표본 (sample) 특정한 상황이 어떻게 발생하는지를 예측하는데 사용되는 자료의 집합.

보기:

클럽 회원 1,000명의 이름을 각각 카드에 적어놓고 이 카드들을 섞었다. 이중에서 100 장의 카드를 뽑아서 이 회원들에게 전화 설문조사를 실시했다. 표본은 전화 설문조사를 받은 100명의 회원들이다.

표본공간 (sample space) 한 실험에서 나올 수 있는 모든 결과의 집합.

보기:

동전 2개를 던졌을 때 나올 수 있는 결과

동전 1	동전 2
앞	뒤
앞	앞
뒤	앞
뒤	뒤

표본공간은 앞, 뒤; 앞, 앞; 그리고 뒤, 뒤이다.

(그래프의) 눈금 (scale (graphical)) 막대그래프나 선그래프에서 막대의 높이를 측정하기 위해 수직축을 따라 동등하게 나누어진 표시.

보기:

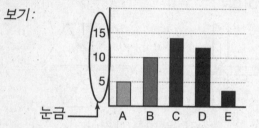

(비례도의) 축척 (scale (in scale drawings)) 비례도와 실제 물체간의 측정비율.

비례도 (scale drawing) 비율을 사용하여 물체를 확대하거나 축소한 그림.

보기:

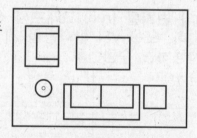

거실의 비례도

축척:
0.1 in. = 1 ft

척도 (scale factor) 비슷한 도형들을 확대하거나 축소하는데 사용하는 비율.

보기:

$\frac{10}{5} = 2$ $\frac{6}{3} = 2$

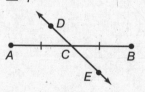

10 cm
6 cm
3 cm
5 cm

확대를 위한 척도는 2이다.

부등변 삼각형 (scalene triangle) 변의 갤이가 모두 다른 삼각형.

보기:

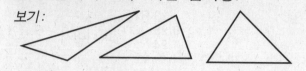

점그래프 (scatterplot) 한쌍의 자료값으로 점의 위치를 잡아 두 자료집합의 관계를 보이는 그래프.

보기:

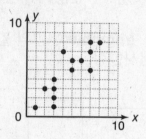

과학적 표기방법 (scientific notation) 1 또는 10 이하의 소수와 10의 승수로 수를 표기하는 방법.

보기: $350{,}000 = 3.5 \times 10^5$

부채꼴 (sector) 원의 일부분으로 부채 또는 쐐기와 같은 모양을 하고 있으며 원 그래프에서 자료집합의 일부가 전체와 어떻게 비교되는지를 보여준다.

보기:

선분 (segment) *선분* (line segment) 참조.

선분의 이등분선 (segment bisector) 선분의 중점을 지나는 선, 반직선 혹은 선분.

보기:

$\overline{DE}$가 C에서 $\overline{AB}$를 이등분한다.

수열 (sequence) 일정한 패턴을 따르는 수의 배열.

보기:

연산수열

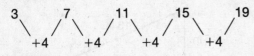

기하수열

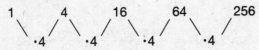

변 (side) 각을 이루는 각각의 반직선. 또한 다각형을 이루는 선분.

보기:

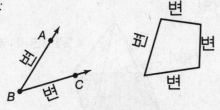

두 각과 끼인 한 변 (SAA Side-Angle-Angle) 대응하는 부분을 비교하여 삼각형들이 서로 합동인지를 판단하는 방법.

보기:

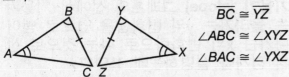

$$\overline{BC} \cong \overline{YZ}$$
$$\angle ABC \cong \angle XYZ$$
$$\angle BAC \cong \angle YXZ$$

SAA 법칙에 의해 $\triangle ABC \cong \triangle XYZ$

세 변 (SAS Side-Angle-Side) 대응하는 부분을 비교하여 삼각형들이 서로 합동인지를 판단하는 방법.

보기:

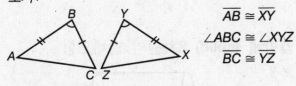

$$\overline{AB} \cong \overline{XY}$$
$$\angle ABC \cong \angle XYZ$$
$$\overline{BC} \cong \overline{YZ}$$

SAS법칙에 의해 $\triangle ABC \cong \triangle XYZ$

세 변 (SSS Side-Side-Side) 대응하는 부분을 비교하여 삼각형들이 서로 합동인지를 판단하는 방법.

보기:

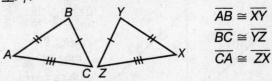

$$\overline{AB} \cong \overline{XY}$$
$$\overline{BC} \cong \overline{YZ}$$
$$\overline{CA} \cong \overline{ZX}$$

SSS 법칙에 의해 $\triangle ABC \cong \triangle XYZ$.

주요 자리수 (significant digits) 측정된 수량에서 실제의 측정치를 나타내는 자리 수.

보기:

380.6700 모든 자리수가 주요 자리수이다.

0.0038 3과 8은 주요 자리수이지만 여기에 나와있는 0은 주요 자리수가 아니다.

닮은꼴 (similar) 모양은 같으나 크기가 같지 않음.

보기:

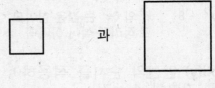

과

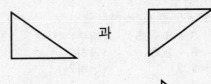

과

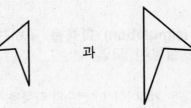

과

닮은 비율 (similarity ratio) 닮은꼴의 도형에서 대응하는 변의 길이들 간의 비율.

보기:

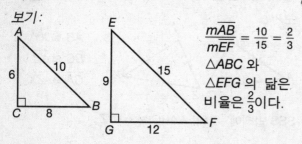

$$\frac{m\overline{AB}}{m\overline{EF}} = \frac{10}{15} = \frac{2}{3}$$

△*ABC* 와 △*EFG* 의 닮은 비율은 $\frac{2}{3}$ 이다.

단순이자 (simple interest) 원금만에 대한 이자.

보기: 레이몬은 이자율이 연 6%인 계좌에 $240 을 5년간 투자했다.

그는 240 · 0.06 · 5 = 72, 즉 5년 후에 $72의 단순이자를 받을 것이다.

정리된 식 (simplified) 같은 항이 없는 다항식.

보기:

$4x^4 + x^3 + x^2 - 8$ 정리된 식

$4x^4 + x^2 + 6x^2 - 8$ x^2 와 $6x^2$ 는 같은 항이므로 정리된 식이 아니다

정리 (simplify) 연산의 순서를 적용하여 복잡한 식을 간단히 하는것.

보기: $3 + 8 \cdot 5^2$ 를 정리하시오

$$3 + 8 \cdot 5^2 = 3 + 8 \cdot 25 \quad (\text{지수})$$
$$= 3 + 200 \quad (\text{곱하기})$$
$$= 203 \quad (\text{더하기})$$

시뮬레이션 (simulation) 확률을 구하는데 사용하는 실험적 모델.

보기:

야구선수의 타율은 .250이다. 이 선수의 타율을 시뮬레이션으로 모형화 하기위해 4등분된 회전판을 돌렸다. 이 시뮬레이션은 타자가 얼마나 자주 연속으로 2를 치거나 연속으로 3을 치는지를 예측하는데 사용될 수 있다.

싸인 (sine) 직각삼각형의 예각 *x*에 대한 싸인 sin(*x*)는 $\frac{\text{마주보는 빗변}}{\text{사변}}$ 의 비율이다.

보기:

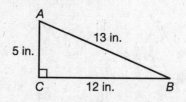

$$\sin \angle CAB = \frac{\text{마주보는 빗변}}{\text{사변}} = \frac{12}{13} \approx 0.92$$

경사면의 높이 (slant height) 피라미드에서 밑면의 모서리부터 꼭지점 까지의 수직거리.

보기:

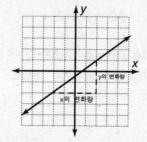

높이   경사면의 높이

미끄러짐 (slide) *이동* 참조.

기울기 (slope) 그래프의 선에서 기울기는 올라가는 y의 변화량을 옆으로 뻗어나가는 x의 변화량으로 나눈 것으로 선의 경사를 설명하는데 쓰인다.

보기:

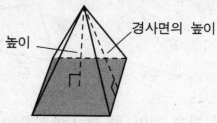

$$\frac{\text{y의 변화량}}{\text{x의 변화량}} = \frac{3}{4}$$

기울기는 $\frac{3}{4}$.

입방체 (solid) 3차원의 입체도형.

보기:

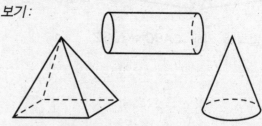

등식 혹은 부등식의 해법 (solutions of an equation or inequality) 등식이나 부등식을 참으로 만드는 값이나 변수.

보기:

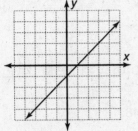

이 선은
$y = x - 1$
의 해법을 나타낸다.

칠해진 부분은
$y > x - 1$
의 해법을 나타낸다.

공식의 해 (solution of a system) 한 체계의 모든 공식들이 참이 될 수 있도록 변수를 대신하는 수.

보기:
$$y = x + 4$$
$$y = 3x - 6$$

(5, 9) 는 위 두 식을 모두 풀어줄 수 있다. 그러므로 (5, 9)는 이 체계의 해이다.

풀기 (solve) 등식 혹은 부등식의 해법을 구하는것.

보기:
$$x + 6 = 13 \text{ 을 풀라.}$$
$$x + 6 = 13$$
$$x + 6 + (-6) = 13 + (-6)$$
$$x + 0 = 7$$
$$x = 7$$

구 (sphere) 모든 점에서 중심까지의 거리가 같은 입방체.

보기:

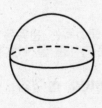

정사각형 (square) 모든 변의 길이가 같고 모든 각이 90도인 사각형.

보기:

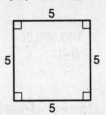

제곱 (squared) 2승으로 올림.

보기: $3 \text{ 의 제곱} = 3^2 = 3 \times 3 = 9$

평방센티미터 (square centimeter) 변의 길이가 1cm인 정사각형의 면적.

보기:

1 평방센티미터

평방인치 (square inch) 변의 길이가 1 인치인 정사각형의 면적.

보기:

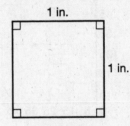

1 평방인치

평방근 (square root) *N*의 평방근은 어떤 수와 그 수를 곱했을 때 *N*이 나오는 수이다. 또한 주어진 수의 평방근은 이 주어진 수와 같은 면적을 가진 정사각형의 한 변의 길이이다.

보기:
$9 \times 9 = 81$, 그러므로
9는 81의 평방근이다.
$9 = \sqrt{81}$

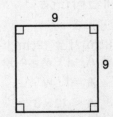

면적은 81 평방단위이다.

표준 양식 (standard form) 자리수를 사용하여 수를 표시하는 법.

보기:

표준 양식: 100,000,000
문자 형식: 일억
수-문자 형식: 1억

줄기-잎 도표 (stem-and-leaf diagram) 자료값의 자리수를 사용하여 자료집합의 모습과 분포를 보여주는 방법.

보기:

도표는 자료 집합을 보여준다: 33, 34, 34, 35, 40, 41, 46, 51, 51, 52, 53, 55, 58.

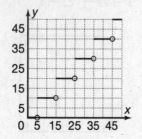

줄기	잎
3	3 4 4 5
4	0 1 6
5	1 1 2 3 5 8

계단식 함수 (step function) 각기 다른 입력값에 각기 다른 법칙이 적용된 함수. 이 함수의 그래프는 서로 연결되지 않은 부분들로 이루어진다.

보기:

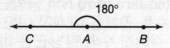

평각 (straight angle) 각도가 180도인 각.

보기:

180°

C　　A　　B

대입 (substitute) 정해진 값으로 변수를 대신하는것.

보기:

가로 8cm, 세로 12cm인 직사각형의 면적을 구하기 위해 $A = l \cdot w$ 공식을 사용한다.

$A = l \cdot w$
$A = 12 \cdot 8$　　　세로와 가로에
$A = 96$　　　　　값을 대입한다.
면적은 96 cm².

뺄셈 (subtraction) 두 수 사이의 차이를 보여주는 연산. 또는 일부를 뺐을 때 얼마가 남는지를 보여주는 연산.

보기:　　　12 − 5 = 7

⊠⊠⊠⊠⊠
○○○○○
○○

합 (sum) 둘 혹은 그 이상의 수를 더한 결과.

보기:　　30 + 18 = 48 ← 합

보각 (supplementary angles) 서로의 합이 180도인 두 각.

보기:

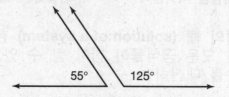

55°　　　125°

표면 면적 (surface area SA) 다면체의 각 면의 면적의 합.

보기:

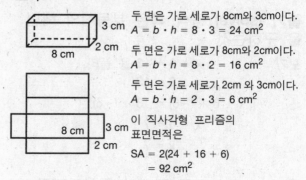

두 면은 가로 세로가 8cm와 3cm이다.
$A = b \cdot h = 8 \cdot 3 = 24$ cm²

두 면은 가로 세로가 8cm와 2cm이다.
$A = b \cdot h = 8 \cdot 2 = 16$ cm²

두 면은 가로 세로가 2cm 와 3cm이다.
$A = b \cdot h = 2 \cdot 3 = 6$ cm²

이 직사각형 프리즘의 표면면적은

SA = 2(24 + 16 + 6)
= 92 cm²

설문조사 (survey) 정보의 수집과 분석이 요구되는 조사.

보기:

학생들이 가장 좋아하는 운동은 무엇인지를 알아보기위해 설문조사를 실시했다.

대칭 (symmetry) 선대칭, 점대칭, 회전대칭 참조.

1차 방정식 체계 (system of linear equations) 함께 취급되는 둘 혹은 그 이상의 1차 방정식.

보기:　　$y = x + 3$
$y = 4x − 15$

T-도표 (T-table) 등식에서 서로 대응하는 x값과 y값을 보여주는 표.

보기:
$$y = 2x + 1$$

x	y
-1	-3
-2	-1
0	1
1	3
2	5

빗줄 눈금 (tally) 조사를 할 때 수를 세어서 이를 빗줄 표시로 기록하는 것.

보기:

차량	빗줄
세단	卌 |||
웨건	||||
서버반	卌	
트럭	卌
밴	|||

빗줄 표시 (tally marks) 큰 자료집합을 정리하는데 사용하는 표시. 한 표시는 자료집합에서 한 번 발생한 것을 뜻한다.

보기: | 1   卌 5

접선 (tangent line) 원의 한 점과 접하는 선.

보기:

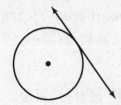

탄젠트 비율 (tangent ratio) 직각삼각형의 예각 x에 대한 탄젠트, $\tan(x)$는 $\dfrac{\text{마주보는 빗변}}{\text{인접한 빗변}}$ 의 비율이다.

보기:

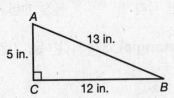

$$\tan \angle CAB = \frac{\text{마주보는 빗변}}{\text{인접한 빗변}} = \frac{12}{5} = 2.4$$

항 (term) 수열의 한 수. 또한 다항식의 한 부분으로 수, 변수, 혹은 변수와 곱한 수를 갖는다. 변수는 0과 자연수의 지수를 가질 수 있다.

보기:

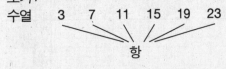

수열   3   7   11   15   19   23

항

다항식 $2x^3 - x^2 + 3x - 5$

항

유한소수 (terminal decimal) 정해진 자리수를 지니는 소수.

보기: 3.5   0.599992   4.05

모자이크식 (tessellation) 서로 겹치거나 중간의 틈을 남기지 않고 면을 모두 덮는 반복되는 도형의 패턴.

보기:

  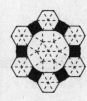

이론상 확률 (theoretical probability) 가능한 결과의 수에 대해 한 경우가 발생할 수 있는 비율.

보기:

$$\frac{\text{하얀색을 가르킬 수 있는 경우}}{\text{전체 경우}} = \frac{3}{6} = \frac{1}{2}$$

이 회전판의 절반은 하얀색이므로 하얀색이 나올 수 있는 이론상 확률은 $\frac{1}{2}$이다.

변형 (transformation) 도형의 크기나 위치의 변화.

보기:

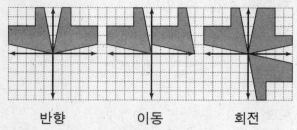

반향   이동   회전

이동 (translation) 뒤집어지거나 회전하지 않고 그대로 새로운 위치로 미끄러지듯이 움직인 도형의 모습. 또한 도형을 미끄러지듯이 움직이는 것 자체.

보기:

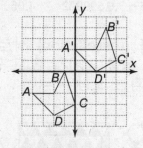

횡단선 (transversal) 둘 혹은 그 이상의 선을 가로지르는 선.

보기:

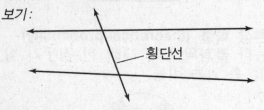

횡단선

사다리꼴 (trapezoid) 정확히 두 변이 평행인 4변형.

보기:

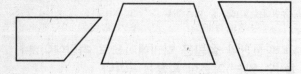

수형도 (tree diagram) 나무의 가지가 뻗어나가는듯한 그림으로, 한 상황의 모든 가능한 결과를 보여준다.

보기:

3개의 동전을 던진다:

동전 1	동전 2	동전 3	모든 가능한 결과:
		앞	앞, 앞, 앞
	앞		
		뒤	앞, 앞, 뒤
앞			
		앞	앞, 뒤, 앞
	뒤		
		뒤	앞, 뒤, 뒤
		앞	뒤, 앞, 앞
	앞		
		뒤	뒤, 앞, 뒤
뒤			
		앞	뒤, 뒤, 앞
	뒤		
		뒤	뒤, 뒤, 뒤

경향 (trend) 점그래프에서 패턴으로 나타난 두 자료 집합의 관계 *정비례관계 반비례관계 관계없음* 참조.

경향선 (trend line) 점그래프에서 경향을 보이고 있는 점들과 어느정도 일치하는 선.

시도 (trial) 한번의 실험.

보기:

주사위 한번 굴리기   동전 한번 던지기

삼각형 (triangle) 3개의 변을 가진 다각형.

보기:

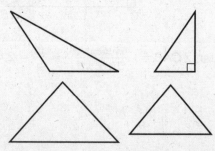

삼각법비율 (trigonometric ratios) 직각 삼각형의 변의 길이와 이 삼각형의 예각의 각도 사이의 비율.

보기:

$$\cos \angle CAB = \frac{\text{인접빗변}}{\text{사변}} = \frac{3}{5} = 0.6$$

$$\sin \angle CAB = \frac{\text{마주보는 빗변}}{\text{사변}} = \frac{4}{5} = 0.8$$

$$\tan \angle CAB = \frac{\text{마주보는 빗변}}{\text{사변}} = \frac{4}{3} \approx 1.3$$

3항식 (trinomial) 항이 세 개있는 다항식.

보기: $2x^3 - x^2 + 3x$ $3x^2 + 2x - 4$

돌기 (turn) 회전 참조.

불공평한 게임 (unfair game) 게임의 참가자 각각이 모두 같은 이길 수 있는 확률을 가지고 있지 않은 게임.

보기:

불공평한 게임: 주사위 두개를 던진다. 각 참가자는 2에서 12까지의 합을 지정받는다. 각 참가자는 자신의 수가 나오면 점수를 받는다. 2에서 12까지의 합이 나올 수 있는 확률은 동일하지 않으므로 참가자들이 이길 수 있는 기회가 동일하지 않고, 따라서 이 게임은 불공평한 것이다.

단가 (unit price) 한 품목의 가격을 나타내는 단위 가격.

보기:

  파운드당 $3.00   상자당 $5.75

단위 (unit) 무엇의 한 개. 측정의 표준으로 쓰이는 수량이나 값.

단위분수 (unit fraction) 분자가 1인 분수.

보기: $\frac{1}{4}$ $\frac{1}{2}$ $\frac{1}{7}$

단위율 (unit rate) 비교를 할 때 두번째 수가 한 단위인 비율.

보기: 분당 25 갈론 $\frac{55 \text{ 마일}}{1시간}$

서로다른 분모 (unlike denominators) 둘 혹은 그 이상의 분수에서 분모가 다른 것.

보기: $\frac{1}{2}$ $\frac{2}{5}$ $\frac{2}{9}$

서로다른 분모

상위 4분위 (upper quartile) 자료집합에서 상위 절반의 중앙값.

보기:

27 27 27 29 32 33 36 38 42 43 62

하위   중앙값   상위
4분위   4분위

변수 (variable) 변하거나 바뀔 수 있는 수량. 보통 문자로 표시한다.

보기: $3x$ y $2t$

변수

벤다이아그램 (Venn diagram) 집합들간의 관계를 보여주기 위해 구역을 사용하는 다이아그램.

보기:

평행사변형
직사각형
정사각형
마름모

꼭지점 (vertex) 각이나 다른 다각형에서 두 변이 교차하는 점. 다면체의 경우 셋 혹은 그 이상의 면이 교차하는 점.

보기:

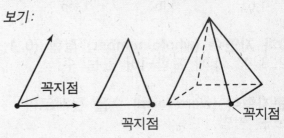

꼭지점   꼭지점   꼭지점

마주보는 각 (vertical angles) 두 선이 교차할 때 서로 마주보는 각.

보기:

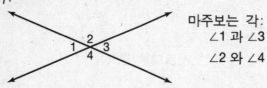

마주보는 각:
∠1 과 ∠3
∠2 와 ∠4

수직 축 (vertical axis) 막대 그래프나 좌표면의 두 선들 중의 수직선.

보기:

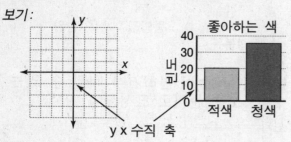

좋아하는 색

y x 수직 축

부피 (volume) 입방체가 차지하는 공간의 양.

보기:

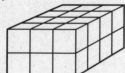

$V = lwh$

$V = 4 \cdot 3 \cdot 2$

$V = 24$ 입방 단위

중량 (weight) 몸체에 중력이 힘을 가하는 양.

보기:

1 oz   1 lb   1 ton

0과 자연수 (whole number) 집합 {0, 1, 2, 3, 4, ...} 에 포함되어 있는 수.

문자형식 (word form) 수를 문자로만 쓰는 방법.

보기:

사십오조   십억   육

x 축 (x-axis) 좌표면의 수평축.

보기:

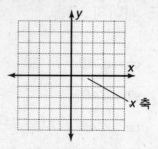

x 축

x 좌표 (x-coordinate) 좌표쌍의 첫 수.

보기:

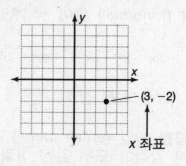

(3, −2)

x 좌표

x 축 교차점 (x-intercept) 등식의 그래프가 x 축을 지나는 지점.

보기:

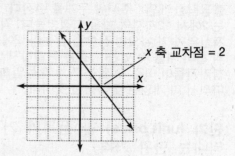

x 축 교차점 = 2

y 축 (y-axis) 좌표면의 수직축.

보기:

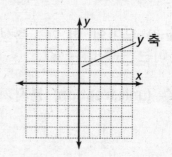

y 축

y 좌표 (y-coordinate) 좌표쌍의 두번째 수.

보기:

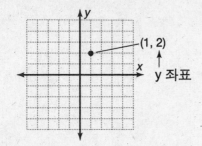

y 축 교차점 (y-intercept) 등식의 그래프가 y 축을 지나는 지점.

보기:

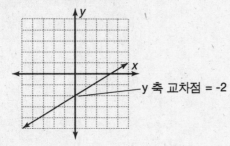

야드 (yard) 관습적 측정법의 한 단위로 3피트와 같다.

보기:

책상의 높이는 약 1 야드이다.

0을 이루는 쌍 (zero pair) 한 수와 그 반대 수.

보기: 7 과 −7   23 과 −23

덧셈의 0의 법칙 (Zero Property of Addition) 자연수와 이 수의 덧셈에 대한 역수의 합은 0이다.

보기:

$$3 + (-3) = 0$$
$$-8 + 8 = 0$$

Spanish Glossary

posición absoluta (absolute position)
Localización dada como coordenadas.

Ejemplo:

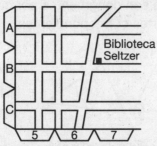

B7 es la posición absoluta para la Biblioteca Seltzer.

valor absoluto (absolute value)
Distancia de un número con respecto a cero. El símbolo para el valor absoluto es $|\ |$.

Ejemplos:

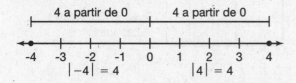

ángulo agudo (acute angle) Un ángulo que mide menos de 90°.

Ejemplos:

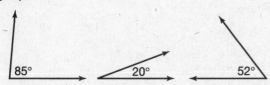

triángulo acutángulo (acute triangle) Un triángulo con tres ángulos agudos.

Ejemplo:

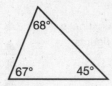

sumando (addend) Un número añadido a uno o más números.

Ejemplo:
$$12 + 19 = 31$$
sumando   sumando

suma (addition) Una operación que da el número total cuando dos o más números se ponen unidos.

Ejemplo:

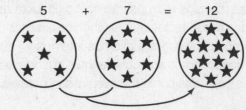

Propiedad de igualdad de la suma (Addition Property of Equality) Si $a = b$, entonces $a + c = b + c$.

Ejemplo:

En la segunda línea del ejemplo a continuación, se añade 1 a ambos lados de la ecuación.

Si $\qquad x - 1 = 2$

entonces $\qquad x - 1 + \mathbf{1} = 2 + \mathbf{1}$

$\qquad\qquad\qquad x = 3$

inverso aditivo (additive inverse)
El opuesto de un número.

Ejemplos:　El inverso aditivo de -2 es 2.

El inverso aditivo de 5 es -5.

lado adyacente (adjacent leg) Para un ángulo agudo en un triángulo rectángulo, es el cateto que se encuentra en uno de los lados de dicho ángulo.

Ejemplos:

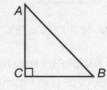

$\overline{AC}$ es el lado adyacente de $\angle CAB$.

$\overline{BC}$ es el lado adyacente de $\angle ABC$.

álgebra (algebra) Es una rama de las matemáticas en la cual se tratan las relaciones aritméticas utilizando variables para representar los números.

expresión algebraica (algebraic expression) Una expresión que contiene al menos una variable.

Ejemplos:　$n - 7$　$2y + 17$　$5(x - 3)$

ángulos alternos (alternate angles) Dos ángulos formados por dos líneas rectas y una transversal, y que están en lados opuestos de la transversal ya sea (1) entre las dos líneas rectas dadas (ángulos alternos internos) o (2) fuera de las dos líneas rectas dadas (ángulos alternos externos). Los ángulos alternos internos y alternos externos son congruentes cuando las líneas cruzadas por la transversal son paralelas.

Ejemplos:

ángulos alternos externos:
∠1 y ∠8
∠2 y ∠7

ángulos alternos internos:
∠3 y ∠6
∠4 y ∠5

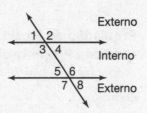

ángulo (angle) Dos líneas con un punto extremo común.

Ejemplo:

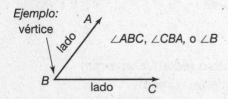

∠ABC, ∠CBA, o ∠B

bisectriz de un ángulo (angle bisector) Una línea que divide un ángulo en dos ángulos congruentes.

Ejemplo:

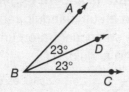

$\overrightarrow{BD}$ es la bisectriz del ángulo ∠ABC.

ángulo de rotación (angle of rotation) El ángulo a través del cual una figura gira durante una rotación.

Ejemplo:

El ángulo de rotación es 90°.

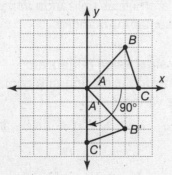

Angulo-Lado-Angulo (Angle-Side-Angle) (ASA) Regla utilizada para determinar si los triángulos son congruentes por comparación de las partes correspondientes.

Ejemplo:

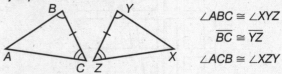

∠ABC ≅ ∠XYZ
$\overline{BC} ≅ \overline{YZ}$
∠ACB ≅ ∠XZY

△ABC ≅ △XYZ por la regla ASA.

área (area) La cantidad de superficie que cubre una figura.

Ejemplo:

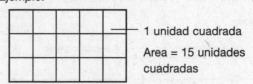

1 unidad cuadrada

Area = 15 unidades cuadradas

progresión aritmética (arithmetic sequence) Una secuencia donde la diferencia entre términos consecutivos es siempre la misma.

Ejemplo:

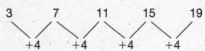

3   7   11   15   19
  +4   +4   +4   +4

ordenación (arrangement) El orden en el cual aparecen personas, letras, números u otras cosas.

Ejemplo:

Todas las configuraciones posibles de tres figuras:

Propiedad asociativa de la suma (Associative Property of Addition) El hecho de cambiar el agrupamiento de los sumandos no altera la suma.

Ejemplos: $a + (b + c) = (a + b) + c$
$5 + (3 + 7) = (5 + 3) + 7$

Propiedad asociativa de la multiplicación (Associative Property of Multiplication) El hecho de que cambie el agrupamiento de los factores no altera el producto.

Ejemplos:
$$a(bc) = (ab)c$$
$$3 \times (4 \times 2) = (3 \times 4) \times 2$$

promedio (average) Vea *la media*.

ejes (axes) Vea *eje "x"* y *eje "y"*.

gráfica de barras (bar graph) Una gráfica que utiliza barras verticales u horizontales para mostrar los datos.

Ejemplos:

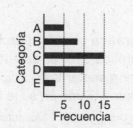

base (de un exponente) (base (of an exponent)) Un número que se multiplica por sí mismo el número de veces que muestra un exponente.

Ejemplo:
base   exponente
$$6^2 = 6 \times 6 = 36$$

base (de un polígono) (base (of a polygon)) Cualquier lado (por lo general el que está en la parte inferior) o la longitud de ese lado.

Ejemplos:

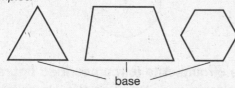

base

base (de un sólido) (base (of a solid)) En un prisma o cilindro, una de las dos caras paralelas y congruentes. En una pirámide, la cara opuesta al vértice. En un cono, la cara circular.

Ejemplos:

base — base — base — base

sistema binario de numeración (binary number system) Un sistema de valores de base 2.

Ejemplo:

En el sistema binario de numeración, 1011 es igual a 11 en el sistema numérico decimal (de base 10).

	Lugar de los ochos	Lugar de los cuatros	Lugar de los dos	Lugar de los unos
Base 2	1	0	1	1
Valor del lugar	8	4	2	1
Producto	$1 \times 8 = 8$	$0 \times 4 = 0$	$1 \times 2 = 2$	$1 \times 1 = 1$

$(1 \times 8) + (0 \times 4) + (1 \times 2) + (1 \times 1) = 8 + 0 + 2 + 1 = 11$

binomio (binomial) Un polinomio de dos términos.

Ejemplos: $4x^3 - 2x^2$ $2x + 5$

bisecar (bisect) Dividir un ángulo o segmento en dos ángulos o segmentos congruentes.

Ejemplos:

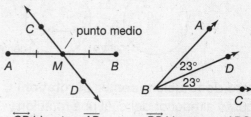

$\overleftrightarrow{CD}$ bisecta a $\overline{AB}$. $\overrightarrow{BD}$ bisecta a $\angle ABC$.

línea de límite (boundary line) En la gráfica de una desigualdad lineal, es la línea que separa los puntos que están en la solución, de los puntos que no lo están.

Ejemplo:

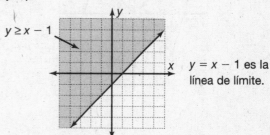

$y \geq x - 1$

$y = x - 1$ es la línea de límite.

gráfica de mediana y rango (box-and-whisker plot) Es una forma visual de mostrar cómo se distribuye una colección de datos. El ejemplo a continuación se basa en las diez siguientes anotaciones de prueba: 52, 64, 75, 79, 80, 80, 81, 88, 92, 99.

Ejemplo:

Anotaciones de prueba

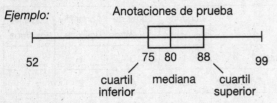

52   75 80   88   99

cuartil inferior   mediana   cuartil superior

capacidad (capacity) El volumen de una figura, dado en términos de medida líquida.

Ejemplos:

500 ml   1 L   1 taza   1 cuarto   1 galón

centro (center) El punto medio exacto de un círculo o esfera.

Ejemplos:

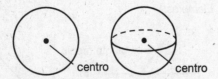

centro   centro

centro de rotación (center of rotation) El punto alrededor del cual una rotación hace girar una figura.

Ejemplo:

El origen es el centro de rotación.

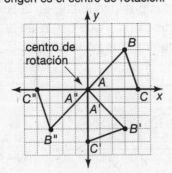

centro de rotación

centi- (centi-) Un prefijo que significa $\frac{1}{100}$.

Ejemplo: 1 centímetro = $\frac{1}{100}$ metro

ángulo central (central angle) Un ángulo cuyo vértice está en el centro de un círculo.

Ejemplo:

El punto *C* es el centro del círculo.

∠*BCA* es un ángulo central

círculo (circle) Una figura plana cuyos puntos se encuentran todos a la misma distancia del centro.

Ejemplo:

gráfica circular (circle graph) Es una gráfica circular que utiliza cuñas para representar las porciones del conjunto de datos. También se le llama gráfica de pastel.

Ejemplo: Mascotas favoritas

Perros 40%   Gatos 25%   Pájaros 20%   Otros 15%

circunferencia (circumference) Es la distancia alrededor de un círculo.

Ejemplo:

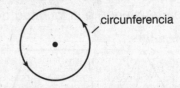

circunferencia

figura circunscrita (circumscribed figure) Es una figura que contiene a otra. Un polígono está circunscrito alrededor de un círculo si el círculo toca a cada uno de sus lados.

Ejemplo:

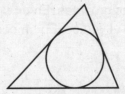

El triángulo está circunscrito con relación al círculo.

en el sentido de las manecillas del reloj (clockwise) Es la dirección de rotación cuando la parte superior de una figura gira hacia la derecha.

Ejemplo:

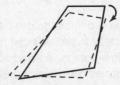

agrupación (clustering) Un método de estimación donde los números que son aproximadamente iguales se tratan como si fueran iguales.

Ejemplo:

26 + 24 + 23 es aproximadamente 25 + 25 + 25, ó 3 × 25.

coeficiente (coefficient) Es una constante por la cual se multiplica una variable.

Ejemplo:

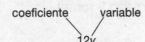

coeficiente   variable

12y

combinación (combination) Es una selección de artículos en la cual el orden no es importante.

Ejemplo:

Dos estudiantes de este grupo serán seleccionados para estar en un comité: David, Juanita, Kim.

Las posibles combinaciones son:

David, Juanita   David, Kim   Juanita, Kim

Nota: La combinación "David, Juanita" es lo mismo que la combinación "Juanita, David".

denominador común (common denominator) Un denominador que es el mismo en dos o más fracciones.

Ejemplo:

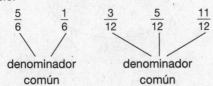

$$\frac{5}{6} \quad \frac{1}{6} \quad \frac{3}{12} \quad \frac{5}{12} \quad \frac{11}{12}$$

denominador   denominador
    común   común

factor común (common factor) Un número que es factor de dos o más números.

Ejemplo:

4 es un factor común de 8, 12 y 20.

$$8 = 4 \times 2$$
$$12 = 4 \times 3$$
$$20 = 4 \times 5$$

múltiplo común (common multiple) Un número que es múltiplo de dos o más números dados.

Ejemplo:

múltiplos de 3: 3 6 9 **12** 15 18 21 **24** 27...

múltiplos de 4: 4 8 **12** 16 20 **24** 28...

12 y 24 son dos de los múltiplos comunes de 3 y 4.

Propiedad conmutativa de la suma (Commutative Property of Addition) El orden no altera la suma de dos o más números.

Ejemplos:
$$a + b = b + a$$
$$18 + 23 = 23 + 18$$

Propiedad conmutativa de la multiplicación (Commutative Property of Multiplication) El órden no altera el producto de dos o más números.

Ejemplos:
$$ab = ba$$
$$4 \times 7 = 7 \times 4$$

números compatibles (compatible numbers) Pares de números que pueden ser computados fácilmente.

Ejemplos: 30 + 70   40 ÷ 4   25 + 75

compensación (compensation) La estrategia matemática mental de escoger números cercanos a los números en un problema y luego ajustar la respuesta para compensar por los números escogidos.

Ejemplo:
$$99 \times 4 = (100 - 1) \times 4$$
$$= (100 \times 4) - (1 \times 4)$$
$$= 400 - 4$$
$$= 396$$

ángulos complementarios (complementary angles) Dos ángulos que al ser medidos suman 90°.

Ejemplo:

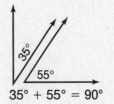

$$35° + 55° = 90°$$

número compuesto (composite number)
Un número entero mayor que 1 y que tiene más de dos factores.

Ejemplos:

factores de 15: 1, 3, 5, 15
   15 es un número compuesto.

factores de 7: 1, 7
   7 no es un número compuesto.

suceso compuesto (compound event)
Evento que es la combinación de dos o más eventos sencillos.

Ejemplo:

 y

La obtención de cara en el lanzamiento de una moneda y de rodar un 1 con un cubo numérico es un suceso compuesto.

interés compuesto (compound interest)
Interés basado en el capital y el interés anterior.

Ejemplo:

Si usted deposita $100 en una cuenta de ahorros que gana un 6% de interés compuesto anual, tendrá
$100 + 0.06 × 100 = $106 el primer año y
$106 + 0.06 × 106 = $112.36 el segundo año.

afirmación compuesto (compound statement)
Un enunciado lógico formado por la unión de dos o más enunciados.

Ejemplos:

10 es mayor que 5 *y* 10 es menor que 21.

10 es mayor que 5 *ó* 10 es menor que 5.

polígono cóncavo (concave polygon)
Un polígono con una o más diagonales que yacen fuera de la figura.

Ejemplo:

probabilidad condicional (conditional probability)
La probabilidad de que un evento B ocurra, dado que el evento A ya haya ocurrido.

Ejemplo:

Si usted sabe que el primero de dos lanzamientos de una moneda es cara, la probabilidad de obtener dos caras es cero. Sin embargo, si usted sabe que el primer lanzamiento es cara, la probabilidad de obtener dos caras es $\frac{1}{2}$.

cono (cone)
Un sólido con una base circular.

Ejemplo:

congruente (congruent)
Que tiene el mismo tamaño y forma.

Ejemplos:

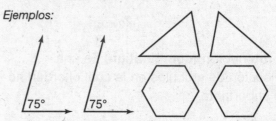

proyección cónica (conic projection)
Es la proyección de mapas en la cual se utiliza una forma de cono para representar una superficie esférica.

Ejemplo:

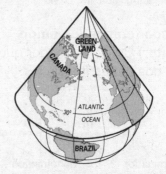

conjunción (conjunction)
Es un conjunto lógico de enunciados unidos por la palabra *y*

Ejemplos:

$x > -2$ y $x < 5$

Un cuadrado tiene cuatro lados de igual longitud *y* un cuadrado es un rectángulo.

constante (constant) Una cantidad que no cambia.

Ejemplo:

En la expresión algebraica $x + 7$, 7 es una constante.

gráfica de una constante (constant graph) Una gráfica en el cual la altura de la línea no cambia.

Ejemplo:

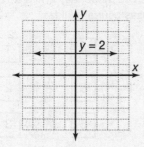

constante de proporcionalidad (constant of proportionality) Es la cantidad $\frac{y}{x}$ para dos variables "x" y "y" cuyo radio es constante. Generalmente se indica por k.

Ejemplo:

x	3	6	9	12
y	5	10	15	20

$k = \frac{5}{3}$

fórmula de conversión (conversion factor) Es una equivalencia de medida que se utiliza para convertir cantidades de una unidad a otra. Se expresa a menudo como una fracción.

Ejemplos:

12 pulgadas = 1 pie $\qquad \frac{12 \text{ pulgadas}}{1 \text{ pie}}$

4 cuartos = 1 galón $\qquad \frac{4 \text{ cuartos}}{1 \text{ galón}}$

polígono convexo (convex polygon) Es un polígono con todas las diagonales yaciendo dentro de la figura.

Ejemplos:

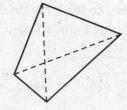

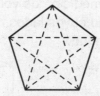

coordenadas (coordinates) Un par de números, en un par ordenado, que se utilizan para localizar un punto en un plano compuesto.

Ejemplo:

(5, 6)
coordenada

plano de coordenadas, sistema de coordenadas (coodinate plane, coordinate system) Un sistema de dos lineas numéricas, vertical y horizontal, que se intersectan y que se utilizan para situar puntos en un plano.

Ejemplo:

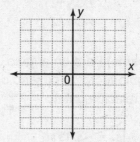

ángulos correspondientes (de rectas) (corresponding angles (for lines)) Son los ángulos que quedan de un mismo lado de una transversal que intersecta dos o más líneas. Los ángulos correspondientes son congruentes cuando la transversal cruza líneas paralelas.

Ejemplo:

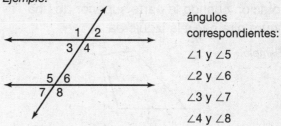

ángulos correspondientes:

$\angle 1$ y $\angle 5$

$\angle 2$ y $\angle 6$

$\angle 3$ y $\angle 7$

$\angle 4$ y $\angle 8$

ángulos correspondientes (de figuras similares) (corresponding angles (in similar figures)) Angulos que combinan en figuras similares.

Ejemplo:

$\triangle ABC \sim \triangle XYZ$

ángulos correspondientes:

$\angle ABC$ y $\angle XYZ$

$\angle BCA$ y $\angle YZX$

$\angle CAB$ y $\angle ZXY$

lados correspondientes (corresponding sides) Lados que combinan en figuras similares.

Ejemplo: $\triangle ABC \sim \triangle XYZ$

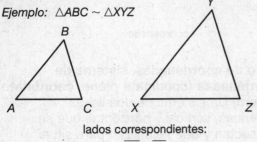

lados correspondientes:
$\overline{AB}$ y $\overline{XY}$
$\overline{BC}$ y $\overline{YZ}$
$\overline{AC}$ y $\overline{XZ}$

coseno (cosine) Para un ángulo agudo x en un triángulo recto, el coseno de x, o $\cos(x)$ es la relación cateto $\frac{\text{adyacente}}{\text{hipotenusa}}$.

Ejemplo:

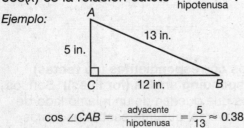

$\cos \angle CAB = \frac{\text{adyacente}}{\text{hipotenusa}} = \frac{5}{13} \approx 0.38$

en sentido contrario de las manecillas del reloj (counterclockwise) Es la dirección de rotación cuando la parte superior de una figura gira hacia la izquierda.

Ejemplo:

contraejemplo (counterexample) Un ejemplo que demuestra que un enunciado es falso.

Ejemplo:
enunciado: Si $x \cdot 0 = y \cdot 0$, entonces $x = y$.
contraejemplo: $3 \cdot 0 = 0$ y $5 \cdot 0 = 0$,
pero $3 \neq 5$.

Principio de conteo (Counting Principle) Si una situación puede ocurrir de m maneras y una segunda situación puede ocurrir de n maneras, entonces ambas cosas pueden ocurrir de $m \times n$ maneras.

Ejemplo:

Hay dos resultados a partir del lanzamiento de una moneda y 6 resultados a partir de la tirada de un cubo numérico. De ese modo, hay 2×6 ó 12 formas de que estas cosas ocurran unidas.

$6 \times 2 = 12$

producto cruzado (cross product) Es el producto del numerador de una relación con el denominador de otra.

Ejemplo:

$\frac{1}{3}$ $\frac{2}{5}$

Productos cruzados
$1 \times 5 = 5$
$3 \times 2 = 6$

cubo (cube) Es un prisma de 6 lados cuyas caras son cuadrados congruentes.

Ejemplo:

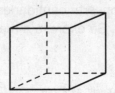

elevado al cubo (cubed) Elevado a la tercera potencia.

Ejemplo:
2 al cubo se escribe 2^3.
$2^3 = 2 \times 2 \times 2 = 8$

unidad cúbica (cubic unit) Es una unidad de medición de volumen, consistente de un cubo cuyos lados miden una unidad de longitud.

Ejemplo:

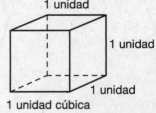

1 unidad
1 unidad
1 unidad
1 unidad cúbica

sistema usual de medidas (customary system of measurement) Es el sistema de medición frecuentemente utilizado en los Estados Unidos: pulgadas, pies, millas, onzas, libras, toneladas, tazas, cuartos, galones, etc.

Ejemplos:

Park City **50** millas

longitud

Leche

1 galón
capacidad

Arroz 1 Libra

peso

cilindro (cylinder) Es un sólido con dos bases circulares paralelas.

Ejemplo:

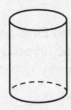

proyección cilíndrica (cylindrical projection) Es una proyección de mapas que utiliza una forma de cilindro para representar una superficie esférica.

Ejemplo:

decágono (decagon) Es un polígono que tiene 10 lados.

Ejemplo:

deci- (deci-) Es un prefijo que significa $\frac{1}{10}$.

Ejemplo: 1 decímetro = $\frac{1}{10}$ metros

decimal (decimal) Cualquier número de base 10 y que se escribe utilizando un punto decimal.

Ejemplos: 6.21   0.59   12.2   5.0

adición decimal (decimal addition) Es la suma de dos o más decimales.

Ejemplo:
$$\begin{array}{r} 1 \\ 12.65 \\ +\ 29.10 \\ \hline 41.75 \end{array}$$

división decimal (decimal division) Es la división de dos decimales.

Ejemplo:
$$\begin{array}{r} 1.25 \\ 0.24\overline{)0.3000} \\ -24 \\ \hline 60 \\ -48 \\ \hline 120 \\ -120 \\ \hline 0 \end{array}$$

multiplicación decimal (decimal multiplication) Es la multiplicación de dos o más decimales.

Ejemplo:
$$\begin{array}{r} 2 \\ 0.13 \\ \times\ 0.7 \\ \hline 0.091 \end{array}$$

2 lugares decimales
1 lugar decimal
3 lugares decimales

sustracción decimal (decimal subtraction) Es la resta de dos decimales.

Ejemplo:
$$\begin{array}{r} {\scriptstyle 13\ 12} \\ 4\ \cancel{3}\ \cancel{7}10 \\ \cancel{5}\cancel{4}\cancel{3}\cancel{0} \\ -\ 16.58 \\ \hline 37.72 \end{array}$$

sistema decimal (decimal system) Sistema de valor de lugar de base 10.

Ejemplo:

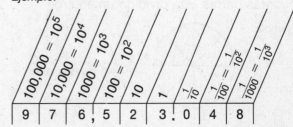

$100{,}000 = 10^5$	$10{,}000 = 10^4$	$1000 = 10^3$	$100 = 10^2$	10	1	$\frac{1}{10}$	$\frac{1}{100} = \frac{1}{10^2}$	$\frac{1}{1000} = \frac{1}{10^3}$
9	7	6,	5	2	3.	0	4	8

gráfica decreciente (decreasing graph) Es
una gráfica en el cual la altura de la línea
disminuye de izquierda a derecha.

Ejemplo:

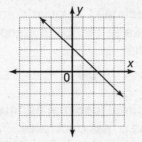

deducción (deductive reasoning)
Utilización de la lógica para llegar a una
conclusión.

Ejemplo:

Cuando añadimos una diagonal a cualquier
cuadrilátero, se forman dos triángulos. Usted sabe
que la suma de las medidas de los ángulos de un
triángulo es 180°. Por consiguiente, la suma de los
medidas de los ángulos de un cuadrilátero es dos
veces la de un triángulo, o $2 \times 180° = 360°$.

grado (°) (degree) Es la unidad de medida
de un ángulo.

Ejemplo: 1° es $\frac{1}{360}$ de un círculo completo.

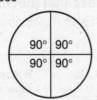

grado (degree) Para un polinomio, es el
valor del mayor exponente de una variable.

Ejemplo: El grado de $5x^3 - 2x^2 + 7x$ es 3.

deka- (deka-) Es un prefijo que significa 10.

Ejemplo: 1 dekámetro = 10 metros

denominador (denominator) Es el número
inferior en una fracción que indica en
cuántas partes está dividido un entero.

Ejemplo:

$\frac{3}{8}$ —— denominador

sucesos dependientes (dependent events)
Eventos en los cuales el resultado de uno
afecta la probabilidad del otro.

Ejemplo:

Los nombres Teresa, Diana y José son escritos en
pedazos de papel separados. Uno de estos pedazos
de papel se extrae y se guarda. Después se extrae
otro. La probabilidad de que el nombre de Diana sea
extraido dado que el nombre de Teresa fue extraido la
primera vez es de $\frac{1}{2}$.

variable dependiente (dependent variable)
Es la variable de salida para una función.

Ejemplo:

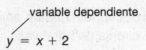

variable dependiente

$y = x + 2$

diagonal (diagonal) Es el segmento que
une dos vértices de un polígono que no
tienen un lado común.

Ejemplo:

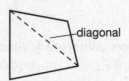

diagonal

diámetro (diameter) Es un segmento de
línea, o su longitud, que pasa a través del
centro de un círculo y tiene ambos puntos
extremos en dicho círculo.

Ejemplo:

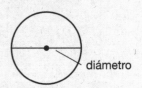

diámetro

diferencia (difference) Es el resultado de
sustraer un número de otro.

Ejemplo: $28 - 15 = 13$

diferencia

dígito (digit) Son los símbolos usados para
escribir los números 0, 1, 2, 3, 4, 5, 6, 7, 8 y 9.

Ejemplo:

En 5847, los dígitos son 5, 8, 4 y 7.

dilación (dilation) Es una reducción o ampliación proporcional de una figura.

Ejemplo:

El factor de escala para la dilatación desde el rectángulo pequeño al rectángulo grande es 3.

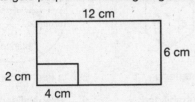

variación directa (direct variation) Cuando dos variables están relacionadas por una razón constante

Ejemplo:

tiempo en horas (x)	1	2	3	4
distancia en millas (y)	55	110	165	220

$$\frac{y}{x} = 55$$

disyunción (disjunction) Es un conjunto lógico de enunciados unidos por la palabra "o".

Ejemplos:

$x > 4$ o $x < -1$

Fuimos al cine o miramos la televisión.

Propiedad distributiva (Distributive Property) Es el hecho mediante el cual $a(b + c) = ab + ac$.

Ejemplo: $3(6 + 5) = 3 \cdot 6 + 3 \cdot 5$

dividendo (dividend) Es el número a ser dividido en un problema de división.

Ejemplo:

dividendo

$8 \div 4 = 2$

divisible (divisible) Que puede ser dividido por otro número sin dejar un residuo.

Ejemplo: 18 es divisible por 6, ya que $18 \div 6 = 3$.

división (division) Una operación que dice cuántos conjuntos iguales hay o cuántos hay en cada conjunto.

Ejemplos:

 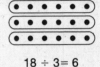

$18 \div 6 = 3$ $18 \div 3 = 6$

18 dividido entre 6 grupos pone 3 en cada grupo.   18 dividido en 3 grupos pone 6 en cada grupo.

divisor (divisor) Un número por el cual se divide otro número.

Ejemplo:

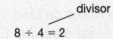
divisor

$8 \div 4 = 2$

dodecágono (dodecagon) Es un polígono con 12 lados.

Ejemplo:

gráfica de doble barra (double bar graph) Es una combinación de gráficas de dos barras, comparando dos juegos de datos relacionados.

Ejemplo:

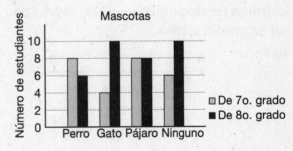

gráfica de doble línea (double line graph)
Es una combinación de gráficas de dos líneas, comparando dos juegos de datos relacionados.

Ejemplo:

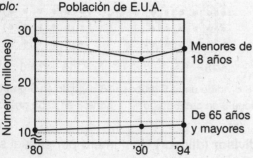

diagrama doble de tallo y hoja (double stem-and-leaf diagram) Es una comparación de tallo y hojas de dos juegos de datos en un solo diagrama.

Ejemplo:

Hoja	Tallo	Hoja
7 2 1	3	0 1 3
5 0 0	4	2 3
9	5	5 6 8
5 2 0	6	1 4

arista (edge) Es un segmento donde se encuentran dos de las caras de un poliedro.

Ejemplo:

extremo (endpoint) Es un punto al final de un segmento o línea.

Ejemplos:

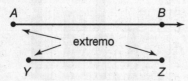

igualdad (equality) Es una relación matemática de que es exactamente lo mismo.

Ejemplos: $16 + 8 = 24$ $25 \div 5 = 5$

resultados igualmente probables (equally-likely outcomes) Resultados que tienen la misma probabilidad.

Ejemplos:

obtener un "1"   que la flecha marque rojo

Probabilidad: $\frac{1}{6}$ Probabilidad: $\frac{1}{6}$

razones iguales (equal ratios) Relaciones que se refieren a la misma cantidad.

Ejemplo: $\frac{2}{6}$, $\frac{1}{3}$, y $\frac{4}{12}$

ecuación (equation) Es una oración matemática que establece que dos expresiones son iguales.

Ejemplos:

$14 = 2x$ $3 + y = 81$ $3 + 4 = 7$

triángulo equilátero (equilateral triangle) Es un triángulo cuyos lados tienen todos la misma longitud.

Ejemplo:

ecuaciones equivalentes (equivalent equations) Son ecuaciones que se cumplen para exactamente las mismas sustituciones de variables.

Ejemplo: $x - 5 = 10$ y $x = 15$

expresiones equivalentes (equivalent expressions) Son dos expresiones que tienen siempre el mismo valor para las mismas sustituciones.

Ejemplo: $5(x + 1)$ y $5x + 5$

fracciones equivalentes (equivalent fractions) Son dos fracciones que representan el mismo número.

Ejemplo: $\frac{1}{2}$ y $\frac{8}{16}$

relaciones equivalentes (equivalent rates)
Relaciones que indican la misma cantidad.

Ejemplo: $\dfrac{40 \text{ millas}}{2 \text{ horas}}$ y $\dfrac{20 \text{ millas}}{1 \text{ hora}}$

razones equivalentes (equivalent ratios)
Ver *razones iguales.*

estimación (estimate) Una aproximación en cuanto al resultado de un cálculo.

Ejemplo:
$$99 \times 21$$
Estimación: $100 \times 20 = 2000$
$$99 \times 21 \approx 2000$$

Fórmula de Euler (Euler's formula) Se trata de una fórmula sobre el número de caras (*F*), vértices (*V*) y aristas (*E*) de un poliedro, que establece que $F + V - E = 2$.

Ejemplo:

Para la pirámide triangular que se muestra,

$$5 + 5 - 8 = 2$$
caras   vértices   aristas

evaluar (evaluate) Sustituir los valores para las variables en una expresión y luego simplificar siguiendo el orden de las operaciones.

Ejemplo: Evaluar $8(x - 3)$ para $x = 10$.
$$8(x - 3) = 8(10 - 3)$$
$$= 8(7)$$
$$= 56$$

número par (even number) Un número entero que tiene 0, 2, 4, 6 u 8 en el lugar de las unidades.

Ejemplos: 16   28   34   112   3000

suceso (event) Un resultado o conjunto de resultados de un experimento o situación.

Ejemplo:

Suceso: La obtención de 3 o un valor más alto cuando se lanza un cubo.

Resultados posibles
para este suceso: 3, 4, 5, 6

notación multiplicativa (expanded form)
Es una forma de escribir un número exponencial mostrando todos los factores individualmente.

Ejemplo: número exponencial 9^3
notación multiplicativa $9 \times 9 \times 9$

experimento (experiment) En probabilidades, toda actividad que implique posibilidad.

Ejemplos:

la tirada de una moneda   la tirada de un cubo numérico   la rotación de una ruleta

probabilidad experimental (experimental probability) Una probabilidad basada en datos de experimentos o encuestas.

Ejemplo:

Se lanza 100 veces una bolsa de frijoles dentro de un aro. Hay 23 aciertos. La probabilidad experimental de un acierto es $\dfrac{23}{100} = 23\%$.

exponente (exponent) Un número elevado que indica una multiplicación repetida.

Ejemplo:
exponente
$$4^3 = 4 \times 4 \times 4 = 64$$

función exponencial (exponential function) Una función no lineal en la cual el exponente es una variable.

Ejemplo: $y = 4^x$

forma exponencial (exponential notation)
Es una forma de escribir la multiplicación repetida de un número, utilizando exponentes.

Ejemplos: 2^8 5^2 9^3

expresión (expression) Es una frase matemática hecha de variables y/o números y operaciones.

Ejemplos: $5(8 + 4)$ $x - 3$ $2x + 4$

ángulos externos (exterior angles) Cuando una transversal cruza dos líneas, los ángulos exteriores a esas dos líneas se denominan ángulos exteriores.

Ejemplo:

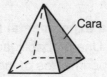

ángulos externos:
∠1, ∠2, ∠7, ∠8

cara (face) Es una superficie plana de un sólido.

Ejemplo:

Cara

factor (factor) Es un número que divide a otro número sin dejar un residuo.

Ejemplo: Como $30 \div 5 = 6$, 5 es un factor de 30.

factorial (factorial) El factorial de un número es el producto de todos los números enteros desde 1 hasta ese número. El símbolo que se utiliza para indicar el factorial es "!".

Ejemplo:

6 factorial $= 6! = 6 \times 5 \times 4 \times 3 \times 2 \times 1 = 720$

árbol de factores (factor tree) Es un diagrama que muestra cómo un número entero se descompone en sus factores primos.

Ejemplo:

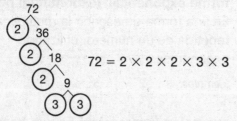

$72 = 2 \times 2 \times 2 \times 3 \times 3$

juego justo (fair game) Un juego en el cual todos los jugadores tienen la misma probabilidad de ganar.

Ejemplo:

Juego justo: Dos jugadores toman turnos en el lanzamiento de un cubo numérico. El Jugador A obtiene un punto para los lanzamientos de 1, 3 ó 5. El Jugador B obtiene un punto para los lanzamientos de 2, 4 ó 6. La probabilidad de obtener un punto es $\frac{1}{2}$ para ambos jugadores.

inversión (flip) Vea *reflexión*.

pie (foot) Una unidad dentro del sistema usual de medidas equivalente a 12 pulgadas.

Ejemplo:

1 pie

fórmula (formula) Una regla que muestra relaciones entre cantidades.

Ejemplos: $A = bh$ $\qquad$ $p = 4s$

fractal (fractal) Se trata de un patrón con autosimilaridad. Si una pequeña parte de un fractal se agranda, la región agrandada luce similar a la figura original.

Ejemplo:

fracción (fraction) Es un número de la forma $\frac{a}{b}$ que describe parte de un todo cuando el todo se corta en piezas iguales.

Ejemplos: $\frac{3}{5}$ $\qquad$ $\frac{2}{7}$ $\qquad$ $\frac{1}{4}$ $\qquad$ $\frac{7}{10}$

adición de fracciones (fraction addition) Es la adición de dos o más fracciones.

Ejemplo: $\frac{1}{3} + \frac{1}{4}$

$$\frac{1}{3} = \frac{1 \times 4}{3 \times 4} = \frac{4}{12}$$

$$\frac{1}{4} = \frac{1 \times 3}{4 \times 3} = \frac{3}{12}$$

$$\frac{1}{3} + \frac{1}{4} = \frac{4}{12} + \frac{3}{12} = \frac{4 + 3}{12} = \frac{7}{12}$$

división de fracciones (fraction division) Es la división de dos fracciones.

Ejemplo:

$$\frac{1}{6} \div \frac{3}{4} = \frac{1}{6} \times \frac{4}{3}$$

$$= \frac{1 \times 4}{6 \times 3}$$

$$= \frac{4}{18} \text{ o } \frac{2}{9}$$

multiplicación de fracciones (fraction multiplication) Es la multiplicación de dos o más fracciones.

Ejemplo:
$$1\frac{1}{2} \times \frac{1}{4} = \frac{3}{2} \times \frac{1}{4}$$
$$= \frac{3 \times 1}{2 \times 4}$$
$$= \frac{3}{8}$$

sustracción de fracciones (fraction subtraction) Es la sustracción de dos fracciones.

Ejemplo: $\frac{3}{4} - \frac{2}{3}$

$$\frac{3}{4} = \frac{3 \times 3}{4 \times 3} = \frac{9}{12}$$
$$\frac{2}{3} = \frac{2 \times 4}{3 \times 4} = \frac{8}{12}$$
$$\frac{3}{4} - \frac{2}{3} = \frac{9}{12} - \frac{8}{12} = \frac{9 - 8}{12} = \frac{1}{12}$$

frecuencia (frequency) Es el número de veces que algo ocurre en una encuesta. Vea *tabla de frecuencia*.

tabla de frecuencia (frequency chart or table) Es una tabla que muestra las clases de cosas y la frecuencia conque ocurren esas cosas.

Ejemplo:

Color de camisa	Frecuencia
Negro	8
Canela	2
Blanco	5
Azul	4

estimación por los primeros dígitos (front-end estimation) Es un método de estimación donde sólo se utiliza el primero o el segundo dígito de cada número para la computación y el resultado se ajusta en base a los dígitos restantes.

Ejemplo: estimación por el extremo delantero

$$
\begin{array}{r}
2{,}485 \\
+\ 3{,}698 \\
\hline
5{,}000 \\
+\ 1{,}200 \\
\hline
6{,}200
\end{array}
$$

Se suman los primeros dígitos. 485 + 698 son aproximadamente 1200.

función (function) Es una relación de entrada-salida que solamente da una salida para cada entrada.

Ejemplos:
$$y = x + 4 \qquad y = 2x \qquad y = x^2$$

Teorema fundamental de la aritmética (Fundamental Theorem of Arithmetic) Todos los enteros mayores de 1 pueden ser escritos como un producto único de números primos.

Ejemplos:
$$24 = 2 \times 2 \times 2 \times 3$$
$$35 = 5 \times 7$$

galón (gallon) Una unidad en el sistema usual de medidas que equivale a 4 cuartos.

Ejemplo:

leche

1 galón

geometría (geometry) Es una rama de las matemáticas en la cual se tratan las relaciones entre puntos, líneas, figuras y sólidos.

probabilidad geométrica (geometric probability) Es una probabilidad basada en la comparación de mediciones de figuras geométricas.

Ejemplo:

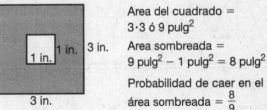

Area del cuadrado = $3 \cdot 3$ ó 9 pulg^2

Area sombreada = 9 pulg^2 − 1 pulg^2 = 8 pulg^2

Probabilidad de caer en el área sombreada = $\frac{8}{9}$

progresión geométrica (geometric sequence) Es una secuencia donde la relación entre términos consecutivos es siempre la misma.

Ejemplo:

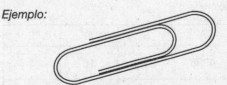

gramo (gram) Es la unidad básica de masa en el sistema métrico.

Ejemplo:

La masa de una presilla de papel grande es de aproximadamente 1 gramo.

gráfica (graph) Es un diagrama que muestra la información en forma organizada.

Ejemplos:

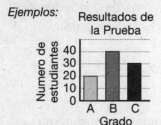

Resultados de la Prueba

tallo	hoja
3	0 1 3
4	2 2
5	6 7 9

máximo factor común (greatest common factor) (GCF) Es el máximo número entero que divide dos o más números enteros sin dejar un residuo.

Ejemplo: 6 es el GCF de 12, 18 y 24.

hecto- (hecto-) Prefijo que significa 100.

Ejemplo: 1 hectometro = 100 metros

altura (height) Es la distancia perpendicular, en un triángulo, cuadrilátero o pirámide, desde la base hasta el vértice o el lado opuesto. En un prisma o un cilindro, es la distancia entre las bases.

Ejemplos:

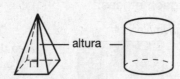

heptágono (heptagon) Es un polígono de siete lados.

Ejemplo:

numeración hexadecimal (hexadecimal number system) Es un sistema de valor de lugar de base 16.

Ejemplo:

Se utilizan las letras A-F para representar los dígitos 10-15. El número de base 16 A3CE es igual a 41,934 (40,960 + 768 + 192 + 14) en el sistema numérico de base 10 (decimal).

Base 16	A	3	C	E
Valor de lugar	4096	256	16	1
Producto	10 × 4096 = 40,960	3 × 256 = 768	12 × 16 = 192	14 × 1 = 14

hexágono (hexagon) Es un polígono con 6 lados.

Ejemplos:

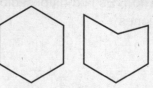

histograma (histogram) Es un tipo de gráfica de barras donde las categorías son rangos de números iguales.

Ejemplo:

Resultados de encuesta

eje horizontal (horizontal axis) Es la línea horizontal o las dos líneas sobre las cuales se construye una gráfica de barras o un plano de coordenadas.

Ejemplos:

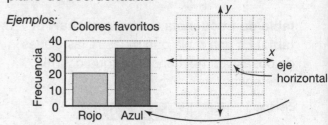

hipotenusa (hypotenuse) Es el lado opuesto del ángulo recto en un triángulo rectángulo.

Ejemplo:

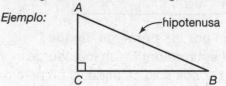

identidad (identity) Para una operación, es el número que mantiene igual a otro número. 0 es la identidad aditiva ya que $a + 0 = a$, 1 es la identidad multiplicativa ya que $a \times 1 = a$.

Ejemplos:
$$6 + 0 = 6$$
$$5 \times 1 = 5$$

enunciado condicional (if-then statement) Es un enunciado lógico que utiliza "*si*" y "*entonces*" para mostrar una relación entre dos condiciones.

Ejemplo:

Si un triángulo es escaleno, *entonces* ninguno de sus lados son congruentes.

fracción impropia (improper fraction) Es una fracción cuyo numerador es mayor que o igual que su denominador.

Ejemplos: $\dfrac{5}{2}$ $\dfrac{8}{8}$ $\dfrac{14}{3}$

gráfica creciente (increasing graph) Es una gráfica en el cual la altura de la línea aumenta de izquierda a derecha.

Ejemplo:

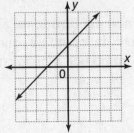

pulgada (inch) Es una unidad de longitud en el sistema usual de medidas.

Ejemplo: La presilla de papel mide $1\frac{3}{8}$ pulgadas o $1\frac{3}{8}"$.

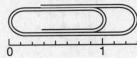

sucesos independientes (independent events) Son sucesos para los cuales la salida de uno no afecta la probabilidad del otro.

Ejemplo:
Los nombres de Teresa, Diana y José están escritos en hojas de papel separadas. Una de las hojas se extrae y se devuelve. Luego se extrae otra. La probabilidad de que el nombre de Diana sea extraido dado que el nombre de Teresa se extrajo en la primera hoja es $\frac{1}{3}$.

variable independiente (independent variable) Es la variable de entrada para una función.

Ejemplo: variable independiente
$$y = x + 2$$

razonamiento inductivo (inductive reasoning) Es utilizar un patrón para llegar a una conclusión.

Ejemplo:
Se extraen muchos cuadriláteros y se miden sus ángulos. En cada caso, la suma de los ángulos es de 360°. La conclusión obtenida es que la suma de los ángulos de un cuadrilátero es igual a 360°.

desigualdad (inequality) Es una sentencia matemática que implica $<$, $>$, $\leq$, o $\geq$.

Ejemplos:
$$6 < 9 \qquad x + 3 \geq 21 \qquad 2x - 8 > 0$$

figura inscrita (inscribed figure) Es una figura que está contenida dentro de otra. Un polígono está inscrito en un círculo si todos sus vértices descansan en dicho círculo.

Ejemplo:

El triángulo está inscrito en el círculo.

números enteros (integers) Es el conjunto de números enteros positivos, sus opuestos y el 0.

Ejemplos: ..., -3, -2, -1, 0, 1, 2, 3, ...

adición entera (integer addition) Es la adición de dos o más enteros.

Ejemplos:
$$-5 + 8 = 3 \qquad\qquad -5 + (-8) = -13$$
$$5 + (-3) = 2 \qquad\qquad 5 + 8 = 13$$

división entera (integer division) Es la división de dos enteros.

Ejemplos:
$$-40 \div 8 = -5 \qquad 40 \div (-8) = -5$$
$$-40 \div (-8) = 5 \qquad 40 \div 8 = 5$$

multiplicación entera (integer multiplication) Es la multiplicación de dos o más enteros.

Ejemplos:
$$-5 \cdot 8 = -40 \qquad -5 \cdot (-8) = 40$$
$$5 \cdot (-8) = -40 \qquad 5 \cdot 8 = 40$$

sustracción entera (integer substraction) Sustracción de dos enteros.

Ejemplos:
$$-5 - 8 = -13 \qquad -5 - (-8) = 3$$
$$5 - (-3) = 8 \qquad 5 - 8 = -3$$

interés (interest) Dinero que se paga por el uso del dinero.

Ejemplo:

David depositó $300 en una cuenta de ahorros. Después de un año, el balance en su cuenta era de $315. El ganó $15 en intereses de su cuenta de ahorros.

ángulos internos (interior angles) Angulos formados por una transversal y las líneas que ésta cruza y que quedan entre dichas líneas.

Ejemplo:

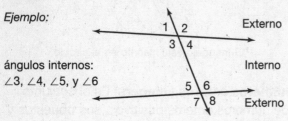

ángulos internos:
∠3, ∠4, ∠5, y ∠6

intersecarse (intersect) Cruzar a través del mismo punto.

Ejemplo:

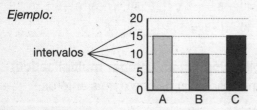

$\overleftrightarrow{AB}$, $\overleftrightarrow{CD}$, y $\overleftrightarrow{EF}$ se intersectan en el punto X.

intervalo (interval) Una de las divisiones de igual tamaño en una gráfica de barras o la escala de la gráfica lineal.

Ejemplo:

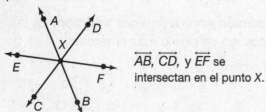

operaciones inversas (inverse operations) Operaciones que se "deshacen" una a otra.

Ejemplos:

adición y sustracción $\quad 2 + 3 = 5 \quad 5 - 3 = 2$

multiplicación y división $\quad 2 \cdot 3 = 6 \quad 6 \div 3 = 2$

variación inversa (inverse variation) Cuando dos variables están relacionadas por un producto constante.

Ejemplo:

x	1	2	3	4	5	6
y	60	30	20	15	12	10

$$x \cdot y = 60$$

número irracional (irrational number) Es un número, tal como $\sqrt{2}$, que no puede expresarse como una repetición o terminación decimal.

Ejemplos: $\quad \sqrt{5} \quad\quad \pi \quad\quad -\sqrt{\frac{1}{2}}$

perspectiva isométrica (isometric drawing) Se trata de un método utilizado para dar perspectiva a un dibujo.

Ejemplo:

triángulo isósceles (isosceles triangle) Es un triángulo que tiene al menos dos lados congruentes.

Ejemplo:

kilo- (kilo-) Prefijo que signfica 1000.

Ejemplo: 1 kilometro = 1000 metros

latitud (latitude) Es una medición en grados norte o sur a partir del ecuador.

Ejemplo:

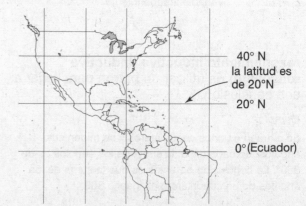

mínimo común denominador (least common denominator) (LCD) Es el mínimo común múltiplo (LCM) de dos o más denominadores.

Ejemplo: $\dfrac{1}{2}$ $\dfrac{2}{3}$ $\dfrac{3}{4}$

El LCM de 2, 3 y 4 es 12, de modo que el LCD de las fracciones es 12.

Las fracciones escritas con el LCD son $\dfrac{6}{12}$, $\dfrac{8}{12}$ y $\dfrac{9}{12}$.

mínimo común múltiplo (least common multiple) (LCM) Es el número más pequeño que es múltiplo común.

Ejemplo:
múltiplos de 3: 3 6 9 **12** 15 18 21 **24**
múltiplos de 4: 4 8 **12** 16 20 **24** 28 32
12 es el LCM de 3 y de 4.

cateto (leg) Uno de los lados del triángulo rectángulo diferente de la hipotenusa.

Ejemplo:

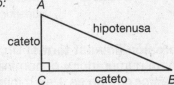

igual denominador (like denominators) Se trata de los denominadores que son iguales en dos o más fracciones.

Ejemplo: $\dfrac{1}{8}$ $\dfrac{3}{8}$ $\dfrac{6}{8}$

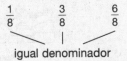

igual denominador

términos similares (like terms) Son término en los cuales la misma variable está elevada al mismo exponente.

Ejemplo: $3x^2$ y $9x^2$ $10y$ y $2y$

recta (line) Es una figura unidimensional que se extiende al infinito en ambas direcciones. Dos puntos denominan una recta.

Ejemplo:

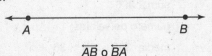

$\overleftrightarrow{AB}$ o $\overleftrightarrow{BA}$

gráfica lineal (line graph) Es una gráfica en el cual una línea muestra los cambios en un dato, generalmente sobre el tiempo.

Ejemplo:

eje de simetría (line of simmetry) La línea que divide una figura con simetría lineal en dos mitades idénticas.

Ejemplos:

1 eje de simetría   4 ejes de simetría

diagrama de puntos (line plot) Un trazado de puntos que muestran la figura de un conjunto de datos mediante la colocación de "x" en columna sobre cada valor en una línea numérica.

Ejemplo:

```
                              x
              x               x
          x   x   x           x
  x   x   x   x       x   x
  |   |   |   |   |   |   |
  0   1   2   3   4   5   6
        Número de estudiantes
```

segmento de recta (line segment) Parte de una línea recta, con dos puntos extremos. Dos puntos denominan un segmento.

Ejemplo:

$\overline{AB}$ o $\overline{BA}$

simetría axial (line symmetry) Una figura tiene simetría axial si puede ser dividida en dos mitades idénticas.

Ejemplo:

Figura con   Figura sin
simetría axial   simetría axial

ecuación lineal (linear equation) Es una ecuación cuya gráfica es una línea recta.

Ejemplo:

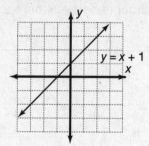

$y = x + 1$

función lineal (linear function) Es una función cuya gráfica es una línea recta.

Ejemplo:

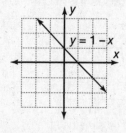

Entrada	Salida
x	y
−2	3
−1	2
0	1
1	0
2	−1
3	−2

$y = 1 - x$

desigualdad lineal (linear inequality) Una expresión matemática que envuelve $<, >, \leq$ o $\geq$ cuya gráfica es una región con una frontera de línea recta.

Ejemplo:

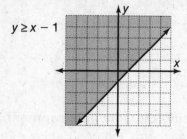

$y \geq x - 1$

litro (liter) La unidad básica de volumen en el sistema métrico.

Ejemplo:

botella de 2 litros

longitud (longitude) Es una medición en grados este u oeste a partir del primer meridiano.

Ejemplo:

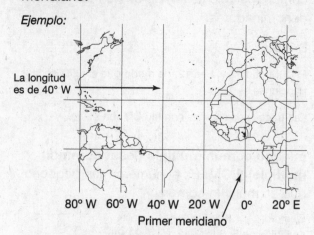

La longitud es de 40° W

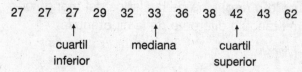

80° W   60° W   40° W   20° W   0°   20° E

Primer meridiano

cuartil inferior (lower quartile) La mediana de la mitad inferior de un conjunto de datos.

Ejemplo:

27   27   27   29   32   33   36   38   42   43   62

cuartil inferior   mediana   cuartil superior

mínima expresión (lowest terms) Una fracción con un numerador y denominador cuyo único factor común es 1 en mínima expresión.

Ejemplos: $\dfrac{1}{2}$ $\dfrac{3}{5}$ $\dfrac{21}{23}$

masa (mass) La cantidad de materia contenida por algo.

Ejemplos:

Una pasa tiene una masa de 1 gramo.   Un par de zapatos atléticos tiene una masa de 1 kilogramo.

media (mean) Es la suma de los valores en un conjunto de datos dividida por el número de valores. También se conoce como el promedio.

Ejemplo:

27   27   27   29   32   33   36   38   42   43   62

suma: 396

número de valores: 11

media: $396 \div 11 = 36$

error en la medición (measurement error)

Es la incertidumbre en una medición. El mayor error posible en una medición es la mitad de la menor unidad utilizada.

Ejemplo:

Como la pulgada es la unidad más pequeña, el mayor error posible es $\frac{1}{2}$ pulgada. De ese modo, la altura real está entre $5'5\frac{1}{2}''$ y $5'6\frac{1}{2}''$.

5' 6"

medida de tendencia central (measure of central tendency) Es un valor sencillo que sumariza un conjunto de datos numéricos.

Ejemplo:

La media, la mediana y el modo son medidas comunes de tendencia central.

27 27 27 29 32 33 36 38 42 43 62

modo   mediana

Media = 396 ÷ 11 = 36

mediana (median) Es el valor medio de un conjunto de datos cuando dichos valores están arreglados en orden numérico.

Ejemplo:

27 27 27 29 32 33 36 38 42 43 62

mediana

cálculo mental (mental math) Es la realización de cálculos en su mente, sin utilizar lápiz ni papel ni una calculadora.

Ejemplo:

$$2000 \times 30$$

3 ceros + 1 cero = 4 ceros

Piense: 2 × 3 = 6, se añaden 4 ceros

2000 × 30 = 60,000

metro (meter) Es la unidad básica de longitud en el sistema métrico.

Ejemplo:

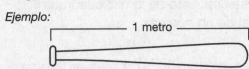

1 metro

El bate de béisbol es de aproximadamente 1 metro de largo.

sistema métrico decimal (metric system)

Es un sistema de medición basado en el metro, el gramo y el litro.

Ejemplos:

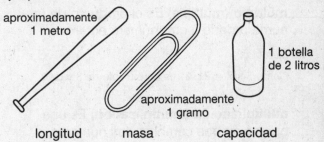

aproximadamente 1 metro

aproximadamente 1 gramo

1 botella de 2 litros

longitud   masa   capacidad

punto medio (midpoint) Es el punto que divide a un segmento en dos segmentos más pequeños.

Ejemplo: C es el punto medio de $\overline{AB}$.

A   C   B

Longitud de $\overline{AC}$ = Longitud de $\overline{CB}$

milla (mile) Es una unidad en el sistema usual de medidas igual a 5280 pies.

Ejemplo:

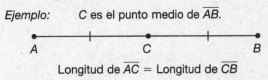

Una milla es la distancia que usted puede caminar en 15 a 20 minutos o correr en aproximadamente 10 minutos.

mili- (milli-) Un prefijo que significa $\frac{1}{1000}$.

Ejemplo: 1 milímetro = $\frac{1}{1000}$ metro

número mixto (mixed number) Es un número hecho de una parte entera y una fracción.

Ejemplos: $3\frac{1}{2}$ $1\frac{3}{4}$ $13\frac{3}{8}$

moda (mode) El(los) valor(es) que ocurren con mayor frecuencia en un conjunto de datos.

Ejemplo:

27 27 27 29 32 33 36 38 42 43 62

Para el conjunto dado de datos, 27 es el modo.

monomio (monomial) Es una expresión algebraica que tiene exactamente un término.

Ejemplos: $2x^2$ $5y$ x^3 -3

múltiplo (multiple) Es el producto de un número dado y otro número entero.

Ejemplo:

Como $3 \times 7 = 21$, 21 es un múltiplo de 3 y de 7.

multiplicación (multiplication) Es una operación que combina dos números, llamados factores, para dar un número, llamado el producto.

Ejemplo:

3 filas de 6

$$3 \times 6 = 18$$

factores   producto

propiedad multiplicativa (multiplication property) Si A y B son eventos independientes, entonces la probabilidad de que ambos ocurran está dada por $P(A$ y $B) = P(A) \times P(B)$.

Ejemplo:

azul | rojo
azul | azul

1er giro: $P(\text{rojo}) = \frac{1}{4}$

2do giro: $P(\text{rojo}) = \frac{1}{4}$

1ro y 2do giros: $P(\text{rojo y rojo}) = \frac{1}{4} \times \frac{1}{4} = \frac{1}{16}$

Propiedad de multiplicativa de la igualdad (Multiplication property of equality) Si $a = b$, entonces $ac = bc$.

Ejemplo:

En la segunda línea del ejemplo a continuación, 2 está multiplicado en ambos lados de la ecuación.

$$\text{Si} \qquad \frac{1}{2}y = 4$$

$$\text{entonces} \qquad \mathbf{2} \times \frac{1}{2}y = \mathbf{2} \times 4$$

inverso mutiplicativo (multiplicative inverse) Si el producto de dos números es 1, cada número es el inverso multiplicativo del otro.

Ejemplo:

$\frac{1}{6}$ y 6 son inversos multiplicativos ya que $\frac{1}{6} \times 6 = 1$.

mutuamente exclusivos (mutually exclusive) Si el evento A o B ocurren, entonces el otro no puede ocurrir.

Ejemplos:

Si la temperatura exterior es 90°, no está nevando.

Si un polígono tiene solamente tres lados, no puede tener 4 ángulos.

números negativos (negative numbers) Números menores que cero.

Ejemplo:

Números negativos   Números positivos

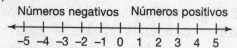

correlación negativa (negative relationship) Dos conjuntos de datos tienen una correlación negativa cuando los valores de datos en un conjunto aumentan a medida que los valores en el otro conjunto disminuyen.

Ejemplo:

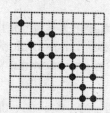

pendiente negativa (negative slope) Es la pendiente de una línea que se inclina hacia abajo.

Ejemplo:

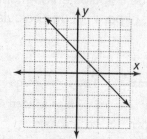

raíz cuadrada negativa (negative square root) Es el opuesto de la raíz cuadrada principal de un número.

Ejemplo:

raíz cuadrada principal: raíz cuadrada negativa:

$$\sqrt{25} = 5 \qquad\qquad -\sqrt{25} = -5$$

desarrollo de un sólido (net) Es un patrón plano que se puede doblar para crear una figura tridimensional tal como un prisma.

Ejemplo:

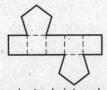

conjunto de intervalos para el prisma pentagonal

prisma pentagonal

nonágono (nonagon) Se trata de un polígono con 9 lados.

Ejemplos:

ecuación no lineal (nonlinear equation) Es una ecuación cuyo gráfico es una curva más que una línea.

Ejemplo:

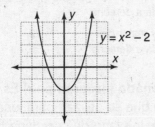

$y = x^2 - 2$

función no lineal (nonlinear function) Una función cuyo gráfico no es una línea recta debido a que cambios iguales en "x" no ocasionan cambios iguales en "y".

Ejemplos:

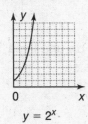 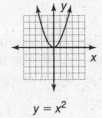 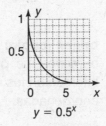

$y = 2^x$ $y = x^2$ $y = 0.5^x$

sin relaciones (no relationship) Dos conjuntos de datos no tienen relaciones cuando no hay relaciones positivas o negativas.

Ejemplo:

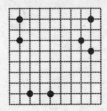

recta numérica (number line) Es una recta que muestra los números en orden.

Ejemplos:

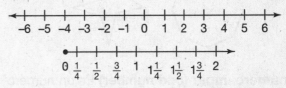

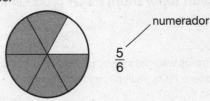

forma de numérica-verbal (number-word form) Es una forma de escribir un número utilizando palabras y números.

Ejemplos: 45 trillones   9 millares

numeral (numeral) Un símbolo que se utiliza para un número.

Ejemplos: 7   58   234

numerador (numerator) Es el máximo número en una fracción que dice cuántas piezas de un todo están siendo denominadas.

Ejemplo:

numerador

$\dfrac{5}{6}$

ángulo obtuso (obtuse angle) Es un ángulo que mide más de 90° y menos de 180°.

Ejemplos:

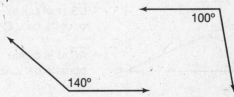

100°

140°

triángulo obtusángulo (obtuse triangle)
Es un triángulo con un ángulo obtuso.

Ejemplos:

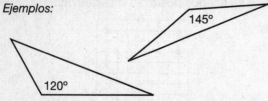

octágono (octagon) Es un polígono con 8 lados.

Ejemplos:

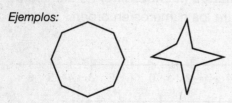

número impar (odd number) Es un número entero que tiene 1, 3, 5,7 ó 9 en los lugares de la unidad.

Ejemplos:

43   225   999   8,007

probabilidades (odds) Es la relación del número de formas en que un evento puede suceder con respecto al número de formas que no puede.

Ejemplo:

Probabilidad para obtener un 3: de 1 a 5.

Probabilidad de no obtener un 3: de 5 a 1.

operación (operation) Es un procedimiento matemático.

Ejemplos:

Hay cuatro operaciones básicas: adición o suma, sustracción o resta, multiplicación y división.

lado opuesto (opposite leg) Para un ángulo agudo en un triángulo recto, el cateto que se encuentra a través del ángulo.

Ejemplo:

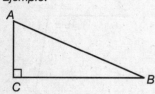

$\overline{CB}$ es el cateto opuesto del $\angle CAB$.

$\overline{AC}$ es el cateto opuesto del $\angle ABC$.

números opuestos (opposite numbers)
Son los números que están a la misma distancia en la línea numérica a partir del cero pero en lados opuestos.

Ejemplo:

7 y −7 son opuestos uno del otro

```
  ├─┼─┼─┼─┼─┼─┼─┼─┼─┼─┼─┼─┼─┤
 −7              0              7
```

orden de las operaciones (order of operations) Las reglas indican en qué orden deben hacerse las operaciones:
(1) simplificar los paréntesis interiores,
(2) simplificar los exponentes, (3) multiplicar y dividir de izquierda a derecha y (4) sumar y restar de izquierda a derecha.

Ejemplo:

Evaluar $2x^2 + 4(x − 2)$ for $x = 3$.

(1) simplificar los paréntesis interiores	$2 \cdot 3^2 + 4(3 − 2)$ $2 \cdot 3^2 + 4(1)$
(2) simplificar los exponentes	$2 \cdot 9 + 4$
(3) multiplicar y dividir de izquierda a derecha	$18 + 4$
(4) sumar y restar de izquierda a derecha	22

par ordenado (ordered pair) Es un par de números que se utilizan para localizar un punto en un plano de coordenadas.

Ejemplo:

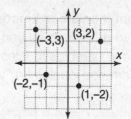

origen (origin) Es el punto cero de una línea numérica o el punto (0, 0) donde se intersectan los ejes de un sistema de coordenadas.

Ejemplos:

dibujo ortogonal (orthographic drawing)
Dibujo de un objeto utilizando vistas delantera, lateral y superior.

Ejemplo:

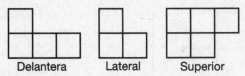

Delantera   Lateral   Superior

onza (ounce) Unidad de peso en el sistema de medición usual.

Ejemplo:

 Una carta pesa aproximadamente una onza.

resultado (outcome) Es la forma en que un experimento o situación puede desarrollarse.

Ejemplo:

Resultados para el lanzamiento de 2 monedas:

moneda 1	moneda 2
cara	cruz
cara	cara
cruz	cara
cruz	cruz

Hay 4 resultados. Un resultado es cara, cara.

valor extremo (outlier) El valor extremo en un conjunto de datos, separado de la mayoría de los otros valores.

Ejemplo:

27 27 27 29 32 33 36 38 42 43 62

↑
valor extremo

parábola (parabola) Es una curva en forma de U o en forma de U invertida que es la gráfica de una función cuadrática.

Ejemplos:

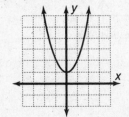 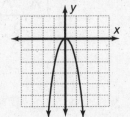

paralelo (parallel) Son dos líneas, segmentos o rayas que nunca se cruzan no importa cuán lejos se extiendan.

Ejemplos:

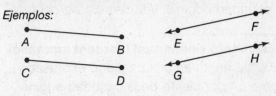

paralelogramo (parallelogram) Es una figura de cuatro lados cuyos lados opuestos son paralelos y congruentes.

Ejemplos:

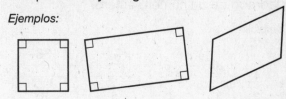

pentágono (pentagon) Es un polígono de 5 lados.

Ejemplos:

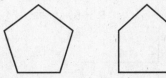

por ciento (percent) Es una relación que compara un número a 100.

Ejemplo:

$$\frac{58}{100} = 0.58 = 58\%$$

porcentaje de cambio (percent change)
La cantidad de cambio, de aumento o disminución, dividida por la cantidad original y expresada como un por ciento de la cantidad original.

Ejemplos:

Encuentre el porcentaje de cambio si se invierten $1500 y se ganan $75 en intereses.

$\frac{75}{1500} = 0.05 = 5\%$ $75 es un 5% de aumento.

Encuentre el porcentaje de cambio si un artículo que cuesta $50 está en venta con un descuento de un 10%.

$\frac{10}{50} = 0.20 = 20\%$ $10 de descuento es un 20% de disminución.

disminución porcentual (percent decrease) Es la disminución en una cantidad expresada como un por ciento de la cantidad original. Vea *cambio porcentual.*

incremento porcentual (percent increase) Es el aumento en una cantidad expresado como un por ciento de la cantidad original. Vea *porcentaje de cambio.*

cuadrado perfecto (perfect square) Es el cuadrado de un número entero.

Ejemplos:

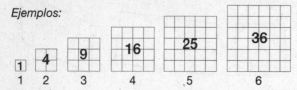

perímetro (perimeter) Es la distancia alrededor del lado exterior de una figura.

Ejemplo:

$P = 5 + 2 + 6 + 4 + 11 + 6$
$= 34$

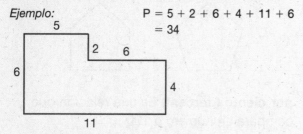

permutación (permutation) Es un arreglo de artículos en el cual el orden es importante.

Ejemplo:

Un estudiante de este grupo será elegido presidente y otro será elegido vicepresidente:

Wendy, Alex, Carlos. Las posibles permutaciones son:

Wendy—presidente, Alex—vicepresidente
Wendy—presidente, Carlos—vicepresidente
Alex—presidente, Wendy—vicepresidente
Alex—presidente, Carlos—vicepresidente
Carlos—presidente, Wendy —vicepresidente
Carlos—preseidente, Alex—vicepresidente

Nota: Cada uno de los resultados anteriores es una permutación diferente.

perpendicular (perpendicular) Son las rayas, líneas o segmentos de línea que se intersectan en ángulos rectos.

Ejemplos:

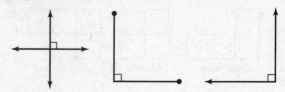

mediatriz (perpendicular bisector) Una raya, línea o segmento que intersecta un segmento en su punto medio y es perpendicular al mismo.

Ejemplo:

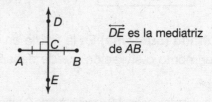

$\overrightarrow{DE}$ es la mediatriz de $\overline{AB}$.

pi (π) (pi) Es la relación de una circunferencia de círculo a su diámetro: 3.14159265.....

Ejemplo:

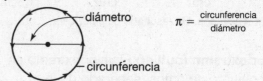

$$\pi = \frac{\text{circunferencia}}{\text{diámetro}}$$

pictografía (pictograph) Es una gráfica que utiliza símbolos para representar los datos.

Ejemplo:

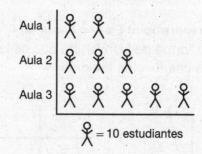

Estudiantes en clase

$\overset{\circ}{\mathord{\text{\Large\Lightning}}}$ = 10 estudiantes

valor posicional (place value) Es el valor dado al lugar que ocupa un dígito.

Ejemplo:

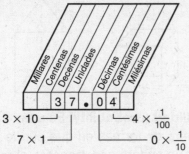

3×10 ——

7×1 ——

—— $4 \times \frac{1}{100}$

$0 \times \frac{1}{10}$

plano (plane) Es una superficie plana que se extiende hasta el infinito.

Ejemplo:

Para visualizar un plano, piense en la extensión de la superficie de la mesa en todas direcciones.

simetría central (point symmetry) Una figura tiene simetría central si luce sin cambios después de una rotación de 180°.

Ejemplo:

La figura parece la misma después de una rotación de 180° o $\frac{1}{2}$ giro.

$\frac{1}{4}$ giro

$\frac{1}{2}$ giro

(90° de rotación)   (180° de rotación)

polígono (polygon) Es una figura cerrada hecha de segmentos de línea.

Ejemplos:

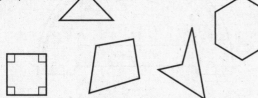

poliedro (polyhedron) Es un sólido cuyas caras son polígonos.

Ejemplos:

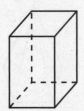

polinomio (polynomial) Expresión algebraica que es la suma de uno o más términos.

Ejemplos:

$$x^2 + 2x - 3 \qquad 5y - 15$$

población (population) Es la recolección de todas las cosas a ser estudiadas en una encuesta.

Ejemplo:

La totalidad de los 1000 nombres de la membresía de un club fue puesta en tarjetas y las tarjetas fueron barajadas. Después se extrajeron 100 tarjetas y a estos miembros de les hizo una encuesta telefónica. La población de la encuesta son todos los 1000 miembros del club.

números positivos (positive numbers) Son los números mayores que cero.

Ejemplo:

Números negativos   Números positivos

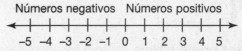

$-5 \quad -4 \quad -3 \quad -2 \quad -1 \quad 0 \quad 1 \quad 2 \quad 3 \quad 4 \quad 5$

correlación positiva (positive relationship) Se dice que dos conjuntos de datos tienen una correlación positiva cuando los valores de sus datos se incrementan los dos o disminuyen los dos.

Ejemplo:

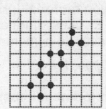

pendiente positiva (positive slope) Es la pendiente de una línea que se inclina hacia arriba.

Ejemplo:

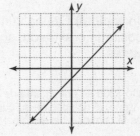

libra (pound) Una unidad en el sistema usual de medidas que es igual a 16 onzas.

Ejemplo:

Arroz
1 libra

potencia (power) Un exponente o el número producido cuando se eleva una base al exponente.

Ejemplo:

$16 = 2^4$ 2 está elevado a la 4ta potencia.

16 es la 4ta potencia de 2.

precisión (precision) Es la exactitud de una medida, determinada por la unidad de medida.

Ejemplo:

La más pequeña unidad de medida, pulgadas, es más precisa que la más grande unidad de medida, pies.

5'1" 61"

factor primo (prime factor) Es un número primo que divide a otro entero sin dejar un residuo.

Ejemplo:

5 es un factor primo de 35 porque $35 \div 5 = 7$.

descomposición factorial (prime factorization) Es la escritura de un número como un producto de números primos.

Ejemplo: $70 = 2 \times 5 \times 7$

número primo (prime number) Es un número entero mayor que 1 cuyos únicos factores son 1 y el propio número.

Ejemplo:

Los números primos comienzan con 2, 3, 5, 7, 11....

principal (principal) Es una cantidad de dinero depositada o extraida, sobre la cual se paga interés.

Ejemplo:

David depositó $300 en una cuenta de ahorros. Después de 1 año, el balance de su cuenta fue de $315. $300 es la cantidad del principal.

raíz cuadrada principal (principal square root) Es la raíz cuadrada positiva de un número.

Ejemplo:

raíz cuadrada principal

$\sqrt{25} = 5$

raíz cuadrada negativa

$-\sqrt{25} = -5$

prisma (prism) Es un poliedro cuyas bases son paralelas y congruentes.

Ejemplo:

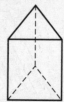

probabilidad (probability) Es una relación del número de formas en que puede suceder un evento con respecto al número total de resultados posibles.

Ejemplo:

La probabilidad de obtener un 3 es $\frac{1}{6}$.

La probabilidad de no obtener un 3 es $\frac{5}{6}$.

producto (product) Es el resultado de multiplicar dos o más números.

Ejemplo:

producto

$2 \times 3 \times 5 = 30$

proporción (proportion) Es una ecuación que establece que dos relaciones son iguales.

Ejemplo: $\frac{12}{34} = \frac{6}{17}$

transportador (protractor) Una herramienta para la medición de ángulos.

Ejemplo:

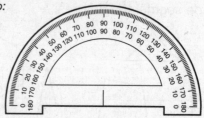

pirámide (pyramid) Es un sólido con una base y cuyos otros lados son triángulos que se unen en un solo punto.

Ejemplos:

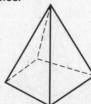

Teorema de Pitágoras (Pythagorean Theorem) En un triángulo rectángulo donde "c" es la longitud de la hipotenusa y "a" y "b" son las longitudes de los catetos, se cumple que $a^2 + b^2 = c^2$.

Ejemplo:

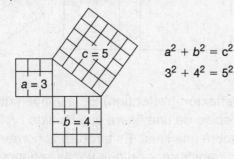

$$a^2 + b^2 = c^2$$
$$3^2 + 4^2 = 5^2$$

cuadrantes (quadrants) Son las cuatro regiones determinadas por los ejes de un plano de coordenadas.

Ejemplo:

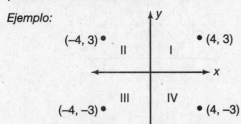

ecuación cuadrática (quadratic equation) Es una ecuación con un término al cuadrado similar a x^2.

Ejemplos:

$$y = x^2 + 3x - 12 \qquad y = 2x^2 + 7$$

función cuadrática (quadratic function) Es una función donde la potencia más alta de x es 2. La gráfica de una función cuadrática es una parábola.

Ejemplo:

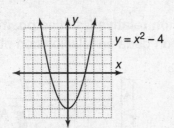

$y = x^2 - 4$

cuadrilátero (quadrilateral) Es un polígono con 4 lados.

Ejemplos:

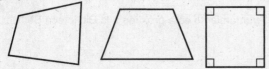

cuarto (quart) Una unidad de volumen en el sistema usual de medidas.

Ejemplo:

Un cuarto de leche

cuartil (quartile) Uno de los números que divide un conjunto de datos en cuartos iguales.

Ejemplo:

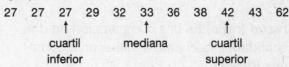

27   27   27   29   32   33   36   38   42   43   62

cuartil inferior   mediana   cuartil superior

27, 33 y 42 son los tres cuartillos para este conjunto de datos.

cociente (quotient) Es el resultado de dividir un número por otro.

Ejemplo:

cociente

$$8 \div 4 = 2$$

radical $\sqrt{}$ **(radical sign)** Utilizado para representar la raíz cuadrada de un número.

Ejemplo: $\sqrt{49} = 7$

radio (radius) Es una línea desde el centro de un círculo hasta cualquier punto en dicho círculo.

Ejemplo:

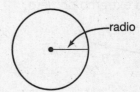

radio

muestra aleatoria (random sample) Es una muestra escogida de forma tal que cada miembro de la población tiene igual probabilidad de ser incluido.

Ejemplo:

La totalidad de los 1000 nombres de la membresía de un club fue puesta en tarjetas y las tarjetas fueron barajadas. Después se extrajeron 100 tarjetas y a estos miembros de les hizo una encuesta telefónica. La muestra es el grupo de 100 miembros tomados para la encuesta telefónica. Todos los miembros del club tuvieron una misma oportunidad de ser llamados de modo que esta fue una muestra aleatoria.

rango (range) Es la diferencia entre los valores más alto y más bajo en un conjunto de datos.

Ejemplo:

27 27 27 29 32 33 36 38 42 43 62

El rango es 62 − 27 = 35.

relación (rate) Es una relación que muestra cómo se relacionan las cantidades con diferentes unidades.

Ejemplos: $\dfrac{72 \text{ dólars}}{28 \text{ horas}}$ $\dfrac{55 \text{ millas}}{1 \text{ hora}}$

razón (ratio) Es una comparación de dos cantidades frecuentemente escrita como una fracción.

Ejemplos: $\dfrac{2}{1}$ 2 a 1   2:1

número racional (rational number) Es un número que puede ser escrito como una relación entre dos enteros. Los enteros, las fracciones y muchos decimales son números racionales.

Ejemplos:

Entero	Fracción	Decimal
$-27 = \dfrac{-27}{1}$	$\dfrac{7}{8}, \dfrac{-1}{2}$	$3.1 = 3\dfrac{1}{10} = \dfrac{31}{10}$

rayo (ray) Una parte de una línea que tiene un punto extremo y se extiende al infinito en la otra dirección. Una línea se denomina por su punto extremo primero.

Ejemplo:

$\overrightarrow{AB}$

números reales (real numbers) Todos los números racionales e irracionales.

Ejemplos:

-27 $\dfrac{1}{2}$ 3.1

$\sqrt{5}$ π $-\sqrt{\dfrac{1}{2}}$

recíprocos (reciprocals) Son dos números cuyo producto es 1.

Ejemplo:

$\dfrac{3}{5}$ y $\dfrac{5}{3}$ son recíprocos ya que $\dfrac{3}{5} \cdot \dfrac{5}{3} = 1$.

rectángulo (rectangle) Es un paralelogramo con lados opuestos de igual longitud y todos los ángulos midiendo 90°.

Ejemplos:

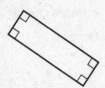

reflexión (reflection) Es la imagen de espejo de una figura que ha sido "volteada" sobre una línea. Es también el nombre para la transformación que voltea la figura sobre la línea.

Ejemplo:

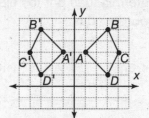

polígono regular (regular polygon) Es un polígono que tiene todos sus lados y ángulos congruentes.

Ejemplos:

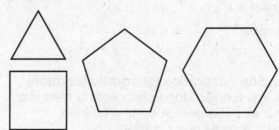

posición relativa (relative position) Posición dada en relación con otro lugar.

Ejemplo:

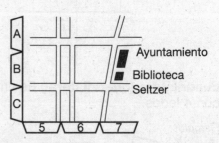

El Ayuntamiento está próximo a la Biblioteca Setltzer.

residuo (remainder) Es el número menor que el divisor y que queda después que se ha completado el proceso de división.

Ejemplo:

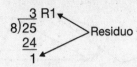

decimal periódico (repeating decimal) Un decimal con un dígito o grupo de dígitos repetitivos a la derecha del punto decimal.

Ejemplos: $0.\overline{6}$ $0.\overline{123}$ $2.1\overline{8}$

rombo (rhombus) Un paralelogramo con los cuatro lados de igual longitud.

Ejemplos:

ángulo recto (right angle) Un ángulo que mide 90°.

Ejemplo:

triángulo rectángulo (right triangle) Un triángulo con un ángulo recto.

Ejemplos:

variación vertical (rise) Para una línea en una gráfica, es el cambio vertical utilizado para un cambio horizontal dado.

Ejemplo:

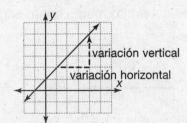

variación vertical
variación horizontal

rotación (rotation) Es la imagen de una figura que ha sido "girada", como en una rueda. Es también el nombre para la transformación que gira la figura.

Ejemplo:

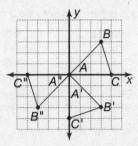

simetría rotacional (rotational symmetry) Una figura tiene simetría rotacional si puede ser rotada menos de un círculo completo y coincide exactamente con su imagen original.

Ejemplos:

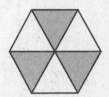

Cada figura tiene simetría rotacional.

redondeo (rounding) Estimación de un número a un valor de lugar dado.

Ejemplo:

2153 redondeado a	
la centena más próxima: 2200	la decena más próxima: 2150

variación horizontal (run) Para una línea en una gráfica, el cambio horizontal utilizado para encontrar el cambio vertical o elevación.

Ejemplo:

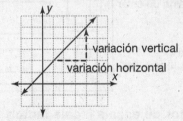

variación vertical
variación horizontal

muestreo (sample) Un conjunto de datos utilizados para predecir cómo pudiera ocurrir una situación en particular.

Ejemplo:

La totalidad de los 1000 nombres de la membresía de un club fue puesta en tarjetas y las tarjetas fueron barajadas. Después se extrajeron 100 tarjetas y a estos miembros de les hizo una encuesta telefónica. El muestreo es el grupo de 100 miembros tomados para la encuesta telefónica.

espacio muestral (sample space) El conjunto de todos los resultados posibles de un experimento.

Ejemplo:

Resultados del lanzamiento de 2 monedas:

moneda 1	moneda 2
cara	cruz
cara	cara
cruz	cara
cruz	cruz

El espacio muestral es cara, cruz; cara, cara, y cruz, cruz.

escala (gráfica) (scale(graphical)) Las marcas uniformemente espaciadas en una gráfica de barras o el eje vertical de la gráfica de línea utilizado para medir la altura de las barras.

Ejemplo:

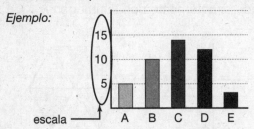

escala (en dibujos a escala) (scale (in scale drawings)) Es la relación de medidas en un plano a escala con relación a las medidas del objeto real. Vea *dibujo a escala.*

dibujo a escala (scale drawing) Un plano que utiliza una escala para hacer un dibujo ampliado o reducido de un objeto.

Ejemplo:

Dibujo a escala del salón de estar

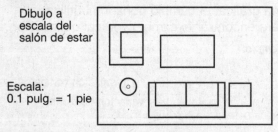

Escala:
0.1 pulg. = 1 pie

factor de escala (scale factor) Es la relación utilizada para agrandar o reducir figuras similares.

Ejemplo:

$\frac{10}{5} = 2$

$\frac{6}{3} = 2$

10 cm
6 cm
3 cm
5 cm

El factor de escala es 2 para la ampliación.

triángulo escaleno (scalene triangle) Es un triángulo cuyos lados tienen longitudes diferentes.

Ejemplos:

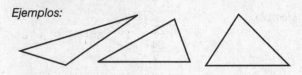

diagrama de dispersión (scatterplot) Una gráfica que utiliza valores de datos pares como puntos para mostrar la relación entre los dos conjuntos de datos.

Ejemplo:

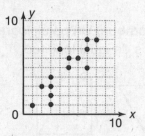

notación científica (scientific notation) Un número escrito como un decimal mayor que o igual a 1 y menor que 10, multiplicado por una potencia de 10.

Ejemplo: $350{,}000 = 3.5 \times 10^5$

sector circular (sector) Una parte de círculo en forma de cuña, utilizada en una gráfica de círculo para mostrar cómo las porciones de un conjunto de datos se comparan con el conjunto completo.

Ejemplos:

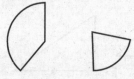

segmento (segment) Vea *segmento de recta.*

bisectriz del segmento (segment bisector) Es una raya, línea o segmento que pasa a través del punto medio de un segmento.

Ejemplo:

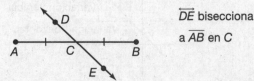

$\overrightarrow{DE}$ bisecciona a $\overline{AB}$ en C

progresión (sequence) Es un arreglo de números que sigue un patrón.

Ejemplos:

progresión aritmética

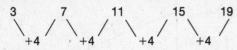

progresión geométrica

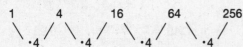

lado (side) Cada una de las líneas que forman un ángulo. También los segmentos de línea que forman un polígono.

Ejemplos:

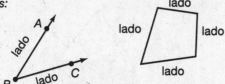

Lado-ángulo-ángulo (Side-Angle-Angle) (SAA) Es una regla utilizada para determinar si los triágulos son congruentes mediante comparación de las partes correspondientes.

Ejemplo:

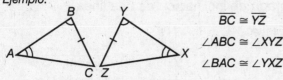

$\overline{BC} \cong \overline{YZ}$

$\angle ABC \cong \angle XYZ$

$\angle BAC \cong \angle YXZ$

$\triangle ABC \cong \triangle XYZ$ por la regla SAA.

Lado-ángulo-lado (Side-Angle-Side) (SAS) Una regla para determinar si los triángulos son congruentes, por comparación de sus partes correspondientes.

Ejemplo:

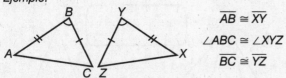

$\overline{AB} \cong \overline{XY}$

$\angle ABC \cong \angle XYZ$

$\overline{BC} \cong \overline{YZ}$

$\triangle ABC \cong \triangle XYZ$ por la regla SAS.

Lado-lado-lado (Side-Side-Side) (SSS) Es una regla utilizada para determinar si los triángulos son congruentes por comparación de las partes correspondientes.

Ejemplo:

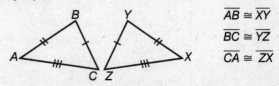

$\overline{AB} \cong \overline{XY}$

$\overline{BC} \cong \overline{YZ}$

$\overline{CA} \cong \overline{ZX}$

$\triangle ABC \cong \triangle XYZ$ por la regla SSS.

dígitos significativos (significatnt digits) En una cantidad medida, son los dígitos que representan la medida real.

Ejemplos:

380.6700   Todos los dígitos son significativos.

0.0038   El 3 y el 8 son significativo, pero ninguno de los ceros son significativos.

similar (similar) Que tienen la misma forma pero no necesariamente el mismo tamaño.

Ejemplos:

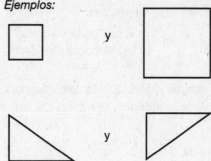

y

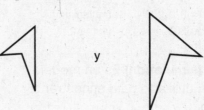

y

relación de similaridad (similarity ratio) Es la relación entre longitudes de lados correspondientes en figuras similares.

Ejemplo:

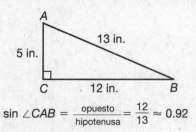

$\dfrac{m\overline{AB}}{m\overline{EF}} = \dfrac{10}{15} = \dfrac{2}{3}$

La relación de similaridad de $\triangle ABC$ y $\triangle EFG$ es de $\dfrac{2}{3}$.

interés simple (simple interest) Interés basado en el capital solamente.

Ejemplo: Ramón invierte $240 en una cuenta que gana un 6% de interés anual durante 5 años.

El ganará $240 \cdot 0.06 \cdot 5 = 72$,

$72 en interés simple después de 5 años.

simplificado (simplified) Un polinomio que no contiene términos semejantes.

Ejemplo:

$4x^4 + x^3 + x^2 - 8$ simplificado

$4x^4 + x^2 + 6x^2 - 8$ no simplificado, ya que x^2 y $6x^2$ son términos semejantes.

simplificar (simplify) Reducir la complejidad de una expresión aplicando el orden de las operaciones.

Ejemplo: Simplificar: $3 + 8 \cdot 5^2$

$3 + 8 \cdot 5^2 = 3 + 8 \cdot 25$ (exponentes)

$= 3 + 200$ (multiplicar)

$= 203$ (sumar)

simulación (simulation) Es un modelo experimental utilizado para encontrar la probabilidad.

Ejemplo:

Un jugador de béisbol batea .250.Para simular cómo este jugador pudiera batear, se hace girar una ruleta de 4 secciones. La simulación puede utilizarse para predecir con qué frecuencia el bateador tendría 2 hits consecutivos o 3 hits consecutivos.

seno (sine) Para un ángulo agudo "x" en un triángulo rectángulo, el seno de "x" o sen(x) es la relación cateto $\frac{\text{opuesto}}{\text{hipotenusa}}$.

Ejemplo:

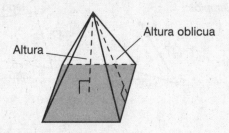

$\sin \angle CAB = \dfrac{\text{opuesto}}{\text{hipotenusa}} = \dfrac{12}{13} \approx 0.92$

altura oblicua (slant height) En una pirámide, la distancia perpendicular desde una arista de la base hasta el vértice.

Ejemplo:

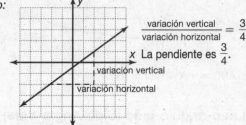

trasladar (slide) Vea *traslación*.

pendiente (slope) Para una línea en una gráfica, la pendiente es la altura dividida por el recorrido y se utiliza para describir el grado de inclinación de una línea.

Ejemplo:

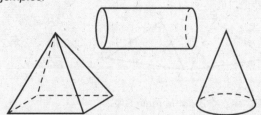

$\dfrac{\text{variación vertical}}{\text{variación horizontal}} = \dfrac{3}{4}$

La pendiente es $\dfrac{3}{4}$.

sólido (solid) Es una figura tridimensional.

Ejemplos:

soluciones de una ecuación o desigualdad (solutions of an equation or inequality) Son los valores de una variable que hacen que una ecuación o desigualdad se cumpla.

Ejemplos:

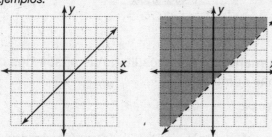

La línea representa la solución para $y = x - 1$.

El área sombreada representa la solución para $y > x - 1$.

solución de un sistema (solution of a system) Las sustituciones de variables que hacen que todas las ecuaciones en un sistema se cumplan.

Ejemplo:
$$y = x + 4$$
$$y = 3x - 6$$

El par ordenado (5, 9) resuelve ambas ecuaciones. Por lo tanto, (5, 9) es una solución del sistema.

resolver (solve) Encontrar las soluciones de una ecuación o desigualdad.

Ejemplo: Solucionar $x + 6 = 13$.
$$x + 6 = 13$$
$$x + 6 + (-6) = 13 + (-6)$$
$$x + 0 = 7$$
$$x = 7$$

esfera (sphere) Es un sólido cuyos puntos están todos a la misma distancia del centro.

Ejemplo:

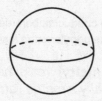

cuadrado (square) Es un cuadrilátero con todos sus lados de la misma longitud y todos sus ángulos midiendo 90°.

Ejemplo:

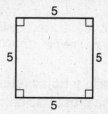

elevado al cuadrado (squared) Elevado a la segunda potencia.

Ejemplo: 3 al cuadrado se escribe 3^2.
$$3^2 = 3 \times 3 = 9$$

centímetro cuadrado (square centimeter) Es el área de un cuadrado con lados de 1 centímetro.

Ejemplo:

1 centímetro cuadrado

pulgada cuadrada (square inch) Es el área de un cuadrado con lados de 1 pulgada.

Ejemplo:

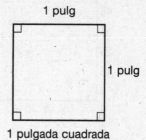

1 pulgada cuadrada

raíz cuadrada (square root) La raíz cuadrada de N es el número que cuando se multiplica por sí mismo da N. También, la raíz cuadrada de un número dado es la longitud de un lado de un cuadrado con un área igual al número dado.

Ejemplo:

$9 \times 9 = 81$, por tanto 9 es la raíz cuadrada de 81.

$9 = \sqrt{81}$

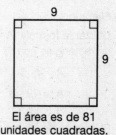

El área es de 81 unidades cuadradas.

forma usual (standard form) Es una forma de escribir un número utilizando dígitos.

Ejemplo:

Forma usual:	100,000,000
Forma en palabras:	cien millones
Forma en palabras y números:	100 millones

diagrama de tallo y hojas (stem-and-leaf diagram) Es una presentación de datos que utiliza los dígitos de los números en el dato para mostrar la forma y distribución del conjunto de datos.

Ejemplo:

El diagrama muestra el conjunto de datos: 33, 34, 34, 35, 40, 41, 46, 51, 51, 52, 53, 55, 58.

Tallo	Hoja					
3	3	4	4	5		
4	0	1	6			
5	1	1	2	3	5	8

función por partes (step function) Es una función en la cual se aplican reglas diferentes a valores de entrada diferentes. La gráfica de una función de escalón está hecho de piezas no conectadas entre sí.

Ejemplo:

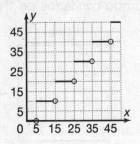

ángulo llano (straight angles) Un ángulo que mide 180°.

Ejemplo:

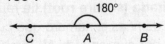

sustituir (substitute) Reemplazar una variable con un valor específico.

Ejemplo:

Utilizar la fórmula $A = l \cdot w$ para encontrar el área de un rectángulo con 12 cm de longitud y 8 cm de ancho.

$A = l \cdot w$

$A = 12 \cdot 8$ — Sustituir los valores para

$A = 96$ — la longitud y el ancho.

El área es de 96 cm².

la resta (subtraction) Una operación que dice la diferencia entre dos números o cuánto queda cuando se toma una parte.

Ejemplo: $12 - 5 = 7$

⊗ ⊗ ⊗ ⊗ ⊗
○ ○ ○ ○ ○
○ ○

suma (sum) Es el resultado de añadir dos o más números.

Ejemplo: $30 + 18 = \underset{\text{suma}}{48}$

ángulos suplementarios (supplementary angles) Dos ángulos cuyas medidas suman 180°.

Ejemplo:

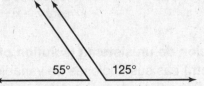

área del superficie (surface area) (SA) La suma de las áreas de cada cara de un poliedro.

Ejemplo:

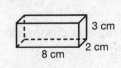

Dos caras son 8 cm por 3 cm.
$A = b \cdot h = 8 \cdot 3 = 24 \text{ cm}^2$

Dos caras son 8 cm por 2 cm.
$A = b \cdot h = 8 \cdot 2 = 16 \text{ cm}^2$

Dos caras son 2 cm por 3 cm.
$A = b \cdot h = 2 \cdot 3 = 6 \text{ cm}^2$

El área de superficie del prisma rectangular es

$SA = 2(24 + 16 + 6)$
$= 92 \text{ cm}^2$

encuesta (survey) Un estudio que requiere recolectar y analizar información.

Ejemplo:

Una encuesta fue conducida para determinar qué deporte era el más popular entre los estudiantes.

simetría (symmetry) Vea *simetría lineal, simetría puntual* y *simetría rotacional*.

sistema de ecuaciones lineales (system of linear equations) Dos o más ecuaciones lineales que se consideran unidas.

Ejemplo:
$y = x + 3$
$y = 4x - 15$

tabla de valores (T-table) Es una tabla que muestra los valores de "x" y de "y" correspondientes para una ecuación.

Ejemplo:

$$y = 2x + 1$$

x	y
− 2	− 3
− 1	− 1
0	1
1	3
2	5

conteo (tally) Anotar, utilizando marcas de contar, la cuenta de los resultados obtenidos durante una encuesta.

Ejemplo:

Vehículo	Cuenta
Sedan	卌 |||
Station Wagon	||||
Suburban	卌	
Truck	卌
Van	|||

marcas de conteo (tally marks) Marcas utilizadas para organizar un conjunto grande de datos. Cada marca indica una vez que un valor aparece en el conjunto de datos.

Ejemplo: | Uno   卌 Cinco

la tangente (tangent line) Es una línea que toca un círculo en un punto solamente.

Ejemplo:

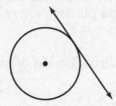

la tangente (tangent ratio) Para un ángulo agudo "x" en un triángulo rectángulo, la tangente de "x", o tan(x), es el $\frac{\text{lado opuesto}}{\text{lado adyacente}}$.

Ejemplo:

A right triangle with vertices A (top), C (bottom left), B (bottom right). AC = 5 in., AB = 13 in., CB = 12 in., right angle at C.

$$\tan \angle CAB = \frac{\text{lado opuesto}}{\text{lado adyacente}} = \frac{12}{5} = 2.4$$

término (term) Es un número en una progresión. También, una parte de un polinomio que es un número con signo, una variable o un número multiplicado por una variable o variables. Las variables pueden tener exponentes numéricos enteros.

Ejemplos:

progresión   3   7   11   15   19   23

términos

polinomio $2x^3 - x^2 + 3x - 5$

términos

decimal finito (terminating decimal) Un decimal con un número de dígitos fijo.

Ejemplos: 3.5   0.599992   4.05

teselado (tesellation) Un patrón de figuras repetido que cubre un plano sin espaciamientos intermedios ni sobreposiciones.

Ejemplos:

probabilidad teórica (theoretical probability) Es la relación del número de formas en que puede ocurrir un evento con respecto al número total de resultados posibles.

Ejemplo:

$$\frac{\text{Número de formas de marcar un blanco}}{\text{Total de formas}} = \frac{3}{6} = \frac{1}{2}$$

Como la mitad de las secciones de la ruleta son blancas, la probabilidad teórica de marcar un blanco es de $\frac{1}{2}$.

transformación (transformation) Es un cambio en el tamaño o posición de una figura.

Ejemplo:

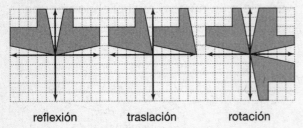

reflexión   traslación   rotación

traslación (translation) Es la imagen de una figura que ha sido desplazada a una nueva posición sin voltearla o girarla. Es también el nombre para la transformación que desplaza la figura.

Ejemplo:

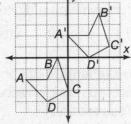

transversal (transversal) Es una línea que cruza dos o más líneas.

Ejemplo:

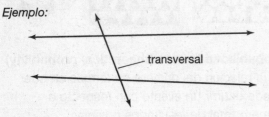

transversal

trapecio (trapezoid) Un cuadrilátero con exactamente dos lados paralelos.

Ejemplos:

diagrama de árbol (tree diagram) Un diagrama de ramas, en forma de árbol, que muestra todos los resultados posibles de una situación.

Ejemplo:

Lanzamiento de 3 monedas:

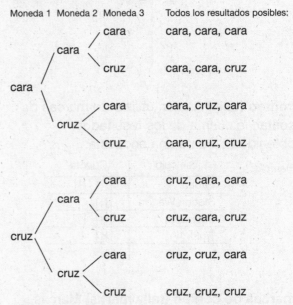

Moneda 1	Moneda 2	Moneda 3	Todos los resultados posibles:
cara	cara	cara	cara, cara, cara
		cruz	cara, cara, cruz
	cruz	cara	cara, cruz, cara
		cruz	cara, cruz, cruz
cruz	cara	cara	cruz, cara, cara
		cruz	cruz, cara, cruz
	cruz	cara	cruz, cruz, cara
		cruz	cruz, cruz, cruz

tendencia (trend) Es una relación entre dos conjuntos de datos que se muestran como un patrón en una dispersión de puntos. Vea *relación positiva*, *relación negativa*, *no relación*.

la tendencia (trend line) Es una línea que "une" los puntos aproximadamente formando una tendencia dentro de una dispersión de puntos. Vea *relación positiva* y *relación negativa*.

de prueba (trial) Un experimento.

Ejemplos:

La tirada de un cubo numérico   El lanzamiento de una moneda

triángulo (triangle) Un polígono con tres lados.

Ejemplos:

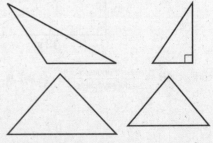

razones trigonométricas (trigonometric ratios) Son las relaciones de las longitudes de los lados de un triángulo rectángulo con respecto a las medidas de los ángulos agudos del triángulo.

Ejemplos:

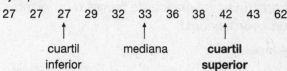

$$\cos \angle CAB = \frac{\text{lado adyacente}}{\text{hipotenusa}} = \frac{3}{5} = 0.6$$

$$\sin \angle CAB = \frac{\text{lado opuesto}}{\text{hipotenusa}} = \frac{4}{5} = 0.8$$

$$\tan \angle CAB = \frac{\text{lado opuesto}}{\text{lado adyacente}} = \frac{4}{3} \approx 1.3$$

trinomio (trinomial) Es un polinomio con tres términos.

Ejemplos: $2x^3 - x^2 + 3x$ $3x^2 + 2x - 4$

giro (turn) Vea *rotación*.

juego no limpio (unfair game) Un juego en el cual no todos los jugadores tienen la misma probabilidad de ganar.

Ejemplo:

Juego no limpio: Se lanza un par de cubos numéricos y a cada jugador se le asigna una suma desde 2 hasta 12. Cada jugador obtiene un punto cuando se tira su suma. Como las sumas desde 2 hasta 12 no tienen iguales oportunidades de ser tiradas, los jugadores no tienen oportunidades iguales de ganar y por eso el juego no es limpio.

precio unitario (unit price) Una razón unitaria que da el costo de un artículo.

Ejemplos:

$3.00 por libra $5.75 por caja

unidad (unit) Uno de algo. Una cantidad utilizada como una norma de medición.

fracción integrante (unit fraction) Una fracción con un numerador de 1.

Ejemplos: $\frac{1}{4}$ $\frac{1}{2}$ $\frac{1}{7}$

razón unitaria (unit rate) Una razón en la cual el segundo número en la comparación es la unidad.

Ejemplos: 25 galones por minuto $\frac{55 \text{ millas}}{\text{hora}}$

distinto denominador (unlike denominators) Denominadores que son diferentes en dos o más fracciones.

Ejemplo:

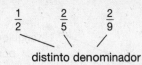

$$\frac{1}{2} \qquad \frac{2}{5} \qquad \frac{2}{9}$$

distinto denominador

cuartil superior (upper quartile) La mediana de la mitad superior de un conjunto de datos.

Ejemplo:

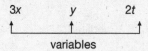

27 27 27 29 32 33 36 38 42 43 62

cuartil inferior   mediana   **cuartil superior**

variable (variable) Una cantidad que puede cambiar o variar, representada frecuentemente por una letra.

Ejemplos: $3x$ y $2t$

variables

diagrama de Venn (Venn diagram) Es un diagrama que utiliza regiones para mostrar las relaciones entre conjuntos de cosas.

Ejemplo:

Paralelogramos
Rectángulo
Cuadrado
Rombo

vértice (vertex) En un ángulo o un polígono, es el punto donde dos lados se intersectan. En un poliedro, es el punto de intersección de dos o más caras.

Ejemplos:

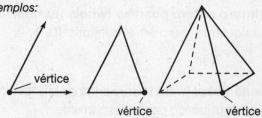

vértice   vértice   vértice

ángulos opuerstos por el vértice (vertical angles) Angulos en los lados opuestos de la intersección de dos líneas.

Ejemplo:

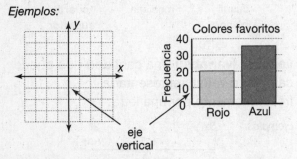

ángulos opuestos por el vértice:
∠1 y ∠3
∠2 y ∠4

eje vertical (vertical axis) Es la línea vertical de las dos líneas sobre las cuales se construye una gráfica de barras o un plano de coordenadas.

Ejemplos:

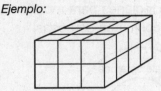

eje vertical

volumen (volume) La cantidad de espacio que ocupa un sólido.

Ejemplo:

$V = lwh$

$V = 4 \cdot 3 \cdot 2$

$V = 24$ unidades cúbicas

peso (weight) Medida de la fuerza que ejerce la gravedad sobre un cuerpo.

Ejemplos:

1 onza   1 lb   1 ton

número entero positivo (whole number) Cualquier número en el conjunto {0, 1, 2, 3, 4, . . .}

forma verbal (word form) Forma de escribir un número utilizando palabras solamente.

Ejemplos:

cuarenta y cinco trillones   un billón   seis

eje de las x (x-axis) El eje horizontal en un plano de coordenadas.

Ejemplo:

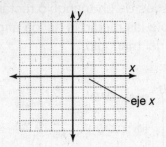

eje x

la abscisa (x-coordinate) El primer número en un par ordenado.

Ejemplo:

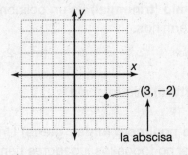

(3, −2)

la abscisa

punto de intersección de x (x-intercept) Un punto donde la gráfica de una ecuación cruza el eje de las x.

Ejemplo:

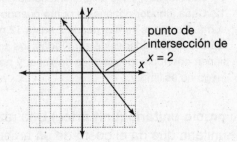

punto de intersección de x = 2

eje de las y (y-axis) El eje vertical en un plano de coordenadas.

Ejemplo:

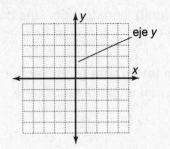

eje y

ordenada (*y*-coordinate) El segundo número en un par ordenado.

Ejemplo:

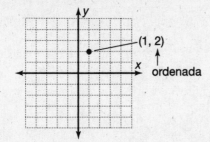

(1, 2)

ordenada

punto de intersección de *y* (*y*-intercept) Un punto donde la gráfica de una ecuación corta el eje de las y.

Ejemplo:

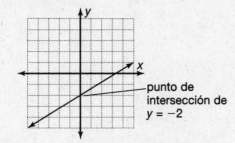

punto de intersección de $y = -2$

yarda (yard) Una unidad en el sistema usual de medidas que es igual a 3 pies.

Ejemplo:

La altura de un escritorio es de aproximadamente una yarda.

par cero (zero pair) Un número y su opuesto.

Ejemplos: 7 y −7 23 y −23

Propiedad cero de la suma (Zero Property of Addition) La suma de un entero y su aditivo inverso es 0.

Ejemplos:
$$3 + (-3) = 0$$
$$-8 + 8 = 0$$

Vietnamese Glossary

vị trí tuyệt đối (absolute position) Địa điểm cho trên tọa độ.

Ví Dụ:

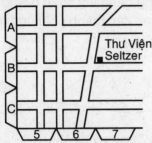

B7 là vị trí tuyệt đối của Thư Viện Seltzer.

trị số tuyệt đối (absolute value) Khoảng cách của một số tính từ số không. Ký hiệu của trị số tuyệt đối là │ │.

Ví Dụ:

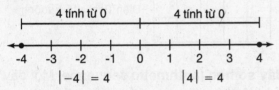

góc nhọn (acute angle) Góc đo được ít hơn 90 độ.

Ví Dụ:

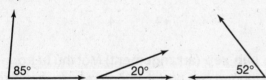

tam giác nhọn (acute triangle) Một tam giác với ba góc nhọn.

Ví Dụ:

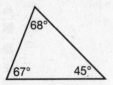

số cộng (addend) Một số được cộng vào một hay nhiều số khác.

Ví Dụ: 12 + 19 = 31
                  số cộng   số cộng

phép cộng (addition) Một phép toán cho ra một tổng số khi hai hay nhiều số gộp chung lại với nhau.

Ví Dụ:

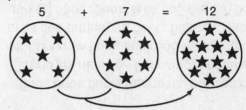

Tính Chất Cộng Một Lượng Bằng Nhau (Addition Property of Equality) Nếu $a = b$, thì $a + c = b + c$.

Ví Dụ:

Trong hàng thứ hai của ví dụ dưới đây, 1 được cộng thêm vào cho cả hai vế của phương trình.

$$\begin{array}{rl} \text{nếu} & x - 1 = 2 \\ \text{thì} & x - 1 + \mathbf{1} = 2 + \mathbf{1} \\ & x = 3 \end{array}$$

số nghịch đảo cộng (additive inverse) Sự trái ngược của một số.

Ví Dụ: Số nghịch đảo cộng của −2 là 2.
             Số nghịch đảo cộng của 5 là −5.

cạnh kề (adjacent leg) Đối với góc nhọn của một tam giác vuông, cạnh kề là một trong hai cạnh của góc vuông.

Ví Dụ:

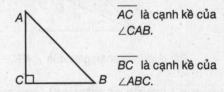

$\overline{AC}$ là cạnh kề của $\angle CAB$.

$\overline{BC}$ là cạnh kề của $\angle ABC$.

đại số (algebra) Một ngành của toán học trong đó những tương quan số học được triển khai bằng những biến số dùng để đại diện cho các số.

biểu thức đại số (algebraic expression) Một biểu thức gồm có ít nhất một biến số.

Ví Dụ: $n - 7$ $2y + 17$ $5(x - 3)$

những góc so le (alternate angles) Hai góc, được lập thành bởi hai đường thẳng và một đường cắt chéo, nằm ở hai phần đối nhau của đường cắt chéo và nằm (1) giữa hai đường thẳng (những góc so le trong) hoặc (2) bên ngoài hai đường thẳng đó (những góc so le ngoài). Những góc so le trong và những góc so le ngoài đồng dạng với nhau khi đường chéo cắt qua hai đường thẳng song song.

Ví Dụ:

Những góc so le ngoài là:
∠1 và ∠8
∠2 và ∠7

Những góc so le trong là:
∠3 và ∠6
∠4 và ∠5

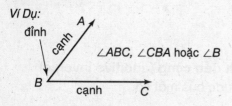

góc (angle) Hai nửa đường thẳng với một điểm gốc chung.

Ví Dụ:

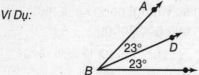

∠ABC, ∠CBA hoặc ∠B

đường phân giác (angle bisector)
Đường chia một góc ra thành hai góc đồng dạng với nhau.

Ví Dụ:

$\overrightarrow{BD}$ là đường phân giác của ∠ABC.

góc quay (angle of rotation) Góc mà một hình chuyển động quét qua trong khi quay.

Ví Dụ:

Góc quay là 90 độ.

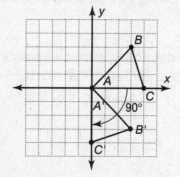

Góc-Cạnh-Góc (Angle-Side-Angle)(ASA)
Một quy tắc dùng để quyết định xem các tam giác có đồng dạng với nhau hay không bằng cách so sánh các thành phần tương ứng.

Ví Dụ:

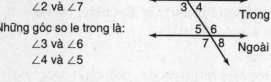

∠ABC ≅ ∠XYZ
$\overline{BC} \cong \overline{YZ}$
∠ACB ≅ ∠XZY

△ABC ≅ △XYZ theo quy tắc ASA.

diện tích (area) Số lượng của bề mặt mà một hình bao phủ.

Ví Dụ:

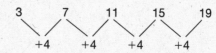

1 ô vuông

Diện Tích = 15 ô vuông

dãy số học (arithmetic sequence) Một dãy mà hiệu số giữa các số hạng liên tiếp nhau luôn luôn bất biến.

Ví Dụ:

3   7   11   15   19
  +4   +4   +4   +4

sự sắp xếp (arrangement) Một thứ tự trong đó, những con người, những mẫu tự, những chữ số, hay những vật thể khác xuất hiện.

Ví Dụ:

Tất cả những sự sắp xếp có thể thực hiện được của ba hình thể:

Tính Chất Nhóm Của Phép Cộng (Associative Property of Addition) Một dãy toán cộng mà sự thay đổi vị trí nhóm của số cộng không làm thay đổi tổng số của phép cộng đó.

Ví Dụ:
$$a + (b + c) = (a + b) + c$$
$$5 + (3 + 7) = (5 + 3) + 7$$

Tính Chất Nhóm Của Phép Nhân (Associative Property of Multiplication) Một dãy toán nhân mà sự thay đổi vị trí nhóm của thừa số không làm thay đổi tích số của phép nhân đó.

Ví Dụ:
$$a(bc) = (ab)c$$
$$3 \times (4 \times 2) = (3 \times 4) \times 2$$

số trung bình (average) Xem *số bình vị.*

trục tọa độ (axes) Xem *trục x* và *trục y.*

biểu đồ thanh (bar graph) Một biểu đồ dùng những thanh ngang hay thanh dọc để biểu thị các dữ kiện.

Ví Dụ:

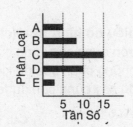

cơ số (của một số mũ) (base of an exponent) Một số nhân với chính nó theo số lần mà số mũ biểu thị.

Ví Dụ:
cơ số   số mũ
$$6^2 = 6 \times 6 = 36$$

cạnh đáy (của một đa giác) (base of a polygon) Bất cứ cạnh nào (thường là cạnh nằm dưới đáy), hay chiều dài của cạnh đó.

Ví Dụ:

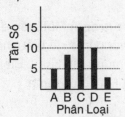

cạnh đáy

mặt đáy (của một hình khối) (base of a solid) Trong hình lăng trụ hay hình ống, nó là một trong hai mặt song song và đồng dạng. Trong hình kim tự tháp, nó là mặt đối diện với đỉnh. Trong hình chóp nón, nó là một mặt tròn.

Ví Dụ:

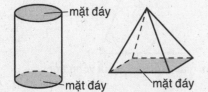

mặt đáy   mặt đáy   mặt đáy

hệ thống số nhị phân (binary number system) Hệ thống trị số vị trí dựa trên 2 cơ số.

Ví Dụ:

Trong hệ thống số nhị phân, 1011 bằng với 11 trong hệ thống số thập phân (dựa trên 10 cơ số).

	Vị trí hàng tám	Vị trí hàng bốn	Vị trí hàng hai	Vị trí hàng một
Cơ Số 2	1	0	1	1
Trị Số Vị Trí	8	4	2	1
Tích Số	$1 \times 8 = 8$	$0 \times 4 = 0$	$1 \times 2 = 2$	$1 \times 1 = 1$

$(1 \times 8) + (0 \times 4) + (1 \times 2) + (1 \times 1) = 8 + 0 + 2 + 1 = 11$

nhị thức (binomial) Một đa thức gồm 2 số hạng.

Ví Dụ: $4x^3 - 2x^2$ $2x + 5$

chia đôi (bisect) Chia một góc hay một đoạn thành hai góc hay hai phân đoạn đồng dạng với nhau.

Ví Dụ:

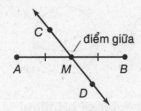

$\overrightarrow{CD}$ chia đôi $\overline{AB}$. $\overrightarrow{BD}$ chia đôi $\angle ABC$.

đường ranh (boundary line) Trên một đồ thị biểu diễn một bất đẳng thức tuyến, nó là đường biểu diễn phân chia các điểm theo hàm số với các điểm không theo hàm số.

Ví Dụ:

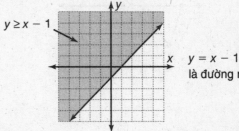

$y \geq x - 1$ $y = x - 1$ là đường ranh.

biểu đồ box-and-whisker (box-and-whisker plot) Một phương pháp biểu thị cho thấy cách thu thập các dữ kiện được trình bày ra sao. Ví dụ sau dựa trên cơ sở mười số điểm thí nghiệm sau đây: 52, 64, 75, 79, 80, 80, 81, 88, 92, 99.

Ví Dụ:

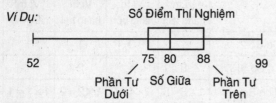

Số Điểm Thí Nghiệm

52   75   80   88   99

Phần Tư Dưới   Số Giữa   Phần Tư Trên

dung tích (capacity) Khối lượng của một hình thể, được biểu thị bằng số đo dưới dạng chất lỏng.

Ví Dụ:

500 ml   1 L   1 cup   1 cuarto   1 ga lông

tâm (center) Điểm ngay giữa của một vòng tròn hay một khối cầu.

Ví Dụ:

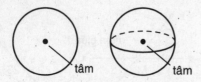

tâm   tâm

tâm của vòng quay (center of rotation) Điểm tại đó một hình quay chung quanh.

Ví Dụ:

điểm gốc của trục x, y là tâm của vòng quay.

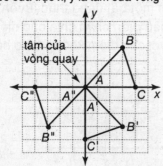

tâm của vòng quay

bách phân- (centi-) Tiếp đầu ngữ có nghĩa là $\frac{1}{100}$.

Ví Dụ: 1 xăng ti mét = $\frac{1}{100}$ mét

góc trung tâm (central angle) Góc mà đỉnh của nó là tâm của vòng tròn.

Ví Dụ:

Điểm C là tâm của vòng tròn.
∠BCA là một góc trung tâm.

vòng tròn (circle) Một hình phẳng mà các điểm trên vòng tròn luôn luôn cách đều với tâm của nó.

Ví Dụ:

biểu đồ hình tròn (circle graph) Một biểu đồ tròn dùng các cung của vòng tròn để biểu thị những phần của dữ kiện muốn trình bày. Biểu đồ này cũng còn được gọi là đồ thị bánh.

Ví Dụ:

Các Thú Cưng

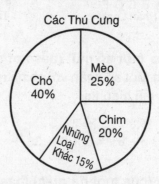

Chó 40%
Mèo 25%
Chim 20%
Những Loại Khác 15%

chu vi (circumference) Chiều dài chung quanh một vòng tròn.

Ví Dụ:

chu vi

hình ngoại tiếp (circumscribed figure) Một hình chứa một hình khác bên trong. Một đa giác ngoại tiếp chung quanh một vòng tròn nếu vòng tròn tiếp xúc với các cạnh của đa giác đó.

Ví Dụ:

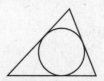

Hình tam giác ngoại tiếp một vòng tròn.

chiều kim đồng hồ (clockwise) Chiều của vòng quay khi đỉnh của hình xoay hướng về phía bên phải.

Ví Dụ:

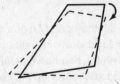

đồng hóa (clustering) Một phương pháp ước tính khi các con số gần bằng nhau được xem như bằng nhau.

Ví Dụ:

26 + 24 + 23 là vào khoảng 25 + 25 + 25, hoặc 3 × 25.

hệ số (coefficient) Một hằng số mà một biến số phải nhân với nó.

Ví Dụ:

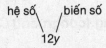

kết hợp (combination) Sự lựa chọn các vật thể mà trong đó thứ tự không quan trọng.

Ví Dụ:

Hai học sinh trong nhóm này sẽ được lựa chọn để thành lập một ủy ban: David, Juanita, Kim.

Những sự kết hợp có thể thực hiện được là: David, Juanita   David, Kim   Juanita, Kim

Chú Ý: Sự kết hợp "David, Juanita" cũng giống như sự kết hợp "Juanita, David."

mẫu số chung (commmon denominator) Một mẫu số giống nhau trong hai hay nhiều phân số.

Ví Dụ:

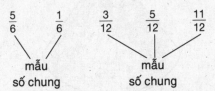

thừa số chung (common factor) Một số là thừa số của hai hay nhiều số khác.

Ví Dụ:

4 là thừa số chung của 8, 12, và 20.

$$8 = 4 \times 2$$
$$12 = 4 \times 3$$
$$20 = 4 \times 5$$

bội số chung (common multiple) Một số là bội số của hai số hay nhiều số khác.

Ví Dụ:

Những bội số của 3: 3 6 9 **12** 15 18 21 **24** 27...

Những bội số của 4: 4 8 **12** 16 20 **24** 28...

12 và 24 là hai trong số những bội số chung của 3 và 4.

Tính Chất Giao Hoán của Phép Cộng (Commutative Property of Addition) Sự thay đổi thứ tự không ảnh hưởng đến tổng số của hai hay nhiều số.

Ví Dụ:
$$a + b = b + a$$
$$18 + 23 = 23 + 18$$

Tính Chất Giao Hoán của Phép Nhân (Commutative Property of Multiplication) Sự thay đổi thứ tự không ảnh hưởng đến tích số của hai hay nhiều số.

Ví Dụ:
$$ab = ba$$
$$4 \times 7 = 7 \times 4$$

những số tương hợp (compatible numbers) Một cặp số được tính toán một cách dễ dàng.

Ví Dụ: 30 + 70   40 ÷ 4   25 + 75

bù trừ (compensation) Tính nhẩm bằng cách chọn những số gần với những số trong bài toán để cho dễ tính, và sau đó chỉnh lại đáp số để bù trừ cho những số đã chọn.

Ví Dụ:
$$99 \times 4 = (100 - 1) \times 4$$
$$= (100 \times 4) - (1 \times 4)$$
$$= 400 - 4$$
$$= 396$$

những góc bù (complementary angles) Hai góc có số đo cộng lại bằng 90 độ.

Ví Dụ:

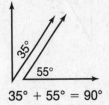

35° + 55° = 90°

số phức hợp (composite number) Một số nguyên lớn hơn 1 có hơn hai thừa số.

Ví Dụ:

những thừa số của 15 : 1, 3, 5, 15
    15 là một số hỗn hợp.

những thừa số của 7: 1, 7
    7 không phải là một số hỗn hợp.

sự kiện kép (compound event) Một sự kiện kết hợp hai hay nhiều sự kiện đơn độc khác.

Ví Dụ:

 và

Thấy một đồng tiền ra được hình đầu và gieo một hột tào cáo ra được số 1 là một sự kiện kép.

lãi kép (compound interest) Lãi tính trên tiền vốn và tiền lãi sinh ra trước đó.

Ví Dụ:

Nếu bạn gởi $100 vào trương mục tiết kiệm với phân lãi kép 6% một năm, bạn sẽ được
$100 + 0.06 × 100 = $106 trong năm đầu và
$106 + 0.06 × 106 = $112.36 trong năm thứ nhì.

lời nói kép (compound statement) Một lời lý luận được thành lập bởi sự kết hợp của hai hay nhiều lời nói khác.

Ví Dụ:

10 lớn hơn 5 *và* 10 nhỏ hơn 21.

10 lớn hơn 5 *hay* 10 nhỏ hơn 5.

đa giác lõm (concave polygon) Một đa giác có một hay nhiều đường chéo nằm bên ngoài đa giác đó.

Ví Dụ:

xác xuất có điều kiện (conditional probability) Một xác xuất mà sự kiện B sẽ xảy ra, khi sự kiện A đã thật sự xảy ra trước đó.

Ví Dụ:

Nếu bạn biết hai lần thấy đầu tiên của đồng tiền ra được hình đuôi, thì xác xuất của việc thấy ra hình đầu là số không. Tuy nhiên, nếu bạn biết lần thấy thứ nhất ra hình đầu, thì xác xuất của việc thấy ra hai hình đầu là $\frac{1}{2}$.

hình nón (cone) Một hình khối với một đáy tròn.

Ví Dụ:

đồng dạng (congruent) Có cùng kích cỡ và hình dạng.

Ví Dụ:

phóng hình theo dạng hình nón (conic projection) Một sự phóng hình bản đồ sử dụng hình nón để trình bày mặt cầu của trái đất.

Ví Dụ:

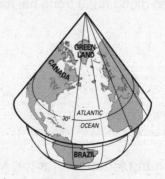

sự liên kết (conjunction) Một nhóm những lời nói được kết hợp bởi chữ *và*.

Ví Dụ:

$x > -2$ và $x < 5$

Một hình vuông có bốn cạnh dài bằng nhau *và* hình vuông là một hình chữ nhật.

6 Vietnamese

hằng số (constant) Một lượng không thay đổi.

Ví Dụ:

Trong biểu thức đại số $x + 7$, 7 là một hằng số.

đồ thị bất biến (constant graph) Một đồ thị mà chiều cao của đường biểu diễn không thay đổi.

Ví Dụ:

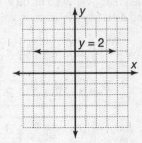

hằng số tỷ lệ (constant of proportionality) Lượng $\frac{y}{x}$ có hai biến số x và y mà tỷ lệ của chúng là một hằng số. Tỷ lệ này thường được biểu thị bằng k.

Ví Dụ:

x	3	6	9	12
y	5	10	15	20

$k = \frac{5}{3}$

hệ số chuyển đổi (conversion factor) Một số đo tương đương dùng để chuyển đổi những lượng từ một đơn vị này sang một đơn vị khác. Hệ số này thường được biểu thị như một phân số.

Ví Dụ:

12 inches = 1 bộ $\dfrac{12 \text{ inches}}{1 \text{ bộ}}$

4 quarts = 1 ga lông $\dfrac{4 \text{ quarts}}{1 \text{ ga lông}}$

đa giác lồi (convex polygon) Một đa giác mà tất cả những đường chéo đều nằm ở bên trong nó.

Ví Dụ:

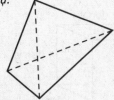

những tọa độ (coordinates) Một cặp số nằm theo thứ tự từng cặp một được dùng để định vị một điểm trên một mặt phẳng tọa độ.

Ví Dụ:

(5, 6)

tọa độ

mặt phẳng tọa độ, hệ thống tọa độ (coordinate plane, coordinate system) Một hệ thống gồm những hàng số ngang và dọc giao nhau dùng để định vị những điểm.

Ví Dụ:

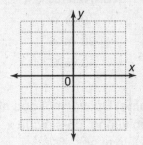

những góc đồng vị (trên những đường thẳng) (corresponding angles for lines) Những góc cùng một phía của một đường chéo cắt qua hai hay nhiều đường thẳng. Những góc đồng vị đồng dạng với nhau khi đường chéo cắt qua hai đường thẳng song song với nhau.

Ví Dụ:

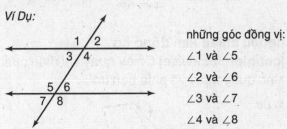

những góc đồng vị:

∠1 và ∠5

∠2 và ∠6

∠3 và ∠7

∠4 và ∠8

những góc đồng vị (trong những hình tương tự) (corresponding angles in similar figures) Những góc trùng với nhau trong những hình tương tự.

Ví Dụ:

△ABC ~ △XYZ

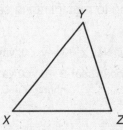

những góc đồng vị:

∠ABC và ∠XYZ

∠BCA và ∠YZX

∠CAB và ∠ZXY

những cạnh đồng vị (corresponding sides) Những cạnh trùng với nhau trong những hình tương tự.

Ví Dụ: △ABC ~ △XYZ

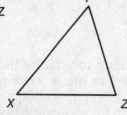

những cạnh đồng vị:
$\overline{AB}$ và $\overline{XY}$
$\overline{BC}$ và $\overline{YZ}$
$\overline{AC}$ và $\overline{XZ}$

cô-sin (cosine) Đối với một góc nhọn *x* trong một tam giác vuông, cô-sin của *x*, hay được viết là cos(*x*), là tỷ số $\frac{\text{cạnh kề}}{\text{cạnh huyền}}$.

Ví Dụ:

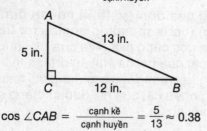

$$\cos \angle CAB = \frac{\text{cạnh kề}}{\text{cạnh huyền}} = \frac{5}{13} \approx 0.38$$

ngược chiều kim đồng hồ (counterclockwise) Chiều quay khi đỉnh của hình quay xoay về phía bên trái.

Ví Dụ:

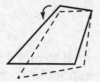

ví dụ phản bác (counterexample) Một ví dụ chứng tỏ một lời nói là sai lầm.

Ví Dụ:
lời nói: Nếu $x \cdot 0 = y \cdot 0$, vậy thì $x = y$.
ví dụ phản bác: $3 \cdot 0 = 0$ và $5 \cdot 0 = 0$, nhưng $3 \neq 5$.

Nguyên Tắc Đếm (Counting Principle) Nếu một tình huống có thể xảy ra trong *m* cách, và một tình huống thứ hai có thể xảy ra trong *n* cách, thì những điều này có thể xảy ra cùng với nhau trong $m \times n$ cách.

Ví Dụ:

Có 2 kết quả xảy ra trong việc thảy một đồng tiền một hào (hai mặt) và 6 kết quả xảy ra trong việc thảy một hột tào cáo (sáu mặt). Vì thế có tất cả 2×6, hay 12, cách khi những điều này xảy ra cùng với nhau.

tích số chéo (cross product) Tích số của tử số của một tỷ số với mẫu số của một tỷ số khác.

Ví Dụ:

$\frac{1}{3}$ ⤢ $\frac{2}{5}$ những tích số chéo:
$1 \times 5 = 5$
$3 \times 2 = 6$

hình lập phương (cube) Một hình khối 6 cạnh có các mặt đều đồng dạng với nhau.

Ví Dụ:

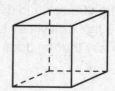

khối (cubed) Tăng lên tới lũy thừa ba.

Ví Dụ:
$2 \text{ khối} = 2^3 = 2 \times 2 \times 2 = 8$

đơn vị khối (cubic unit) Một đơn vị đo thể tích gồm có một hình lập phương với các cạnh dài một đơn vị tính.

Ví Dụ:

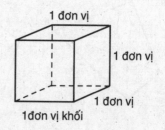

1 đơn vị
1 đơn vị
1 đơn vị
1 đơn vị khối

hệ thống đo lường thông dụng (customary system of measurement) Hệ thống đo lường thường được dùng tại Hoa Kỳ: inches, feet, miles, ounces, pound, tons, cup, quart, gallons, v.v..

Ví Dụ:

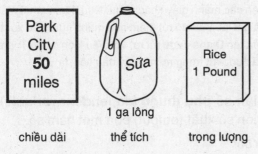

chiều dài   thể tích   trọng lượng

hình trụ (cylinder) Một hình khối với hai đáy tròn song song với nhau.

Ví Dụ:

phóng hình theo dạng hình trụ (cylindrical projection) Sự phóng ảnh bản đồ sử dụng hình dáng của hình trụ để trình bày mặt cầu của trái đất.

Ví Dụ:

hình thập giác (decagon) Một đa giác với 10 cạnh.

Ví Dụ:

đề xi- (deci-) Một tiếp đầu ngữ có nghĩa là $\frac{1}{10}$.

Ví Dụ: 1 đề xi mét = $\frac{1}{10}$ mét

số thập phân (decimal) Bất cứ những số dựa trên 10 đơn vị khi viết sử dụng một dấu chấm thập phân.

Ví Dụ: 6.21   0.59   12.2   5.0

phép cộng số thập phân (decimal addition) Cộng hai hay nhiều số thập phân lại với nhau.

Ví Dụ:

$$\begin{array}{r} 1 \\ 12.65 \\ + \ 29.10 \\ \hline 41.75 \end{array}$$

phép chia số thập phân (decimal division) Chia hai số thập phân.

Ví Dụ:

$$\begin{array}{r} 1.25 \\ 0.24\overline{)0.3000} \\ -24 \\ \hline 60 \\ -48 \\ \hline 120 \\ -120 \\ \hline 0 \end{array}$$

phép nhân số thập phân (decimal multiplication) Nhân hai hay nhiều số thập phân.

Ví Dụ:

$$\begin{array}{rl} 2 & \\ 0.13 & \text{2 vị trí thập phân} \\ \times \ 0.7 & \text{1 vị trí thập phân} \\ \hline 0.091 & \text{3 vị trí thập phân} \end{array}$$

phép trừ số thập phân (decimal subtraction) Trừ hai số thập phân.

Example

$$\begin{array}{r} {}^{13}\ {}^{12} \\ 4\ \cancel{3}\ \cancel{2}10 \\ 5\cancel{4}.\cancel{3}\cancel{0} \\ -\ 16.58 \\ \hline 37.72 \end{array}$$

hệ thống thập phân (decimal system) Một hệ thống dựa trên giá trị vị trí của 10 cơ số.

Ví Dụ:

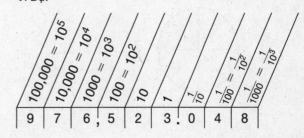

đồ thị giảm (decreasing graph) Một đồ thị trong đó chiều cao của đường biểu diễn giảm xuống từ trái qua phải.

Ví Dụ:

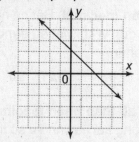

lý luận suy diễn (deductive reasoning) Sử dụng lý luận hợp lý để rút ra một kết luận.

Ví Dụ:

Khi một đường chéo được vẽ thêm vào một hình tứ giác, thì ta có hai hình tam giác. Bạn biết rằng tổng số đo của các góc trong hình tam giác là 180 độ. Do đó, tổng số đo của các góc trong hình tứ giác gấp đôi số đo các góc của hình tam giác, hay 2 x 180° = 360°.

độ (°) (degree(°)) Một đơn vị đo lường của góc.

Ví Dụ: 1° là $\frac{1}{360}$ của một vòng tròn kín.

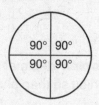

cấp (degree) Đối với một đa thức, nó là giá trị của số mũ lớn nhất của biến số.

Ví Dụ: Cấp của $5x^3 - 2x^2 + 7x$ là 3.

đề ka- (deka-) Một tiếp đầu ngữ có nghĩa là 10.

Ví Dụ: 1 đề ka mét = 10 mét

mẫu số (denominator) Số bên dưới của một phân số cho biết một tổng thể được chia làm mấy phần.

Ví Dụ:

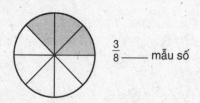

$\frac{3}{8}$ —— mẫu số

những sự kiện phụ thuộc (dependent events) Những sự kiện mà sự xuất hiện của nó ảnh hưởng đến xác xuất của những sự kiện khác.

Ví Dụ:

Các tên Therese, Diane, và José được viết riêng rẽ trên các mảnh giấy khác nhau. Người ta rút một mảnh và giữ lại. Sau đó rút thêm một mảnh nữa. Xác xuất của tên Diane được rút ra, với điều kiện là tên Therese đã được rút trong mảnh giấy đầu tiên, là $\frac{1}{2}$.

biến số phụ thuộc (dependent variable) Biến số xuất (output) của một hàm số.

Ví Dụ:

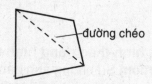

biến số phụ thuộc
$y = x + 2$

đường chéo (diagonal) Trong một đa giác, nó là một đoạn thẳng nối liền hai đỉnh không có chung một cạnh nào.

Ví Dụ:

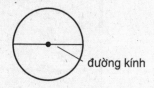

đường chéo

đường kính (diameter) Một đoạn thẳng, hoặc chiều dài của nó, chạy xuyên qua tâm của một vòng tròn và có cả hai điểm chấm dứt trên vòng tròn đó.

Ví Dụ:

đường kính

hiệu số (difference) Kết quả của việc trừ một số từ một số khác.

Ví Dụ: 28 − 15 = 13

hiệu số

con số (digit) Những ký hiệu được sử dụng để viết các số tự 0, 1, 2, 3, 4, 5, 6, 7, 8, và 9.

Ví Dụ:

Trong số 5,847, các con số là 5, 8, 4, và 7.

sự co giãn (dilation) Một sự co rút hay giãn nở theo tỷ lệ của một hình.

Ví Dụ:

Thừa số tỷ lệ giãn nở của một hình chữ nhật nhỏ lên một hình chữ nhật lớn là 3.

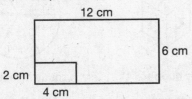

sự biến thiên trực tiếp (direct variation) Khi hai biến số liên quan với nhau bằng một tỷ số bất biến.

Ví Dụ:

thời gian tính bằng giờ (*x*)	1	2	3	4
khoảng cách tính bằng dặm (*y*)	55	110	165	220

$$\frac{y}{x} = 55$$

sự tách biệt (disjunction) Một số những câu lý luận hợp lý được nối với nhau bằng chữ hoặc.

Ví Dụ:

$x > 4$ hoặc $x < -1$

Chúng ta đã đi xem phim hoặc chúng ta đã xem TV.

Tính Chất Phân Phối (Distributive Property) Sự kiện $a(b + c) = ab + ac$.

Ví Dụ: $3(6 + 5) = 3 \cdot 6 + 3 \cdot 5$

số bị chia (dividend) Số bị đem chia trong một bài toán chia.

Ví Dụ:

số bị chia

$8 \div 4 = 2$

chia chẵn (divisible) Có thể được chia chẵn bởi một số khác mà không còn thừa lại số nào.

Ví Dụ: 18 chia chẵn cho 6, bởi vì $18 \div 6 = 3$.

phép chia (division) Một phép toán cho biết có bao nhiêu phần bằng nhau hoặc có bao nhiêu cái trong mỗi phần bằng nhau.

Ví Dụ:

$18 \div 6 = 3$ $18 \div 3 = 6$

18 được chia thành 6 nhóm mỗi nhóm gồm 3 cái.

18 được chia thành 3 nhóm mỗi nhóm gồm 6 cái.

ước số (divisor) Một số dùng để chia một con số khác (số chia).

Ví Dụ:

ước số (số chia)

$8 \div 4 = 2$

đa giác 12 cạnh (dodecagon) Một đa giác có 12 cạnh.

Ví Dụ:

đồ thị thanh đôi (double bar graph) Một sự kết hợp của hai đồ thị thanh, dùng để so sánh hai loại dữ kiện liên quan với nhau.

Ví Dụ:

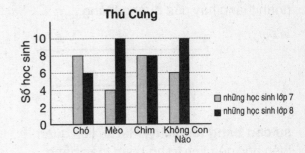

đồ thị biểu diễn đôi (double line graph)
Một sự kết hợp của hai đồ thị đường thẳng, dùng để so sánh hai loại dữ kiện có liên quan với nhau.

Ví Dụ:

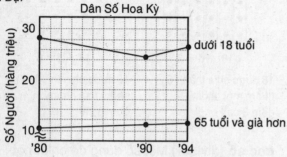

biểu đồ thân-và-lá đôi (double stem-and-leaf diagram) Một sự so sánh thân-và-lá của hai loại dữ kiện trong một biểu đồ đơn.

Ví Dụ:

Lá	Thân	Lá
7 2 1	3	0 1 3
5 0 0	4	2 3
9	5	5 6 8
5 2 0	6	1 4

cạnh (edge) Một đoạn thẳng nơi hai mặt của một đa giác gặp nhau.

Ví Dụ:

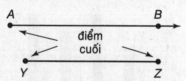

điểm cuối (endpoint) Một điểm tại cuối một đoạn thẳng hay nửa đường thẳng.

Ví Dụ:

sự cân bằng (equality) Một sự liên quan toán học của tình trạng hoàn toàn bằng nhau.

Ví Dụ: $16 + 8 = 24$ $25 \div 5 = 5$

những kết quả có khả năng bằng nhau (equally-likely outcomes) Những kết quả có cùng một xác xuất giống nhau.

Ví Dụ:

thấy được số "1"   quay ra màu đỏ

Xác xuất: $\frac{1}{6}$ Xác Xuất: $\frac{1}{6}$

tỷ số bằng nhau (equal ratios) Những tỷ số dùng để chỉ những lượng bằng nhau.

Ví Dụ: $\frac{2}{6}$, $\frac{1}{3}$, và $\frac{4}{12}$

phương trình (equation) Một biểu thức toán cho thấy hai vế bằng nhau.

Ví Dụ:

$14 = 2x$ $3 + y = 81$ $3 + 4 = 7$

tam giác đều (equilateral triangle) Một tam giác có tất cả các cạnh dài bằng nhau.

Ví Dụ:

những phương trình tương đương (equivalent equations) Những phương trình hoàn toàn bằng nhau khi thay thế những biến số giống y nhau.

Ví Dụ: $x - 5 = 10$ và $x = 15$

những biểu thức tương đương (equivalent expressions) Hai biểu thức luôn luôn có trị số giống nhau khi thay thế một lượng giống nhau.

Ví Dụ: $5(x + 1)$ và $5x + 5$

những phân số tương đương (equivalent fractions) Hai phân số đại diện một số bằng nhau.

Ví Dụ: $\frac{1}{2}$ và $\frac{8}{16}$

những tỷ lệ tương đương (equivalent rates) Những tỷ số nêu ra một lượng bằng nhau.

Ví Dụ: $\dfrac{40 \text{ dặm}}{2 \text{ giờ}}$ và $\dfrac{20 \text{ dặm}}{1 \text{ giờ}}$

những tỷ số tương đương (equivalent ratios) xem *những tỷ số bằng nhau*.

ước tính (estimate) Sự phỏng định kết quả của một sự tính toán.

Ví Dụ:
$$99 \times 21$$
Ước tính: $100 \times 20 = 2000$
$$99 \times 21 \approx 2000$$

công thức Euler (Euler's formula) Một công thức về số lượng của các mặt (F), các đỉnh (V), và các cạnh (E) của một đa giác cho biết rằng $F + V - E = 2$.

Ví Dụ:

Đối với một tháp hình tam giác ta thấy

$$\underset{\text{các mặt}}{5} + \underset{\text{các đỉnh}}{5} - \underset{\text{các cạnh}}{8} = 2$$

đánh giá (evaluate) Thay thế những biến số trong một biểu thức bằng các trị số và sau đó đơn giản hóa bằng cách tính theo thứ tự các phép toán.

Ví Dụ: Đánh giá $8(x - 3)$ cho biết $x = 10$.
$$8(x - 3) = 8(10 - 3)$$
$$= 8(7)$$
$$= 56$$

số chẵn (even number) Một số nguyên có những số 0, 2, 4, 6, hay 8 ở vị trí hàng đơn vị.

Ví Dụ: 16   28   34   112   3000

sự kiện (event) Một kết quả hay một nhóm những kết quả của một sự thử nghiệm hay của một tình huống.

Ví Dụ:

Sự kiện: Đạt được số 3 hay số lớn hơn khi gieo một hột tào cáo.

Những kết quả có thể xảy ra cho sự kiện này: 3, 4, 5, 6

dạng triển khai (expanded form) Cách viết một số có số mũ cho thấy tất cả những thừa số riêng rẽ.

Ví Dụ: số có số mũ 9^3
           dạng triển khai $9 \times 9 \times 9$

thử nghiệm (experiment) Trong xác xuất, bất cứ hoạt động nào liên quan đến cơ hội.

Ví Dụ:

thảy đồng tiền   gieo hột tào cáo   quay dĩa số

xác xuất thử nghiệm (experimental probability) Xác xuất dựa trên dữ kiện của những thử nghiệm hay những cuộc thăm dò.

Ví Dụ:

Ném một hột đậu vào trong chiếc nhẫn 100 lần. Có 23 lần ném trúng. Xác xuất thử nghiệm của việc ném trúng vào chiếc nhẫn là $\dfrac{23}{100} = 23\%$.

số mũ (exponent) Một số ở trên cao nằm bên phải một số khác cho thấy số lần nhân lập lại.

Ví Dụ:
số mũ
$$4^3 = 4 \times 4 \times 4 = 64$$

hàm số mũ (exponential function) Một hàm số phi tuyến (cong) trong đó một số mũ là biến số.

Ví Dụ: $y = 4^x$

ký hiệu số mũ (exponential notation) Một cách viết số lần nhân lập lại của một số bằng những số mũ.

Ví Dụ: 2^8 5^2 9^3

biểu thức (expression) một biểu thị toán học gồm những biến số và/hoặc những con số và những phép toán.

Ví Dụ: $5(8 + 4)$ $x - 3$ $2x + 4$

những góc ngoài (exterior angles) Khi một đường chéo cắt qua hai đường thẳng, những góc nằm bên ngoài hai đường thẳng đó được gọi là những góc ngoài.

Ví Dụ:

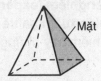

những góc ngoài:
∠1, ∠2, ∠7, ∠8

mặt (face) Bề mặt phẳng trên một hình khối.

Ví Dụ:

Mặt

thừa số (factor) Một số chia một số khác mà không để lại số dư.

Ví Dụ: Vì 30 ÷ 5 = 6, 5 là thừa số của 30.

giai thừa (factorial) Giai thừa của một số là tích số của tất cả những số nguyên từ 1 đến số đó. Ký hiệu của giai thừa là "!".

Ví Dụ:

6 giai thừa = 6! = 6 × 5 × 4 × 3 × 2 × 1 = 720

cây thừa số (factor tree) Một đồ hình cho thấy một số nguyên được phân tách ra thành những số nguyên tố của nó.

Ví Dụ:

72
2 36
2 18   72 = 2 × 2 × 2 × 3 × 3
2 9
3 3

trò chơi công bình (fair game) Một trò chơi trong đó tất cả những người tham dự đều có cùng một xác xuất để thắng cuộc.

Ví Dụ:

Trò chơi công bình: Hai người tham dự một trò chơi thay phiên nhau gieo một hột tào cáo. Người A được một điểm khi gieo ra được số 1, 3 hay 5. Người B được một điểm khi gieo ra được số 2, 4, hay 6. Xác xuất để được một điểm là $\frac{1}{2}$ cho cả hai người.

lật ngược lại (flip) Xem *phản chiếu*.

bộ (foot) Một đơn vị trong hệ thống đo lường thông thường có chiều dài bằng 12 inches.

Ví Dụ:

1 bộ

công thức (formula) Một quy tắc cho thấy những sự liên hệ giữa các lượng.

Ví Dụ: $A = bh$ $p = 4s$

mẫu thức tự giống (fractal) Một mẫu thức với sự tự giống như chính nó. Nếu một phần nhỏ của mẫu thức này được phóng rộng ra, vùng được phóng rộng đó trông tương tự như hình nguyên thủy.

Ví Dụ:

phân số (fraction) Một số trong dạng $^a/_b$ diễn tả một phần của tổng thể khi tổng thể bị cắt ra là nhiều phần bằng nhau.

Ví Dụ: $\frac{3}{5}$ $\frac{2}{7}$ $\frac{1}{4}$ $\frac{7}{10}$

phép cộng phân số (fraction addition) Cộng hai hay nhiều phân số lại với nhau.

Ví Dụ: $\frac{1}{3} + \frac{1}{4}$

$$\frac{1}{3} = \frac{1 \times 4}{3 \times 4} = \frac{4}{12}$$

$$\frac{1}{4} = \frac{1 \times 3}{4 \times 3} = \frac{3}{12}$$

$$\frac{1}{3} + \frac{1}{4} = \frac{4}{12} + \frac{3}{12} = \frac{4+3}{12} = \frac{7}{12}$$

phép chia phân số (fraction division) Chia hai phân số.

Ví Dụ: $\frac{1}{6} \div \frac{3}{4} = \frac{1}{6} \times \frac{4}{3}$

$$= \frac{1 \times 4}{6 \times 3}$$

$$= \frac{4}{18} \text{ hoặc } \frac{2}{9}$$

phép nhân phân số (fraction multiplication) Nhân hai hay nhiều phân số.

Ví Dụ:
$$1\frac{1}{2} \times \frac{1}{4} = \frac{3}{2} \times \frac{1}{4}$$
$$= \frac{3 \times 1}{2 \times 4}$$
$$= \frac{3}{8}$$

phép trừ phân số (fraction subtraction) Trừ hai phân số với nhau.

Ví Dụ: $\frac{3}{4} - \frac{2}{3}$

$$\frac{3}{4} = \frac{3 \times 3}{4 \times 3} = \frac{9}{12}$$
$$\frac{2}{3} = \frac{2 \times 4}{3 \times 4} = \frac{8}{12}$$
$$\frac{3}{4} - \frac{2}{3} = \frac{9}{12} - \frac{8}{12} = \frac{9-8}{12} = \frac{1}{12}$$

tần số (frequency) Số lần một sự việc xảy ra trong một cuộc thăm dò nghiên cứu. Xem *biểu đồ tần số*.

biểu đồ hay bảng tần số (frequency chart or table) Một bảng cho thấy những loại sự việc và tần số qua đó những sự việc này xảy ra.

Ví Dụ:

Màu Áo	Tần số
Đen	8
Nâu Lạt	2
Trắng	5
Xanh	4

ước tính số đầu (front-end estimation) Một phương pháp ước tính chỉ tính một hay hai số đầu của những số phải tính, sau đó điều chỉnh lại dựa trên những số còn lại của số phải tính đó.

Ví Dụ: Ước tính một số đầu

$$
\begin{array}{ll}
\;\;\;2,485 & \\
+\;3,698 & \\
\hline
\;\;\;5,000 & \text{Cộng một số đầu.} \\
+\;1,200 & 485 + 698 \text{ là vào khoảng} \\
\hline
\;\;\;6,200 & 1,200.
\end{array}
$$

hàm số (function) Sự tương quan giữa hai vế nhập-xuất (input-output) chỉ có một vế xuất cho mỗi vế nhập mà thôi.

Ví Dụ:
$$y = x + 4 \qquad y = 2x \qquad y = x^2$$

Định Lý Căn Bản của Số Học (Fundamental Theorem of Arithmetic) Tất cả những số nguyên lớn hơn 1 đều có thể được viết như một tích số độc nhất của những số nguyên tố.

Ví Dụ:
$$24 = 2 \times 2 \times 2 \times 3$$
$$35 = 5 \times 7$$

ga lông (gallon) Một đơn vị đo lường thông dụng bằng 4 quart.

Ví Dụ:

1 ga lông

hình học (geometry) Một ngành của toán học trong đó những sự liên hệ giữa các điểm, các đường thẳng, các hình, và các khối được triển khai.

xác xuất hình học (geometric probability) Một xác xuất dựa trên việc so sánh những số đo của các hình hình học.

Ví Dụ:

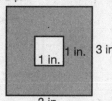

Diện tích của hình vuông lớn = $3 \cdot 3$ hay 9 in^2

Vùng xám = $9 \text{ in}^2 - 1 \text{ in}^2 = 8 \text{ in}^2$

Xác xuất của việc rơi vào vùng xám là $= \frac{8}{9}$

dãy số hình học (geometric sequence) Một dãy số mà tỷ lệ giữa những số hạng liên tiếp nhau luôn luôn bất biến.

Ví Dụ:

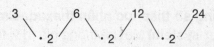

gam (gram) Đơn vị đo lường khối lượng căn bản trong hệ mét.

Ví Dụ:

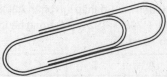

Khối lượng của một cái kẹp giấy lớn là vào khoảng 1 gam.

biểu đồ (graph) Một đồ hình cho thấy những thông tin được trình bày một cách có tổ chức.

Ví Dụ:

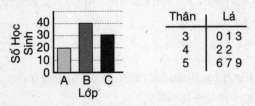

thừa số chung lớn nhất (greatest common factor) (GCF) Số nguyên lớn nhất chia cho hai hay nhiều số nguyên khác mà không để lại số dư nào.

Ví Dụ: 6 là GCF của 12, 18, và 24.

héc tô- (hecto-) Tiếp đầu ngữ có nghĩa là 100.

Ví Dụ: 1 héc tô mét = 100 mét

chiều cao (height) Trong một tam giác, tứ giác, hoặc hình tháp, nó là khoảng cách thẳng đứng từ đáy đến đỉnh đối diện hay cạnh đối diện. Trong một hình khối hay hình lăng trụ, nó là khoảng cách giữa hai đáy.

Ví Dụ:

hình thất giác (heptagon) Một đa giác có 7 cạnh.

Ví Dụ:

hệ thống số thập lục phân (hexadecimal number system) Một hệ thống giá trị vị trí dựa trên 16 cơ số.

Ví Dụ:

Những mẫu tự từ A đến F được dùng để đại diện cho những số từ 10 đến 15. Số thập lục phân A3CE là số 41,934 (40,960 + 768 + 192 + 14) trong hệ thống thập phân (dựa trên 10 cơ số).

Cơ Số 16	A	3	C	E
Giá Trị Vị Trí	4096	256	16	1
Tích Số	10 × 4096 = 40,960	3 × 256 = 768	12 × 16 = 192	14 × 1 = 14

hình lục giác (hexagon) Một đa giác có 6 cạnh.

Ví Dụ:

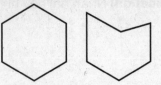

biểu đồ ngang (histogram) Một loại biểu đồ thanh nơi những dữ kiện cùng loại nằm trong những khoản số bằng nhau.

Ví Dụ:

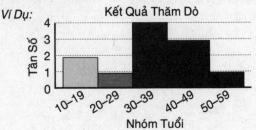

trục hoành (horizontal axis) Đường nằm ngang của hai đường thẳng giao nhau, lập thành một đồ thị hay một mặt phẳng tọa độ.

Ví Dụ:

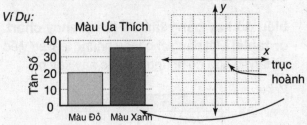

cạnh huyền (hypotenuse) Cạnh đối diện với góc vuông.

Ví Dụ:

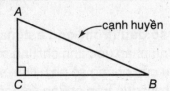

đồng nhất thức (identity) Đối với bất cứ phép tính nào, nó là con số giữ cho một con số khác bất biến. 0 là một đồng nhất thức cộng, bởi vì $a + 0 = a$, 1 là một đồng nhất thức nhân bởi vì $a \times 1 = a$.

Ví Dụ: $6 + 0 = 6$
              $5 \times 1 = 5$

lời nói nếu-thì (if-then statement) Một lời nói hợp với lý luận dùng chữ nếu và thì để cho thấy sự tương quan giữa hai điều kiện.

Ví Dụ:

Nếu là một tam giác lệch, *thì* sẽ không có cạnh nào đồng dạng cả.

phân số không hợp cách (improper fraction) Một phân số mà tử số lớn hơn hay bằng với mẫu số.

Ví Dụ: $\dfrac{5}{2}$ $\dfrac{8}{8}$ $\dfrac{14}{3}$

đồ thị tăng (increasing graph) Một đồ thị trong đó chiều cao của đường biểu diễn tăng cao từ trái qua phải.

Ví Dụ:

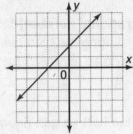

in (inch) Một đơn vị đo chiều dài trong hệ thống đo lường thông dụng.

Ví Dụ: Cái kẹp giấy đo được $1\frac{3}{8}$ in, hay $1\frac{3}{8}''$.

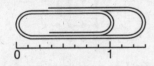

những sự kiện độc lập (independent events) Những sự kiện mà kết quả của một cái không ảnh hưởng đến xác xuất của những cái khác.

Ví Dụ:
Những tên Therese, Diane, và José được viết riêng rẽ trên các mảnh giấy rời. Người ta rút một mảnh giấy đó ra và bỏ trở vào lại. Sau đó người ta rút thêm một mảnh giấy nữa. Xác xuất mà tên Diane sẽ rút được, với điều kiện là tên Therese đã rút ra được trong lần rút đầu tiên, là $\frac{1}{3}$.

biến số độc lập (independent variable) Biến số đưa vào trong một hàm số.

Ví Dụ:
$$\text{biến số độc lập}$$
$$y = x + 2$$

lý luận quy nạp (inductive reasoning) Dùng một mẫu thức để rút ra một kết luận.

Ví Dụ:
Người ta vẽ nhiều tứ giác và đo các góc của chúng. Trong tất cả các lần tổng số các góc là 360 độ. Người ta rút ra được kết luận rằng tổng số các góc của một đa giác là 360 độ.

sự bất bình đẳng (inequality) Một biểu thị toán học gồm có các ký hiệu $<$, $>$, $\le$, hoặc $\ge$.

Ví Dụ:
$$6 < 9 \qquad x + 3 \ge 21 \qquad 2x - 8 > 0$$

hình nội tiếp (inscribed figure) Một hình nằm ở bên trong một hình khác. Một đa giác nội tiếp trong một hình tròn nếu tất cả các đỉnh của nó nằm trên vòng tròn đó.

Ví Dụ:

Một tam giác nội tiếp trong một hình tròn.

những số nguyên (integers) Một nhóm những số dương nguyên vẹn, những số đối nghịch của chúng, và số 0.

Ví Dụ: ..., -3, -2, -1, 0, 1, 2, 3, ...

$$\xleftarrow{\qquad}\underset{-4}{\bullet}\;\underset{-3}{\bullet}\;\underset{-2}{\bullet}\;\underset{-1}{\bullet}\;\underset{0}{\bullet}\;\underset{1}{\bullet}\;\underset{2}{\bullet}\;\underset{3}{\bullet}\;\underset{4}{\bullet}\xrightarrow{\qquad}$$

cộng số nguyên (integer addition) Cộng hai hay nhiều số nguyên lại với nhau.

Ví Dụ:
$$-5 + 8 = 3 \qquad\qquad -5 + (-8) = -13$$
$$5 + (-3) = 2 \qquad\qquad 5 + 8 = 13$$

chia số nguyên (integer division) Chia hai số nguyên.

Ví Dụ:
$$-40 \div 8 = -5 \qquad\qquad 40 \div (-8) = -5$$
$$-40 \div (-8) = 5 \qquad\qquad 40 \div 8 = 5$$

nhân số nguyên (integer multiplication) Nhân hai hay nhiều số nguyên với nhau.

Ví Dụ:
$$-5 \cdot 8 = -40 \qquad\qquad -5 \cdot (-8) = 40$$
$$5 \cdot (-8) = -40 \qquad\qquad 5 \cdot 8 = 40$$

trừ số nguyên (integer subtraction) Trừ hai số nguyên.

Ví Dụ:
$$-5 - 8 = -13 \qquad\qquad -5 - (-8) = 3$$
$$5 - (-3) = 8 \qquad\qquad 5 - 8 = -3$$

lãi (interest) Tiền trả cho việc sử dụng tiền.

Ví Dụ:

Dave gởi $300 vào trương mục tiết kiệm. Sau 1 năm kết số trương mục của anh là $315. Anh đã kiếm được $15 tiền lãi trong trương mục tiết kiệm của mình.

những góc trong (interior angles) Những góc được thành lập bởi một đường cắt chéo và hai đường thẳng bị cắt qua, nằm giữa hai đường thẳng đó.

Ví Dụ:

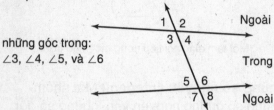

những góc trong:
$\angle 3$, $\angle 4$, $\angle 5$, và $\angle 6$

giao nhau (intersect) Cắt xuyên qua cùng một điểm.

Ví Dụ:

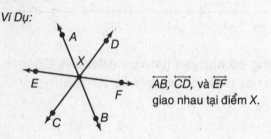

$\overleftrightarrow{AB}$, $\overleftrightarrow{CD}$, và $\overleftrightarrow{EF}$ giao nhau tại điểm *X*.

khoảng cách (interval) Một trong những phần chia đều trên một đồ thị thanh hay trên một biểu đồ ngang.

Ví Dụ:

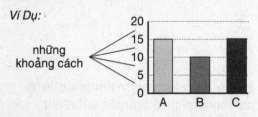

những khoảng cách

những phép toán nghịch đảo (inverse operations) Những phép toán "tự giải" lẫn nhau.

Ví Dụ:

phép cộng và phép trừ $2 + \mathbf{3} = 5$ $5 - \mathbf{3} = 2$

phép nhân và phép chia $2 \cdot \mathbf{3} = 6$ $6 \div \mathbf{3} = 2$

sự biến thiên nghịch đảo (inverse variation) Khi hai biến số có liên quan với nhau bởi một tích số bất biến.

Ví Dụ:

x	1	2	3	4	5	6
y	60	30	20	15	12	10

$$x \cdot y = 60$$

số vô tỷ (irrational number) Một số, chẳng hạn như $\sqrt{2}$, không thể biểu diễn bằng một số thập phân có số lẻ hay số thập phân chẵn.

Ví Dụ: $\sqrt{5}$ π $-\sqrt{\dfrac{1}{2}}$

vẽ không theo luật xa gần (isometric drawing) Một phương pháp được dùng để vẽ phối cảnh trên mặt phẳng một hình có ba chiều.

Ví Dụ:

tam giác cân (isosceles triangle) Một tam giác có ít nhất hai cạnh đồng dạng.

Ví Dụ:

18   18

14

kí lô- (kilo-) Một tiếp đầu ngữ có nghĩa là 1000.

Ví Dụ: 1 kí lô mét = 1000 mét

vĩ tuyến (latitude) Một sự đo đạt bằng độ về hướng bắc và hướng nam tính từ đường xích đạo.

Ví Dụ:

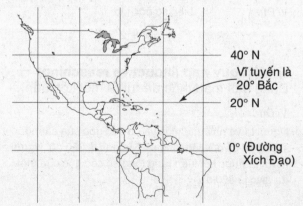

40° N

Vĩ tuyến là 20° Bắc

20° N

0° (Đường Xích Đạo)

mẫu số chung nhỏ nhất (least common denominator (LCD)) Bội số chung nhỏ nhất (LCM) của hai hay nhiều mẫu số.

Ví Dụ: $\frac{1}{2}$ $\frac{2}{3}$ $\frac{3}{4}$

LCM của 2, 3, và 4 là 12, vì thế LCD của các phân số là 12.

Các phân số được viết với LCD là $\frac{6}{12}, \frac{8}{12}$ và $\frac{9}{12}$.

bội số chung nhỏ nhất (least common multiple (LCM)) Một số nhỏ nhất là bội số chung cho các số.

Ví Dụ:
Những bội số của 3: 3 6 9 **12** 15 18 21 **24** ...
Những bội số của 4: 4 8 **12** 16 20 **24** 28 32 ...
12 là LCM của 3 và 4.

cạnh (leg) Một cạnh, không phải là cạnh huyền, của một tam giác vuông.

Ví Dụ:

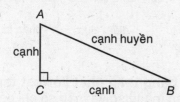

những mẫu số giống nhau (like denominators) Những mẫu số giống như nhau trong hai hay nhiều phân số.

Ví Dụ: $\frac{1}{8}$ $\frac{3}{8}$ $\frac{6}{8}$

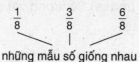

những mẫu số giống nhau

những số hạng giống nhau (like terms) Những số hạng trong đó những biến số giống nhau có số mũ bằng nhau.

Ví Dụ: $3x^2$ và $9x^2$ $10y$ và $2y$

đường thẳng (line) Một hình một chiều kéo dài vô tận trong cả hai hướng. Hai điểm đặt tên một đường thẳng.

Ví Dụ:

$\overleftrightarrow{AB}$ hay $\overleftrightarrow{BA}$

đồ thị đường thẳng (line graph) Một đồ thị trong đó một đường thẳng biểu diễn những sự thay đổi trong dữ kiện, thường là qua thời gian.

Ví Dụ:

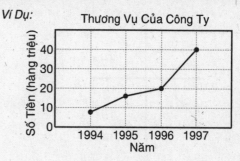

đường cắt đối xứng (line of symmetry) Đường thẳng chia một hình có đường đối xứng ra làm hai nửa giống nhau.

Ví Dụ:

1 đường cắt đối xứng   4 đường cắt đối xứng

biểu đồ đường thẳng (line plot) Một biểu đồ cho thấy hình dạng của một dữ kiện được thiết lập bởi việc chồng những chữ x lên mỗi trị số trên một hàng số.

Ví Dụ:

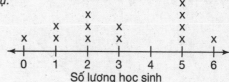

Số lượng học sinh

đoạn thẳng (line segment) Một phần của một đường thẳng, với hai điểm cuối. Hai điểm đặt tên một đoạn thẳng.

Ví Dụ:

$\overline{AB}$ hay $\overline{BA}$

đường đối xứng (line symmetry) Một hình có đường đối xứng nếu nó có thể chia được ra làm hai nửa giống nhau.

Ví Dụ:

Hình với đường   Hình không có
đối xứng   đường đối xứng

phương trình tuyến (linear equation) Một phương trình có đường biểu diễn là một đường thẳng.

Ví Dụ:

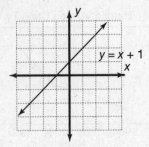

hàm số tuyến (linear function) Một hàm số có đường biểu diễn là một đường thẳng.

Ví Dụ:

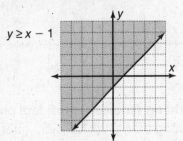

Lượng Nhập	Lượng Xuất
x	y
-2	3
-1	2
0	1
1	0
2	-1
3	-2

$y = 1 - x$

bất đẳng thức tuyến (linear inequality) Một biểu thị toán học gồm có những ký hiệu $<$, $>$, $\leq$ hay $\geq$ có đường biểu diễn là một vùng với một đường ranh giới thẳng.

Ví Dụ:

$y \geq x - 1$

lít (liter) Đơn vị căn bản của thể tích trong hệ thống mét.

Ví Dụ:

chai 2 lít

kinh tuyến (longitude) Một sự đo lường bằng độ về hướng đông và hướng tây tính từ kinh tuyến gốc.

Ví Dụ:

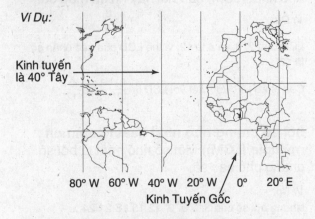

Kinh tuyến là 40° Tây

80° W   60° W   40° W   20° W   0°   20° E

Kinh Tuyến Gốc

phần tư thấp (lower quartile) Điểm giữa của một phân nửa phần thấp của một nhóm dữ kiện.

Ví Dụ:

27 27 27 29 32 33 36 38 42 43 62

phần tư thấp   điểm giữa   phần tư cao

những số hạng thấp nhất (lowest terms) Một phân số mà tử số và mẫu số chỉ có một thừa số chung là 1 là phân số thuộc những số hạng thấp nhất.

Ví Dụ: $\dfrac{1}{2}$ $\dfrac{3}{5}$ $\dfrac{21}{23}$

khối lượng (mass) Số lượng vật chất mà một vật chứa đựng.

Ví Dụ:

Một hột nho khô có khối lượng 1 gam.

Một đôi giày thể thao có khối lượng 1 kí lô gam.

số bình vị (mean) Tổng số những trị số của một nhóm dữ kiện được chia cho số lượng của những trị số đó. Cũng được gọi là số trung bình.

Ví Dụ:

27 27 27 29 32 33 36 38 42 43 62

tổng số: 396

số lượng những trị số: 11

số bình vị: $396 \div 11 = 36$

sai số đo lường (measurement error)
Phần không chắc chắn trong sự đo lường. Sai số lớn nhất có thể xảy ra trong sự đo lường là phân nửa đơn vị đo lường nhỏ nhất được sử dụng.

Ví Dụ:

Vì in (inch) là đơn vị nhỏ nhất, sai số lớn nhất có thể xảy ra là $\frac{1}{2}$ in Vì thế chiều cao thật sự là khoảng giữa $5'5\frac{1}{2}"$ và $5'6\frac{1}{2}"$.

5' 6"

đo lường theo xu hướng trung tâm (measure of central tendency)
Một trị số đơn độc tóm tắt một nhóm những dữ kiện số.

Ví Dụ:

Số bình vị, số giữa, và số thường xảy ra là những số đo thông thường theo xu hướng trung tâm.

27 27 27 29 32 33 36 38 42 43 62

số thường xảy ra   số giữa

Số bình vị = 396 ÷ 11 = 36

số giữa (median)
Trị số giữa của một nhóm dữ kiện khi những trị số của những dữ kiện đó được sắp xếp theo thứ tự của số hạng.

Ví Dụ:

27 27 27 29 32 33 36 38 42 43 62

số giữa

tính nhẩm (mental math)
Thực hiện các phép tính trong đầu của bạn, mà không sử dụng đến giấy bút hay máy tính.

Ví Dụ:

2000 × 30

3 số không + 1 số không = 4 số không

Hãy suy nghĩ: 2 × 3 = 6, cộng thêm 4 số không

2000 × 30 = 60,000

mét (meter)
Đơn vị đo lường căn bản của chiều dài trong hệ thống mét.

Ví Dụ:

1 mét

Cây gậy đánh bóng chày dài khoảng 1 mét.

hệ thống mét (metric system)
Một hệ thống đo lường đặt cơ sở trên mét, gam, và lít.

Ví Dụ:

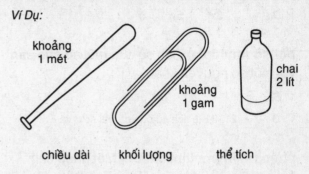

khoảng 1 mét   khoảng 1 gam   chai 2 lít

chiều dài   khối lượng   thể tích

điểm giữa (midpoint)
Điểm chia một đoạn thẳng ra làm hai phân đoạn đồng dạng với nhau.

Ví Dụ: C là điểm giữa của $\overline{AB}$.

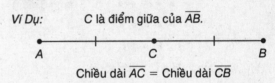

A   C   B

Chiều dài $\overline{AC}$ = Chiều dài $\overline{CB}$

dặm (mile)
Một đơn vị trong hệ thống đo lường thông thường bằng 5280 bộ Anh.

Ví Dụ:

Một dặm là khoảng cách bạn có thể đi bộ trong 15 đến 20 phút hay chạy trong khoảng 10 phút.

mi li- (milli-)
Một tiếp đầu ngữ có nghĩa là $\frac{1}{1000}$.

Ví Dụ: 1 mi li mét = $\frac{1}{1000}$ mét

số hỗn hợp (mixed number)
Một số được tạo thành bởi một số nguyên và một phân số.

Ví Dụ: $3\frac{1}{2}$ $1\frac{3}{4}$ $13\frac{3}{8}$

số thường xảy ra (mode)
Một (hay những) trị số thường xảy ra nhất trong một nhóm dữ kiện.

Ví Dụ:

27 27 27 29 32 33 36 38 42 43 62

Trong một nhóm dữ kiện nêu trên, 27 là số thường xảy ra.

đơn thức (monomial) Một biểu thức đại số chỉ có một số hạng.

Ví Dụ: $2x^2$ $5y$ x^3 -3

bội số (multiple) Tích số của một số cho sẵn với một số nguyên khác.

Ví Dụ:

Vì $3 \times 7 = 21$, 21 là tích số của cả hai số 3 và 7.

phép nhân (multiplication) Một phép tính kết hợp hai số, được gọi là những thừa số, để cho ra một số khác, được gọi là tích số.

Ví Dụ:

• • • • • •
• • • • • •   3 hàng 6 điểm
• • • • • •

$$3 \times 6 = 18$$

những thừa số   tích số

tính chất của phép nhân (multiplication property) Nếu A và B là những sự kiện độc lập, thì xác xuất xảy ra của cả hai sự kiện này được tính như sau $P(A$ và $B) = P(A) \times P(B)$.

Ví Dụ:

Lần quay thứ nhất: $P(\text{đỏ}) = \frac{1}{4}$

Lần quay thứ nhì: $P(\text{đỏ}) = \frac{1}{4}$

Lần quay thứ nhất và lần quay thứ nhì:
$P(\text{đỏ và đỏ}) = \frac{1}{4} \times \frac{1}{4} = \frac{1}{16}$

Tính Chất Bình Đẳng của Phép Nhân (Multiplication Property of Equality) Nếu $a = b$, thì $ac = bc$.

Ví Dụ:

Trong hàng thứ nhì của ví dụ dưới đây, người ta nhân 2 cho cả hai vế của phương trình.

Nếu $\frac{1}{2}y = 4$

thì $2 \times \frac{1}{2}y = 2 \times 4$

số nhân đảo ngược (multiplicative inverse) Nếu tích số của hai số là 1, thì mỗi một số là số nhân đảo ngược của số kia.

Ví Dụ:

$\frac{1}{6}$ và 6 là những số nhân đảo ngược vì $\frac{1}{6} \times 6 = 1$.

độc quyền hổ tương (mutually exclusive) Nếu sự kiện A hay B xảy ra, thì sự kiện khác không thể xảy ra.

Ví Dụ:

Nếu nhiệt độ ngoài trời là 90°, thì tuyết không thể rơi được.

Nếu một đa giác chỉ có ba cạnh, thì nó không thể có bốn góc được.

những số âm (negative numbers) Những số nhỏ hơn số không.

Ví Dụ:

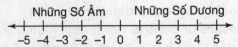

Những Số Âm   Những Số Dương

−5 −4 −3 −2 −1 0 1 2 3 4 5

sự liên hệ nghịch chiều (negative relationship) Hai nhóm dữ kiện có một sự liên hệ nghịch chiều khi những trị số dữ kiện trong một nhóm gia tăng thì trị số dữ kiện của nhóm kia tụt xuống.

Ví Dụ:

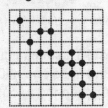

độ dốc âm (negative slope) Độ dốc của một đường thẳng nghiêng xuống phía dưới.

Ví Dụ:

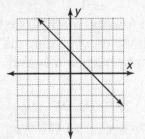

căn bậc hai âm (negative square root) Số ngược lại của căn bậc hai chính của một số.

Ví Dụ:

căn bậc hai chính: căn bậc hai âm:

$\sqrt{25} = 5$ $-\sqrt{25} = -5$

mạng (net) Một mẫu hình phẳng có thể gấp lại thành một hình ba chiều chẳng hạn như một hình khối.

Ví Dụ:

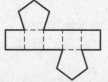

Mạng của một hình khối ngũ giác   Hình khối ngũ giác

hình cửu giác (nonagon) Một hình đa giác có chín cạnh.

Ví Dụ:

phương trình cong (phi tuyến) (nonlinear equation) Một phương trình có đường biểu diễn là một đường cong mà không phải là một đường thẳng.

Ví Dụ:

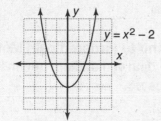

$$y = x^2 - 2$$

hàm số cong (phi tuyến) (nonlinear function) Một hàm số có đường biểu diễn không phải là một đường thẳng bởi vì những sự thay đổi bằng nhau trong trị số x không dẫn đến sự thay đổi bằng nhau trong trị số y.

Ví Dụ:

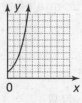 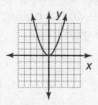

$y = 2^x$ $y = x^2$ $y = 0.5^x$

không có sự liên hệ (no relationship) Hai nhóm dữ kiện không có sự liên hệ với nhau khi không có sự liên hệ thuận chiều hay sự liên hệ nghịch chiều giữa hai nhóm.

Ví Dụ:

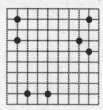

hàng số (number line) Một hàng cho thấy các số hạng theo thứ tự.

Ví Dụ:

hình thức số-chữ (number-word form) Cách viết một số bằng con số và chữ viết.

Ví Dụ: 45 ngàn tỷ   9 ngàn

chữ số (numeral) Một ký hiệu cho một con số.

Ví Dụ: 7   58   234

tử số (numerator) con số trên của một phân số cho thấy bao nhiêu phần của một tổng thể được chỉ định.

Ví Dụ:

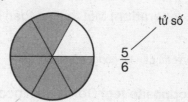

góc tù (obtuse angle) Một góc đo được lớn hơn 90° và nhỏ hơn 180°.

Ví Dụ:

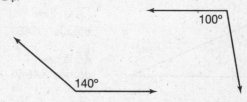

tam giác tù (obtuse triangle) Một tam giác có một góc tù.

Ví Dụ:

hình bác giác (octagon) Một hình đa giác có 8 cạnh.

Ví Dụ:

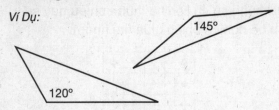

số lẻ (odd number) Một số nguyên có số 1, 3, 5, 7, hay 9 ở hàng đơn vị.

Ví Dụ:

43   225   999   8,007

tỷ số (odds) Tỷ lệ của số lần có thể xảy ra của một sự kiện đối với số lần mà nó không thể xảy ra.

Ví Dụ:

Tỷ số của việc thảy ra số 3 là: 1 trên 5.

Tỷ số của việc thảy không ra số 3 là: 5 trên 1.

phép toán (operation) Một thủ tục toán học.

Ví Dụ:

Bốn phép toán căn bản là: cộng, trừ, nhân, chia.

cạnh đối (opposite leg) Đối với một góc nhọn trong một tam giác vuông, cạnh đối là cạnh nằm ngang qua trước mặt góc đó.

Ví Dụ:

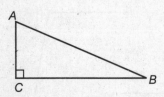

$\overline{CB}$ là cạnh đối của $\angle CAB$.

$\overline{AC}$ là cạnh đối của $\angle ABC$.

những số đối nghịch (opposite numbers) Những số có cùng khoảng cách trên một hàng số tính từ số không nhưng nằm ở phía đối nghịch.

Ví Dụ:

7 và -7 là những số đối nghịch nhau.

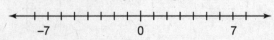

thứ tự của các phép toán (order of operations) Những quy tắc cho biết về thứ tự để tính các phép toán: (1) đơn giản hóa bên trong ngoặc đơn, (2) tính các số mũ, (3) nhân và chia từ trái qua phải, và (4) cộng và trừ từ trái qua phải.

Ví Dụ:

Tính trị số $2x^2 + 4(x - 2)$ cho $x = 3$.

(1) đơn giản hóa bên trong ngoặc đơn	$2 \cdot 3^2 + 4(3 - 2)$
	$2 \cdot 3^2 + 4(1)$
(2) tính các số mũ	$2 \cdot 9 + 4$
(3) nhân và chia từ trái qua phải	$18 + 4$
(4) cộng và trừ từ trái qua phải	22

cặp số thứ tự (ordered pair) Một cặp số dùng để định vị một điểm trên một mặt phẳng tọa độ.

Ví Dụ:

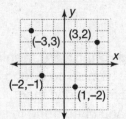

gốc (origin) Điểm số không trên một hàng số, hoặc điểm (0, 0) nơi những trục của một hệ thống tọa độ giao nhau.

Ví Dụ:

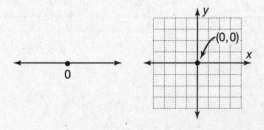

phép vẽ trực giao (orthographic drawing)
Phép vẽ một vật bằng cách nhìn từ phía trước, bên hông, và từ bên trên nhìn xuống một vật.

Ví Dụ:

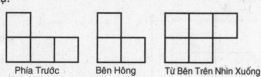

Phía Trước   Bên Hông   Từ Bên Trên Nhìn Xuống

lạng (ounce) Một đơn vị đo trọng lượng trong hệ thống đo lường thông thường.

Ví Dụ:

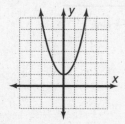 Một lá thư cân nặng vào khoảng một lạng.

kết quả (outcome) Cách mà một thử nghiệm hay một tình huống có thể xảy ra.

Ví Dụ:

Những Kết Quả của việc Thảy 2 Đồng Tiền:

đồng tiền 1	đồng tiền 2
hình đầu	hình đuôi
hình đầu	hình đầu
hình đuôi	hình đầu
hình đuôi	hình đuôi

Có 4 kết quả. Một kết quả là hình đầu, hình đầu.

số ngoại hạng (outlier) Một trị số cực đại trong một nhóm dữ kiện, khác xa hầu hết những trị số khác.

Ví Dụ:

27   27   27   29   32   33   36   38   42   43   62
                                                  ↑
                                          số ngoại hạng

ba ra bol (parabola) Một hình cong chữ U hay chữ U lộn ngược là đường biểu diễn của một hàm số bậc hai.

Ví Dụ:

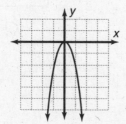

song song (parallel) Hai đường thẳng, đoạn thẳng hay nửa đường thẳng không bao giờ giao nhau, cho dù kéo dài đến vô tận.

Ví Dụ:

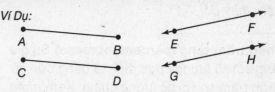

hình bình hành (parallelogram) Một hình bốn cạnh có các cạnh đối diện song song và đồng dạng với nhau.

Ví Dụ:

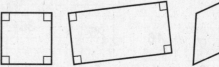

hình ngũ giác (pentagon) Một hình đa giác có năm cạnh.

Ví Dụ:

phần trăm (percent) Một tỷ lệ sánh với số 100.

Ví Dụ:

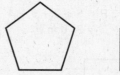 $\frac{58}{100} = 0.58 = 58\%$

số phần trăm thay đổi (percent change)
Số lượng của một sự thay đổi, tăng hay giảm, được chia bởi số lượng nguyên thủy, được diễn tả như là số phần trăm thay đổi so với số lượng nguyên thủy.

Ví Dụ:

Hãy tìm số phần trăm thay đổi nếu đầu tư $1500 và tiền lời kiếm được là $75.

$\frac{75}{1500} = 0.05 = 5\%$ $75 là một sự gia tăng 5%.

Hãy tìm số phần trăm thay đổi nếu một vật có giá $50 đang bán giảm bớt $10.

$\frac{10}{50} = 0.20 = 20\%$ $10 bớt là một sự sụt giảm 20%.

phần trăm giảm (percent decrease) Sự sụt giảm với số lượng được diễn tả bằng con số phần trăm so với số lượng chính. Xem *phần trăm thay đổi*.

phần trăm tăng (percent increase) Sự gia tăng với số lượng được diễn tả bằng con số phần trăm so với dố lượng chính. Xem *phần trăm thay đổi*.

số bình phương hoàn chỉnh (perfect square) Bình phương của một số nguyên.

Ví Dụ:

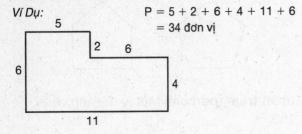

chu vi (perimeter) Khoảng cách chung quanh bên ngoài của một hình.

Ví Dụ:

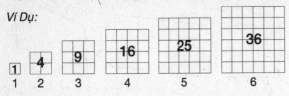

$$P = 5 + 2 + 6 + 4 + 11 + 6$$
$$= 34 \text{ đơn vị}$$

phép hoán vị (permutation) Một sự sắp xếp những sự vật trong đó thứ tự rất quan trọng.

Ví Dụ:

Một học sinh trong nhóm này sẽ được bầu làm chủ tịch và một học sinh sẽ được bầu làm phó chủ tịch: Wendy, Alex, Carlos. Những sự hoán vị có thể xảy ra là:

Wendy—chủ tịch, Alex—phó chủ tịch
Wendy—chủ tịch, Carlos—phó chủ tịch
Alex—chủ tịch, Wendy—phó chủ tịch
Alex—chủ tịch, Carlos—phó chủ tịch
Carlos—chủ tịch, Wendy—phó chủ tịch
Carlos—chủ tịch, Alex—phó chủ tịch

Ghi chú: Mỗi một hàng trên là một sự hoán vị khác nhau.

đường trực giao (perpendicular) Những đường thẳng, nửa đường thẳng, hay những đoạn thẳng giao nhau tại những góc vuông.

Ví Dụ:

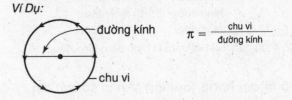

đường trung trực (perpendicular bisector) Một đường thẳng, nửa đường thẳng, hay một đoạn thẳng cắt một đoạn thẳng khác tại điểm giữa và thẳng góc với đoạn thẳng đó.

Ví Dụ:

$\overleftrightarrow{DE}$ là đường trung trực của $\overline{AB}$.

pi (π) (pi (π)) Tỷ lệ của chu vi một vòng tròn với đường kính của nó: 3.14159265...

Ví Dụ:

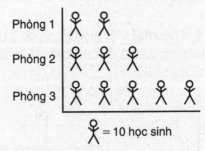

$$\pi = \frac{\text{chu vi}}{\text{đường kính}}$$

biểu đồ hình (pictograph) Một biểu đồ dùng những ký hiệu để đại diện những dữ kiện.

Ví Dụ:

Những học sinh trong lớp học

Phòng 1
Phòng 2
Phòng 3

= 10 học sinh

trị số vị trí (place value) Trị số được ban cho một vị trí mà một số chiếm ngụ.

Ví Dụ:

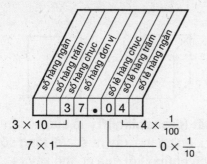

$$3 \times 10 \qquad 4 \times \frac{1}{100}$$
$$7 \times 1 \qquad 0 \times \frac{1}{10}$$

mặt phẳng (plane) Một bề mặt phẳng kéo dài đến vô tận.

Ví Dụ:

Để hình dung một mặt phẳng, hãy nghĩ đến việc kéo dài một mặt bàn ra ở khắp tất cả các hướng.

điểm đối xứng (point symmetry) Một hình có điểm đối xứng nếu sau khi quay 180° mà nhìn vẫn không thay đổi.

Ví Dụ:

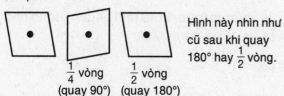

Hình này nhìn như cũ sau khi quay 180° hay $\frac{1}{2}$ vòng.

$\frac{1}{4}$ vòng (quay 90°) $\frac{1}{2}$ vòng (quay 180°)

đa giác (polygon) Một hình kín được tạo thành bởi nhiều đoạn thẳng.

Ví Dụ:

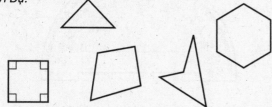

khối đa diện (polyhedron) Một hình khối có các mặt là những hình đa giác.

Ví Dụ:

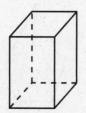

đa thức (polynomial) Một biểu thức đại số là tổng số của một hay nhiều số hạng.

Ví Dụ:

$$x^2 + 2x - 3 \qquad 5y - 15$$

dân số (population) Sự tập hợp tất cả các sự vật được nghiên cứu trong một cuộc thăm dò.

Ví Dụ:

Người ta viết tất cả 1000 tên của hội viên câu lạc bộ lên trên các thẻ khác nhau, và những thẻ này được xáo trộn đều. Sau đó người ta rút ra 100 thẻ và người ta tiếp xúc bằng điện thoại với những hội viên có tên trong những thẻ đó để thực hiện một cuộc thăm dò. Dân số của cuộc thăm dò này là 1000 hội viên câu lạc bộ.

số dương (positive number) Những số lớn hơn số không.

Ví Dụ:

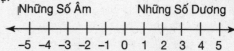

Những Số Âm   Những Số Dương

$$-5 \quad -4 \quad -3 \quad -2 \quad -1 \quad 0 \quad 1 \quad 2 \quad 3 \quad 4 \quad 5$$

sự liên hệ thuận chiều (positive relationship) Hai nhóm dữ kiện có một sự liên hệ thuận chiều khi những trị số của chúng cùng tăng hay cùng giảm.

Ví Dụ:

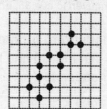

độ dốc dương (positive slope) Độ dốc của một đường thẳng hướng lên trên.

Ví Dụ:

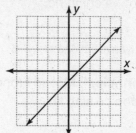

cân Anh (pound) Một đơn vị trong hệ thống đo lường thông thường bằng 16 lạng.

Ví Dụ:

Gạo
1 cân Anh

lũy thừa (power) Số mũ hay một số được tạo thành bởi sự gia tăng số lần của cơ số đến số mũ của nó.

Ví Dụ:

$16 = 2^4$ 2 được gia tăng đến lũy thừa 4.

16 là lũy thừa 4 của 2.

sự chính xác (precision) Chi tiết đúng của một sự đo lường, được quyết định bởi đơn vị đo lường.

Ví Dụ:

Đơn vị đo lường nhỏ, như in (inche), chính xác hơn đơn vị đo lường lớn hơn nó, như bộ Anh (feet).

5'1" 61"

thừa số nguyên tố (prime factor) Một số nguyên tố chia một số nguyên khác mà không để lại số thừa.

Ví Dụ:

5 là một thừa số nguyên tố của 35, bởi vì $35 \div 5 = 7$.

thừa số hóa nguyên tố (prime factorization) Viết một số như là một tích số của những số nguyên tố.

Ví Dụ:

$70 = 2 \times 5 \times 7$

số nguyên tố (prime number) Một số nguyên lớn hơn 1 mà chỉ có những thừa số duy nhất là 1 và chính nó.

Ví Dụ:

Những số nguyên tố bắt đầu từ 2, 3, 5, 7, 11, ...

tiền vốn (principal) Một số lượng tiền ký gởi hay vay mượn có sinh lãi.

Ví Dụ:

Dave ký gởi $300 trong trương mục tiết kiệm. Sau một năm kết số trương mục của anh là $315. $300 là tiền vốn.

căn số bậc hai chính (principal square root) Căn số dương của một số.

Ví Dụ:

căn số bậc hai chính

$\sqrt{25} = 5$

căn số bậc hai âm

$-\sqrt{25} = -5$

hình lăng trụ (prism) Một hình đa giác có hai đáy đồng dạng và song song với nhau.

Ví Dụ:

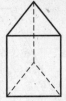

xác xuất (probability) Tỷ lệ của số lần mà một sự kiện có thể xảy ra so với tổng số lần mà tất cả những kết quả có thể xảy ra.

Ví Dụ:

Xác xuất của việc thảy ra con số 3 là $\frac{1}{6}$.

Xác xuất của việc thảy không ra con số 3 là $\frac{5}{6}$.

tích số (product) Kết của của việc nhân hai hay nhiều số khác với nhau.

Ví Dụ:

tích số

$2 \times 3 \times 5 = 30$

tỷ lệ thức (proportion) Một phương trình cho thấy hai tỷ số bằng nhau.

Ví Dụ:

$\frac{12}{34} = \frac{6}{17}$

thước đo góc (protractor) Một dụng cụ dùng để đo góc.

Ví Dụ:

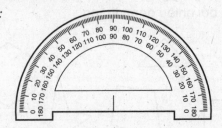

hình tháp (pyramid) Một hình khối với một đáy có những mặt khác đều là những hình tam giác cùng gặp nhau tại một điểm.

Ví Dụ:

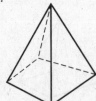

Định Lý Pytago (Pythagorean Theorem)
Trong một tam giác vuông c là chiều dài của cạnh huyền và a, b là những chiều dài của các cạnh của góc vuông, thì $a^2 + b^2 = c^2$.

Ví Dụ:

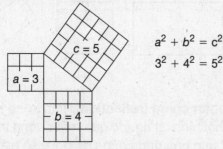

$$a^2 + b^2 = c^2$$
$$3^2 + 4^2 = 5^2$$

những góc phần tư (quadrants) Bốn vùng được chia bởi các trục của một mặt phẳng tọa độ.

Ví Dụ:

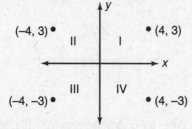

phương trình bậc hai (quadratic equation) Một phương trình với một số hạng bình phương như x^2.

Ví Dụ:
$$y = x^2 + 3x - 12 \qquad y = 2x^2 + 7$$

hàm số bậc hai (quadratic function) Một hàm số có lũy thừa cao nhất của x là 2. Đường biểu diễn của hàm số bậc hai là một hình ba-ra-bol.

Ví Dụ:

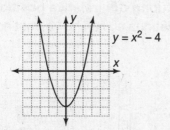

$$y = x^2 - 4$$

hình tứ giác (quadrilateral) Một hình đa giác có 4 cạnh.

Ví Dụ:

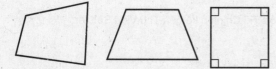

quạt (quart) Một đơn vị đo thể tích trong hệ thống đo lường thông thường.

Ví Dụ:

Một quạt sữa

phần tư (quartile) Một trong các số chia một nhóm dữ kiện ra làm bốn phần bằng nhau.

Ví Dụ:

27   27   27   29   32   33   36   38   42   43   62

phần tư thấp   số giữa   phần tư cao

27, 33, và 39 là ba cái phần tư của nhóm dữ kiện này.

thương số (quotient) Kết quả của việc chia một số cho một số khác.

Ví Dụ:

thương số
$$8 \div 4 = 2$$

dấu căn (radical sign $\sqrt{}$) dùng để biểu thị một căn bậc hai của một số.

Ví Dụ:
$$\sqrt{49} = 7$$

bán kính (radius) Một đường từ tâm của một vòng tròn đến bất cứ một điểm nào trên vòng tròn đó.

Ví Dụ:

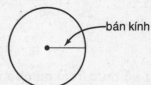

bán kính

mẫu ngẫu nhiên (random sample) Một mẫu được chọn theo một cách mà tất cả những thành viên dân số (trong nhóm) đều có cơ hội đồng đều để được chọn.

Ví Dụ:

Người ta viết tất cả 1000 tên của các hội viên câu lạc bộ lên các thẻ khác nhau, và các thẻ này được xáo trộn đều. Sau đó người ta rút ra 100 thẻ và người ta tiếp xúc bằng điện thoại với những hội viên có tên trong những thẻ đó để thực hiện một cuộc thăm dò. Tất cả những hội viên của câu lạc bộ đều có cơ hội đồng đều để được tiếp xúc bằng điện thoại vì thế người ta gọi đó là một mẫu ngẫu nhiên.

khoảng biến thiên (range) Hiệu số giữa những trị số cao nhất và những trị số thấp nhất trong một nhóm dữ kiện.

Ví Dụ:

27 27 27 29 32 33 36 38 42 43 62

khoảng biến thiên là 62 − 27 = 35.

tỷ suất (rate) Một tỷ số cho thấy các số lượng trong những đơn vị khác nhau liên hệ với nhau như thế nào.

Ví Dụ: $\dfrac{72 \text{ mỹ kim}}{28 \text{ giờ}}$ $\dfrac{55 \text{ dặm}}{1 \text{ giờ}}$

tỷ số (ratio) Một sự so sánh giữa hai số lượng.

Ví Dụ: $\dfrac{2}{1}$ 2 đối với 1 2:1

số hữu tỷ (rational number) Một số có thể được viết như một tỷ số của hai số nguyên. Những số nguyên, những phân số, và nhiều số thập phân khác là những số hữu tỷ.

Ví Dụ:

Số Nguyên	Phân Số	Số Thập Phân
$-27 = \dfrac{-27}{1}$	$\dfrac{7}{8}$	$3.1 = 3\dfrac{1}{10} = \dfrac{31}{10}$

nửa đường thẳng (ray) Một phần của một đường thẳng có một điểm cuối và một chiều kia có thể kéo dài đến vô tận. Nửa đường thẳng được gọi tên bắt đầu từ điểm cuối trước.

Ví Dụ:

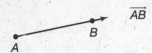

$\overrightarrow{AB}$

những số thực (real numbers) Tất cả những số hữu tỷ và những số vô tỷ là những số thực.

Ví Dụ:

-27 $\dfrac{1}{2}$ 3.1

$\sqrt{5}$ π $-\sqrt{\dfrac{1}{2}}$

những số đảo (reciprocals) Hai số có tích số bằng 1.

Ví Dụ:

$\dfrac{3}{5}$ và $\dfrac{5}{3}$ là những số đảo vì $\dfrac{3}{5} \cdot \dfrac{5}{3} = 1.$

hình chữ nhật (rectangle) Một hình bình hành với các cạnh đối diện có chiều dài bằng nhau và tất cả các góc đo được 90°.

Ví Dụ:

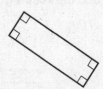

phản chiếu (reflection) Hình trong kính của một hình lật ngược qua một đường thẳng. Cũng còn được dùng để gọi việc biến đổi lật ngược một hình qua một đường thẳng.

Ví Dụ:

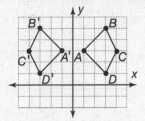

đa giác đều (regular polygon) Một đa giác với tất cả các cạnh và các góc đồng dạng với nhau.

Ví Dụ:

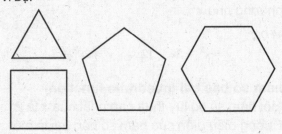

vị trí tương đối (relative position) Địa điểm cho biết qua sự liên hệ với một nơi chốn khác.

Ví Dụ:

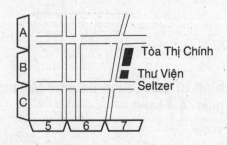

Tòa Thị Chính ở kế bên Thư Viện Seltzer.

số dư (remainder) Số ít hơn số chia (ước số) còn lại sau khi chia xong.

Ví Dụ:

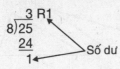

số thập phân lập lại với số lẻ (repeating decimal) Một số thập phân với một hay một nhóm số lập lại nằm bên mặt của dấu chấm thập phân.

Ví Dụ: $0.\overline{6}$ $0.\overline{123}$ $2.\overline{18}$

hình thoi (rhombus) Một hình bình hành với bốn cạnh có chiều dài bằng nhau.

Ví Dụ:

góc vuông (right angle) Một góc đo được 90°.

Ví Dụ:

tam giác vuông (right triangle) Một tam giác có một góc vuông.

Ví Dụ:

sự tăng lên (rise) Đối với một đường thẳng trên một đồ thị, đó là sự thay đổi dọc để cho một sự thay đổi ngang được thực hiện.

Ví Dụ:

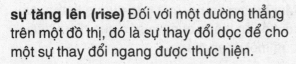

quay (rotation) Ảnh của một hình đang "quay" như nằm trên một trục quay. Cũng còn dùng để gọi một sự biến đổi làm quay một hình.

Ví Dụ:

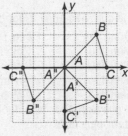

đối xứng quay (rotational symmetry) Một hình có đối xứng quay nếu nó có thể quay ít hơn một vòng tròn mà vẫn hoàn toàn trùng với hình nguyên thủy.

Ví Dụ:

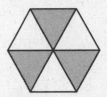

Mỗi hình đều có đối xứng quay.

quy tròn (rounding) Ước tính một số đến một trị số vị trí cho sẵn.

Ví Dụ:

2153 quy tròn thành	
gần với số hàng trăm 2200	gần với số hàng chục 2150

sự tiến tới (run) Đối với một đường thẳng trên một đồ thị, đó là sự thay đổi ngang để bắt được một sự thay đổi dọc, hay tăng lên.

Ví Dụ:

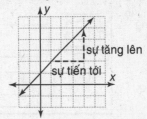

mẫu (sample) Một nhóm dữ kiện dùng để tiên đoán một tình huống đặc biệt có thể xảy ra như thế nào.

Ví Dụ:

Người ta viết tất cả 1000 tên của hội viên câu lạc bộ lên các tấm thẻ riêng biệt và xào trộn các tấm thẻ ấy. Sau đó người ta rút ra 100 thẻ và tiếp xúc bằng điện thoại với những hội viên có tên trên những thẻ này để thực hiện một cuộc thăm dò. Người ta gọi 100 hội viên nghe điện thoại thăm dò đó là mẫu.

mẫu cách khoảng (sample space) Một loạt tất cả những kết quả có thể xảy ra của một thử nghiệm.

Ví Dụ:

Kết Quả của Việc Thảy 2 Đồng Tiền:

Đồng tiền 1	Đồng Tiền 2
hình đầu	hình đuôi
hình đầu	hình đầu
hình đuôi	hình đầu
hình đuôi	hình đuôi

Mẫu cách khoảng là hình đầu , hình đuôi; hình đầu, hình đầu; hình đuôi, hình đầu; hình đuôi, hình đuôi.

chia độ (trong đồ thị) (scale (graphical)) Những khoảng cách đều nhau trên trục tung của một biểu đồ thanh hay biểu đồ đường thẳng. Được dùng để đo chiều cao của các thanh biểu diễn.

Ví Dụ:

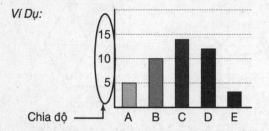

tỷ lệ vẽ (trong việc vẽ theo tỷ lệ) (scale (in scale drawings)) Tỷ lệ số đo trong việc vẽ theo tỷ lệ so với số đo thật sự của vật đó bên ngoài. Xem *vẽ theo tỷ lệ.*

vẽ theo tỷ lệ (scale drawing) Cách vẽ sử dụng tỷ lệ vẽ để phóng đại ra hay thu nhỏ lại hình ảnh của một vật.

Ví Dụ:

Vẽ theo tỷ lệ một phòng khách

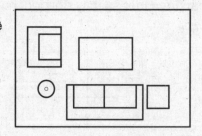

Tỷ lệ vẽ:
0.1 in. = 1 bộ

thừa số tỷ lệ (scale factor) Tỷ lệ dùng để phóng đại hay thu nhỏ những hình tương tự.

Ví Dụ:

$\frac{10}{5} = 2$ $\frac{6}{3} = 2$

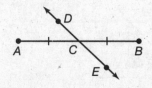

Thừa số tỷ lệ để phóng đại ra là 2

tam giác lệnh (scalene triangle) Một tam giác với các cạnh có chiều dài khác nhau.

Ví Dụ:

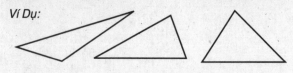

biểu đồ rải rác (scatterplot) Một đồ thị dùng những cặp trị số dữ kiện như là những điểm để trình bày những sự liên hệ giữa hai nhóm dữ kiện.

Ví Dụ:

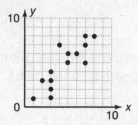

ký hiệu khoa học (scientific notation) Một số được viết như là một số thập phân lớn hơn hay bằng 1 và nhỏ hơn 10, được nhân lên với một lũy thừa của số 10.

Ví Dụ: $350{,}000 = 3.5 \times 10^5$

hình quạt (sector) Một phần của hình tròn giống như một cái nêm, dùng trong một biểu đồ tròn để cho thấy những phần của một nhóm dữ kiện so với toàn bộ nhóm dữ kiện đó.

Ví Dụ:

đoạn (segment) Xem *đoạn thẳng.*

đường trung đoạn (segment bisector) Một đường thẳng, một nửa đường thẳng, hay một đoạn thẳng chạy xuyên qua điểm giữa của một đoạn thẳng.

Ví Dụ:

$\overrightarrow{DE}$ chia đôi $\overline{AB}$ tại điểm C.

dãy số (sequence) Một sự sắp xếp các số theo một mẫu thức.

Ví Dụ:

dãy số theo cấp số cộng

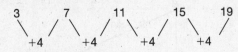

dãy số theo cấp số nhân

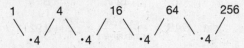

cạnh (side) Mỗi một cặp nửa đường thẳng tạo thành một góc. Cũng vậy, những đoạn thẳng tạo thành một đa giác.

Ví Dụ:

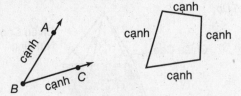

Cạnh-Góc-Góc (Side-Angle-Angle (SAA)) Một quy tắc áp dụng để xem hai tam giác có đồng dạng với nhau hay không bằng cách so sánh các thành phần tương ứng của nó.

Ví Dụ:

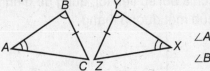

$\overline{BC} \cong \overline{YZ}$

$\angle ABC \cong \angle XYZ$

$\angle BAC \cong \angle YXZ$

$\triangle ABC \cong \triangle XYZ$ theo quy tắc SAA.

Cạnh-Góc-Cạnh (Side-Angle-Side (SAS)) Một quy tắc áp dụng để xem hai tam giác có đồng dạng với nhau hay không bằng cách so sánh các thành phần tương ứng của nó.

Ví Dụ:

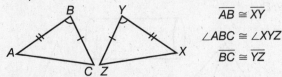

$\overline{AB} \cong \overline{XY}$

$\angle ABC \cong \angle XYZ$

$\overline{BC} \cong \overline{YZ}$

$\triangle ABC \cong \triangle XYZ$ theo quy tắc SAS.

Cạnh-Cạnh-Cạnh (Side-Side-Side (SSS)) Một quy tắc áp dụng để xem hai tam giác có đồng dạng với nhau hay không bằng cách so sánh các thành phần tương ứng của nó.

Ví Dụ:

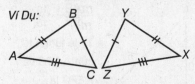

$\overline{AB} \cong \overline{XY}$

$\overline{BC} \cong \overline{YZ}$

$\overline{CA} \cong \overline{ZX}$

$\triangle ABC \cong \triangle XYZ$ theo quy tắc SSS.

những con số có ý nghĩa (significant digits) Trong một số lượng đo lường, những con số đại diện cho số đo thật sự.

Ví Dụ:

380.6700   Tất cả những con số này đều có ý nghĩa.

0.0038   và 8 là số có ý nghĩa, nhưng không có con số không nào có ý nghĩa cả.

tương tự (similar) Có cùng một hình dạng nhưng không cần thiết phải cùng kích thước.

Ví Dụ:

 và

 và

 và

tỷ lệ tương tự (similarity ratio) Tỷ lệ giữa những chiều dài tương ứng trong những hình tương tự.

Ví Dụ:

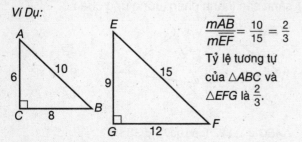

$$\frac{m\overline{AB}}{m\overline{EF}} = \frac{10}{15} = \frac{2}{3}$$

Tỷ lệ tương tự của △ABC và △EFG là $\frac{2}{3}$.

lãi đơn (simple interest) Tiền lãi được trả chỉ căn cứ trên tiền vốn mà thôi.

Ví Dụ: Ramon đầu tư $240 trong một trương mục có lãi suất hằng năm là 6% trong năm năm. Anh sẽ kiếm được 240 · 0.06 · 5 = 72, $72 là lãi đơn sau 5 năm.

đã đơn giản hoá (simplified) Một đa thức không có những số hạng giống nhau.

Ví Dụ:

$4x^4 + x^3 + x^2 - 8$ đã đơn giản hóa

$4x^4 + x^2 + 6x^2 - 8$ chưa đơn giản hoá, bởi vì x^2 và $6x^2$ là những số hạng giống nhau.

đơn giản hoá (simplify) Làm giảm sự phức tạp của một biểu thức bằng cách áp dụng phép tính toán theo thứ tự.

Ví Dụ: Đơn giản hoá: $3 + 8 \cdot 5^2$

$$3 + 8 \cdot 5^2 = 3 + 8 \cdot 25 \quad \text{(các số mũ)}$$
$$= 3 + 200 \quad \text{(nhân)}$$
$$= 203 \quad \text{(cộng)}$$

giả cách (simulation) Một mẫu thử nghiệm dùng để tìm xác xuất.

Ví Dụ:

Một cầu thủ bóng chày đánh .250. Để giả cách đánh của cầu thủ này, (để biết cầu thủ này có thể đánh như thế nào) người ta quay một hộp quay số có 4 phần. Việc giả cách này có thể được dùng để tiên đoán xem người đánh banh có thể đánh trúng một loạt 2 hay 3 cái với mức độ thường xuyên như thế nào.

sin (sine) Đối với một góc nhọn x trong một tam giác vuông, sin của x, hay sin(x), là tỷ lệ $\frac{\text{cạnh đối}}{\text{cạnh huyền}}$.

Ví Dụ:

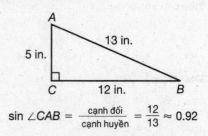

$$\sin \angle CAB = \frac{\text{cạnh đối}}{\text{cạnh huyền}} = \frac{12}{13} \approx 0.92$$

chiều cao nghiêng (slant height) Trong một khối hình tháp, nó là khoảng cách thẳng đứng từ cạnh rìa của đáy lên đến đỉnh.

Ví Dụ:

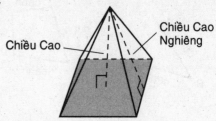

trượt (slide) Xem *sự tịnh tiến*.

độ nghiêng (slope) Đối với một đường thẳng trên một đồ thị, độ nghiêng là một sự tăng lên bị chia bởi sự tiến tới, dùng để diễn tả độ dốc của một đường thẳng.

Ví Dụ:

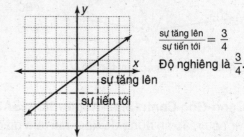

$$\frac{\text{sự tăng lên}}{\text{sự tiến tới}} = \frac{3}{4}$$
Độ nghiêng là $\frac{3}{4}$.

khối (solid) Một hình ba chiều.

Ví Dụ:

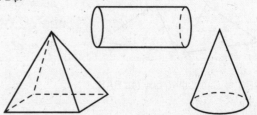

những lời giải của một phương trình hay bất đẳng thức (solutions of an equation or inequality) Những trị số của một biến số làm một phương trình hay một bất đẳng thức đúng với sự thật.

Ví Dụ:

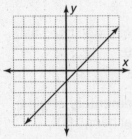

Đường thẳng đại diện cho lời giải của phương trình $y = x - 1$.

Vùng xám đại diện cho lời giải của bất đẳng thức $y > x - 1$.

lời giải của một hệ thống (solution of a system) Những sự thay thế của biến số làm tất cả những phương trình trong một hệ thống đúng với sự thật.

Ví Dụ:
$$y = x + 4$$
$$y = 3x - 6$$

Cặp số thứ tự $(5, 9)$ giải đúng cả hai phương trình trên. Vì thế $(5, 9)$ là một lời giải của hệ thống.

giải (solve) Tìm những lời giải của một phương trình hay một bất đẳng thức.

Ví Dụ: Giải $x + 6 = 13$.
$$x + 6 = 13$$
$$x + 6 + (-6) = 13 + (-6)$$
$$x + 0 = 7$$
$$x = 7$$

khối cầu (sphere) Một hình khối mà các điểm trên đó cách đều với trung tâm.

Ví Dụ:

hình vuông (square) Một tứ giác với tất cả các cạnh có cùng một chiều dài và tất cả các góc đều đo được 90°.

Ví Dụ:

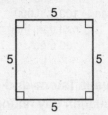

bình phương (squared) tăng lên tới lũy thừa hai.

Ví Dụ: 3 bình phương $= 3^2$.
$$3^2 = 3 \times 3 = 9$$

xen ti mét vuông (square centimeter) Diện tích một hình vuông có mỗi cạnh là 1 xen ti mét.

Ví Dụ:

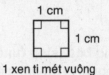

1 cm

1 cm

1 xen ti mét vuông

in vuông (square inch) Diện tích một hình vuông có các cạnh là 1 in.

Ví Dụ:

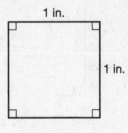

1 in.

1 in.

1 in vuông

căn số bậc hai (square root) Căn số bậc hai của *N* là một số mà khi nhân với chính nó sẽ cho ra *N*. Cũng vậy, căn số bậc hai của của một số cho sẵn là chiều dài một cạnh của một hình vuông có diện tích bằng với số cho sẵn đó.

Ví Dụ:

$9 \times 9 = 81$, vì thế 9 là căn số bậc hai của 81.

$9 = \sqrt{81}$

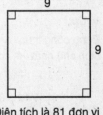

9

9

Diện tích là 81 đơn vị vuông.

hình thức tiêu chuẩn (standard form)
Cách viết của một số bằng những con số.

Ví Dụ:

Hình thức tiêu chuẩn: 100,000,000
Hình thức chữ: một trăm triệu
Hình thức số-chữ: 100 triệu

đồ hình thân-và-lá (stem-and-leaf diagram) Một sự trình bày những dữ kiện bằng cách dùng những con số của những số dữ kiện để cho thấy đồ hình và sự phân phối của nhóm dữ kiện đó.

Ví Dụ:

Đồ hình sau đây cho thấy nhóm dữ kiện: 33, 34, 34, 35, 40, 41, 46, 51, 51, 52, 53, 55, 58.

Thân	Lá					
3	3	4	4	5		
4	0	1	6			
5	1	1	2	3	5	8

hàm số thang bậc (step function) Một hàm số trong đó người ta áp dụng những quy luật khác nhau cho những trị số nhập vào khác nhau. Đồ thị của hàm số thang bậc bao gồm những mảnh rời rạc không dính liền nhau.

Ví Dụ:

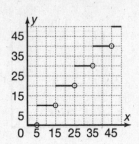

góc bẹt (straight angle) Một góc đo được 180°.

Ví Dụ:

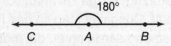

thế trị (substitute) Thay thế một biến số bằng một trị số riêng biệt.

Ví Dụ:

Dùng công thức $A = l \cdot w$ để tìm diện tích của một hình chữ nhật với chiều dài 12 cm và chiều rộng 8 cm.

$$A = l \cdot w$$
$$A = 12 \cdot 8 \qquad \text{Thế những trị số cho}$$
$$A = 96 \qquad \text{chiều dài và chiều rộng.}$$

Diện tích là 96 cm².

trừ (subtraction) Một phép toán cho biết hiệu số của hai số, hoặc còn lại bao nhiêu khi một số lượng bị lấy đi.

Ví Dụ: $12 - 5 = 7$

⌧ ⌧ ⌧ ⌧ ⌧
○ ○ ○ ○ ○
○ ○

tổng số (sum) Kết quả của việc cộng hai hay nhiều số lại với nhau.

Example: $30 + 18 = 48$ ⟵ tổng số

những góc phụ (supplementary angles) Hai góc có số đo cộng lại bằng 180°.

Ví Dụ:

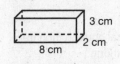

55°   125°

diện tích bề mặt (surface area (SA)) Tổng số những diện tích các mặt của một hình đa giác.

Ví Dụ:

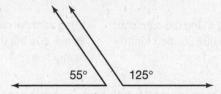

Hai mặt có một chiều là 8cm và một chiều là 3cm.
$A = b \cdot h = 8 \cdot 3 = 24$ cm²
Hai mặt có một chiều là 8cm và một chiều là 2cm.
$A = b \cdot h = 8 \cdot 2 = 16$ cm²
Hai mặt có một chiều là 2cm và một chiều là 3cm.
$A = b \cdot h = 2 \cdot 3 = 6$ cm²
Diện tích bề mặt của khối hình chữ nhật là
$SA = 2(24 + 16 + 6)$
$= 92$ cm²

cuộc thăm dò (survey) Một cuộc nghiên cứu đòi hỏi phải thu lượm thông tin và phân tích các thông tin đó.

Ví Dụ:

Người ta tổ chức một cuộc thăm dò để xác định môn thể thao nào phổ thông nhất trong giới học sinh.

đối xứng (symmetry) Xem *đường đối xứng, điểm đối xứng, và đối xứng quay.*

hệ thống của những phương trình tuyến (system of linear equations) Hai hay nhiều phương trình tuyến được xem xét chung với nhau.

Ví Dụ: $y = x + 3$
$y = 4x - 15$

bảng-T (T-table) Một bảng cho thấy những trị số tương ứng của x và y trong một phương trình.

Ví Dụ:

$$y = 2x + 1$$

x	y
-2	-3
-1	-1
0	1
1	3
2	5

kiểm đếm (tally) Dùng dấu đếm để ghi lại việc đếm thực hiện trong một cuộc thăm dò.

Ví Dụ:

Xe Cộ	Kiểm Đếm
Xe du lịch	ⅢⅢ Ⅲ
Xe có chỗ để hành lý	‖‖
Xe chạy ở ngoại ô	ⅢⅢ ‖
Xe trắc	ⅢⅢ
Xe Van	Ⅲ

dấu đếm (tally marks) Những dấu dùng để tổ chức một nhóm dữ kiện lớn. Mỗi dấu cho biết một lần hiện diện của một trị số trong nhóm dữ kiện.

Ví Dụ:

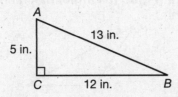

đường tiếp tuyến (tangent line) Một đường thẳng chỉ tiếp xúc với một điểm của một vòng tròn.

Ví Dụ:

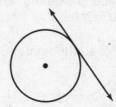

tỷ số tan (tangent ratio) Đối với một góc nhọn x trong một tam giác vuông, tan của x, hay là tan(x), là $\frac{\text{cạnh đối}}{\text{cạnh kề}}$.

Ví Dụ:

A — 13 in. — B, 5 in., C, 12 in.

$$\tan \angle CAB = \frac{\text{cạnh đối}}{\text{cạnh kề}} = \frac{12}{5} = 2.4$$

số hạng (term) Số trong một dãy số. Cũng là một phần của đa thức mà đa thức này là một ký số, một biến số, hay một số được nhân bởi một hay nhiều biến số. Những biến số đó có thể có những số mũ là số nguyên.

Ví Dụ:

secuencia 3 7 11 15 19 23

những số hạng

polinomio $2x^3 - x^2 + 3x - 5$

những số hạng

số thập phân chấm dứt (terminating decimal) Một số thập phân với một số lượng cố định các con số.

Ví Dụ: 3.5 0.599992 4.05

sự lát hoa (tessellation) Sự lập lại mẫu thức những hình ảnh bao phủ một mặt phẳng một cách liên tục không có sự gián đoạn hay trùng lặp.

Ví Dụ:

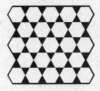

xác xuất lý thuyết (theoretical probability) Tỷ lệ của số lần một sự kiện có thể xảy ra đối với tổng số lần của những kết quả có thể xảy ra.

Ví Dụ:

$$\frac{\text{Số lần quay ra màu trắng}}{\text{tổng số lần quay}} = \frac{3}{6} = \frac{1}{2}$$

Bởi vì một nửa mặt của đĩa quay có màu trắng, nên xác xuất lý thuyết của việc quay ra màu trắng là $\frac{1}{2}$.

phép biến đổi (transformation) Một sự thay đổi trong kích cỡ hay vị trí của một hình.

Ví Dụ:

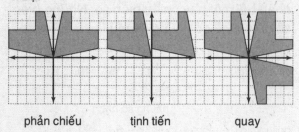

phản chiếu   tịnh tiến   quay

sự tịnh tiến (translation) Hình ảnh một hình trượt đến một vị trí mới mà không lật ngược lại hay quay. Cũng còn được dùng để gọi sự biến đổi làm trượt một hình.

Ví Dụ:

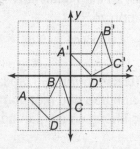

đường cắt chéo (transversal) Một đường thẳng cắt qua hai hay nhiều đường thẳng khác.

Ví Dụ:

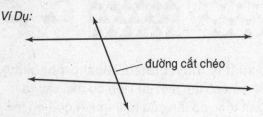

đường cắt chéo

hình thang (trapezoid) Một hình tứ giác chỉ có hai cạnh song song với nhau mà thôi.

Ví Dụ:

biểu đồ cây (tree diagram) Một biểu đồ giống hình cây, hình nhánh cho thấy tất cả những kết quả của một tình huống có thể xảy ra.

Ví Dụ:
Thảy 3 đồng tiền:

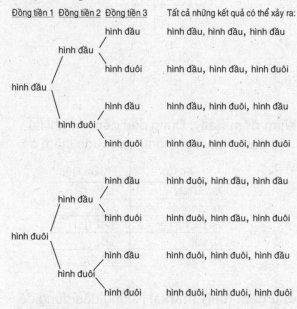

Đồng tiền 1	Đồng tiền 2	Đồng tiền 3	Tất cả những kết quả có thể xảy ra:

xu hướng (trend) Sự liên hệ giữa hai nhóm dữ kiện được thấy như là một mẫu thức trong một biểu đồ rải rác. Xem *sự liên hệ thuận chiều*, *sự liên hệ nghịch chiều*, *không có sự liên hệ*.

đường hướng (trend line) Một đường thẳng gần "nối" những điểm tạo thành một xu hướng trong một biểu đồ rải rác. Xem *sự liên hệ thuận chiều*, *sự liên hệ nghịch chiều*, *không có sự liên hệ*.

thử (trial) Một sự thử nghiệm.

Ví Dụ:

Một lần gieo một hột tào cáo   Một lần thảy một đồng tiền

hình tam giác (triangle) Một hình đa giác có ba cạnh.

Ví Dụ:

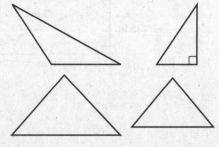

những tỷ số lượng giác (trigonometric ratios) Những tỷ số của chiều dài các cạnh của một tam giác vuông, có liên quan tới số đo của các góc nhọn của tam giác đó.

Ví Dụ:

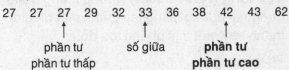

$$\cos \angle CAB = \frac{\text{cạnh kề}}{\text{cạnh huyền}} = \frac{3}{5} = 0.6$$

$$\sin \angle CAB = \frac{\text{cạnh đối}}{\text{cạnh huyền}} = \frac{4}{5} = 0.8$$

$$\tan \angle CAB = \frac{\text{cạnh đối}}{\text{cạnh kề}} = \frac{4}{3} \approx 1.3$$

tam thức (trinomial) Một đa thức có ba số hạng.

Ví Dụ: $2x^3 - x^2 + 3x$ $3x^2 + 2x - 4$

xoay (turn) Xem *quay.*

trò chơi bất công (unfair game) Một trò chơi trong đó tất cả những người tham dự đều không có cơ hội đồng đều để thắng cuộc.

Ví Dụ:

Trò chơi bất công: Trong trò chơi gieo một cặp hột tào cáo, mỗi người tham dự được chỉ định một tổng số từ 2 đến 12. Mỗi người sẽ được một điểm khi gieo ra được tổng số của họ. Vì không có những cơ hội bằng nhau để gieo ra những tổng số từ 2 đến 12, những người tham dự không có cơ hội đồng đều để thắng và như vậy trò chơi này không công bình.

giá đơn vị (unit price) Tỷ lệ đơn vị cho biết chi phí của một món đồ.

Ví Dụ:

$3.00 một cân Anh $5.75 một hộp

đơn vị (unit) Một của cái gì. Một số hay lượng dùng làm tiêu chuẩn cho sự đo lường.

phân số đơn vị (unit fraction) Một phân số có tử số bằng 1.

Ví Dụ: $\frac{1}{4}$ $\frac{1}{2}$ $\frac{1}{7}$

tỷ lệ đơn vị (unit rate) Một tỷ lệ trong đó số thứ nhì trong chuỗi so sánh là một đơn vị.

Ví Dụ: 25 ga lông một phút $\frac{55 \text{ dặm}}{1 \text{ giờ}}$

những mẫu số khác nhau (unlike denominators) Những mẫu số khác nhau trong hai hay nhiều phân số.

Ví Dụ:

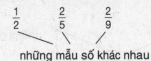

$\frac{1}{2}$ $\frac{2}{5}$ $\frac{2}{9}$

những mẫu số khác nhau

phần tư cao (upper quartile) Số giữa của một nửa phần trên của một nhóm dữ kiện.

Ví Dụ:

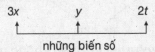

27 27 27 29 32 33 36 38 42 43 62

phần tư   số giữa   phần tư
phần tư thấp   phần tư cao

biến số (variable) Một lượng có thể thay đổi hay biến đổi, thường được đại diện bằng một mẫu tự.

Ví Dụ: $3x$ y $2t$

những biến số

biểu đồ Venn (Venn diagram) Một biểu đồ dùng những vùng để trình bày những sự liên hệ giữa những nhóm vật.

Ví Dụ:

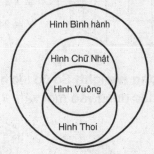

đỉnh (vertex) Trong một góc hay trong một đa giác, nó là điểm nơi hai cạnh giao nhau. Trong một khối đa diện, nó là điểm giao nhau của ba hay nhiều mặt.

Ví Dụ:

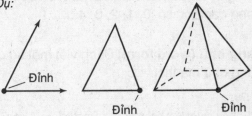

những góc đối đỉnh (vertical angles)
Những góc nằm ở hai bên đối nhau tại giao điểm của hai đường thẳng.

Ví Dụ:

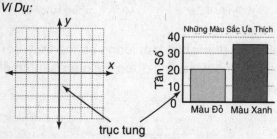

những góc đối đỉnh:
∠1 và ∠3
∠2 và ∠4

trục tung (vertical axis) Đường thẳng đứng trong hai đường thẳng lập thành một biểu đồ thanh hay một mặt phẳng tọa độ.

Ví Dụ:

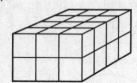

trục tung

thể tích (volume) Khoảng không gian mà một hình khối chiếm hữu.

Ví Dụ:

$V = lwh$

$V = 4 \cdot 3 \cdot 2$

$V = 24$ đơn vị khối

trọng lượng (weight) Số đo lực hút của trọng lực tác dụng vào một vật.

Ví Dụ:

1 oz   1 lb   1 ton

số nguyên (whole number) Bất cứ số nào trong các con số {0, 1, 2, 3, 4,......}

dạng chữ (word form) Cách viết một số chỉ dùng chữ mà thôi.

Ví Dụ:

bốn mươi lăm ngàn tỷ   một tỷ   sáu

trục-*x* (*x*-axis) Trục hoành trên một mặt phẳng tọa độ.

Ví Dụ:

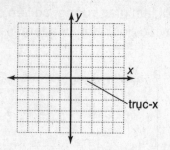

trục-x

tọa độ-*x* (*x*-coordinate) Con số đầu tiên trong một cặp số thứ tự.

Ví Dụ:

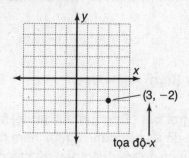

(3, −2)

tọa độ-x

điểm chắn-*x* (*x*-intercept) Một điểm nơi mà đường biểu diễn của một phương trình cắt qua trục-*x*.

Ví Dụ:

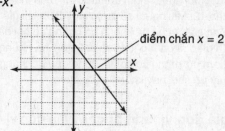

điểm chắn x = 2

trục-*y* (*y*-axis) Trục tung của một mặt phẳng tọa độ.

Ví Dụ:

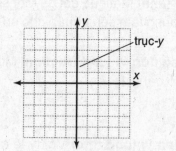

trục-y

tọa độ-y (y-coordinate) Con số thứ nhì trong một cặp số thứ tự.

Ví Dụ:

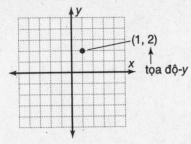

điểm chắn-y (y-intercept) Một điểm nơi đường biểu diễn của một phương trình cắt qua trục-y.

Ví Dụ:

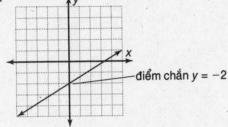

điểm chắn $y = -2$

thước Anh (yard) Một đơn vị trong hệ thống đo lường thông dụng có chiều dài bằng 3 bộ (feet).

Ví Dụ:

Chiều cao của cái bàn vào khoảng một thước Anh.

cặp số triệt tiêu (zero pair) Một số và số đối nghịch của nó.

Examples: 7 và −7   23 và −23

Tính Chất Triệt Tiêu của Phép Cộng (Zero Property of Addition) Tổng số của một số nguyên và số đảo ngược cộng của nó bằng 0.

Ví Dụ:
$$3 + (-3) = 0$$
$$-8 + 8 = 0$$

Hmong Glossary

qhov chaw tseeb ntsiab (absolute position) Thaj chaw uas uas muaj qhov los sib tshuam kom paub tseeb.

Piv txwv:

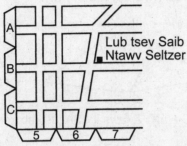

B7 yog thaj chaw qhia tu ntawm lub Tsev Saib Ntawv Seltzer.

tus nqi tu nrho (absolute value) Yog ib tus leb txawv nrug lub zej. Tus cim qhia txog tsiaj tu yog | |.

Piv txwv:

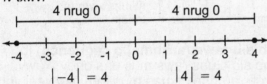

$|-4| = 4$ $|4| = 4$

ntsais kaum ti (acute angle) Ib lub ntsais kaum ntsuas tau me dua 90°.

Piv txwv:

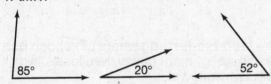

lub duab peb ceg ti (acute triangle) Ib lub peb ceg muaj ntsais kaum ti.

Piv txwv:

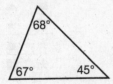

tus los ntxiv (addend) Ib tug leb muaj los ntxiv rau ib tug lossis ntau tus leb.

Piv txwv: 12 + 19 = 31

tus los ntxiv   tus los ntxiv

kev sib txiv (addition) Ib qho kev ua uas tshwm tau ib tug leb thaum muab ob lossis ntau tus leb los tso ua ke.

Piv txwv:

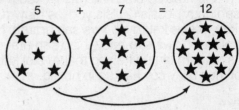

Yam Ntxwv kev Tso Ntxiv kom Sib Npaug (Addition Property of Equality) Yog hais tias a = b, thaum ntawd a + c = b + c.

Piv txwv:
Nyob rau kab thib ob hauv tus piv txwv hauv qab, 1 muab los ntxiv rau ob sab ntawm tus equation.

Yog tias	$x - 1 = 2$
Thaum ntawd	$x - 1 + 1 = 2 + 1$
	$x = 3$

tus los ntxiv tig rov (additive inverse) yog tus leb rov qab.

Piv txwv: Tus los ntxiv tig rov ntawm -2 yog 2.

Tus los ntiv tig rov ntawm 5 yog -5.

txoj ces nyob sib ze (adjacent leg) Hais txog lub kaum ti nyob sab xis ntawm lub peb ceg, tus ces nyob rau sab pw rau lub ces kaum.

Piv txwv:

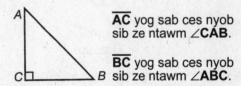

$\overline{AC}$ yog sab ces nyob sib ze ntawm ∠**CAB**.

$\overline{BC}$ yog sab ces nyob sib ze ntawm ∠**ABC**.

algebra (algebra) Yog ib yam txuj ci hauv mathematics uas tej kev suav leb arithmetic tau muab tshawb tawm uas yog siv cov pauv qhia cim los tam rau cov leb.

kev sau leb raws algebraic (algebraic expression) Yog ib qho kev sau tawm uas muaj qhov tsawg tshaj plaws yog ib tug pauv.

Piv txwv: n - 7   2y + 17   5(x - 3)

ntsais kaum hloov tau (alternate angles)

Ob lub ntsais kaum uas tau los ntawm ob txog kab thiab ib txog kab tav uas nyob rau sab cuab tim rau txoj kab tav toj uas (1) nyob rau hauv nruab nrab ob txog kab (ntsais kaum sib xws sab hauv) lossis (2) tsis yog los ntawm ob txog kab (ntsais kaum sib xws sab nraud). Ntsais kaum sib xws sab hauv thiab sab nraud yuav sib haum tau ua ke yog thaum txoj kab tav toj mus txiav cov kab ua ib ntxaig.

Piv txwv:

Cov ntsais kaum
sib xws sab nraud: Sab nraud
   ∠1 thiab ∠8
   ∠2 thiab ∠7   Sab hauv
Cov ntsais kaum
sib xws sab hauv: Sab nraud
   ∠3 thiab ∠6
   ∠4 thiab ∠5

ntsais kaum (angle) Ob txog kab uas mus xaus ua ke rau ib qho.

Piv txwv:

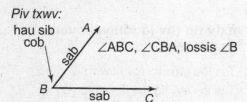

∠ABC, ∠CBA, lossis ∠B

txoj kab phua ntshais kaum (angle bisector) Ib txog kab uas faib lub ntsais kaum mus ua ob lub ntxais kaum sib puab.

Piv txwv:

$\overline{BD}$ yog txoj kab phua lub ntsais kaum ntawm ∠ABC.

ntsais kaum kiv tig (angle of rotation) Lub ntsais kaum uas ua rau ib tug leb pauv thaum kiv tig.

Piv txwv:

Lub ntsais kaum kiv tig yog 90°.

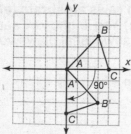

Ntsais kaum-Sab-Ntsais kaum (Angle-Side-Angle) (ASA) Tus kab ke muab siv kom qhia saib cov peb ceg xab xeeb kaum puas sib haum ua ke uas yog muab cov teeb ua nws coj los sib piv.

Piv txwv:

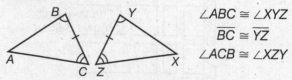

∠ABC ≅ ∠XYZ
$\overline{BC}$ ≅ $\overline{YZ}$
∠ACB ≅ ∠XZY

△ABC ≅ △XYZ raws li ASA tus kab ke.

npoo av (area) Thaj tsam npoo av uas ib lub duab khav puag txog.

Piv txwv:

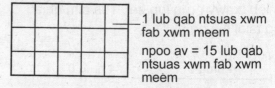

1 lub qab ntsuas xwm fab xwm meem

npoo av = 15 lub qab ntsuas xwm fab xwm meem

leb sib raws (arithmetic sequence) Ib qho sib txuas raws mus uas qhov txawv nyob rau qhov txuas mus tom ntej yeej yog deb tib yam tag mus li.

Piv txwv:

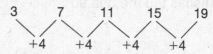

kev teeb tso (arrangement) Txoj qab qua uas tib neeg, niam ntawv, leb, lossis lwm yam tshwm tawm.

Piv txwv:

Kev teeb tso tuaj yeem
ua tau tag nrho ntawm
peb lub duab:

Yam Ntxwv Raws ntawm kev Ua Leb Sib ntxiv (Associative Property of Addition) Qhov kev uas thaum hloov pauv cov pawg tus los ntxiv yuav tsis ua rau muaj kev hloov qhov tau txais.

Piv txwv: a + (b + c) = (a + b) + c
                   5 + (3 + 7) = (5 + 3) + 7

Yam Ntxwv Raws ntawm kev Ua leb npaug (Associative Property of Multiplication) Qhov kev uas thaum hloov pauv cov pawg ntawm factors yuav tsis ua rau muaj kev hloov qhov tau txais.

Piv txwv:
$$a(bc) = (ab)c$$
$$3 \times (4 \times 2) = (3 \times 4) \times 2$$

pes nrab (average) Saib *mean*

cov kab sib lig (axes) Saib *x-axis* thiab *y-axis*.

daim graph ua ib tug (bar graph) Daim graph uas siv cov kab sawv ntsug los yog tav toj coj los tam qhia cov data.

Piv txwv:

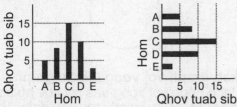

hauv paus pib (ntawm ib tug exponent) (base (of an exponent)) Tus leb uas muab coj los suav tshooj rov rau nws raws cov zauv uas muab sau ua tus leb exponent.

Piv txwv:

hauv paub pib   tus exponent
$$6^2 = 6 \times 6 = 36$$

hauv paus pib (ntawm ib lub duab ces kaum) (base (of a polygon)) Sab (feem ntau yog sab nyob hauv qab), los yog xeem ntev ntawm sab ntawd.

Piv txwv:

hauv paus pib

hauv paus pib (ntawm ib yam khoom tawv) (base (of a solid)) Nyob rau ib lub raj muaj lub qab ua ces kaum los yog raj kheej, ib qhov nyob rau ntawm ob sab yiag ncaj qha thiab sab sib haum nyob ua ke. Nyob rau ib lub pyramid (duab peb ceg muaj hau), nws yog sab uas nyob tim rau lub hau kawg. Nyob rau lub duab yias yeeb khwb, yog lub ncauj voj voog kheej.

Piv txwv:

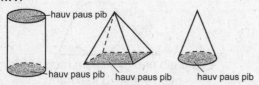

hauv paus pib   hauv paus pib   hauv paus pib   hauv paus pib

kabke siv leb lav ob pib qab (binary number system) Yog system uas siv lav 2 coj los ntaus nqi.

Piv txwv:
Nyob rau kev siv lav 2, 1011 yog npaum ib yam li 11 nyob rau kev siv leb lav kaum (base 10).

	Thaj chaw rau cov yim	Thaj chaw rau cov plaub	Thaj chaw rau cov ob	Thaj chaw rau cov ib
Qab pib lav 2	1	0	1	1
Thaj chaw tsim nuj	8	4	2	1
Yam tau txais	$1 \times 8 = 8$	$0 \times 4 = 0$	$1 \times 2 = 2$	$1 \times 1 = 1$

$(1 \times 8) + (0 \times 4) + (1 \times 2) + (1 \times 1) = 8 + 0 + 2 + 1 = 11$

muaj ob lub npe (binomial) Yog yam muaj ob lub npe sib txuas ua ke.

Piv txwv: $4x^3 - 2x^2$ $2x + 5$

ua ob tog (bisect) Phua ib lub ntsais kaum los yog ib tog mus ua ob lub ntsais kaum sib haum ua ke lossis ob tog.

Piv txwv:

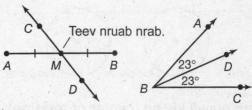

$\overleftrightarrow{CD}$ phua $\overline{AB}$. $\overrightarrow{BD}$ phua $\angle ABC$.

txoj kab npoo (boundary line) nyob rau ib lub graph ntawm txoj xov tsis xwm yeem, txoj kab uas cais cov teev uas yog qhov tau txais los ntawm cov teev uas tsis yog qhov tau txais.

Piv txwv:

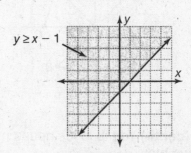

$y = x - 1$ yog txoj kab tom npoo.

box-and-whisker plot (box-and-whisker plot)
Kev muab cov data yus sau tau coj los tso saib. Qhov piv txwv hauv qab no yog tau los ntawm kev kaum tus khab nee (scores) uas tau ntsuas tawm: 52, 64, 75, 79, 80, 80, 81, 88, 92, 99.

Piv txwv:

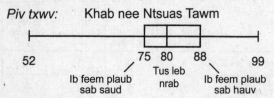

Khab nee Ntsuas Tawm

52   75 80   88   99

Ib feem plaub sab saud / Tus leb nrab / Ib feem plaub sab hauv

ntim tau ntau tsawg (capacity)
Kev yeem ntim tau ntau tsawg tej yam khoom ua kua.

Piv txwv:

500 ml   1 L   1 khob   1 quart   1 thawv gallon

teev plawv (center)
Teev uas nyob ncaj ncaj hauv nruab nrab lub voj voog los yog lub rog pob khoob.

Piv txwv:

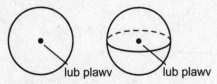

lub plawv   lub plawv

nrab plawv kiv tig (center of rotation)
Teev nyob rau qhov uas muaj kev tig mus ua ib lub duab.

Piv txwv:

Lub chaw chiv keeb yog lub nrab plawv kiv tig.

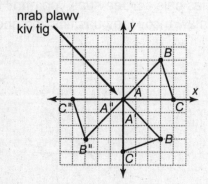

nrab plawv kiv tig

centi- (centi-)
Yog ib lo lus npuas nyob rau tom hauv ntev $\frac{1}{100}$.

Piv txwv: 1 centimeter = $\frac{1}{100}$ meter

ntsais kaum plawv (central angle)
Lub ntsais kaum uas muaj lub hau nyob rau hauv nrab plawv voj voog.

Piv txwv:

Teev C yog nruab nrab ntawm lub voj voog.
∠BCA yog lub ntsais kaum nrab plawv

voj voog (circle)
Daim npoo uas cov kab tawm hauv nrab plawv rau tom ntug ntev tib yam tag nrho.

Piv txwv:

txoj kab graph voj voog (circle graph)
Yog daim npoo voj voog uas siv cov nplais ntsais kaum los sawv cev rau cov data. Nws tseem hu tau hais tias lub pie chart thiab.

Piv txwv: Cov tsiaj yug hauv tsev yus nyiam heev

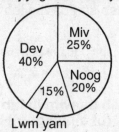

Dev 40%   Miv 25%   Noog 20%   15% Lwm yam

txoj kab ncig ntug voj voog (circumference)
Yog ncua kab ntev ncig lub voj voog.

Piv txwv:

txoj kab ncig ntug voj voog

lub duab sib qhwv (circumscribed figure)
Ib lub duab uas qhwv ib lub nyob nws sab hauv. Lub duab ua ces kaum raug qhwv rau sab hauv yog tias lub voj voog tau mus txhuam raug txhua txhua sab duab.

Piv txwv:

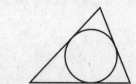

Lub duab peb ceg kaum raug qhwv nyob voj voog sab hauv.

mus raws li koob moos khiav (clockwise)
Yog kev kiv tig mus thaum lub hau duab kiv mus sab xis.

Piv txwv:

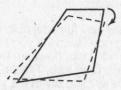

kev tso yam sib xws nyob ua ke (clustering) Kev ntaus nqi uas saib cov leb yuav luag sib npaug muab saib tias yam li yog sib npaug.

Piv txwv:
26 + 24 + 23 yuav luag npaum 25 + 25 + 25, los yog 3 x 25.

tus leb siv los npuab (coefficient) Yog tus leb uas muab coj los multiply rau lwm tus.

Piv txwv: tus leb siv los npuab   tus pauv

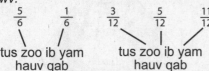

12y

kev koom ua ke (combination) Kev xaiv cov khoom uas tsis paus rau ntsis saib ua qhov tseem ceeb.

Piv txwv:
Yuav tau xaiv ob tug tub ntxhais kawm ntawv hauv pawg neeg no los nyob rau hauv lub koom haum: David, Juanita, Kim.
Kev muaj peev xwm sib koom ua ke yog:
David, Juanita   David, Kim   Juanita, Kim
Qhia paub: Qhov kev koom "David, Juanita" kuj yog tib yam li qhov kev koom "Juanita, David."

tus leb zoo ib yam hauv qab (common denominator) Tus leb uas zoo ib yam nyob rau hauv qab ob tug fractions (leb faib)

Piv txwv:

$\frac{5}{6}$ $\frac{1}{6}$ $\frac{3}{12}$ $\frac{5}{12}$ $\frac{11}{12}$

tus zoo ib yam   tus zoo ib yam
hauv qab   hauv qab

tus factor sib koom (common factor) Tus leb uas yog factor rau ob tug lossis ntau tus leb.

Piv txwv:
4 yog tus factor koom ntawm 8, 12, thiab 20.
8 = **4** x 2
12 = **4** x 3
20 = **4** x 5

tus leb koom ua npaug (common multiple) Tus leb uas yog tus ua npaug rau txhua txhua ob tug lossis ntau tus leb.

Piv txwv:
multiples ntawm 3: 3 6 9 **12** 15 18 21 **24** 27 ...
multiples ntawm 4: 4 8 **12** 16 20 **24** 28 ...
12 thiab 14 yog ob tug multiples koom ntawm 3 thiab 4.

Tus Yam Ntxwv kev muab Sib ntxiv (Commutative Property of Addition) Hais txog tias kev muaj qab muaj hau tsis ua rau muaj qhov txawv txav rau tus sum los ntawm ob tug los yog ntau tus leb.

Piv txwv: $a + b = b + a$
18 + 23 = 23 + 18

Yam Ntxwv kev Ua leb Tshooj Npaug (Commutative Property of Multiplication) Hais txog tias kev ua ntej ua qab tsis ua rau muaj qhov txawv txav ntawm tus sum ob tug los yog ntau tus leb.

Piv txwv: $ab = ba$
4 x 7 = 7 x 4

cov leb nyob tau ua ke (compatible numbers) Nkawm leb uas tuaj yeem muab sib xam ua ke tau yoojyim.

Piv txwv: 30 + 70   40 ÷ 4   25 + 75

kev them rau (compensation) Yog kev siv lub hlwb ua leb uas xaiv cov leb kom ze rau cov leb ntawm qhov teebmeem, ntxiv ntawd mam kho qhov lus teb los kho rau cov leb uas tau xaiv.

Piv txwv: 99 x 4 = (100 - 1) x 4
= (100 x 4) - (1 x 4)
= 400 - 4
= 396

ntsais kaum sib txhawb (complementary angles) Ob lub ntsais kaum uas sib nxtiv ua ke muaj 90°.

Piv txwv:

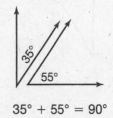

35° + 55° = 90°

leb muaj tus tshooj (composite number)
Tus leb loj dua 1 uas muaj ntau tshaj ob tug leb uas tshooj npaug tau.

Piv txwv:
factors ntawm 15: 1, 3, 5, 15
       15 yog leb muaj tshooj npaug.
factors ntawm 7: 1, 7
       7 tsis yog leb muaj tshooj npaug.

txheej xwm sib tshooj (compound event)
Txheej xwm uas yog koom los ntawm ob los yog ntau qhov txheej xwm ua ke.

Piv txwv:

Ntxeev sab muaj tob hau thaum pov txiaj npib thiab ntxeev sab muaj leb 1 yog txheej xwm sib tshooj.

paj sib tshooj (compound interest) Paj uas tau txais los ntawm cov nyiaj tso ntxiv rau cov paj yav tag los ua ke.

Piv txwv:
Yog tias koj muab $100 coj mus tso rau tus account khaws nyiaj uas yuav muaj paj sib tshooj yog 6% rau ib xyoos, koj yuav tau txais nyiaj $100 + (0.06 x 100) = $106 nyob xyoo thib ib thiab txais $106 + (0.06 x 106) = $112.36 rau xyoo thib ob.

zaj lus tshooj (compound statement) Zaj lus hais muaj qab muaj hau uas yog tau los ntawm muab ob zaj los yog ntau zaj lus los ua ke.

Piv txwv:
      10 ntau dua 5 thiab 10 tsawg dua 21.
      10 ntau dua 5 los yog 10 tsawg dua 5.

lub duab ces kaum (concave polygon)
Lub duab ua ces uas muaj ib los yog ntau txoj kab hla ces kaum pw tawm nyob sab nraud.

Piv txwv:

kev tej zaum yuav tshwm sim tau (conditional probability) Kev tej zaum txheej xwm B yuav tawm tau, yog hais tias txheej xwm A twb tshwm sim ua ntej lawm.

Piv txwv:
Yog koj paub tias pov lub txiaj npib thawj zaug ntawm ob zaug pov tawm los yog ko tw, qhov yuav tshwm sim tau tias dov kom tawm ob lub tob hau ces yog zero (zej) xwb. Tabsis, yog koj paub hais tias pov thawj zaug tawm los yog tob hau, qhov yuav tshwm sim ob lub tob hau yog $\frac{1}{2}$.

duab ua yias yeeb (cone) Lub duab yias yeeb uas muaj lub qab npoo kheej ua voj voog.

Piv txwv:

sib xws (congruent) Qhov loj me thiab tus yam ntxwv zoo sib luag zos.

Piv txwv:

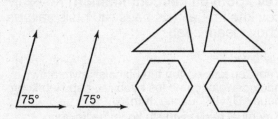

tsom ua duab yias yeeb (conic projection) daim tsom tawm uas siv lub duab yias yeeb los tam rau lub pob khoob kheej.

Piv txwv:

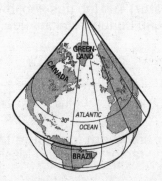

lus txuas (conjunction) Zaj lus muaj qab muaj qua uas muaj lo lus thiab los txuas.

Piv txwv:
    x > -2 thiab x < 5

Lub duab xwm fab xwm meem muaj 4 sab ntev ib yam thiab lub duab yog duab plaub ceg sib nte.

qhov tsis hloov pauv (constant) Yog qhov ntau tsawg uas tsis hloov li.

Piv txwv:

Nyob rau qhov kev sau tawm x + 7, 7 yog tus tsis hloov li.

txoj kab graph tsis hloov (constant graph) Txoj kab qhia uas nws lub hau ntawm cov kab tsis hloov pauv.

Piv txwv:

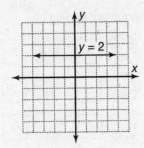

qhov tsis hloov pauv yam los sib piv (constant of proportionality) qhov ntau tsawg $\frac{y}{x}$ ntawm ob tug pauv x thiab y uas muaj qhov sib piv tsis hloov. Qhov no seem ntau yog siv tus niam ntawm k sau rau.

Piv txwv:

x	3	6	9	12
y	5	10	15	20

$k = \frac{5}{3}$

tus leb siv cia ntxeev (conversion factor) tus ntsuas kev sib npaug uas yog siv ntxeev yam ntau tsawg ntawm ib qho mus rau ib qho. Qhov no feem ntau yuav sau tawm ua leb faib.

Piv txwv:

12 inches = 1 foot; $\frac{12\ inches}{1\ foot}$

4 quarts = 1 gallon; $\frac{4\ quarts}{1\ gallon}$

duab ces kaum muaj kab lo (convex polygon) Lub duab ces kaum muaj cov kab lo lub duab sab hauv.

Piv txwv:

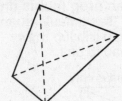

cov kab los sib txiav (coordinates) ib nkawm leb teeb kom muaj qab luag uas siv nrhiav cov kab sib txiav hauv daim npoo kab sib txiav.

Piv txwv:

(5, 6)
cov kab sib txiav

daim npoo cov kab sib txiav, ntsauv kab sib txiav (coordinate plane, coordinate system) ntsauv sib txiav ntawm cov kab tav toj thiab kab sawv ntsug thiab kab tav toj siv nrhiav thaj tsam.

Piv txwv:

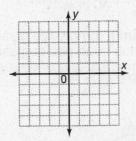

cov ntsais kaum sib xws (rau cov kab) (corresponding angles (for lines)) Cov ntsais kaum nyob rau tib sab ntawm txoj kab txiav uas mus tshuam rau ob los yog ntau txoj kab. Cov ntsais kaum sib xws yog sib haum thaum yog tias txoj kab txiav tav cov kab ua ib ntxiag.

Piv txwv:

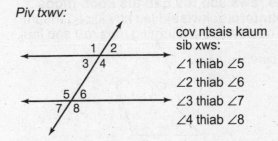

cov ntsais kaum sib xws:
∠1 thiab ∠5
∠2 thiab ∠6
∠3 thiab ∠7
∠4 thiab ∠8

cov ntsais kaum sib xws (nyob rau cov duab yuav luag zoo ib yam) (corresponding angles (in similar figures)) Kev muab cov ntsais kaum los tso rau cov duab yuav luag zoo sib xws.

Piv txwv:
△ABC ~ △XYZ

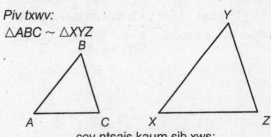

cov ntsais kaum sib xws:
∠ABC thiab ∠XYZ
∠BCA thiab ∠YZX
∠CAB thiab ∠ZXY

cov sab sib xws (corresponding sides)
Muab cov sab mus tso rau cov duab yuav luag zoo tib yam.

Piv txwv:

$\triangle ABC \sim \triangle XYZ$

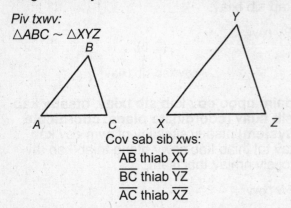

Cov sab sib xws:
$\overline{AB}$ thiab $\overline{XY}$
$\overline{BC}$ thiab $\overline{YZ}$
$\overline{AC}$ thiab $\overline{XZ}$

cosine (cosine)
Yog rau lub ntsais kaum ti x nyob rau lub duab peb ceg sab xis, lub cosine ntawm x, lossis cos(x), yog qhov ratio ntawm $\frac{\text{ces nyob sib ze}}{\text{hypotenuse}}$.

Piv txwv:

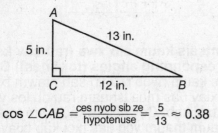

$$\cos \angle CAB = \frac{\text{ces nyob sib ze}}{\text{hypotenuse}} = \frac{5}{13} \approx 0.38$$

mus raws sab rov qab tus koob moos (counterclockwise)
Hau kev kiv tig thaum lub hau daim duab lem tig mus rau sab lauj.

Piv txwv:

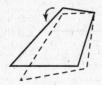

piv txwv ntaus rov qab (counterexample)
Qhov piv txwv uas qhia txog tias ib zaj lus tsis yog li hais.

Piv txwv:

zaj lus: Yog tias x • 0 = y • 0, thaum ntawd x = y.

piv txwv ntaus rov qab: 3 • 0 = 0 thiab 5 • 0 = 0, tab sis 3 ≠ 5.

Tus Kab ke Suav (Counting Principle)
Yog hais tias ib qhov txheej xwm tshwm sim tawm ua *m*, thiab qhov txheej xwm thib ob tuaj yeem tshwm sim ua *n*, thaum ntawd ob qho no tuaj yeem tshwm sim tawm ua ke yog *m* x *n*.

Piv txwv:

Muaj 2 txog kev tawm ntawm kev pov txiaj npib kom ntxeev thiab muaj 6 txoj kev tawm ntawm kev tig lub pob rau fab xab xeeb kaum. Lintawd yuav muaj 2 x 6, los yog 12, txog kev tawm rau ob yam khoom no tshwm sim ua ke.

yam tau txais sib tig (cross product)
Qhov tau txais los ntawm tus leb numerator nyob sab saum txoj kab quas ntawm ib tug ratio mus rau ib tug leb denominator sab hauv qab ntawm lwm tus ratio.

Piv txwv:

yam tau txais sib tig:

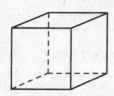

$1 \times 5 = 5$
$3 \times 2 = 6$

lub duab rau sab (cube)
Ib lub pob duab uas muaj 6-sab hu ua prism uas sab nraud ua ces xwm fab xwm meem sib haum ua ke.

Piv txwv:

peb tshooj (cubed)
Nce txog peb tshooj.

Piv txwv: 2 nce peb tshooj = 2^3 = 2 x 2 x 2 = 8

ntsuas txog yam nruab nrog (cubic unit)
Qhov ntsuas txog ntau tsawg hauv nruab nrog puag ncig, uas nyob li ib lub thawv xwm fab xwm meem siab ib unit.

Piv txwv:

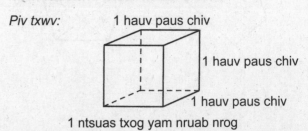

1 hauv paus chiv
1 hauv paus chiv
1 hauv paus chiv
1 ntsuas txog yam nruab nrog

yam kev ntsuas raws li yav thaud (customary system of measurement) Kev ntsuas keev siv nyob rau Teb Chaw Amesliskas xws li: inches, feet, miles, ounces, pounds, tons, cups, quarts, gallons, lossis lwm yam.

Piv txwv:

Lub Zos Park 50 Mais
Ncua ntev

Mis Nyuj
ntim taus 1 gallon

Mov 1 pound
qhov nyhav

lub duab ua tog raj (cylinder) Ib lub tog raj ob tog sib luag, ob lub qab ua voj voog kheej.

Piv txwv:

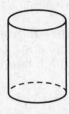

kev tsom duab ua voj voog (cylindrical projection) Kev tsom duab ntawv qhia toj roob hauv pes uas siv lub duab ua tog raj coj los sawv cev lub npoo pob khoob.

Piv txwv:

duab muaj kaum ces (decagon) Lub duab muaj 10 ces.

Piv txwv:

deci- (deci-) Yog ib lo lus qhia txuas tom hau ntev.

Piv txwv: 1 decimeter = $\frac{1}{10}$ meter

decimal (decimal) Kev siv leb nyob rau base-10 uas sau tom qab teev quas tus leb.

Piv txwv: 6.21 0.59 12.2 5.0

kev ntxiv rau tom qab teev quas (decimal addition) Kev sau ob lossis ntau tus leb ntxiv rau sab tom qab teev quas.

Piv txwv:

$$
\begin{array}{r}
1 \\
12.65 \\
+\ 29.10 \\
\hline
41.75
\end{array}
$$

kev sib faib leb muaj teev quas (decimal division) Faib ob tug leb uas muaj teev quas.

Piv txwv:

$$
\begin{array}{r}
1.25 \\
0.24\,)\overline{0.3000} \\
-24 \\
\hline
60 \\
-48 \\
\hline
120 \\
-120 \\
\hline
0
\end{array}
$$

kev tso npaug ntxiv (decimal multiplication) Kev suav npaug ntxiv ntawm ob lossis ntau tshaj tus leb uas muaj teev quas.

Piv txwv:

$$
\begin{array}{r}
2 \\
0.1\,3 \quad \text{2 tug leb tom qab ntxiv} \\
\times\ \ 0.7 \quad \text{1 tug leb tom qab ntxiv} \\
\hline
0.0\,9\,1 \quad \text{3 tug leb tom qab ntxiv}
\end{array}
$$

kev rho tawm tom qab teev quas (decimal subtraction) Kev rho tawm ob tug leb tom qab teev quas.

Piv txwv:

$$
\begin{array}{r}
13\ 12 \\
4\ \cancel{3}\ \cancel{2}\,10 \\
\cancel{5}\cancel{4}.\cancel{3}\cancel{0} \\
-\ 16.58 \\
\hline
37.72
\end{array}
$$

kev sau leb tom qab teev quas (decimal system) Kev siv tus base-10.

Piv txwv:

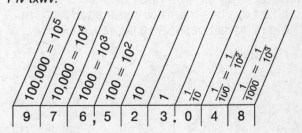

$100,000=10^5$	$10,000=10^4$	$1000=10^3$	$100=10^2$	10	1	$\frac{1}{10}$	$\frac{1}{100}=\frac{1}{10^2}$	$\frac{1}{1000}=\frac{1}{10^3}$
9	7	6,	5	2	3.	0	4	8

txoj kab qhia nqis zuj zus (decreasing graph) Txoj kab qhia uas lub hau qis zuj zus ntawm sab lauj mus rau sab xis.

Piv txwv:

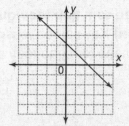

kev muab tswv yim los ntawm lwm qhov (deductive reasoning) Siv kev qab hau kom teeb ncauj lug tau zoo.

Piv txwv:
Yog muab ib txoj kab ces kaum rub mus phua ib lub duab plaub ceg xwm fab xwm meem, yuav tau txais ob lub duab peb ceg. Koj yuav paub lawm tias tag nrho peb lub ntsais kaum ntawm ib lub duab peb ceg coj los sib ntxiv yuav muaj 180°. Yog lintawd, ntsuas tag nrho cov ntsais kaum ntawm lub duab plaub ceg xwm fab xwm meem uas muaj kab phua natwd yuav muaj tshaj ob zaug ntawm lub duab peb ceg, los yog 2 x 180° = 360°.

teev cim siab qis (°) (degree) (°) Qhov kev ntsuas ntsais kaum.

Piv txwv: 1° yog $\frac{1}{360}$ ntawm tas nrho ib lub duab voj voog kiag xwb.

teev cim siab qis (degree) txog lub polynomial, nws qhov ntau tsawg ntawm tus exponent loj tshaj plaws ntawm tus hloov pauv.

Piv txwv:
Teev cim siab qis ntawm $5x^3 - 2x^2 + 7x$ yog 3.

deka- (deka-) Qhov npuas tom hau ntej uas muaj ntsiab tias 10.

Piv txwv: 1 dekameter =10 meters

tus leb nyob sab hauv leb faib (denominator) Tus leb sab hauv qab leb faib uas qhia txog tias muab cov sab saud faib rau tag nrho rau pes tsawg pawg.

Piv txwv:

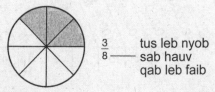

$\frac{3}{8}$ — tus leb nyob sab hauv qab leb faib

xwm txheej sib rub (dependent events) Xwm txheej uas thaum qhov tshwm sim tawm ntawm ib qho ua rau tuaj yeem muaj lwm qhov tshwm sim tau.

Piv txwv:
Lub npe Therese, Diane, thiab Jose raug muab nyias sau nyias rau ib daim menyuam ntawv. Ib daim menyuam ntawv raug nrho tawm khaws tseg. Ntxiv ntawd ho nrho ib daig thiab. Muaj qhov yuav tshwm sim tau tias daim ntawv muaj Diane's lub npe yuav raug rho tawm, yog tias daim muaj Therese npe twb raug rho tawm thawj zaug lawm, yog $\frac{1}{2}$.

tus hloov pauv sib rub (dependent variable) Tus hloov pauv uas tshwm sim nyob rau ib lub function.

Piv txwv:

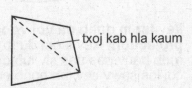

tus hloov pauv sib rub

$y = x + 2$

txoj kab hla kaum (diagonal) Nyob rau lub duab muaj ces kaum, txoj kab uas cab ib lub kaum rau ib lub kaum uas tsis nyob sib npuab.

Piv txwv:

txoj kab hla kaum

txoj kab hla plawv voj voog (diameter) Txoj kab, los yog txoj ncua, uas mus txiav hla lub plawv voj voog thiab nws ob tog kawg mus xaus rau lub ntug voj voog.

Piv txwv:

Txoj kab hla plawv voj voog

qhov sib txawv (difference) Qhov tau txais los ntawm kev rho ib tug leb tawm mus ntawm ib tug.

Piv txwv: 28 - 15 = 13

qhov sib txawv

cov zauv (digit) Cov cim uas siv los sau cov leb 0, 1, 2, 3, 4, 5, 6, 7, 8, thiab 9.

Piv txwv:
Nyob rau 5,847, cov zauv yog 5, 8, 4, thiab 7.

kev txav loj me (dilation) Kev txav ib lub duab kom loj los yog kom me xwm yeem ib yam.

Piv txwv:
Tus ncua leb siv txav lub duab plaub fab me kom loj tuaj yog 3.

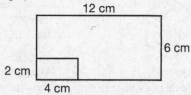

kev txawv txav raws ncaj (direct variation) Yog ob tug hloov pauv sib rub ua ke tau vim muaj ib tug ratio tsis pauv.

Piv txwv:

Sijhaum ua xuab moos (x)	1	2	3	4
ncua deb ua miles (y)	55	110	165	220

$$\frac{y}{x} = 55$$

kev xaiv ib qho (disjunction) Zaj lus muaj qab qua uas yog muaj lo lus lossis no los txuas.

Piv txwv:
x > 4 or x < -1
Peb tau mus saib yeeb duab lossis peb tau saib TV.

Yam ntxwv nthuav tawm (Distributive Property) Qhov tseeb tias a(b + c) = ab + ac.

Piv txwv: 3(6 + 5) = 3 · 6 + 3 · 5

tus cia faib (dividend) Tus leb uas los faib rau nyob hauv kev ua leb faib.

Piv txwv:

tus cia faib
8 ÷ 4 = 2

faib tu tau (divisible) Tuaj yeem muab faib raws lwm tus leb kom tau du lug tsis seem.

Piv txwv: 18 tuaj yeem faib tau rau 6, rau qhov 18 ÷ 6 = 3.

kev faib (division) Qhov kev ua leb uas qhia paub tias yuav muaj pes tsawg pob sib npaug zos los yog muaj pes tsawg nyob rau ib pob sib npaug.

Piv txwv:

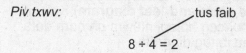

18 ÷ 6 = 3   18 ÷ 3 = 6
18 faib tau ua 6 pawg   18 faib tau ua 3 pawg
ib pawg yuav muaj 3.   ib pawg yuav muaj 6.

tus faib (divisor) Tus leb uas siv cia lwm tus muab coj los faib rau.

Piv txwv:

tus faib
8 ÷ 4 = 2

duab kaum ob ces (dodecagon) Duab ua ces kaum uas muja 12 sab.

Piv txwv:

daim graph qhia ob tshooj (double bar graph) Kev tso ob tug graphs, uas sib piv txog ob hom data.

Piv txwv:

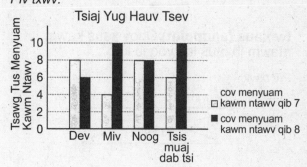

daim graph ob txog kab (double line graph) Ob txog kab graph sib koom, los sib piv ob hom data uas sib rub ua ke.

Piv txwv:

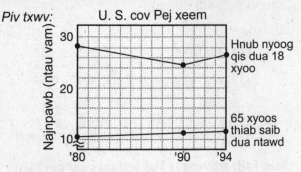

U. S. cov Pej xeem

Najnpawb (ntau vam)

Hnub nyoog qis dua 18 xyoo

65 xyoos thiab saib dua ntawd

daim diagram ob tshooj ceg thiab nplooj (double stem-and-leaf diagram) Kev sib piv nplooj-ceg-nplooj ntawm ob hom data nyob rau ib tug diagram.

Piv txwv:

Nplooj	Ceg	Nplooj
7 2 1	3	0 1 3
5 0 0	4	2 3
9	5	5 6 8
5 2 0	6	1 4

npoo (edge) Txoj kab uas ob sab duab los xaus ua ke.

Piv txwv:

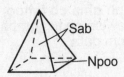

Sab

Npoo

tw xaus (endpoint) Qhov xaus kawg ntawm ib ntus los yog ib kab.

Piv txwv:

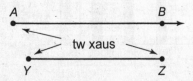

A   B

tw xaus

Y   Z

kev sib npaug (equality) Kev ua leb mathematical uas muaj sib npaug zos.

Piv txwv: 16 + 8 = 24   25 ÷ 5 = 5

qhov yam li yuav muaj tawm sib npaug (equally-likely outcomes) Qhov yuav muaj peev xwm tshwm sim tawm tau tib yam nkaus.

Piv txwv:

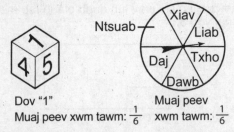

Ntsuab

Xiav
Liab
Txho
Dawb
Daj

Dov "1"
Muaj peev xwm tawm: $\frac{1}{6}$

Muaj peev xwm tawm: $\frac{1}{6}$

cov ratios sib npaug (equal ratios) Cov ratios rau npe qhov ntau tsawg tib yam.

Piv txwv: $\frac{2}{6}$, $\frac{1}{3}$, thiab $\frac{4}{12}$

tus sau ob sab sib npaug (equation) Tus sau txog kev tso xam leb mathematical uas qhia hais tias muaj ob sab sib npuag zos.

Piv txwv:

$14 = 2x$ $3 + y = 81$ $3 + 4 = 7$

duab peb ceg muaj sab sib npaug (equilateral triangle) Lub duab peb ceg uas nws cov sab sib nte ib yam tag nrho.

Piv txwv:

4   4

4

cov sau ob sab sib npaug sib xws (equivalent equations) Cov sau ob sab sib npaug uas yog muab tus hloov tib yam coj los pauv rau nws puav leej raug tib yam nkaus.

Piv txwv: x - 5 = 10 thiab x = 15

zaj sau sib xws (equivalent expressions) Ob zaj sau uas puav leej muaj qhov tau txais tib yam yog muab tus los txauv tib yam.

Piv txwv: 5(x + 1) thiab 5x + 5

fractions sib xws (equivalent fractions) Ob tug fractions uas sawv cev rau tib tug leb.

Piv txwv: $\frac{1}{2}$ thiab $\frac{8}{16}$

cov rates sib xws (equivalent rates) Cov rates rau npe rau tib tug amount (khoom ntsuas).

Piv txwv:

$$\frac{40 \text{ mais (miles)}}{2 \text{ xuabmoos}} \quad \text{thiab} \quad \frac{20 \text{ mais (miles)}}{1 \text{ xuabmoob}}$$

cov ratios sib xws (equivalent ratios) Saib *cov ratios sib npaug*.

kev kwv yees (estimate) Kev tsom xam kwv yees.

Piv txwv:

$$99 \times 21$$
$$\text{Kwv yees: } 100 \times 20 = 2000$$
$$99 \times 21 \approx 2000$$

Euler's formula (Euler's formula) Tus formula hais txog najnpawb cov phab (F), cov hau xaus (V), thiab cov npoo (E) ntawm ib lub duab ces kaum uas hais tias F + V- E =2.

Piv txwv:

Nyob rau lub duab peb ceg pyramid uas pom ntawm no,

$$\underset{\text{Phab}}{5} \quad + \quad \underset{\substack{\text{Cov hau} \\ \text{xaus}}}{5} \quad - \quad \underset{\substack{\text{Cov} \\ \text{npoo}}}{8} \quad = 2$$

ntaus nqi (evaluate) Txauv cov leb rau tus hloov pauv nyob rau zaj sau thiab tom qab ntawd ua kom yoojyim ntxiv uas yog ua raw sib teem zuj zus ntawm kev ua leb.

Piv txwv: Ntaus nqi 8(x - 3) thaum x = 10.

$$8(x - 3) = 8(10 - 3)$$
$$= 8(7)$$
$$= 56$$

leb khub (even number) Tus leb uas yog muaj 0, 2, 4, 6, los yog 8 nyob rau ib qho chaw twg.

Piv txwv: 16   28   34   112   3000

xwm txheej (event) Qhov tshwm sim tawm lossis ib co kev tshwm sim tawm los ntawm kev sim ua los yog txheej xwm.

Piv txwv:

Xwm txheej: Tau txais 3 lossis saib dua ntawd thaum muab ib lub pob rau fab xab xeeb kaum dov.

Qhov tuaj yeem yuav tshwm sim tawm tau ntawm qhov xwm txheej no: 3, 4, 5, 6

kev nthuav dav (expanded form) Kev sau ib tug leb exponential uas qhia kom pom tag nrho cov factors ib tug zuj zus.

Piv txwv: tus leb exponential 9^3
kev nthuav dav $9 \times 9 \times 9$

kev sim paub (experiment) Nyob rau probability (kev tuaj yeem tshwm sim tau), ib qho kev ua dab tsi yuav muaj qhov hais txog seb puas muaj hmoo tshwm sim tau.

Piv txwv:
lub kauj kiv tig   pov txiaj npib   cov sab pov lub pob rau fab

kev sim paub txog qhov tuaj yeem tshwm sim tau (experimental probability) Qhov tuaj yeem tshwm sim tau uas paub los ntawm data kev sim lossis nrhiav paub.

Piv txwv:
Muab ib hlab noob taum pov rau ib lub kauj 100 zaus. Raug tag nrho 23 zaug. Qhov kev sim paub txog yam tuaj yeem tshwm sim tau raug yog muaj $\frac{23}{100}$ = 23%.

exponent (exponent) Tus leb tshooj qhia txog kev tshooj rau zaum tas zaum dua.

Piv txwv: exponent
$$4^3 = 4 \times 4 \times 4 = 64$$

exponential function (exponential function) Lub function tsis ua kab ncaj uas tus leb exponent yog tus hloov pauv.

Piv txwv: $y = x^4$

tus sau cim exponential (exponential notation) Yog txoj kev sau tshooj ib tug najnpawb zaum tas zaum dua uas siv exponents.

Piv txwv: 2^8 5^2 9^3

kev sau expression (expression) Kab leb mathematical uas tau los ntawm cov hloov pauv thiab/los yog najnpawb thiab kev ua leb.

Piv txwv: 5(8 + 4)x - 3   2x + 4

cov ntsais kaum sab nraud (exterior angles) Thaum txoj kab tav toj mus txiav ob txog kab, cov ntsais kaum uas nyob rau sab nraum qaum ob txog kab no hu ua ntsais kaum sab nraud.

Piv txwv:

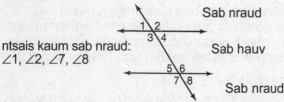

ntsais kaum sab nraud: ∠1, ∠2, ∠7, ∠8

phab (face) Ib phab npoo ntawm tej yam khov.

Piv txwv:

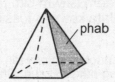

phab

factor (factor) Tus leb uas muab lwm tus leb faib tau du lug tsis seem.

Piv txwv:
Rau qhov 30 ÷ 5 = 6, 5 yog tus factor ntawm 30.

factorial (factorial) Tus factorial ntawm ib tug leb yog qhov tau txais sib ntshooj ntawm tus leb no rau tag nrho cov leb suav pib leb 1 los txog rau tus leb ntawd. Tus tsiaj cim factorial yog "!".

Piv txwv: 6 factorial = 6! = 6 x 5 x 4 x 3 x 2 X 1 = 720

ceg ncau factor (factor tree) Daim diagram qhia txog tus leb loj uas tawg ncau mus ua nws cov factors tseem ceeb.

Piv txwv:

72

② 36

② 18

② 9

③ ③

$72 = 2 \times 2 \times 2 \times 3 \times 3$

kev sib tw ncaj nrab (fair game) Kev sib tw uas cov koom sib tw txhua leej muaj peev xwm tuaj yeem yuav yeej sib npaug zos.

Piv txwv:
Kev sib tw ncaj nrab: Ob tug los sib tw sib pauv pov ib co pob rau fab xab xeeb kaum. Tus sib tw A tau txais khab nee rau qhov nws pov zaum 1, 3, los yog 5. Tus sib tw B tau txais khab nee rau qhov nws pov zaum 2, 4, los yog 6. Qhov kev tuaj yeem tau txais khab nee tshwm sim ntawm ob leeg yog $\frac{1}{2}$ rau tag nrho ob tug sib tw ntawd.

14   Hmong

pov (flip) Saib *reflection (kev pom rov)*.

foot (foot) Kev siv ntsuas ncua ntev luv raws li yav thaud uas yog muaj li 12 nti (inches).

Piv txwv:

1 foot

formula (formula) Tus kab ke qhia txog kev sib tshuam nyob rau yam muaj ntau tsaug.

Piv txwv: $A = bh$ $p = 4s$

fractal (fractal) Ib qho saib uas muaj qhov zoo sib xws. Yog muab ib qho piv txwv me coj mus rub kom loj tuaj, thaj tsam raug muab rub loj no yuav zoo xws li qhov piv txwv qub ua ntej muab los rub ntawd.

Piv txwv:

ib qho me (fraction) Tus leb muaj yam ntxwv $\frac{a}{b}$ uas hais txog ib qho me nyob rau ntawm qhov loj uas yog thaum muab qhov loj ntawv txiav phua ua ntau daim.

Piv txwv: $\frac{3}{5}$ $\frac{2}{7}$ $\frac{1}{4}$ $\frac{7}{10}$

kev muab qhov me los sib ntxiv (fraction addition) Kev ntxiv ob qho los yog ntau qhov me ua ke.

Piv txwv: $\frac{1}{3} + \frac{1}{4}$

$$\frac{1}{3} = \frac{1 \times 4}{3 \times 4} = \frac{4}{12}$$

$$\frac{1}{4} = \frac{1 \times 3}{4 \times 3} = \frac{3}{12}$$

$$\frac{1}{3} + \frac{1}{4} = \frac{4}{12} + \frac{3}{12} = \frac{4 + 3}{12} = \frac{7}{12}$$

kev muab qho me sib faib (fraction division) Kev faib ob qho me.

Piv txwv: $\frac{1}{6} \div \frac{3}{4} = \frac{1}{6} \times \frac{4}{3}$

$$= \frac{1 \times 4}{6 \times 3}$$

$$= \frac{4}{18} \quad \frac{2}{9}$$

kev muab qhov me ua tshooj (fraction multiplication) Kev ua tshooj ob qho los yog ntau qho me.

Piv txwv:

$$1\tfrac{1}{2} \times \tfrac{1}{4} = \tfrac{3}{2} \times \tfrac{1}{4}$$
$$= \tfrac{3 \times 1}{2 \times 4}$$
$$= \tfrac{3}{8}$$

kev muab qhov me rho tawm (fraction subtraction) Kev rho ob qho me.

Piv txwv:

$$\tfrac{3}{4} - \tfrac{2}{3}$$
$$\tfrac{3}{4} = \tfrac{3 \times 3}{4 \times 3} = \tfrac{9}{12}$$
$$\tfrac{2}{3} = \tfrac{2 \times 4}{3 \times 4} = \tfrac{8}{12}$$
$$\tfrac{3}{4} - \tfrac{2}{3} = \tfrac{9}{12} - \tfrac{8}{12} = \tfrac{9-8}{12} = \tfrac{1}{12}$$

kev ntxug (frequency) Cov zaus uas ib yam dab tsi tau tshwm sim tawm nyob hauv kev nrhiav paub. Saib *daim frequency chart.*

Daim chart los yog table kev ntxug (frequency chart or table) Lub table qhia txog leej khoom thiab kev ntxug uas tej khoom ntawd muaj tawm.

Piv txwv:

Kob ntawm lub Tsho	Kev ntxug
Dub	8
Av	2
Dawb	5
Xiav	4

kev kwm yees tom hauv ntej-tom qab (front-end estimation) Kev kwv yees uas tsuas yog tus zauv thib ib los yog thib ob ntawm ib tug leb tau muab los sib ntxiv, thiab qhov tau txais los tau muab kho uas yog ua raws li cov zauv tshuav seem.

Piv txwv:

Kev kwv yees ib-tug zauv tom hauv ntej-tom qab

```
   2,485
 + 3,698
 ─────────
   5,000   Muab cov zauv thib ib los sib ntxiv.
 + 1,200   485 + 698      1,200.
 ─────────
   6,200
```

function (function) Kev sib tshuam ntawm tus muab rau-tus tau txais uas yuav tau txais ib qho los ntawm qhov muab ib qho mus xwb.

Piv txwv:

$$y = x + 4 \qquad y = 2x \qquad y = x^2$$

tus Theorem (Fundamental Theorem of Arithmetic) Txhua tus leb loj dua 1 tuaj yeem muab sau tau li ib qho tau txais los ntawm cov leb chiv hauv paus.

Piv txwv:

$$24 = 2 \times 2 \times 2 \times 3$$
$$35 = 5 \times 7$$

gallon (gallon) Lub cuab yeej ntsuas li yav thaud uas muaj npaum li 4 quarts.

Piv txwv:

1 gallon

geometry (geometry) Ib ceg kev kawm paub ntawm leb mathematics uas kev sib tshuam ntawm cov teev, kab, duab, thiab cov duab khov tau muaj tshawb paub.

kev tuaj yeem tshwm sim geometric (geometric probability) Ib qhov kev tuaj yeem tshwm sim tau los ntawm kev ntsuas piv ob lub duab geometric.

Piv txwv:

Npoo ntawm ib lub duab xab xeeb kaum loj = 3 • 3 los yog 9 in²

Cheeb tsam npoo zas dub = 9 in² - 1 in² = 8 in²

Kev tuaj yeem tshwm sim tawm mus rau cheeb tsam zas dub = $\tfrac{8}{9}$

kev sib txuas geometric (geometric sequence) Kev sib txuas uas tus ratio ntawm tus cov leb txuas mus puav leej yog tib yam xwb li.

Piv txwv:

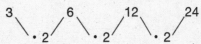

gram (gram) Qhov luj ntau tsawg nyob rau kev siv tus luj raws metric system.

Piv txwv:

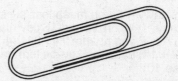

Qhov nyhav ntawm cov koob tais ntawv loj luj tau muaj kwv yees 1 gram.

graph (graph) Daim diagram uas qhia paub txog xov xwm uas tau muab teeb.

Piv txwv:

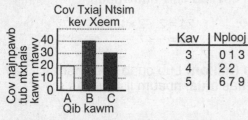

Cov Txiaj Ntsim kev Xeem

Kav	Nplooj
3	0 1 3
4	2 2
5	6 7 9

greatest common factor (greatest common factor (GCF)) Tus leb loj tshaj plaws uas siv faib ob tug los yog ntau tus leb tau du lug tsis seem dab tsi.

Piv txwv: 6 yog tus leb GCF loj tshaj plaws ntawm 12, 18, thiab 24.

hecto- (hecto-) Lo lus nyob ua ntej muaj lub ntsiab yog 100.

Piv txwv: 1 hectometer = 100 meters

ncua siab (height) Nyob rau lub duab peb ceg, duab plaub ceg, los yog duab pyramid, txoj kab sawv ntsug ncua ntawm lub qab uas cuab tim rau lub hau los yog sab hau. Nyob rau lub duab prism los yog duab tog raj, yog txoj kab ncua ntawm ob sab qab.

Piv txwv:

heptagon (heptagon) Lub duab muaj 7 ces kaum.

Piv txwv:

hexadecimal number system (hexadecimal number system) Kev siv leb nyob rau tus base-16.

Piv txwv:

Cov niam ntawv A-F yog muab loss siv sawv cev rau cov zauv 10-15. Tus base-16 cov niam ntawv najnpawb A3CE yog npaum li 41,934 (40,960 + 768 + 192 + 14) nyob rau kev siv tom qab teev quas (base-10).

Base 16	A	3	C	E
Leb qhia chaw	4096	256	16	1
Qhov tau txais	10 × 4096 = 40,960	3 × 256 = 768	12 × 16 = 192	14 × 1 = 14

hexagon (hexagon) Lub duab muaj 6 ces kaum.

Piv txwv:

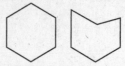

histogram (histogram) Daim bar graph uas cov hom kev xav paub muaj npaum ib yam li qhov kev loj me ntawm cov najnpawb.

Piv txwv:

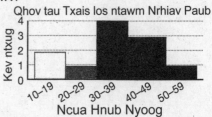

txoj kab tav toj (horizontal axis) Txoj kab tav toj ntawm ob txog kab uas daim bar graph pw rau los yog chaw ua cov kab sib txiav natwd nyob.

Piv txwv:

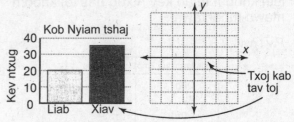

hypotenuse (hypotenuse) Sab cuab tim rau lub ntsais kaum sab xis ntawm lub duab peb ces sab xis.

Piv txwv:

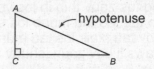

kev qhia (identity) Nyob rau ib qho kev ua leb, tus leb uas ua rau lwm tus leb nyob zoo li qub. yog tus qhia uas muab los ntxiv, vim tias a + 0 = a, yog tus qhia uas tshooj npaug vim tias a x 1 = a.

Piv txwv: 6 + 0 = 6
5 x 1 = 5

zaj lus hais yog tias-thaum ntawd (if-then statement) Ib zaj lus muaj qab muaj hau uas siv lo lus yog tias thiab thaum ntawd coj los qhia txog kev sib tshuam xeeb ntawm ob qho txheej xwm.

Piv txwv:

Yog tias ib lub duab peb ceg sab tsis sib luag, thaum ntawd nws cov sab yuav tsis muaj qhov sib xws.

leb fraction tsis yog (improper fraction)

Tus fraction uas nws tus leb nyob sab saud loj dua los yog sib npaug li tus leb sab hauv qab.

Piv txwv: $\dfrac{5}{2}$ $\dfrac{8}{8}$ $\dfrac{14}{3}$

daim graph nce zuj zus (increasing graph)

Daim graph uas ncua siab ntawm txoj kab nce zuj zus sab laug mus rau sab xis.

Piv txwv:

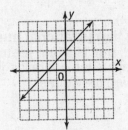

inch (inch)

qhov ntsuas ntev luv nyob rau kev ntsuas li yav thaud.

Piv txwv: Tub koob tais ntawv ntev $1\frac{3}{8}$ in. los yog $1\frac{3}{8}$".

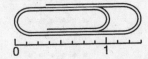

xwm txheej ywj siab (independent events)

Xwm txheej uas qhov tau txais los ntawm ib tug tsis ua licas rau qhov lwm tus tuaj yeem yuav tshwm sim tau.

Piv txwv:

Sau npe Therese, Diane, thiab Jose nyias rau nyias ib daim ntawv. Rho ib daim ntawv tawm thiab tso rov qab rau. Tas ntawd ho rho dua ib daig. Qhov tuaj yeem yuav tswm sim tau tias yuav rho tau Diane lub npe, vim hais tias Therese lub npe twb raug rho thawj zaug lawm, yog $\frac{1}{3}$.

tus hloov pauv ywj siab (independent variable)

Tus hloov pauv uas muab ntsaws rau ib tus function.

Piv txwv:

tus hloov pauv ywj siab
|
$y = x + 2$

kev muab tswv yim (inductive reasoning)

Kev siv tej pattern (yam saib pom) mam coj los ntaus nqi hais qhov kawg tau.

Piv txwv:

Kos ntau lub duab plaub ces kaum thiab ho ntsuas nws cov ntsais kaum.Txhua zaus ntsuas nws cov ntsais kaum puav leej muaj 360°. Qhov los hais tau kawg hais tias tas nrho cov ntsais kaum ntawm ib lub duab plaub ceg yog 360°.

kev tsis koob pheej (inequality)

Qhov sau raws kev leb mathematical uas siv <, >, ≤, los yog ≥.

Piv txwv:

$6 < 9$ $x + 3 \geq 21$ $2x - 8 > 0$

lub duab pw sab hauv ib lub (inscribed figure)

Lub duab uas nyob rau sab hauv ib lub thiab. Ib lub duab muaj ntau ces kaum yuav nyob sab hauv ib lub duab voj voog yog hais tias tag nrho nws cov hau kaum pw raws txoj kab voj voog ntawd.

Piv txwv:

Lub duab peb ceg kaum no
pw rau hauv lub voj voog.

integers (integers)

Cov leb tag nrho, nws cov ntxeev rov, thiab lub 0.

Piv txwv: ..., -3, -2, -1, 0, 1, 2, 3, ...

| -4 | -3 | -2 | -1 | 0 | 1 | 2 | 3 | 4 |

kev ntxiv integer (integer addition)

Kev muab ob los yog ntau tus leb los sib ntxiv.

Piv txwv:

$-5 + 8 = 3$ $-5 + (-8) = -13$

$5 + (-3) = 2$ $5 + 8 = 13$

Kev faib leb integer (integer division)

Kev muab ob tug leb faib.

Piv txwv:

$-40 \div 8 = -5$ $40 \div (-8) = -5$

$-40 \div (-8) = 5$ $40 \div 8 = 5$

kev tshooj npaug integer (integer multiplication)

Kev tshooj npaug ob tug los yog tshaj ob tug integers.

Piv txwv:

$-5 \cdot 8 = -40$ $-5 \cdot (-8) = 40$

$5 \cdot (-8) = -40$ $5 \cdot 8 = 40$

Kev rho tawm integer (integer subtraction)

Kev rho ob tug integers.

Piv txwv:

$-5 - 8 = -13$ $-5 - (-8) = 3$

$5 - (-3) = 8$ $5 - 8 = -3$

paj (interest) Nyiaj them rau kev siv nyiaj.

Piv txwv:
Dave tau tso $300 rau ib tug account khaws nyiaj. Dhau mus 1 xyoos muaj nyiaj tshaj ntxiv rau nws qhov nyiaj khaws yog $315. Hias tau tias nws tau txais $15 yog paj los ntawm qhov nyiaj nws tso khaws cia rau account.

ntsais kaum sab hauv (interior angles)
Yog txoj kab tav toj mus txiav ob txoj kab ib ntxaig, cov ntsais kaum nyob rov sab hauv ob txog kab no yog hu ua ntsais kaum sab hauv.

Piv txwv:

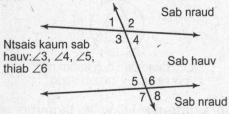

Ntsais kaum sab hauv: ∠3, ∠4, ∠5, thiab ∠6

Sab nraud
Sab hauv
Sab nraud

kab txiav koom (intersect) Kab mus txiav koom rau tib teev xwb.

Piv txwv:

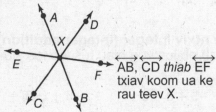

AB, CD *thiab* EF txiav koom ua ke rau teev X.

kem sib luag (interval) Ib kem nyob rau hauv cov kem dav sib luag ntawm daim bar graph los yog kab ntsuas graph.

Piv txwv:

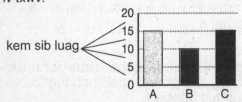

kem sib luag

kev ua leb rov qab (inverse operations)
Kev ua leb uas "rov tig" nws rov qab dua.

Piv txwv:

kev sib ntxiv thiab rho tawm

$2 + 3 = 5$
$5 - 3 = 2$

kev tshooj npaug thiab kev faib

$2 \cdot 3 = 6$
$6 \div 3 = 2$

kev hloov rov (inverse variation) Thaum ob tug hloov pauv muaj qhov sib tshuam xeeb los ntawm qhov tau txais uas tsis txawv txav.

Piv txwv:

x	1	2	3	4	5	6
y	60	30	20	15	12	10

$$x \cdot y = 60$$

leb tsis yog tiag (irrational number) Tus leb, xws li $\sqrt{2}$, uas tsis tuaj yeem yuav sau tau kom muaj tus leb seem los yog kawg tom qab ntawm teev quas.

Piv txwv: $\sqrt{5}$ π $-\sqrt{\frac{1}{2}}$

kev kos duab isometric (isometric drawing) Ib yam kev siv kos duab uas ua kev pom tseeb rau tus duab ntawd.

Piv txwv:

duab peb ceg sab sib nte (isosceles triangle) Lub duab peb ceg uas muaj qhov tsawg yog ob sab sib xws.

Piv txwv:

18   18
14

kilo- (kilo-) lo lus nyob tom hau ntej txhais tias 1000.

Piv txwv: 1 kilometer = 1000 meters

kab ib ntxaig (latitude) Kev ntsuas ua degrees qaum ntiaj teb los yog qab ntiaj teb suav mus ntawm txoj kab ruab rab lub ntiaj teb.

Piv txwv:

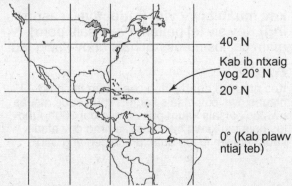

40° N
Kab ib ntxaig yog 20° N
20° N

0° (Kab plawv ntiaj teb)

© Scott Foresman Addison Wesley 6-8

least common denominator (LCD) (least common denominator (LCD)) The least common multiple (LCM) Tus tshooj npaug ua ke me tshaj plaws ntawm ob tug los yog ntau tus leb nyob sab hauv qab fraction.

Piv txwv: $\frac{1}{2}$ $\frac{2}{3}$ $\frac{3}{4}$

Tus LCM ntawm 2, 3, thiab 4 yog 12, lintawd tus LCD ntawm tus fractions yog 12.

Tus fractions muab LCD sau yog $\frac{6}{12}$, $\frac{8}{12}$ thiab $\frac{9}{12}$.

least common multiple (LCM) (least common multiple (LCM)) Tus leb ua ke uas me tshaj plaws ntawm kev tshooj npaug.

Piv txwv:
Tshooj npaug ntawm 3:3 6 9 12 15 18 21 24 ...
tshooj npaug ntawm 4:4 8 12 16 20 24 28 32 ...
12 yog tus LCM ntawm 3 thiab 4.

ces (leg) Txoj kab nyob raws sab xis ntawm lub duab peb ceg uas tsis yog txoj kab sab cuab tim hypotenuse.

Piv txwv:

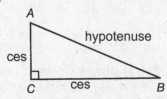

leb denominators sib xws (like denominators) Tus leb sab hauv qab fraction uas zoo tib yam nyob rau ob los yog ntau tshaj ob tug fractions.

Piv txwv:

$\frac{1}{8}$ $\frac{3}{8}$ $\frac{6}{8}$

leb denominators sib xws

tus leb sib xws (like terms) Tus leb uas tus hloov pauv tib yam tau muab tshooj rau tus exponent zoo tib yam.

Piv txwv: $3x^2$ thiab $9x^2$ 10y thiab 2y

txoj kab (line) Kab sau uas pib ib qho chaw mus tsis muaj qab xaus rau tog twg li. Ob teev sau tau ib txog kab.

Piv txwv:

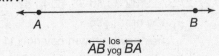

$\overleftrightarrow{AB}$ los yog $\overleftrightarrow{BA}$

graph kab (line graph) Txoj graph uas muaj txoj kab qhia txog kev txawv txav ntawm cov data, suam ntau yog piv rau lub sijhawm.

Piv txwv:

Company Kev muag Khoom

txoj kab sib xws (line of symmetry) Txoj kab uas txiav lub duab muaj kab sib xws raug faib ua ob nrab zoo ib yam.

Piv txwv:

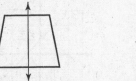

1 txoj kab sib xws   4 txog kab sib xws

kab nraj (line plot) Kev sau uas qhia txog tus yam ntxwv ntawm cov data uas muaj x nyob rau saum toj tus nqi raws txoj kab leb.

Piv txwv:

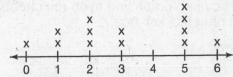

Najnpawb tub ntxhais kawm ntawv

ib ntu ntawm txoj kab (line segment) Ib ntu nyob rau txoj kab ncaj, uas muaj ob teev kawg. Ob teev hu tau ua ib ntu ntawm txoj kab.

Piv txwv:

$\overline{AB}$ los yog $\overline{BA}$

sib xws raws txoj kab (line symmetry) Ib lub duab muaj kev sib xws raws txoj kab yog hais tias nws tuaj yeem muab faib ua tau ob sab zoo ib yam.

Piv txwv:

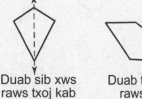

Duab sib xws   Duab tsis sib xws
raws txoj kab   raws txoj kab

equation ua kab (linear equation) Tus equation uas muaj txoj graph ua ib txog kab ncaj.

Piv txwv:

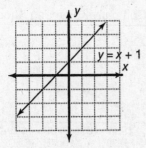

$y = x + 1$

function ua kab (linear function) lub function uas muaj txoj graph ua kab ncaj.

Piv txwv:

Qhov muab mus	Qhov tau txais
x	y
−2	3
−1	2
0	1
1	0
2	−1
3	−2

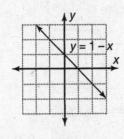

$y = 1 - x$

kev tsis koob pheej ua kab (linear inequality) Kab sau leb mathematical sentence uas muaj cov <, >, ≤ los yog ≥ uas lawv cov kab graph yog nyob rau cheeb tsam ntug txoj kab ncaj.

Piv txwv:

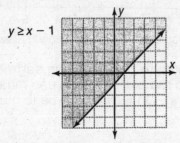

$y \geq x - 1$

liter (liter) Lub hauv paus yeem yam ua kua uas siv nyob rau kev ntsuas metric system.

Piv txwv:

Lam hwj 2-liter

txoj kab nqi raws lub ntiaj teb (longitude) Kev ntsuas ua degrees hnub tuaj los yog hnub poob piv rau txoj kab ncig sawv ntsug nruab nrab lub ntiaj teb.

Piv txwv:

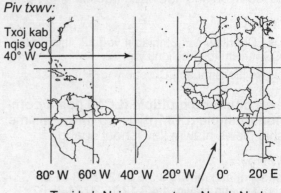

Txoj kab nqis yog 40° W

| 80° W | 60° W | 40° W | 20° W | 0° | 20° E |

Txoj kab Ncig sawv ntsug Nruab Nrab

ib feem plaub ncua nqis (lower quartile) Tus nqi nruab nrab ncua qis ntawm cov data.

Piv txwv:

27 27 27 29 32 33 36 38 42 43 62

↑ ib feem plaub ncua nqis   ↑ nqi nruab nrab   ↑ nqi ib feem plaub sab siab

tus leb qis tshaj plaws (lowest terms) Tus fraction uas muaj tus leb sab saud thiab tus leb sab hauv uas muaj tus tshooj ua ke tib tug nkaus xwb uas yog 1.

Piv txwv: $\frac{1}{2}$ $\frac{3}{5}$ $\frac{21}{23}$

ntau tsawg (mass) Qhov ntau tsawg uas ib lub dabtsi ntim tau.
Piv txwv:

Ib lub txiv raisin (txiv hmab ua cawv) muaj ntau tsawg 1 gram.

Ib nkawm khau ua kis las muaj ntau tsawg 1 kilogram.

qhov nrab (mean) Tag nrho cov nqi ntawm pawg data faib rau cov najnpawb ntawm cov nqi. Hu tau ua qhov nruab nrab thiab.

Piv txwv:

27 27 27 29 32 33 36 38 42 43 62

tag nrho: 396

najnpawb ntawm cov nqi: 11

qhov nrab: 396 ÷ 11 = 36

kev ntsuas txhaum (measurement error)

Kev tsis paub tseeb ntawm kev ntsuas. Qhov kev ntsuas txhaum loj tshaj plaws yog ib nrab ntawm qhov pib qab me tshaj plaws uas tau siv.

Piv txwv:

Rau qhov tias inch yog tus pib qab ntsuas me tshaj plaws, kev ntsuas txhaum loj tshaj plaws yog $\frac{1}{2}$ inch. Lintawd qhov ncua siab kom yog tiag yog nyob rau $5'5\frac{1}{2}''$ thiab $5'6\frac{1}{2}''$.

5' 6"

measure of central tendency (measure of central tendency)

Yog ib tug nqi uas muaj tag nrho pawg data ua tus leb.

Piv txwv:

Qhov nrab, nruab nrab, thiab mode yog kev ntsuas uas pom siv ntau ntsuas central tendency.

27 27 27 29 32 33 36 38 42 43 62

mode   nruab nrab

Qhov nrab = 396 ÷ 36 = 11

qhov nrab (median)

Tus nqi nyob nruab nrab ntawm pawg data uas muab teeb ua ib kab raws tus leb.

Piv txwv:

27 27 27 29 32 33 36 38 42 43 62

Qhov nrab

leb siv kev cim xeeb (mental math)

Kev tsom xam leb cim hauv nruab siab, uas tsis siv cwj mem thiab ntawv lossis lub tshuab laij leb.

Piv txwv:

2000	x	30
3 lub zej	+	1 lub zej = 4 lub zej
Xav: 2	x	3 = 6, ntxiv 4 zej
2000	x	30 = 60,000

meter (meter)

Lub qab ntsuas ntev luv nyob rau kev siv metric system.

Piv txwv:

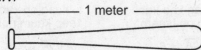

1 meter

Tus pas ntaus baseball ntev kwv yees yog 1 meter.

metric system (metric system)

Tus system kev ntsuas uas siv raws meter, gram, thiab liter.

Piv txwv:

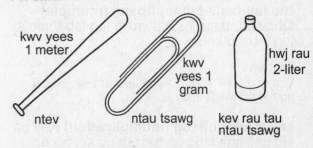

kwv yees 1 meter

kwv yees 1 gram

hwj rau 2-liter

ntev   ntau tsawg   kev rau tau ntau tsawg

teev nrab (midpoint)

Teev uas faib ib ntus mus ua ob ntus sib xws me dua qub.

Piv txwv: C yog teev nrab ntawm $\overline{AB}$.

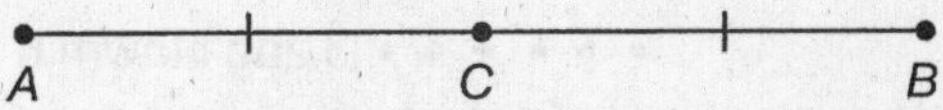

A   C   B

Ncua ntev ntawm $\overline{AC}$ = Ncua ntev ntawm $\overline{CB}$.

mile (mile)

Qhov pib qab ntsuas nyob rau kev ntsuas yav thaud uas muaj txog 5280 feet.

Piv txwv:

Ib mile yog ncua kev deb uas koj mus ko taw siv sijhawm 15 txog 20 nas this los yog khiav li 10 nas this.

milli- (milli-)

Lo lus nyob rau tom hauv ntej uas muaj $\frac{1}{1000}$.

Piv txwv: 1 millimeter = $\frac{1}{1000}$ meter

najnpawb sib xyaws (mixed number)

Ib tus najnpawb uas tau los ntawm tus leb thiab ib tus fraction.

Piv txwv: $3\frac{1}{2}$ $1\frac{3}{4}$ $13\frac{3}{8}$

mode (mode)

Tus nqi uas pom tawm heev tshaj nyob rau ntawm ib pawg data.

Piv txwv:

27 27 27 29 32 33 36 38 42 43 62

Nyob rau pawg data muab los no, 27 yog tus mode.

monomial (monomial) Kev sau leb algebraic uas muaj kiag ib lub npe xwb.

Piv txwv: $2x^2$ $5y$ x^3 -3

tus tau txais tshooj npaug (multiple) Qhov tau txais los ntawm ib tug leb thiab ib tug leb sib koom.

Piv txwv:

Vim yog 3 x 7 = 21, 21 yog tus tau txais tshooj npaug ntawm 3 thiab 7.

kev tshooj npaug (multiplication) Kev ua leb uas sua txog ob tug leb ua ke, hu ua factors, kom tau txais ib tug leb koom, hu ua qhov tau txais.

Piv txwv:

3 zag ntawm 6

$3 \times 6 = 18$

factors   qhov tau txais

yam ntxwv kev ua tshooj npaug (multiplication property) Yog tias *A* thiab *B* yog xwm txheej ywj siab, thaum ntawd qhov tuaj yeem yuav tshwm sim tawm tau ntawm ob tug niam ntawv tau muab sau ua $P(A$ thiab $B) = P(A) \times P(B)$.

Piv txwv:

tig zaum 1st: $P(\text{liab}) = \frac{1}{4}$

tig zaum 2nd: $P(\text{liab}) = \frac{1}{4}$

tig zaum 1st thiab zaum 2nd;

$P(\text{liab thiab liab}) = \frac{1}{4} \times \frac{1}{4} = \frac{1}{16}$

Yam Ntxwv kev Ua Tshooj Npaug (Multiplication Property of Equality) Yog tias a = fa, thaum ntawd ac - bc.

Piv txwv:

Nyob rau kab thib ob ntawm tus piv txwv hauv qab no, 2 yog tus tshooj npaug tag nrho rau ob sab tib si ntawm tus equation.

yog tias $\frac{1}{2}y = 4$

thaum ntawd $2 \times \frac{1}{2}y = 2 \times 4$

tus tshooj npaug rov qab (multiplicative inverse) Yog tias qhov tau txais ntawm ob tug leb yog 1, txhia tus leb yuav yog tus tshooj npaug rov qab rau lwm tus.

Piv txwv:

$\frac{1}{6}$ thiab 6 yog tus tshooj npaug rov qab vim tias $\frac{1}{6} \times 6 = 1$.

sib nyom (mutually exclusive) Yog hais tias ib tug nyob rau xwm txheej A los yog B tshwm sim tawm, thaum ntawd lwm tus yuav tsis muaj peev xwm tshwm tawm tau.

Piv txwv:

Yog tias huab cua sab nraud kub txog 90°, nws yuav tsis tuaj yeem los daus tau.

Yog tias ib lub duab ces kaum tsuas muaj peb sab ntug xwb, nws yuav tsis tuaj yeem muaj 4 lub ntsais kaum tau.

cov leb nqis (negative numbers) Cov leb me dua lub zej.

Piv txwv:

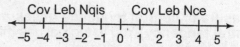

kev sib tshuam xeeb nqis (negative relationship) Ob pawg data muaj kev sib tshuam xeeb sab lauv yog thaum cov nqi data nyob rau ib pawg muaj qhov nce ua rau cov nqi lwm pawg nqis.

Piv txwv:

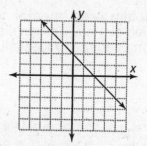

txoj kab nqis (negative slope) Txoj kab uas muaj qhov nqis zuj zus rau hauv.

Piv txwv:

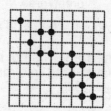

tus cag ob xab xeeb kaum nqis (negative square root) Tus tim cuab ntawm tus cag ob xab xeeb kaum tseem ntawm ib tug leb.

Piv txwv:

tus cag xab xeeb   tus cag ob xab
kaum ob tseem: xeeb kaum nqis:

$\sqrt{25} = 5$ $-\sqrt{25} = -5$

net (net) Ib daim npoo uas tuaj yeem muab kauv kom ua tau daim duab siab tau ua peb fab ib yam li lub prism.

Piv txwv:

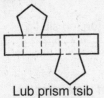

Lub prism tsib ceg kaum

Net ntawm lub prism tsib ceg kaum

nonagon (nonagon) Lub duab muaj 9 ces kaum.

Piv txwv:

equation tsis ua kab ncaj (nonlinear equation) Tus equation uas nws txoj graph ua txoj kab nkhaus tsis yog txoj kab ncaj.

Piv txwv:

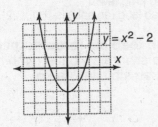

$y = x^2 - 2$

function tsis ua kab ncaj (nonlinear function) Lub function uas nws txoj graph tsis ua txoj kab ncaj vim tias yog hloov pauv sib npaug ntawm tus x tsis ua rau muaj kev hloov pauv tib yam ntawm qov tau txais nyob y.

Piv txwv:

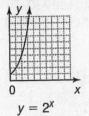
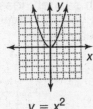
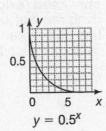

$y = 2^x$ $y = x^2$ $y = 0.5^x$

tsis muaj kev sib tshuam xeeb (no relationship) Ob pawg data tsis sib muaj kev sib tshuam xeeb yog tias nws tsis muaj kev sib tshuam xeeb nce los yog nqis li.

Piv txwv:

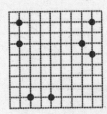

txoj kab muaj najnpawb (number line) Ib txog kab uas muaj najnpawb sau sib raws mus.

Piv txwv:

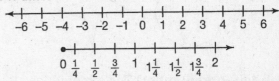

kev siv najnpawb-lus (number-word form) Kev sau najnpawb uas yog siv zauv leb sau thiab sau ua lus.

Piv txwv: 45 trillion (vam vam)   9 txhiab

sau ua najnpawb (numeral) Tus tsiaj cim ib tug najnpawb.

Piv txwv: 7   58   234

tus leb saum toj (numerator) Tus leb sab saum toj nyob rau tus fraction uas qhia paub tias qhov ntawd muaj pes tsawg npaug nyob rau tag nrho yam uas tau muaj los hais ntawd.

Piv txwv:

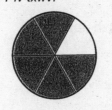

tus leb saum toj

$\frac{5}{6}$

ntsais kaum nthuav (obtuse angle) Lub ntsais kaum uas ntsuas tau ntau tshaj 90° thiab me tshaj 180°.

Piv txwv:

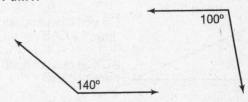

100°

140°

duab peb ceg nthuav (obtuse triangle)
Lub duab peb ceg uas muaj ntsais kaum nthuav.

Piv txwv:

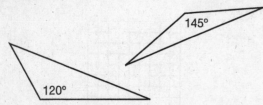

octagon (octagon) Lub duab muaj 8 ces kaum.

Piv txwv:

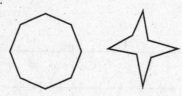

leb tab (odd number) Tus leb puv uas yog muaj 1,3,5, 7, los yog 9 nyob rau qhov chaw twg.

Piv txwv:

43   225   999   8,007

odds (odds) Tus ratio ntawm cov kev yuav tuaj yeem tshwm sim tau ntawm ib tug xwm txheej piv rau qhov kev yuav tsis tshwm sim tau.

Piv txwv:

Odds ntawm kev dov tau 3: 1 ntawm 5

Odds uas dov tsis tau 3: 5 ntawm 1

kev ua (operation) txheej txheem ua leb mathematics.

Piv txwv:

Plaub qho kev ua yoojyim: sib ntxiv, rho tawm, tshooj npaug, faib tawm

ces tim cuab (opposite leg) Nyob rau lub ntsais kaum ti sab ncaj, nws yog ces pw rov tav ntawm lub ntsais kaum los.

Piv txwv:

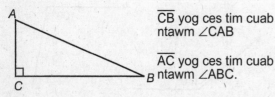

$\overline{CB}$ yog ces tim cuab ntawm $\angle CAB$

$\overline{AC}$ yog ces tim cuab ntawm $\angle ABC$.

leb sib tig (opposite numbers) Cov leb uas muaj ncua deb tim yam nrug ntawm lub zej (zero) nyob rau txoj kab leb tabsis nyias nyob rau nyias ib sab.

Piv txwv:

7 thiab -7 yog ob tug leb sib tig.

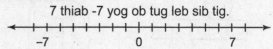

kab ke ua leb (order of operations)
Tus kab ke uas qhia txog qab luag kev ua leb nyob rau:
(1) ua cov leb nyob hauv lub kauj kaw kom tsawg,
(2) ua kom cov exponents tsawg, (3) tshooj npaug thiab faib ntawm sab laug mus rau sab xis, thiab
(4) ntxiv thiab nrho tawm ntawm sab laug mus rau sab xis.

Piv txwv:

Ntsuas $2x^2 + 4(x - 2)$ yog $x = 3$.

(1) ua qhov nyob hauv lub kauj kaw kom tsawg	$2 \cdot 3^2 + 4(3 - 2)$ $2 \cdot 3^2 + 4(1)$
(2) ua cov exponents kom tsawg	$2 \cdot 9 + 4$
(3) tshooj npaug thiab faib ntawm sab laug rau sab xis	$18 + 4$
(4) ntxiv thiab nrho tawm ntawm sab laug rau sab xis	22

nkawm leb teeb cia (ordered pair) Ib nkawm leb siv nrhiav ib tee nyob rau daim npoo cov kab sib txiav ua ke.

Piv txwv:

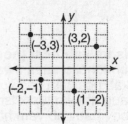

chiv keeb (origin) Teev ntawm lub zej nyob rau txoj kab sau leb, lossis teev (0, 0) uas ob txoj kab nyob rau ntawm coordinate system los sib txiav ua ke.

Piv txwv:

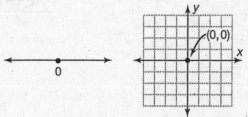

daim duab cov sab ncaj (orthographic drawing) Daim duab ib yam khoom uas saib tom sab hauv ntej, tom ib sab, thiab sab saud tuaj.

Piv txwv:

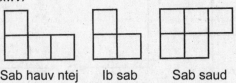

Sab hauv ntej   Ib sab   Sab saud

fiab (ounce) Ib qho pib kev ntsuas nyhav sib nyob rau kev ntsuas li yav thaud.

Piv txwv:

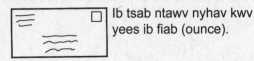

Ib tsab ntawv nyhav kwv yees ib fiab (ounce).

qhov tshwm tawm (outcome) Ib qho kev tuaj yeem tshwm tawm los ntawm kev sim lossis txheej xwm.

Piv txwv:

qhov tshwm tawm ntawm kev pov 2 lub Txiaj Npib:

lub txiaj 1	lub txiaj 2
tob hau	ko tw
tob hau	tob hau
ko tw	tob hau
ko tw	ko tw

Muaj 4 qho tshwm tawm tau. Ib qho yog tob hau, tob hau.

outlier (outlier) Ib tus nqi nyob rau ntawm ib pawg data, uas seem ntau nws txawv cov nqi lwm tus.

Piv txwv:

27   27   27   29   32   33   36   38   42   43   62
↑
outlier

txoj kab parabola (parabola) Txoj kab nkhaus zoo li tus niam ntawv U los yog nkhaus li tus U khwb saud rov hauv uas yog txoj graph ntawm lub function tshooj ob.

Piv txwv:

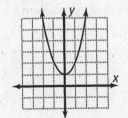 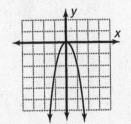

txoj kab ib ntxaig (parallel) Ob txog kab, ntu, los yog txoj kab nyob rau hauv daim npoo uas tsis los sib txiav.

Piv txwv:

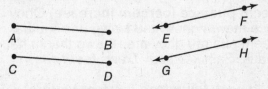

lub duab (parallelogram) Lub duab plaub fab uas nws cov sab sib tim cuab ncaj ib ntxaig thiab zoo sib xws.

Piv txwv:

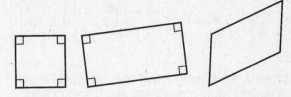

pentagon (pentagon) Lub duab muaj 5 ces kaum.

Piv txwv:

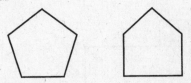

feem pua (percent) Tus ratio sib piv tus leb ua npaug rau 100.

Piv txwv:

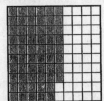

$$\frac{58}{100} = 0.58 = 58\%$$

qhov txawv raws feem pua (percent change) Qhov txawv ntau tsawg, nce los yog nqis, muab faib rau qhov ntau tsawg thaum hauv paus, uas sau ua feem pua piv rau qhov ntau tsawg thaum chiv keeb.

Piv txwv:

Nrhiav feem pua qhov hloov yog hais tias muab $1500 mus nqi luam thiab $75 yog qhov paj tau txais.

$\frac{75}{1500} = 0.05 = 5\%$ $75 yog 5% nce ntxiv.

Nrhiav feem pua qhov hloov yog hais tias ib qho khoom muaj nqi $50 coj mus muag luv nqi $10.

$\frac{10}{50} = 0.20 = 20\%$ $10 luv nqi yog 20% nqis.

feem pua nqis (percent decrease) Qhov nqis ntawm qhov ntau tsawg uas sau ua feem pua rau qhov ntau tsawg thaum hauv paus. Saib *kev pauv txawv feem pua*.

feem pua nce (percent increase) Qhov nce ntawm qhov ntau tsawg uas sau ua feem pua rau qhov ntau tsawg thaum hauv paus. Saib *kev pauv txawv feem pua*.

xab xeeb kaum zoo (perfect square) Kev xab xeeb kaum rau tag nrho ib tug leb.

Piv txwv:

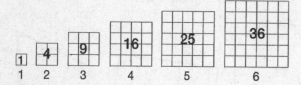

cheeb tsam ncig ntug (perimeter) Ncua ib ncig sab ntug ntawm lub duab sab nraud.

Piv txwv:

$$P = 5 + 2 + 6 + 4 + 11 + 6$$
$$= 34 \, \text{units}$$

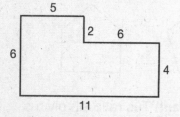

kev teeb tso (permutation) Kev teeb tso khoom uas qhov twg ua ntej qhov twg lawv qab yog qhov tseem ceeb.

Piv txwv:

Ib tug tub ntxhais kawm ntawv nyob rau ntawm pab no yuav raug xaiv tsa ua tus thawj coj hos muaj ib tug yauv raug xaiv tsa ua tus lwm thawj coj: Wendy, Alex, Carlos. Qhov kev teeb tso uas tuaj yeem ua tau yog:

Wendy—thawj coj, Alex—lwm thawj coj
Wendy— thawj coj, Carlos— lwm thawj coj
Alex— thawj coj, Wendy— lwm thawj coj
Alex— thawj coj, Carlos— lwm thawj coj
Carlos— thawj coj, Wendy— lwm thawj coj
Carlos— thawj coj, Alex— lwm thawj coj

Qhia paub: Nyias leej nyob saum toj no yog muab teeb tso sib txawv.

txoj kab sawv ntsug ncaj (perpendicular) Kab, ya kab, los yog ib ntu kab, uas mus sib txiav nyob rau lub ntsais kaum ncaj.

Piv txwv:

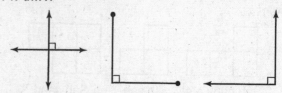

txoj kab teeb ncaj txiaj nruab nrab (perpendicular bisector) Txoj kab, ya kab, los yog ib ntu kab uas mus txiav ib ntu kab nyob rau ntu nruab nrab thiab teeb ncaj rau nws.

Piv txwv:

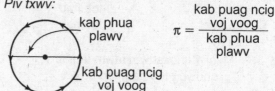

$\overleftrightarrow{DE}$ yog txoj kab teeb ncaj rau $\overline{AB}$.

pi (π) (pi (π)) Tus ratio ntawm txoj kab puag ncig voj voog rau nws txoj kab phua plawv voj voog uas yog: 3.14159265....

Piv txwv:

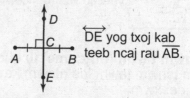

$$\pi = \frac{\text{kab puag ncig voj voog}}{\text{kab phua plawv}}$$

daim graph siv duab (pictograph) Daim graph uas siv tsiaj cim coj los sawv cev rau cov data.

Piv txwv:

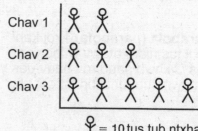

Tub Ntxhais Kam Ntawv hauv Chav

Chav 1
Chav 2
Chav 3

= 10 tus tub ntxhais kawm

tus nqi qhov chaw (place value) Tus nqi uas muab tso rau qhov chaw ntawm tug zauv leb.

Piv txwv:

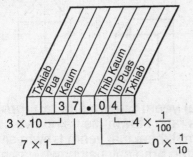

3×10

7×1

$4 \times \frac{1}{100}$

$0 \times \frac{1}{10}$

daim npoo (plane) Daim npoo tiaj uas ntev tsis muaj qhov kawg.

Piv txwv:

Txhim rau xav tawm daim npoo zoo licas, kom xav txog kev rub daim npoo table mus rau txhua txhia sab.

teev sib xws (point symmetry) Ib lub duab muaj teev sib xws yog hais tias nws tsis muaj qhov txawv txav tom qab muab tig mus rau 180° lawm.

Piv txwv:

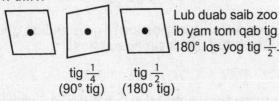

Lub duab saib zoo ib yam tom qab tig 180° los yog tig $\frac{1}{2}$.

tig $\frac{1}{4}$ (90° tig)

tig $\frac{1}{2}$ (180° tig)

polygon (polygon) Lub duab koo nyob sab hauv uas muaj cov kab txiav nyob rau nws qhov xaus kawg xwb.

Piv txwv:

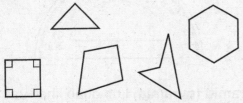

polyhedron (polyhedron) Lub duab khov uas nws cov sab ntsej muag yog lub duab polygons.

Piv txwv:

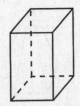

polynomial (polynomial) Nyob rau kev sau leb algebraic uas yog tag nrho cov npe nyob rau hauv.

Piv txwv: $x^2 + 2x - 3$ $5y - 15$

population (population) Tag nrho tej khoom sau ua ke nyob rau ib qho kev nrhiav paub.

Piv txwv:

Tag nrho 1000 lub npe ntawm cov neeg koom nyob koom haum raug muab sau rau daim ntawv me es muab coj los sib xyaws. Tas ntawd 100 daim ntawv me raug muab coj los rho xaiv thiab cov neeg ib puas leej no tau muab hu xov tooj mus nug kom paub. Cov neeg nyob rau qhov kev nug no tseem yog tag nrho 1000 leej ntawm lub koom haum.

cov leb nce (positive numbers) Cov leb loj dua zej.

Piv txwv:

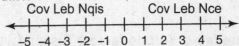

Cov Leb Nqis   Cov Leb Nce

−5 −4 −3 −2 −1 0 1 2 3 4 5

kev tshuam xeeb nce (positive relationship) Ob pawg data uas muaj kev tshuam xeeb nce yog thaum nws nkawd cov nqi data puav leej nce los yog puav leej nqis.

Piv txwv:

txoj kab qaij nce (positive slope) Txoj kab uas muaj qhov qaij nce rov saud.

Piv txwv:

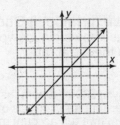

pound (pound) Qhov pib qab kev ntsuas raws li yav thaud uas yog muaj 16 ounces (fiab).

Piv txwv:

Mov 1 pound

tus leb tshooj (power) Tus leb exponent los yog tus leb tau txais los ntawm kev tshooj npaug rau tub leb pib qab kom ua exponent.

Piv txwv:

$16 = 2^4$ 2 yog tshooj npaug txog 4 zaug. 16 yog tau los ntawm 4 tshooj npaug ntawm 2.

qhov tseeb (precision) Kev raug tseeb ntawm kev ntsuas, uas yog tau txais los ntawm ib tus pib qab kev ntsuas los.

Piv txwv:

5'1" 61"

Tus pib qab kev ntsuas, inches, yuav raug tseeb dua tus pib qab kev ntsuas loj, feet.

prime factor (prime factor) Tus leb loj uas faib lwm tus leb kom tsis tshuav dab tsi seem.

Piv txwv: 5 yog tus factor tseem ceeb ntawm 35, vim tias 35 ÷ 5 = 7.

prime factorization (prime factorization) Kev sau ib tug leb uas yog qhov tau txais los ntawm cov leb tseem ceeb.

Piv txwv: 70 = 2 x 5 x 7

prime number (prime number) Tag nrho cov leb loj dua 1 uas muaj tus factors yog 1 thiab nws tus kheej xwb.

Piv txwv:

Cov leb primes pib txij 2, 3, 5, 7, 11, ...

peev chiv qab (principal) Qhov nyiaj muab coj mus khaws cia los yog muab qiv, uas tau txais them paj rau.

Piv txwv:

Dave tau tso nyiaj $300 rau tom tus account khaws nyiaj cia. Tom qab 1 xyoos qhov nyiaj txawv ntxiv ntawm nws tus account muaj yog $315. $300 yog cov nyiaj peev chiv keeb.

tus cag xab xeeb kaum nce (principal square root) Tus cag xab xeeb kaum ntawm ib tug leb nce.

Piv txwv:

cag xab xeeb kaum nce   cag xab xeeb kaum nqis

$\sqrt{25} = 5$ $-\sqrt{25} = -5$

---

prism (prism) Lub duab ua ces kaum ntev thiab cov sab ib ntxaig sib xws tag nrho.

Piv txwv:

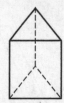

kev tuaj yeem tshwm sim tau (probability) Tus ratio ntawm tus najnpawb uas ib qho xwm txheej tuaj yeem tshwm sim tawm piv rau tag nrho cov najnpawb uas muaj peev xwm tawm tau.

Piv txwv:

Qhov tuaj yeem tshwm sim tawm ntawm kev tig tus leb 3 yog $\frac{1}{6}$.

Qhov tuaj yeem tshwm sim tawm ntawm qhov tsis tig tus leb 3 yog $\frac{5}{6}$.

qhov tau txais (product) Qhov tau txais ntawm kev tshooj npaug los ntawm ob tug leb los yog ntau tus leb.

Piv txwv:

Qhov tau txais

2 x 3 x 5 = 30

proportion (proportion) Tus equation qhia tias ob tug ratios sib npaug zos.

Piv txwv: $\frac{12}{34} = \frac{6}{17}$

protractor (protractor) Lub cuab yeej ntsuas ntsais kaum.

Piv txwv:

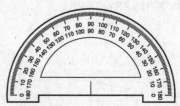

pyramid (pyramid) Lub duab khov uas muaj lub qab npoo ua ces kaum thiab cov phab sawv ntsug tag nrho puav leej yog daim peb ceg uas mus sib koom rau ib lub hau ua ke.

Piv txwv:

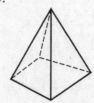

Pythagorean Theorem (Pythagorean Theorem) Nyob rau lub duab peb ceg uas muaj ntsais kaum ncaj uas muaj c yog ncua ntev ntawm txoj kab hla sab tim cuab hypotenuse hos a thiab b yog ncua ntev ntawm ob tug ceg duab, yuav muaj tias $a^2 + b^2 = c^2$.

Piv txwv:

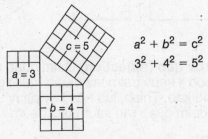

$$a^2 + b^2 = c^2$$
$$3^2 + 4^2 = 5^2$$

quadrants (quadrants) Plaub sab npoo tau los ntawm kev sib txiav ntawm cov kab tav toj thiab ntsug.

Piv txwv:

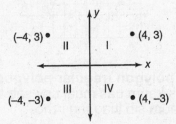

equation ob tshooj (quadratic equation) Tus equation uas muaj tus leb tshooj yog x^2.

Piv txwv:

$$y = x^2 + 3x - 12 \qquad y = 2x^2 + 7$$

function ob tshooj (quadratic function) Lub function uas muaj tus leb tshooj siab tshaj plaws ntawm x yog 2. Txoj graph ntawm lub function ob tshooj yog txoj kab parabola.

Piv txwv:

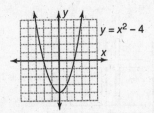

$y = x^2 - 4$

quadrilateral (quadrilateral) Lub duab uas muaj 4 sab kaum.

Piv txwv:

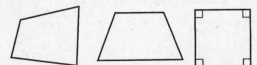

quart (quart) Qab pib kev ntsuas yam khoom ua kua ntau tsawg raws li thaum ub.

Piv txwv:

Ib quart mis nyuj

ib feem plaub (quartile) Ib nyob rau cov najnpawb uas faib ib pawg data ua plaub feem sib npaug zos.

Piv txwv:

27 27 27 29 32 33 36 38 42 43 62

ib feem plaub qis   nruab nrab   ib feem plaub siab

27, 33, thiab 42 yog peb qhov feem plaub ntawm pawg data no.

qhov tau los ntawm kev faib (quotient) Qhov tau txais los ntawm kev muab ib tug najnpawb los faib rau lwm tug najnpawb.

Piv txwv: qhov tau los ntawm kev faib

$$8 \div 4 = 2$$

tus cim cag (radical sign) Siv sawv cev rau tus leb muaj cag ob tshooj.

Piv txwv: $\sqrt{49} = 7$

radius (radius) Txoj kab tawm ntawm lub plawv ntawm lub voj voog mus rau ib teev twg nyob rau txoj kab voj voog.

Piv txwv:

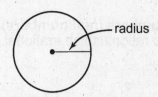

radius

kev lam cia li xaiv (random sample) Qhov piv txwv xaiv yuav uas hais tias ntxhua yam khoom nyob rau qhov yuav xaiv ntawd puav leej muaj peev xwm yuav raug xaiv tau tib yam nkaus.

Piv txwv:
Tag nrho 1000 lub npe cov neeg koom nyob rau lub koom haum raug muab sau rau daim ntawv me thiab muab cov ntawv me ntawd los sib xyaws. Tas ntawd muab 100 daim ntawv los rho thiab hu xov tooj mus nug paub cov neeg raug rho tau no. Tas nrho cov neeg nyob lub koom haum no puav leej muaj peev xwm yuav raug hu txhua tus yog li qhov no hu ua kev lam cia li xaiv.

ncua (range) Qhov txawv txav ntawm qhov siab tshaj plaws thiab qhov qis tshaj plaws nyob rau ib pawg data.

Piv txwv:

27 27 27 29 32 33 36 38 42 43 62

Tus ncua yog 62 - 27 = 35.

rate (rate) Tus ratio qhia txog tias qhov ntau tsawg thiab qhov kev ntsuas sib txawv ntawv muaj qho sib tshuam xeeb licas.

Piv txwv: $\dfrac{72 \text{ dollars}}{28 \text{ xuabmoos}}$ $\dfrac{55 \text{ miles}}{1 \text{ xuabmoos}}$

ratio (ratio) Ib qho kev sib piv ntawm ob qho ntau thiab tsawg, seem ntau sau ua fraction.

Piv txwv: $\dfrac{2}{1}$ 2 rau 1   2 : 1

rational number (rational number) Tus leb uas sau ua tau ib tug ratio ntawm ob tug leb. Cov leb, fractions, thiab ntau tus leb seem tom qab teev quas puav leej yog leb rational numbers.

Piv txwv:

Leb	Fraction	Leb seem tom qab teev quas
$-27 = \dfrac{-27}{1}$	$\dfrac{7}{8}$	$3.1 = 3\dfrac{1}{10} = \dfrac{31}{10}$

ray (ray) Ib ya txoj kab uas muaj ib tog xaus thiab ntev mus tsis kawg rau ib tog. Txoj ray yog hu raws nws lub hauv paus xaus.

Piv txwv:

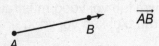

$\overrightarrow{AB}$

real numbers (real numbers) Tag nrho cov leb rational thiab irrational.

Piv txwv:

-27 $\dfrac{1}{2}$ 3.1

$\sqrt{5}$ π $-\sqrt{\dfrac{1}{2}}$

reciprocals (reciprocals) Ob tug leb uas muaj qhov tau txais ua ke yog 1.

Piv txwv:

$\dfrac{3}{5}$ thiab $\dfrac{5}{3}$ yog leb reciprocals vim tias $\dfrac{3}{5} \cdot \dfrac{5}{3} = 1$.

duab plaub ces ob sab ntev (rectangle) Lub duab plaub ces ob sab ntev sib tim cuab thiab cov ntsais kaum muaj 90°.

Piv txwv:

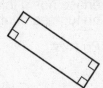

pom rov qab (reflection) Daim duab uas pom zoo li hauv daim iav muab "qaij tig" raw sib txog kab. Thiab, lub npe kev pauv uas tau yaws daim duab rau saum txoj qaum kab.

Piv txwv:

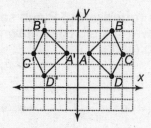

regular polygon (regular polygon) Lub duab ces kaum uas muaj cov sab thiab cov ntsais kaum sib luag tag nrho.

Piv txwv:

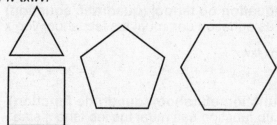

thaj chaw sib piv (relative position) Ib thaj chaw uas qhia tawm uas piv rau lwm thaj chaw.

Piv txwv:

City Lub Tsev Koom nyob ze rau Lub tsev saib ntawv Seltzer.

qhov seem (remainder) Tus leb uas me dua tus muaj coj los faib tom qab thaum kev ua leb faib tau tiav lawm.

Piv txwv:

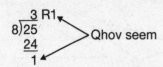

repeating decimal (repeating decimal) Tus leb seem uas muaj zoo ib yam tom qab teev quas los yog ib pawg zauv leb ib yam mus rau sab xis.

Piv txwv: $0.\overline{6}$ $0.\overline{123}$ $2.\overline{18}$

rhombus (rhombus) Lub duab plaub ceg plaub sab ntev tib yam.

Piv txwv:

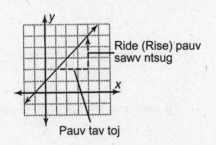

ntsais kaum ncaj (right angle) Lub ntsais kaum uas muaj 90 °.

Piv txwv:

duab peb ces ncaj (right triangle) lub duab peb ceg uas muaj ib lub ntsais kaum ncaj.

Piv txwv:

pauv sawv ntsug (rise) Ib txog kab nyob ib daim graph, kev pauv txoj kab sawv ntsug thaum txoj kab tav toj tau muaj ib qho pauv.

Piv txwv:

Ride (Rise) pauv sawv ntsug

Pauv tav toj

kiv tig (rotation) Lub duab uas tau muab "kiv tig," xws li lub log tsheb. Kuj tseem yog lub npe siv rau kev qhov hloov pauv uas tig lub duab.

Piv txwv:

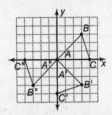

kev sib xws kiv tig (rotational symmetry) Ib lub duab uas muaj qhov sib xws thaum kiv tig yog hais tias tuaj yeem muab nws kiv yuav luag thoob ib ncig voj voog es tseem raug raws li nws tus qub duab.

Piv txwv:

Txhua lub duab puav leej muaj qhov sib xws kiv tig.

rounding (rounding) Kev kwv yees muab ib tug leb txav mus kom raug ib qho chaw muaj leb pauv kiag.

Piv txwv:

2153 muab txav kom mus rau	
Tus leb nyob ze kaum: 2150	Tus leb nyob ze ib puas: 2200

pawv tav toj (run) Nyob ib txog kab nyob rau daim graph, qhov pauv tav toj uas siv nrhiav qhov pauv sawv ntsug, los yog rise.

Piv txwv:

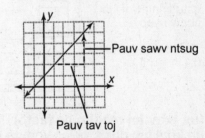

Pauv sawv ntsug

Pauv tav toj

piv txwv khaws sim (sample) Ib pawg data siv cia nrhiav paub tias ib qhov txheej xwm licas yuav tshwm sim tawm rau yav tom ntej.

Piv txwv:

Tag nrho 1000 lub npe ntawm cov neeg koom nyob rau lub koom haum raug muab sau rau daim ntawv me thiab muab cov ntawv me ntawd los sib xyaws. Tas ntawd muab 100 daim ntawv los rho thiab hu xov tooj mus nug paub cov neeg raug rho tau no. Qhov khaws cia sim yog 100 tus neeg uas tau raug hu xov tooj mus nug ntawd.

cov piv txwv tau txais tag nrho (sample space) Pawg uas tuaj yeem tau txais los ntawm ib qho kev sim paub.

Piv txwv:

Qhov tau txais ntawm kev pov 2 lub txiaj npib:

Lub txiaj 1	Lub txiaj 2
tob hau	ko tw
tob hau	tob hau
ko tw	tob hau
ko tw	ko tw

Qhov cov piv txwv tau txais tag nrho yog tob hau, ko tw; tob hau, tob hau; thiab ko tw, ko tw.

cim suav (nyob rau graphical) (scale (graphical)) Ntu cim sib luag zos nyob raws tus bar graph los yog txoj kab graph sawv ntsug, siv ntsuas ncua siab ntawm cov bars los yog cov kab.

Piv txwv:

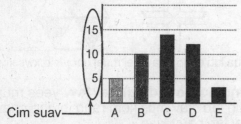

ntu ntev luv (scale (in scale drawings)) Tus ratio ntawm kev ntsuas ua raws kev kos duab mus piv rau qhov khoom tiag. Saib *tus ntsuas kev kos duab.*

tus ntsuas kev kos duab (scale drawing) Daim duab kos uas siv tus ntsuas kom ua daim duab loj ntxiv los yog me ntxiv tau nyob rau ib yam khoom.

Piv txwv:

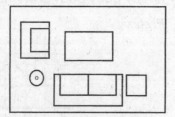

Kev kos duab nstuas ntawm lub chaw nyob

Tus ntsuas Ntsuas: 0.1 in. = 1 ft

tus txav loj me (scale factor) Tus ratio siv ua kom lub duab loj los yog ua kom me zoo ib yam.

Piv txwv:

$$\frac{10}{5} = 2$$
$$\frac{6}{3} = 2$$

10 cm
6 cm
3 cm
5 cm

Tus scale factor yog 2 rau qhov ua kom loj.

duab peb ces sab tsis sib luag (scalene triangle) Lub duab peb ceg uas muaj sab tsis sib nte ib yam.

Piv txwv:

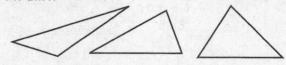

kev tso ri (scatterplot) Daim graph uas siv khawm data coj los ua teev qhia txog kev tshuam xeeb ntawm ob pawg data.

Piv txwv:

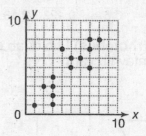

scientific notation (scientific notation) Tus leb sau ua tus seem tom qab teev quas loj dua los yog sib npaug li 1 thiab tsawg dua 10, muab tshooj npaug rau 10.

Piv txwv: $350,000 = 3.5 \times 10^5$

txauj (sector) Daim nplais duab uas los ntawm lub duab voj voog, siv nyob rau lub graph duab voj voog cia qhia cov suam pawg data piv rau tag nrho cov data ntawd.

Piv txwv:

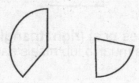

ntu txoj kab (segment) Saib *ib ntu ntawm txoj kab.*

txoj kab los txiav nruab nrab (segment bisector) Ib txoj kab, yav kab, los yog ntu txoj kab mus rau teev plawv ntawm ib ntu txoj kab.

Piv txwv:

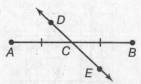

$\overleftrightarrow{DE}$ mus txiav nruab nrab $\overline{AB}$ nyob rau C.

kev sib txuas (sequence) Kev teeb tso cov leb uas mus kom raws paus ntsis.

Piv txwv:
kev sib txuas arithmetic

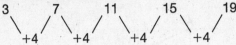

kev sib txuas geometric

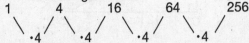

sab (side) Txhua yav kab uas los mus ua lub ntsais kaum. Thiab, txoj kab ntu nyob nruab nrab uas ua tau lub duab ces kaum.

Piv txwv:

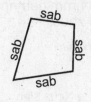

Sab-Ntshais Kaum-Ntsais Kaun (Side-Angle-Angle (SAA)) Tus kab ke siv los qhia tias cov duab peb ceg zoo sib xws uas yog muab nws cov sab ib yam los sib piv.

Piv txwv:

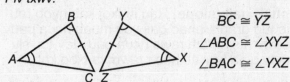

$$\overline{BC} \cong \overline{YZ}$$
$$\angle ABC \cong \angle XYZ$$
$$\angle BAC \cong \angle YXZ$$

ΔABC ≅ ΔXYZ Raws li tus kab ke ntawm SAA.

Sab-Ntsais Kaum-Sab (Side-Angle-Side (SAS)) Tus kab ke qhia txog saib cov duab peb ceg kaum puas zoo sib xws raws li kev sib piv nws cov sab zoo ib yam.

Piv txwv:

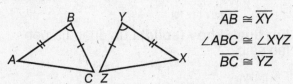

$$\overline{AB} \cong \overline{XY}$$
$$\angle ABC \cong \angle XYZ$$
$$\overline{BC} \cong \overline{YZ}$$

ΔABC ≅ ΔXYZ Raws li tus kab ke ntawm SAS.

Sab-Sab-Sab (Side-Side-Side (SSS)) Tus kab ke siv qhia seb lub duab peb ceg puas zoo sib xws uas yog muab cov sab sib xws los sib piv.

Piv txwv:

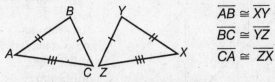

$$\overline{AB} \cong \overline{XY}$$
$$\overline{BC} \cong \overline{YZ}$$
$$\overline{CA} \cong \overline{ZX}$$

ΔABC ≅ ΔXYZ raws tus kab ke SSS.

cov zauv tseem ceeb (significant digits) Nyob rau qhov kev ntau tsawg uas tau ntsuas, yog cov zauv uas sawv cev rau kev ntsuas ntawd.

Piv txwv:

380.6700	Tag nrho cov zauv puav leej tseem ceeb.
0.0038	3 thiab 8 tseem ceeb, tabsis tsis muaj lub zej twg tseem ceeb li.

sib xws (similar) Muaj tus yam ntxwv zoo tib yam tabsis tsis yog yuav tsum muaj qhov loj me tib yam.

Piv txwv:

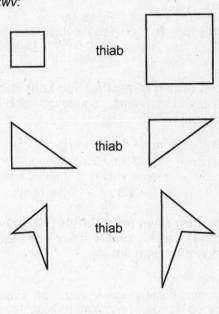

tus ratio uas sib xws (similarity ratio)
Tus ratio ntawm ncua sab ntev luv nyob rau cov duab sib xws tib yam.

Piv txwv:

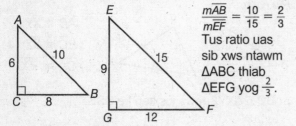

$$\frac{m\overline{AB}}{m\overline{EF}} = \frac{10}{15} = \frac{2}{3}$$

Tus ratio uas sib xws ntawm $\triangle ABC$ thiab $\triangle EFG$ yog $\frac{2}{3}$.

paj ncaj (simple interest)
Paj tau los ntawm cov nyiaj tso chiv thaum hauv paus xwb.

Piv txwv:

Ramon tso $240 nyob rau tus account uas muaj paj yog 6% tauj ib lub xyoo rau sijhawm 5 xyoos.

Nws yuav tau txais 240 • 0.06 • 5 = 72; $72 yog nyiaj paj ncaj tom qab 5 xyoos.

muab sib sau (simplified)
Kab leb sau uas tsis muaj cov tsiaj ntawv zoo tib yam nyob hauv.

Piv txwv:
$4x^4 + x^3 + x^2 - 8$	muab sib sau
$4x^4 + x^2 + 6x^2 - 8$	tsis muab sib sau, vim x^2 thiab $6x^2$ yog tsiaj ntawv zoo tib yam

ua kom tsawg (simplify)
Tso kom kab leb sau yoojyim ntxiv uas yog siv cov qab luag kev ua leb.

Piv txwv: Ua kom $3 + 8 \cdot 5^2$ tsawg.
$$3 + 8 \cdot 5^2 = 3 + 8 \cdot 25 \quad \text{(tshooj)}$$
$$= 3 + 200 \quad \text{(tshooj npaug)}$$
$$= 203 \quad \text{(siv ntxiv)}$$

kev xyaum raws (simulation)
Ib qhov kev sim xyuas uas siv nrhiav qhov kev muaj peev xwm tshwm sim tau.

Piv txwv:
Ib tug tub ua baseball ntaus .250. Yuav xyaum seb tus tub ua no tuaj yeem ntaus licas, tau muab ib lub kauj vab muaj plaub kem tig. Kev xyaum raws yuav raug siv los twv ua ntej tias tus pas ntaus pob yuav raug 2 lub nyob hauv kab lossis 3 nyob hauv kab.

sine (sine)
Rau lub ntsais kaum ti x nyob rau a lub duab peb ceg ncaj, lub sine ntawmf x, los yog $\sin(x)$, yog tus ratio ntawm $\frac{\text{ces sab tim cuab}}{\text{hypotenuse}}$.

Piv txwv:

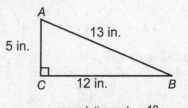

$$\sin \angle CAB = \frac{\text{ces sab tim cuab}}{\text{hypotenuse}} = \frac{12}{13} \approx 0.92$$

ncua siab qaij (slant height)
Nyob rau lub duab pyramid, txoj kab teeb ncaj rau ncua deb nram qab npoo kab rov lawm saum lub hau xaus.

Piv txwv:

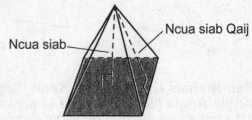

Ncua siab   Ncua siab Qaij

swb (slide)
Saib *translation*.

phab qaij (slope)
Rau ib txoj kab nyob rau ib tug graph, phab qaij yog muab ncua pauv sawv ntsug faib raws ncua pauv tav toj, siv piav qhia kev ntxhab ntawm ib txog kab.

Piv txwv:

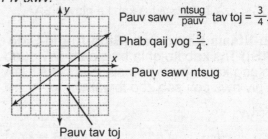

Pauv sawv $\frac{\text{ntsug}}{\text{pauv}}$ tav toj = $\frac{3}{4}$.

Phab qaij yog $\frac{3}{4}$.

Pauv sawv ntsug

Pauv tav toj

lub duab khov (solid)
Lub duab ua peb fab saib.

Piv txwv:

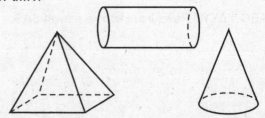

kev daws rau tus equation los yog qhov tsis sib npaug (solutions of an equation or inequality) Tus nqi leb ntawm ib tug pauv hloov uas ua rau ib tug equation los yog tus tsis sib npaug raug tau.

Piv txwv:

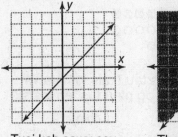 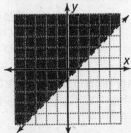

Txoj kab sawv cev los ntawm tus solutions rau y = x - 1.

Thaj tsam tsaus sawv cev tus solutions rau y > x - 1.

kev daws rau tus system (solution of a system) Tus hloov pauv uas ua rau tag nrho cov equations nyob rau tus system raug.

Piv txwv: y = x + 4
                y = 3x - 6

Nkawm leb (5, 9) daws tag nrho ob tug equations. Li ntawd, (5, 9) yog qhov daws nyob rau qhob leb system no.

daws (solve) Nrhiav kom tau kev daws ntawm tus equation lossis tus tsis sib npaug.

Piv txwv: Daws x + 6 = 13.
            x + 6 = 13
            x + 6 + (-6) = 13 + (-6)
            x + 0 = 7
            x = 7

duab pob kheej khov (sphere) Lub duab khov uas nws cov teev puav leej muaj ncua nrug deb lub plawv tib yam tas nrho.

Piv txwv:

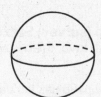

duab plaub fab xab xeeb kaum (square) Ib lub duab tag nrho plaub sab sib ncag thiab ncua ntev tib yam thiab muaj cov ntsais kaum yog 90°.

Piv txwv:

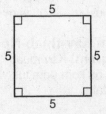

tshooj npaug (squared) Tau muab tshooj txog ob npaug.

Piv txwv: 3 tshooj npaug ob yog sau 3^2.
                $3^2 = 3 \times 3 = 9$

centimeter xwm fab xwm meem (square centimeter) Npoo ntsuas ua xwm fab xwm meem uas muaj cov sab yog 1-centimeter.

Piv txwv:

1 centimeter xwm fab xwm meem

inch xwm fab xwm meem (square inch) Npoo ntsuas xwm fab xwm meem uas muaj 1-inch ntawm cov sab.

Piv txwv:

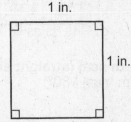

1 inch xwm fab xwm meem

cag tshooj ob (square root) Tus cag tshooj ob ntawm N yog tus leb uas thaum muab tshooj ob rau nws tus kheej yuav tau txais N. Thiab, tus cag tshooj ob ntawm ib tug leb twg yog ncua ntev ntawm ib sab ntawm ib lub duab plaub fab xwm fab xwm meem uas muaj npoo sib npaug li tus leb ntawd.

Piv txwv:

$9 \times 9 = 81$, lintawd 9 yog tus cag tshooj ob ntawm 81

$9 = \sqrt{81}$

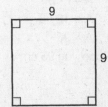

Npoo yog 81 square units.

daim foo standard (standard form) Txoj kev sau ib tug leb uas siv zauv.

Piv txwv:

Daim foo standard:	100,000,000
Foo lus:	Ib puas vam
Foo Najnpawb-lus:	100 vam

daim diagram Kav-thiab-Nplooj (stem-and-leaf diagram) Kev muab data tso saib uas siv zauv coj los ua kom pom tus yam ntxwv thiab kev faib pawg data.

Piv txwv:
Tus diagram qhia txog cov data: 33, 34, 34, 35, 40, 41, 46, 51, 51, 52, 53, 55, 58.

Kav	Nplooj					
3	3	4	4	5		
4	0	1	6			
5	1	1	2	3	5	8

Function txawv tu (step function) Lub function uas muab cov kab ke txawv coj los siv rau cov nqi input sib txawv. Txoj graph ntawm lub step function yog tau los ntawm kev muaj cov kab tsis sib txuas ua ke.

Piv txwv:

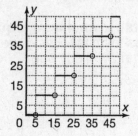

ntsais kaum ncaj (straight angle) Lub ntsais kaum muaj 180°.

Piv txwv:

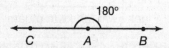

tus hloov (substitute) Kev hloov chaw ib tug pauv kom muab kiag tus nqi rau.

Piv txwv:
Siv tus formula A = l • w nrhiav npoo lub duab plaub fab muaj ncua ntev 12 cm thiab dav 8 cm.

A = l • w

A = 12 • 8   Hloov tso tus nqi rau

A = 96   ncua ntev thiab dav.

Npoo yog 96 cm².

kev rho tawm (subtraction) Kev ua leb uas qhia txog qhov txawv ntawm ob tug leb, los yog tias muaj pes tsawg tus seem nyob thaum muaj ib cov rho tawm lawm.

Piv txwv:

$$12 - 5 = 7$$

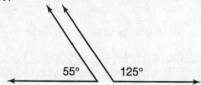

tag nrho (sum) Tus tau txais los ntawm qhov muab ob los yog ntau tus leb los sib ntxiv ua ke.

Piv txwv:

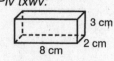

ntsais kaum ntxiv (supplementary angles) Ob lub ntsais kaum uas muab los sib ntsuas ua ke muaj txog 180°.

Piv txwv:

55°   125°

npoo (surface area (SA)) Cov npoo tag nrho ntawm txhua sab ntawm lub duab ces kaum tso ua ke.

Piv txwv:

Ob sab yog 8 cm rau 3 cm.
A = b • h = 8 • 3 = 24 cm²

Ob sab yog 8 cm rau 2 cm.
A = b • h = 8 • 2 = 16 cm²

Ob sab yog 2 cm rau 3 cm.
A = b • h = 2 • 3 = 6 cm²

Npoo ntawm lub duab rectangular prism (ntev puam fab) yog:

SA = 2(24 + 16 + 6)
    = 92 cm²

kev rhiav paub (survey) Saib sib xws raws txoj kab, teev sib xwb, thiab kev sib xws kiv tig.

Piv txwv:
Ib qho kev nrhiav paub uas tau ua tawm kom nrhiav tau tias hom kis las dab tsi yog hom tsoom tub txhais kawm ntawv nyiam dua ntais.

kev sib xws teeb tim (symmetry) Saib *line symmetry, point symmetry,* thiab *rotational symmetry.*

tus system ntawm cov equations ua kab (system of linear equations) Ob los yog ntau tus linear equations tsom xam ua ke.

Piv txwv:

y = x + 3
y = 4x - 15

lub T-table (T-table) Lub table qhia txog x- thiab y- tus nqi sib koos nyob rau ib tug equation.

Piv txwv:

$$y = 2x + 1$$

x	y
−2	−3
−1	−1
0	1
1	3
2	5

tus cim (tally) Tus record, siv kev kos, suav thaum ua kev nrhiav paub.

Piv txwv:

Tsheb	Tus cim
Tsheb Vaubkib	||||| |||
Tsheb Thauv	||||
Tsheb Xa Neeg	|||||	
Tsheb Thauj khoom	|||||
Tsheb Tub	|||

tsiaj cim (tally marks) Tus tsiaj cim siv rau kev khaws pawg data ntau cia. Ib tus tsiaj cim qhia txog tias tus nqi ntawd tau tawm ib zaug nyob rau ntawm pawg data.

Piv txwv: ||Ib ||||| Tsib

txoj kab tangent (tangent line) Txoj kab uas los txhuam rau lub voj voog nyob rau ib teev qhov twg.

Piv txwv:

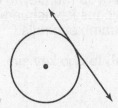

tangent ratio (tangent ratio) Ib lub ntsais kaum ti x nyob rau sab lub duab peb ceg ncaj, lub tangent ntawm x, los yog tan(x), yog tus ceg tim $\frac{cuab}{nyob}$ ze.

Piv txwv:

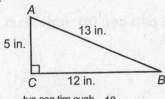

$$\tan \angle CAB = \frac{\text{tus ceg tim cuab}}{\text{nyob ze}} = \frac{12}{5} = 2.4$$

tus leb (term) Ib tug najnpawb nyob rau hauv kab leb. Thiab, yog ib tug nyob rau hauv tus polynomial uas yog tus najnpawb cim paub, tus pauv, los yog tus leb muab ntshooj npaug rau tus pauv los yog cov pauv. Cov pauv ntawd tuaj yeem muaj cov leb puv-leb exponents.

Piv txwv:

qab luag   3   7   11   15   19   23

leb

polynomial $2x^3 - x^2 + 3x - 5$

leb

tus leb kawg (terminating decimal) Tus leb sau kawg tom qab teev quas uas muaj cov leb zauv zoo li qub tas li.

Piv txwv: 3.5   0.599992   4.05

kev tso ua tsheej leej (tessellation) Kev tso ua tsheej leej mus los ntawm cov duab uas nyob rau hauv daim npoo kom tsis muaj qhov nrug los yog sib tshooj.

Piv txwv:

kev xav tias tuaj yeem tshwm sim tau (theoretical probability) Tus ratio ntawm cov najnpawb uas yuav tuaj yeem muaj qhov tshwm sim tau piv rau cov najnpawb tag nrho ntawm qhov yuav tawm tau.

Piv txwv:

Najnpawb kev kiv kauj tawm dawb/Tas nrho qhov yuav tawm tau = $\frac{3}{6} = \frac{1}{2}$

Vim tias ib nrab ntawm cov kem lub kauj tig yog dawb, qhov kev xav tias yuav tsum tawm tau dawb thiaj li yog $\frac{1}{2}$.

kev hloov txauv (transformation) Ib qhov kev pauv ntawm tus txheej xwm ntawm ib lub duab.

Piv txwv:

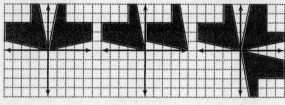

pom rov qab   txhais mus   kiv tig

txhais mus (translation) Daim duab uas tau swb dhau mus rau thaj chaw tshiab uas tsis vau lossis tsis tig rov. Thiab, lub npe ntawm qhov kev hloov txauv uas swb daim duab mus.

Piv txwv:

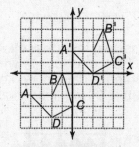

txoj kab tav toj (transversal) Ib txoj kab uas mus txiav ob txog kab lossis ntau txoj kab.

Piv txwv:

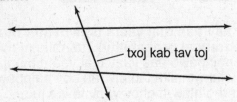

txoj kab tav toj

lub duab (trapezoid) Lub duab plaub ces uas muaj ob sab ib ntxaig sib luag zos.

Piv txwv:

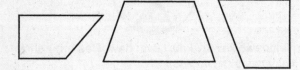

diagram tsob ntoo (tree diagram) Qhov diagram ua ceg tawm, zoo li tsob ntoo qhia txog qhov tau txais ntawm ib qho txheej xwm.

Piv txwv:

Pov 3 txiaj npib:

Txiaj 1	Txiaj 2	Txiaj 3	Cov kev yuav tshwm tawm tau yog:

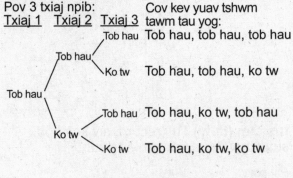
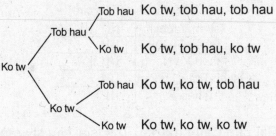

Tob hau   Tob hau, tob hau, tob hau

Ko tw   Tob hau, tob hau, ko tw

Tob hau   Tob hau, ko tw, tob hau

Ko tw   Tob hau, ko tw, ko tw

Tob hau   Ko tw, tob hau, tob hau

Ko tw   Ko tw, tob hau, ko tw

Tob hau   Ko tw, ko tw, tob hau

Ko tw   Ko tw, ko tw, ko tw

xws li (trend) Tus kev tshuam xeeb ntawm ob pawg data uas qhia paub txog nyob rau hauv tus kev tso ri. Saib tus kev tshuam xeeb nce, kev tshuam xeeb nqis, tsis muaj kev tshuam xeeb.

txoj kab xws li (trend line) Txoj kab uas yuav luag "haum" rau teev uas ua kom mus rau tus xws li nyob rau ntawm daim graph kev tso ri. Saib tus kev tshuam xeeb nce thiab kev tshuam xeeb nqis.

kev sim (trial) Ib qho kev sim.

Piv txwv:

Tig lub kauj xab   Pov lub txiaj
xeeb kaum ib zaug   npib ib zaug

duab muaj peb ceg (triangle) Lub duab ua peb ceg.

Piv txwv:

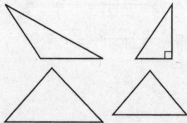

trigonometric ratios (trigonometric ratios)

Tus ratios ntawm sab ncua ntev ntawm lub duab peb ceg ncaj, npuas txog rau kev ntsuas cov ntsais kaum ti ntawm lub duab peb ceg.

Piv txwv:

$$\cos \angle CAB = \frac{\text{Ces nyob ze}}{\text{hypotenuse}} = \frac{3}{5} = 0.6$$

$$\sin \angle CAB = \frac{\text{Ces tim cuab}}{\text{hypotenuse}} = \frac{4}{5} = 0.8$$

$$\tan \angle CAB = \frac{\text{Ces tim cuab}}{\text{Ces nyob ze}} = \frac{4}{3} \approx 1.3$$

peb lub npe (trinomial)

Lub duab polynomial uas muaj peb lub npe.

Piv txwv: $2x^3 - x^2 + 3x$ $3x^2 + 2x - 4$

tig (turn)

saib *kev kiv tig*.

kev sib tw tsis ncaj nrab (unfair game)

Kev sib tw uas tsis yog txhua leej muaj peev xwm yuav yeej tau tib yam.

Piv txwv:

Kev sib tw tsis ncaj nrab: Muab ib nkawm pob xab xeeb kaum dov thiab muab qhov suav khab nee rau ib tug sib tw yog 2 txog 12. Ib tus sib tw yuav tau txais khab nee yog thaum muab nws qhov khab nee koom tig. Vim tias qhov khab nee tag nrho yog 2 txog 12 tsis muaj peev xwm yuav tig tau kom sib xws, cov sib tw thiaj li tsis muaj peev xwm yuav tau txais kev yeej sib npaug thiab yog li ntawd qhov ke sib tw no tsis ncaj nruab nrab.

hauv paus nqi (unit price)

lub hauv paus nqi uas tab rau ib yam khoom dab tsi.

Piv txwv:

$3.00 tauj pound $5.75 tau ib pob

hauv paus chiv (unit)

Kev tab rau ib yam dab tsi. Ib yam ntau tsawg lossis qhov ntau tsawg uas siv ua hauv paus ntawm kev ntsuas.

fraction pib (unit fraction)

Ib tug fraction uas muaj tus leb sab saum toj yog 1.

Piv txwv: $\frac{1}{4}$ $\frac{1}{2}$ $\frac{1}{7}$

rate pib (unit rate)

Ib tug rate uas tus leb thib ob ntawm qhov los sib piv ntawd yog ib tug unit.

Piv txwv: 25 gallons tauj 1 nasthis $\frac{55 \text{ miles tauj}}{1 \text{ xuab moos}}$

denominators tsis sib thooj (unlike denominators)

Tus denominators uas sib txawv nyob rau ob tug los yog ntau tus leb fractions.

Piv txwv:

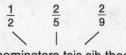

$\frac{1}{2}$ $\frac{2}{5}$ $\frac{2}{9}$

Denominators tsis sib thooj

ib feem plaub sab saud (upper quartile)

Tus leb nruab nrab ntawm ib nrab ntawm pawg data set rov saud.

Piv txwv:

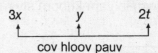

27   27   27   29   32   33   36   38   42   43   62

ib feem plaub   nruab nrab   ib feem plaub
sab hauv   sab saud

tus hloov pauv (variable)

Qhov ntau tsawg uas tuaj yeem pauv los yog txawv tau, seem ntau yog muaj ib tug niam ntawv los sawv cev rau.

Piv txwv:

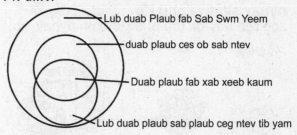

$3x$ y $2t$

cov hloov pauv

Venn diagram (Venn diagram)

Tus diagram uas siv thaj tsam duab los qhia txog kev tshuam xeeb ntawm yam khoom.

Piv txwv:

Lub duab Plaub fab Sab Swm Yeem

duab plaub ces ob sab ntev

Duab plaub fab xab xeeb kaum

Lub duab plaub sab plaub ceg ntev tib yam

hau sib cob (vertex)

Nyob rau lub ntsais kaum los yog lus duab ces kaum, teev uas ob sab ntug duab los sib txiav ua ke. Nyob rau lub duab ces kaum qhwv sab hauv, nws yog qhov sib txiav ntawm peb los yog ntau phab.

Piv txwv:

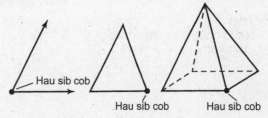

Hau sib cob   Hau sib cob   Hau sib cob

ntsais kaum sawv ntsug (vertical angles) Cov ntsais kaum nyob rau sab tim cuab ntawm qhov ob txog kab los sib txiav.

Piv txwv:

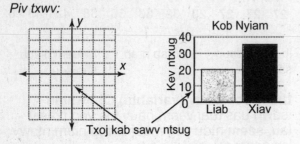

Ntsais kaum sawv ntsug:
∠1 thiab ∠3
∠2 thiab ∠4

txoj kab sawv ntsug (vertical axis) Txoj kab sawv ntsug ntawm ob txog kab uas muaj tus bar graph los yog tus npoo uas teeb cov kab sib txiav.

Piv txwv:

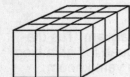

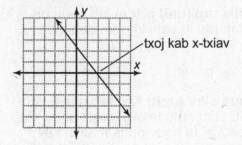

Txoj kab sawv ntsug

qhov ntim tau (volume) Qhov chaw ntau tsawg ntawm ib yam khoom siv rau.

Piv txwv:

$V = lwh$
$V = 4 \cdot 3 \cdot 2$
$V = 24$ cubic units

nyhav sib (weight) Kev ntsuas txog lub zog rub uas ua rau qhov khoom nyhav sib.

Piv txwv:

1 oz   1 lb   1 ton

leb pauv (whole number) Txhua tus leb nyob rau pawg {0,1,2,3,4,...}.

hom lus (word form) Txoj kev sau ib tus leb uas siv lus.

Piv txwv:

plaub caug   ib txhiab   rau
   tsib vam   vam

txoj kab x (x-axis) Txoj kab tav toj nyob rau daim npoo cov kab sib tshuam.

Piv txwv:

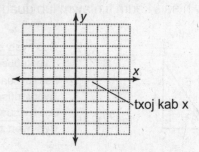

txoj kab x

txoj kab x-sib txiav (x-coordinate) Tus leb thib ib nyob ntawm txwm leb teem muaj qab muaj luag.

Piv txwv:

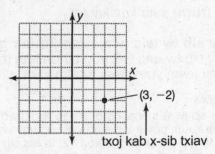

(3, −2)

txoj kab x-sib txiav

txoj kab x- mus txiav (x-intercept) Teev uas txoj graph ntawm ib tug equation los txiav txoj kab x tav toj.

Piv txwv:

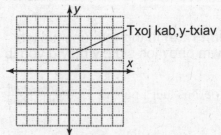

txoj kab x-txiav

txoj kab y (y-axis) Txoj kab sawv ntsug nyob rau hauv daim npoo kab sib txiav.

Piv txwv:

Txoj kab,y-txiav

txoj kab y-sib txiav (y-coordinate) Tus leb thib ob nyob rau txwm leb muaj qab muaj hau.

Piv txwv:

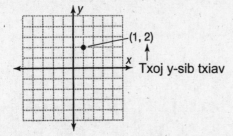

txoj kab y-mus txiav (y-intercept) Teev uas daim graph ntawm ib tus equation mus txiav txoj kab y.

Piv txwv:

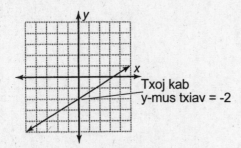

nrab daj (yard) Lub qab pib kev ntsuas raws li yav thaud uas yog muaj 3 feet.

Piv txwv:

txwm zej (zero pair) Tus leb thiab nws tus tig sab rov ntawm nws.

Piv txwv: 7 thiab -7   23 thiab -23

Yam Ntxwv Kev Sib Ntxiv ntawm lub Zej (Zero Property of Addition) Qhov tau txais los ntawm ib tus leb thiab nws tus leb tig rov qab yog 0.

Piv txwv: 3 + (-3) = 0

                    -8 + 8 = 0

Pilipino (Tagalog) Glossary

tiyak na posisyon (absolute position)
Ang kinalalagyan na ibinibigay bilang mga coordinate.

Halimbawa:

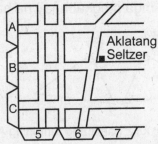

Ang B7 ay ang tiyak na posisyon ng Aklatang Seltzer.

tiyak na halaga (absolute value)
Ang layo ng isang bilang mula sa sero. Ang simbolo ng tiyak na halaga ay | |.

Mga halimbawa:

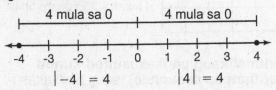

$|-4| = 4$ $|4| = 4$

anggulong agudo (acute angle)
Isang anggulo na ang sukat ay mas maliit sa 90°.

Mga halimbawa:

tatsulok na agudo (acute triangle)
Isang tatsulok na may tatlong anggulong agudo.

Halimbawa:

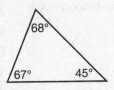

addend (addend)
Isang bilang na idinaragdag sa isa o mas marami pang mga bilang.

Halimbawa: 12 + 19 = 31

    addend   addend

pagdaragdag (addition)
Isang operasyon na nagbibigay ng kabuuang bilang kapag ipinagsasama-sama ang dalawa o mas maraming mga bilang.

Halimbawa:

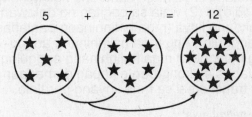

Katangiang Pagdaragdag ng Pagkaka-tumbas (Addition Property of Equality)
Kung ang a = b, samakatwid ay ang a + c = b + c.

Halimbawa:

Sa pangalawang linya ng halimbawa sa ibaba, ang 1 ay idinaragdag sa magkabilang panig ng equation.

Kung $x - 1 = 2$

samakatwid ay ang $x - 1 + 1 = 2 + 1$

                    $x = 3$

kabaligtaran ng pagdaragdag (additive inverse)
Ang kasalungat ng isang bilang.

Mga halimbawa: Ang kabaligtaran ng pagdaragdag ng -2 ay 2. Ang kabaligtaran ng pagdaragdag ng 5 ay -5.

katabing binti (adjacent leg)
Sa isang anggulong agudo ng isang tatsulok na may anggulong kwadrado (right triangle), ang binti na nasa isa sa mga panig ng anggulo.

Mga halimbawa:

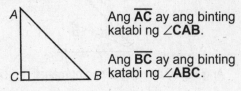

Ang $\overline{AC}$ ay ang binting katabi ng $\angle$**CAB**.

Ang $\overline{BC}$ ay ang binting katabi ng $\angle$**ABC**.

alhebra (algebra)
Isang sangay ng matematika kung saan ang mga kaugna-yang aritmetika ay sinasaliksik gamit ang mga variable (bilang na may iba't-ibang halaga) na kumakatawan sa mga bilang.

pagpapahayag sa alhebra (algebraic expression)
Isang pagpapahayag na naglalaman ng isang variable man lamang.

Mga halimbawa: n - 7   2y + 17   5(x - 3)

mga halinhinang anggulo (alternate angles)
Dalawang anggulong nilikha ng dalawang linya at ng isang transversal na nasa mga magkatunggaling panig ng transversal na (1) nasa pagitan ng dalawang itinakdang linya (mga kahaliling halinhinang anggulo) o (2) wala sa pagitan ng dalawang itinakdang linya (mga halinhinang panlabas na anggulo). Ang mga halinhinang anggulong panloob at mga halinhinang anggulong panlabas ay kongruente kapag dumadaan ang transversal sa mga linyang paralelo.

Mga halimbawa:

mga halinhinang anggulong panlabas:
Panlabas
∠1 at ∠8
Panloob
∠2 at ∠7

mga halinhinang anggulong panloob:
Panlabas
∠3 at ∠6
∠4 at ∠5

anggulo (angle)
Dalawang ray na may iisang dulo.

Halimbawa:

∠ABC, ∠CBA, o ∠B

anggulong humahati (angle bisector)
Isang ray na naghahati sa isang anggulo at ginagawa itong dalawang mga kongruenteng anggulo.

Halimbawa:

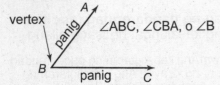

Ang $\overline{BD}$ ay ang anggulong humahati ng ∠ABC.

anggulo ng pag-ikot (angle of rotation)
Ang anggulo kung saan umiikot ang isang katawan sa panahon ng pag-ikot.

Halimbawa:

Ang anggulo ng pag-ikot ay 90°.

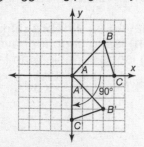

Anggulo-Panig-Anggulo (Angle-Side-Angle) (ASA)
Isang tuntuning ginagamit upang tiyakin kung ang mga tatsulok ay kongruente sa pamamagitan ng paghambing ng mga magkabagay na bahagi.

Halimbawa:

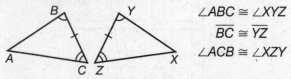

$∠ABC ≅ ∠XYZ$
$\overline{BC} ≅ \overline{YZ}$
$∠ACB ≅ ∠XZY$

ΔABC ≅ ΔXYZ gamit ang tuntuning ASA.

lawak (area)
Ang kalakihan ng kalatagan na tinatakpan ng isang katawan.

Halimbawa:

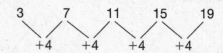

1 square unit

Lawak = 15 square units

aritmetikang pagkakasunod-sunod (arithmetic sequence)
Isang pagkakasunod-sunod kung saan ang pagkakaiba sa pagitan ng mga magkakasunod na termino ay palaging magkapareho.

Halimbawa:

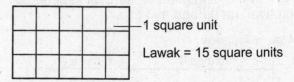

pagsasaayos (arrangement)
Ang ayos ng paglabas ng mga tao, mga titik, mga bilang o mga ibang bagay.

Halimbawa:

Ang lahat ng mga posibleng pagsasaayos ng tatlong hugis:

Pagsama-samang Katangian ng Pagdaragdag (Associative Property of Addition)
Ang katotohanan na ang pagbago ng pagkakagrupo-grupo ng mga addend ay hindi makababago sa kabuuan.

Mga halimbawa:

$$a + (b + c) = (a + b) + c$$
$$5 + (3 + 7) = (5 + 3) + 7$$

Pagsama-samang Katangian ng Multiplikasyon (Associative Property of Multiplication) Ang katotohanan na ang pagbago ng pagkakagrupo-grupo ng mga factor ay hindi makababago sa resulta matapos magmultiplika.

Mga halimbawa:
$$a(bc) = (ab)c$$
$$3 \times (4 \times 2) = (3 \times 4) \times 2$$

karaniwan (average) Tingnan ang *mean*.

axes (axes) Tingnan ang *x-axis* at *y-axis*.

talaguhitang may baras (bar graph) Isang talaguhitan na gumagamit ng mga patayo o pahalang na mga baras upang ipakita ang mga datos.

Mga halimbawa:

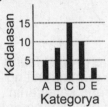 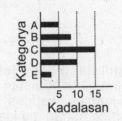

base (ng isang exponent) (base (of an exponent) Isang bilang na minultiplika sa kanyang sarili gamit ang bilang ng mga beses na ipinakita ng isang exponent.

Halimbawa:

base   exponent
$$6^2 = 6 \times 6 = 36$$

base (ng isang polygon) (base (of a polygon) Anumang panig (karaniwan ang panig na nasa ilalim), o ang haba ng panig na iyon.

Mga halimbawa:

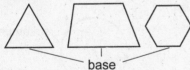

base

base (ng isang solido) (base (of a solid) Sa isang prism o silindro, ang isa sa dalawang paralelo at mga kongruenteng mukha. Sa isang piramide, ang mukha na nasa harap ng vertex. Sa isang kono, ang pabilog na mukha.

Mga halimbawa:

binary na sistema ng bilang (binary number system) Isang base-2 na sistema ng halaga ng puwesto (place value system).

Halimbawa:

Sa binary na sistema ng bilang, ang 1011 ay katumbas ng 11 sa decimal (base 10) na sistema ng bilang.

	Puwesto para sa mga walo	Puwesto para sa mga apat	Puwesto para sa mga dalawa	Puwesto para sa mga isa
Base 2	1	0	1	1
Halaga ng puwesto	8	4	2	1
Resulta matapos magmultiplika	$1 \times 8 = 8$	$0 \times 4 = 0$	$1 \times 2 = 2$	$1 \times 1 = 1$

$(1 \times 8) + (0 \times 4) + (1 \times 2) + (1 \times 1) = 8 + 0 + 2 + 1 = 11$

binomial (binomial) Isang polynomial na may dalawang termino.

Mga halimbawa: $4x^3 - 2x^2$ $2x + 5$

hatiin sa gitna (bisect) Hatiin ang isang anggulo o segment sa dalawang kongruenteng anggulo o segment.

Mga halimbawa:

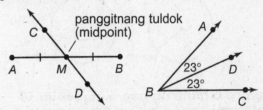

Hinahati ng $\overleftrightarrow{CD}$ ang $\overline{AB}$. Hinahati ng $\overrightarrow{BD}$ ang $\angle ABC$.

linyang hanggahan (boundary line) Sa isang talaguhitan ng isang linear inequality, ang linyang naghihiwalay sa mga tuldok na siyang mga kalutasan mula sa mga tuldok na hindi mga kalutasan.

Halimbawa:

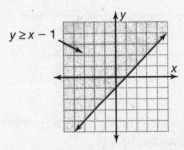

Ang $y = x - 1$ ay ang linyang hanggahan

box-and-whisker plot (box-and-whisker plot) Isang paraan ng pagpapakita kung paano ipinamamahagi ang isang koleksiyon ng mga datos. Ang halimbawa sa ibaba ay batay sa mga sumusunod na sampung iskor sa iksamen: 52, 64, 75, 79, 80, 80, 81, 88, 92, 99.

Halimbawa: Mga Iskor sa Iksamen

52   75 80   88   99

Ibabang quartile   Median   Itaas na quartile

kapasidad (capacity) Ang bolumen ng isang katawan, ibinibigay bilang likidong sukat.

Mga halimbawa:

500 ml   1 L   1 tasa   1 quart   1 galon

sentro, gitna (center) Ang tuldok na nasa hustong gitna ng isang bilog o globo.

Mga halimbawa:

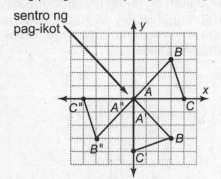

sentro   sentro

sentro o gitna ng pag-ikot (center of rotation) Ang tuldok kung saan pinaiikot ng pag-ikot ang isang katawan.

Halimbawa:

Ang pinagsimulan ay ang sentro ng pag-ikot.

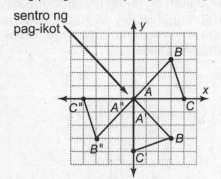

sentro ng pag-ikot

senti- (centi-) Isang unlapi (prefix) na nangangahulugang $\frac{1}{100}$.

Halimbawa: 1 sentimetro = $\frac{1}{100}$ metro

panggitnang anggulo (central angle) Isang anggulo na ang vertex ay nasa gitna ng isang bilog.

Halimbawa:

Ang tuldok C ay ang gitna ng bilog.

Ang ∠BCA ay isang panggitnang anggulo

bilog (circle) Isang patag na katawan na ang mga tuldok ay lahat magkaparehong layo mula sa kanyang gitna.

Halimbawa:

talaguhitang bilog (circle graph) Isang pabilog na talaguhitan na gumagamit ng mga kunyas (wedges) upang katawanin ang mga bahagi ng isang pangkat ng datos (data set). Ito'y tinatawag ding pie chart.

Halimbawa: Mga Paboritong Alagang Hayop

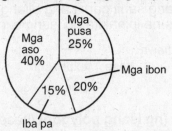

Mga pusa 25%

Mga aso 40%

Mga ibon

15% 20%

Iba pa

sirkumperensiya (circumference) Ang sukat paikot sa isang bilog.

Halimbawa:

sirkumperensiya

katawang nakapaikot (circumscribed figure) Isang katawang nagtataglay ng iba. Ang isang polygon ay nakapaikot sa isang bilog kung nakadikit ang bilog sa bawat panig nito.

Halimbawa:

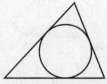

Ang tatsulok ay nakapaikot sa bilog.

pakanan (clockwise) Ang direksiyon ng pag-ikot kapag ang ibabaw ng isang katawan ay lumiliko sa kanan.

Halimbawa:

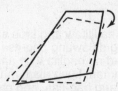

pagkumpul-kumpol (clustering) Isang paraan ng pagtantiya kung saan ang mga bilang na humigit-kumulang na pareho ay tinuturing na wari sila'y pareho.

Halimbawa:
26 + 24 + 23 ay humigit-kumulang na 25 + 25 + 25, o 3 x 25.

katuwang (coefficient) Isang palagian (constant) na ginagamit sa pagmultiplika ng isang variable.

Halimbawa: katuwang (coefficient)   variable

12y

kombinasyon (combination) Isang grupo ng mga piniling bagay kung saan ang pagkakaayos ay hindi mahalaga.

Halimbawa:
May dalawang estudyanteng pipiliin mula sa grupong ito upang maging miyembro ng lupon: David, Juanita, Kim.

Ang mga posibleng kombinasyon ay:
David, Juanita   David, Kim   Juanita, Kim

Pansinin: Ang kombinasyon na "David, Juanita" ay katulad ng kombinasyon na "Juanita, David."

panlahat na panghatimbilang (common denominator) Isang panghatimbilang na magkapareho sa dalawa o higit pang mga hatimbilang.

Halimbawa:

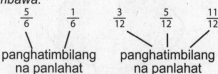

$$\frac{5}{6} \quad \frac{1}{6} \quad \frac{3}{12} \quad \frac{5}{12} \quad \frac{11}{12}$$

panghatimbilang   panghatimbilang
na panlahat   na panlahat

panlahat na factor (common factor) Isang bilang na isang factor ng dalawa o higit pang mga bilang.

Halimbawa:
Ang 4 ay isang panlahat na factor ng 8, 12 at 20.
$$8 = \mathbf{4} \times 2$$
$$12 = \mathbf{4} \times 3$$
$$20 = \mathbf{4} \times 5$$

panlahat na multiple (common multiple) Isang bilang na isang multiple ng bawat isa sa dalawa o higit pang takdang mga bilang.

Halimbawa:
mga multiple ng 3: 3 6 9 **12** 15 18 21 **24** 27 ...
mga multiple ng 4: 4 8 **12** 16 20 **24** 28 ...
Ang 12 at 24 ay dalawang mga panlahat na multiple ng 3 at 4.

Pagpalit-palit na Katangian ng Pagdaragdag (Commutative Property of Addition) Ang katotohanan na ang ayos ay walang epekto sa kabuuan ng dalawa o higit pang mga bilang.

Mga halimbawa $a + b = b + a$
$$18 + 23 = 23 + 18$$

Pagpalit-palit na Katangian ng Multiplikasyon (Commutative Property of Multiplication) Ang katotohanan na ang ayos ay walang epekto sa resulta ng multiplikasyon ng dalawa o higit pang mga bilang.

Mga halimbawa: $ab = ba$
$$4 \times 7 = 7 \times 4$$

mga magkabagay na bilang (compatible numbers) Mga pares ng mga bilang na maaaring kuwentahin nang madali.

Mga halimbawa: 30 + 70   40 ÷ 4   25 + 75

pagpupunan (compensation) Ang estratehiya ng pang-isip na matematika kung saan pinipili ang mga bilang na malapit sa mga bilang sa isang problema, at pagkatapos ay inaakma ang sagot upang pagpunan ang mga piniling bilang.

Halimbawa: $99 \times 4 = (100 - 1) \times 4$
$$= (100 \times 4) - (1 \times 4)$$
$$= 400 - 4$$
$$= 396$$

mga magkakabagay na anggulo (complementary angles) Dalawang anggulo na kapag dinagdag ang kanilang sukat ay 90° ang makukuha.

Halimbawa:

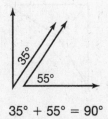

$$35° + 55° = 90°$$

composite na bilang (composite number)
Isang buong bilang na mas malaki sa 1 at
may higit sa dalawang factor.

Mga halimbawa:

Ang mga factor ng 15: 1, 3, 5, 15
　　　Ang 15 ay isang composite na bilang.
Ang mga factor ng 7: 1, 7
　　　Ang 7 ay hindi isang composite na bilang.

pinagsama-samang pangyayari (compound event) Isang pangyayari na siyang
kombinasyon ng dalawa o higit pang nag-
iisang mga pangyayari.

Halimbawa:

 at

Ang makakuha ng kara sa pag-itsa ng barya at
ang paglitaw ng 1 sa pag-itsa ng dice ay isang
pinagsama-samang pangyayari.

**pinagsama-samang interes (compound
interest)** Interes batay sa puhunan at sa
dating interes.

Halimbawa:

Kung nagdeposito ka ng $100 sa isang savings
account sa bangko na kumikita ng 6% na ang
interes ay pinagsasama-sama taun-taon, magkakaroon ka ng $100 + (0.06 x 100) = $106 sa
unang taon at ng $106 + (0.06 x 106) = $112.36
sa pangalawang taon.

**pinagsama-samang pahayag (compound
statement)** Isang may lohikang pahayag na
nilikha sa pamamagitan ng pagdugtong ng
dalawa o higit pang mga pahayag.

Mga halimbawa:

　　　Ang 10 ay mas malaki sa 5 *at* ang 10 ay
　　　mas maliit sa 21.

　　　Ang 10 ay mas malaki sa 5 *o* ang 10 ay
　　　mas maliit sa 5.

**malukong na polygon (concave poly-
gon)** Isang polygon na may isa o higit pang
mga diyagonal na nasa labas ng pigura.

Halimbawa:

**may-pasubaling probabilidad (condi-
tional probability)** Ang probabilidad na
mangyayari ang isang pangyayari B, dahil
nangyari na ang pangyayari A.

Halimbawa:

Kung alam mo na lilitaw ang krus sa panguna
hing pag-itsa ng dalawang pag-itsa ng barya,
ang probabilidad ng paglitaw ng dalawang kara
ay sero. Gayunman, kung alam mo na lilitaw
ang kara sa unang pag-itsa, ang probabilidad na
lilitaw ang dalawang kara ay $\frac{1}{2}$.

kono (cone) Isang solido na may isang
bilog na base.

Halimbawa:

magkatumbas (congruent) May magkaparehong laki at hugis.

Mga halimbawa:

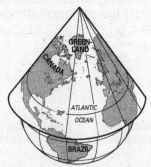

conic projection (conic projection) Isang
projection ng mapa na gumagamit ng hugis
kono upang kumatawan sa isang kalata-
gang globo (spherical surface).

Halimbawa:

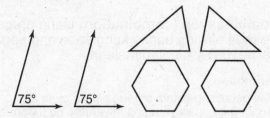

pagkakasabay (conjunction) Isang may
lohikang grupo ng mga pahayag na pinag-
durugtong ng salitang *at*.

Mga halimbawa:

　　　x > -2 at x < 5

　　　Ang isang parisukat ay may 4 na panig
　　　na pantay-pantay ang haba *at* ang isang
　　　parisukat ay isang rektanggulo.

palagian (constant) Isang dami na hindi nagbabago.

Halimbawa:

Sa pagpapahayag sa alhebra na x + 7, ang 7 ay isang hindi nagbabagong bilang.

palagiang talaguhitan (constant graph) Isang talaguhitan kung saan ang taas ng linya ay hindi nagbabago.

Halimbawa:

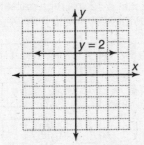

palagian ng proporsiyonalidad (constant of proportionality) Ang dami na $\frac{y}{x}$ para sa dalawang variable na x at y na ang pagkakaugnay (ratio) ay hindi nagbabago. Ang titik na k ay karaniwang palatandaan nito.

Halimbawa:

x	3	6	9	12
y	5	10	15	20

$k = \frac{5}{3}$

paktor ng pagpapalit (conversion factor) Isang pagkakatumbas sa pagsusukat na ginamit upang palitan ang mga dami mula sa isang yunit papunta sa iba. Ito'y kadalasang ipinapahayag bilang hatimbilang.

Mga halimbawa:

12 pulgada = 1 talampakan; $\frac{12\ pulgada}{1\ talampakan}$

4 quart = 1 galon; $\frac{4\ quart}{1\ galon}$

maumbok na polygon (convex polygon) Isang polygon na ang lahat ng diyagonal ay nasa loob ng pigura.

Mga halimbawa:

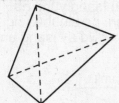 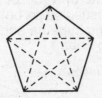

mga coordinate (coordinates) Isang pares ng mga bilang sa isang pinag-ayus-ayos na pares na ginagamit upang mahanap ang isang tuldok sa isang coordinate plane.

Halimbawa:

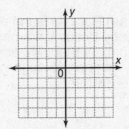

coordinate plane, coordinate system (coordinate plane, coordinate system) Isang sistema ng mga nagsasalikop na pahalang at patayong linya ng bilang (number lines) na ginamit upang mahanap ang mga tuldok.

Halimbawa:

mga magkatugong na anggulo (para sa mga linya) (corresponding angles (for lines)) Ang mga anggulo na nasa parehong panig ng isang transversal na bumabagtas sa dalawa o higit pang mga linya. Ang mga magkatugong na anggulo ay magkatumbas (congruent) kapag ang transversal ay bumabagtas sa mga linyang paralelo.

Halimbawa:

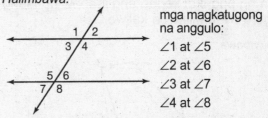

mga magkatugong na anggulo:

∠1 at ∠5

∠2 at ∠6

∠3 at ∠7

∠4 at ∠8

mga magkatugong na anggulo (sa mga magkatulad na pigura) (corresponding angles (in similar figures)) Mga magkabagay na anggulo sa mga magkatulad na pigura.

Halimbawa:

△ABC ~ △XYZ

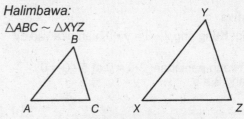

mga magkatugong na anggulo:

∠ABC at ∠XYZ

∠BCA at ∠YZX

∠CAB at ∠ZXY

mga magkatugong na panig (corresponding sides) Mga magkabagay na panig sa mga magkatulad na pigura.

Halimbawa:

$\triangle ABC \sim \triangle XYZ$

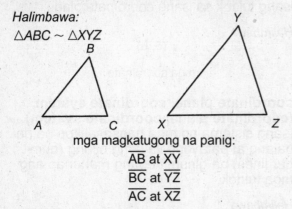

mga magkatugong na panig:
$\overline{AB}$ at $\overline{XY}$
$\overline{BC}$ at $\overline{YZ}$
$\overline{AC}$ at $\overline{XZ}$

cosine (cosine) Para sa isang anggulong agudo x sa isang tatsulok na may anggulong kwadrado (right triangle), ang cosine ng x, o cos(x), ay ang pagkakaugnay na (ratio) $\frac{\text{katabing binti (adjacent leg)}}{\text{hypotenuse}}$.

Halimbawa:

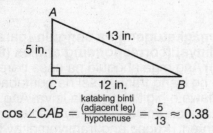

$$\cos \angle CAB = \frac{\substack{\text{katabing binti} \\ \text{(adjacent leg)}}}{\text{hypotenuse}} = \frac{5}{13} \approx 0.38$$

pasaliwa (counterclockwise) Ang direksiyon ng pag-ikot kapag ang ibabaw ng isang pigura ay lumiliko sa kaliwa.

Halimbawa:

halimbawang panlaban (counterexample) Isang halimbawang nagpapakita na ang isang pahayag ay mali.

Halimbawa:

pahayag: Kung ang x • 0 = y • 0, samakatwid ay ang x = y.

halimbawang panlaban: 3•0 = 0 at 5 • 0 = 0, ngunit ang 3 ≠ 5.

Prinsipyo ng Pagbilang (Counting Principle) Kung ang isang kalagayan ay maaaring mangyari nang *m* na paraan, at ang pangalawang kalagayan ay maaaring mangyari nang *n* na paraan, samakatwid ay maaaring mangyari ang mga bagay na ito nang magkasama nang *m* x *n* na mga paraan.

Halimbawa:

May 2 kinalabasan para sa pag-itsa ng byara at 6 na kinalabasan para sa pag-itsa ng dice. Samakatwid ay may 2 x 6, o 12, na mga paraan na mangyayari nang magkasama ang mga bagay na ito.

kinalabasang resulta ng pagmultiplika (cross product) Ang resulta ng pagmultiplika ng numerator ng isang pagkakaugnay (ratio) sa panghatimbilang ng iba.

Halimbawa:

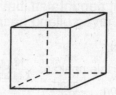

mga resulta ng pagmultiplika:
$1 \times 5 = 5$
$3 \times 2 = 6$

cube (cube) Isang prismang may 6 na panig na ang mga mukha ay mga konguenteng parisukat.

Halimbawa:

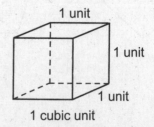

cubed (cubed) Paramihin nang tatlong beses ang sarili.

Halimbawa: 2 cubed = 2^3 = 2 x 2 x 2 = 8

cubic unit (cubic unit) Isang yunit na nagsusukat sa bolumen, na binubuo ng isang cube na ang mga gilid ay isang unit ang haba.

Halimbawa:

1 unit
1 unit
1 unit
1 cubic unit

kinaugaliang sistema ng pagsusukat (customary system of measurement)

Ang sistema ng pagsusukat na kadalasang ginagamit sa Estados Unidos: pulgada, talampakan, milya, onsa, libra, tonelada, tasa, quart, galon, atb.

Mga halimbawa:

haba   1 galon kapasidad   timbang

silindro (cylinder) Isang solido na may dalawang paralelo at bilog na base.

Halimbawa:

cylindrical projection (cylindrical projection) Isang projection ng mapa na gumagamit ng hugis silindro upang katawanin ang isang kalatagang globo (spherical surface).

Halimbawa:

dekagon (decagon) Isang polygon na may 10 panig.

Halimbawa:

desi- (deci-) Isang unlapi na nanganga-hulugang $\frac{1}{10}$.

Halimbawa: 1 desimetro = $\frac{1}{10}$ metro

decimal (decimal) Anumang base-10 na pambilang na isinusulat gamit ang isang decimal point.

Mga halimbawa: 6.21   0.59   12.2   5.0

decimal addition (decimal addition) Ang pagdaragdag ng dalawa o higit pang mga decimal.

Halimbawa:

$$\begin{array}{r} 1 \\ 12.65 \\ + 29.10 \\ \hline 41.75 \end{array}$$

decimal division (decimal division) Ang paghahati ng dalawang decimal.

Halimbawa:

$$\begin{array}{r} 1.25 \\ 0.24\overline{)0.3000} \\ -24 \\ \hline 60 \\ -48 \\ \hline 120 \\ -120 \\ \hline 0 \end{array}$$

decimal multiplication (decimal multiplication) Ang pagmultiplika ng dalawa o higit pang mga decimal.

Halimbawa:

$$\begin{array}{r} 2 \\ 0.13 \\ \times \ 0.7 \\ \hline 0.091 \end{array}$$

0.13   2 decimal places
× 0.7   1 decimal place
0.091   3 decimal places

decimal substraction (decimal subtraction) Pagbabawas ng dalawang decimal.

Halimbawa:

$$\begin{array}{r} 13\,12 \\ 4\,\cancel{3}\,\cancel{2}10 \\ 5\cancel{4}.\cancel{3}\cancel{0} \\ -16.58 \\ \hline 37.72 \end{array}$$

decimal na sistema (decimal system) Isang base-10 na sistema ng halaga ng puwesto (place value).

Halimbawa:

talaguhitang lumiliit (decreasing graph) Isang talaguhitan kung saan ang taas ng linya ay lumiliit mula kaliwa hanggang kanan.

Halimbawa:

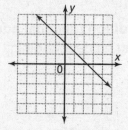

pangangatwirang may-batayan (deductive reasoning) Gumagamit ng lohika upang makarating sa isang pasiya.

Halimbawa:

Kapag ang isang diyagonal ay idinagdag sa anumang quadrilateral, may dalawang tatsulok na nabubuo. Alam mo na ang kabuuan ng mga sukat ng mga anggulo sa isang tatsulok ay 180°. Samakatwid, ang kabuuan ng mga sukat ng mga anggulo ng isang quadrilateral ay doble ng sa isang triyanggulo, o 2 x 180° = 360°.

grado (degree (°)) Isang unit ng sukat ng anggulo.

Halimbawa: Ang 1° ay $\frac{1}{360}$ ng isang kumpletong bilog.

antas (degree) Para sa isang polynomial, ang halaga ng pinakamalaking exponent ng isang variable.

Halimbawa: Ang antas ng $5x^3 - 2x^2 + 7x$ ay 3.

deka- (deka-) Isang unlapi na nangangahulugang 10.

Halimbawa: 1 dekametro =10 metro

panghatimbilang (denominator) Ang pang-ibabang bilang sa isang hatimbilang na nagsasabi kung gaano karaming mga bahagi nahahati ang kabuuan.

Halimbawa:

$\frac{3}{8}$ ——panghatimbilang

mga nababatay ng pangyayari (dependent events) Mga pangyayari kung saan ang kinalabasan ng isa ay may epekto sa probabilidad noong isa.

Halimbawa:

Ang mga pangalang Therese, Diane at Jose ay nakasulat sa mga magkahiwalay na piraso ng papel. Kinuha at itinago ang isang piraso. Pagkatapos ay kinuha pa ang isa pang piraso. Ang probabilidad na ang pangalang Diane ay makukuha, dahil ang pangalang Therese ay nakuha sa unang piraso, ay $\frac{1}{2}$.

nababatay na variable (dependent variable) Ang kinalabasang variable para sa isang function.

Halimbawa: nababatay na variable na
$$y = x + 2$$

diyagonal (diagonal) Sa isang polygon, isang bahaging nagkakabit sa dalawang vertices na hindi nagbabahagi na isang panig sa isa't-isa.

Halimbawa:

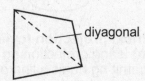

diyametro (diameter) Isang bahaging linya, o ang haba nito, na dumadaan sa sentro ng isang bilog at na ang dalawang pinkadulong tuldok ay nasa bilog.

Halimbawa:

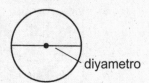

pagkakaiba (difference) Ang resulta ng pagbabawas ng isang bilang mula sa iba.

Halimbawa: 28 - 15 = 13
ang pagkakaiba

tambilang (digit) Ang mga simbolong ginamit upang isulat ang mga pambilang na 0, 1, 2, 3, 4, 5, 6, 7, 8 at 9.

Halimbawa:

Sa 5,847, ang mga tambilang ay 5, 8, 4 at 7.

pagluwang (dilation) Isang proporsiyunadong pagbabawas o paglaki ng isang pigura.

Halimbawa:

Ang paktor ng iskala (scale factor) ng pagluwang mula sa maliit na rektanggulo hanggang sa malaking rektanggulo ay 3.

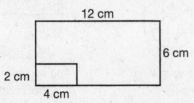

tuwirang pagkakaiba (direct variation) Kapag ang dalawang variable ay may kaugnayan sa pamamagitan ng isang palagiang pagkakaugnay.

Halimbawa:

panahon sa oras (x)	1	2	3	4
layo sa milya (y)	55	110	165	220

$$\frac{y}{x} = 55$$

disjunction (disjunction) Isang may lohikang grupo ng mga pahayag na pinagdugtong ng salitang o.

Mga halimbawa:

x > 4 o x < -1

Pumunta kami sa sine o nanood kami ng telebisyon.

Katangian ng Pamamahagi (Distributive Property) Ang katotohanan na ang $a(b + c) = ab + ac$.

Halimbawa: $3(6 + 5) = 3 \cdot 6 + 3 \cdot 5$

ang hahatiin (dividend) Ang bilang na hahatiin sa isang problema ng paghahati.

Halimbawa:

ang hahatiin

$8 \div 4 = 2$

mahahati (divisible) Maaaring hatiin ng ibang bilang nang walang natitira.

Halimbawa: Ang 18 ay mahahati ng 6, dahil ang $18 \div 6 = 3$.

paghahati (division) Isang operasyong nagsasabi kung gaano kadaming pantay-pantay na grupo o gaano kadami ang nasa bawat pantay-pantay na grupo.

Mga halimbawa:

$18 \div 6 = 3$
Kapag pinaghati-hati ang 18 sa 6 na grupo, magkakaroon ng 3 sa bawat grupo.

$18 \div 3 = 6$
Kapag pinaghati-hati ang 18 sa 3 grupo, magkakaroon ng 6 sa bawat grupo.

ang panghati (divisor) Isang bilang na naghahati sa ibang bilang.

Halimbawa:

ang panghati

$8 \div 4 = 2$

dodecagon (dodecagon) Isang polygon na may 12 panig.

Halimbawa:

talaguhitang may dobleng baras (double bar graph) Isang kombinasyon ng dalawang talaguhitang may baras, na naghahambing sa dalawang magkaugnay na pangkat ng datos.

Halimbawa:

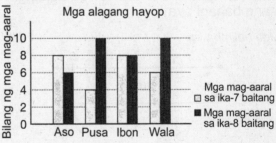

Mga alagang hayop

Mga mag-aaral sa ika-7 baitang
Mga mag-aaral sa ika-8 baitang

talaguhitang may dobleng linya (double line graph) Isang kombinasyon ng dalawang talaguhitang linya, na naghahambing sa dalawang magkaugnay na pangkat ng datos.

Halimbawa:

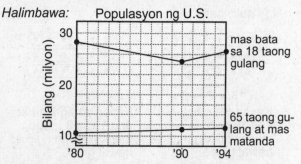

Populasyon ng U.S.

mas bata sa 18 taong gulang

65 taong gulang at mas matanda

dobleng dayagram na may sanga't dahon (double stem-and-leaf diagram) Isang sanga't dahon na paghahambing ng dalawang pangkat ng datos sa iisang dayagram.

Halimbawa:

Dahon	Sanga	Dahon
7 2 1	3	0 1 3
5 0 0	4	2 3
9	5	5 6 8
5 2 0	6	1 4

gilid (edge) Isang bahagi kung saan nagsasalubong ang dalawang mukha ng isang polyhedron.

Halimbawa:

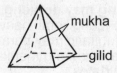

mukha

gilid

dulo (endpoint) Isang tuldok sa dulo ng isang bahagi o ray.

Mga halimbawa:

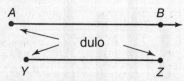

dulo

pagkakatumbas (equality) Isang kaugnayang pangmatematika ng pagiging hustong magkapareho.

Mga halimbawa: 16 + 8 = 24   25 ÷ 5 = 5

mga kinalabasang pantay-pantay ang pagiging malamáng na mangyari (equally-likely outcomes) Mga kinalabasan na may magkaparehong probabilidad.

Mga halimbawa:

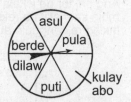

asul

pula

berde

dilaw

kulay abo

puti

Ang paglitaw ng "1"
Probabilidad: $\frac{1}{6}$

Ang paglitaw ng pula
Probabilidad: $\frac{1}{6}$

mga pantay-pantay na pagkakaugnay (equal ratios) Mga pagkakaugnay na nagsasabi ng magkaparehong halaga.

Halimbawa: $\frac{2}{6}, \frac{1}{3}$, at $\frac{4}{12}$

equation (equation) Isang pangmatematikang pangungusap na naglalahad na ang dalawang pagpapahayag ay pantay-pantay.

Mga halimbawa:
14 = 2x   3 + y = 81   3 + 4 = 7

equilateral triangle (equilateral triangle) Isang tatsulok na ang lahat ng mga panig ay may magkaparehong haba.

Halimbawa:

4   4

4

mga magkatumbas na equation (equivalent equations) Ang mga equation na totoo para sa mga gayon ding variable na kapalit.

Halimbawa: x - 5 = 10 at x = 15

mga magkatumbas na pagpapahayag (equivalent expressions) Dalawang pagpapahayag na palaging may magkaparehong halaga para sa mga magkaparehong kapalit.

Halimbawa: 5(x + 1) at 5x + 5

mga magkatumbas ng hatimbilang (equivalent fractions) Dalawang hatimbilang na kumakatawan sa gayon ding bilang.

Halimbawa: $\frac{1}{2}$ at $\frac{8}{16}$

mga magkatumbas na halaga (equivalent rates) Mga halagang tumutukoy sa gayon ding halaga.

Halimbawa:

$$\frac{40 \text{ milya}}{2 \text{ oras}} \quad at \quad \frac{20 \text{ milya}}{1 \text{ oras}}$$

mga magkatumbas na pagkakaugnay (equivalent ratios) Tingnan ang mga pantay-pantay na pagkakaugnay (equal ratios).

pagtantiya (estimate) Isang pagkamalapit (approximation) para sa resulta ng isang kalkulasyon.

Halimbawa:

$$99 \times 21$$
Pagtantiya: $100 \times 20 = 2000$
$$99 \times 21 \approx 2000$$

pormula ni Euler (Euler's formula) Isang pormula tungkol sa bilang ng mga mukha (F), vertices (V) at mga gilid (E) ng isang polyhedron na nagsasabi na F + V - E = 2.

Halimbawa:

Para sa tatsulok na piramide na ipinapakita,

5	+	5	-	8	= 2
Mga mukha		Mga vertex		Mga gilid	

suriin (evaluate) Palitan ang mga halaga ng mga variable sa isang pagpapahayag at pagkatapos ay gawing simple ito sa pamamagitan ng paggamit ng ayos ng mga operasyon.

Halimbawa: Suriin ang 8(x - 3) para sa x = 10.

$$8(x - 3) = 8(10 - 3)$$
$$= 8(7)$$
$$= 56$$

bilang na tukol (even number) Isang buong bilang na may 0, 2, 4, 6 o 8 sa puwesto ng mga isa.

Mga halimbawa: 16 28 34 112 3000

pangyayari (event) Isang kinalabasan o grupo ng mga kinalabasan ng isang eksperimento o kalagayan.

Halimbawa:

Pangyayari: Ang paglitaw ng 3 o mas mataas na bilang kapag initsa ang dice.

Ang mga posibleng kinalabasan ng pangyayaring ito: 3, 4, 5, 6

pinalawak na anyô (expanded form) Isang paraan ng pagsulat ng isang exponential na bilang na nagpapakita sa lahat ng mga paktor nang isa-isa.

Halimbawa: exponential na bilang 9^3
pinalawak na anyô $9 \times 9 \times 9$

eksperimento (experiment) Sa probabilidad, ang anumang gawain kung saan may pagsasapalaran.

Mga halimbawa:

pag-itsa
ng barya

pag-itsa
ng dice

pag-ikot
ng turumpo

pang-eksperimentong probabilidad (experimental probability) Isang probabilidad na batay sa mga datos galing sa mga eksperimento o mga palatanungan.

Halimbawa:

Inihahagis ang isang supot ng patani (bean bag) sa isang sirkulo nang 100 beses. 23 beses tumama ito. Ang pang-eksperimentong probabilidad ng isang pagtama ay $\frac{23}{100}$ = 23%

exponent (exponent) Isang pinataas na bilang (raised number) na nagpapakita ng paulit-ulit na multiplikasyon.

Halimbawa: exponent

$$4^3 = 4 \times 4 \times 4 = 64$$

exponential function (exponential function) Isang nonlinear function kung saan ang isang exponent ay isang variable.

Halimbawa: $y = x^4$

exponential notation (exponential notation) Isang paraan ng pagsulat ng paulit-ulit na multiplikasyon ng isang bilang gamit ang mga exponent.

Mga halimbawa: 2^8 5^2 9^3

pagpapahayag (expression) Isang pang-matematikang prase na binubuo ng mga variable at/o mga bilang at mga operasyon.

Mga halimbawa: 5(8 + 4)   x - 3   2x + 4

mga anggulong panlabas (exterior angles) Kapag bumabagtas ang isang transversal sa dalawang linya, ang mga anggulong nasa labas ng dalawang linyang ito ay tinatawag na mga anggulong panlabas.

Halimbawa:

mga anggulong panlabas: ∠1, ∠2, ∠7, ∠8

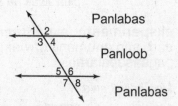

Panlabas
Panloob
Panlabas

mukha (face) Isang patag na kalatagan sa isang solido.

Halimbawa:

mukha

paktor (factor) Isang bilang na naghahati sa ibang bilang nang walang natitira.

Halimbawa:
Dahil ang 30 : 5 = 6, ang 5 ay isang paktor ng 30.

factorial (factorial) Ang factorial ng isang bilang ay ang resulta ng pagmultiplika (product) ng lahat ng mga buong bilang mula 1 hanggang sa bilang na ito. Ang simbolo ng factorial ay "!".

Halimbawa:
6 factorial = 6! = 6 x 5 x 4 x 3 x 2 X 1 = 720

puno ng paktor (factor tree) Isang dayagram na nagpapakita kung paano hinihiwahiwalay ang isang buong bilang sa kanyang mga gansal na paktor (prime factors).

Halimbawa:

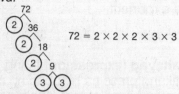

$72 = 2 \times 2 \times 2 \times 3 \times 3$

makatarungang laro (fair game) Isang laro kung saan ang lahat ng mga manlalaro ay may pare-parehong probabilidad na manalo.

Halimbawa:
Makatarungang laro: Naghahali-halili ang dalawang manlalaro sa pag-itsa ng isang dice. Ang manlalaro A ay nakakakuha ng isang punto kung lumitaw ang 1, 3 o 5. Ang manlalaro B ay nakakakuha ng isang punto kung lumitaw ang 2, 4 o 6. Ang probabilidad na makakakuha ng isang punto ay $\frac{1}{2}$ para sa dalawang manlalaro.

pitikin (flip) Tingnan ang pagsasalamin (reflection).

talampakan (foot) Isang yunit sa kinaugaliang sistema ng pagsusukat na katumbas ng 12 pulgada.

Halimbawa:

1 talampakan

pormula (formula) Isang tuntuning nagpapakita ng mga kaugnayan ng mga dami.

Mga halimbawa: $A = bh$ $p = 4s$

fractal (fractal) Isang huwaran na may pagkakatulad sa sarili. Kung ang maliit na bahagi ng isang fractal ay pinalaki, ang pinalaking lugar ay katulad ng orihinal na pigura.

Halimbawa:

hatimbilang (fraction) Isang bilang na nasa anyong $\frac{a}{b}$ na naglalarawan sa bahagi ng isang buo kapag ang buo ay hiniwa at ginawang mga pantay-pantay na bahagi.

Mga halimbawa: $\frac{3}{5}$ $\frac{2}{7}$ $\frac{1}{4}$ $\frac{7}{10}$

pagdaragdag ng hatimbilang (fraction addition) Ang pagdaragdag ng dalawa o higit pang mga hatimbilang.

Halimbawa: $\frac{1}{3} + \frac{1}{4}$

$$\frac{1}{3} = \frac{1 \times 4}{3 \times 4} = \frac{4}{12}$$

$$\frac{1}{4} = \frac{1 \times 3}{4 \times 3} = \frac{3}{12}$$

$$\frac{1}{3} + \frac{1}{4} = \frac{4}{12} + \frac{3}{12} = \frac{4+3}{12} = \frac{7}{12}$$

paghahati ng hatimbilang (fraction division) Ang paghahati sa dalawang hatimbilang.

Halimbawa: $\frac{1}{6} \div \frac{3}{4} = \frac{1}{6} \times \frac{4}{3}$

$$= \frac{1 \times 4}{6 \times 3}$$

$$= \frac{4}{18} \text{ o } \frac{2}{9}$$

multiplikasyon ng hatimbilang (fraction multiplication) Ang pagpaparami ng dalawa o higit pang mga hatimbilang.

Halimbawa: $1\frac{1}{2} \times \frac{1}{4} = \frac{3}{2} \times \frac{1}{4}$

$$= \frac{3 \times 1}{2 \times 4}$$

$$= \frac{3}{8}$$

pagbabawas ng hatimbilang (fraction subtraction) Ang pagbabawas ng dalawang hatimbilang.

Halimbawa: $\frac{3}{4} - \frac{2}{3}$

$$\frac{3}{4} = \frac{3 \times 3}{4 \times 3} = \frac{9}{12}$$

$$\frac{2}{3} = \frac{2 \times 4}{3 \times 4} = \frac{8}{12}$$

$$\frac{3}{4} - \frac{2}{3} = \frac{9}{12} - \frac{8}{12} = \frac{9 - 8}{12} = \frac{1}{12}$$

kadalasan (frequency) Ang bilang ng beses na ang isang bagay ay nangyayari sa isang palatanungan. Tingnan ang talangguhit ng kadalasan (frequency chart).

talangguhit ng kadalasan o talaan ng kadalasan (frequency chart or table) Isang talaang nagpapakita ng mga klase ng bagay at ang kadalasan na nangyayari ang mga bagay.

Halimbawa:

Kulay ng Kamisadentro	Kadalasan
Itim	8
Tan	2
Puti	5
Asul	4

pagtantiya ng nasa harapang dulo (front-end estimation) Isang paraan ng pagtantiya kung saan ang una o pangalawang tambilang lamang ng bawat bilang ang ginagamit para sa kalkulasyon, at inaakma ang resulta batay sa mga natitirang tambilang.

Halimbawa:

Pagtantiya ng nasa harapang dulo gamit ang isang tambilang (one-digit front-end estimation)

$$\begin{array}{r} 2,485 \\ + \ 3,698 \\ \hline 5,000 \\ + \ 1,200 \\ \hline 6,200 \end{array}$$

Idagdag ang mga unang tambilang. Ang 485 + 698 ay humigit-kumulang sa 1,200.

function (function) Isang kaugnayan ng ipinasok/inilabas (input/output) na nagbibigay ng isang inilabas (output) lamang para sa bawat ipinasok (input).

Mga halimbawa: $y = x + 4$ $\qquad y = 2x$ $\qquad y = x^2$

Saligang Teyoriya ng Aritmetika (Fundamental Theorem of Arithmetic) Ang lahat ng mga integer (buong numero) na mas mataas sa 1 ay maaaring isulat bilang isang bukod-tanging resulta ng pagmultiplika ng mga gansal na bilang.

Mga halimbawa: $\qquad$ 24 = 2 x 2 x 2 x 3
$\qquad\qquad\qquad$ 35 = 5 x 7

galon (gallon) Isang yunit sa kinaugaliang sistema ng pagsusukat na katumbas ng 4 na quart.

Halimbawa:

1 galon

heometriya (geometry) Isang sangay ng matematika kung saan sinasaliksik ang mga kaugnayan ng mga tuldok, linya, pigura at solido.

geometric probability (geometric probability) Ang probabilidad na batay sa paghahambing ng mga sukat ng mga pangheometriyang hugis.

Halimbawa:

Ang lawak ng malaking parisukat = 3x3 o 9 in²

Lugar na may kulay = 9 in² - 1 in² = 8 in²

Probabilidad na tatama sa lugar na may kulay = $\frac{8}{9}$

geometric sequence (geometric sequence) Isang pagkakasunod-sunod kung saan ang pagkakaugnay ng mga magkakasunod na termino ay palaging magkapareho.

Halimbawa:

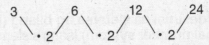

gramo (gram) Ang saligang unit ng mass sa metrikong sistema.

Halimbawa:

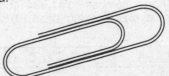

Ang mass ng isang malaking paperclip ay humigit-kumulang na 1 gramo.

talaguhitan (graph) Isang dayagram na nagpapakita ng impormasyon sa isang maayos na paraan.

Mga halimbawa:

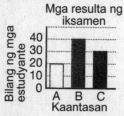

pinakamalaking sangkap na panlahat (greatest common factor (GCF)) Ang pinakamalaking buong bilang na naghahati-hati sa dalawa o mas higit na buong bilang nang walang natitira.

Halimbawa: Ang 6 ay ang GCF ng 12, 18 at 24.

hekto- (hecto-) Isang unlapi na may kahulugang 100.

Halimbawa: 1 hektometro = 100 metro

taas (height) Sa isang triyanggulo, apatang-gilid o piramide, ang layong patayo mula sa base hanggang sa katunggaling tuktok o panig. Sa isang prisma o silindro, ang layo sa pagitan ng mga base.

Mga halimbawa:

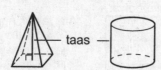

pituhang-gilid (heptagon) Isang polygon na may 7 panig.

Halimbawa:

heksadesimal na sistema ng bilang (hexadecimal number system) Isang sistema ng halaga ng puwesto na ang base ay 16.

Halimbawa:

Ang mga titik na A-F ay ginagamit upang katawanin ang mga tambilang 10-15. Ang bilang na A3CE na batay sa 16 ay katumbas ng 41,934 (40,960 + 768 + 192 + 14) sa panampuang (base 10) sistema ng bilang.

Base 16	A	3	C	E
Halaga ng puwesto	4096	256	16	1
Kinala-basan	10 × 4096 = 40,960	3 × 256 = 768	12 × 16 = 192	14 × 1 = 14

animang-gilid (hexagon) Isang polygon na may 6 panig.

Mga halimbawa:

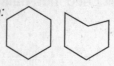

histogram (histogram) Isang uri ng talaguhitang may baras kung saan ang mga kategorya ay mga pantay-pantay na hanay ng mga bilang.

Halimbawa: Mga resulta ng palatanungan

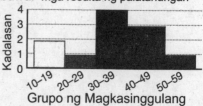

pahalang na aksis (horizontal axis) Ang pahalang na linya ng dalawang linya kung saan nakatayo ang isang talaguhitang may baras o isang coordinate plane.

Mga halimbawa:

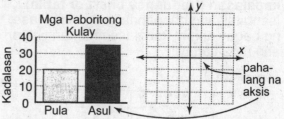

hypotenuse (hypotenuse) Ang panig na katunggali ng panulukang ayos (right angle) sa isang triyanggulong ayos (right triangle).

Halimbawa:

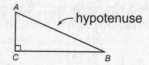

pagkakakilanlan (identity) Sa anumang operasyon, ang bilang na nagpapanatili sa ibang bilang na maging magkapareho. 0 ay ang pagkakakilanlang idinadagdag (additive identity), sapagkat a + 0 = a, 1 ay ang pagkakakilanlang nagpaparami (multiplicative identity) sapagkat ang a x 1 = a.

Halimbawa: 6 + 0 = 6   5 x 1 = 5

pahayag na kung-samakatwid (if-then statement) Isang panlohikong pahayag na gumagamit ng "kung" at "samakatwid" upang ipakita ang kaugnayan ng dalawang kalagayan.

Halimbawa:

Kung ang isang triyanggulo ay iskalino, samakatwid ay wala sa mga panig nito ang magkatumbas.

hindi nararapat na hatimbilang (improper fraction) Isang hatimbilang na ang kabilangan (numerator) ay mas mataas o katumbas ng kanyang panghatimbilang (denominator).

Mga halimbawa: $\frac{5}{2}$ $\frac{8}{8}$ $\frac{14}{3}$

tumataas na talaguhitan (increasing graph) Isang talaguhitan kung saan ang taas ng linya ay tumataas mula kaliwa hanggang kanan.

Halimbawa:

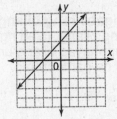

pulgada (inch) Isang yunit ng haba sa kaugaliang sistema ng pagsusukat.

Halimbawa: Ang sukat ng paperclip ay $1\frac{3}{8}$ in. o $1\frac{3}{8}$".

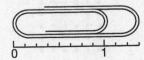

mga nagsasariling pangyayari (independent events) Mga pangyayari kung saan ang kinalabasan ng isa ay hindi umaapekto sa probabilidad ng iba.

Halimbawa:
Ang mga pangalang Therese, Diane at Jose ay isinulat sa mga magkahiwalay na piraso ng papel. Iginuhit at ibinalik ang isang piraso. Ang isa namang piraso ay iginuhit. Ang probabilidad na ang pangalang Diane ay mapipili, na kung saan ang pangalang Therese ay iginuhit sa unang piraso, ay $\frac{1}{3}$.

nagsasariling variable (independent variable) Ang variable na ipinasok para sa isang function.

Halimbawa:

nagsasariling variable
|
$y = x + 2$

pangangatwirang batay sa partikular na katotohanan (inductive reasoning) Gumagamit ng isang huwaran upang makadating sa isang pasiya.

Halimbawa:
Maraming apatang-gilid ang iginuhit at ang kanilang mga anggulo ay sinukat. Sa bawat panahon ang kabuuan ng mga anggulo ay 360°. Ang pangwakas ng pangungusap ay ang kabuuan ng mga anggulo ng isang apatang-gilid ay 360°.

di-pagkakatumbas (inequality) Isang pangmatematikang pangungusap na sumasaklaw sa <, >, ≤, o ≥.

Mga halimbawa:

$6 < 9$ $x + 3 \geq 21$ $2x - 8 > 0$

iniukit na pigura (inscribed figure) Isang pigura na nasa loob ng iba. Iniukit ang isang polygon sa isang bilog kung ang lahat ng mga tuktok nito ay nasa bilog.

Halimbawa:

Iniukit ang triyanggulo sa bilog.

mga numerong buo (integers) Ang pangkat ng mga positibo at buong bilang, ang kanilang katunggali at ang 0.

Mga halimbawa: ..., -3, -2, -1, 0, 1, 2, 3, ...

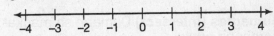

pagdaragdag ng numerong buo (integer addition) Pagdaragdag ng dalawa o mas higit na mga numerong buo.

Mga halimbawa:

$-5 + 8 = 3$ $-5 + (-8) = -13$

$5 + (-3) = 2$ $5 + 8 = 13$

paghahati ng numerong buo (integer division) Paghahati ng dalawang numerong buo.

Mga halimbawa:

$-40 \div 8 = -5$ $40 \div (-8) = -5$

$-40 \div (-8) = 5$ $40 \div 8 = 5$

multiplikasyon ng numerong buo (integer multiplication) Pagpaparami ng dalawa o mas higit na mga numerong buo.

Mga halimbawa:

$-5 \cdot 8 = -40$ $-5 \cdot (-8) = 40$

$5 \cdot (-8) = -40$ $5 \cdot 8 = 40$

pagbabawas ng numerong buo (integer subtraction) Pagbabawas ng dalawang numerong buo.

Mga halimbawa:

$-5 - 8 = -13$ $-5 - (-8) = 3$

$5 - (-3) = 8$ $5 - 8 = -3$

tubo (interest) Ang salaping ibinayad upang makagamit ng salapi.

Halimbawa:
Idineposito ni Dave ang $300 sa isang savings account. Pagkatapos ng 1 taon ang balanse sa kanyang lagak sa bangko ay umabot sa $315. Kumita siya ng $15 bilang tubo sa kanyang savings account.

mga anggulong panloob (interior angles) Kapag dinadaanan ng isang transversal ang dalawang linya, ang mga anggulong nasa loob nitong dalawang linya ay tinatawag na mga anggulong panloob.

Halimbawa:

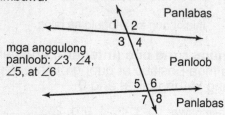

mga anggulong panloob: ∠3, ∠4, ∠5, at ∠6

bumagtas (intersect) Dumaan sa magkaparehong punto.

Halimbawa:

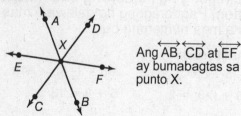

Ang $\overleftrightarrow{AB}$, $\overleftrightarrow{CD}$ at $\overleftrightarrow{EF}$ ay bumabagtas sa punto X.

pagitan (interval) Isa sa mga dibisyong may pantay-pantay na laki sa isang talaguhitang may baras o iskala ng talaguhitang linya (line graph scale).

Halimbawa:

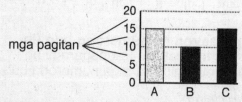

mga pagitan

mga operasyong pabaligtad (inverse operations) Mga operasyong "sumasaliwa" sa isa't-isa.

Mga halimbawa:
pagdaragdag at pagbabawas	2 + **3** = 5
	5 - **3** = 2
multiplikasyon at paghahati	2 · **3** = 6
	6 ÷ **3** = 2

pabaligtad na pag-iiba-iba (inverse variation) Kapag magkaugnay ang dalawang variable sa pamamagitan ng isang hindi nagbabagong kinalabasan ng pagpaparami.

Halimbawa:

x	1	2	3	4	5	6
y	60	30	20	15	12	10

$$x \cdot y = 60$$

di-napangangatwirang bilang (irrational number) Isang bilang, tulad ng √2, na hindi maaaring mapahayag bilang umuulit-ulit o nagwawakas na panampuan.

Mga halimbawa: $\sqrt{5}$ $\qquad \pi \qquad -\sqrt{\frac{1}{2}}$

isometric drawing (isometric drawing) Isang paraang ginagamit upang bigyan ng perspektibo ang isang larawang-guhit.

Halimbawa:

triyanggulong isosiles (isosceles triangle) Isang triyanggulo na may di-kukulangin sa dalawang magkatumbas na panig.

Halimbawa:

kilo- (kilo-) Isang unlapi na may kahulugang 1000.

Halimbawa: 1 kilometro = 1000 metro

latitude (latitude) Isang pagsusukat sa antas sa hilaga o timog ng ekwador.

Halimbawa:

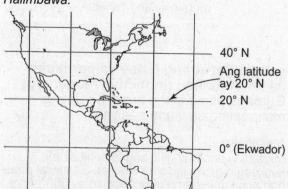

40° N

Ang latitude ay 20° N

20° N

0° (Ekwador)

pinakamaliit na panghatimbilang na panlahat (least common denominator (LCD))

Ang pinakamaliit na multiple na panlahat (least common multiple (LCM)) ng dalawa o mas higit na mga panghatimbilang.

Halimbawa: $\frac{1}{2}$ $\frac{2}{3}$ $\frac{3}{4}$

Ang LCM ng 2, 3 at 4 ay 12, samakatwid ang LCD ng mga hatimbilang ay 12.

Ang mga hatimbilang na isinulat nang kasama ang LCD ay $\frac{6}{12}$ $\frac{8}{12}$ at $\frac{9}{12}$.

pinakamaliit na multiple na panlahat (least common multiple (LCM))

Ang pinakamaliit na bilang na isang multiple na panlahat (common multiple).

Halimbawa:

mga multiple ng 3: 3 6 9 **12** 15 18 21 **24** ...
mga multiple ng 4: 4 8 **12** 16 20 **24** 28 32 ...
Ang 12 ay ang LCM ng 3 at 4.

binti (leg)

Isang panig ng isang triyanggulong ayos (right triangle) na kakaiba sa hypotenuse.

Halimbawa:

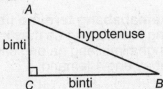

mga katulad na panghatimbilang (like denominators)

Mga panghatimbilang na magkapareho sa dalawa o mas higit na mga hatimbilang.

Halimbawa:

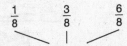

$\frac{1}{8}$ $\frac{3}{8}$ $\frac{6}{8}$

mga katulad na panghatimbilang

mga katulad na termino (like terms)

Mga termino kung saan ang kaparehong variable ay itinatataas sa kaparehong exponent.

Halimbawa: $3x^2$ at $9x^2$ $10y$ at $2y$

linya (line)

Isang pigura na may isang dimensiyon na umaabot nang walang wakas sa dalawang dako. Hinihirang ng dalawang punto ang isang linya.

Halimbawa:

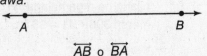

$\overleftrightarrow{AB}$ o $\overleftrightarrow{BA}$

talaguhitang linya (line graph)

Isang talaguhitan kung saan ipinapakita ng isang linya ang mga pagbabago ng impormasyon, kadalas sa paglipas ng panahon.

Halimbawa: Pagbebenta ng Kompanya

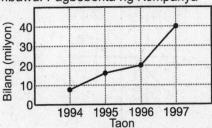

linya ng simetriya (line of symmetry)

Ang linya na naghahati-hati sa isang pigura na may simetriya sa linya sa dalawang magkatulad na kalahati.

Mga halimbawa:

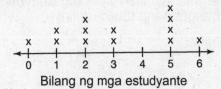

1 linya ng simetriya   4 na linya ng simetriya

line plot (line plot)

Isang plot na nagpapakita sa hugis ng isang pangkat ng datos sa pamamagitan ng pagpatong ng mga x sa itaas ng bawat halaga sa isang linya ng bilang.

Halimbawa:

Bilang ng mga estudyante

bahagi ng linya (line segment)

Bahagi ng isang tuwid na linya, na may dalawang pinakadulong punto. Hinihirang ng dalawang punto ang isang bahagi.

Halimbawa:

$\overline{AB}$ o $\overline{BA}$

simetriya sa linya (line symmetry)

Ang isang pigura ay may simetriya sa linya kung ito ay maaaring paghati-hatiin sa dalawang magkatulad na kalahati.

Halimbawa:

Pigura na may simetriya sa linya   Pigura na walang simetriya sa linya

linear equation (linear equation) Isang equation na ang talaguhitan ay isang tuwid na linya.

Halimbawa:

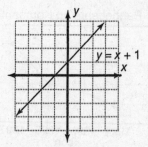

linear function (linear function) Isang function na ang talaguhitan ay isang tuwid na linya.

Halimbawa:

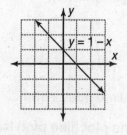

Ipinasok (input)	Nagawa (output)
x	y
−2	3
−1	2
0	1
1	0
2	−1
3	−2

di-pagkakatumbas-tumbas ng guhit (linear inequality) Isang pangmatematikang pangungusap na sumasaklaw sa <, >, ≤ o ≥ na ang talaguhitan ay isang rehiyon na may hanggahang tuwid na linya.

Halimbawa:

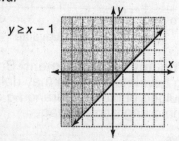

litro (liter) Ang saligang yunit ng bolumen sa metrikong sistema.

Halimbawa:

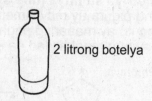

2 litrong botelya

longitude (longitude) Isang pagsusukat sa antas sa silangan o kanluran mula sa prime meridian.

Halimbawa:

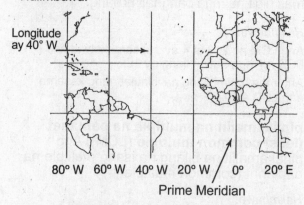

Prime Meridian

mas mababang quartile (lower quartile) Ang median ng mas mababang kalahati ng isang pangkat ng datos.

Halimbawa:

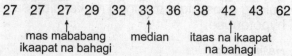

27 27 27 29 32 33 36 38 42 43 62

mas mababang ikaapat na bahagi   median   itaas na ikaapat na bahagi

mga pinakamababang termino (lowest terms) Isang hatimbilang na may kabilangan at panghatimbilang na ang sangkap na panlahat ay ang 1 lamang.

Mga halimbawa: $\frac{1}{2}$ $\frac{3}{5}$ $\frac{21}{23}$

mass (mass) Ang dami ng materiya (matter) na itinataglay ng isang bagay.

Mga halimbawa:

Ang isang pasas ay may mass na 1 gramo.

Ang isang pares ng sapatos na pantakbo ay may mass na 1 kilo.

mean (mean) Ang kabuuan ng mga halaga sa isang pangkat ng datos na pinaghatihati ng bilang ng mga halaga. Tinatawag ding average.

Halimbawa:

27 27 27 29 32 33 36 38 42 43 62

kabuuan: 396

bilang na mga halaga: 11

mean: 396 ÷ 11 = 36

kamalian sa pagsusukat (measurement error) Ang pag-aalinlangan sa isang pagsusukat. Ang pinakamalaking posibleng kamalian sa isang pagsusukat ay kalahati ng pinakamaliit na yunit na ginamit.

Halimbawa:

Dahil ang pulgada ay ang pinakamaliit na yunit, ang pinakamala-king posibleng kamalian ay $\frac{1}{2}$ pulgada. Samakatwid, ang totoong taas ay nasa pagitan ng 5' $5\frac{1}{2}$" at $5'6\frac{1}{2}$".

5' 6"

sukat ng gitnang pagkahilig (measure of central tendency) Ang iisang halaga na lumalagom sa isang pangkat ng datos batay sa bilang (numerical data).

Halimbawa:
Ang mean, median at mode ay mga karaniwang sukat ng gitnang pagkahilig.

27 27 27 29 32 33 36 38 42 43 62

‹—mode—›   ↑ median

Mean = 396 ÷ 36 = 11

median (median) Ang gitnang halaga ng isang pangkat ng datos kapag ang mga halaga ay may ayos batay sa bilang.

Halimbawa:
27 27 27 29 32 33 36 38 42 43 62

↑ Median

matematika sa isip (mental math) Ang paggawa ng mga kalkulasyon sa iyong isip, nang walang ginagamit na lapis at papel o kalkiyuletor.

Halimbawa:

2000	x	30
3 sero	+	1 sero = 4 na sero
Isipin: 2	x	3 = 6, ikabit ang 4 na sero
2000	x	30 = 60,000

metro (meter) Ang saligang yunit ng haba sa metrikong sistema.

Halimbawa:

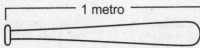
1 metro

Ang baseball bat ay may humigit-kulumang na 1 metrong haba.

metrikong sistema (metric system) Isang sistema ng pagsusukat batay sa metro, gramo at litro.

Mga halimbawa:

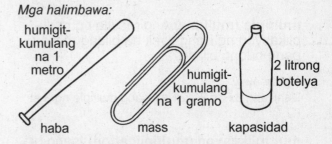

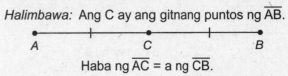

humigit-kumulang na 1 metro

humigit-kumulang na 1 gramo

2 litrong botelya

haba   mass   kapasidad

gitnang puntos (midpoint) Ang punto na naghahati-hati sa isang bahagi upang makakuha ng dalawang magkatumbas na mas maliit na bahagi.

Halimbawa: Ang C ay ang gitnang puntos ng $\overline{AB}$.

A   C   B

Haba ng $\overline{AC}$ = a ng $\overline{CB}$.

milya (mile) Isang unit sa kinaugaliang sistema ng pagsusukat na katumbas ng 5280 talampakan.

Halimbawa:

Ang isang milya ay ang layo na kaya mong lakarin sa loob ng 15 hanggang 20 minuto o takbuhin sa loob ng humigit-kumulang sa 10 minuto.

milli- (mili-) Isang unlapi na nangangahulugang $\frac{1}{1000}$.

Halimbawa: 1 milimetro = $\frac{1}{1000}$ metro

magkahalong bilang (mixed number) Isang bilang na binubuo ng isang buong bilang at isang hatimbilang.

Mga halimbawa: $3\frac{1}{2}$ $1\frac{3}{4}$ $13\frac{3}{8}$

mode (mode) Ang (mga) halaga na pinakamadalas na nangyayari sa isang pangkat ng datos.

Halimbawa:
27 27 27 29 32 33 36 38 42 43 62

Para sa isang tiyak na pangkat ng datos, ang 27 ay ang mode.

monomial (monomial) Isang pagpapahayag sa alhebra na may iisang termino.

Mga halimbawa: $2x^2$ $5y$ x^3 -3

multiple (multiple) Ang resulta ng multiplikasyon ng isang tiyak na bilang at isa pang buong bilang.

Halimbawa:
Dahil ang 3x7 = 21, 21 ay isang multiple ng 3 at ng 7.

multiplikasyon (multiplication) Isang operasyon na nagsasama-sama sa dalawang bilang, na tinatawag na factors, upang makarating sa isang bilang, na tinatawag na resulta ng multiplikasyon.

Halimbawa:

3 hanay ng 6

$$3 \times 6 = 18$$

factors   resulta ng multiplikasyon

katangiang multiplikasyon (multiplication property) Kung ang A at B ay mga nagsasariling pangyayari, ang probabilidad na mangyayari ang dalawa ay ibinibigay ng P(A at B) = P(A) x P(B).

Halimbawa:
Unang pag-ikot: $P(pula) = \frac{1}{4}$
Pangalawang pag-ikot: $P(pula) = \frac{1}{4}$
Una at pangalawang pag-ikot:
$P(pula\ at\ pula)= \frac{1}{4} \times \frac{1}{4} = \frac{1}{16}$

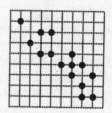

Multiplikasyon na Katangian ng Pagkakatumbas (Multiplication Property of Equality) Kung ang a = b, samakatwid ay ang ac = bc.

Halimbawa:
Sa pangalawang linya ng halimbawa sa ibaba, ang 2 ay minumultiplika sa magkabilang panig ng equation.

Kung $\frac{1}{2}y = 4$

samakatwid ay ang $2 \times \frac{1}{2}y = 2 \times 4$

kabaligtaran ng multiplikasyon (multiplicative inverse) Kung ang resulta ng pagmultiplika ng dalawang bilang ay 1, ang bawat bilang ay ang kabaligtaran ng multiplikasyon noong isa.

Halimbawa:
Ang $\frac{1}{6}$ at ang 6 ay mga kabaligtaran ng pagpaparami sapagkat $\frac{1}{6} \times 6 = 1$.

kapwa kumakansela (mutually exclusive) Kung ang pangyayari A o B ay nangyayari, yung isa ay hindi maaaring mangyari.

Mga halimbawa:
Kung ang temperatura sa labas ay 90°, samakatwid ay hindi nagniniyebe.
Kung ang isang polygon ay may tatlong panig lamang, hindi ito maaaring magkaroon ng 4 na anggulo.

mga negatibong bilang (negative numbers) Mga bilang na mas mababa sa sero.

Halimbawa:
Mga Negatibong Bilang   Mga Positibong Bilang

$$-5\ -4\ -3\ -2\ -1\ \ 0\ \ 1\ \ 2\ \ 3\ \ 4\ \ 5$$

negatibong kaugnayan (negative relationship) Ang dalawang pangkat ng datos ay may negatibong kaugnayan kapag ang mga halaga ng datos sa isang pangkat ay tumataas habang ang mga halaga doon sa isa ay bumababa.

Halimbawa:

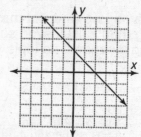

negatibong tarik (negative slope) Ang tarik ng isang linya ay nakahilis nang pababa.

Halimbawa:

negatibong square root (negative square root) Ang kasalungat ng pangunahing square root ng isang bilang.

Halimbawa:

pangunahing   negatibong
square root: square root:
$\sqrt{25} = 5$ $-\sqrt{25} = -5$

net (net) Isang patag na huwaran na maaaring tiklupin upang lumikha ng isang pigura na may tatlong dimensiyon tulad ng isang prisma.

Halimbawa:

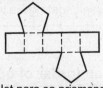

Net para sa prismang may limang gilid

Prismang may limang gilid

nonagon (nonagon) Isang polygon na may 9 na panig.

Mga halimbawa:

nonlinear equation (nonlinear equation) Isang equation na ang talaguhitan ay isang kurba sa halip na isang linya.

Halimbawa:

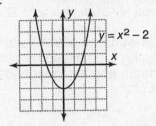

$$y = x^2 - 2$$

nonlinear function (nonlinear function) Isang function na ang talaguhitan ay hindi tuwid na linya sapagka't ang mga pantay-pantay na pagbabago sa x ay hindi nagreresulta sa mga pantay-pantay na pagbabago sa y.

Mga halimbawa:

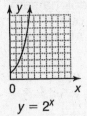 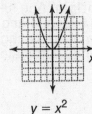 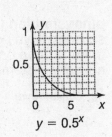

$y = 2^x$ $y = x^2$ $y = 0.5^x$

walang kaugnayan (no relationship) Ang dalawang pangkat ng datos ay walang kaugnayan kapag walang positibo o negatibong kaugnayan.

Halimbawa:

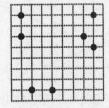

linya ng bilang (number line) Isang linyang nagpapakita ng mga bilang na nasa ayos.

Mga halimbawa:

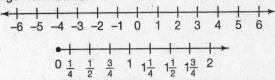

anyô ng bilang at salita (number-word form) Isang paraan ng pagsulat ng bilang gamit ang mga tambilang at mga salita.

Mga halimbawa: 45 trilyon   9 na libo

pambilang (numeral) Isang simbolo para sa isang bilang.

Mga halimbawa: 7   58   234

kabilangan (numerator) Ang itaas na bilang sa isang hatimbilang na nagsasabi kung gaano karaming parte ng buo ang tinutukoy.

Halimbawa:

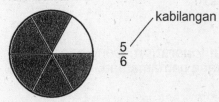

kabilangan

$\frac{5}{6}$

anggulong bika (obtuse angle) Isang anggulo na ang sukat ay mas malaki sa 90° at mas maliit sa 180°.

Mga halimbawa:

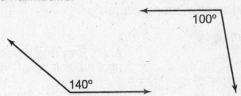

100°

140°

tatsulok na bika (obtuse triangle) Isang tatsulok na may isang anggulong bika.

Mga halimbawa:

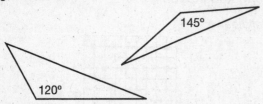

octagon (octagon) Isang polygon na may 8 panig.

Mga halimbawa:

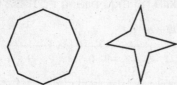

bilang na may butal kapag pinagdalawa (odd number) Isang buong bilang na may 1,3,5, 7 o 9 sa puwesto ng mga isa.

Mga halimbawa:
     43   225   999   8,007

kalamangan (odds) Ang pagkakaugnay ng bilang ng mga paraan kung paano maaaring mangyari ang isang pangyayari sa bilang ng mga paraan kung paano ito hindi maaaring mangyari.

Halimbawa:

 Gaano kalamang na lilitaw ang 3: 1 sa 5

Gaano kalamang na hindi lilitaw ang 3: 5 sa 1

operasyon (operation) Isang pang-matematikang pamamaraan.

Mga halimbawa:
Apat na saligang operasyon: pagdaragdag, pag-babawas, multiplikasyon, paghahati

kasalungat na binti (opposite leg) Para sa isang anggulong agudo sa isang tatsu-lok na may anggulong kwadrado, ang bin-ting kasalungat ng anggulo.

Halimbawa:

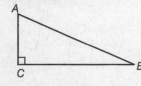

Ang $\overline{CB}$ ay ang kasalu-ngat na binti ng $\angle CAB$

Ang $\overline{AC}$ ay ang kasalu-ngat na binti ng $\angle ABC$.

mga kasalungat na bilang (opposite numbers) Mga bilang na ang layo sa isang linya ng bilang ay pareho mula sa sero ngunit nasa mga kasalungat na panig.

Halimbawa:
Ang 7 at ang -7 ay mga kasalungat ng isa't-isa.

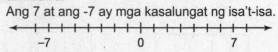

ayos ng mga operasyon (order of operations) Ang mga alituntuning nagsasabi kung anong ayos dapat gawin ang mga operasyon sa: (1) gawing simple sa loob ng mga panaklong, (2) gawing simple ang mga exponent, (3) multiplikahin at paghati-hatiin mula kaliwa hanggang kanan, at (4) magdagdag at magbawas mula kaliwa hanggang kanan.

Halimbawa:
Suriin ang $2x^2 + 4(x - 2)$ para sa $x = 3$.

(1) gawing simple sa loob ng mga panaklong	$2 \cdot 3^2 + 4(3 - 2)$ $2 \cdot 3^2 + 4(1)$
(2) gawing simple ang mga exponent	$2 \cdot 9 + 4$
(3) multiplikahin at paghati-hatiin mula kaliwa hanggang kanan	$18 + 4$
(4) magdagdag at magbawas mula kaliwa hanggang kanan	22

pinag-ayus-ayos na pares (ordered pair) Isang pares ng mga bilang na ginagamit upang hanapin ang isang lugar sa isang coordinate plane.

Halimbawa:

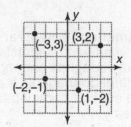

pinagsimulan (origin) Ang tuldok na sero sa isang linya ng bilang, o ang puntong (0, 0) kung saan bumabagtas ang mga aksis ng isang sistemang coordinate.

Mga halimbawa:

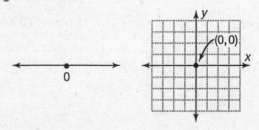

ortograpikong larawang-guhit (ortho-graphic drawing) Isang larawang-guhit ng isang bagay gamit ang mga anyô mula sa harap, sa tabi at sa itaas.

Halimbawa:

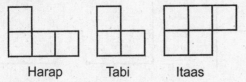

Harap   Tabi   Itaas

onsa (ounce) Isang unit ng bigat sa kaugaliang sistema ng pagsusukat.

Halimbawa:

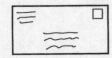

Ang bigat ng isang sulat ay humigit-kumulang sa isang onsa.

kinalabasan (outcome) Isang paraan kung saan maaaring tumungo ang isang eksperimento o kalagayan.

Halimbawa:

Mga kinalabasan para sa Pag-itsa ng 2 Barya:

barya 1	barya 2
kara	krus
kara	kara
krus	kara
krus	krus

May 4 na kinalabasan. Ang isang kinalabasan ay kara, kara.

outlier (outlier) Isang labis na halaga sa isang pangkat ng datos, na hiwalay sa karamihan ng ibang mga halaga.

Halimbawa:

27   27   27   29   32   33   36   38   42   43   62
                                                ↑
                                            outlier

parabola (parabola) Isang hugis U o nakataob na hugis U na kurba na talaguhitan ng isang quadratic function.

Mga halimbawa:

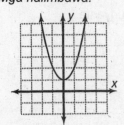
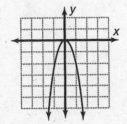

paralelo (parallel) Dalawang linya, mga bahagi o mga ray sa parehong patag na hindi bumabagtas.

Halimbawa:

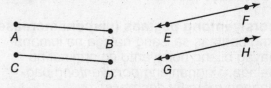

paralelogramo (parallelogram) Isang pigura na may apat na panig na ang mga magkasalungat na panig ay paralelo at kongruente.

Mga halimbawa:

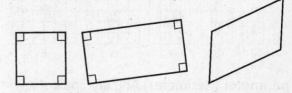

pentagon (pentagon) Isang polygon na may 5 panig.

Mga halimbawa:

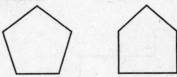

porsiyento (percent) Ang pagkakaugnay na naghahambing ng isang bilang sa 100.

Halimbawa:

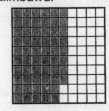

$$\frac{58}{100} = 0.58 = 58\%$$

porsiyentong pagbabago (percent change) Ang halaga ng isang pagbabago, pagtaas o pagbaba, na hinahati ng orihinal na halaga, at ipinapahayag bilang isang porsiyento ng orihinal na halaga.

Mga halimbawa:

Hanapin ang porsiyentong pagbabago kung $1500 ay ipinamumuhunan at $75 ang kinita bilang tubo.

$\frac{75}{1500} = 0.05 = 5\%$ $75 ay isang 5% pagtaas.

Hanapin ang porsiyentong pagbabago kung ang isang bagay na may halagang $50 ay ipinagbibili nang may $10 diskuwento.

$\frac{10}{50} = 0.20 = 20\%$ Ang $10 diskuwento ay isang 20% pagbaba.

porsiyentong pagbaba (percent decrease) Ang pagbabawas sa isang halaga na ipinapahayag bilang porsiyento ng orihinal na halaga. Tingnan ang *porsiyentong pagbabago (percent change)*.

porsiyentong pagtaas (percent increase) Ang pagtaas sa isang halaga na ipinapahayag bilang porsiyento ng orihinal na halaga. Tingnan ang *porsiyentong pagbabago (percent decrease)*.

perfect square (perfect square) Ang square ng isang buong bilang.

Mga halimbawa:

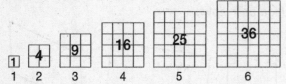

perimeter (perimeter) Ang layo paikot sa labas ng isang pigura.

Halimbawa:

$$P = 5 + 2 + 6 + 4 + 11 + 6$$
$$= 34 \text{ unit}$$

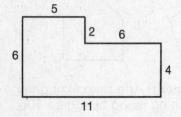

permutation (permutation) Isang pagsasaayos ng mga bagay kung saan ang ayos ay mahalaga.

Halimbawa:

Ang isang estudyante mula sa grupong ito ay ihahalal bilang presidente at ang isa naman ay ihahalal bilang bise presidente: Wendy, Alex, Carlos. Ang mga posibleng permutation ay:

Wendy—presidente, Alex—bise presidente
Wendy—presidente, Carlos—bise presidente
Alex—presidente, Wendy—bise presidente
Alex—presidente, Carlos—bise presidente
Carlos—presidente, Wendy—bise presidente
Carlos—presidente, Alex—bise presidente

Pansinin: Ang bawat isa sa itaas ay isang naiibang permutation.

patayo (perpendicular) Mga linya, rays o bahaging linya na bumabagtas sa anggulong kwadrado.

Mga halimbawa:

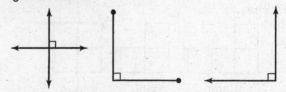

patayong tagahati (perpendicular bisector) Isang linya, ray o bahagi na bumabagtas sa isang bahagi sa kanyang kalagitnaan at ito'y patayo dito.

Halimbawa:

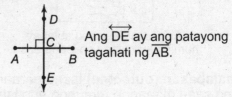

Ang $\overleftrightarrow{DE}$ ay ang patayong tagahati ng $\overline{AB}$.

pi (π) (pi (π)) Ang pagkakaugnay ng sirkumperensiya ng isang bilog sa kanyang diyametro: 3.14159265....

Halimbawa:

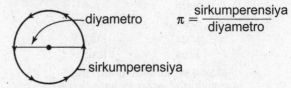

$$\pi = \frac{\text{sirkumperensiya}}{\text{diyametro}}$$

pictograph (pictograph) Isang talaguhitang gumagamit ng mga simbolo upang katawanin ang datos.

Halimbawa:

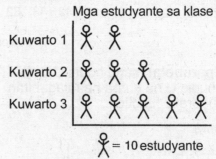

halaga ng puwesto (place value) Ang halagang ibinibigay sa puwestong kinaroroonan ng isang tambilang.

Halimbawa

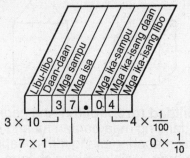

$$3 \times 10 \qquad 4 \times \frac{1}{100}$$
$$7 \times 1 \qquad 0 \times \frac{1}{10}$$

patag (plane) Isang patag na kalatagan na umaabot nang walang-hanggan.

Halimbawa:

Upang isaisip ang isang patag, isipin na pinaaabot ang kalatagan ng lamesa sa lahat ng direksyon.

point symmetry (point symmetry) Ang isang pigura ay may point symmetry kung ito'y waring di nagbabago pagkatapos ikutin nang 180°.

Halimbawa:

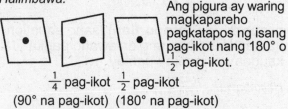

Ang pigura ay waring magkapareho pagkatapos ng isang pag-ikot nang 180° o $\frac{1}{2}$ pag-ikot.

$\frac{1}{4}$ pag-ikot $\frac{1}{2}$ pag-ikot
(90° na pag-ikot) (180° na pag-ikot)

polygon (polygon) Isang saradong pigura sa isang patag na binubuo ng mga bahaging linya na bumabagtas lamang sa kanilang mga dulong tuldok.

Mga halimbawa:

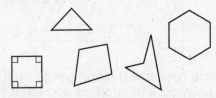

polyhedron (polyhedron) Isang solido na ang mga mukha ay mga polygon.

Mga halimbawa:

polynomial (polynomial) Isang pagpapahayag sa alhebra na kabuuan ng isa o higit pang mga termino.

Mga halimbawa: $\qquad x^2 + 2x - 3 \qquad 5y - 15$

populasyon (population) Ang koleksiyon ng lahat ng mga bagay na susuriin sa isang palatanungan.

Halimbawa:
Ang lahat ng 1000 pangalan ng mga miyembro ng isang klub ay inilagay sa mga kard at pinaghaluhalo ang mga kard. Pagkatapos ay kumuha ng 100 kard at ang mga miyembrong ito ay binigyan ng isang palatanungang pangtelepono. Ang populasyon ng palatanungan ay ang lahat ng 1000 miyembro ng klub.

mga positibong bilang (positive numbers) Mga bilang na mas malaki sa sero.

Halimbawa:

Mga Negatibong Bilang   Mga Positibong Bilang

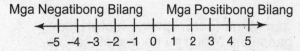

positibong kaugnayan (positive relationship) Ang dalawang pangkat ng datos ay may positibong kaugnayan kapag ang kanilang mga halaga ng datos ay parehong tumataas o parehong bumababa.

Halimbawa:

positibong tarik (positive slope) Ang tarik ng isang linyang nakahilis nang pataas.

Halimbawa:

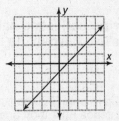

libra (pound) Isang unit sa kinaugaliang sistema ng pagsusukat na katumbas ng 16 onsa.

Halimbawa:

Bigas
1 libra

antas (power) Isang exponent o ang bilang na resulta ng pagtaas ng isang base sa exponent.

Halimbawa: $16 = 2^4$

2 ay pinataas sa ika-4 na antas (4th power).

Ang 16 ay ang ika-4 na antas ng 2.

pagkatiyak (precision) Ang pagiging eksakto ng isang pagsusukat, na tiniyak ng unit ng sukat.

Halimbawa:

5'1" 61" Ang mas maliit na unit ng sukat, mga pulgada, ay mas tiyak kaysa sa mas malaking unit ng sukat, ang talampakan.

gansal na factor (prime factor) Isang gansal na bilang na naghahati-hati sa ibang numerong buo nang walang natitira.

Halimbawa: Ang 5 ay isang gansal na factor ng 35, sapagka't $35 \div 5 = 7$.

prime factorization (prime factorization) Ang pagsulat ng isang bilang bilang resulta ng pagmultiplika ng mga gansal na bilang.

Halimbawa: $70 = 2 \times 5 \times 7$

gansal na bilang (prime number) Isang buong bilang ma mas mataas sa 1 na ang mga kaisa-isang factor ay 1 at ang kanyang sarili.

Halimbawa:

Ang mga gansal na bilang ay nag-uumpisa sa 2, 3, 5, 7, 11, ...

puhunan (principal) Isang halaga ng salaping idineposito o hiniram, na binabayaran ng tubo.

Halimbawa:

Idineposito ni Dave ang $300 sa isang savings account. Pagkatapos ng 1 taon ang balanse sa kanyang account ay umabot sa $315. $300 ang halaga ng puhunan.

pangunahing square root (principal square root) Ang positibong square root ng isang bilang.

Halimbawa:

pangunahing square root   negatibong square root

$\sqrt{25} = 5$ $-\sqrt{25} = -5$

prisma (prism) Isang polyhedron na ang mga base ay kongruente at paralelo.

Halimbawa:

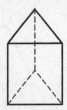

probabilidad (probability) Ang pagkakaugnay ng dami ng mga paraan na ang isang bagay ay maaaring mangyari sa kabuuang dami ng mga posibleng kinalabasan.

Halimbawa:

Ang probabilidad na lilitaw ang 3 sa pag-itsa ay $\frac{1}{6}$.

Ang probabilidad na hindi lilitaw ang 3 sa pag-itsa ay $\frac{5}{6}$.

resulta ng pagmultiplika (product) Ang resulta ng pagmultiplika ng dalawa o higit pang mga bilang.

Halimbawa:

resulta ng pagmultiplika

$2 \times 3 \times 5 = 30$

proporsiyon (proportion) Isang equation na naglalahad na ang dalawang pagkakaugnay ay pantay-pantay.

Halimbawa: $\frac{12}{34} = \frac{6}{17}$

protractor (protractor) Isang kasangkapang pangsukat ng mga anggulo.

Halimbawa:

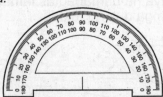

piramide (pyramid) Isang solido na may isang polygonal base at na ang lahat ng mga ibang panig ay mga tatsulok na nagsasalubong sa iisang punto.

Mga halimbawa:

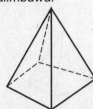

Pythagorean Theorem (Pythagorean Theorem) Sa isang tatsulok na may anggulong kwadrado, kung saan ang *c* ay ang haba ng hypotenuse at ang *a* at *b* ay ang mga haba ng mga binti, $a^2 + b^2 = c^2$.

Halimbawa:

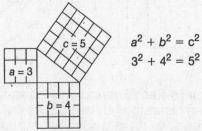

$$a^2 + b^2 = c^2$$
$$3^2 + 4^2 = 5^2$$

mga quadrant (quadrants) Ang apat na rehiyon na tiniyak ng mga aksis ng isang coordinate plane.

Halimbawa:

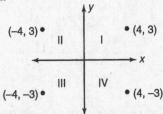

quadratic equation (quadratic equation) Isang equation na may isang squared term katulad ng x^2.

Mga halimbawa:
$$y = x^2 + 3x - 12 \qquad y = 2x^2 + 7$$

quadratic function (quadratic function) Isang function kung saan ang pinaka-mataas na antas (power) ng *x* ay 2. Ang talaguhitan ng isang quadratic function ay isang parabola.

Halimbawa:

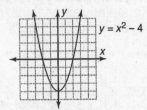

$y = x^2 - 4$

quadrilateral (quadrilateral) Isang polygon na may 4 na panig.

Mga halimbawa:

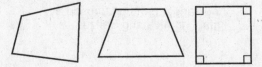

quart (quart) Isang unit ng bolumen sa kaugaliang sistema ng pagsusukat.

Halimbawa:

Isang quart ng gatas

quartile (quartile) Isa sa mga bilang na naghahati sa isang pangkat ng datos at ginagawa itong mga pantay-pantay na ika-apat na bahagi.

Halimbawa:

27 27 27 29 32 33 36 38 42 43 62

mas mababang   median   pinakamataas
quartile   na quartile

Ang 27, 33 at 42 ay ang tatlong quartile ng pangkat ng datos na ito.

quotient (quotient) Ang resulta kapag hinati ng isang bilang ang ibang bilang.

Halimbawa:

quotient
$$8 \div 4 = 2$$

radical sign (radical sign) ginagamit upang katawanin ang square root ng isang bilang.

Halimbawa: $\sqrt{49} = 7$

radius (radius) Isang linya mula sa gitna ng isang bilog papunta sa anumang lugar sa bilog.

Halimbawa:

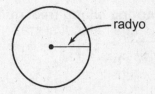

radyo

sapalarang muwestra (random sample) Isang muwestrang pinili sa isang paraan na ang bawat miyembro ng populasyon ay may pantay-pantay na pagkakataong maisama.

Halimbawa:
Ang lahat ng 1000 pangalan ng mga miyembro ng isang klub ay inilagay sa mga kard at pinaghalu-halo ang mga kard. Pagkatapos ay kumuha ng 100 kard at ang mga miyembrong ito ay binigyan ng isang palatanungang pangtelepono. Ang lahat ng mga miyembro ng klub ay nagkaroon ng pantay-pantay na pagkakataong matawagan, sama-katwid ay isa itong sapalarang muwestra.

hanay (range) Ang pagkakaiba ng mga pinakamataas at pinakamababang halaga sa isang pangkat ng datos.

Halimbawa:
        27 27 27 29 32 33 36 38 42 43 62
        Ang hanay ay 62 - 27 = 35.

rate (rate) Isang pagkakaugnay na nagpapakita kung paano magkakaugnay ang mga daming may iba't-ibang unit.

Mga halimbawa: $\dfrac{72 \text{ dolyar}}{28 \text{oras}}$ $\dfrac{55 \text{ milya}}{1 \text{ oras}}$

pagkakaugnay (ratio) Isang paghahambing ng dalawang dami, madalas na isinusulat bilang hatimbilang.

Mga halimbawa: $\dfrac{2}{1}$ 2 sa 1 2 : 1

rational na bilang (rational number) Isang bilang na maaaring isulat bilang pagkakaugnay ng dalawang numerong buo. Ang mga numerong buo, mga hatimbilang, at maraming decimal ay mga rational na bilang.

Mga halimbawa:

Numerong buo Hatimbilang Decimal
$-27 = \dfrac{-27}{1}$ $\dfrac{7}{8}$ $3.1 = 3\dfrac{1}{10} = \dfrac{31}{10}$

ray (ray) Isang bahagi ng isang linya na may isang dulong tuldok at umaabot nang walang-hanggan sa kabilang direksiyon. Ang isang ray ay pinangangalanan muna gamit ang kanyang dulong tuldok.

Halimbawa:

 $\overrightarrow{AB}$

mga totoong bilang (real numbers) Ang lahat ng mga rational at irrational na bilang.

Mga halimbawa:

   -27 $\dfrac{1}{2}$ 3.1

   $\sqrt{5}$ π $-\sqrt{\dfrac{1}{2}}$

reciprocals (reciprocals) Dalawang bilang na ang resulta ng pagmultiplika ay 1.

Halimbawa:
Ang $\dfrac{3}{5}$ at $\dfrac{5}{3}$ ay mga reciprocal sapagkat $\dfrac{3}{5} \cdot \dfrac{5}{3} = 1$.

rektanggulo (rectangle) Isang paralelogramo na ang mga magkasalungat na panig ay may parehong haba at ang lahat ng mga anggulo ay may sukat na 90°.

Mga halimbawa:

  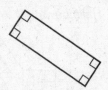

larawan (reflection) Ang imahen sa salamin ng isang pigura na "ibinaligtad" sa ibabaw ng isang linya. Ito rin ang pangalan ng pagpapanibagong-anyô na nagbabaligtad sa pigura sa ibabaw ng linya.

Halimbawa:

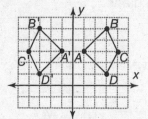

regular polygon (regular polygon) Isang polygon na kongruente ang lahat ng mga panig at anggulo.

Mga halimbawa:

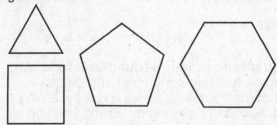

may-kaugnayang posisyon (relative position) Kinalalagyan na ibinibigay nang may kaugnayan sa ibang lugar.

Mga halimbawa:

Ang Tanggapan ng Lungsod ay katabi ng Aklatang Seltzer.

ang natitira (remainder) Ang bilang na mas kaunti sa panghati (divisor) na nananatili pagkatapos makumpleto ang proseso ng paghahati.

Halimbawa:

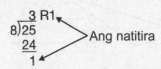

umuulit-ulit na decimal (repeating decimal) Isang decimal na may isang umuulit-ulit na tambilang o grupo ng tambilang sa kanan ng decimal point.

Mga halimbawa: $0.\overline{6}$ $0.\overline{123}$ $2.\overline{18}$

rombus (rhombus) Isang paralelogramo na may apat na panig na pantay-pantay ang haba.

Mga halimbawa:

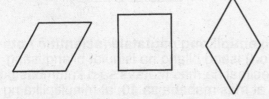

anggulong kwadrado (right angle) Isang anggulo na ang sukat ay 90°

Halimbawa:

tatsulok na may anggulong kwadrado (right triangle) Isang tatsulok na may isang anggulong kwadrado.

Mga halimbawa:

rise (rise) Sa isang linya sa isang talaguhitan, ang patayong pagbabago para sa isang tiyak na pahalang na pagbabago.

Halimbawa:

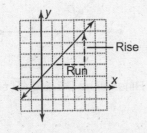

pag-ikot (rotation) Ang imahen ng isang pigura na "inikot", tila ba nasa isang gulong. Ito rin ang pangalan ng pagpapanibagong-anyô na nagpapaikot sa pigura.

Halimbawa:

simetriya sa pag-ikot (rotational symmetry) Ang isang pigura ay may simetriya sa pag-ikot kung maaari itong ikutin nang mas kakaunti sa isang buong bilog at hustong tinutumbasan nito ang kanyang orihinal na imahen.

Mga halimbawa:

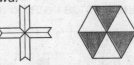

Ang bawat pigura ay may simetriya sa pag-ikot.

pagbubuo (rounding) Pagtatantiya ng isang bilang hanggang umabot ito sa isang tiyak na halaga ng puwesto.

Halimbawa:

binuo ang 2153 hanggang sa	
Pinaka-malapit na daan: 2200	Pinaka-malapit na sampu; 2150

run (run) Sa isang linya sa isang talaguhitan, ang pahalang na pagbabago na ginagamit upang hanapin ang patayong pagbabago, o rise.

Halimbawa:

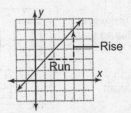

muwestra (sample) Isang pangkat ng datos na ginagamit upang hulaan kung paano maaaring mangyari ang isang tiyak na sitwasyon.

Halimbawa:
Ang lahat ng 1000 pangalan ng mga miyembro ng isang klub ay inilagay sa mga kard at pinaghaluhalo ang mga kard. Pagkatapos ay kumuha ng 100 kard at ang mga miyembrong ito ay binigyan ng isang palatanungang pangtelepono. Ang muwestra ay ang 100 miyembro na sumagot sa palatanungang pangtelepono.

halimbawang espasyo (sample space)
Ang pangkat ng lahat ng mga posibleng kinalabasan ng isang eksperimento.

Halimbawa:

Mga kinalabasan para sa Pag-itsa ng 2 barya:

barya 1	barya 2
kara	krus
kara	kara
krus	kara
krus	krus

Ang halimbawang espasyo ay kara, krus; kara, kara; at krus, krus.

iskala (sa talaguhitan) (scale (graphical))
Ang mga tanda na may pare-parehong agwat sa isa't-isa sa patayong aksis ng isang talaguhitang may baras o isang talaguhitang may linya, na ginamit upang sukatin ang mga taas ng mga baras o mga linya.

Halimbawa:

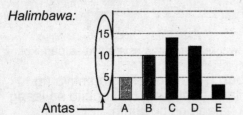

iskala (sa mga larawang-guhit na may iskala) (scale (in scale drawings)) Ang pagkakaugnay ng mga sukat sa isang larawang-guhit na may iskala sa mga sukat ng tunay na bagay. Tingnan ang iskalang larawang-guhit.

iskalang larawang-guhit (scale drawing)
Isang larawang-guhit na gumagamit ng isang iskala upang gumawa ng isang pinalaki o pinaliit na larawan ng isang bagay.

Halimbawa:

Iskalang larawang-guhit ng isang sala

Antas:
0.1 pulgada =
1 talampakan

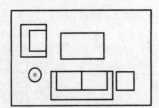

iskalang factor (scale factor) Ang pagkakaugnay na ginagamit upang palakihin o paliitin ang mga magkatulad na pigura.

Halimbawa:

$\frac{10}{5} = 2$

$\frac{6}{3} = 2$

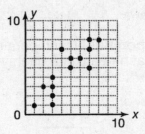

Ang iskalang factor ay 2 para sa pagpapalaki.

scalene triangle (scalene triangle) Isang tatsulok na ang mga panig ay may mga iba't-ibang haba.

Mga halimbawa:

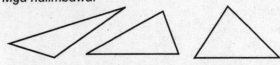

scatterplot (scatterplot) Isang talaguhitang gumagamit ng mga pinagpares na halaga ng datos bilang mga tuldok upang ipakita ang kaugnayan ng dalawang pangkat ng datos.

Halimbawa:

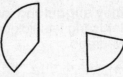

siyentipikong pagtatala (scientific notation) Isang bilang na isinulat bilang isang decimal na mas mataas sa o katumbas ng 1 at mas mababa sa 10, at minultiplika ng isang antas (power) ng 10.

Halimbawa: $350{,}000 = 3.5 \times 10^5$

sektor (sector) Isang hugis-kunyas na bahagi ng isang bilog, ginagamit sa isang talaguhitang bilog upang ipakita kung paano humahambing ang mga bahagi ng isang pangkat ng datos sa buong pangkat.

Mga halimbawa:

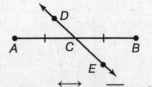

bahagi (segment) Tingnan ang *bahagi ng linya (line segement)*.

segment bisector (segment bisector)
Isang linya, ray o bahagi na dumadaan sa kalagitnaan ng isang bahagi.

Halimbawa:

Hinahati ng $\overleftrightarrow{DE}$ ang $\overline{AB}$ sa C.

pagkakasunod-sunod (sequence) Isang pagsasaayos ng mga bilang na sumusunod sa isang huwaran.

Mga halimbawa:

aritmetikang pagkakasunod-sunod

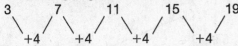

3   7   11   15   19
  +4   +4   +4   +4

geometric sequence

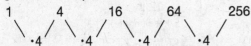

1   4   16   64   256
  ·4   ·4   ·4   ·4

panig (side) Ang bawat isa sa mga ray na bumubuo ng isang anggulo. Ito rin ang mga bahaging linya na bumubuo sa isang polygon.

Mga halimbawa:

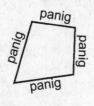

Panig-Anggulo-Anggulo (Side-Angle-Angle (SAA)) Isang tuntuning ginagamit upang tiyakin kung kongruente ang mga tatsulok sa pamamagitan ng pagham-bing ng mga magkatugong na bahagi.

Halimbawa:

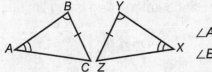

$\overline{BC} \cong \overline{YZ}$
$\angle ABC \cong \angle XYZ$
$\angle BAC \cong \angle YXZ$

$\triangle ABC \cong \triangle XYZ$ ayon sa tuntuning PAA.

Panig-Anggulo-Panig (Side-Angle-Side (SAS)) Isang tuntuning ginagamit upang tiyakin kung kongruente ang mga tatsulok sa pamamagitan ng paghambing ng mga magkatugong na bahagi.

Halimbawa:

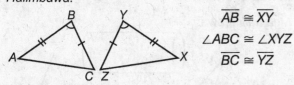

$\overline{AB} \cong \overline{XY}$
$\angle ABC \cong \angle XYZ$
$\overline{BC} \cong \overline{YZ}$

$\triangle ABC \cong \triangle XYZ$ ayon sa tuntuning PAP.

Panig-Panig-Panig (Side-Side-Side (SSS)) Isang tuntuning ginagamit upang tiyakin kung magkatumbas ba ang mga tatsulok sa pamamagitan ng paghambing ng mga magkatugong na bahagi.

Halimbawa:

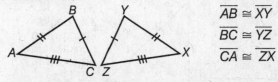

$\overline{AB} \cong \overline{XY}$
$\overline{BC} \cong \overline{YZ}$
$\overline{CA} \cong \overline{ZX}$

$\triangle ABC \cong \triangle XYZ$ ayon sa tuntuning PPP.

mga makahulugang tambilang (significant digits) Sa isang nasukat na dami, ang mga tambilang na kumakatawan sa totoong sukat.

Mga halimbawa:

380.6700   Ang lahat ng mga tambilang ay makahulugan.

0.0038   Ang 3 at 8 ay makahulugan, ngunit ni isa sa mga sero ay makahulugan.

magkatulad (similar) May magkapare-hong hugis ngunit hindi naman dapat may magkaparehong laki.

Mga halimbawa:

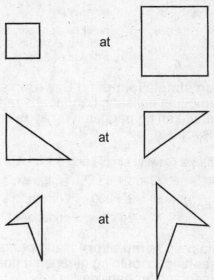

at

at

at

pagkakaugnay ng pagkakatulad (similarity ratio) Ang pagkakaugnay ng mga magkatugong na haba ng panig sa mga magkatulad na pigura.

Halimbawa:

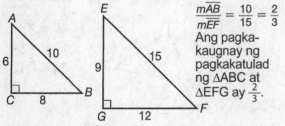

$$\frac{m\overline{AB}}{m\overline{EF}} = \frac{10}{15} = \frac{2}{3}$$

Ang pagkakaugnay ng pagkakatulad ng $\triangle ABC$ at $\triangle EFG$ ay $\frac{2}{3}$.

simpleng tubo (simple interest) Tubong batay sa puhunan lamang.

Halimbawa:

Si Ramon ay namumuhunan ng $240 sa isang account na kumikita ng 6% na tubo taun-taon sa loob ng 5 taon.

Kikita siya ng $240 \cdot 0.06 \cdot 5 = 72$; $72 bilang simpleng tubo pagkatapos ng 5 taon.

pinasimple (simplified) Isang polynomial na nagtataglay ng walang mga magkatulad na termino.

Halimbawa:

$4x^4 + x^3 + x^2 - 8$	pinasimple
$4x^4 + x^2 + 6x^2 - 8$	hindi pinasimple, sapagkat ang x^2 at $6x^2$ ay mga magkatulad na termino

gawing simple (simplify) Bawasan ang kasalimuutan ng isang pagpapahayag sa pamamagitan ng paggamit ng ayos ng mga operasyon.

Halimbawa: Gawing simple ang $3 + 8 \cdot 5^2$.

$$3 + 8 \cdot 5^2 = 3 + 8 \cdot 25 \quad \text{(mga exponent)}$$
$$= 3 + 200 \quad \text{(imultiplika)}$$
$$= 203 \quad \text{(idagdag)}$$

simulasyon (simulation) Isang pang-eksperimentong modelo ng ginagamit upang malaman ang probabilidad.

Halimbawa:

Ang isang manlalaro ng baseball ay pumapalo nang .250. Upang gayahin kung paano maaaring pumalo sa bat ang manlalarong ito, ipinaiikot ang isang "spinner" na may 4 na bahagi. Ang simulasyon ay maaaring gamitin upang hulaan kung gaano kadalas tatamaan ng manlalaro ang bola nang 2 magkakasunod o 3 magkakasunod na beses.

sine (sine) Sa isang anggulong agudo x sa isang tatsulok na may anggulong kwadrado, ang sine ng x, o sin(x), ay ang pagkakaugnay ng $\frac{\text{kasalungat na binti}}{\text{hypotenuse}}$.

Halimbawa:

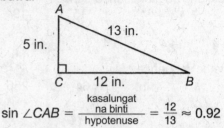

$$\sin \angle CAB = \frac{\text{kasalungat na binti}}{\text{hypotenuse}} = \frac{12}{13} \approx 0.92$$

pahilig na taas (slant height) Sa isang piramide, ang patayong layo mula sa isang gilid ng base hanggang sa tuktok.

Halimbawa:

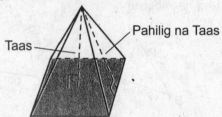

Pahilig na Taas

Taas

ipadausdos (slide) Tingnan ang *pagsalin (translation)*.

tarik (slope) Sa isang linya sa isang talaguhitan, ang tarik ay ang rise na pinaghati-hati ng "run", ito'y ginagamit upang isalarawan kung gaano katarik ang isang linya.

Halimbawa:

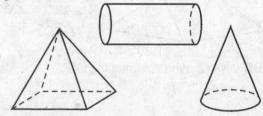

$$\frac{\text{rise}}{\text{run}} = \frac{3}{4}$$

Ang tarik ay $\frac{3}{4}$.

Rise

Run

solido (solid) Isang pigurang may tatlong dimensiyon.

Mga halimbawa:

mga kalutasan ng isang equation o inequality (solutions of an equation or inequality) Ang mga halaga ng isang variable na nagpapatotoo sa isang equation o inequality.

Mga halimbawa:

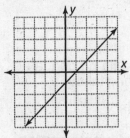 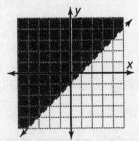

Kinakatawan ng linya ang mga kalutasan sa y = x - 1.

Ang lugar na may lilim kulay ay kumakatawan sa kalutasan sa y > x - 1.

kalutasan ng isang sistema (solution of a system) Ang mga iba't-ibang kapalit na nagpapatotoo sa lahat ng mga equation sa isang sistema.

Halimbawa: y = x + 4
y = 3x - 6

Linulutas ng pinag-ayus-ayos na pares (5, 9) ang dalawang equation. Samakatwid, ang (5, 9) ay isang kalutasan ng sistema.

lutasin (solve) Hanapin ang mga kalutasan ng isang equation o inequality.

Halimbawa: Lutasin ang x + 6 = 13.

$$x + 6 = 13$$
$$x + 6 + (-6) = 13 + (-6)$$
$$x + 0 = 7$$
$$x = 7$$

globo (sphere) Isang solido na ang lahat ng mga tuldok ay magkapareho ang layo mula sa gitna.

Halimbawa:

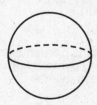

parisukat (square) Isang quadrilateral na ang lahat ng mga panig ay may magkaparehong haba at ang lahat ng mga anggulo ay may sukat na 90°.

Halimbawa:

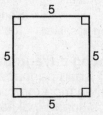

squared (squared) Pinataas sa pangalawang antas (power).

Halimbawa:
Ang 3 squared ay isinusulat bilang 3^2.
$$3^2 = 3 \times 3 = 9$$

sentimetrong parisukat (square centimeter) Ang lawak ng isang parisukat na ang mga panig ay 1 sentimetro ang haba.

Halimbawa:

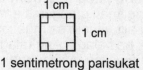

1 sentimetrong parisukat

pulgadang parisukat (square inch) Ang lawak ng isang parisukat na ang mga panig ay may 1 pulgada ang haba.

Halimbawa:

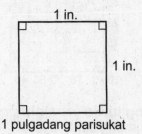

1 pulgadang parisukat

square root (square root) Ang square root ng N ay ang bilang na kapag minultiplika sa kanyang sarili ay nagreresulta sa N. Gayon din, ang square root ng isang tiyak na bilang ay ang haba ng isang panig ng isang parisukat na may isang lawak na katumbas ng tiyak na bilang.

Halimbawa:

9 × 9 = 81, kaya't ang 9 ay ang square root ng 81.
$$9 = \sqrt{81}$$

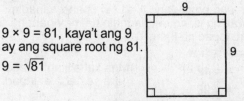

Ang lawak ay 81 square unit

pamantayang paraan (standard form)
Isang paraan ng pagsulat ng isang bilang na gumagamit ng mga tambilang.

Halimbawa:

Pamantayang paraan: 100,000,000
Paraang salita: isang daang milyon
Paraan ng bilang at salita: 100 milyon

sanga-at-dahong dayagram (stem-ang-leaf diagram) Isang pagpapakita ng datos na gumagamit ng mga tambilang ng mga bilang ng datos upang ipakita ang hugis at pamamahagi ng pangkat ng datos.

Halimbawa:

Ipinapakita ng dayagram ang pangkat ng datos: 33, 34, 34, 35, 40, 41, 46, 51, 51, 52, 53, 55, 58.

Sanga	Dahon				
3	3	4	4	5	
4	0	1	6		
5	1	1	2	3	5	8

step function (step function) Isang function na kung saan ginagamit ang mga iba't-ibang alituntunin sa mga iba't-ibang ipinapasok na halaga. Ang talaguhitan ng isang step function ay binubuo up mga walang-kaugnayang bahagi.

Halimbawa:

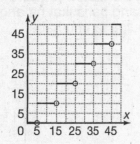

anggulong tuwid (straight angle) Isang anggulo na ang sukat ay 180°.

Halimbawa:

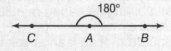

kahilili (substitute) Palitan ang isang variable ng isang tiyak na halaga.

Halimbawa:

Gamitin ang pormulang A = l • w upang hanapin ang lawak ng isang rektanggulo na may habang 12 cm at lapad na 8 cm.

A = l • w
A = 12 • 8   Mga kahaliling halaga
A = 96   para sa haba at lapad.

Ang lawak ay 96 cm².

pagbabawas (subtraction) Isang operasyon na nagsasabi kung ano ang pagkakaiba ng dalawang bilang, o kung gaano karami ang naiiwan kapag inalis ang ilan dito.

Halimbawa: 12 − 5 = 7

⊠ ⊠ ⊠ ⊠ ⊠
○ ○ ○ ○ ○
○ ○

kabuuan (sum) Ang resulta ng pagdaragdag ng dalawa o higit pang bilang.

Halimbawa: 30 + 18 = 48 —kabuuan

supplementary angles (supplementary angles) Dalawang anggulo na ang mga sukat kapag idinagdag ay 180°.

Halimbawa:

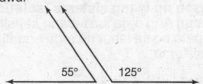

lawak ng kalatagan (surface area [SA]) Ang kabuuan ng mga lawak ng bawat mukha ng isang polyhedron.

Halimbawa:

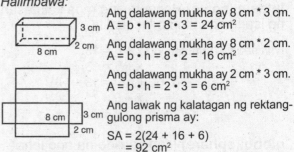

Ang dalawang mukha ay 8 cm * 3 cm.
A = b • h = 8 • 3 = 24 cm²

Ang dalawang mukha ay 8 cm * 2 cm.
A = b • h = 8 • 2 = 16 cm²

Ang dalawang mukha ay 2 cm * 3 cm.
A = b • h = 2 • 3 = 6 cm²

Ang lawak ng kalatagan ng rektangulong prisma ay:

SA = 2(24 + 16 + 6)
= 92 cm²

palatanungan (survey) Isang pagsusuri na nag-aatas ng paglikom at pag-analisa ng impormasyon.

Halimbawa:

Isinagawa ang isang palatanungan upang tiyakin kung anong larong pampalakasan ang pinaka-popular sa mga estudyante.

simetriya (symmetry) Tingnan ang *simetriya ng linya (line symmetry), point symmetry* at *simetriya sa pag-ikot (rotational symmetry).*

sistema ng mga linear equation (system of linear equations) Dalawa o higit pang mga linear equation na itinuturing na magkasama.

Halimbawa: y = x + 3
                y = 4x - 15

talaang T (T-table) Isang talaang nagpa-pakita sa mga magkatugon na halagang x at halagang y para sa isang equation.

Halimbawa:

$$y = 2x + 1$$

x	y
-2	-3
-1	-1
0	1
1	3
2	5

talaan (tally) Isang tala, na gumagamit ng mga marka ng talaan, ng isang pagbilang na ginawa sa isang palatanungan.

Halimbawa:

Sasakyan	Talaan
Sedan	IIII III
Station Wagon	IIII
Suburban	IIII I
Trak	IIII
Van	III

mga marka ng talaan (tally marks) Mga markang ginagamit upang isaayos ang isang malaking pangkat ng datos. Ipinapa-kita ng bawat marka ang isang beses kung kailan lumilitaw ang isang halaga sa pang-kat ng datos.

Halimbawa: | Isa   IIII Lima

tangent line (tangent line) Isang linyang dumidikit sa isang bilog sa iisang lugar lamang.

Mga halimbawa:

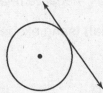

tangent na pagkakaugnay (tangent ratio) Sa isang anggulong agudo x sa isang tatsulok na may anggulong kwadrado, ang tangent ng x, o tan(x), ay $\frac{\text{kasalungat na binti}}{\text{katabing binti}}$.

Halimbawa:

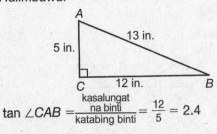

$$\tan \angle CAB = \frac{\text{kasalungat na binti}}{\text{katabing binti}} = \frac{12}{5} = 2.4$$

termino (term) Isang bilang sa isang pag-kakasunod-sunod. Ito rin ang isang bahagi ng isang polynomial na isang bilang na may senyas (signed number), isang vari-able o isang bilang na minultiplika ng isang variable o mga variable. Ang mga variable ay maaaring magkaroon ng mga exponent na mga numerong buo.

Mga halimbawa:

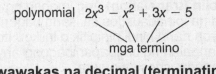

pagkakasunod-sunod   3   7   11   15   19   23
mga termino

polynomial $2x^3 - x^2 + 3x - 5$
mga termino

nagwawakas na decimal (terminating decimal) Isang decimal na may itinakdang dami ng mga tambilang.

Mga halimbawa: 3.5   0.599992   4.05

tessellation (tessellation) Isang umuulit-ulit na huwaran ng mga pigura na tumat-akip sa isang patag nang walang kakulan-gan o mga pagkakasanib.

Mga halimbawa:

teoretikal na probabilidad (theoretical probability) Ang pagkakaugnay ng dami ng mga paraan na ang isang bagay ay maaaring mangyari sa kabuuang dami ng mga posibleng kinalabasan.

Halimbawa:

$$\frac{\text{Dami ng mga paraan kung paano makakarating sa puti}}{\text{mga kabuuang paraan}} = \frac{3}{6} = \frac{1}{2}$$

Dahil ang kalahati ng mga seksiyon sa spinner ay puti, ang teoretikal na probabilidad na makakara-ting sa puti ay $\frac{1}{2}$.

pagpapanibagong-anyô (transformation)
Isang pagbabago sa posisyon ng isang pigura.

Halimbawa:

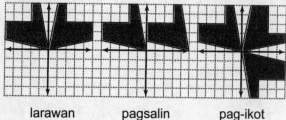

larawan   pagsalin   pag-ikot

pagsalin (translation)
Ang imahen ng isang pigura na ipinadausdos sa isang bagong posisyon nang hindi pinipitik o iniikot. Ito rin ang pangalan ng pagpapanibagong-anyô na nagpapadausdos sa pigura.

Halimbawa:

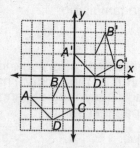

transversal (transversal)
Isang linya na bumabagtas sa dalawa o higit pang mga linya.

Halimbawa:

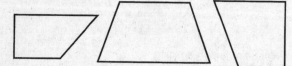

transversal

trapezoid (trapezoid)
Isang quadrilateral na may hustong dalawang panig na paralelo.

Mga halimbawa:

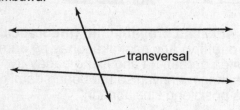

dayagram ng puno (tree diagram)
Isang nagsasangang dayagram na katulad ng puno na nagpapakita ng lahat ng mga posibleng kinalabasan ng isang sitwasyon.

Halimbawa:

Pag-itsa ng 3 barya: Ang lahat ng mga
Barya 1 Barya 2 Barya 3 posibleng kinalabasan:

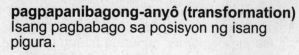

kara	kara	kara	kara, kara, kara
		krus	kara, kara, krus
	krus	kara	kara, krus, kara
		krus	kara, krus, krus
krus	kara	kara	krus, kara, kara
		krus	krus, kara, krus
	krus	kara	krus, krus, kara
		krus	krus, krus, krus

pagkahilig (trend)
Isang kaugnayan sa pagitan ng dalawang pangkat ng datos na lumilitaw bilang huwaran sa isang scatterplot. Tingnan ang *positibong kaugnayan (positive relationship), negatibong kaugnayan (negative relationship), walang kaugnayan (no relationship).*

linya ng pagkahilig (trend line)
Isang linya na humigit-kumulang na "nagbabagay" sa mga punto upang bumuo ng isang pagkahilig sa isang scatterplot. Tingnan ang *positibong kaugnayan (positive relationship)* at *negatibong kaugnayan (negative relationship).*

pagsubok (trial)
Isang eksperimento.

Mga halimbawa:

Isang pag-itsa   Isang pag-itsa
ng isang dice   ng isang barya

tatsulok (triangle)
Isang polygon na may tatlong panig.

Mga halimbawa:

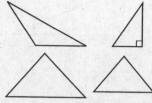

mga pagkakaugnay pang-trigonometriya (trigonometric ratios) Mga pagkakaugnay ng mga haba ng panig ng isang tatsulok na may anggulong kwadrado, na kaugnay ng mga sukat ng mga anggulong agudo ng tatsulok.

Mga halimbawa:

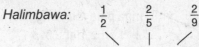

$$\cos \angle CAB = \frac{\text{katabing binti}}{\text{hypotenuse}} = \frac{3}{5} = 0.6$$

$$\sin \angle CAB = \frac{\text{kasalungat na binti}}{\text{hypotenuse}} = \frac{4}{5} = 0.8$$

$$\tan \angle CAB = \frac{\text{kasalungat na binti}}{\text{katabing binti}} = \frac{4}{3} \approx 1.3$$

trinomial (trinomial) Isang polynomial na may tatlong termino.

Mga halimbawa: $2x^3 - x^2 + 3x$ $3x^2 + 2x - 4$

ibaligtad (turn) Tingnan ang *pag-ikot (rotation)*.

di-makatarungang laro (unfair game) Isang laro kung saan hindi lahat ng mga manlalaro ay may pare-parehong probabilidad na manalo.

Halimbawa:
Di-makatarungang laro: Iniitsa ang isang pares ng dice at itinalaga sa bawat manlalaro ang isang kabuuan mula 2 hanggang 12. Ang bawat manlalaro ay binibigyan ng isang punto kapag lumitaw ang kanyang kabuuan. Dahil ang mga kabuuan mula 2 hanggang 12 huwag ay walang pantay-pantay na pagkakataong lumitaw, ang mga manlalaro ay walang pantay-pantay na pagkakataong manalo at sa gayon ay di-makatarungan ang laro.

presyo ng isa (unit price) Halaga ng isa na ibinibigay sa halaga ng isang bagay.

Mga halimbawa:

$5.75 bawat libra $3.00 bawat kahon

unit (unit) Anumang isang bagay. Isang halaga o daming ginagamit bilang pamantayan ng pagsusukat.

unit na hatimbilang (unit fraction) Isang hatimbilang na ang kabilangan ay 1.

Mga halimbawa: $\frac{1}{4}$ $\frac{1}{2}$ $\frac{1}{7}$

unit rate (unit rate) Isang rate kung saan ang pangalawang bilang sa paghahambing ay isang unit.

Mga halimbawa: 25 galon bawat minuto $\frac{55\ \text{milya}}{1\ \text{oras}}$

mga di-magkatulad na panghatimbilang (unlike denominators) Mga panghatimbilang na kakaiba sa dalawa o higit pang mga hatimbilang.

Halimbawa:

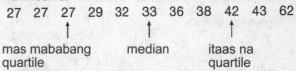

mga di-magkatulad na panghatimbilang

itaas na quartile (upper quartile) Ang median ng itaas na kalahati ng isang pangkat ng datos.

Halimbawa:

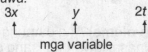

27   27   27   29   32   33   36   38   42   43   62

mas mababang quartile   median   itaas na quartile

variable (variable) Isang dami na maaaring magbago o mag-iba-iba, madalas na kinakatawan ng isang titik.

Mga halimbawa:
$3x$ y $2t$
mga variable

Venn diagram (Venn diagram) Isang dayagram na gumagamit ng mga rehiyon upang ipakita ang mga kaugnayan ng mga pangkat ng mga bagay.

Halimbawa:

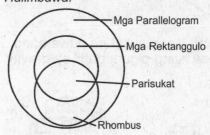

Mga Parallelogram
Mga Rektanggulo
Parisukat
Rhombus

vertex (vertex) Sa isang anggulo o isang polygon, ang lugar kung saan bumabagtas ang dalawang panig. Sa isang polyhedron, ang tuldok na bagtasan ng tatlo o higit pang mukha.

Mga halimbawa:

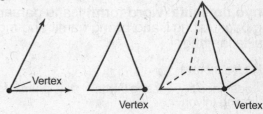

Vertex   Vertex   Vertex

mga patayong anggulo (vertical angles)
Ang mga anggulong nasa mga kasalungat na panig ng bagtasan ng dalawang linya.

Halimbawa:

mga patayong anggulo:
∠1 at ∠3
∠2 at ∠4

patayong aksis (vertical axis)
Ang patayong linya ng dalawang linya kung saan nakabatay ang isang talaguhitang may baras o isang coordinate plane.

Mga halimbawa:

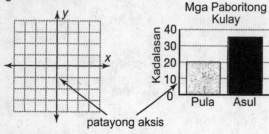

patayong aksis

bolumen (volume)
Ang dami ng espasyong sinasaklawan ng isang solido.

Halimbawa:

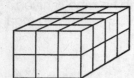

$V = lwh$
$V = 4 \cdot 3 \cdot 2$
$V = 24$ cubic unit

bigat (weight)
Isang sukat ng puwersang umaapekto sa isang pigura dahil sa gravity.

Mga halimbawa:

1 oz   1 lb   1 tonelada

buong bilang (whole number)
Anumang bilang sa pangkat {0,1,2,3,4,...}.

anyô ng salita (word form)
Isang paraan ng pagsulat ng isang bilang gamit ang mga salita lamang.

Mga halimbawa:

apatnapu't-limang trilyon   isang bilyon   anim

x-aksis (x-axis)
Ang pahalang na aksis sa isang coordinate plane.

Halimbawa:

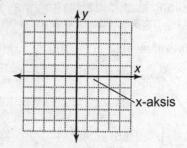

x-aksis

x-coordinate (x-coordinate)
Ang unang bilang sa isang pinag-ayus-ayos na pares.

Halimbawa:

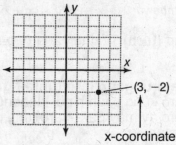

(3, −2)

x-coordinate

x-intercept (x-intercept)
Ang lugar kung saan bumabagtas ang isang talaguhitan ng isang equation sa x-aksis.

Halimbawa:

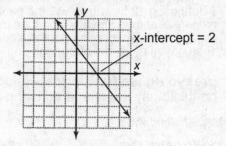

x-intercept = 2

y-aksis (y-axis)
Ang patayong aksis sa isang coordinate plane.

Halimbawa:

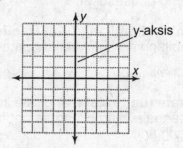

y-aksis

y-coordinate (y-coordinate) Ang pangalawang bilang sa isang pinag-ayus-ayos na
pares.

Halimbawa:

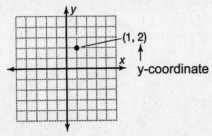

y-intercept (y-intercept) Ang lugar kung
saan bumabagtas ang talaguhitan ng isang
equation sa y-aksis.

Halimbawa:

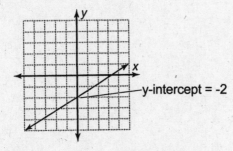

yarda (yard) Isang unit sa kinaugaliang
sistema ng pagsusukat na katumbas ng 3
talampakan.

Halimbawa:

Ang taas ng isang
mesang sulatan ay
humigit-kumulang
sa isang yarda.

serong pares (zero pair) Isang bilang at
ang kanyang kasalungat.

Mga halimbawa: 7 at -7   23 at -23

**Katangiang Sero ng Pagdaragdag (Zero
Property of Addition)** Ang kabuuan ng
isang integer at ang kanyang kabaligtaran
ng pagdaragdag ay 0.

Mga halimbawa: $3 + (-3) = 0$

$-8 + 8 = 0$

Mandarin Glossary

绝对位置 (absolute position) 按坐标给定的位置。

例子：

B7 是 Seltzer 图书馆的绝对位置。

绝对值 (absolute value) 从零到某个数的距离。绝对值的符号是 ｜ ｜ 。

例子：

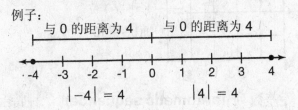

锐角 (acute angle) 测量值小于 90° 的角。

例子：

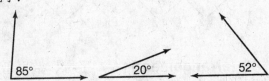

锐角三角形 (acute triangle) 具有三个锐角的三角形。

例子：

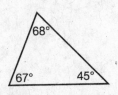

加数 (addend) 与一个或一个以上的其它数相加的数。

例子：
$$12 + 19 = 31$$

加数　　加数

加法 (addition) 将两个或两个以上的数放在一起求出总和的运算。

例子：

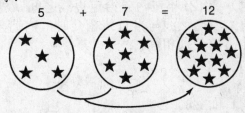

方程式的加法性质 (Addition Property of Equality) 如果 a = b，那么 a + c = b + c。

例子：
在以下例子的第二行中，把方程式的两侧各加 1。

如果　　　　　x - 1 = 2
那么　　　　　x - 1 + 1 = 2 + 1
　　　　　　　x = 3

加法逆元 (additive inverse) 一个数的相反数。

例子：　-2 的加法逆元是 2。
　　　　5 的加法逆元是 -5。

直角边 (adjacent leg) 与直角三角形的锐角相对，位于锐角的两侧之一的那条边。

例子：

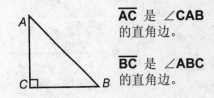

$\overline{AC}$ 是 ∠CAB 的直角边。

$\overline{BC}$ 是 ∠ABC 的直角边。

代数 (algebra) 数学的一个分支，它通过使用变量来表示数字，从而研究其中的算术关系。

代数式 (algebraic expression) 至少含有一个变量的表达式。

例子：　n - 7　　　　2y + 17　　　　5(x - 3)

错角 (alternate angles) 由两条直线和一条截线形成的两个角，这两个角在截线的相对两侧，在 (1) 两条给定直线之间（内错角）或 (2) 不在两条给定直线之间（外错角）。当截线与平行线相交时，内错角和外错角分别相等。

例子：

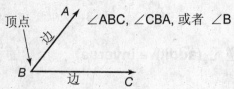

外错角：
    ∠1 和 ∠8
    ∠2 和 ∠7
内错角：
    ∠3 和 ∠6
    ∠4 和 ∠5

外部

内部

外部

角 (angle) 具有一个公共端点的两条射线。

例子：

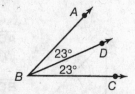

∠ABC, ∠CBA, 或者 ∠B

顶点
边
边

角平分线 (angle bisector) 把一个角分成两个相等角的一条射线。

例子：

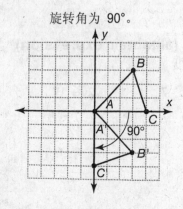

$\overline{BD}$ 是 ∠ABC 的角平分线

旋转角 (angle of rotation) 图形在旋转期时所转过的角度。

例子：

旋转角为 90°。

角边角 (Angle-Side-Angle (ASA)) 用于通过比较相应部分确定三角形是否全等的定律。

例子：

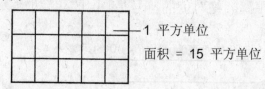

∠ABC ≅ ∠XYZ
$\overline{BC}$ ≅ $\overline{YZ}$
∠ACB ≅ ∠XZY

根据 △ASA 定律，△ABC ≅ △XYZ。

面积 (area) 某图形所覆盖的表面的测量。

例子：

1 平方单位
面积 = 15 平方单位

等差数列 (arithmetic sequence) 一种特殊的数列，从第二项起，每一项与前一的项差始终相等。

例子：

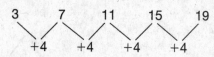

3   7   11   15   19
  +4   +4   +4   +4

排列 (arrangement) 人、字母、数字或其它事件出现的顺序。

例子：
三个形状所有可能的排列：

加法结合律 (Associative Property of Addition) 改变加数的分组，而总和不变的定律。

例子：   a + (b + c) = (a + b) + c
        5 + (3 + 7) = (5 + 3) + 7

乘法的结合律 (Associative Property of Multiplication) 改变乘数的分组，而乘积不变的定律。

例子：
$$a(bc) = (ab)c$$
$$3 \times (4 \times 2) = (3 \times 4) \times 2$$

平均数 (average) 见平均数。

轴 (axes) 见 x 轴和 y 轴。

条形图 (bar graph) 使用垂直或水平条以显示数据的图。

例子：

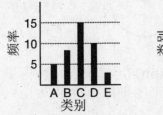

（指数的）底数 (base (of an exponent)) 以指数所显示的数为倍数、与自身相乘的数。

例子：

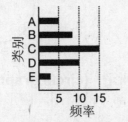

底数　指数
$$6^2 = 6 \times 6 = 36$$

（多边形的）底边 (base (of a polygon)) 任何一边（通常指底部的边），或者这个边的边长。

例子：

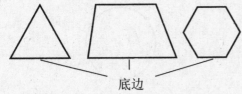

底边

（立体的）底面 (base (of a solid)) 棱柱或圆柱体中两个平行且相等的面中的一面。棱椎中与顶角相对的面。圆锥体中的圆形面。

例子：

底面　　底面　　底面

二进制 (binary number system) 逢 2 进 1 的进位制。

例子：
在二进制中，1011 等于十进位（逢 10 进 1）数制中的 11。

	八位	四位	二位	个位
逢 2 进一	1	0	1	1
制值	8	4	2	1
乘积	1×8=8	0×4=0	1×2=2	1×1=1

$(1 \times 8) + (0 \times 4) + (1 \times 2) + (1 \times 1) = 8 + 0 + 2 + 1 = 11$

二项式 (binomial) 两项的多项式。

例子：　$4x^3 - 2x^2$　　　$2x + 5$

平分 (bisect) 把一个角或线段分成两个相等的角或线段。

例子：

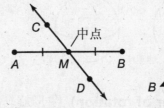
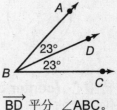

$\overleftrightarrow{CD}$ 平分 $\overline{AB}$。　　　$\overrightarrow{BD}$ 平分 $\angle ABC$。

分界线 (boundary line) 在线性不等式的图上，将是解的点与不是解的点分隔开的线。

例子：

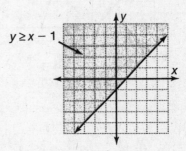

$y = x - 1$ 是分界线。

盒须图 (box-and-whisker plot) 显示数据集如何分布的视觉方法。下面的例子以下列十次测验分数为根据：52、64、75、79、80、80、81、88、92、99

例子：

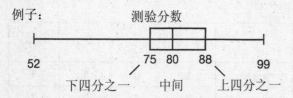

测验分数

下四分之一　中间　上四分之一

容量 (capacity) 容器的液体测量体积。

例子：

500 ml　1 L　1 杯　1 夸脱　1 加仑

球心 (center) 圆或球形正中间的点。

例子：

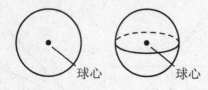

旋转中心 (center of rotation) 图形旋转所围绕的点。

例子：

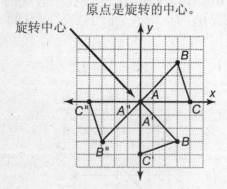

原点是旋转的中心。

旋转中心

厘 (centi-) 表示 $\frac{1}{100}$ 的前缀。

例子：1 厘米 = $\frac{1}{100}$ 米

圆心角 (central angle) 顶点在圆心的角。

例子：

点 C 是圆心。

∠BCA 是圆心角

圆 (circle) 所有点距其中心都相等的平面图。

例子：

圆形图 (circle graph) 用楔形表示数据集各部分的圆图。圆形图也称为饼图。

例子：

喜欢的宠物

狗 40%　猫 25%　鸟 20%　15% 其它

圆周 (circumference) 围绕圆周围的距离。

例子：

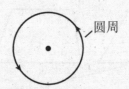

圆周

外切图形 (circumscribed figure) 一个图形包含另一图形。多边形包围圆，其中圆与多边形的每条边相切。

例子：

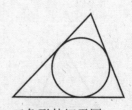

三角形外切于圆。

顺时针 (clockwise) 图形的顶部向右转时的旋转方向。

例子：

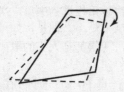

归类 (clustering) 一种把大约相等的数作为相等的数处理的估算方法。

例子：
26 + 24 + 23 约为 25 + 25 + 25，或者 3 x 25。

系数 (coefficient) 与变量相乘的常量。

例子：

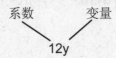

系数　　　变量

12y

组合 (combination) 项的集合，其中的顺序无关紧要。

例子：
将从这组学生中选两个作为委员会成员：David、Juanita、Kim。
可能的组合有：
David、Juanita　David、Kim　Juanita、Kim
注意：组合"David、Juanita"与组合"Juanita、David"相同。

公分母 (common denominator) 两个或两个以上分数中相同的分母。

例子：

$$\frac{5}{6} \quad \frac{1}{6} \qquad \frac{3}{12} \quad \frac{5}{12} \quad \frac{11}{12}$$

公分母　　　　　公分母

公因数 (common factor) 作为两个或两个以上数的共同因数的数。

例子：
4 是 8、12 和 20 的公因数。
$$8 = 4 \times 2$$
$$12 = 4 \times 3$$
$$20 = 4 \times 5$$

公倍数 (common multiple) 作为两个或两个以上给定数中每个数的倍数的数。

例子：
3的倍数：3　6　9　**12**　15　18　21　**24**　27 ......
4的倍数：4　8　**12**　16　20　**24**　28 ......
12 和 24 是 3 和 4 的两个公倍数。

加法交换律 (Commutative Property of Addition) 在加法运算中，加数的顺序不影响总和的定律。

例子：
$$a + b = b + a$$
$$18 + 23 = 23 + 18$$

乘法交换律 (Commutative Property of Multiplication) 在乘法运算中，乘数的顺序不影响乘积的定律。

例子：
$$ab = ba$$
$$4 \times 7 = 7 \times 4$$

相配的数 (compatible numbers) 容易进行计算的一对数。

例子：　30 + 70　　　40 ÷ 4　　　25 + 75

补偿法 (compensation) 选择与题目中的数接近的这些数，然后调整答案以对选定的数进行补偿的心算策略。

例子：　$99 \times 4 = (100 - 1) \times 4$

$$= (100 \times 4) - (1 \times 4)$$

$$= 400 - 4$$

$$= 396$$

互余角 (complementary angles) 角度相加等于 90° 的两个角。

例子：

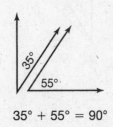

$$35° + 55° = 90°$$

合数 (composite number) 具有多于两个约数的、大于 1 的整数。

例子:
15 的约数为: 1, 3, 5, 15
　　　　15 是合数。
7 的约数为: 1, 7
　　　　7 不是合数。

复合事件 (compound event) 由两个或两个以上单个事件组合起来的事件。

例子:

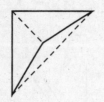 和

硬币抛掷中出现人头的一面且丢骰子出现 1 是一个复合事件。

复利 (compound interest) 在本金和先前利息的基础上计算出的利息。

例子:
如果你在储蓄帐户上存入 $100, 每年复利 6%, 第一年你将拥有 $100 + (0.06 x 100) = $106, 而第二年你将拥有 $106 + (0.06 x 106) = $112.36。

复合语句 (compound statement) 通过把两个或多个语句连在一起形成的逻辑语句。

例子:
　　10 大于 5 且 10 小于 21。
　　10 大于 5 还是 10 小于 5。

凹多边形 (concave polygon) 存在一条或一条以上的对角线位于图形外部的多边形。

例子:

条件概率 (conditional probability) 假定事件 A 已经发生, 事件 B 发生的概率。

例子:
如果你知道两次硬币投掷当中第一次是背面, 则投掷两次人头的概率是零。但是, 如果你知道第一次投掷的是人头, 两次都是人头的概率则为 $\frac{1}{2}$。

圆锥 (cone) 具有一个圆形底面的立体。

例子:

全等 (congruent) 具有相同的尺寸和形状。

例子:

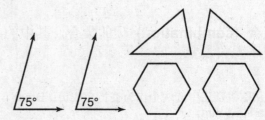

圆锥投影 (conic projection) 使用圆锥形表示球形的图形投影。

例子:

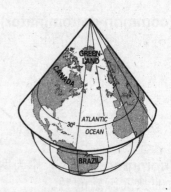

合取词 (conjunction) 使用文字 "和"、 "且"、 "与" 等连接的逻辑语句集合。

例子:
　　x > -2 且 x < 5
　　正方形有 4 个等长的边, 且正方形是矩形。

常数 (constant) 一个不改变的量。

例子：
在代数式 x + 7 中，7 是常数。

常数图 (constant graph) 线的高度恒定的图。

例子：

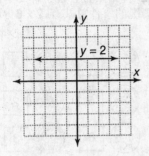

比例常数 (constant of proportionality) 对于两个变量 x 和 y 量，数值 $\frac{x}{y}$ 恒定。通常由 k 表示。

例子：

x	3	6	9	12
y	5	10	15	20

$k = \frac{5}{3}$

换算因子 (conversion factor) 用于把量值从一个单位换算成另一个单位的恒等性。它经常用分数来表示。

例子：

12 英寸 = 1 英尺； $\frac{12 \text{ 英寸}}{1 \text{ 英尺}}$

4 夸脱 = 1 加仑； $\frac{4 \text{ 夸脱}}{1 \text{ 加仑}}$

凸多边形 (convex polygon) 所有对角线都在图形内部的多边形。

例子：

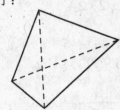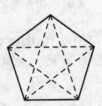

坐标 (coordinates) 用于定位坐标平面上一点的、有序对中的一对数。

例子：

(5, 6)
| |
坐标

坐标平面、坐标系 (coordinate plane, coordinate system) 用于定位点的垂直和水平数值轴相交的系统。

例子：

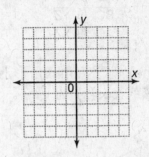

同位角 (对于多条线来说) (corresponding angles (for lines)) 截线与两条或两条以上直线相交时，与截线同侧的角。当截线与平行线相交时同位角相等。

例子：

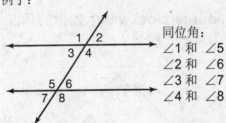

同位角：
∠1 和 ∠5
∠2 和 ∠6
∠3 和 ∠7
∠4 和 ∠8

对应角（在相似图形中）(corresponding angles (in similar figures)) 相似图形上的匹配角。

例子：
△ABC ~ △XYZ

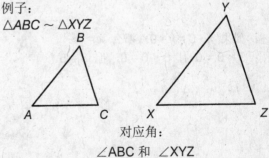

对应角：
∠ABC 和 ∠XYZ
∠BCA 和 ∠YZX
∠CAB 和 ∠ZXY

对应边 (corresponding sides) 相似图形上的匹配边。

例子：

△ABC ~ △XYZ

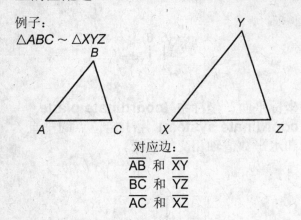

对应边：
$\overline{AB}$ 和 $\overline{XY}$
$\overline{BC}$ 和 $\overline{YZ}$
$\overline{AC}$ 和 $\overline{XZ}$

余弦 (cosine) 对于直角三角形上的锐角 x，x 的余弦或 cos(x) 为 $\frac{邻边}{斜边}$。

例子：

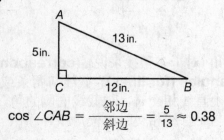

$$\cos \angle CAB = \frac{邻边}{斜边} = \frac{5}{13} \approx 0.38$$

逆时针 (counterclockwise) 图形的顶部向左转时的旋转方向。

例子：

反例 (counterexample) 显示陈述不正确性的例子。

例子：

陈述：如果 x • 0 = y • 0，那么 x = y。
反例：3 × 0 = 0 且 5 × 0 = 0，但 3 ≠ 5。

计数原理 (Counting Principle) 如果一个情况可以通过 m 种方式出现，第二个情况可以通过 n 种方式出现，那么包含两种情况的事件总共可以通过 m x n 种方式出现。

例子：

投掷硬币有 2 种结果且丢骰子有 6 种结果。因此包含这两种情况的事件总共有 2 x 6 或者 12 种方式出现。

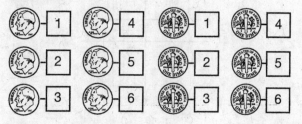

交叉乘积 (cross product) 一个比率的分子与另一个比率的分母的乘积。

例子：

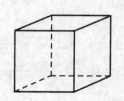

交叉乘积：

$1 \times 5 = 5$
$3 \times 2 = 6$

立方体 (cube) 6 个面都是全等正方形的棱柱。

例子：

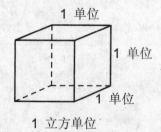

三次方 (cubed) 提升到三次幂。

例子：2 的三次方 = 2^3 = 2 x 2 x 2 = 8

立方单位 (cubic unit) 测量体积的单位，由边长等于一个单位的立方体组成。

例子：

1 单位
1 单位
1 单位

1 立方单位

常用测量系统 (customary system of measurement) 美国的常用测量系统：英寸、英尺、英里、盎司、英镑、吨、杯、夸脱、加仑等。

例子：

长度　　　1 加仑 容积　　　重量

圆柱体 (cylinder) 具有两个平行的圆形底面的立体。

例子：

圆柱投影 (cylindrical projection) 使用圆柱形表示球形表面的图形投影。

例子：

十边形 (decagon) 具有十个边的多边形。

例子：

十分之一 (deci-) 表示 $\frac{1}{10}$ 的前缀。

例子：　　　　　1 分米 $= \frac{1}{10}$ 米

小数 (decimal) 用小数点写出的任何基于 10 进制的数。

例子：　6.21　0.59　12.2　5.0

小数加法 (decimal addition) 两个或两个以上的小数相加。

例子：

```
      1
   12.65
 + 29.10
   41.75
```

小数除法 (decimal division) 两个小数相除。

例子：

```
              1.25
   0.24 )0.30 0 0
         - 24
           60
         - 48
          1 2 0
        - 1 2 0
              0
```

小数乘法 (decimal multiplication) 两个或多个小数相乘。

例子：

```
       2
    0.13    2 位小数位
  ×  0.7    1 位小数位
  0.091     3 位小数位
```

小数减法 (decimal subtraction) 两个小数相减。

例子：

```
      1312
    4 3 210
   54.30
 - 16.58
   37.72
```

十进制 (decimal system) 逢 10 进 1 的进位制。

例子：

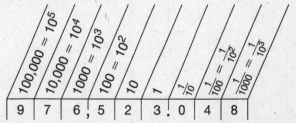

递减图 (decreasing graph) 线的高度从左到右逐步下降的图形。

例子：

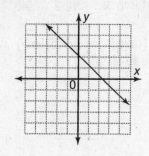

演绎推理 (deductive reasoning) 运用逻辑来得出结论。

例子：
当把一条对角线添加到任何四边形时，就形成两个三角形。三角形的角度之和为 180°。因此，四边形的角度之和是三角形的两倍，即：2 x 180° = 360°。

度(°) (degree) 角度的测量单位。

例子：1° 是整个圆的 $\frac{1}{360}$。

最高次幂 (degree) 在多项式中，变量的最大指数值。

例子：$5x^3 - 2x^2 + 7x$ 的最高次幂是 3。

十 (deka-) 表示 10 的前缀。

例子：1 十米 = 10 米

分母 (denominator) 分数中分数线下面的数字，以显示整体被分成了多少份。

例子：

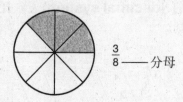

$\frac{3}{8}$ —— 分母

相依事件 (dependent events) 一个事件结果影响另一个事件结果的概率。

例子：
把 Therese、Diane 和 José 的名字分别写在几个纸条上。抽出并保存一个纸条。接着抽出另一纸条。假设抽出的第一个纸条上写的是 Therese 的名字，那么抽出 Diane 名字的概率是 $\frac{1}{2}$。

因变量 (dependent variable) 一个函数的输出变量。

例子：

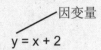

因变量

$y = x + 2$

对角线 (diagonal) 在一个多边形上，连接两个不在同一条边上的顶点的线段。

例子：

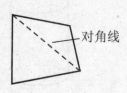

对角线

直径 (diameter) 经过圆心且其两端点在圆上的线段或其长度。

例子：

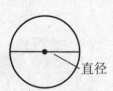

直径

差 (difference) 一个数与另一个数相减的结果。

例子：

28 - 15 = 13

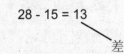

差

阿拉伯数字 (digit) 用于写数字 0、1、2、3、4、5、6、7、8 和 9 的符号。

例子：

在 5,847 中，阿拉伯数字是 5、8、4 和 7。

伸缩 (dilation) 图形按一定比例缩小或扩大。

例子：
小矩形对大矩形的伸缩比例系数为 3。

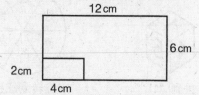

正变分 (direct variation) 两个变量的比例恒定。

例子：

时间以小时计 (x)	1	2	3	4
距离以英里计 (y)	55	110	165	220

$$\frac{y}{x} = 55$$

析取 (disjunction) 由词"或"连接的逻辑语句集。

例子：

x > 4 or x < -1
我们去看电影或看电视。

分配律 (Distributive Property)
a(b + c) = ab + ac 的定律。

例子：3(6 + 5) = 3 · 6 + 3 · 5

被除数 (dividend) 在除法运算中被除的那个数。

例子：

被除数
8 ÷ 4 = 2

整除 (divisible) 可以被另一个数相除而无余数。

例子：18 可被 6 整除，因为 18 ÷ 6 = 3。

除法 (division) 把一个整体分割成多少相等组或每个所分割的相等组中有多少的运算。

例子：

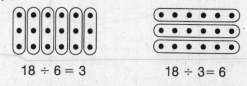

18 ÷ 6 = 3   18 ÷ 3 = 6

18 分成 6组每组有3个。18 分成3组每组有6个。

除数 (divisor) 用来除另一个数的数。

例子：

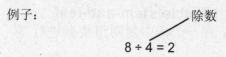

除数
8 ÷ 4 = 2

十二边形 (dodecagon) 具有十二个边的多边形。

例子：

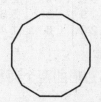

双条图 (double bar graph) 比较两个相关数据集的两个条形图的组合。

例子：

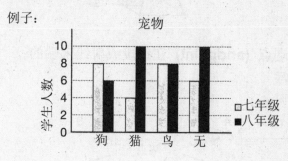

双线图 (double line graph) 两个线形图的组合，对两个相关数据集进行比较。

例子：

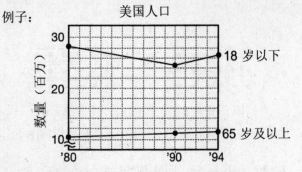

美国人口

双茎叶图 (double stem-and-leaf diagram) 在一个图中对两组数据进行茎叶比较。

例子：

叶	茎	叶
7 2 1	3	0 1 3
5 0 0	4	2 3
9	5	5 6 8
5 2 0	6	1 4

边 (edge) 多边形的两个面相交的线段。

例子：

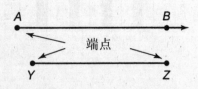

面
边

端点 (endpoint) 在线段或射线末端的点。

例子：

A B
端点
Y Z

等式 (equality) 完全相同的数学关系。

例子： 16 + 8 = 24   25 ÷ 5 = 5

等可能的结果 (equally-likely outcomes) 具有相同概率的结果。

例子：

丢到"1"
概率：$\frac{1}{6}$

蓝 红
绿 灰
黄 白

旋转到红色的
概率：$\frac{1}{6}$

等比 (equal ratios) 指定相同量的比率。

例子： $\frac{2}{6}$、$\frac{1}{3}$ 和 $\frac{4}{12}$

等式 (equation) 表示两个表达式相等的数学句子。

例子：

$14 = 2x$ $3 + y = 81$ $3 + 4 = 7$

等边三角形 (equilateral triangle) 三边具有相同长度的三角形。

例子：

4   4
4

等价方程 (equivalent equations) 具有完全相同的置换变量的方程。

例子： $x - 5 = 10$ 和 $x = 15$

等价表达式 (equivalent expressions) 对于相同的置换，两个表达式始终具有相同值。

例子： $5(x + 1)$ 和 $5x + 5$

相等的分数 (equivalent fractions) 表示相同的数的两个分数。

例子： $\frac{1}{2}$ 和 $\frac{8}{16}$

等同速率 (equivalent rates) 速率相同的量。

例子：

$$\frac{40英里}{2小时} \quad 和 \quad \frac{20英里}{1小时}$$

等比率 (equivalent ratios) 见等比。

估计 (estimate) 计算结果的近似值。

例子：

$$99 \times 21$$
$$估计：100 \times 20 = 2000$$
$$99 \times 21 \approx 2000$$

欧拉方程 (Euler's formula) 有关多面体中面 (F)、顶点 (V) 和边 (E) 的数量的方程，表示为 F + V - E = 2。

例子：

对于所示三棱锥，
$$5 + 5 - 8 = 2$$
面　顶点　边

求值 (evaluate) 替换表达式中的变量值，然后利用运算顺序进行简化。

例子：对于 x = 10，求 8(x − 3) 的值。
$$8(x - 3) = 8(10 - 3)$$
$$= 8(7)$$
$$= 56$$

偶数 (even number) 个位数字为 0、2、4、6 或 8 的整数。

例子：　16　　28　　34　　112　　3000

事件 (event) 试验或情况的结果或结果的集合。

例子：
事件：　　　　　　　丢一个骰子时获得 3
　　　　　　　　　　或更大的数。
这个事件的
可能结果：　　　　　3, 4, 5, 6

展开式 (expanded form) 写出显示所有单个因子的指数的方法。

例子：　　　指数　　　　9^3
　　　　　　展开式　　　$9 \times 9 \times 9$

试验 (experiment) 在概率中，涉及偶然性的任何行为。

例子：
投币　　　　　丢骰子　　　　纺纱机纺纱

试验概率 (experimental probability) 以试验或调查的数据为根据的概率。

例子：
豆袋投入环中 100 次。有 23 次投中。投中的试验概率为 $\frac{23}{100}$ = 23%。

指数 (exponent) 一个显示重复倍数的提升的数。

例子：　　　　指数
$$4^3 = 4 \times 4 \times 4 = 64$$

指数函数 (exponential function) 其中指数为变量的非线性函数。

例子：　　　　$y = x^4$

指数计数法 (exponential notation) 使用指数写出一个数的重复倍数的方法。

例子：　2^8　　　5^2　　　9^3

表达式 (expression) 由变量和/或数字及运算符号组成的数学短语。

例子：　$5(8 + 4)$　　　$x - 3$　　　$2x + 4$

外角 (exterior angles) 当一条截线穿过两条直线时，在这两条直线外部的角叫做外角。

例子：

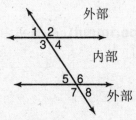

外角：∠1、∠2、∠7、∠8

面 (face) 立体上的平面。

例子：

面

因数 (factor) 可将另一个数整除而无余数的数。

例子：因为 30 ÷ 5 = 6，所以 5 是 30 的因数。

阶乘 (factorial) 数的阶乘是从 1 到那个数的所有整数的乘积。阶乘的符号是"！"。

例子：6 的阶乘 = 6! = 6 x 5 x 4 x 3 x 2 x 1 = 720

因数树图 (factor tree) 显示一个整数如何分解成它的质因数的图。

例子：

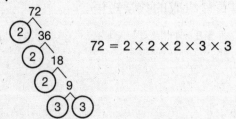

$$72 = 2 \times 2 \times 2 \times 3 \times 3$$

公平游戏 (fair game) 游戏中各方均有相同获胜概率的游戏。

例子：
公平游戏：游戏双方轮流丢骰子。A 方丢到 1、3 或 5 时各得一分。B 方丢到 2、4 或 6 时各得一分。得一分的概率对于游戏双方都是 $\frac{1}{2}$。

翻转 (flip) 见反射。

英尺 (foot) 常用测量系统中一个等于 12 英寸的单位。

例子：

1 英尺

公式 (formula) 显示量与量之间关系的规则。

例子：　A = bh　　　p = 4s

分形体 (fractal) 具有自我相似的图案。如果放大分形体中的一个小部分，放大的区域看上去与原来的图形相似。

例子：

分数 (fraction) 当整体分割成多个相等部分时，描述整体一部分的、以 $\frac{a}{b}$ 形式表示的数。

例子：　$\frac{3}{5}$　　$\frac{2}{7}$　　$\frac{1}{4}$　　$\frac{7}{10}$

分数加法 (fraction addition) 两个或多个分数相加。

例子：　$\frac{1}{3} + \frac{1}{4}$

$$\frac{1}{3} = \frac{1 \times 4}{3 \times 4} = \frac{4}{12}$$

$$\frac{1}{4} = \frac{1 \times 3}{4 \times 3} = \frac{3}{12}$$

$$\frac{1}{3} + \frac{1}{4} = \frac{4}{12} + \frac{3}{12} = \frac{4+3}{12} = \frac{7}{12}$$

分数除法 (fraction division) 两个分数相除。

例子：

$$\frac{1}{6} \div \frac{3}{4} = \frac{1}{6} \times \frac{4}{3}$$

$$= \frac{1 \times 4}{6 \times 3}$$

$$= \frac{4}{18} \text{或} \frac{2}{9}$$

分数乘法 (fraction multiplication) 两个或多个分数相乘。

例子：

$$1\frac{1}{2} \times \frac{1}{4} = \frac{3}{2} \times \frac{1}{4}$$

$$= \frac{3 \times 1}{2 \times 4}$$

$$= \frac{3}{8}$$

分数减法 (fraction subtraction) 两个分数相减。

例子：$\frac{3}{4} - \frac{2}{3}$

$$\frac{3}{4} = \frac{3 \times 3}{4 \times 3} = \frac{9}{12}$$

$$\frac{2}{3} = \frac{2 \times 4}{3 \times 4} = \frac{8}{12}$$

$$\frac{3}{4} - \frac{2}{3} = \frac{9}{12} - \frac{8}{12} = \frac{9-8}{12} = \frac{1}{12}$$

频率 (frequency) 在一次调查中某个事件发生的次数。见频率图。

频率图或频率表 (frequency chart or table) 显示事件分类和事件发生频率的表。

例子：

衬衫颜色	频率
黑色	8
褐色	2
白色	5
蓝色	4

前端估计 (front-end estimation) 仅用每个数的第一或第二位数进行计算的估算方法，且结果根据尾数进行调整。

例子：一位数的前端估计

```
  2,485
+ 3,698
  5,000    第一位数相加。
+ 1,200    485 + 698 的值约为 1,200。
  6,200
```

函数 (function) 对于每个输入，只有一个输出的输入输出关系。

例子：

$$y = x + 4 \qquad y = 2x \qquad y = x^2$$

算术基础理论 (Fundamental Theorem of Arithmetic) 所有大于 1 的整数可以被写成质数的唯一乘积。

例子： $24 = 2 \times 2 \times 2 \times 3$
$35 = 5 \times 7$

加仑 (gallon) 常用测量系统中一个等于 4 夸脱的单位。

例子：

1 加仑

几何 (geometry) 研究点、线、图形和立体之间的关系的一个数学分支。

几何概率 (geometric probability) 以比较几何图形测量为基础的概率。

例子：

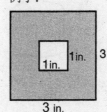

大正方形的面积 = 3 x 3 或 9 平方英寸

阴影的面积 = 9 平方英寸 - 1 平方英寸 = 8 平方英寸

落入阴影区域的概率 = $\frac{8}{9}$

等比数列 (geometric sequence) 其相邻两项之比始终相等的数列。

例子：

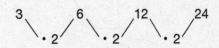

克 (gram) 在公制中重量的基本单位。

例子：

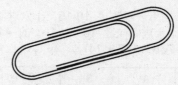

一个大回形针的重量约为 1 克。

图表 (graph) 有条不紊地显示信息的图。

例子：

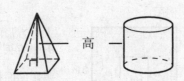

最大公因数 (greatest common factor (GCF)) 可以除两个或两个以上的整数而无余数的最大整数。

例子：6 是 12、18 和 24 的 GCF。

百 (hecto-) 表示 100 的前缀。

例子：1 百米 = 100 米

高 (height) 在三角形、四边形或棱锥上，指从底面到相对顶点或对边的垂直距离。在棱柱或圆柱体上，指两底面之间的距离。

例子：

七边形 (heptagon) 具有七个边的多边形。

例子：

十六进制 (hexadecimal number system) 逢 16 进 1 的进位制。

例子：
字母 A-F 用于表示数字 10-15。十六进制数 A3CE 等于十进制（逢 10 进 1 ）的 41,934 (40,960 + 768 + 192 + 14)。

逢16进一	A	3	C	E
位值	4096	256	16	1
乘积	10 × 4096 = 40,960	3 × 256 = 768	12 × 16 = 192	14 × 1 = 14

六边形 (hexagon) 具有六个边的多边形。

例子：

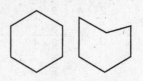

柱形图 (histogram) 一类条形图，其中的各个类别具有相等的数字范围。

例子：

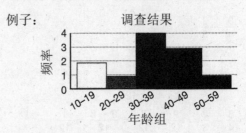

水平轴 (horizontal axis) 在其上建立条形图或坐标平面的两条线中的水平线。

例子：

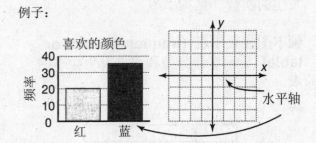

斜边 (hypotenuse) 在直角三角形中与直角相对的边。

例子：

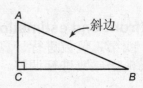

单位元素 (identity) 任何运算中，使另一个数保持不变的数。0 是加法的单位元素，因为 $a + 0 = a$。1 是乘法的单位元素，因为 $a \times 1 = a$。

例子：   6 + 0 = 6
         5 × 1 = 5

如果–那么语句 (if-then statement) 用"如果"和"那么"来表示两个条件之间的关系的逻辑语句。

例子：
如果三角形是不等边三角形，那么它的边不相等。

假分数 (improper fraction) 分子大于或等于分母的分数。

例子： $\frac{5}{2}$ $\frac{8}{8}$ $\frac{14}{3}$

递增图 (increasing graph) 线的高度从左到右逐步增加的图。

例子：

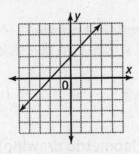

英寸 (inch) 常用测量体系中的一个长度单位。

例子：回形针测量的值为 $1\frac{3}{8}$ 英寸或 $1\frac{3}{8}''$。

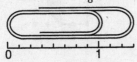

独立事件 (independent events) 一个事件的结果不影响另一个事件的结果的概率。

例子：
Therese、Diane 和 José 的名字分别写在几个纸条上。抽出一个纸条并放回。接着抽出另一纸条。假设抽出 Therese 的名字在第一个纸条上，那么将抽出 Diane 名字的概率是 ⅓。

自变量 (independent variable) 一个函数的输入变量。

例子：

自变量
|
$y = x + 2$

归纳推理 (inductive reasoning) 运用模型得出结论。

例子：
画出多个四边形并测量它们的角度。每个多边形的角度之和是 360°。得出的结论是四边形的角度之和是 360°。

不等式 (inequality) 数学语句中包含 <, >, ≤, 或 ≥。

例子：
6 < 9 $x + 3 \geq 21$ $2x - 8 > 0$

内接图形 (inscribed figure) 包含在另一个图形内的图形。如果多边形的所有顶点都在圆上，那么称多边形内接于圆。

例子：

多边形内接于圆。

整数 (integers) 正整数、负整数和 0 的集合。

例子：   ......, -3, -2, -1, 0, 1, 2, 3, ...

-4 -3 -2 -1 0 1 2 3 4

整数加法 (integer addition) 两个或两个以上的整数相加。

例子：
$-5 + 8 = 3$ $-5 + (-8) = -13$
$5 + (-3) = 2$ $5 + 8 = 13$

整数除法 (integer division) 两个整数相除。

例子：
$-40 \div 8 = -5$ $40 \div (-8) = -5$
$-40 \div (-8) = 5$ $40 \div 8 = 5$

整数乘法 (integer multiplication) 两个或两个以上的整数相乘。

例子：
$-5 \cdot 8 = -40$ $-5 \cdot (-8) = 40$
$5 \cdot (-8) = -40$ $5 \cdot 8 = 40$

整数减法 (integer subtraction) 两个整数相减。

例子：
$-5 - 8 = -13$ $-5 - (-8) = 3$
$5 - (-3) = 8$ $5 - 8 = -3$

利息 (interest) 为用钱而支付的钱。

例子：
Dave 在存储帐户上存了 $300。1 年后他的帐户结余为 $315。他在自己的存储帐户上获得 $15 的利息。

内角 (interior angles) 当一条截线穿过两条直线时，两条直线内部的角称作内角。

例子：

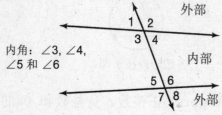

内角：∠3, ∠4, ∠5 和 ∠6

相交 (intersect) 图形穿过同一点。

例子：

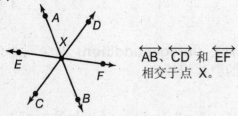

$\overleftrightarrow{AB}$、$\overleftrightarrow{CD}$ 和 $\overleftrightarrow{EF}$ 相交于点 X。

间隔 (interval) 条形图或线形图比例上等尺寸分隔的一个单位。

例子：

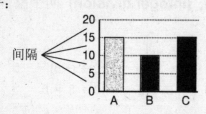

逆运算 (inverse operations) 每一步都"相反"的运算。

例子：
加法和减法　　2 + 3 = 5　　5 - 3 = 2
乘法和除法　　2 · 3 = 6　　6 ÷ 3 = 2

逆变分 (inverse variation) 两个变量的乘积恒定。

例子：

x	1	2	3	4	5	6
y	60	30	20	15	12	10

$$x \cdot y = 60$$

无理数 (irrational number) 不能表示为循环小数或有限小数的数，例如 $\sqrt{2}$。

例子：

$\sqrt{5}$ 　　　 π 　　　 $-\sqrt{\dfrac{1}{2}}$

等距画法 (isometric drawing) 用于给图作透视的方法。

例子：

等腰三角形 (isosceles triangle) 至少两边相等的三角形。

例子：

18　　18
14

千 (kilo-) 表示 1000 的前缀。

例子：1 千米 = 1000 米

纬度 (latitude) 赤道以北或以南的度数的测量。

例子：

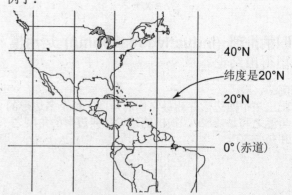

40°N
纬度是 20°N
20°N
0°（赤道）

最小公分母 (least common denominator (LCD)) 两个或两个以上的分母的最小公倍数（LCM）。

例子： $\frac{1}{2}$　$\frac{2}{3}$　$\frac{3}{4}$

2、3 和 4 的最小公倍数是 12，因此分数的最小公分母是 12。

以最小公分母写出的分数是 $\frac{6}{12}$、$\frac{8}{12}$ 和 $\frac{9}{12}$。

最小公倍数 (least common multiple (LCM)) 公倍数中最小的数。

例子：
3 的倍数：3、6、9、**12**、15、18、21、**24**…
4 的倍数：4、8、**12**、16、20、**24**、28、32…
12 是 3 和 4 的最小公倍数。

直角边 (leg) 直角三角形中不是斜边的一个边。

例子：

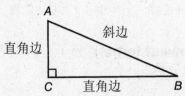

同分母 (like denominators) 两个或两个以上分数中分母相同的分母。

例子：

同类项 (like terms) 具有相同变量且指数相同的项。

例子：$3x^2$ 和 $9x^2$　　　　$10y$ 和 $2y$

线 (line) 沿两个方向延伸而无端点的一维图形。两点确定一条直线。

例子：

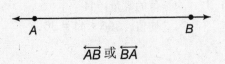

线形图 (line graph) 用一条线表示数据（通常随时间推移）变化的图。

例子：

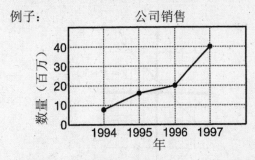

对称线 (line of symmetry) 将图形对称地分成相同的两部分的线。

例子：

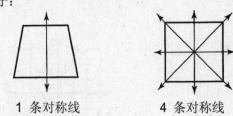

1 条对称线　　　　4 条对称线

线图 (line plot) 通过在一条数值轴上在每个值上堆叠 x 表示数据集形状的图。

例子：

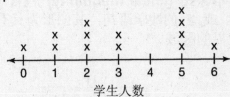

线段 (line segment) 直线的一部分，具有两个端点。两点确定一条线段。

例子：

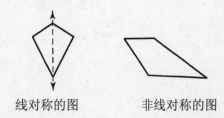

线对称 (line symmetry) 如果图形可以分成相同的两部分，那么称这个图形线对称。

例子：

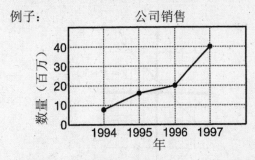

线对称的图　　　　非线对称的图

线性方程 (linear equation) 其图解为直线的方程。

例子：

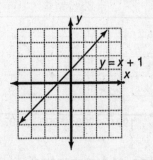

线性函数 (linear function) 其图形为直线的函数。

例子：

输入	输出
x	y
-2	3
-1	2
0	1
1	0
2	-1
3	-2

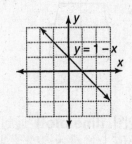

线性不等式 (linear inequality) 包含 <, >, ≤ 或 ≥ 的数学语句，其图形为具有直线边界的区域。

例子：

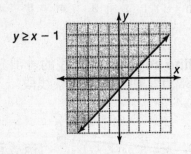

升 (liter) 在公制中容积的基本单位。

例子：

2 升的瓶子

经度 (longitude) 本初子午线以东或以西的度数的测量。

例子：

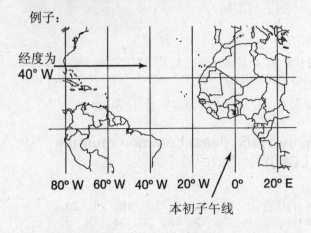

经度为 40° W

80° W 60° W 40° W 20° W 0° 20° E

本初子午线

下四分位数 (lower quartile) 数据集下一半的中值。

例子：

27 27 27 29 32 33 36 38 42 43 62

↑ 下四分位数   ↑ 中值   ↑ 上四分位数

最低项 (lowest terms) 分子分母仅有公因数 1 的分数。

例子： $\frac{1}{2}$ $\frac{3}{5}$ $\frac{21}{23}$

质量 (mass) 物体包含的物质量。

例子：

一个葡萄干的质量为 1 克。一双运动鞋的质量为 1 千克。

平均值 (mean) 数据集合中的值的总和除以值的数量。也称作平均数。

例子：

27 27 27 29 32 33 36 38 42 43 62

总数：396

值的数量：11

均值：396 ÷ 11 = 36

测量误差 (measurement error) 测量中的不确定度。测量中最大可能误差为所使用的最小单位的一半。

例子：

因为英寸为最小单位，最大可能误差为 $\frac{1}{2}$ 英寸。所以实际高度在 $5'5\frac{1}{2}''$ 与 $5'6\frac{1}{2}''$ 之间。

5'6"

集中趋势数 (measure of central tendency) 对一组数值数据求和的单一值。

例子：
均值、中值和众数是常见的集中趋势数。

27 27 27 29 32 33 36 38 42 43 62
<u>众数</u>　　　　　　中值↑

均值 = 396 ÷ 36 = 11

中值 (median) 当值按数字顺序排列时一组数据的中间值。

例子：

27 27 27 29 32 33 36 38 42 43 62
　　　　　　　　　↑
　　　　　　　　　中值

心算 (mental math) 不用铅笔和纸或计算器，在心中计算。

例子：

　　2000 x 　30
　3 个零 + 1 个零 = 4 个零
想一想：2 x 3 = 6，加 4 个零
　　2000 x 30 = 60,000

米 (meter) 在公制中长度的基本单位。

例子：

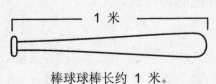

棒球球棒长约 1 米。

公制 (metric system) 以米、克和升为基础单位的测量体系。

例子：

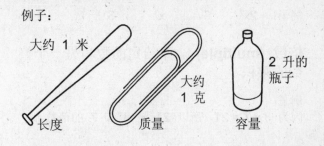

大约 1 米
长度　　质量　　容量
大约 1 克　　2 升的瓶子

中点 (midpoint) 把线段分成相同的两小段的点。

例子：

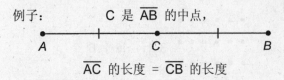

C 是 $\overline{AB}$ 的中点，

$\overline{AC}$ 的长度 = $\overline{CB}$ 的长度

英里 (mile) 常用测量体系中一个等于 5280 英尺的单位。

例子：

一英里是你可以在 15 到 20 分钟内走完或在大约 10 分钟内跑完的距离。

千分之一 (milli-) 表示 $\frac{1}{1000}$ 的前缀。

例子：1 毫米 = $\frac{1}{1000}$ 米

带分数 (mixed number) 由一个整数和一个分数构成的数。

例子：　　$3\frac{1}{2}$　　$1\frac{3}{4}$　　$13\frac{3}{8}$

众数 (mode) 数据集合中出现最多的值。

例子：
27 27 27 29 32 33 36 38 42 43 62

对于给出的数据集合，27 是众数。

单项式 (monomial) 只具有一项的代数表达式。

例子： $2x^2$ $5y$ x^3 -3

倍数 (multiple) 一个给定的数和另一个整数的乘积。

例子：
因为 $3 \times 7 = 21$，所以 21 是 3 和 7 的倍数。

乘法 (multiplication) 把称作因数的两个数组合得出一个被称作乘积的数的运算。

例子：

· · · · · ·
· · · · · ·   3 行，每行 6 个
· · · · · ·

$3 \times 6 = 18$
因数   乘积

乘法的性质 (multiplication property) 如果 A 和 B 是独立事件，那么两者发生的概率由 P(A 和 B) = P(A) x P(B) 给定。

例子：

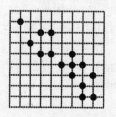

第一次旋转： $P(红) = \frac{1}{4}$
第二次旋转： $P(红) = \frac{1}{4}$
第一次和第二次旋转：$P(红和红) = \frac{1}{4} \times \frac{1}{4} = \frac{1}{16}$

等式的乘法性质 (Multiplication Property of Equality) 如果 a = b 那么 ac = bc。

例子：
在以下例子的第二行中，将方程式的两边各乘以 2。

如果 $\frac{1}{2}y = 4$

那么 $2 \times \frac{1}{2}y = 2 \times 4$

乘法逆元 (multiplicative inverse) 如果两个数的乘积是 1，那么一个数是另一个数的乘法逆元。

例子：
$\frac{1}{6}$ 和 6 是乘法逆元，因为 $\frac{1}{6} \times 6 = 1$。

互斥 (mutually exclusive) 如果事件 A 或 B 中的一个发生，那么另一个不会发生。

例子：
如果外部温度为 90°，那么现在不下雪。
如果多边形仅有三条边，那么它不会有 4 个角。

负数 (negative numbers) 小于零的数。

例子：

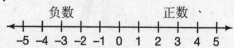

负相关 (negative relationship) 当一个数据集合中的数值增加时而另一个数据集合中的值减少，那么称这两个数据集为负相关。

例子：

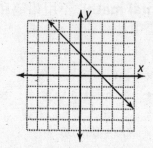

负斜率 (negative slope) 一条向下倾斜的线的斜率。

例子：

负平方根 (negative square root) 一个数的平方根的相反数。

例子：

平方根：   负平方根：
$\sqrt{25} = 5$ $-\sqrt{25} = -5$

© Scott Foresman Addison Wesley 6-8

网格 (net) 可以折叠以形成诸如棱柱的三维图形的平面图案。

例子：

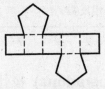

形成五棱柱的网格　　　　五棱柱

九边形 (nonagon) 具有九个边的多边形。

例子：

非线性方程 (nonlinear equation) 其图解是一条曲线而不是直线的方程。

例子：

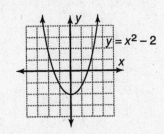

$y = x^2 - 2$

非线性函数 (nonlinear function) 其图解不是一条直线的函数，因为在 x 轴上进行的相等的改变不能在 y 轴上产生相等的改变。

例子：

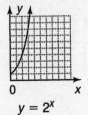 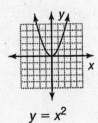 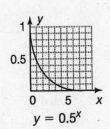

$y = 2^x$　　　　$y = x^2$　　　　$y = 0.5^x$

不相关 (no relationship) 当两个数据集不存在正相关或负相关时，那么称它们不相关。

例子：

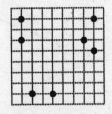

数轴 (number line) 按顺序显示数的一条线。

例子：

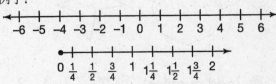

数–字形式 (number-word form) 使用数字和文字写出数值的方法。

例子：　45 万亿　　　　9 千

数字 (numeral) 数的符号。

例子：　7　　　58　　　234

分子 (numerator) 分数中上面的数，它表示在整体中占多少部分。

例子：

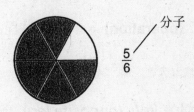

分子

$\dfrac{5}{6}$

钝角 (obtuse angle) 测量值大于 90° 且小于 180° 的角。

例子：

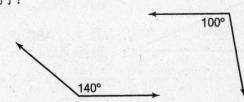

100°

140°

钝角三角形 (obtuse triangle) 具有一个钝角的三角形。

例子：

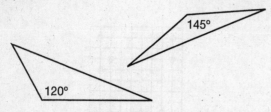

八边形 (octagon) 具有八个边的多边形。

例子：

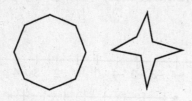

奇数 (odd number) 个位数字为 1、3、5、7或 9 的整数。

例子：

43   225   999   8,007

机率 (odds) 一个事件可能发生的次数与不能发生的次数的比率。

例子：

丢到 3 的机率：1 比 5

丢不到 3 的机率：5 比 1

运算 (operation) 一种数学过程。

例子：
四种基本运算：加、减、乘、除

相对的直角边 (opposite leg) 直角三角形的一个锐角所对的直角边。

例子：

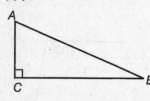

$\overline{CB}$ 是 ∠CAB 的相对直角边。

$\overline{AC}$ 是 ∠ABC 的相对直角边。

相反数 (opposite numbers) 在数值轴上到零点具有相同的距离但在不同侧的数。

例子：

7 和 -7 互为相反数。

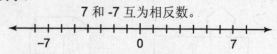

运算顺序 (order of operations) 按什么顺序进行运算的规则说明：
(1) 括号内的化简，(2) 指数化简，(3) 乘除从左到右，(4) 加减从左到右。

例子：
求值：$2x^2 = 4(x - 2)$，其中 $x = 3$。
(1) 括号内的化简， $2 \cdot 3^2 + 4(3 - 2)$
                      $2 \cdot 3^2 + 4(1)$

(2) 指数化简 $2 \cdot 9 + 4$
(3) 乘除从左到右 $18 + 4$
(4) 加减从左到右 22

有序对 (ordered pair) 用于定位坐标平面上的点的一对数。

例子：

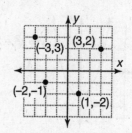

原点 (origin) 数值轴上的零点，或坐标系的两轴相交的点 (0, 0)。

例子：

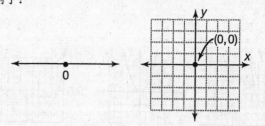

正投影图 (orthographic drawing) 物体的正视、侧视和俯视图。

例子:

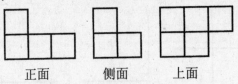

正面　　　　侧面　　　　上面

盎司 (ounce) 常用测量体系中的重量单位。

例子:

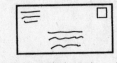

一封信的重量大约为一盎司。

结果 (outcome) 某种试验或情况可能出现的一种结果。

例子:

投掷 2 枚硬币的结果:

硬币 1	硬币 2
人头	背面
人头	人头
背面	人头
背面	背面

有 4 种结果。一种结果是人头、人头。

异常值 (outlier) 一个数据集中的极值,与其它大多数值有一定的差距。

例子:

27　27　27　29　32　33　36　38　42　43　62

↑

异常值

抛物线 (parabola) 二次函数图形,一般为 U 形或倒 U 形曲线。

例子:

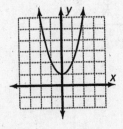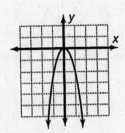

平行线 (parallel) 在同一平面内不相交的两条线、线段或射线。

例子:

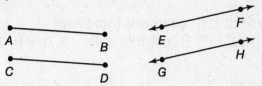

平行四边形 (parallelogram) 对边平行且相等的四边形。

例子:

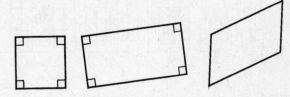

五边形 (pentagon) 具有五个边的多边形。

例子:

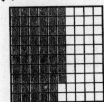

百分比 (percent) 一个数与 100 相比得到的比率。

例子:

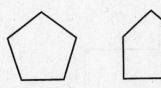

$$\frac{58}{100} = 0.58 = 58\%$$

百分比变化 (percent change) 将增加或减少的改变量与原始量相除,表示为原始量的百分比。

例子:

如果投资 $1500,且获得 $75 的利润,找出百分比变化。

$\frac{75}{1500} = 0.05 = 5\%$　　　$75 是增加 5%。

如果一件东西花费 $50,折扣 $10 廉售,找出百分比变化。

$\frac{10}{50} = 0.20 = 20\%$折扣 $10 为降价 20%。

百分比下降 (percent decrease) 表示为原始量的百分比的数量下降。见百分比变化。

百分比上升 (percent increase) 表示为原始量的百分比的数量上升。见百分比变化。

完全平方 (perfect square) 整数的平方。

例子：

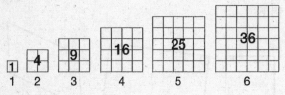

周长 (perimeter) 围绕图形外部的距离。

例子：

$$P = 5 + 2 + 6 + 4 + 11 + 6$$
$$= 34 单位$$

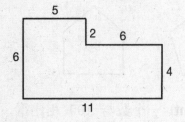

排列 (permutation) 一种项的安排，其中顺序很重要。

例子：

将从这组学生中选出一个作为会长，且另一个学生作为副会长：Wendy、Alex、Carlos。可能的排列是：

Wendy—会长，Alex—副会长；
Wendy—会长，Carlos—副会长；
Alex—会长，Wendy—副会长；
Alex—会长，Carlos—副会长；
Carlos—会长，Wendy—副会长；
Carlos—会长，Alex—副会长

注意：以上每一组都是一个不同的排列。

垂直 (perpendicular) 相交成直角的直线、射线或线段。

例子：

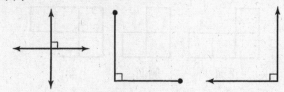

垂直平分 (perpendicular bisector) 直线、射线或线段与一条线段的中点相交并与其垂直，则称为垂直平分。

例子：

$\overleftrightarrow{DE}$ 是 $\overline{AB}$ 的垂直平分线。

圆周率 (π) (pi (π)) 圆的周长与其直径的比率：3.14159265....

例子：

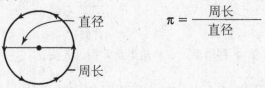

$$\pi = \frac{周长}{直径}$$

象形图 (pictograph) 使用符号表示数据的图形。

例子：

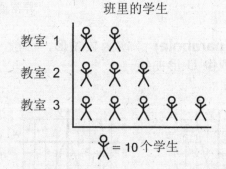

班里的学生

👤 = 10 个学生

位值 (place value) 数字占据的位的值。

例子：

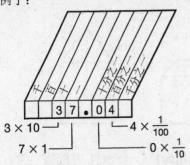

3 × 10 ——⌐   ⌐—— 4 × $\frac{1}{100}$

7 × 1 ——┘   └—— 0 × $\frac{1}{10}$

平面 (plane) 始终延伸的水平表面。

例子：

 为了使平面形象化，想象桌面向所有方向延伸。

点对称 (point symmetry) 如果图形在旋转 180° 后，看上去没有变化，则图形为点对称。

例子：

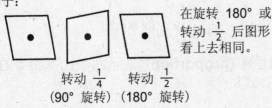 在旋转 180° 或转动 $\frac{1}{2}$ 后图形看上去相同。

转动 $\frac{1}{4}$ （90° 旋转）   转动 $\frac{1}{2}$ （180° 旋转）

多边形 (polygon) 在一个平面内由仅在其端点相交的线段组成的封闭图形。

例子：

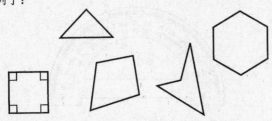

多面体 (polyhedron) 各个面是多边形的立体。

例子：

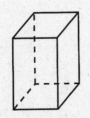

多项式 (polynomial) 一项或一项以上求和的代数表达式。

例子： $x^2 + 2x - 3$ $5y - 15$

对象总体 (population) 在调查中被研究的所有物体的集合。

例子：
将所有 1000 个俱乐部成员的名字都写在卡上，且打乱这些卡的顺序。接着随机抽取 100 张卡，并对这些成员进行电话调查。调查的对象总体是所有 1000 名俱乐部成员。

正数 (positive numbers) 大于零的数。

例子：

正相关 (positive relationship) 当两个数据集的数值同时增加或减少时，这两个数据集称为正相关。

例子：

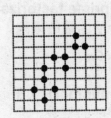

正斜率 (positive slope) 一条向上倾斜的线的斜率。

例子：

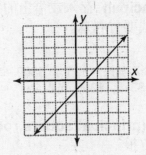

镑 (pound) 常用测量体系中一个等于 16 盎司的单位。

例子：

幂 (power) 指数或由底数升到指数次方运算所得的数。

例子：

$$16 = 2^4$$ 2 升到 4 次方。
16 是 2 的 4 次幂。

精度 (precision) 由测量单位确定的测量的精确度。

例子：

较小的测量单位"英寸"比较大的测量单位"英尺"的精度要高。

5'1" 61"

质因数 (prime factor) 除另一个整数而无余数的一个因数，且因数为质数。

例子：5 是 35 的一个质因数，因为 35 ÷ 5 = 7。

质因数分解 (prime factorization) 把一个数写成几个质因数的乘积。

例子：70 = 2 x 5 x 7

质数 (prime number) 大于 1 且只能被 1 和其自身整除的整数。

例子：
质数开始于 2、3、5、7、11 …… 。

本金 (principal) 存入或借出的钱的数量，这些钱要付利息。

例子：
Dave 在一个存储帐户上存了 $300。1 年后他的帐户余额为 $315。$300 是本金。

主平方根 (principal square root) 一个数的正平方根。

例子：

主平方根
$\sqrt{25} = 5$

负平方根
$-\sqrt{25} = -5$

棱柱 (prism) 两个底面全等且平行的多面体。

例子：

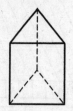

概率 (probability) 一个事件可能发生的次数与所有可能结果的数目的比率。

例子：

丢到 3 的概率是 $\frac{1}{6}$。
丢不到3 的概率是 $\frac{5}{6}$。

乘积 (product) 两个或两个以上的数相乘的结果。

例子：

乘积
|
2 x 3 x 5 = 30

比例 (proportion) 表示两个比率相等的等式。

例子： $\frac{12}{34} = \frac{6}{17}$

量角器 (protractor) 一种测量角的工具。

例子：

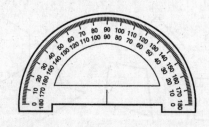

棱锥 (pyramid) 具有一个多边形底面，且所有其它面都是三角形并在一个点相遇的立方体。

例子：

© Scott Foresman Addison Wesley 6-8

勾股定理 (Pythagorean Theorem) 在直角三角形中，其中 c 为斜边的长度，且 a 和 b 是直角边的长度，那么 $a^2 + b^2 = c^2$

例子：

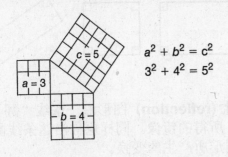

$$a^2 + b^2 = c^2$$
$$3^2 + 4^2 = 5^2$$

象限 (quadrants) 由坐标平面的两个轴确定的四个区域。

例子：

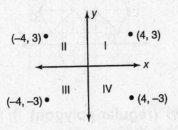

二次方程 (quadratic equation) 具有象 x^2 这样的平方项的方程。

例子：

$$y = x^2 + 3x - 12 \qquad y = 2x^2 + 7$$

二次函数 (quadratic function) x 的最高次幂为 2 的函数。二次函数的图形是抛物线。

例子：

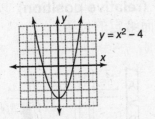

$$y = x^2 - 4$$

四边形 (quadrilateral) 具有四个边的多边形。

例子：

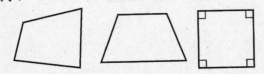

夸脱 (quart) 常用测量体系中的体积单位。

例子：

牛奶　一夸脱牛奶

四分位数 (quartile) 把一个数据集分成相等的四部分的数中的一个。

例子：

27　27　27　29　32　33　36　38　42　43　62
　　　　↑　　　　　　↑　　　　　　↑
　　下四分位数　　中值　　上四分位数
27、33 和 42 是这个数据集的三个四分位数。

商 (quotient) 一个数与另一个数相除的结果。

例子：

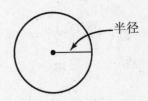

商
$$8 \div 4 = 2$$

根号 (radical sign) 用于表示一个数的平方根。

例子：
$$\sqrt{49} = 7$$

半径 (radius) 从圆的中心到圆上任意一点的线段。

例子：

半径

随机样本 (random sample) 通过一种让对象总体内的每个成员都有相等机会的方式选取出来的样本。

例子：
将所有 1000 个俱乐部成员的名字都写在卡上，且打乱这些卡的顺序。接着抽取 100 张卡，并对这些成员进行电话调查。俱乐部的所有成员都有相等的机会被调查

值域 (range) 在一个数据集合中最大值与最小值之间的区域。

例子：

27 27 27 29 32 33 36 38 42 43 62

值域是 62 - 27 = 35。

比率 (rate) 表示具有不同单位的量的相关关系的比。

例子： $\dfrac{72\ 美元}{28\ 小时}$ $\dfrac{55\ 英里}{1\ 小时}$

比 (ratio) 两个量的比较，通常写成一个分数。

例子： $\dfrac{2}{1}$ 2 比 1   2 : 1

有理数 (rational number) 能够写成两个整数的比的数。整数、分数和许多小数都是有理数。

例子：

整数	分数	小数
$-27 = \dfrac{-27}{1}$	$\dfrac{7}{8}$	$3.1 = 3\dfrac{1}{10} = \dfrac{31}{10}$

射线 (ray) 直线的一部分，具有一个端点，另一端无线延伸。射线首先由其端点命名。

例子：

 $\overrightarrow{AB}$

实数 (real numbers) 所有的有理数和无理数。

例子：

-27 $\dfrac{1}{2}$ 3.1

$\sqrt{5}$ π $-\sqrt{\dfrac{1}{2}}$

倒数 (reciprocals) 其乘积为 1 的两个数。

例子：

$\dfrac{3}{5}$ 和 $\dfrac{5}{3}$ 互为倒数，因为 $\dfrac{3}{5} \cdot \dfrac{5}{3} = 1$。

矩形 (rectangle) 对边相等且四个角都是 90° 的平行四边形。

例子：

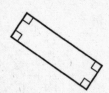

反射 (reflection) 图形沿一条线"翻转"所得的镜像。同样也称沿这条线翻转此图形所产生的变换。

例子：

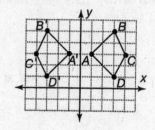

正多边形 (regular polygon) 所有边和角都相等的多边形。

例子：

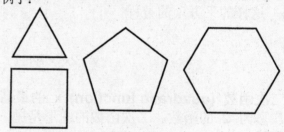

相对位置 (relative position) 以另一个地点为参考而给定的位置。

例子：

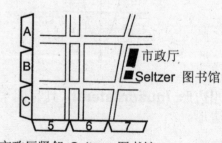

市政厅紧邻 Seltzer 图书馆。

余数 (remainder) 除法完成后所保留的、小于除数的数。

例子：

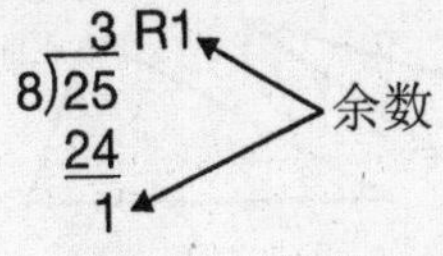

循环小数 (repeating decimal) 小数点右侧具有一个循环数字或一组循环数字的小数。

例子： $0.\overline{6}$　$0.\overline{123}$　$2.\overline{18}$

菱形 (rhombus) 四个边边长都相等的平行四边形。

例子：

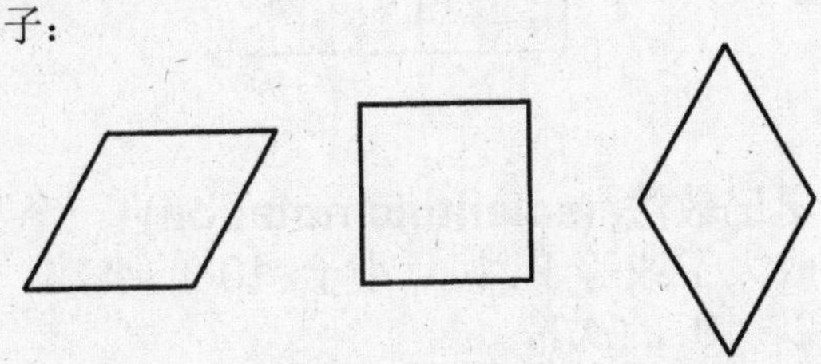

直角 (right angle) 测量值为 90° 的角。

例子：

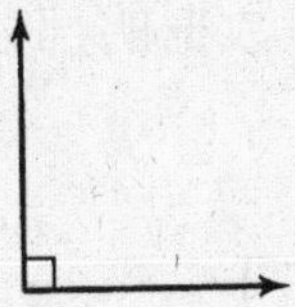

直角三角形 (right triangle) 具有一个直角的三角形。

例子：

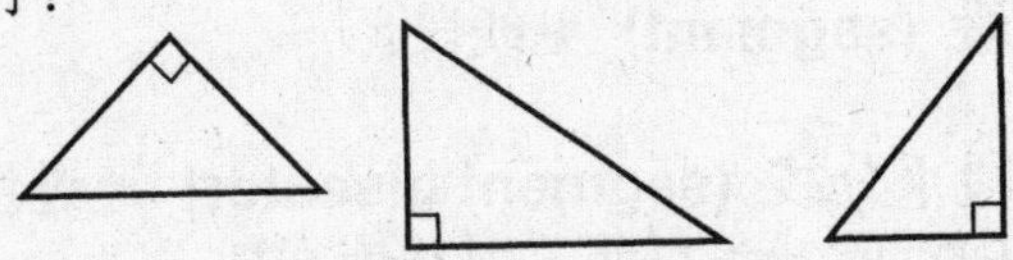

上升的高度 (rise) 对于图上的一条线，因给定的水平方向发生的变化而引起的垂直方向发生的变化。

例子：

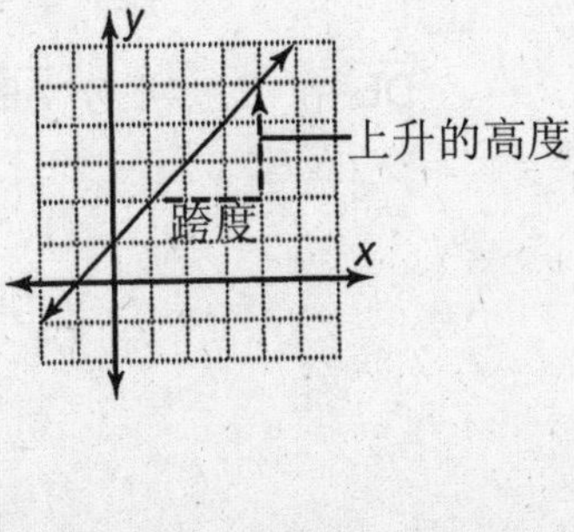

旋转 (rotation) 已经“转动”的图形的图像，就如在车轮上转动一样。同样也指，沿这条线转动此图形所产生的变换的名称。

例子：

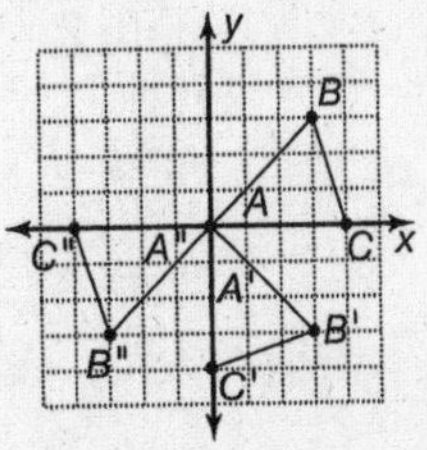

轴向对称 (rotational symmetry) 如果图形在旋转小于一圈时可与其原有图形匹配，那么就称这个图形轴向对称。

例子：

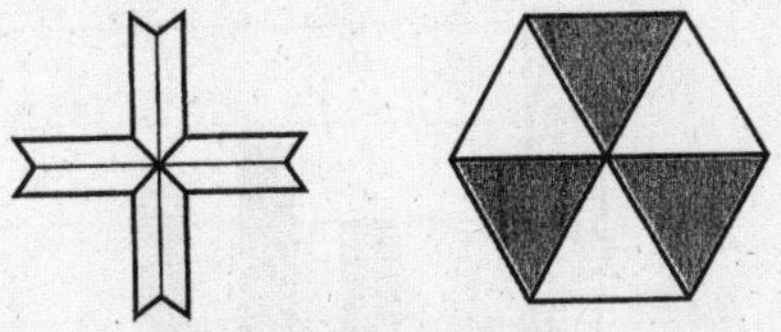

每个图形都轴向对称。

四舍五入 (rounding) 把一个数估算到给定的位值。

例子：

2153 四舍五入到	
最近的十位：2200	最近的百位：2150

跨度 (run) 对于图上的一条线，用于找出垂直方向的变化或者上升的高度的水平方向的变化幅度。

例子：

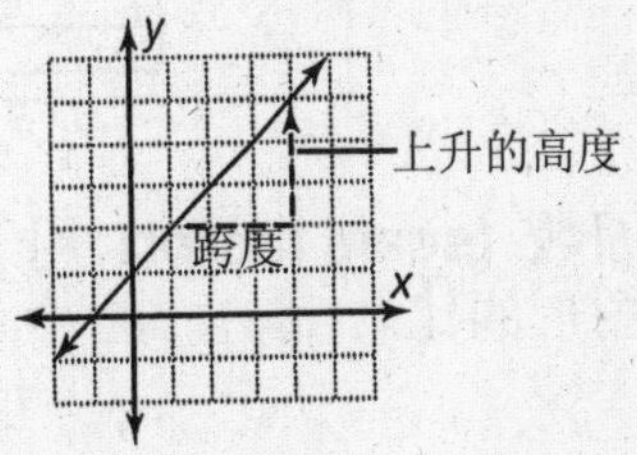

样本 (sample) 用于预测特定情况如何发生的一组数据。

例子：
将俱乐部所有成员的1000 个名字都写在卡上，且打乱这些卡的顺序。接着随机抽取 100 张卡，并对这些成员进行电话调查。样本就是进行电话调查的 100 名成员。

样本空间 (sample space) 一个试验的所有可能结果的集合。

例子：

投掷 2 枚硬币的结果：

硬币 1	硬币 2
人头	背面
人头	人头
背面	人头
背面	背面

样本空间是人头、背面；人头、人头；和背面、背面。

刻度（图形的） (scale (graphical)) 在条形图或线形图的竖轴上均匀间隔开的标记，用于测量条或线的高度。

例子：

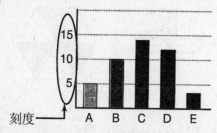

比例（在比例图中） (scale (in scale drawings)) 在比例图中的尺寸与实物尺寸的比。见比例图。

比例图 (scale drawing) 使用比例制成的物体放大图或缩小图。

例子：

客厅的比例图

比例：
0.1 英寸 = 1 英尺

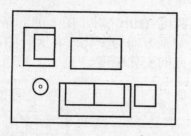

比例因数 (scale factor) 用于放大或缩小相似图形的比。

例子：

$$\frac{10}{5} = 2$$

$$\frac{6}{3} = 2$$

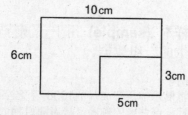

放大比例因数是 2。

不等边三角形 (scalene triangle) 三个边边长不等的三角形。

例子：

散点图 (scatterplot) 使用成对的数值作为点来显示两个数据集的关系的图。

例子：

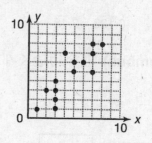

科学记数法 (scientific notation) 一个数写成大于或等于 1 且小于 10 的小数乘以 10 的次幂。

例子：　　　　　　$350,000 = 3.5 \times 10^5$

扇形 (sector) 一个圆的扇形部分，用于圆图以表示一组数据的部分与全部相比所占的比例。

例子：

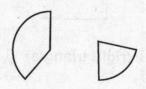

线段 (segment) 见线段。

线段平分线 (segment bisector) 通过线段中点的一条直线、射线或线段。

例子：

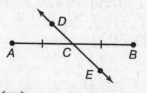

$\overleftrightarrow{DE}$ 在 C 点平分 $\overline{AB}$。

数列 (sequence) 遵循某种特定模式的数的排列。

例子：

等差数列

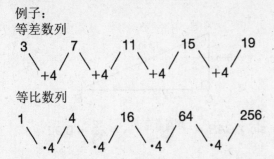

等比数列

边 (side) 形成一个角的两条射线中的每一条。同样指组成多边形的线段。

例子：

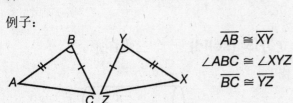

边角角 (Side-Angle-Angle (SAA)) 通过比较相应部分来确定三角形是否全等的定律。

例子：

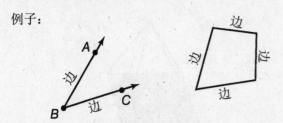

$\overline{BC} \cong \overline{YZ}$
$\angle ABC \cong \angle XYZ$
$\angle BAC \cong \angle YXZ$

根据 SAA 定律，△ABC ≅ △XYZ。

边角边 (Side-Angle-Side (SAS)) 通过比较相应部分来确定三角形是否全等的定律。

例子：

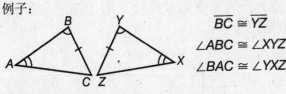

$\overline{AB} \cong \overline{XY}$
$\angle ABC \cong \angle XYZ$
$\overline{BC} \cong \overline{YZ}$

根据 SAS 定律，△ABC ≅ △XYZ。

边边边 (Side-Side-Side (SSS)) 通过比较相应部分来确定三角形是否全等的定律。

例子：

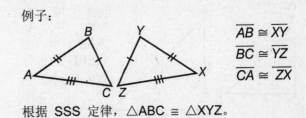

$\overline{AB} \cong \overline{XY}$
$\overline{BC} \cong \overline{YZ}$
$\overline{CA} \cong \overline{ZX}$

根据 SSS 定律，△ABC ≅ △XYZ。

有效数字 (significant digits) 在某个测量值中表示实际测量的数字。

例子：

380.6700   所有数字都是有效的。

0.0038   3 和 8 是有效的，但零是无效的。

相似 (similar) 图形之间形状相同，但尺寸不一定相等。

例子：

和

和

和

相似比 (similarity ratio) 相似图形之间对应边边长的比。

例子：

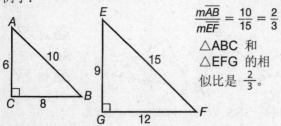

$$\frac{m\overline{AB}}{m\overline{EF}} = \frac{10}{15} = \frac{2}{3}$$

△ABC 和 △EFG 的相似比是 $\frac{2}{3}$。

单利 (simple interest) 只按本金计算的利息。

例子： Ramon 在一个帐户上投入 \$240，每年获得 6% 的利息，共投入 5 年。
他将获得 240 · 0.06 · 5 = 72；5 年后单利是 \$72。

化简 (simplified) 不含有同类项的多项式。

例子：
$4x^4 + x^3 + x^2 - 8$ 已经化简
$4x^4 + x^2 + 6x^2 - 8$ 未化简，因为 x^2 和 $6x^2$ 是同类项。

简化 (simplify) 通过运算顺序的应用来降低表达式的复杂性。

例子：简化 $3 + 8 \cdot 5^2$。

$$
\begin{aligned}
3 + 8 \cdot 5^2 &= 3 + 8 \cdot 25 \quad &(\text{指数})\\
&= 3 + 200 \quad &(\text{乘法})\\
&= 203 \quad &(\text{加法})
\end{aligned}
$$

模拟 (simulation) 用于找出概率的试验模型。

例子：
棒球运动员击球 .250。为了模拟这个运动员如何击球，旋转一个四部分的旋转器。这种模拟可用于预测击球手连续击中 2 次或 3 次的频率。

正弦 (sine) 对于直角三角形的锐角 x，x 的正弦或 sin(x) 是 $\frac{\text{相对直角边}}{\text{斜边}}$。

例子：

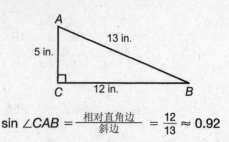

$$\sin \angle CAB = \frac{\text{相对直角边}}{\text{斜边}} = \frac{12}{13} \approx 0.92$$

斜高 (slant height) 在棱锥上，从底面的一边到顶点的垂直距离。

例子：

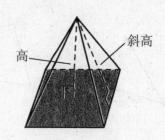

滑动 (slide) 见平移。

斜率 (slope) 对于图上的一条直线，斜率是上升的高度除以跨度，用于描述一条线的陡度。

例子：

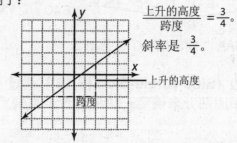

$$\frac{\text{上升的高度}}{\text{跨度}} = \frac{3}{4}。$$

斜率是 $\frac{3}{4}$。

立方体 (solid) 一个三维图形。

例子：

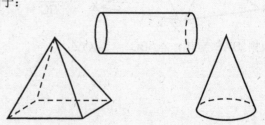

方程式或不等式的解 (solutions of an equation or inequality) 使方程或不等式成立的变量的值。

例子：

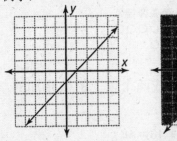

这条线表示 y = x – 1 的解。   阴影区域表示 y > x – 1 的解。

方程组的解 (solution of a system) 使系统中的所有方程成立的变量代换。

例子：

$$y = x + 4$$
$$y = 3x - 6$$

有序对 (5, 9) 是两个方程的解。因此，(5, 9) 是方程组的解。

解答 (solve) 找出方程式或不等式的解。

例子：解方程 x + 6 = 13。
x + 6 = 13
x + 6 + (-6) = 13 + (-6)
x + 0 = 7
x = 7

球体 (sphere) 所有点到中心的距离都相等的立体。

例子：

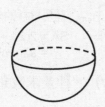

正方形 (square) 所有边的边长都相等且四个角都是 90° 的平行四边形。

例子：

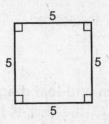

平方 (squared) 提升到二次幂。

例子： 3 的平方写成 3^2。
$3^2 = 3 \times 3 = 9$

平方厘米 (square centimeter) 边长为 1 厘米的正方形的面积。

例子：

1 厘米
1 厘米
1 平方厘米

平方英寸 (square inch) 边长为 1 英寸的正方形的面积。

例子：

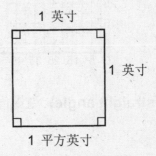

1 英寸
1 英寸
1 平方英寸

平方根 (square root) N 的平方根是与其自身相乘得到N 的数。同样，一个给定数的平方根是面积与这个给定数相等的正方形的边长。

例子：

$9 \times 9 = 81$, 所以
9 是 81 的平方根。
$9 = \sqrt{81}$

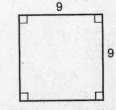

面积为 81 平方单位。

标准形式 (standard form) 使用数字写出一个数的方法。

例子：

标准形式： 100,000,000
文字形式： 一亿
数-字形式： 1 亿

茎叶图 (stem-and-leaf diagram) 用数字位数来显示数据集合的形状和分布的一种数据表示方法。

例子：

该图表示数据集合：33, 34, 34, 35, 40, 41, 46, 51, 51, 52, 53, 55, 58。

茎	叶			
3	3	4	4	5
4	0	1	6	
5	1	1	2	3	5	8

阶梯函数 (step function) 不同规则用于不同输入值的函数。阶梯函数的图由不相连的线段组成。

例子：

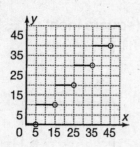

平角 (straight angle) 测量值为 180° 的角。

例子：

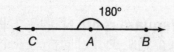

替代 (substitute) 由一个指定的值来替换一个变量。

例子：

使用公式 $A = l \cdot w$ 得出长为 12 cm 且宽为 8 cm 的矩形的面积。

$$A = l \cdot w$$
$$A = 12 \cdot 8$$
$$A = 96$$

替代长度和宽度的值。

面积是 96 cm²。

减法 (subtraction) 能得出两个数之间的差或拿掉一些还剩多少的运算。

例子：

$$12 - 5 = 7$$

⊠⊠⊠⊠⊠⊠⊠
○○○○○
○○

总数 (sum) 两个或两个以上的数相加的结果。

例子：

$$30 + 18 = 48$$ ——总数

互补角 (supplementary angles) 角度之和为 180° 的两个角。

例子：

55° 125°

表面积 (surface area (SA)) 多面体每个表面的面积之和。

例子：

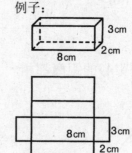

两个面是 8 cm 乘 3 cm。
$A = b \cdot h = 8 \cdot 3 = 24$ cm²

两个面是 8 cm 乘 2 cm。
$A = b \cdot h = 8 \cdot 2 = 16$ cm²

两个面是 2 cm 乘 3 cm。
$A = b \cdot h = 2 \cdot 3 = 6$ cm²

直角棱柱的表面积是：

$$SA = 2(24 + 16 + 6)$$
$$= 92 \text{ cm}^2$$

调查 (survey) 一种要求收集和分析信息的研究方法。

例子：
进行一项调查，以确定什么体育活动最受学生欢迎。

对称 (symmetry) 见线对称、点对称和轴向对称。

线性方程组 (system of linear equations) 放在一起考虑的两个或两个以上的线性方程。

例子：
$$y = x + 3$$
$$y = 4x - 15$$

T 形表 (T-table) 显示方程对应的 x 和 y 的值的表。

例子：

$$y = 2x + 1$$

x	y
−2	−3
−1	−1
0	1
1	3
2	5

短线 (tally) 在调查期间使用短线标记计数的记录。

例子：

汽车	短线
轿车	卌 ⦀
旅行车	⦀⦀
多功能运动车	卌 ∣
卡车	卌
面包车	⦀∣

短线标记 (tally marks) 用于组织较大数据集合的标记。每个标记表示在数据集合中某值出现了一次。

例子： ∣ 一　　　卌 五

切线 (tangent line) 仅在一点与圆接触的一条线。

例子：

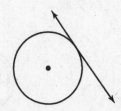

正切比 (tangent ratio) 对于直角三角形上的一个锐角 x，x 的正切或 tan(x) 为 $\frac{相对直角边}{相邻直角边}$。

例子：

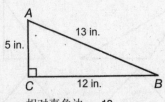

$$\tan \angle CAB = \frac{相对直角边}{相邻直角边} = \frac{12}{5} = 2.4$$

项 (term) 数列中的一个数。同样也指多项式的一部分，这个多项式为带正负号的数、与一个或几个变量相乘的数。变量可以包含整数的次方。

例子：

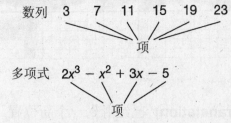

数列 3　7　11　15　19　23
　　　　　　　　项

多项式 $2x^3 - x^2 + 3x - 5$
　　　　　　　　项

有限小数 (terminating decimal) 具有一定量的位数的小数。

例子：　3.5　　0.599992　　4.05

镶嵌 (tessellation) 将一个平面完全覆盖而不含缺口或重叠部分的图形的重复模式。

例子：

理论概率 (theoretical probability) 一个事件可能发生的次数与所有可能结果的次数的比。

例子：

$$\frac{旋到白色的次数}{总次数} = \frac{3}{6} = \frac{1}{2}$$

因为旋转器上的一半是白色，所以旋到白色的理论概率是 $\frac{1}{2}$。

变换 (transformation) 图形位置的改变。

例子:

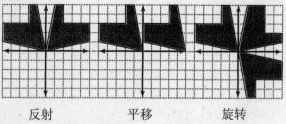

反射　　　　平移　　　　旋转

平移 (translation) 已经滑到一个新位置而没有翻转或转动的图形的图像。同样,图形滑动所产生的变换也是这个名称。

例子:

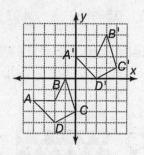

截线 (transversal) 与两条或两条以上的其它直线相交的直线。

例子:

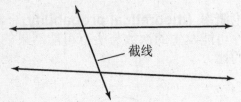

截线

梯形 (trapezoid) 只有两个边平行的四边形。

例子:

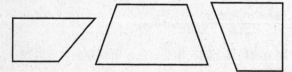

树图 (tree diagram) 表示一种情况的所有可能的结果的分支、树状图。

例子:
投掷 3 个硬币:

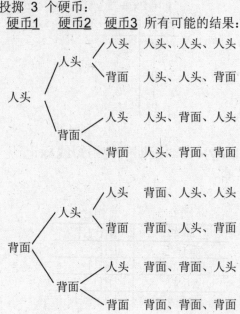

趋势 (trend) 在散点图中以图案的形式出现的两组数据之间的关系。见正相关、负相关、不相关。

趋势线 (trend line) 与形成散点图中一个趋势的点大致"符合"的线。见正相关和负相关。

试验 (trial) 一次实验。

例子:

丢一次骰子　　　　掷一次硬币

三角形 (triangle) 具有三个边的多边形。

例子:

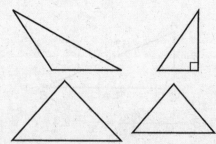

三角比 (trigonometric ratios) 直角三角形边长的比，与三角形锐角的角度有关。

例子：

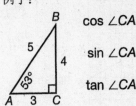

$$\cos \angle CAB = \frac{相邻直角边}{斜边} = \frac{3}{5} = 0.6$$

$$\sin \angle CAB = \frac{相对直角边}{斜边} = \frac{4}{5} = 0.8$$

$$\tan \angle CAB = \frac{相对直角边}{相邻直角边} = \frac{4}{3} \approx 1.3$$

三项式 (trinomial) 具有三项的多项式。

例子：　　　　$2x^3 - x^2 + 3x$　　　$3x^2 + 2x - 4$

转动 (turn) 见旋转。

不公平游戏 (unfair game) 并非所有参加游戏者都有相同获胜概率的游戏。

例子：

不公平游戏：丢一对骰子，并为参加的每个人指定从 2 到 12 的总数。当丢到他/她的总数时，就得一分。因为丢到 2 到 12 的总数机会不相等，那么所有人获胜的机会也都不相等，因此这个游戏不公平。

单价 (unit price) 一个物品的单位价格。

例子：

　　　每磅 $3.00　　　每盒 $5.75

单位 (unit) 一件物品。用作测量标准的一个量或数量。

单分数 (unit fraction) 分子为 1 的分数。

例子：　　$\frac{1}{4}$　　　$\frac{1}{2}$　　　$\frac{1}{7}$

单位比率 (unit rate) 一组比例中第二个数是一个单位的比率。

例子：每分钟 25 加仑　　　$\dfrac{55\ 英里}{1\ 小时}$

不同分母 (unlike denominators) 两个或两个以上分数中不相同的分母。

例子：

$$\frac{1}{2} \qquad \frac{2}{5} \qquad \frac{2}{9}$$

不同分母

上四分位数 (upper quartile) 数据集合上一半的中值。

例子：

27　27　27　29　32　33　36　38　42　43　62

下四分位数　　　中值　　　上四分位数

变量 (variable) 可以改变或变动的量，通常由字母表示。

例子：

3x　　　　　y　　　　　2t

变量

维恩图 (Venn diagram) 使用区域表示事件集合之间的关系的图。

例子：

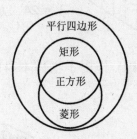

顶点 (vertex) 在一个角或一个多边形上，两个边相交的点。在一个多面体上，三个或三个以上的面相交的点。

例子：

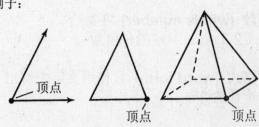

顶点　　　　　　顶点　　　　　顶点

对顶角 (vertical angles) 两条线相交，相对的角。

例子：

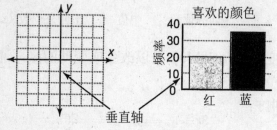

顶角：
∠1 和 ∠3
∠2 和 ∠4

垂直轴 (vertical axis) 在其上建立条形图或坐标平面的两条线中的垂线。

例子：

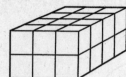

喜欢的颜色

垂直轴

体积 (volume) 立体所占的空间量。

例子：

$V = lwh$
$V = 4 \cdot 3 \cdot 2$
$V = 24$ 立方单位

重量 (weight) 作用于物体本身的重力的测量值。

例子：

1 盎司　　1 磅　　　　1 吨

整数 (whole number) 在集合 {0,1,2,3,4,......} 中的任何数。

字格式 (word form) 只使用文字来写出一个数的方法。

例子：

四十五万亿　　十亿　　六

x 轴 (x-axis) 坐标平面上的水平轴。

例子：

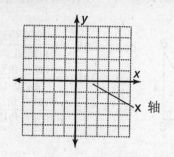

x 轴

x 坐标 (x-coordinate) 有序对的第一个数。

例子：

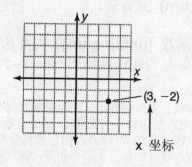

(3, −2)

x 坐标

x 轴截距 (x-intercept) 方程的图形与 x 轴相交的点。

例子：

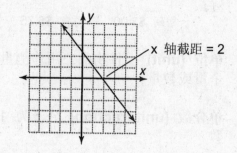

x 轴截距 = 2

y 轴 (y-axis) 坐标平面上的垂直轴。

例子：

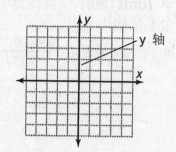

y 轴

y 坐标 (y-coordinate) 有序对的第二个
数。

例子：

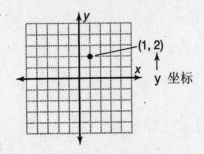

y 轴截距 (y-intercept) 方程的图形与 y
轴相交的点。

例子：

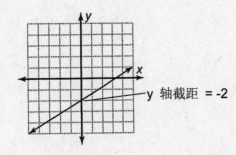

码 (yard) 常用测量体系中一个等于 3 英
尺的单位。

例子：

桌子的高度大
约为一码。

成零对 (zero pair) 一个数和它的相反
数。

例子： 7 和 -7   23 和 -23

**加法的成零特性 (Zero Property of
Addition)** 一个整数和它的相反数的和总
是 0。

例子： $3 + (-3) = 0$

         $-8 + 8 = 0$